Native California Guide
Native California Guide
Native California Guide

EDITION 2000 EDITION 2000 EDITION 2000 EDITION 2000

Dolan H. Eargle, Jr.

Trees Company Press
San Francisco

First printing, March, 2000
Library of Congress Catalog Card Number: 99-93868
ISBN: 0-937401-10-2 (softcover)

Editing:
Sheryl Fullerton

Editing and Art Direction:
Fred Dodsworth

Book Design, Production, & Packaging:
The Pirate's Paradigm
510-548-0697

Maps:
Mike Mosher and Dolan Eargle
Baskektry Design Illustrations:
Nancy Record (Ojibway)

Printed in Canada by Transcontinental Printing

Photographs are by the author, unless otherwise credited in the captions

NATIVE CALIFORNIA GUIDE
NATIVE CALIFORNIA GUIDE
NATIVE CALIFORNIA GUIDE

BOOK ONE

THE EVOLUTION OF NATIVE CULTURES IN THE LAND THAT BECAME CALIFORNIA

INCLUDING THEIR EARLY HISTORY

AND THEIR ARTISTIC AND CULTURAL EXPRESSIONS

Dolan H. Eargle, Jr.
Trees Company Press
San Francisco

ARRANGEMENT of the BOOK

THIS BOOK CONSISTS OF SEVERAL PARTS:
Book One is an early history of Native Californians, covering topics common to most parts of the state, including the development of the various cultures, followed by the tragic story of the effects of the European and American invasions. At the end of Book One you'll find some information on the large Native American population from out of state.

Books Two and Three are regional guides of the peoples and tribes of Northern and Southern California, respectively, including their environments, and broad sketches of their characteristics. Some treatment is given to the more specific characteristics of each tribal group, accompanied by current accounts of some of the happenings, successes, and aspirations of the groups. Each reservation, rancheria, and tribal organization (Federally recognized or not) is given some attention.

Incorporated throughout the book are a series of short essays on the many facets of Indian life in California, from art to food to casinos.

The first half of Book Four looks at social services and education for Indians, while the second half is comprised of a group of appendices, featuring long lists of where to go for information or experiences of Indian life, museums, missions, even old forts. Finally are two Calendars of Events, one for events with mainly California Indian orientation, the other a Powwow calendar of intertribal events. Remember that the information in both of these can, and does change, although most events have attempted to establish themselves on a regular basis

MORE THAN THIRTY PERSONS HAVE
generously offered their time and knowledge to tell us of their situation, be it tribal or administrative. These interviews, describing nearly every type of Native situation found in California, accompany the sketches of the locations or organizations.

Contributors:
American Indian Council of Mariposa County (Miwok)
Danny Ammon, Member, Tsnungwe Tribe
Larry Banegas, Member, Tribal Council, Barona Reservation (Kumeyaay)
David Belardes, Tribal Chair, Ajachemem Nation
Dore Bietz, Director, California Indian Lands Office
Marvin Brown, Spiritual Leader, E'lem Indian Colony (Pomo)
Wayne Burrell, Jr., Chief, United Lumbee Nation
California Indian Health Service Directory
Gregg Castro, Tribal Council Vice Chair, Salinan Nation
Roberto Dansie, Pit River Health Service
Dee Dominguez, Tribal Chair, Kitanemuk Tribe of Tejon Indians

Lorrie Frazier, Cultural Resources Chair, Mooretown Rancheria (Konkow Maidu)
Isidore Garfield & Louise Williams, Elders, Tule River Reservation
Aggie Garnicke, Hutash Consultant, Coastal Band of Chumash Nation
John Green, Chair, Elk Valley Tribal Council (Tolowa)
Stacey Greer, Member, Redding Rancheria
Gloria Grimes, Tribal Chair, Calaveras Band of Mi-wuk Indians
Betty Hall, Tribal Historian, Shasta Nation
Rick Heredia, Public Information Officer, D-Q University
Carol Irvine, Director, Chapa-De Indian Health Services (Auburn)
Jessica Jim, Member, Ajumawi Pit River Tribe
John Johnson, Tribal Administrator, Auburn Rancheria (Nisenan Maidu)
Linda Knight, member, Middletown Miwok Rancheria
Frank LaPena, Nomtipom Wintu, permission to reproduce his painting, "Deer Spirit"
Alan Leventhal, Tribal Ethnohistorian, & Concha Rodriguez, Lawrence Marine, Kathy Perez, Rosemary Cambra, Tribal Council Members, Muwekma Tribe (Ohlone)
Jennifer Malone, Tribal Member, Wukchumni Tribe (Yokuts)
Carol Martin, Secretary, Wintu Tribe
Kenny Meza, Tribal Chair, Jamul Indian Village (Kumeyaay)
Anthony Morales, Chief, & Mark Acuña, Captain, Tongva Dancers, Tongva Nation
Ron Morales, Spokesman, Honey Lake Maidu
Chris Moser & the Riverside Municipal Museum, permission to use redrawn designs from California Indian Basketry (3 volumes)
Tom Little Bear Nason, Spiritual Leader, Esselen Nation
Little Bear Rudy Ortega, Sr., Chief, Fernandeño/Tataviam Tribe
Bob Pennell, Tribal Cultural Resource Director, Table Mountain Rancheria (Chukchansi & other Yokotch)
Jim Penney, Business Manager, Ewiiaapaayp (Cuyapaipe) Reservation (Kumeyaay)
Paul Peterson, archaeologist, for sketches of Anderson Marsh
Pete Ramirez, Chair, Mechoopda Maidu Tribe
Eva Silver Star Reed, National Head Chief, United Lumbee Nation
Ann Marie Sayers, Tribal Leader, Mutsun: Indian Canyon Nation
Caleen Sisk-Franco, 4-Winds Charter School (Wintu)
Charlene Storr & Janice Bowen, Council Members, Tolowa Nation
Timbisha Shoshone Tribe
Cornelio Tristan, Azteca, permission to use his poem, "Prison Life", & artwork, "History Unity Strength Peace"
Dion Wood, Karuk Tribal Office
Irene Zweirlein, Tribal Council Chair & Elvis A. Castillo & Amah-Mutsun Tribal Council (Ohlone)

Plus many other persons who have written, spoken, and otherwise contributed information to the public or myself. Without your cooperation and contributions, this book could not have been possible. Many thanks.

Opposite: Mr. and Mrs. Jim Pepper prepare acorns above their home on the Klamath River.

(photo A.W. Erickson, 1894, State Parks)

TABLE of CONTENTS

TABLE OF CONTENTS

THE PEOPLES OF CALIFORNIA

THE INDIAN PEOPLES OF CALIFORNIA ARE STILL HERE, AS THEY have been for many thousands of years. How many are here now is not that important. Where they are and what they are doing is important.

Just where they came from is a curiosity that has not been resolved with any certainty by archaeologists or anthropologists. The various tribes' tales of creation do not suggest migration, an idea that is dear in the minds of the anthropologists. For speculation purposes (and grant funding), there is the old notion that some bands managed to sneak across the 40-odd miles of the Bering Strait between Russia and Alaska during a warm and dry spell when the ground was not submerged, nor the sea ice blockading the Strait. When? Maybe ten or twelve thousand years before the present (BP). Efforts to find evidence of animal bones in the Alaska-Canada region before 13,000 years BP have failed. But reputable archaeologists have wood and leather and bone fragments and charcoal and arrowheads dating back to at least 10-14,000 years BP, right here in several different locations within California. While it seems that there is no record of Siberians before approximately 25,000 years ago, some pieces of stone found in the Mojave Desert appear to have been chipped (by one estimate) much longer ago than that.

HOW EVER THEY ARRIVED, THE EARLIEST CALIFORNIANS SETTLED HERE. THEY FOUND THE LIFE~SUSTAINING FOOD, WATER, AND SHELTER THEY NEEDED. THEIR LANDS WERE, AND ARE, PRETTY RUGGED IN CHARACTER, RESTRICTING TRAVEL AND MOVEMENT, EXCEPT FOR THE MOST ADVENTURESOME TRADERS.

APPARENTLY WE NEED A NEW THEORY. THE RED EARTH People left specific patterns of red ochre and stones in their ceremonial grounds in Michigan, Wisconsin, Nova Scotia (eastern Canada), Norway, Sweden, and Finland that go back about 25,000 years. Where are they now? The Lapps of northern Scandinavia have the same ceremonial practices today. Did a few of the earliest Michiganders pick up and journey west? Are we related?

Early Ainu (a Caucasoid people) from northern Japanese islands were probably excellent boat builders. Maybe some of them or their friends went on fishing and colonizing expeditions early on. Recently, a village in central Chile was unearthed, disclosing 12,800-year-old human bones. Why not? Maybe they came from Africa, only a few hundred miles to the east of South America. That is, if you require that all humans came from Africa. Thor Heyerdahl showed that he could sail from South American to Polynesia on a balsa raft. Some DNA comparisons have been made between Asian (Siberian) and North American Natives, and between Europeans and North Americans. The results point to an Asian connection, but not with a perfect match.

Maybe we should begin to listen to the ancients here in North America. They tell their own stories. (*See p.21*).

How ever they arrived, the earliest Californians settled here. They found the life-sustaining food, water, and shelter which they needed. Their lands were, and are, pretty rugged in character, restricting travel and movement, except for the most adventuresome traders.

THIS BOOK IS THE STORY OF THE PERSISTENCE OF THESE PEOPLES. There is an important concept framed by the people who study peoples: cultural imperative. The term implies that a culture (or strong tribal tradition) will endure in spite of tremendous adversity. Adversity was what California's native peoples received; persistence of their cultures is what they offer the world.

Remnants or blends of the earliest tribes do indeed exist. Most are now organized as they may have never been before. Most are finding the threads of their existence in language and family customs, recovering their relation to the lands where they live.

You will find here a brief story of the earliest peoples, their development into tribes, their encounters with various alien cultures, and how their descendants survive, adapt, and thrive in a dominant culture not their own.

Bill Franklin, elder of the Calaveras Band of Mi-wuk
Indians, helped design two well-known roundhouses,
one at Chaw-Se Indian Grinding Rocks State Park,
and the one, here, at the Band's home in West Point.

(dhe, 1995)

LANGUAGE TELLS US SOMETHING ABOUT TRIBAL ORIGINS & TRIBAL RELATIONSHIPS

LANGUAGE IS the most commonly used method of distinguishing the tribal peoples of California. The colors of Map I, Ancestral Lands (opposite page) show the relationships among the tribes of California, to the best of the knowledge of linguists and anthropologists who have studied languages of the original peoples.

How do we know of these relationships? —from the known language vocabularies of the original peoples, their tribal histories, and artifacts. Linguists have long known that early California was one of the richest language centers of the world. Map I shows the relation (or non-relation) of most of these.

We know from their accounts that the first European explorers and settlers recognized that the tribes spoke many diverse and also many similar languages. How did this come about?

The theory (and it is not at all proven) is that in the earliest times, these peoples had come here from a common source (probably from the east), slowly populating vacant areas. As time passed, most of the groups settled themselves among the remote valleys, deserts, and, and plains of the state. Languages that these people brought with them slowly changed over the millenia and became different from their nearby, but separated relatives.

MANY VOCABULARIES, EARLIER THOUGHT TO HAVE BEEN LOST, HAVE BEEN RECOVERED; AND MANY TRIBES HAVE INSTITUTED LANGUAGE CLASSES FOR THEIR TRIBAL MEMBERS, BOTH YOUNG AND OLD.

Even though separated, there were always relatives, friends, and traders who brought new words or exchanged the names for things and concepts.

One glance at the relationships suggests that the earliest Hokan speakers (blue colors) may have became somehow separated by the Penutian speakers (green colors), who also occupied Central Valley land west of the Sacramento River. The Uto-Aztecan speakers (shown in yellows) apparently found their way into California from the east, settling east of the Sierras, the Owens Valley, and into the western Mojave and Los Angeles/San Fernando Basins.

MEANWHILE, in the far northern parts of California, Athapascan and Lutuamian speakers from further north became permanent residents. Other languages seem to have originated solely in isolated areas.

Studies of these languages have increased immensely in the last few years. Many vocabularies, earlier thought to have been lost, have been recovered; and many tribes have instituted language classes for their tribal members, both young and old. Knowledge of your ancestral language will greatly strengthen your pride in your roots. (*Also see p.57, Tribal Cultures— section on languages.*)

THE LANGUAGE FAMILIES that have been identified by linguists are given here along with their present-day tribal groups*:

Several of the tribal languages and dialects listed here have merged with others or have been lost. The names used here, both tribes and dialects, are the ones most commonly used in 2000.

ALGIC, related somewhat to Algonkian languages from the upper midwest and east (browns); *Yurok* and *Wiyot*

ATHAPASKAN, related to languages of the northwest (pinks); *Tolowa, Hupa/Chilula/Whilkut, Tsnungwe, Wailaki/Nongatl/Lassik/Sinkyone/ Mattole (Eel River tribes), Cahto*

YUKIAN, not closely related to any outside group, but possibly Siouan (grays); *Yuki, Coast Yuki, Huchnom, Wappo (?)*

HOKAN, described as "the oldest *in situ* California language family" [Hokan is the Atsugewi word for "two"], but not closely related to other outside groups (blues); *Karuk, Shasta, Chimariko, Yana, Pit River* (11 bands, including *Atsugewi*), *Pomo* (7 groups), *Esselen, Salinan, Chumash* (6 groups), *Ipai, Tipai, Kumeyaay, Mohave, Quechan*

PENUTIAN, a very early, probably original California language group, not closely related to other outside groups [Penutian is also a made-up word for "two"] (greens); *Wintun (Wintu, Nomlaki, Patwin), Maidu* (including *Konkow* and *Nisenan*), *Yokuts* or *Yokotch* (several dialects, including *Chukchansi, Choinumni, Wukchumni, Yowlumni, Tachi*), *Miwok (Coast, Lake, Plains, Northern Sierra, Central Sierra, Southern Sierra), Ohlone (Costanoan)* (including *Muwekma, Amah, Mutsun, Rumsen* or *Rumsien, Karkin, Chochenyo,* others), *Washoe.*   (*continued*)

This classification is largely from the Smithsonian Institution's Handbook of North American Indians, Vol. 8, California (1978), "Native Languages of California", by William Shipley. It varies somewhat from the map, "Native Languages and Language Families of North America", by Ives Goddard, in App.VII, Vol.11, (1996). which refers to some California Hokan and Penutian relationships as "super-families", but ignores differences among the Uto-Aztecan groups.

ANCESTRAL HOMELANDS
MAP 1

OREGON

Tolwa
Karuk
CRESCENT CITY
Yurok
DOCTOR ROCK
Modoc
Goose Lake
Medicine Lake
Shastans
Chilula
Hupa
MT. SHASTA
Pit River
ALTURAS
Whilkut
Wiyot
Tsnungwe
Chimariko
Atsugewi Eagle Lake
MT. LASSEN
Northern Paiute
Nongatl
Wintu
Yana
Mountain Maidu
Mattole Lo Lahnko
Lassik
REDDING
Honey Lake
Pyramid Lake
Sinkyone To Cho Be
Wailaki
Nomlaki
ISHI'S VILLAGE
QUINCY
Cahto
Yuki
CHICO
Konkow Maidu
Pomo
Clear Lake
Patwin
SUTTER BUTTES
Washoe
Lake Tahoe
MT. KONOCTI
Lake Miwok
Nisenan Maidu
Wappo
SACRAMENTO
Northern Paiute
Coast Miwok
Plains Miwok
Bay Miwok
SAN FRANCISCO
STOCKTON
Sierra Miwok
Eastern Mono (Northern Paiute)
MT. DIABLO
Mono Lake
NEVADA
Muwekma
Northern Valley Yokuts
MERCED
Chukchansi North Fork
Western Mono (Monache)
Owens Valley Paiute
Ohlone (Costanoan)
Mutsun
FRESNO
Tachi
Dunlap
Rumsen
Esselen
VENTANA PEAKS
Owens Lake
Panamint and Coso Shoshone
Salinan
Foothill Yokuts tribes
Tubatulabal
Wukchumni
Chemehuevi
Southern Valley Yokuts
Tule Lake
BAKERSFIELD
Kawaiisu
SAN LUIS OBISPO
Kitanemuk
Mt. Pinos
VICTORVILLE
Mohave
Chumash
Tataviam
SANTA BARBARA
Fernandeño/Tataviam
Vanyume/Serrano
TWENTY-NINE PALMS
VENTURA
Tongva (Gabrielino)
LOS ANGELES
Acjachmem (Juaneño/Luiseño)
Cahuilla
MT. SAN JACINTO (Taquitz)
Halchidhoma
Salton Sea
MT. PALOMAR
Cupeño
Ipai
MT. LAGUNA
Quechan
SAN DIEGO
Kumeyaay (Tipai)
YUMA
Cócopa
Tipai
BAJA CALIFORNIA NORTE

Hokan								
Penutian								
Yukian								
Uto-Aztecan								
Athapascan								
Algic								

Shared or unoccupied

LUTUAMIAN (probably Penutian-related) (purple); *Modoc, Klamath*

UTO-AZTECAN, or **SHOSHONEAN***, related to many languages to the east of California and into Mexico. There are three branches: TAKIC, TUBATULABAL (both in California), and NUMIC, the latter found also in the Great Basin and southern plains (yellows); *Northern Paiute, Eastern Mono, Western Mono* or *Monache, Owens Valley Paiute, Panamint* and *Coso Shoshone, Kitanemuk, Tataviam (Fernandeño), Tongva (Gabrieleno), Ajachemem* and *Luiseño, Serrano/Vanyume, Cahuilla, Cupeño, Tubatulabal*

For the purposes of oversimplification, or relating things, I will with some hesitancy, almost equate the following: Uto-Aztecan=Shoshonean=Paiute

Above: Anthropomorphic and animal figures, solar diagrams in their original bright colors are seen on the ceiling stones of the Tule River Reservation Painted Rock. (Permission to visit obtainable at the Tribal Offices.) (dhe, 1985)

Below: Designs at "Red Rock" in the Owens Valley near Bishop. The site is a large reddish granite outcrop in a desert mesa. Hundreds of designs, figures, and symbols are carved here dating from about 1000 BC to 1000 AD—as religious aids to hunting and other rituals. The Owens Valley and nearby desert areas were a favorite location for many such petroglyphs, probably because its wetter climate attracted game, which made for many hunting opportunities. (dhe, 1984)

On the high cliffs of a dry wash, ancestors of Paiute hunters carved these designs in the Owens Valley. The central figure appears to be someone wearing a skirt, but has been more appropriately described as the sun seen above clouds, causing rain. To the sides, the series of vertical lines indicate falling rain. (dhe, 1982)

Within the Lava Beds National Monument is a very long wall of petroglyphs, carved by the early ancestors of the Modoc poeple on an ancient cliff of ancient lakeshore. These designs are only a very few of the hundreds: shield (protection), fallen shield, lines with circles denote a counting of something, zig-zag lines show going back and forth, human-like figures are women wearing basket caps. (dhe, 1982)

INTRODUCTION

THE INDIAN PEOPLE of California have shown their will and ability to survive, to grow, to perpetuate their heritage, and to demonstrate it to all the world, whether that world watches or not. Survival is not yet guaranteed—it never is—but it is easier. The hearts and minds of all the people, Native and non-Native, are not yet won to the obligations of cultural survival.

arts, poetry, Indian pride, and self-determination are coming into view. Everyone can now honor the Native American efforts by celebrating and participating in the public ceremonies and by sharing with others what is learned from the many tribal cultures. All persons should go into a culture well-informed about what they are witnessing, and who these people are who have survived to a new century.

SOME USEFUL ANTHROPOLOGICAL TERMS:

"Archaeology" consists of studies of the records of human life and activities from as far back as earliest humans, and can take us up to even recent times (last century). But this term blends into another, favored by many Indians themselves, that is, "cultural anthropology," which might best be described as a study of the development of the cultural and social patterns and customs of the various peoples. A simpler term is "ethnography."

Terms that anthropologists use for this earliest period are "prehistoric" and "protohistoric." "Prehistoric" simply means any time before written records or recalled memory. There are few very old oral histories in California tribal life, and the first written or recalled stories are from the Spanish explorers.

"Protohistoric" is the time or events immediately before the historic period in which patterns of life were rather well-formed—a period usually just before contact with the white man. Protohistoric information and facts can often be obtained from written accounts of people living in "historic" times or from relatively recent archaeological sources. Nevertheless, many histories of tribes and peoples before European contact are well-known from the passing down of oral traditions. Others, tragically, have been lost.

The more recent we get, however, the more touchy the subject of archaeology becomes. Many present Indian peoples and tribes are as understandably reluctant to have persons of any descent poking around their ancestors' graves as, say, whites would be to have "urban archaeologists" digging up Arlington Cemetery or Colma, California.

So our conjectures on early life of the first people of California must come from several sources: archaeology (diggings revealing tools, burials, etc.); from study of modes of life of other cultures living under similar circumstances; and, to some extent, from the historical knowledge of the ways of early Indian life, especially in language differences.

CONTINUITY AND COHERENCE of time, ancestors, spirit, and customs infuse the life of Native Americans, more than most other cultures, despite attempts to compartmentalize and analyze their ways. Archaeologists and anthropologists, sociologists, linguists, and others have attempted to segment these peoples' lives, supposedly to understand them better. But for them, life is a continuous thread woven not only from what can be seen and heard and sensed but also from unseen and unfelt sources. All of us, of any race, realize that our own lives, our own "history", is the sum of all that has influenced our lives, not least of which is our own parents and ancestors. So it is with Native peoples, who know well that life is this thread, woven into a fabric of other past and present and future lives, not distinct strands to be examined fiber by fiber.

It is this continuity of Native life, though changed, modified, and adapted through the years, that I wish to emphasize in this book. Here, today, are the descendants of the original Native peoples of California, and here is their origins and history.

•Readers may feel that some of the patterns or phrases in this book are repeats. True. This is because *Native California Guide* is in part an update, a remake, and a vastly expanded *Earth Is Our Mother* (updated every 2 years from 1986-1996), blended and combined with the essence of *California Indian Country* (1992). More than 40 interviews with contributions from tribal leaders and service-providers in just about every imaginable situation are new to this work. So much progress and so many changes have occurred within the Indian communities that they deserve a fresh look. Just trying to keep up is, in that worn phrase, really exciting. The Calendar of Events used to be about three pages. Look at it now. Space is being left to add new items as they occur. Expect *Native California Guide* to be updated every two years. You all know the reasons for the increased Indian presence: a realization that the past was almost lost and there has been a way to regain it through money and interest.

The difficulties of the future will not be the burdens of the past but the difficulties of stimulating enthusiasm among the young, maintaining continuity, and reweaving the threads of the ancient ways into the fabric of new patterns.

Enthusiasm is everywhere. The reader can experience the new Native American reality and dreams with visits to Indian country, and look deep, beyond the casinos. In all parts of the state, cultures are emerging from obscurity, with able and proud leaders; scores of inspired young dancers are led by elders who carefully teach the old ways; the results of the efforts by determined tribal and spiritual leaders in housing, health,

THE WEAVE of LIFE: THE FABRIC of HISTORY

IT IS AS IF THE FABRIC of Indian history, woven with the many designs of all the tribes, had been folded over and over many times, then laid away for a while. Only in the recent years has the fabric begun to unfold again, revealing patterns that had been hidden. Some seem to be upside down as we peek deep into the folds. Most appear to be faded, some more than others. Some are completely decayed, while others disclose their ancient patterns even through the tatters of the original fabric. Some appear to us only as fossils—the imprint remains, but the fabric has disintegrated.

Patterns of some strands are still with us, but the fabric is unravelled, awaiting a master weaver who can work it back into a semblance of the pattern that was there before. Some of the patterns seem to have changed in an eery way. The original colors and values and shapes aren't as before. But new weavers can make beautiful patterns with old fibers, too. What is their meaning—these patterns? Some are obvious, some are puzzling, discernable only with the help of the elders, who participated in the weaving. Some are interpreted by younger persons, who learned the arrangements from earlier weavers.

Eventually, these patterns of the past come to be seen as legitimate parts of the whole. Each tribe possesses fragments of the entire quiltwork of the weaving. Where parts are missing, once in a while it becomes necessary for weavers to make their own tradition from what they believe is true, then go on.

THE EARLY CALIFORNIA INDIANS were not
designers of imperial kingdoms or powerful hierarchies of jade and gold and stone. They were not people of the thundering of horse or bison hooves or of booming drums. They did not require a single fortress or defensive fortification. They were and are people of many quiet cultures, very colorful in special ways, and highly respectful of the land and their people. They have dispersed and settled over the entire land. They left no monuments to class oppression or bristling defenses. They were self-governing and free. They have been the most equitable and democratic of people.

IN THE NEXT CENTURY we will see a grand reweaving of the Native peoples' fabric; the threads and leaves and roots and shoots will not only be reconstructed from older concepts, but original patterns will be formed. The future will not be as it would have been without the tearing or fraying of the fabric, but it is made whole by weavers with new knowledge of their past and an exuberant imagination for the future.

Above Right: Pajaro Valley Ohlone dancers at the Honoring of the Elders Gathering, Mt. Madonna, near present day Gilroy: Yana-hea (Patrick Orozco); Monsoom, "Gray Fox", (Marcus Rodriguez); Tru-la La-che-amk "Thunder Woman", (Teresa Renaga); and Summer (no other name given)

(dhe, 1699)

Above Left: Depiction of prehistoric Anderson Marsh, Clear Lake.

(by archaeologist Paul Peterson 1995)

NATIVE AMERICAN WISDOM says that the land is a living part of creation. Given proper concern for the interconnections that permeate all things—the air, the water, the rocks, the creatures, the humans—creation will survive and all its parts will exist in harmony. If we truly know the earth, we are prepared to care for it.

This book is a presentation in word and picture of that California that has been the home of the Native California American.

THE EARLIEST TIMES
THE FiRST WEAViNG

THREE FACTORS profoundly affect life in any setting. The oldest of these is *geology*. The very structure of the earth under us governs our concepts of life and how we will live. Do we live on rocks, on soil, on sand, on mud, near rivers or lakes, near seas? Are they red rocks or grey rocks or green? Is our soil acid or basic? Are our waters acid or salty or full of minerals?

The structure of the geology then determines the *geography*. Are our slopes steep and tall and mountainous, or just hilly, or do they slope at all? Are they drenched with rains, or blanketed with snow in winter, or do mountains block the rains and give us a desert, or something in between?

The interplay of all the geographic and geologic forces upon us, acting upon the millions of living species around us, then form our *habitat*. Are we residents of a coastal town where we have salt-water fish, crabs, shellfish? Or do we live along a huge river, where eons ago floods gave us terraces which support deciduous trees and willows and bushes? Or do we live in a desert where we get our water from a well, and create much of our own habitat with irrigation?

These three features shape the requirements for existence. Redwoods and alders don't grow in the Mojave Desert. Joshua trees and yucca don't grow in Del Norte County. Gila lizards don't thrive along the Klamath River, and trout are hard to find in the Mojave River.

The forces that shape the conditions for living are like the pieces of a "living quilt". Most segments are different, but all are sewn together into a whole. Let us consider the parts and how they are put together, as well as how they change.

Humans have lived all over California, in all kinds of settings, for countless generations. The first people chose their places carefully—not just because of water and flat land, but for their intrinsic power and the special relation they would have with the geology, geography, and habitat. Whether village sites, burial grounds, hunting grounds, fishing spots, gathering grounds, places for prayer and vision, Native peoples saw each one as special in some some way, even sacred. Even protected spots in the desert, seemingly no different from others, were chosen for their inherent qualities. This sensitivity to their surroundings extended to plants for medicine or nourishment, to forests and the wood they provide for fuel, to animals. Through the centuries these places became recognized for their exceptional qualities and are known as sacred sites or power places (*p.48*).

Even among Native peoples, not everyone can determine or sense the exquisite relation of the forces in a particular spot or the powers inherent in a particular habitat. Early peoples and their descendants have recognized that certain people do possess this special ability. We call them today by many names: men and women with powerful medicine, shamans, holy persons, spiritual persons, doctors, priests.

Nevertheless, almost any of us who is sensitive to the earth and its forces, using quiet concentration, can feel and accept the power of these places.

VILLAGE SiTES OR HUNTING CAMPS had to be chosen carefully to provide sources of water and food and shelter. We will see later in this book how different peoples made use of the variety of materials in

An Indian doctor always carried his or her bag of curing supplies. This is the kit of Thomas Smith, a Coast Miwok singing doctor; the kit is maintained as a Smith family heirloom. His supplies are: clapper sticks with quartz crystals, with the largest crystals used for the most serious illnesses; four pouches, two of buckskin and two woven with Maru religious designs—the contents (laid out) are charmstones for various pains, herbs, beads, pigments; mortars and pestles for grinding the pigments and herbs; small obsidian blades for cutting to suck out pains (illnesses); a large blade for hide scraping; a decorated bamboo whistle (music always accompanies doctoring); pegs from a "ghost house"; golden eagle and flicker feathers; a beaded flicker wing to brush away soreness of the joints; a cocoon rattle with ant hill gravel and buzzard quill handle.   (State Parks , 1950)

the habitat available to them. (Anthropologists call this use the "material culture" of a culture.)

Finding good water isn't always as easy as you might think. Even in the wet north, a deluge can silt up or muddy a normally quiet creek. It might even wipe out a poorly sited village. In dry California, much water isn't even visible. Some Cahuilla villages, for example, dug deep walk-in wells to get access to the precious stuff. The first Indians were very good at finding springs and water sources, but unfortunately usually lost them to those who invaded and took over their lands. Across the Mojave Desert in the 1850s, the U.S. Army set up a series of forts, each a day's ride apart, from Ft. Mojave to Barstow. Each fort occupied a water source that had been located by the ancient ancestors of Paiute, Mohave, or Serrano/Vanyume peoples. (*Appendix IV*)

Village sites also had to be near a sources of fiber for clothing and other uses such as basket-making. Even if the earliest peoples had to use animal skins (because early California weather could become very cold), they still had to stitch up their clothes. Some clothes were made of cotton-like fiber, and containers like bags and baskets were made of fibers. Some homes were even woven from thatching. In the desert, yucca and willow make excellent fibers, whereas in other places, grasses, tule reeds, soft tree twigs, roots serve (*p.64*).

It is therefore no surprise that for many tribes the regular spawning run of the fish became a sort of New Year's event symbolizing the renewal of the world every year—signaling a celebration. Imagine how the people thought of fishing… They would wait from a perch on a boulder by the rushing stream—in a place their grandfathers told them had always been the best spot. Somehow, the fish were always there.

In the old days Indians wove their own nets from

Tule reed was the material of choice for weaving boats—in marshlands of lakes and estuaries. This fisher was photographed in 1880 in Clear Lake. Replicas of these can be seen in several museums today; a few are waterworthy. (Southwest Museum, 1880)

IN MANY PARTS OF CALIFORNIA, along the coast, rivers, and the streams that flow into lakes, the salmon run regularly every year—like a calendar. They struggle upstream right through Indian reservations: the Yurok, the Hupa, the Smith River, the Karuk, the Pit River, the Resighini, the Big Lagoon, the Manchester, the Kashaya, the Round Valley, the Colusa, the Grindstone, the Paskenta, the Yo-Ka-Yo, the Cloverdale.

Other fish swim near or alongside the Tsurai, the Quartz Valley, the Table Bluff, the Blue Lake, the Ft. Bidwell, the Maidu ceremonial grounds at Roxie Peconum, the Alpine Washoe, the Redding, the Rumsey, the Hopland, E-lem, Big Valley, the Robinson, the Upper Lake, Ya-Ka-Ama, the North Fork, the Cold Springs, the Tule River, the Santa Ynez, the Bridgeport, the Bishop, the Kern Valley Ceremonial Site, the Ft. Mojave, the Chemehuevi, the Colorado River Tribes, the Ft. Yuma, the Rincon, the Pala, the La Jolla, the Agua Caliente. Smaller streams run through many more, though some are dry much of the year.

rushes or iris stalks or grasses, or they chipped obsidian spear points and shaped wooden shafts for spear fishing. That's what the grandfathers had done, and what their grandfathers had done before them.

How many grandfathers told how many grandchildren where to fish? Maybe those tales go all the way back to when Coyote or one of the other Great Spirits created the world. So far as they knew, the people had always gone fishing in these spots and in this way—for in their ancient oral histories, there were no tales or myths of any wandering tribe who finally settled in this valley.

TODAY, some of the families who live along the river get out their rods and reels, maybe a small boat. A few men who have a large family to provide for bring out nets with their boats, to do a pleasant chore that has been done for as far back as anyone can remember. Swarming around the Indians like wasps, the white man comes, too; with fancy gear, campers, and boats. Hopefully, there will be enough for all. But village celebrations are fewer and different now.

CHARACTERISTIC of most of the native peoples of California, there were no written calendars as such kept, just the seasonal changes that happened every year about same time. The people had great oral traditions and histories. As a matter of fact, when an outsider asked an elder when some great event took place (a flood, an earthquake, or even family births), that elder could recall dates up to five generations earlier with some accuracy.

Making fire beside the Klamath River. The sharp long stick is twirled in a pit pushed into the dry flat tinder. Friction ignites the combustible material and fire is at hand.   (State Parks)

The elders could not know that their very distant ancestors had not always been fishing in these places and had migrated there several millennia earlier. (They couldn't know that these ancestors might not have even liked fish.) If their people were living in northern California along the Klamath, they might go back as far as 3,000-5,000 years. If they were living along a fishing stream in southern California, the people might go back another thousand years. Either way, four or five millennia might as well be "since creation," as they knew it.

And who were these ancestors? How did they come to be here in "Alta California"? A few recent archaeological finds (not without considerable controversy

and indefinite dating) put humans in such varied parts of California as Santa Rosa Island off Santa Barbara and the Calico Hills near Barstow possibly as far back as 40,000 years ago. Who these people were can only be guessed, as we know very little about their origins and their mode of life. But they were forming the first bits of the fabric of Native life

ASSEMBLING THE MATERIAL
~12,000~2,000 BC

LET US GO FAR BACK in prehistory to the time when the great glaciers were melting, geologically called the late Pleistocene, about 12,000 BC, California's climate was remarkably different from what it is now. No one had to fight over water rights; the whole state was either wet or frozen, and now-extinct animals roamed the land—camels, tigers, sloths, tiny horses, and huge mammoths. Immense lakes covered places that are desert today.

SOME SPECTACULAR INDIAN COUNTRY today is to be found at archaeological and geological sites of the very earliest Indian land:
Cedarville Rancheria and Fort Bidwell Reservation look out on salt lakes that once were fresh-water tributaries to the great ancient Lake Lahontan, which covered eastern California and western Nevada. Two nearby Nevada Paiute reservations are at Pyramid Lake and Walker Lake, other remnants of that great lake. The Timbi-Sha Shoshone Tribe occupies the very bottom of an ancient lake bed in Death Valley. Large parts of the Torres-Martinez Reservation lie flooded under the salty waters of the Salton Sea, a residue of ancient Lake Cahuilla, which covered the Coachella Valley, while other parts border its extinct beaches. Lone Pine Reservation sits on the former shore of Owens Lake, which dried up because Los Angeles pirated the water. At Calico, near Barstow, once on the wooded shore of ancient Lake Mohave, some early, unknown tribe ran a factory, shaping thousands of arrows and lances and scrapers for hundreds of years. Dr. Richard Leakey, of African anthropology fame, suggested that this Early Man site may go back as far as 40,000 years!

ABOUT THE SAME TIME, as early as 5,000 BC, others of these Early Peoples were crafting objects for living on Santa Rosa Island, off Santa Barbara. Most anthropologists speculate where these early peoples came from—maybe from Asia hop-skipping alongside the ice sheet by boat, maybe across the Bering Strait by a land or ice bridge, and then southeastward, if the ice melted enough to permit passage across Alaska and the Yukon. Or maybe they came westward across the continent from a frozen north Atlantic, or northward from who knows where. These are the theories about a race of people offered by another race who arrived late in California: "We came in late, but we weren't the first. Others must have come in, too, as we did."

But these are only theories, which come from those who are educated in devising theories to fit their facts, and believe in the importance of them. These are not the stories of the Native peoples.

TRIBAL STORYTELLERS can narrate the stories of their origin; moreover, some elders can point out actual places that the stories tell about. The Kawaiisu people of the southern Sierras revere the Coso Hot Springs (located within the China Lake Naval Station), a place where the earth can be heard to continuously rumble and gurgle. This place obviously bears a close relation to Mother Earth, and her geyser outpourings of vapors and gases vividly demonstrate the powers of creation. The sacred creation place of the Cahuilla people of the southern California deserts and mountains is the conical massif of *Tahquitz* (Tákwish), far up on the southwestern summit of San Jacinto Peak (near Idyllwild). This mountain, the tallest in the area, is a spectacular creator of storms, lightning, and thunder.

Not all creation places are so awesome. A Konkow Maidu story tells of Earth-Initiate (creator), who took a bit of mud and slime from Turtle's fingernails and created Earth. His first landfall was a hillock in the Sacramento River floodplain just south of Chico. The Yurok world center is a small pyramidal mountain which causes dangerous rapids in the Klamath River, at its confluence with the Salmon River. From such stories of origins, we see the tremendous power of the great spirits in transforming otherwise insignificant places into places of great power. Perhaps the lesson is that no place is truly insignificant.

In the stories of their beginnings, these peoples make no specific reference to time, but do we really need one? Do we need to know the composer and year of a song to appreciate its beauty?

Whatever their origin, the best archaeological evi-

In 1914, University of California anthropologist A.L. Kroeber took Ishi on a field trip back to his homeland on Deer Creek, above Chico. The purposes of the trip were to re-acquaint Ishi with his ancestral land, and to observe his survival skills. Here, he shows harpooning. (photo by A.L. Kroeber, Phoebe Apperson Hearst Museum of Anthropology, University of California, Berkeley)

dence shows that around 11,000 or 12,000 years ago, several bands of very early Indians were making ornate and well designed lance points and arrowheads—finely-shaped like leaves, with fluted center depressions to fit into the arrow shaft. These early works of art have been found along the San Dieguito River (near the San Diego Mission), the Calico site, and Borax Lake in Lake County.

Somewhat more recently (7,000-6,000 BC), people were settling all over the state: from Oroville (Butte County) to Tulare Lake (west of Bakersfield), Diablo Canyon (San Luis Obispo County coast), and Topanga Canyon (Los Angeles County). These are the earliest known peoples who settled California Indian country. Some of their artifacts may be seen at the Lakeport Museum (Lake County), the Morro Bay State Park Museum (near San Luis Obispo), and in other, larger archaeological museums of the state. The materials for the weaving were being assembled.

BEFORE EARLY HUMANS grouped into tribes, small bands were exploring the land to find permanent places to live. As mentioned before, the earliest artifacts found in California are projectile points—probably for use with the atlatl (a sling-like stick for throwing arrows or spears), or for use as spears and stone tools (for scraping and working hides and wood). These have all come from sources in southern California and the Central Valley. The lack of seed-grinding tools seems to tell us that these peoples subsisted mostly by hunting—deer, birds, and fish, and also now-extinct early California animals like camel, bison, and horse. Some archaeologists think that the hunting techniques were so efficient that these animals may have been *driven to extinction*.

By 6,000 BC, milling stones for grinding seeds were

The cyclorama at the Santa Barbara Museum of Natural History gives a good idea of the activities in an ancient Chumash coastal community. (dhe, 1992)

Throughout the state, conflicts between tribes were rare and usually resolved by negotiation. In the absence of large scale tribal warfare, armor such as this worn by a Pomo warrior was seldom utilized and remarkably ineffective against U.S. Cavalry weapons. This photo demonstration was staged around 1900. (State Parks)

being used, which means that more food was being collected from plants than before. People began to settle into more permanent communities, especially in southern California, as their discard piles (middens) show.

Later, by 3,000 BC, food sources were much more diversified, and included fishing on both land and sea, as well as hunting and plant gathering. Northern California was just being settled, but more distinctive cultures were developing in such widely varied places as the Cosumnes-Mokolumne River basin, coastal Santa Barbara-San Luis Obispo Counties, coastal Los Angeles County and San Diego County, and the cool, damp land soon to become desert (especially Owens Valley).

BURIALS became more elaborate, with offerings to the dead, indicating belief in an after-life. Basketry became well-developed, even elegant, and the household and village cache of utensils and implements was plenteous and varied—sharpening stones, cooking vessels, smoking pipes, fire drills, shell and bone ornaments, whistles.

THE WEAVING OF TRIBAL PATTERNS ~2000 BC TO 1500 AD

By this point, the glaciers had retreated and melted, the climate had grown warmer, and many of the larger lakes were evaporating and disappearing—in general, the ecology was becoming more static and as we know it today. This is the protohistorical era, in which differences in peoples became more pronounced.

Large numbers of peoples had by now settled into their valleys, mountain retreats, and coastal villages. They improved on tools, and made more ornate and elegant baskets, woodwork, and regalia. Hundreds of years of relative isolation allowed for more diversity to develop. Languages became increasingly divergent, even unique. It has been estimated that in 1760, California natives spoke more than sixty different languages and dialects, most of which were mutually unintelligible. (*See section on languages, p.12*)

Great religions arose and spread, artwork increased in complexity and beauty, family relations and governance became more definite. Peoples maximized their relation with the local ecology and learned to manage the land and food sources.

Along the Colorado River, groups adopted the tech-

niques of pottery-making from nearby Hakataya peoples in Arizona.* They began to farm the land with beans, corn, and squash as major crops. They adopted other Hakataya strategies of living and their religion.

Groups everywhere developed special characteristics—sometimes borrowed and adapted, but mostly invented for their own ecological niche. In an unusual flowering along the Santa Barbara coast, the peoples began to develop an extraordinarily complex culture, to become the Chumash.

Overall, two other important things happened. Someone, probably from the northeast, brought in bows and arrows around 2,000 years ago. Hunting was, of course, already well-developed, and the introduction of this new missile-launcher increased both the number and kinds of animals hunted.

At the same time, many more acorn-grinding tools were made, which tells us that acorn eating ("balanophagy" is the fancy word) had become a major part of their diets. Once the technique of leaching out the bitter tannin was discovered, acorns became popular and healthy, and have remained to this day.

TO SAY THAT THESE BANDS became settled doesn't mean that they necessarily were immobilized. In general, the peoples of the various cultures adapted well to their situations and surroundings, but from all evidence, some disruptions of populations took place from other bands wandering in. However, no large-scale "invasion" of hordes of tribes took place.

California terrain is rather rugged in most parts, and where it isn't rough, it can be dry (at least before irrigation) and difficult. For the early natives it was geographically divided in this way—once settled, the local tribes or peoples developed rather independently, and it seems obvious that the multilingual divergence only

Arrow points about 10,000 years old have been found here at Borax Lake, just over the hill behind E-lem. The lake is unusual in that it has no surface outlet, but is not salty. The water level varies only a little, indicating that the lava rock on all sides must be quite porous. The site must have been ideal for its Pomo ancestors. (dhe, 1998)

*"Hakataya" is the archaeological name for the ancient culture to the east of the Colorado River, mostly in Arizona and partly contemporaneous with the "Anazsazi".

A lady of the desert engaged in the ancient and necessary art of basketweaving, practiced throughout California. (Huntington Library, San Marino)

heightened the continuing sense of difference and mild hostilities between groups. (In a somewhat contradictory attitude, we tend to hold uniqueness and distinctiveness in peoples as a positive attribute.)

It is true, too, that in the absence of any large overall threat of invasion, war, or incursions (as in Maya and Aztec Central America or Inca Peru), internal and external cohesiveness of groups simply wasn't necessary. We will see how this separateness worked to disastrous consequences later. Nevertheless, there was much social intercourse between these many groups—in religion, trade, and alliances. (*See "Trade" later*)

EARLY EUROPEAN EXPLORERS (those who had any kind of ear for languages) found a confusing mix of languages and peoples. Corroborating suppositions of language relationships among people are secondary bits of evidence in the form of cultural paraphernalia: similarities or differences in beadwork, mortuary practices, arrowhead design, dietary preferences, value systems, and the like.

These are the assumptions and theories about these early peoples that the anthropologists tell us. From the tribes, though, there are other stories—dreamlike stories from great oral traditions of how their earth or their tribe was created. Sometimes the story tells that the first people emerged from under the earth; others say that they drifted in on a raft from the north; still others relate how man was sort of hatched from substances in the darkness. Stories from these sources have something to tell; they must not be dismissed as fiction or pure imagination.

IT WAS THIS FABRIC of ecology, tribes, and people* and their customs that existed entering the era of contact with Europeans. Short sketches of these peoples, based on the various regions of the state and the languages they speak, appear in this book just before the descriptions of the various Indian reservations and communities of today.

TRADE

A wide-ranging trade network was set up around California, much like those in Aztec Mexico and along the Mississippi River tributaries. Although trading in some northwestern California neighborhoods was considered a dangerous occupation (mistrust of outsiders), there were literally dozens of trade routes and trails found in protohistorical California—in all parts of the state. Many of these old trails are still known; some have even become highways. Traveling professional multilingual traders with diplomatic immunity passed from territory to territory over this well-known trade network, using an elaborate money system.

How do we know? First-hand historic accounts of routes tell us (some traces still exist), but we also have thousands of objects, mostly shell-bead money, hides, obsidian, and ornaments that ended up hundreds of miles from their origins.

As defined later, a "tribe" usually refers to a smaller community, while "people" refers to a larger linguistic or culture group.

THE RELIGIONS

AS THE GREAT RELIGIONS* of the various areas developed—the *World Renewal*, the *Kuksu*, the *toloache*†—each tribe or people traditionally invited neighboring groups to its ceremonies. Obviously, this was a great chance to exchange goods, ideas, gossip, potential mates, and ornaments. The mutual feasting and dancing also served unconsciously as a means of minimizing rivalries and intergroup conflict.

Most of the rituals were supervised by a specially chosen (by inheritance or spiritual inclination) member belonging to a secret society. These persons had considerable secular or "political" power within the community. In California, the dance leaders were either priests of a secret society or shamans (individuals with exceptional religious and medical powers). Fragments of these practices survive today.

Deer Dance Spirit, a painting by Frank LePena, Wintu. *As with many Native artists, Mr. LaPena's creative vision derives from a respect for traditional Indian religion and spiritual values.*

(painting courtesy of the artist)

The *World Renewal*, which is found mostly in the northwestern part of the state, is based largely on seasonal events, especially the salmon run in the rivers and obvious climatic and celestial changes in the seasons. Each year the world is renewed, as provided by the Creator, and the dances are thanksgiving for this. It is important to distinguish a celebration from a worship—there are no deities as such in California Native religions, rather spirits who look after us, guide us, or sometimes trick us.

The *Kuksu* (a powerful spirit) and the derivative *Bole-Maru* have a rather different orientation—originally honoring the persons gone before, but also honoring and celebrating all the spirits that sustain us. Their beautiful and fanciful regalia ("costumes" are clothing) were conceived "many, many years ago, before the knowledge of anyone alive," by dreamer-shamans. Humans dance the regalia and take upon themselves the spirit, much as do the Pueblo kachina dancers. We find *Kuksu* ceremonies mainly, but not exclusively, in the tribal groups who have roundhouses, in the central part of the state.

In the southwestern and south central parts of California, the powerful spirit is *Chi-ngich-ngish*. The shamans of this region were powerful doctor-priests who employed hypnosis and toloache, and even transformed themselves when necessary. The shamans in the south today are generally doctors, and lead ceremonies of healing. To the Chumash, the dolphin spirit is very powerful.

The tribes along the Colorado River had yet a different, more diffuse approach to religion, called *dreaming*. It was less structured, relying largely on *toloache* use for effective "dreaming". Doctoring of the sick and distressed was powerful, and is such to this day.

Unfortunately, most southern California Native communities lost many elements of their early religions during the time when the Spanish missionaries suppressed and nearly eradicated their beliefs and practices (*more on this later*). Nevertheless, the dance, songs, and important ceremonies are being revived in a number of areas; we can expect to see more of them in the near future, as peoples begin to emerge from their suppression and obscurity.

The early shamans, like those of the Great Basin and the north, whether under the influence of herbal potions or not, did undertake extraordinary artistic activities in connection with their work—rock art. California is blessed with the largest number of examples of painting, carving, and chipping on rocks in all of the United States. Most of these works were done in the period from 500 BC to 1500 AD. In most cases, the art was undertaken for a purpose, that is, by the shamans to enhance success in the hunt, fertility, the magnificence of a ceremony, or, occasionally, the power of the rain spirit. (*See the section on Rock Art, p.62.*)

* *The term "cult" was early assigned to the California Native religions. It has nothing to do with the term as used by modern media to denote small groups of extremist sects.*

† *Toloache is the Spanish term for datura, jimsonweed, loco weed. It is a common vine with white, trumpet-like flowers that flourishes over a large part of warmer California. Preparations made from any part of this plant are hallucinogenic, and fatally toxic in overdose. Early California cultures used this plant, as their neighbors use peyote, to sharpen perceptions, to dream, to gain insights, and occasionally to find lost objects. This is the plant used by the shaman Don Juan in the books by Carlos Castañeda.*

BIG HEAD DANCE

Look! in the doorway
as if coming out
of your dream
the huge figure
of the dancer
head covered
in starburst of feathers
wider than
reach of arms
dandelion puff
plumes shaking out
on willow wands
You hear before see him
plaintive cry
of reed whistle
held in teeth
moaning sigh
of the singers
shaking of wooden clackers
echo of woodpecker
in old oaks outside
Big Head shuffles
onto wet-down dirt
the only light
the rising flicker of fire
The singers pound
board-over-hole drum
on roundhouse floor
Big Pomo women
dark haired girls
shuffle step
at edge of circle
toss pennies
to feed the Big Head
Anglo children
eyes round with wonder
watch him dance
into their Santa Claus dreams
Reed whistle howls
like dying cry of lost locomotive
gone over dark pine rise of Sierra foothills
Big Head spins slowly around the circle
leaving now
backs out the door
firelight
on feathered headdress
smoke curling up
through roof hole
Ho! the women
Ho! the tiny children
Girls scoop pennies
from the floor
Big Head recedes into the place
where visions come from
The world of your dreams
will never be
the same
           —*Kathy Goss*

The singers and dancers here are seen in a 1910 Hesi ceremony of Wintu or Maidu origin, in the Central Valley.   (photo by A.L. Kroeber, Phoebe Apperson Hearst Museum
of Anthropology, University of California, Berkeley)

RIPPING & SHREDDING OF THE FABRIC
THE EUROPEAN INVASIONS

History is the propaganda of the victors.
The ultimate truth is that history ought to
consist of the anecdotes of the little people
who are caught up in it.
—Louis de Bernières, 1994

WHEN IT COMES TO those "historical" accounts of the early European presence in California, we hear of the adventurers' and explorers' exploits, but we never are told of their attitudes, their reasons, their belligerent and destructive behavior. But we do get their names in heroic headline size. During this period of less than 40 years the Spanish, English, Russian, Mexican, and Anglo-American powers slowly but relentlessly invaded Native California.

For 200 years before the fateful Spanish invasion in 1769, the Native population of Alta California had been paid only sporadic visits by European sailors, most of whom were rather rude to their hosts. The first, repairing his damaged boat near Point Reyes, was Sir Francis Drake (1579), followed by Sebastian Vizcaino (1602) and Juan de Oñate (1604). Other Spanish, English, Russian, and French ships put in along the coast for provisions, and the European penchant for arrogant behavior and violence gave the white man a deservedly bad reputation.

Toward the end of the 1700s, pressures from the east were beginning to have an impact on Alta California. The Quechan of southeastern California were already being stricken by European disease transmitted from the Spanish occupation of Pueblo country to the east. They lost one-fourth of their 4,000 people between 1740 and 1770. In eastern California, Utes from further east raided their Paiute cousins, capturing slaves to sell to New Mexican Spanish (Santa Fe, 1609). Agriculture and dietary customs were rapidly upset by the introduction of wheat into the Colorado River area in 1702. The horse came into use in eastern areas, although for many tribes it served mainly as food.

Up to this time California had been benignly ignored—too little gold, too much greenery, it didn't look enough like Spain, and military supply lines were already stretched far in México. It was into this milieu that Spanish authorities in Mexico dispatched Padre Fray Junípero Serra and his company to save souls, to explore, to claim the land for Spain, and to try to discourage Russian and English expansion. Rumors of gold "out there" helped raise his military escort.

SPANISH (1769~1825) & MEXICAN (1825~1846) SETTLEMENT
THE JUAN BAUTISTA DE ANZA EXPEDITION

IN 1759 Carlos III became King of Spain, and Alta California was part of the Spanish colony of Nueva España. Unrest was brewing in México, owing in large part to the extreme difference in levels of wealth between the Viceroyalty and bureaucrats and the miserable (Indian) peasants. In 1765, Carlos sent from Madrid a Visitador General (Inspector General), José de Galvez, to México to try to calm the situation.

Galvez tried numerous programs—new schools, new roads, and new explorations northwestward to find an overland route for settlers. This Spanish form of "pioneering" also served to take the pressure off a Spanish-Indian population, expanding beyond its resources.

Spanish expeditions were being organized for two other reasons: The first was to extend direct Spanish influence into the region, countering the push southward by Russian otter fur hunters and the British Hudson's Bay Company. (Later, the Russian-American Company set up shop at Ft. Ross in Pomo territory, and Hudson's Bay opened a post in Yerba Buena [San Francisco] in Ohlone territory.)

The other reason was to extend the reach of the Catholic Church into Alta California in the form of Franciscan missions.

Modern vaqueros re-enact the Rancho Era at Covarrubias Rancho in the Chumash-built Presidio of Santa Barbara. (dhe, 1985)

SEVERAL SPANIARDS were eager to be adventurous explorers. Some were known to be attracted by the prospect of gold and plunder. In 1769, Father Junípero Serra and Capitán Gaspar de Portolá set out into Alta California to further Church and military control. Then in 1774, Capitán Juan Bautista de Anza, from Sinaloa, México, received permission and funds to lead an expedition of 2,000 miles northwestward to find a colonizing route. He took with him 240 persons: soldiers, "servants", wives, settler families (including 128 children), 23 animal handlers, 3 Indian interpreters, 2 friars (Frays Pedro Font and Francisco Garcés), and more than 1,000 pack animals and cattle.

Spanish explorers of the 1700s were especially good at keeping records, so we know much of what happened to this expedition. Of course, all these expeditions were bound to impact the Native populations enroute. A mission trail had already been established from San Diego to Monterey; it had an immense impact on the tribes. To add an immigrant trail only increased the stress.

In anticipation of larger wagon trains from México, the deAnza expedition had to find a route with sufficient water to cross long stretches of both the Sonoran Desert and the Salton Depression desert west of Yuma. As they progressed they contacted many tribes in Sonoran México: Yaqui, Pima, Seri, and O'odham peoples; in Arizona: Apaches, other O'odham, Maricopa, and Cúcupa.

The expedition arrived in Tubac, Arizona (present-day United States), in October, 1775, eventually taking 5 days (November 28-December 2) to cross the Colorado into California. Tribes affected in this area included: Quechan, Kumeyaay, Cupeño, Cahuilla, Gabielino/Tongva, Chumash, Salinan, Esselen, and Ohlone. Their presence (piddling in comparison to the American hordes in 1849) doubled the European population of Alta California in 1776.

THE DE ANZA NATIONAL HISTORIC TRAIL

BECAUSE OF THIS expedition's immense effect on the destiny of the U.S. and California, the National Park Service has designated their route(s) as an important historical trail. The Trail itself touches on many more historic places: missions, early adobes and Spanish/Mexican settler homes, presidios, roads, and publicly-known Indian sites. Natural environments, especially those with endangered species, were also considered in the designation.

Keeping in mind that very sensitive Indian places and areas are adjacent as well, the Park Service has been careful to contact as many tribal representatives as possible for their input on impact. Since the route does pass through private lands and even military posts, the economic and other kinds of effects on such places have been considered. A large volume on management and use plan and environmental impact has been prepared, considering these ethnographical, economic, and culturally sensitive situations.

It is likely in the near future that the public will be seeing the familiar "bent triangle" trail markers bearing silhouettes of Anza with Indian guide logos along southern California (and Arizona highways). Some 96 sites have been chosen for designation from Ft. Yuma to San Francisco. Look for them, and be mindful of our history.

More information: JUAN BAUTISTA DE ANZA NATIONAL HISTORIC TRAIL, U.S. Department of the Interior, National Park Service, Pacific West Field Area, 600 Harrison St., Ste. 600, San Francisco, CA 94107-1372. (415) 427-1438.

Spanish ranchero roundup of Natives for enslaved farm labor. (depiction by F. Peterson, WPA, 1954)

EFFECT OF THE SPANISH INCURSIONS

OVER A PERIOD OF only fifty-six years, the Spanish invasion and colonization completely ripped apart the Native fabric of the southern coastal half of California. With 250 years of experience in cultural extermination in the heart of México, the Spanish occupiers began to apply their methods northward. The padres' method was to approach a village, in a place that appeared to be reasonably self-sustaining, with water, food supply, and a fair-sized population. The peoples received them with attitudes ranging from curious to frigid to hostile. A few natives, seeking to possess some of these strangers' "power," would allow themselves to be baptized. After dedicating the place [for instance, the Serra landing site in Monterey], the padre would spend a few months in residence, then move on, leaving the chore of actually building a mission to his subordinates. (*See Missions, Appendix II*)

The hard labor of adobe and stonemasonry, earth moving, Spanish-style farming with plows and oxen, and heavy tasks was done by the "neophytes", that is, newly converted Natives, who zealously took to their labor, voluntarily at first, then under the prodding of the soldiers as the labor became forced. Under the rules of the Church of Rome, a harsh new regime replaced the former free and open life of the people.

They were compelled to live in the mission compound, segregated by sex, restrained from their earlier life styles, forbidden to use their language, religion, and dances. They were told what new food to eat, and roughly commanded to raise wheat, weave, make olive oil and wine for officials in Mexico.

Native Californians were not overly impressed with the joys promised by the padres. Nearly every mission experienced at least one major rebellion over these 50 years. Indeed, in 1781 the Quechans of Yuma, to show their appreciation of their serfdom, killed the padre, threw out the army, and remained independent until overpowered by American army forces many decades later.

THROUGHOUT THE HISTORY of Europe, the Middle East, Africa, and Asia, many diseases swept the populations, often reducing towns to one-third of their former size. Such epidemics had left the people with a fairly strong genetic immunity to many afflictions. They nevertheless carried the germs of these terrible plagues with them when they arrived in the Western Hemisphere. But the American Indian had no resistance to the sword of these armies of viruses. Whatever other societal treatment the Native Californians were offered, they were helpless before the onslaught of disease.

VILLAGE LIFE, WORK ROUTINES, family life, hunting, fishing—none can be carried on in the usual manner when disease strikes. Of all the devastating alterations to Indian life in the New World, the introduction of European diseases was the worst. Whether endemic (in small areas) or epidemic, the diseases—measles, smallpox, cholera, pneumonia, diphtheria, scarlet fever, syphilis, dysentery, tuberculosis, and typhoid—exacted a genocidal toll. Colds, fevers, and diarrhea affected nearly all the Indian populations at one time or another. Their immunological susceptibility made the spread of disease possible, but missionization made it worse. Once the people were forced into the mission compounds, not even modern medicine could have prevented the epidemics that followed.

It is unlikely that the padres were blind to the havoc they were causing. When their labor force became depleted, they called upon the soldiers to range ever wider in their search for able-bodied workers. Rebellion or flight prompted stern measures from the Church—lashing, chopping off of toes, imprisonment; escapees risked death if caught. Luís Peralta, Gervásio Argüello, and Father L.A. Martinez, Spaniards commemorated in California place names, were noted for their enthusiasm in gathering in "apostates." They were known to brag about their entrapment or killing of fugitives. (Recall that the Spanish Inquisition ended

JUANA MARIA,
THE "LONE WOMAN OF SAN NICOLAS ISLAND"

In Heizer and Whipple's Indians of California *there is a 12-page account by Emma Hardacre, packed with extravagantly romantic writing, of this extraordinary woman.*

Briefly, a group of Kodiak (Alaska) otter hunters were brought by Spaniards to this outermost of the Channel Islands, some 70 miles out from the mainland, in the mid-1700s. Abandoned by their ship, they eventually murdered all the native Gabrielino men on the island. Over the years, a small community of some 20 persons survived, but the Franciscan fathers of the mainland demanded their removal.

In 1835, while a huge storm hampered the removal process, one woman screamed that her child had remained on the island. She jumped overboard, seemingly lost. Several attempts at returning to find either the child or the mother were frustrated, each time by huge storms. (Read Richard Henry Dana's Two Years Before the Mast *to get some idea of their magnitude.)*

Finally, 18 years later, in 1853, a woman speaking a language unknown by the mainlanders was found on the island (mother or child?). She was brought to live at the home of the rescuing ship captain, was given the name Juana Maria, died a short time later, and was buried in the Indian graveyard of Misión Santa Barbara. It is problematic that this is really her in the photograph, taken some years later. But the real story is touching.

(Photograph #N 22587, described as "Juana Maria",
courtesy of the Southwest Museum, Los Angeles, by Hawas & Mulzell)

only in 1821, the year of the independence of México.)

Though the specter of death was ever-present in the mission, few Indians thought of flight. Traditionally, most Indians had never ventured far beyond tribal territory; to go further into alien tribal territory meant capture and sometimes death. The courage to flee and brave the unknown had to outweigh the fear. The birth rate declined precipitously, as the fabric of original cultures was lost forever.*

LiFE iN THE MiSSiONS was not idyllic, despite much of the romantic propaganda. During this 60-year period, 56,000 Indians had been baptized, but by 1834 the mission population was only 15,000. Mexican independence in 1821 had as one of goals to free all Mexican Indians of mission control. By the 1830s, much of the California mission population had died, and upon independence, many of the remainder fled at the first chance of escape, carrying the microbes of death to remote villages.

Perhaps life in those 60 years could have become routine for those who had adjusted to the new ways, or had been permitted to live adjacent to missions in countryside villages, as was the case in the south, especially in Luiseño territory. Nevertheless, the missions were built with four walls for a reason—which, contrary to poplar belief, was not to keep people out.

THE RANCHO ERA & MEXICAN GOVERNMENT

MÉXICO'S MOVE toward independence from Spain, begun by Fray Hidalgo in 1811, was achieved in 1821, although few waves of change reached Alta California. Nevertheless, from all over México came the cry of the captive Indian to be released from the bondage of the Church. The year 1834 finally brought the "secularization" (control by civilian authority) of the missions, and their downfall as a power source. There is but one thing to note to the romanticizers of mission life: Within only two years of secularization, nearly the entire Indian population had fled. By 1848 the mission system no longer existed.

Since the early period of Mexican independence did not change mission life much, Indian rebellion continued. Even as late as 1837, José María Amador was out on a "recapturing" expedition. He found 200 Indians, half of them already baptized. His party marched the Christians down a road, murdering each with four arrows. With the others, he poured a bottle of water on their heads in a mock baptism, then shot them in the back. Amador city and county are named after this man's family. Recapturing fugitive Indians must have been a popular sport, since so many prominent men did it: Luís Peralta (Santa Clara, 1805) killed ten and brought back twenty-five "head" on one expedition. Gervásio Argüello (Santa Clara, 1806)

Many Indian women resorted to natural herbal abortive drugs, saying that they would not care to subject their children to the life which they themselves had lived.

found 42 apostates and 47 unconverted out in the bush. Father L. A. Martinez (San Luis Obispo, 1816), with soldiers, brought back "only five persons."

IT WAS THE iNTENTiON, though weakly expressed, of the new Mexican government to make the mission lands into Indian pueblos, while retaining some land for the padres. What actually happened was that the missions and their lands were sacked and seized by greedy and powerful rancheros. In 1823, the year of the founding of the first Mexican republic, there were only 20 secular land grants in Alta California; by 1845 the number had increased to nearly 800; a few actually were Indian.

The main square in the pueblo of Nuestra Señora de Los Angeles still bears some resemblance to its 200-year-old ancestor. (dhe, 1988)

Thus, the Indian once again became the pawn in the land grab that solidly entrenched the hacienda-peón system. The Indian became the peón.

In the rancho system, several men rose to prominence: General Mariano Vallejo had a rancho in Petaluma that spread over nearly 100,000 acres, and had his luxurious life supported by his Indian mercenaries. His troops raided nearby and distant tribes for laborers, and in one battle killed over 200 protesting Wappos.

José Andrés Sepúlveda managed to acquire a large rancho from former San Juan Capistrano (ex-Luiseño Indian) land. He used, of course, Indian vaqueros to maintain the life-style of the ranchero.

Outsiders began to move in: John Temple into Los Cerritos (1844); Hugo Reid into Santa Anita Rancho (1839)—largely San Gabriel Mission, ex-Gabrielino and Tongva—territory.

AT THE END OF THE FIRST HALF of the 19th century, the big land-grab was getting more agitated as missions declined and immigrants from México, the United States, and Europe arrived. Eventually, the missions fell into disrepair as most were abandoned. Control of the churches proper was returned to the Catholic Church by the U.S. government in the 1860s (by a law signed by Abraham Lincoln), while most of the buildings remaining in the 20th century were restored by the State Parks Department, in cooperation with the local parishes.

RESISTANCE TO THE SUPERIOR FORCE OF THE SPANIARDS PROVED FUTILE.

Nearly all of former mission land in California from San Diego to Sonoma Counties was divided up—most became huge ranchos, others not so big. The owners of these extensive lands founded extremely powerful families, whose influence lasted to the present day. (*Appendix III*) Then they too eventually disappeared, as did their labor force and their lifestyle.

RESISTANCE

WHEN THEY COULD, the Natives employed guerrilla tactics to defend their lands. Estánislao (Stanislaus) escaped Misión San José, organized a band of resistance fighters in the Central Valley, defeated his Mexican army pursuers in 1829, and fought on until 1838.

In southern California those tribes to the east (Colorado River) were the least affected, though they were subjected to secondary pressures from the Spanish occupation of Arizona and New Mexico, which involved migration and raids by Ute and Paiute refugees pushed westward. The Kumeyaay and, to some extent, the Cahuilla in the South Coast Range managed to stay independent through stiff resistance and clever avoidance of pitched battles with Spanish/Mexican troops.

Over all of southern California, resistance most often took the more personal form of defiance of orders and brusque force by troops. Organized protest was difficult and suppressed by the troops guarding the missions.

Mission tactics invited rebellion as the only means of protest. California Indians had never known European military tactics and had never undergone massive invasions, as had several Native American cultures (Central American and Andean tribes, for instance). Kumeyaay of Misión San Diego mounted a revolt after six years of repression, destroying the mission. It was rebuilt.

In 1781, the Quechan, having had only one year of mistreatment by Serra's successor, permanently destroyed both the Spanish mission and army, maintaining their independence until the American invasion. As a consequence of their separateness, the California tribes had never learned the stategies of cooperation in warfare.

Other rebellions: San Gabriel (1785); San Francisco and San José (1793 and 1797), serious forays to capture and return "apostates". In 1824, when some 2,000 Chumash took over La Puríssima (Lompoc), they were soon joined by other revolts at Santa Ynez and Santa Barbara as the word spread. The revolt lasted a month, and was put down only with concentrated Spanish troop action and cannonades. Nearly all the missions, at one time or another, incurred the wrath of the Natives, but resistance to the superior force of the Spaniards proved futile. In the San Francisco Bay area in 1821, three "apostates" made their names known by their rebellious exploits: Pompónio, Marín, and Quintín. The latter two are today immortalized with place names elevating them to a peculiar status—San Marin and San Quentin.

ONE REFLECTION must be offered concerning this period of California history. Although the Spanish attitude (created by Church dogma and practice) towards the Indian was often patronizing and excessively stern, it at least recognized the Native as human and deserving of certain rights. This approach differed markedly from that the incoming American, whose attitude could only be described as detestable. The average American immigrant considered the Indian as something approaching that of a pest to be exterminated, or at best, to be put to use as forced labor. It took over 75 years to overcome this sentiment. (*Missions are listed and described briefly in Appendix II. Prominent ranchos of Northern and Southern California are listed in Appendix III.*)

TEARS IN THE FABRIC BEYOND THE MISSIONS

THE INFLUENCE of the missions on Indian life in the rest of the state depended, of course, on the distance from the missions, or upon the demands the missions and presidios (fortified Spanish garrisons) made on the resources and materials they required. The established Indian trading networks were excellent means of obtaining most needed goods, but this network also unwittingly extended the unseen reach of disease. Being the most remote and distant, most northern California tribes did manage to evade the worst epidemics until the American invasion, but the Central Valley tribes were inevitably decimated.

Most of the resources sought were for laborers—men, women and children to be stoneworkers, metalworkers, and farmworkers. The soldiers and the rancheros reached out in ever-widening waves, kidnapping and condemning the Indians they caught to serfdom. Johann Sutter and Mariano Vallejo (and family) were among the most notorious for establishing Indian mercenary armies to subdue nearby tribes.

In southeastern California, the great Mojave and Upper Sonoran Deserts insulated the more eastern tribes from occupation, but the effect of the great Spanish mission system in the west was a constant threat.

Sticks & Stones

To illustrate the personal insults that California Indians had to endure around 1890-1910, I wish to include a short section from a book entitled *Our Own Country*, by James Cox, published in St. Louis, Missouri, in 1894. This was one of a set of books of the same title, written by authors from a number of countries. These books were widely distributed and used in schools. I recently have heard comments like this on talk radio.

Difficult as it is to appreciate the fact, the picture of a California 'Digger' Indian on this page* is nothing more than the photograph of one of several hundred human beings who resemble each other so much in feature, filth and wretchedness that when they are mixed up in a group the average white man cannot, by any process of examination or reasoning, distinguish one from the other.

Men who have traveled around the world and visited the poorer sections and the slums of the principal countries in each, agree that for absolute misery the "Digger" Indian in California holds the blue ribbon, and is likely to do so until the race dies out on general principles and ceases to exist.

This idea [that the Californian tribes "descended from the residents of Eastern Asia"] is very prevalent among writers on California, who believe that some hundreds of years ago Chinese and Japanese junks were from time to time wrecked on the Californian coast, and that the castaways mingled with the aboriginal races and introduced into them all the peculiarities, not to say vices, of the Orient.

Certain it is that the lower grade of Californian Indians have peculiarities not generally with in Red Men, as American Indian are rather illogically called, seeing that they are not red. The "Digger" Indian heralds his approach by a distinctly unpleasant perfume… The term "Digger" as applied to these unfortunate creatures, has been denounced as inappropriate. Various sources have been assigned for the nickname, the most absurd being that it results from the use made of these diminutive specimens of humanity of tubers…

Mr. Cox calls this man "Digger" obviously to infer the epithet used towards African Americans. Until Cox's slur, the term "Digger" had been applied only to Sierra foothill Indians who dug roots and tubers with adroitly designed digging sticks.

The photograph referred to is not identically the same as the State Parks photo below, although the setting, the unknown photographer, and even the person depicted are probably the same.

DISMEMBERING & DESTROYING THE FABRIC
THE AMERICAN INVASION

...it was reckless without hardihood, greedy without audacity, and cruel without courage; there was not an atom of foresight or of serious intention in the whole batch of them, and they did not seem aware those things are wanted for the work of the world. To tear treasure out of the bowels of the land was their desire, with no more moral purpose at the back of it than there is in burglars breaking into a safe.
—Joseph Conrad, *Heart of Darkness*

ON A DRY AND DUSTY DAY IN 1841, the first American immigrant train, the Bidwell-Bartleson company, clattered into Mexican Alta California. Already, for thirty years American sailboat skippers had been assisting coastal pueblos in a way that Spain and México could not—trading for essential supplies. The stage was being set for the drama that was to demolish the Native American way of life forever. American Manifest Destiny—the march to the western sea—was about to reach California. Manifest Destiny told the American public that all land from Atlantic to the Pacific, not otherwise claimed by American landholders, could be had just for the taking. Never mind that it was already occupied by other nations, both Indian and European.

On the pretense of "scientific surveys" in 1844 and a more blatant military operation in 1846, Capt. John C. Frémont freely roamed central California, eventual-ly raising the American flag on a peak near Gilroy. Along with American ground forces from Santa Fe under General Stephen Kearny and naval Commodores Robert Stockton and John Sloat, Frémont forced the Mexican Army of Alta California to capitulate in 1847. Alta California was ceded to the U.S. by the Treaty of Guadalupe Hidalgo on February 2, 1848.* A few days before, at a sawmill owned by Johann Sutter, a Swiss ranchero who had founded a small empire at Sacramento, a New Jersey wagon builder found a small gold nugget. Gold fever, among other fevers, ran rampant, and the mass American immigration began.

Here are some numbers: In 1845, the Mexican population of Alta California was 4,000. In 1847, the Americans numbered 15,000; in 1850, they were 93,000; in 1860, 380,000. Estimates of the Native population in 1776 range from at least 300,000 to one million. (Estimates, then or now, for heavily-populated areas, such as San Francisco, San Diego, and

*The Treaty of Guadalupe Hidalgo included Alta California, Arizona, New Mexico, Nevada, Utah, parts of Colorado and Wyoming, and recognized formerly independent Texas as part of the U.S. The treaty left in place Mexican land grants and recognition of indigenous land and rights, but American law was now supreme, and all such legal structures and treaty affirmations were ignored and became worthless.

The California end of the Oregon Trail, at the Truckee River, circa 1850. As settlers descended upon the soon to be state of California, Indian lives and lands were no longer safe. (from a print by H.S. Crocker, in *A Pictorial History of California*, Bancroft Library, UC Berkeley)

Los Angeles are impossible to fix.) By 1850, the Indian populations, already severely affected by the massive influx of disease, could no longer resist the rending of their cultures.

The immigrants arrived with a frenzied greed for gold or land. Most of this horde had come from poverty in the East or the slave culture of the South, passing through midwestern lands occupied by a thoroughly hostile Indian population. They were in no mood for such distractions as "primitive" Indians who protested the seizure and spoilage of their lands and homes. The Indian was pushed aside and ignored, and if there was protest, punished by the sternest measures, including extermination.

By 1854, only five years later, the gold supply was dwindling rapidly and the best lands had been taken or depleted. A general financial depression settled upon the pioneers. There was work to be sought, crooks and ruffians to be dealt with, land and survival to be considered, and soon, a Civil War to be fought. There was no time for any interference.

No doubt most of these seekers had some moral sense, but in the general mêlée, it was overwhelmed by the outrageous behavior of the worst of the lot. Right behind them followed the pioneers—families who usually followed a moral inclination, but who picked up anti-Indian sentiment quickly. Into the confusion trooped the U.S. Cavalry and the U.S. Infantry. They were the only source of law and order, but they were also white—convinced of the "right" of U.S. citizens to settle wherever they pleased.

IN 1850, California was admitted to the Union as a "free" state—an appellation that didn't extend to the Indian population. Until mid-century the eastern United States had had a policy of Indian "removal" further and further west, but this policy could hardly be used anymore. Certainly something had to be done with the Native Californians, but what?

In 1851 a delegation of three commissioners was sent from Washington to make "peace" treaties with the tribes—the treaties were to consist of removing the Indians to reservations in order to reduce Indian-white friction. The commissioners, though sweeping rapidly through most of the Central Valley and much of northern California, actually negotiated randomly with eighteen groups (not tribes), or whatever apparently important individual they might grasp in an area. They promised to furnish teachers, farm advisers and implements, blacksmiths, seed, cloth, and to guarantee 7.5 million acres of reservation lands (*see Map 2*) in exchange for the Indians' relinquishing claim to most

of the state. In reality most of the signers had no "claim" to any land outside their own local clan. (*See p.46, A Short History of Land, and p.168, on Yokotch*)

NEVERTHELESS, THE NATIVES began to honor their part of the treaties they had signed, withdrawing to the designated lands and refraining from armed confrontation. Congress, however, refused to acknowledge the treaties and the responsibilities in them, under pressure from greedy California legislators.

After shrinking the claims to a tiny fraction of originally promised lands, a number of large reservations (the largest less than a ten mile square) were established between 1853 and 1887. The majority of them were either in uninhabitable locations, or in climates totally unsuitable for the inhabitants. Of the original ten reservations, parts of five remain today. Over the next 75 years, a large number of rancherias (small residential villages) were established, often on or near the original tribal lands, by executive order or Congressional bill, but total reservation lands never exceeded 500,000 acres.

Where disease had not exterminated the Indian populations, the next sixty years brought mutilation of their cultures.

IN 1850, CALIFORNIA WAS ADMITTED TO THE UNION AS A "FREE" STATE—AN APPELLATION THAT DIDN'T EXTEND TO THE INDIAN POPULATION.

GENOCIDE

I believe [the Government] was made by white men and their posterity forever, and I am in favor of conferring citizenship to white men, men of European birth and descent, instead of conferring it upon negroes, Indians, and other inferior races.
—*Stephen A. Douglas, Senator from Illinois, 1858, in debate with Abraham Lincoln*

I speak advisedly when I say that killing a slave, or any colored person, was not treated as a crime, either by the courts or the community...
—*Frederick Douglass, 1845, statesman, and ex-slave*

THE CENTRAL VALLEY and northern California received the brunt of the gold fever. By 1850 disease had already terribly weakened and debilitated the people there through pneumonia, influenza, tuberculosis, and venereal diseases. In addition to the murderous callousness of miners and settlers, the Indians' food sources were devastated—their staple of acorns, fish, game, seeds. Much of the countryside appeared as though a thousand tornadoes had passed—the aftereffects of mining operations. Almost every fishing stream flowing from the Sierras was laden with silt and rubble; the foothill valleys were gouged out; settlers

Ft. Churchill was built near Reno in 1860 to subdue the Paiutes of Nevada and eastern California, who were loathe to lose their territory. The rectangular adobe structures, now dissolving back into the earth, were constructed using local labor, Paiute. (dhe, 1982)

fenced off "their" land and turned cattle loose on the abundant grasses of formerly open fields. (What you see today is countryside that has undergone massive repair and reconfiguration since that first invasion.)

What resistance the Indians could muster to the depletion of their food sources and the threat of starvation took the form of drawing upon the white man's larder, stealing cattle, food, and wood for fuel and shelter. This, in turn, aroused reprisal and vengeance far in excess of the "injury" done. Occasionally, the Indian would react violently and the vicious cycle began.

Here, as in all the West, the Army was called upon ostensibly to "protect and restrain" the Indians. "Protection" was minimal, and "restraint" was enthusiastic to the point of pursuit. From 1849 to the 1880s, nearly 200 military forts and posts were erected in California for Indian control, some directly on the reservations (*App. IV*). Although it persisted elsewhere until 1900, Indian resistance in California culminated in the Modoc War of 1872-73, said to be the single most expensive campaign in the West.

AN ACCUSATION OF GENOCIDE can be sustained only by citation upon citation of criminal acts. The feeling of the lawlessness of the times can only be supported by a citing of the reports of horror and terror. The following accounts are drawn from Cook, Forbes, Gillis, Hart (1965), Heizer (1978), and Rawls (*see Bibliography, App. VII*), all of which detail other tragedies.

• General Kibbe reported a policy to drive the Achumawi into the mountains to starve during food-gathering seasons. *1850, Siskiyou County*

• Two settlers, Charles Stone and Andrew Kelsey, tormented many Clear Lake Pomos held in serfdom on their rancho to the point of lashing, rape, slavery, and murder. Incensed by this treatment, Stone and Kelsey were executed by two Natives incensed by this inhuman treatment. The other Indians, fearing certain reprisal, fled to an island at the north end of the lake. But the Army was called out to mete vengeance, and in an organized campaign, brought boats to reach the island, and massacred 60 of the 400 there, now called "Bloody Island". Women and especially children were easy prey. Active pursuit took another 75 Indian lives, including some "hanged and burnt". A Treaty of Peace and Friendship followed, in which the Pomo relinquished their lands for a gift of "10 head of beef, three sacks of bread, and sundry clothing." *1850-51, Lake County*

• Juan Antonio Garrá, Cupeño, organized a successful revolt of several southern California desert peoples. The Colorado River and parts of the Mojave came under Indian control, but the movement collapsed when Garrá was betrayed by disloyal Indians. In retaliation, the Army destroyed the food supplies of the people involved. Garrá was executed, and the chief Cupeño village was burned. *1851-52, San Diego, Imperial, Riverside Counties*

• At a feast given by whites for 300 Wintu, all Indians present were ambushed one-by-one by soldiers and volunteers. *1850s, Shasta County*

• At another "feast" for the Shasta tribe, to celebrate a treaty of peace, the food was laced with poison. Nearly all the men of the tribe died. *1850s, Shasta County*

• Shasta City (government) offered $5 for every Indian head presented at city headquarters. Shortly thereafter several mules were seen bearing 8-12 Indian heads. *1855, Shasta County*

• On the Trinity River, some Hupa were displaced by white settlers. Upon returning to fish their waters, they were shot. *1855, Humboldt County*

• Numerous accounts from the northwest of the state report many of the worst depredations—nearly 50 rancherias and encampments attacked, burned, ambushed, inhabitants slaughtered. *1855-63, Humboldt and Trinity Counties*

• In retaliation for attacking an immigrant train, a detail of 58 dragoons and infantry killed 20 Indians near Ft. Mojave, quickly retreating to San Bernardino (1858). The Army returned and took the land, this time without bloodshed, by taking six chieftains hostage. Hostilities again erupted, with the Army killing 23 Mohaves and destroying their crops. *1859, San Bernardino County*

•Survivors of three Eel River tribes were encamped on Indian Island in Humboldt Bay, Eureka, attempting to avoid white contact. While the men were away fishing, the local whites descended upon the women, children, and elderly, literally butchering them all. (Author Bret Harte denounced the raid in print, for which he was fired from his journalist post.)

1860, Humboldt County

•The good citizens of Honey Lake paid 25¢ apiece for Indian scalps. *1863, Lassen County*

•Nearly 100 Yuma and Mohave were drowned in an alkali lake in retaliation for raids on cattle and immigrant trains. *1865, Inyo County*

REPORTS OF INDIAN SLAVES, kidnapped in the countryside for sale elsewhere, were common. Only three arrests were made and no convictions for these or other similar crimes. Until 1867, an estimated 10,000 California Indians, including 4,000 children were held as chattel.

•Kidnapping children in Sacramento. *1854*

•Kidnapping children for southern ranchos. *1857, Chico*

•Enslaving children for San Francisco. *1858*

•Enslaving children after the U.S. Army raids villages. *1861, Humboldt and Mendocino Counties*

•White settlers in the Sierra kidnap Maidu children and women. The offering rate is $50-60 for a cook or servant, and $100 for a "likely young girl". *1861, Nevada County*

In an 1864 Army roundup of Indians in northern California and southern Oregon, long-unfriendly neighbors Modocs and Klamaths were thrown onto a reservation near Klamath Falls, Oregon.
Modocs were particularly unhappy with their forced proximity and soon decamped, heading for the rugged Lava Beds, where they could protect themselves. The Army pursued them, and beseiged them in the Modoc War of 1872-73. Some 60 Modocs held off an Army of 600 for four months. The eventually victorious Army took revenge and hanged Kintpuash (Captain Jack) with five warriors. Three captives photographed by the Army are, left to right, Curley-Headed Jack, Wheum, and Buckskin Doctor. (State Parks) [*See p.115*]

•Enslaving children for San Francisco. *1863*

•"General" Bidwell (abolitionist) accused of vile treatment of his "serfs". *1864, Chico*

•Killing adults to get the children.

1867, Round Valley

MURDER AND slavery were not the only depredations inflicted on the Indian community, far more debilitating were the effects of diseases, not infrequently deliberately introduced—an early version of genocidal, biologic warfare.

•One hundred of nearly 500 villagers near Yuba City died of cholera. *1849, Yuba County*

•At one of Sutter's farms, 40 of 48 residents died of an epidemic. The next year 500 died.

1852, Placer County

IN A TRAIL OF TEARS, the weary and bedraggled remnants of these once-happy peoples were rounded up, removed from their homelands and forced on long marches, bereft of food or shelter, to reservations that were inhospitable and worthless. Much loss of life occurred en route.

• Inhabitants of the sparsely-populated Southern Sierra Tehachapi Mountains of Ventura, Los Angeles, Kern, and Santa Barbara Counties were rounded up and marched to Ft. Tejon.

1853, Kern/Los Angeles Counties,

• Achumawi and Maidu of the northeast were driven hundreds of miles to Round Valley

1869, Mendocino County

• A roundup of the Sacramento Valley drove what peoples could be found to the Nome Lackee Reservation.

1863, Tehama County

• Cupeños were removed from Warner Springs to Pala.

1903, San Diego County

RESERVATIONS often proved to be little better than concentration camps. The miserable inhabitants fell victim to fraud, appropriation of supplies, maltreatment, and gross neglect. The Army's protection proved worthless. In 1862, 45 Indians of Round Valley were murdered in camp by neighboring whites; a year later 20 Wailaki were murdered in the same place. Some persons disappeared into the most remote areas, some banded together gypsy-like in camps at the rural edge of white society. Others took refuge with settled Indian groups, still others were befriended by whites or ranchers. Most denied their heritage and tried to pass as "Mexican" or African-American. A census of 1900 reported less than 16,000 Native Americans, though it is known that many thousands of Natives chose not to be recognized. (Many still do not choose this recognition.)

A Maidu camp in Plumas Co. with shelters from scrap. 1900 (State Parks)

*Many Pomo people fled to an island in Clear Lake to escape a revenge invasion by the U.S. Army in 1850. The Army came in boats to massacre men, women, and children. The high ground was diked off to create agricultural fields, but an effort is being made to re-create the island. (Landmark **427**, Highway 20)* (dhe, 1998)

RESISTANCE

Short-lived and sporadic resistance by Indians arose in several places, but none were successful:

1851-52, Klamath War
1850-1860s, Hamakhavas (Mohaves)
1850s-1865, Owens Valley Paiutes and Shoshones
1856, Kern River War
1860s, Northern Paiutes
1867, Pit River "Massacres"
1872-73, Modoc War

PROMINENT BATTLES SITES OR MASSACRE SITES IN WHICH INDIAN AND SETTLER OR ARMY FORCES CONTENDED (1829-73)

1829 Vallejo vs. San Joaquin Valley Indians

San Joaquin County **214**

1850 Bloody Island Massacre. *Lake County* **427**

1850 Fandango Pass/Bloody Point.

Modoc County **8,546**

1850 James Savage Battalion in Yosemite Valley.

Mariposa County **527,790**

1855 Battle Rock (Castle Crags). *Shasta County* **116**

1862 Bishop Creek Battle. *Imperial County* **811**

1862 Mayfield Canyon Battle. *Inyo County* **211**

1867 Infernal Caverns Battleground.

Modoc County **16**

1867 Chimney Rock. *San Bernardino County* **737**

1872 Land's Ranch Battle. *Modoc County* **108**

1873 Captain Jack's Stronghold. *Modoc County* **9**

[*Throughout the book, the numbers in boldface refer to State Historical Landmark numbers.*]

Only the barest threads of the original culture remained, but a difficult and painful restoration of some of the fabric was to prove possible.

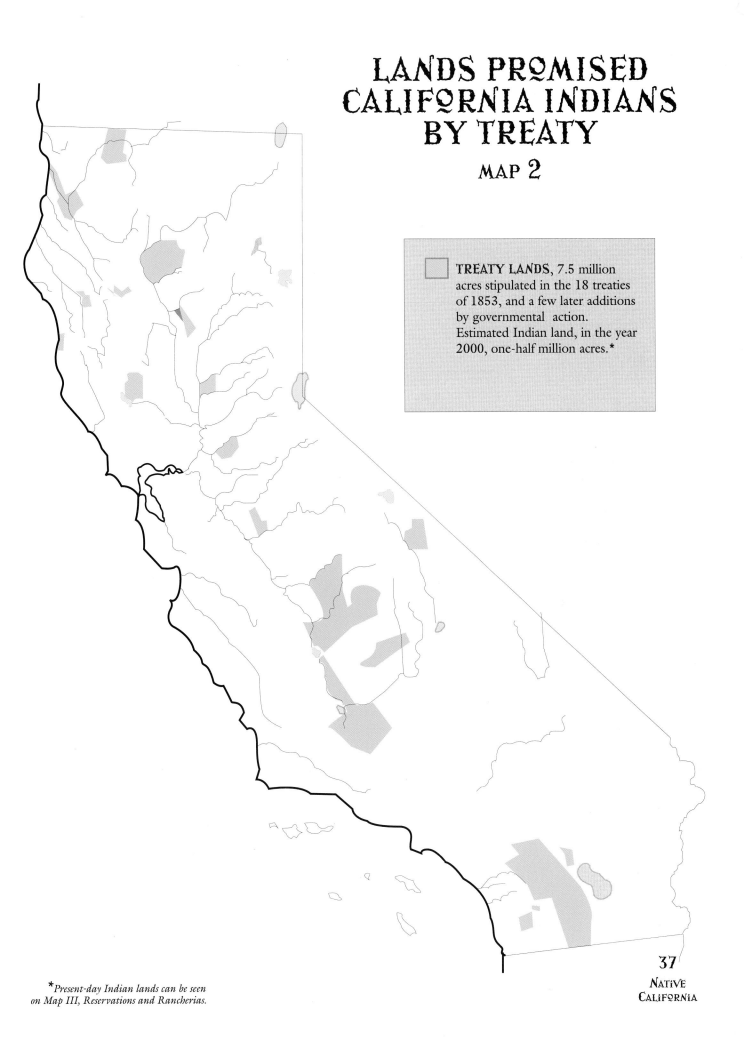

LANDS PROMISED CALIFORNIA INDIANS BY TREATY

MAP 2

TREATY LANDS, 7.5 million
acres stipulated in the 18 treaties
of 1853, and a few later additions
by governmental action.
Estimated Indian land, in the year
2000, one-half million acres.*

*Present-day Indian lands can be seen
on Map III, Reservations and Rancherias.

REWEAVING THE FABRIC
SURVIVAL, ENDURANCE, & REGENERATION

We have survived the 4 BCs:
before Christ,
before Columbus,
before Custer,
before casinos.
—an unidentified Indian elder seen on TV

SOME OUTCAST PEOPLES of this world possess a power and will to survive. Though incredibly beleaguered, decimated, dispersed, and alone, the Native peoples of California faced their challenge, and very slowly, found this power within themselves.

Retreating from the settlers, these Yokuts people used cast off lumber to build their traditional cedar bark tipi homes. Frémont Rancheria of the Central Valley, 1870.

(State Parks)

A first need is shelter—finding and acquiring available materials, from discarded lumber or adobe. Another first need is food—planting or harvesting native plants in a manner based on what one remembers from earlier times, or adapting newly introduced seeds and plants. Another need is health—very difficult to maintain in a land where the healthful food and medicinal herbs were devastated and facilities of the dominant society were denied. Another need is a stubborn faith in what is right. Somehow, most of the people found these things.

When one is concerned with the basics of survival, issues of human rights seldom appear to be primary concerns. Civil and human rights of Indians had been extinguished—no private property, no recourse to the justice system, no vote, no education. These rights were not recovered until the 20th century—voting rights were not restored until 1924. With the vote came the others, but only grudgingly.

As mentioned in the section "Short History of Land", p.46, over the past 75 years Indians have acquired land in the form of small rancherias through Presidential and Congressional acts, but even this miserly generosity has sometimes been reversed in strangely contradictory governmental behavior. In the 1950s, Congress sought to eliminate some "Indian problems" simply by eliminating Indian land and requiring Indians to "assimilate". Several rancherias were illegally "terminated" from "trust" status through this process. Fortunately, most have been partially restored, but some land was irrevocably lost. (*Also see Termination, p.80*)

INDIAN EDUCATION has gone through some bizarre twists during the last 100 years. Serious efforts at providing Indian schooling was not begun by either state or local authorities until the turn of the century. Some larger reservations provided day schools or boarding schools, but many of these were closed, due to poor attendance. For decades, the rampant epidemics continued to take huge tolls on the numbers of Indian students, who were affected more than the white population. Many times, Indian parents perceiving the insidious destruction of their cultures, withdrew their children from cruel and racist schools. Pupils at such schools were forcibly prevented from using their language or customs, and were taken long distances from their parents to attend these institutions.

For a time in the last century, federal authorities tried a new tack—Christian church (Protestant and Catholic) administration of whole reservations. Schools here, too, often turned out to be cruelly run and corrupt, and once again Indian cultural values were suppressed. Church administration was removed early in the 20th century; nevertheless, missionaries have been allowed to continue upon the reservations and have introduced schooling within their own denomination.

Eventually, students seeking secondary education, in the values of the dominant society, were offered the Indian School in Carlisle, Pennsylvania, Chemawa School in Oregon, or Sherman Indian High School, a boarding school in Riverside, California. (*For a description, see p.263.*) Indian secondary education for California students is today also available at the private school in Pala, Sherman High School in Riverside, and at an increasing number of casino-funded reservations—elsewhere, pupils attend local schools. Instruction in tribal and cultural history and customs remains a task for the tribe itself, sometimes on a released-time basis. D-Q University near Davis, California's only Native American institution of higher education, offers courses in social sciences, the sciences, humanities, and agriculture. Its approach to course offerings in indigenous studies are uniquely

Native American, though some Native American studies programs are to be found at several campuses in the State.

Only within the last ten years of the 20th century has Indian health received adequate attention in California. The impoverished peoples of the preceding 100 years had to find medical and health care where they could. At first, public health programs in the Indian communities were as expected—nonexistent. The people had to rely on their traditional herbal and shamanic medicine—which too often had no means of coping with the European-introduced epidemics. The Indian doctors tried, and when they failed, often lost the peoples' confidence.

It was not until 1901 that the Indian people had a hospital, at Sherman School in Riverside. One can well imagine what health was in the distant rural areas. Since the 1970s, the Indian Health Service has been trying to establish clinics in all the major areas of need, so that several of the more rural reservations and rancherias now have at least an itinerant doctor, nurse, dentist, and optician. (*See Health Services, p.252*) As in most government programs, stingy, nearsighted budgeteers offer the least to those most in need.

INDIAN POWER? Heroes are those who struggle against intimidating odds. So many unnamed Indian heroes arose during the painful times of recovery—those who protested the extermination of people and culture, those who demanded rights, those who wanted only justice for their people. Then came the anti-bureaucracy heroes who could badger and manipulate the bureaucracy and cut the "white tape" for the betterment of their people.

IF THESE LAST PAGES seem to the reader to be a chronicle of unmitigated grief and struggle, I have but one thing to say: It is so.

Through all of this incredible debasement of a race, somehow there was a will to survive, to perpetuate, even to grow. It seems phenomenal that the strength of these peoples maintained as much of the ancient customs and heritage as they did. Probably their determination along with the cultural remoteness of this civilization allowed them to persist, to regenerate, to exist even today among us, around us, almost without our knowledge. Modern civilization is so caught up in itself that it pays little attention to its undercurrents—to the minor cultures that continue to propagate in spite of the overall ignorance or indifference of the "dominant society".

Finally, Cultural Imperative meets Manifest Destiny. It looks as though both will survive—changed and adapted to coexistence.

No doubt casino issues have brought California Indians to the attention of the public; at last the public has a glimpse of the existence of the people. But what does the public really know about the tribes, the people, the struggle, the problems and issues?

NOTES ON POPULATION FIGURES

In 1900, almost no Indian wanted to be known as such, owing to the intense stigma and possible danger of that identity, so the census people found only tiny groups. Maybe as many as three or four times these numbers hid out, called themselves "Mexican", or otherwise disappeared. Since these numbers are known to be extremely low, it is not useful to quote the published figures; even the estimates of anthropologists are admittedly low. There may be a pity factor in quoting low numbers, but then someone may raise the question of the gene pool being being exceedingly shallow.

Today the situation on census is entirely different. Many benefits and entitlements, though grudgingly released by the Federal government, are available to all the Indian public. The number of descendants of original California tribes, if truly known, would probably reach nearly a million, three times published figures. There are several reasons for this discrepancy today: families have been growing faster than they have been identified; Indian people tend to live in areas undercounted by Census Bureau; the unrecognized peoples out there are never toted up in BIA figures, even though each of the tribes that have petitioned for re-recognition is required to have a goodly number of verified descendants; and there are thousands who have not petitioned, because they were never "officially" recognized in the first place. Although descendants of the "18 treaties" tribes or the mission rolls, they simply weren't found or visited by the treaty commissioners because they weren't near "sensitive" white settlement areas. And then there are the thousands who still don't want anything at all to do with the Federal government, having already survived decades of being oppressed and cheated, and thousands more of assimilated people who simply choose to ignore the whole thing.

Hundreds of thousands of U.S. Native American "immigrants" have come to California from tribes north and south, east, and, yes, west (Hawaii and Samoa). They have come here because the weather, jobs, and tolerance are reasonably good. Sometimes they marry into families of U.S. tribes. Even more, there are millions of California-resident Native Americans whose roots lie south of the border. Indeed, many of these tribal peoples maintain direct contact with their home ethnic groups—consider Aztecs (who dance just about everywhere there is a festival); Yaquis (who also have a U.S. Federal reservation, Pasqua, in Tucson, and keep up other home ties in México); the Oaxacan groups, who broadcast in their own languages in the Central Valley, p.43. On a few reservations in southern California, some residents maintain dual citizenship, since political border lines were drawn across their ancestral tribal areas (Campo, Jamul).

Happy times for the Indian? Far back, maybe now, for those not weary or spiritless or caught up in mindless pursuits. But maybe there were happy times even a hundred years ago, when it was possible to spend a night gaming with friends, exchanging tales with family, or simply to spending a few hours in a remote desert or forest, listening and waiting.

LATTER-DAY MIGRATIONS INTO CALIFORNIA

THE MAGNET that is California has attracted people of all races, and Native Americans are no exception. As early as the 1930s, the Depression encouraged the migration of many Indian people from parts of the U.S. hit by drought and unemployment. World War II drew Indian workers to California's shipyards, agricultural fields, and urban-based industries. These peoples came from Indian and Aleut Alaska, from Oklahoma and the Dakotas and the upper Midwest, from Arizona and New Mexico, from Hawaii, and from as far away as New York. These new arrivals brought with them their tribal customs and yearnings for their rituals and ceremonies.

Consequently, the centers where these peoples settled became nuclei for the organization of powwow societies and drums. [A drum is not just the actual large, horizontal "bass" drum, but the society of singers and drummers as well.] The drums are based on the music and rituals of Plains, Great Basin, and some Southwest and Southeast tribes. Their style is frequently called Intertribal or "Pan-Indian", reflecting an amalgam of different customs.

At powwows we are presented with the regalia and dancing styles of many different peoples from all over the U.S. At powwows, distinctive songs and dancing may be invited, such as Pueblo White Eagle, Cherokee Corn Dance, Hoop Dance, or Navajo (*Diné*) clan

dances. Even displaced Iroquois (originally from New York) have organized in Long Beach as the Iroquois Social Dancers (doing traditional storytelling and dancing). Although occasionally dancing at powwows, Hawaiian Native peoples hold their own annual dance and Hula festivals in the San Francisco Bay and Los Angeles areas.

The agricultural fields and employment opportunities of California have attracted millions of Native Americans, often transient, from Mexican, Central, and South American homelands. If there are tribal rituals for the people of Yaqui, Aztec, Zapotec, Maya, Garifuna, and other Native origins, they are usually to be found only at home, not in the barrios and bracero camps of California—with some important exceptions. In Sacramento, San Francisco, Los Angeles, Orange County, and San Diego groups of Aztec Dancers (Nahuatl speakers) have organized. They will tell you that they dance because they must; and so it seems. On certain feast days, they gather and dance all day; spectators are invited, but these are not always public.

UNITED LUMBEE NATION OF NORTH CAROLINA & AMERICA

THIS IS A CULTURAL ASSOCIATION originating from tribal peoples of the Lumber River, North Carolina. The following information has been contributed by Eva Silver Star Reed, National Head Chief and Chief Wayne Burrell, Jr. (from *The Hawk Society of the United Lumbee Nation*, 1995). The State of California is privileged to be the present home of the National Tribal Office of the United Lumbee Nation (ULN), since the National Head Chief, Eva Silver Star Reed, resides here.

"The first white contacts with the Indians of Robeson County, North Carolina, came in the early 1700s. Several cultural groups were resident at that time, speaking dialects from Algonquian, Siouan, and Iroquoian language families. Upheavals and tribal decimations followed contact with European white settlers, initially through disease and land seizure. Intertribal warfare followed, caused by pressures from the invaders. The Chowan, the Tuscarora, and the Cherokee peoples all suffered major conflicts.

Although the majority of the Tuscarora migrated northward to join the Iroquois Federation, some families remained. Despite the fact that the Cherokee people continued to be the most powerful Indian group, the Cherokee Nation began to disintegrate. One group migrated to East Texas around 1800, others to Arkansas in "Indian Territory". Still others of the Lumber River area (central and eastern North Carolina) attempted to assimilate through purchase of land. In 1830 the Indian Removal Act was passed by Congress, and the infamous Trail of

Mural art of and about Native Americans has appeared in many California cities. This work is in a playground in San Francisco's Mission District on 24th Street, a street well-known for its many murals. (dhe, 1985)

Tears removed some 16,000 Cherokees westward.

Nevertheless, through various means, about a third of the people managed to remain in North Carolina. Some of these people are ancestors of the present-day Lumbee. As early as 1913, and again in 1953, the Cherokees of Robeson County set up a formal organization. Seeing their traditions and ways disappearing rapidly, these peoples and remnants of other peoples of North Carolina (the groups of Cape Fear, Hattaras, Keyauwee, Shakori, Sissipahow, Waccamaw, and Waxhow) became known as the Lumbee People. Even though Congress recognized the Lumbee People in 1956, rights and privileges of Federally recognized tribes through the BIA have not been forthcoming. The combined California membership is a little over 2,000. (7,000 nationally).

Dispersal of the Lumbee throughout the U.S. is well-known, through earlier and later migrations, with concentrations of people in Texas, Oklahoma, Oregon, Missouri, and California. Surviving are many clans (bands) within the United Lumbee: Bear, War Hawk, Deer, Desert Sage, Coyote, Thunderstar, Red Tailed Hawk, Eagle, Black Bear, Cougar, Wind, Blue Feather, Great Lakes, Woodland, Beaver, Grey Wolf, Three Lakes. Within California, the first seven on this list are represented. The Hawk Society of the Lumbee is charged with the preservation of traditions —the skills and knowledge for daily survival, recreation, and artistic expression. Ceremonies, both at the national and state level are observed. The Hawk Society holds a Green Corn Festival each summer. In California, the ULN Bear Clan presents an annual Powwow on Mother's Day weekend, and the Deer Clan has an annual camp-out on Father's Day weekend. The location and dates of all of these events are given in their publication, the *United Lumbee Nation Times*."
—Eva Silver Star Reed, National Head Chief and Chief Wayne Burrell, Jr.

scholarly lectures in schools, churches, colleges, and public meetings in northern California, especially in the Yuba City-Marysville area.

These presentations are always given by well-known respected leaders, who may be from eastern Cherokee or Oklahoma groups, as well as other bands throughout the country.

In association with the Cherokees of Northern California Club (see below), there is an annual June Campout.

CHEROKEES OF CALIFORNIA
Information: Barbara Summerall,
P.O. Box 202, Sheridan CA 95681
(530) 633-4038

The Stanford Powwow attracts dancers from all over Native America. Among many others seen here are representatives from midwestern Plains, Pueblos, and Seminole tribes.

(dhe, 1997)

UNITED LUMBEE NATION OF NORTH CAROLINA AND AMERICA
P.O. Box 512, Fall River Mills, CA 96028-0512
Also publishers of the *United Lumbee Nation Times*, a tri-monthly publication.

CHEROKEES OF CALIFORNIA
THIS GROUP MAINTAINS TRIBAL AFFINITY (membership and lineage) directly with their parent organization in Tahlequah, Oklahoma. In addition, they serve a social and cultural function through sponsorship of numerous presentations of tribal histories, demonstrations of Cherokee cultural traditions (dance, stories, music, etc. —*see Culture, p.56*), and

CHEROKEES OF NORTHERN CALIFORNIA CLUB
THE CHEROKEE PEOPLE in Central/Northern California use a common heritage as the basis for a club for social and cultural gatherings. This club is loosely affiliated with the "home" tribe in Tahlequah, Oklahoma, but not necessarily through direct lineages. They draw their membership of some 150 persons from Bakersfield to Oregon; they meet four times a year. They encourage traditional craft and artwork, especially in basketry and beadwork.

CHEROKEES OF NO. CALIFORNIA CLUB
9643 Kent St., Elk Grove, CA 95624
(916) 726-8655

continued

IROQUOIS SOCIAL DANCERS
IROQUOIS CONFEDERATION AND OTHERS
Los Angeles and Orange Counties

THIS GROUP of about 120 tribal émigrés from New York State, organized to carry on their tribal traditions, meeting monthly in the spring. "Social Dancers" means more than it says—it includes storytelling and traditional dancing to an Iroquois singer.

Info: Lou Doxtater (213) 532-7504 (Long Beach)

When he is not creating, arranging, or selling craftwork, Airi Hua (Ecuadoriano of Otavalo, left) is playing music with friends. At his vendor stall at the San Juan Bautista Indian Market, Labor Day, 1999.

(dhe)

TLINGIT~HAIDA CALIFORNIA COUNCIL
Tlingit & Haida (Alaska)
Alameda County

INDIGENOUS PEOPLES from many other places have found California a good place to live and work, and to gather with other of their displaced tribal members. Alaskan peoples have organized into a 490-member statewide council. Every two months this group gathers at the Urban Indian Health Board, 3124 14th St. in Oakland.

Info: Bill Martin,
4634 Chateau Park Ct., Fremont, CA 94538
(510) 651-9046

LATIN AMERICAN INDIGENOUS GROUPS IN CALIFORNIA

AS IS WELL~KNOWN, California attracts immigrants from the south as well as from the east and north, making California temporary or permanent home for hundreds of thousands of persons of Native descent from nearly all countries south of the border. The history of their indigenous populations has had many parallels to that of the U.S.—persecution, subjugation, economic privation, personal oppression, land loss. Yet, as in the U.S., many islands of tribal identity manage to maintain their cultures.

For the same social and economic reasons as those in the U.S., many Hispanics have been reluctant to acknowledge their Native heritage. These attitudes are slowly diminishing, as Native pride and consciousness and power builds.

In California, a surprising number of Latin American immigrants and workers identify with an ethnic group (tribe), such as Aztec, Mixtec, Mayan, Yaqui, etc. The vast majority of these people must return to their ethnic territories in order to take part in festivals, dances, and other tribal occasions. However, today in California, a few of the better represented Mexican ethnic groups have organized to sponsor regular fiestas and gatherings. Four centers with such activities are Sacramento, San Francisco, Los Angeles, and San Diego. These groups present dances primarily from (but not restricted to) the central region of Mexico— Aztec, Mixtec, etc. Sharing in or attendance at one of these events is to participate in an intensely satisfying and exciting ceremony.
[NOTE: Latin American groups generally prefer identification as Indigenous (rather than Indian), and ethnic group or pueblo (rather than tribe)].

AZTEC

AZTEC DANCERS are usually found at almost any public function of indigenous people in the Sacramento, San Francisco Bay, San Diego, or Los Angeles areas. Their headdresses of very long peacock (formerly quetzal) feathers are easily spotted from a distance. Their very strong and unusually rhythmic drums are easily heard from a distance. And their devotion to and concentration upon dancing is outstanding and renowned. Powwows may feature special dances by the Aztecs, and individuals may also take part in the intertribal dances.

Aztec dance groups must be granted the privilege of dancing directly from established groups in México. The dances performed have been handed down for generations from Nahuatl-speaking groups in México, many of which require extraordinary physical skill.

MAYA
GRUPO MAYA QUSAMEJ JUNAN
San Francisco

GRUPO MAYA Qusamej Junan is a loose organization of some 200-300 volunteers, centered in St. Peter's Church in San Francisco's Mission District.

The people have organized to provide a vital cultural center for the preservation of traditions and the promotion and support of peace initiatives in Guatemala. Workshops on the spiritual traditions of Cakchiquel, Quiché, Kanjobal, Tzu'tuhil, Ladino, Mam, and Xinca peoples are observed. It is estimated that some 20,000 Maya people, some refugees, some residents, live in the San Francisco Bay area.

Music classes in marimba, with maracas, chirimia, xul, and drum are offered; arrangements to host visiting speakers from the homeland are made. A Sunrise public event is held on the Maya New Year (a 9-month calendar), usually in Dolores Park at the hidden spring in the center of the Park. Marimba and drums are used here, and prayers are led by a Maya elder. A commemoration of the massacre of Tz'utuhil Mayas of Santiago Atitlán by the Guatemalan Army is held in December.

The group participates in local Dia de Los Muertos functions. There is also some association with Grupos Cohales in Los Angeles and Seventh Generation in Arcata.

GRUPO MAYA CENTER, 24th St. and Florida, P.O. Box 40892, San Francisco, CA 94140
(415) 824-2534
TEMPLO FLOR (Los Angeles)
Josefina Gallardo, *capitana*
(Mayan dances, songs, healing counsel)
GRUPOS COHALES are organized in Los Angeles, *no other information available*

Oaxaca: Mixteca, Zapoteca, Chinanteca,
other Indigenous groups from Oaxaca state, México
The organization "Asociación Cívica Benito Juarez" in Fresno exists to assist the many residents and workers in California and Oregon from Oaxaca. Since 1984, this group has helped disseminate information on workers rights, health, housing, and the many facets of U.S. immigrant documentation. Information concerning music and cultural activities are not forgotten. Groups in Santa Barbara, Los Angeles, and San Diego frequently present their indigenous dances.

From public radio station KIDE, FM 91.5 (and other nearby frequencies), Fresno, Radio Bilingüe announcer Silimon López broadcasts in Mixteca for two hours on Sundays.

ASOCIACIÓN CÍVICA BENITO JUAREZ
5005 E. Belmont Av., Fresno, CA 93720

ZAÁCHILA GRUPO *DANZA DE LA PLUMA*
presents Zapotecan dances in the San Diego area. Their leader is Tomás Martinez. (760) 736-4587

South & Meso American Indian Rights & Information Center (SAIIC)
Among its several activities, SAIIC publishes the highly informative magazine *ABYA YALA*, a unique and invaluable source of news of interest from Native Americans south of the U.S. border.

SAIIC
1714 Franklin, Box 28703, Oakland, 94604,
(510) 834-4263

Aztec dancers dedicate their energetic movements and rhythms to many California events. Here they dance at the Indian Market in San Juan Bautista. (dhe, 1982)

AZTEC DANCERS OF CALIFORNIA
SACRAMENTO
Danza Quetzalcoatl, Chuy Ortiz, capitán
SAN FRANCISCO BAY AREA
Xitlallí (San Francisco, Daly City)
Francisco Camplis, capitán, Macuil Ortiz, maestra
WATSONVILLE
White Hawk, Guillerma Arranda, capitán
LOS ANGELES & ORANGE CO.
Xipe Totec (Anaheim), Lazaro Arvizu, capitán
Aztec Dancers without Borders (Downey)
Sonia & Hector Sanchez, leaders
(The Sanchez also publish an Aztec newsletter)
Yunculc Tletl (Pasadena), Margarita Esparza, leader
SAN DIEGO
Danza Mexicayotl, Mario Aguilar, capitán

GARIFUNA
The word "Garifuna" is not well-known as a reference to a cultural group. Garifuna are a loosely-associated mix of peoples from Africa, Native America, Spain, England. They live in villages along the Caribbean coastlines—México, Honduras, Belize, Nicaragua, Costa Rica, and Panama. The immigrant group in Los Angeles alone is some 25,000 strong. Their tribal customs and traditions derive from African and indigenous American sources. Their language is a

mix of all of the above, though most speak an English dialect, since many are descendants of escaped slaves from English islands of the Caribbean—Jamaica, Trinidad, Tobago, Bahamas, and others. Information for Garifuna activities is best obtained from local newspapers in Los Angeles or from members.

OTHER ORGANIZATIONS
PACIFIC ISLANDERS CULTURAL ASSOC.
450 Sutter St., Ste. 1112, San Francisco, CA 94108

INTERNAT'AL INDIAN TREATY COUNCIL
(*See Bibliography, Appendix VII*)
IITC, 2390 Mission St., Ste. 301, San Francisco, CA 94110 (415) 641-4482, (FAX 415.641.1298)

PRISON LIFE

Our Nights are dark
No Stars to Light our way
No Moon to shine for our Hearts
or Sunshine to Welcome our days......
    The shadows of a Poisoned Past
    Made us live life so wild & fast......
  The Poisoned Mentality
Has done away with our Freedom & Peace
Now Darkness & Madness never seem to cease......
But the struggles of the Moment
Have made us stronger & wiser for a better Day
For People like some that are now present
Have Given us Light with their kind & wise ways......
    Good Brothers of Motherearth
    It is Good to have you near
For your Good ways Give us the strength we do Feel......
Your leaves always bring strong spirit for us to hear......
    And our relations make life real......
    Words spoken from my heart
      Honor and Respect...
      —Soaring Eagle (Cornelio Tristan)
      Pelican Bay State Prison— July, 1996

COPING

NEARLY EVERY BOOK and article on California Indians emphasizes coping with some aspect of the "dominant society" that has impacted Native life, customs, or well-being. In the late 20th century, the theme has been Indian gaming, or how to cope with the rules laid down by the dominant society for the conduct of economics on the reservation. For 150 years, the economic state of the Indian in California has been governed almost entirely by the outcome of the treaty abrogation of 1851. These treaties set up the Indian as legal "wards of the state", that is, under the care and protection of the United States Government. The government has since done almost nothing to improve the welfare of its wards, and the result has been extreme poverty and extreme unemployment. The resources of the reservations and surrounding communities were grossly insufficient.

The failure of the government as "guardian" has necessitated coping with the lack of health facilities, adequate educational facilities free of racist and classist attitudes, proper environmental protection. Land, as inadequate in size and resources as it was, suffered appropriation, forfeiture, and deceitful sale to the white community.

Congressional vicissitudes, reversals, oscillations, indecision, and contemptible behavior have required very extreme coping skills. Were Federal entitlements, both by treaty and laws applying to all citizens, toward reservations, recognized members, and deserving individuals being observed? Who's to monitor this?

Let's say you're brought up in Indian tradition, but the local church says "Do it OUR way!" Cope. The school teacher puts the Indian kids in a group in the back of the room. Cope. The sheriff says you're under his jurisdiction, not the tribe's. Cope.

Indian survival strategies developed over the last few decades have finally resulted in major improvements. Legal and ethical pressure on state and Federal authorities on gaming is one. Incessant demands and requests in the right places have resulted in a vastly improved Indian Health Service. Almost all reservations and rancherias have learned to write and receive Federal HUD grants for housing. The result is that hundreds of formerly scattered tribal members are once again gathered into a community, a source of power that can be exercised at local, county, state, and Federal levels. Law enforcement can be made just, though much is yet to be done through Federal recognition of deserving tribes. Respect for the people can be equalized. Business and administrative activities can be exercised as a community, a township. Relationships with other Federal agencies such as the Bureau of Land Management, the Forest Service, and the National Park Service have markedly improved. The "dominant society" is slowly coming to terms with the term "sovereignty". The comeback, the rejuvenation of California Indian society is with us.

Coping has been worth it.

FACES
OF NATIVE CALIFORNIA
PAST AND PRESENT

from top, left to right:
Portrait of Mary Shiape (Maidu) State Parks
Washoe child in cradleboard

1903, State Parks

Chief Truckee (Washoe)

bas-relief in Murphys CA, E Clampus Vitus

SF State Powwow   1979, dhe
Son of Pascual (Quechan)   State Parks
Portrait of Paiute Lady   State Parks
Stirring acorn for a Maidu Feast

1910, State Parks

"Old" Gabriel" of Carmel Mission
  (probably Rumsien or Esselen) State Parks

45
NATIVE
CALIFORNIA

A SHORT HISTORY OF CALIFORNIA INDIAN LAND

IN THE BEGINNING, all 101,120,000 acres of California belong to the Natives; at the end of 1999, only 500,000 acres (1/2%). Spanish troops and padres under direction of Father Junípero Serra in 1769 take the first land. Native possession disappears mission by mission until 1821 (*Appendix II*).

México declares independence in 1822, and the serfdom condition of Indians is declared at an end in 1833. Indians are supposed to have their land returned, but it doesn't happen that way.

Rancheros and foreign settlers appear (1812-45) (*Appendix III*), seizing more land from Central Valley people now debilitated by pandemics. Some tribes sign a few "agreements", but lose land anyway. California's Mexican government is in revolt in 1841, and so land-taking stops, temporarily.

Almost on cue, the American Army (John C. Frémont) and Navy (John D. Sloat) appear (1846) and California becomes part of the U.S. (The Donner Party rejects help from Washoes and end up devouring each other.)

GOLD IS DISCOVERED near Columbia (1848); the gold rush mob begins taking land (1849). The territorial legislature passes a law to protect the rights of Indians (1850). Rights? Major (a self-appointed rank) James D. Savage seizes Yosemite Valley (1851).

Congress sees a need to remove Indians from contact with the white mob; so southerners O. M. Wozencraft, Redick McKee, and George Barbour are appointed commissioners to arrange treaties throughout the new state (1850-51), then to become Indian agents. Seeing the need to move rapidly, as conflict is escalating, they separate. They manage to gain signatures on 18 "treaties", each of which sets out specific tracts as sole occupancy land. The Indians' total is 7.5 million acres. (*See Map 2, also examples of Shasta people, p.98 & 169*) No Native signatures, only "X"es, some have only Spanish given names. Few "interpreters" know what is going on.

The 18 treaties go to Congress, but California legislators successfully lobby for defeat in secret session and results are hidden until 1905. Meanwhile, Indian

Williams Butte (here) is the site of the old Paskenta Rancheria. The tribal village was once bought and destroyed by a local lumber company, has been recovered by the Paskenta Tribe, and soon will be their home again.

(dhe, 1997)

NATIVE CALIFORNIA

land almost completely disappears. In 1926, in an attempt to specifically identify the "tribes", most are found to have been small bands or only villages, pertaining to only 56 of the 126 tribes known at the time (by anthropologists).

IN 1928 INDIANS are allowed to sue Congress, $5M is awarded, but lawyers get most of it. Thousands of people are rounded up and deposited in ten larger reservations beginning in the 1850s-60s, but five are completely worthless and are closed. The residents are left to wander, usually back to their homes. Nothing much happens until the early 1900s, when small rancherias are acquired by presidential executive order or by congressional action, "for landless California Indians", when wretched conditions of several bands are identified. Most rancherias are established on or very near original tribal territories. At the 1900 census, the government manages to identify only 15,000+ Indians in California. (*See p.38 on Populations.*) In this book you will see dates accompanying the reservation descriptions indicating the year(s) it is founded.

The government finally takes an Indian census, called the Baker Roll (1928-33). As a result, it gives supposed cash compensation (a piddling $1.25/ acre) for the 1851 treaties land, nothing for the other 92M acres. Again, lawyers take most. Some tribes don't go for the swindle, but have to wait 20 years for legalities to turn to drivel and their hopes of some recompense to evaporate.

Meanwhile, the Federal BIA in 1936 and 1938, the California BIA in 1944, 1949, and 1950, then Congress in 1958 have the brilliant idea to abolish all Indian lands, thus solving everything. "Assimilation" is the doublespeak, "termination" is the action, which intends to give all Indians a deed to the land they are living on, and then sign off. Sign-off would be worth $670 per person in California. All reservations would be abolished. The idea does not become reality in most states, since almost all Indian lands are held in common by the tribe, not by individuals.*

MOST RANCHERIA RESIDENTS don't fall for the this swindle, either; but many rancherias are terminated around 1958-60 anyway, setting the rancheria residents adrift. Finally, a complicated lawsuit called simply **Tillie Hardwicke** requires the government to reinstate the terminated rancherias (1983). This is a long time for the people to be without Federal assistance. The grounds for reinstatement are "illegal representations to residents as to what expectations

would be from termination", like loss of benefits for health, education, utility connections, tax exemptions, unemployment benefits, welfare, etc. At this point, some rancherias disappear, since all residents are required to accept the deal, go broke, sell out, and move away. Most rancherias survive, at least as communities, none without some damage. A few are only "skeletal" remains, but sue for major reinstatement of their rancherias, even if at another location nearby. New land allows housing and casinos. A few are successful (1997-99).

Two old homes (abandoned) in the town of Paskenta were occupied by tribal members displaced from the old rancheria.   (dhe, 1997)

SOME GOOD NEWS is that the Bureau of Land Management has deeded some of its "unused" acreage in southern California to a few bordering reservations (1995). The BLM and some forestry companies agree to Indian purchase and management of the Sinkyone Wilderness (1997). (*See p.97.*) The Forest Service is listening to suggestions that some of the northern tribes assume land and/or forest management of their nearby or adjacent ancestral lands. USFS also agrees to Indian monitoring of land used for growing traditional basketry materials on a continuing basis. USFS also recognizes quite a few dedicated ceremonial areas for tribal use throughout the state (also disregards a few, too).

THE NATIONAL PARK SERVICE accepts Indian ceremonial use claim in some Parks (Yosemite, 1998; Point Reyes, 1989; Santa Monica Mountains National Recreation Area, mid-1990s), but tries to prohibit descendants of the original lands residence within the park (so far unsuccessful in Death Valley, partly in Yosemite).

*The National Indian Law Library (NILL) of the Native American Rights Fund (NARF, p.257) can offer interested readers a long list of titles which it holds on the subject of termination: books, articles, reports, to a copy of the law itself, by Congressman Morris Thompson. NARF, 1506 Broadway, Boulder, CO 80302

THE PLACES THAT ARE DUE RESPECT

SACRED SITES, MOUNTAINS & LANDFORMS, SPECIAL PLACES, BURIAL GROUNDS

"To us, the ashes of our ancestors are sacred,
and their resting place is hallowed ground."
—Chief Seattle (*Sealth*), *Duwamish*, 1855

THE OLDEST PLACES, the ones that were touched and worked by human hands ages ago—so long ago that we cannot know when—demand our reverent respect. A special appreciation comes to me when I realize I am witnessing the artistic or even everyday work of a human being who lived a thousand or more years ago. Such work is not likely to have been "art for art's sake" nor grafitti; the effort is an expression of the inseparable relation of religion and survival, thus becoming a useful and attractive piece of work.

In California, the oldest artistic places are nearly all rock art sites: carvings chipped into the surface (petroglyphs) or paintings (pictographs) (*Rock Art, p.62 and App. VII.*). A few known sites are of stones laid out in a pattern. All these places were selected by their artists for special purposes. Spiritual leaders tell us that the places themselves chose to be so honored because they are "power places". In a quiet visit to such sites, you should be able to feel the uniqueness of the place. Go to them with an attitude of respect and reverence, not levity or triviality.

Most locations, especially those with numerous figures or designs, are deeply religious in nature, much as paintings, sculpture, stained glass, or symbols are used in other cultures or times. Imagine a religious leader by torchlight using symbolic petroglyphs to illustrate a point, to recall a very special event, or to teach his/her students how to remember a certain religious rite. Imagine that certain symbols are there to be remembered at an initiation into a clan or society.

In many sites the artists used religious* symbols oriented to hunting—we must recall that the hunt, survival, and religion are all part of the same unbroken fabric of life. In these places we may see drawings of recognizable animals, and sometimes depictions of fanciful ones. These drawings were often used to help summon animal spirits to the place so that the hunt might be used to provide sustenance for the group.

A few sites have been found in California of astronomical significance, that enabled those entrusted with knowing the seasons to forecast the time to plant or to move camp. It was also important to know the time to prepare for certain festivals or rituals of invocation or thanksgiving.

Sometimes we find rather isolated instances of rock art—these may be trail directions (a spiral saying look up or down for something important—a spring or a landmark), or sometimes they are a simple invocation of help to a spirit (a "shrine"). The burial sites of the ancestors are sacred also. Many tribes believe that spirits do not rest unless the bones remain and return to the earth whence they came. Everyone must respect this belief; this respect is due all our ancestors, regardless of origin. Some tribes, such as the Maidu and the Paiute/Shoshone, hasten the return, preferring to practice cremation.

In the Native American cultures or religions, some sacred places are not marked by rock art or any external structure, no "edifice complex". These are the most powerful places—where one can go to receive inspiration, a "vision", direction in one's life, or to meditate. These are natural places, where the ideas of nature embedded in the Indian culture become most evident. Frequently, but not always, they are mountaintops or summits, remote places that bring one closer to the spirits. Several mountains are well-known as "sacred" mountains (*Map 1*), others are held more like "revered" mountains (Mt. Tamalpais, Mt. Boney, Mt. St. Helena, Cuyamaca Peak, Mt. Laguna). Within the natural places are the birds of the air, the fish of the waters, the rocks and soil and trees of the mountains—all belong to the family.

Indian people have a very difficult time preserving such places from desecration—someone always seems to want to put in a road, a beacon, or radar, or microwave, or a lookout. Unfortunately, not all these sites are under Indian control. Nevertheless, everyone must learn to respect these places by going there and sensing the delight of being in a unique and sacred place. People are not poor who respect the land, especially the unspoiled land.

The most sacred places within the Native world are burial grounds. The burial ground at Misión San Juan Bautista is well-marked, but the wall surrounds only a fraction of the estimated 2,000 Indians interred here. (dhe, 1988)

THE CAMPOSANTO
(CEMETERY)

THIS CEMETERY WAS USED FOR BURIALS FROM 1778 TO 1865, AND FADED ARCHIVES REVEAL THAT c. 6,000 INDIANS WERE INTERRED HERE DURING THAT PERIOD. MANY OF THEM WERE STRICKEN IN THE DEVASTATING CHOLERA AND SMALL POX EPIDEMICS OF 1825.

THE CEMETERY WAS FIRST CONSECRATED IN 1778, THREE YEARS AFTER THE MISSION WAS MOVED TO THIS SITE.

IN JANUARY 29, 1939, THE CAMPOSANTO WAS REDEDICATED BY HIS EXCELLENCY........THE ARCHBISHOP CANTWELL.

Misión San Gabriel

These are not "magic" symbols, for summoning the spirits to our attention is a religious, not a magical or miraculous act.

continued

On a high mesa at the narrows of the Colorado River at Needles, ancient Mohave fashioned the Rock Maze in the desert pebbles. The site is used in association with mourning ceremonies by the Mohave tribe. Souls at death travel downstream to this region, where they may continue to live yet again. However, they may be pursued by evil spirits. As souls travel the maze, the evil ones are confused and become lost, leaving good ones to live on in peace.   (dhe, 1982)

This is the environment of the famous Painted Rock of the Carrizo (reed grass) Plain. Fantastic triangular shapes, animals, suns, and webs are both carved and painted on the walls of a huge cleft in the rock. An inscription is carved in a nearby stone—a relic of an early Spanish expedition.   (dhe, 1989)

The most sacred places in Indian country are the places where the remains of those passed on lie. Some are marked, as is this one of the Robinson Rancheria near Clear Lake, although many burials are not marked. Other cemeteries, traditionally, are not marked at all, making it difficult to know their location until some disturbance of the ground occurs. Absence of markers at least lessens the disrespectful, ghoulish, and illegal practices of raiding Indian burials.   (dhe, 1997)

The future of the culture and traditions of the Tongva, as with all peoples, lies in teaching the young the sacredness of their young. (This is the Kuruvungna Spring beside University High School in Westwood, Los Angeles County.   (dhe, 1999)

Lastly, we must respect the ancient archaeological village sites themselves, aside from the fact that they are protected by state and Federal laws. A place where humans resided for hundreds or thousands of years must have some special significance. These village sites are the places where the fabric of Indian history was first designed. Once they are destroyed, our knowledge, realization, and imagination of what has gone before are diminished.

No person may excavate, remove, damage, or otherwise alter or deface any archaeological resource located on public lands or Indian lands...
—*Archaeological Resources Protection Act of 1979,*
Public Law 96-95

San Miguel Mission (along U.S. 101) gives public recognition to the hundreds of Salinans lost at the Mission. (dhe, 1999)

NATIVE AMERICAN GRAVES PROTECTION AND REPATRIATION ACT (NAGPRA)

UNTIL VERY RECENT TIMES, archaeologists dug up skeletons and bones along with the artistry the early people had created, with the aim to "study" them. Most modern Indian people properly objected to this desecration of the bones of their ancestors. Specifically, state and federal laws have been passed that require respect for the dead—the most stringent laws pertain to any government-owned property; however, in California all ancient bones found in digging (of whatever origin and for whatever reason), must be reburied under the auspices of the local Native American Heritage Commission (Sacramento). Rock art and archaeological sites, including village sites, are also protected from destruction. Heavy penalties have resulted from violation of these laws. Anyone noticing violation of these statutes are requested to report the situation to law enforcement and the Commission.

A monument to the Nome Lackee (Nomlaki) people stands in a barren field, pierced by a tiny stream, dry eight months of the year. Thousands of Central Valley Indians were taken from their homes and put here to try to make a living. Most went back home as soon as they could, if they could. (dhe, 1998)

SACRED SITES

BURIAL GROUNDS (OFTEN UNMARKED)
POWER PLACES (USUALLY UNMARKED)
SACRED MOUNTAINS (SOME PROMINENT, OTHERS UNMARKED)
ROUNDHOUSES
DANCE ARENAS
ANCIENT ROCK ART
ANCIENT VILLAGE SITES
SPRINGS AND WATER SOURCES
UNSPOILED NATURAL PLACES

A roundhouse site is always chosen with great care for its sacred power. The roundhouse shown at left is located in Calaveras county's Mi-wuk community at West Point. The most sacred dances of California Indians are held in these. (dhe, 1994)

THE PROBLEM WITH NAMES

PLACES OR GEOGRAPHICAL features often bear the names of persons whose memories and deeds are to be honored. That's only reasonable. But who gets to do the naming?

THE BESTOWAL of a name on a place normally is the privilege of the first European to encounter it. The name he (never she) selects can be that of a saint (San José), a place he remembers in the east, like Washington, or that of some well-known hero of military or political fame (Sheridan, Gavilan, Miranda).

It was common to give simple descriptive names (in Spanish or English): Encino, Live Oak, Chico, Willows, Coyote, Hermosa Beach, Greenfield, etc.

The most common names for people are the hundreds of places given the name of the first European landowner or adventurer: Pico, Pacheco, Irvine, Woodfords, Patrick.

MOST CALIFORNIA TRIBES gave names to just about every conceivable feature of the landscape—hills and mountains, passes, creeks, towns, significant clumps of trees. These were the oral maps, which also designated the sacred sites and power places*. California is unusual in the large number of Indian names left upon the landscape, except in the northeast, where Indian names were often translated into English.

IN THIS BOOK you will find a portion of each regional description devoted to the original Indian name for many sites and features. Even a few names of outstanding Indians are honored. Marin and Quintín (Indians given Italian names, from San Marin and San Quintín), for example, were actually Miwok rebels from Misión San Rafael. These two won considerable fame for their protests of harsh Spanish rule. Stanislaus, a Yokuts man, led a vigorous rebellion against Spanish domination in the Central Valley, before being defeated. Joaquin Murietta, part Sonora, Mexico Indian, is no doubt the most famous of those honored with a place named after him.

WHEN IT IS TIME to put a name on public works—roads and streets, buildings, neighborhoods, and the like, persons ignorant of history often take the mentally lazy or simply prejudiced path. They find it easiest to choose a name that has been around the longest, without giving a thought to the association of this name.

A rather appalling number of such names honor the memories of men who had dreadfully adverse effects on the fabric of the Native population.

Thus, we have names to honor the memories of…

*Bean, Lowell, et al., The Cahuilla Landscape. Appendix VII

JUNÍPERO SERRA (1769, arrived in California; many sites named for him). Founder of the mission chain, responsible for nearly extinguishing the cultures of two dozen tribes of southern California and destroying thousands of Indian lives by disease.

GASPAR DE PORTOLÁ (1769, arrived with Serra; sites, streets named for him). Serra's army captain, who carried out his orders.

JEDEDIAH SMITH (1828, explored Smith River). Rather brutal leader of the first American expeditions through northern California rivers and forests, spreading European diseases and shooting Indians opposing his trek.

U.S. Army Capt. John C. Frémont

JOSÉ MARIA AMADOR (1837; Amador County named for him). Butcher of dozens of escapees from coastal missions.

MARIANO GUADALUPE VALLEJO (1830s; Vallejo city and streets). Brother of Salvador Vallejo. Established a huge rancho, some of it still extant, in Petaluma (Sonoma County) using Wappo (*Satiyomi*) indentured servants, workers, and mercenaries. The Satiyomi had been "pacified" by his killing 200 and taking 300 others prisoner in 1834.

SALVADOR VALLEJO (1841). Established a ranch on Clear Lake (Lake County) using kidnapped Pomo ranch hands, after murdering several in a sweatlodge.

Johann (John A.) Sutter

ANDREW KELSEY (1840s; Kelseyville, Lake County). and Charles Stone, bought out Salvatore Vallejo's ranch. He was eventually murdered by ungrateful Pomos in 1849. U.S Army revenged this with the1850 Bloody Island Massacre.

GEORGE C. YOUNT (1832; Yountville). Friend of the Vallejos, used Patwin Wintun as mercenaries and indentured ranch hands.

JUAN JOSÉ WARNER (1850; Warner's Ranch, San Diego County). His harsh mishandling of Cupeño Indians on "his" land, along with the levy of illegal taxes caused a Cupeño uprising in 1850. *continued*

JOHANN (JOHN A.) SUTTER (1840s; Sutter Buttes, many sites in Sacramento area). Militant founder of a large fort and farm system called New Helvetia (later Sacramento), built and entirely worked with Konkow and Nisenan Maidu, and Miwok mercenary labor.

PEARSON B. READING (1846; place names near Redding, no relation). Carved a huge land grant of Wintun land in northern Sacramento Valley. Wintu and Maidu Indian labor.

JOHN C. FRÉMONT (1849; Fremont city, Peak). Captain, U.S. Army who hired Tulare and Gabrielino/Tongva mercenaries to prey on their own people. On other exploits slaughtered 174 Wintu and Yana who protested his presence on his "fact finding" expedition.

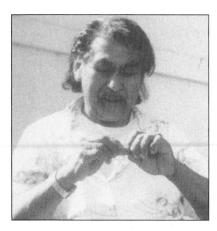

"Bun" Lucas, Teacher and Friend (Kashaya)

ROBERT F. STOCKTON (1846; Stockton city, streets, schools). Navy commander who led an attack from his ship on the Mexican army of indigenous citizens in San Pedro, led by Andrés Pico and Antonio Castro, wealthy landowners in L.A. area.

JOHN BIDWELL (1841; Ft. Bidwell, parts of Chico). Leader of first wagon train into California into Paiute, Pit River, and Maidu territory. Established a refuge in Chico for Maidu made homeless by settler immigrants.

Fred Nason, Wrangler, Teacher & Friend (Esselen)

PETER LASSEN (1844; Lassen County, Lassen Park and Peak). In 1844 obtained a land grant, then became a ruthless gold miner in 1850. Evicted and killed many Maidu. He was eventually murdered and mourned by no one.

BRAXTON BRAGG (1865; Ft. Bragg). This Confederate general had earlier invaded northern México with the U.S. Army.

KIT CARSON (1860s ; Carson City, Sierra mountain Pass). This famous scout led the U.S. army to massacre many Navajo (Diné) who were protecting their land.

PERHAPS IT IS TIME to rename some places with their original names, or honor more honorable citizens, real heroes:

THE REBEL:
JUAN ANTONIO GARRÁ (*Cupeño*), who fought against his captors (*p.34*),

THE HEALERS:
ESSIE PARRISH (*Kashaya*),
SEMU HUAUTE (*Chumash*),
JAY JOHNSON (*Miwok*),

THE WEAVERS:
ELSIE ALLEN (*Pomo*),
MABEL MCKAY (*Pomo*),
JUANITA CENTENO (*Chumash/Yaqui*),
VIVIEN HAILSTONE (*Yurok/ Karuk/Hupa*),
VERA REYERSON (*Yurok*),

THE TEACHERS & LEADERS:
MILTON "BUN" LUCAS (*Kashaya*),
BERNICE TORREZ (*Kashaya*),
HENRY AZBILL (*Maidu*),
RUPERT COSTO (*Cahuilla*),
ISHI (*Yahi*),
BILL FRANKLIN (*Mi-wuk*),
BERNEICE HUMPHREY (*Tolowa*),
SPARKY MORALES (*Tongva*),
FLORENCE JONES (*Winemem Wintu*),
KATHERINE SIVA SAUBEL (*Cahuilla*),
FRANCISCA PATENCIO (*Cahuilla*)...

This list must remain incomplete. There is space to add the names of your own heroes who ought to be honored.

Bernice Torrez, Spiritual Leader & Friend (Kashaya)

THE ECOLOGICAL ENVIRONMENT OF NATIVE CALIFORNIA

IN THE YEAR 2000, Indian trust land occupies a little more than 500,000 acres, but this land touches three of the four corners of the state, and all ecological niches in between.

Much of this land treasure has never been touched except by the Native owners, and much of that has never been exploited. What the California Native American communities uniquely possess, then, are in effect large ecological preserves, a form of wilderness. Additionally, the State Park, National Park, and some National Forest systems are in many places integrating into their parks an awareness of the earliest inhabitants—an awareness of Indian presence. These areas embrace deeply forested coastal zones, high mountain fastnesses, chaparral-scattered hills, unspoiled desert terrain. Not having made a careful survey of this countryside, I cannot make a detailed account of the flora and fauna contained there, but let me describe some of the places.

In the searing, sandy Coachella Valley, one Reservation stands out as an ecological preserve, the Augustine. Its one square mile has no residents and no developed agriculture. The land is not really disturbed. A few dirt tracks lead to trash heaps, that's all. (dhe, 1988)

The Chemehuevi Reservation occupies nearly twenty miles of Colorado River bank, and some four miles of it is devoted to an intensely-developed marina. However, two hundred yards up the bank is a desert land inhabited largely by one alien species—the wild burro (which tramples the local springs, and is undesirable to the Indian game officers). The other life and countryside is almost undisturbed. Why? It is fiercely ovenlike in summer, and, to most humans, devoid of interest. But it is there, and hopefully will remain as it is, a protected desert nature reserve.

The upper reaches of the Tule River Reservation have been sporadically lumbered, but not clearcut. Today, timber is seldom harvested here. This area is a magnificently forested stretch of the southern Sierra, with stark rock outcroppings towering over river valleys. It is rich in wild animals, fish, and beautiful plant life. As Indian land it will persevere in its splendor, under tribal guidance and management of the Natural Resources Director.

The Augustine Reservation is a square mile of the Coachella Valley desert. Some say "nothing is there". Others say that this reserve of greasewood and desert scrub, occasionally hit by fires and sometimes abused by the locals, is a slightly blemished remnant of the early Valley; never irrigated or settled upon, it is still almost pristine. The same can be said for several sections of the nearby checkerboard Torres-Martinez Reservation. Some sections of that reservation were submerged under the Salton Sea many years ago. The Sea level rises and falls with wet or dry seasons, and it suffers pollution from agricultural runoff. Whether or not this underwater land is an ecological preserve continues to be the subject of debate.

Portions of the Agua Caliente Reservation have been quite purposefully set aside as ecological preserves—the palm canyons and their adjacent lands. These are of especially vital scientific, biological, visual, historical, and planetary interest, have been protected in the past by the tribe, and will continue to be so. These beautiful places, preserves of green nature and water in the exotic desert, are today tourist destinations.

Not far from Agua Caliente, the Campo Reservation has established the Campo Environmental Protection Agency (CEPA), aggressively attacking the problems of land destruction and erosion by traditional methods of replanting arroyos, reviving marshes and wetlands, and restablishing fisheries.

Cholla cactus is a decorative element of the desert here in the Agua Caliente Tribe's Palm Springs desert washes. (dhe, 1991)

Pachepus (a private ranch) is part of the ancestral homeland of the Esselen people. Never under government domination, the 1200-acre ranch is being kept in the family of descendants of an Esselen member of the Carmel Mission. Adjacent to the Ventana Wilderness, it is true wilderness itself, intriguing with ancient acorn grinding rocks, village sites, and painted caves. Pack trips by horseback and hikes, supervised by the tribe, explore this network of ecological preserves of immense proportions in the coastal mountains of Big Sur.

For over fifty miles upstream from the Pacific Ocean the Yurok and the Hoopa Reservations follow the Klamath and Trinity Rivers. Along this luxuriant and wild stretch of river, it is possible to see inglorious patches of clearcut forest, the land exposed like a wound. But the majority of the margins are old, if not ancient forest, especially in the vicinity of the few villages (where logging was rare). Most of the villages along these banks have been there for several thousand years, excepting the present houses, of course. The lands around these villages are some of California's best examples of ecological preservation in which both nature and man exist in harmony—not as "wilderness". The Indian peoples have used the riverine margins and the forests for all their subsistence needs, yet the land continues to produce appropriately, if not abused.

In some places, however, in order to provide a reasonable standard of living for its people, a tribe has found it necessary to develop the land. Such development usually takes the form of agriculture. Owing to successful retention of irrigation rights, large-scale land-lease farming has been brought to the Fort Mojave, Colorado River Tribes, and the Fort Yuma and Torres-Martinez Reservations in the southland. To a much lesser extent, some farming is found at Fort Bidwell and Round Valley. Though it need not be abusive, agriculture does introduce a wholly different form of ecology to the land, and it no longer can be considered an ecological preserve.

Through some recent unsavory and urgent governmental financial inducements, some tribal administrations have been under pressure to devote lands to hazardous waste dumps and other projects harmful to the earth and its beings. In its refusal to offer tribes reasonable means to a reasonable living standard, the government has thrust upon them a most degrading situation— threatened systematic degeneration and destruction of the land itself! Fortunately, at least three such recent proposals have been put down by aware tribal administrations, and most Indian land remains fairly pristine.

TRIBAL ETHNOZOOLOGICAL ACTIVITIES

WHAT: The well-being of the overall coastal environment and its flora and fauna is occupying the concerns of a group of Chumash environmental activists—includes whales, dolphins, otters. Salmon runs, both in sea and riverine environments are the concerns of a number of Klamath/Trinity and Smith River tribes, since the health of these runs directly influences religious and survival fisheries. Clear Lake fishers: concerns over mercury poisoning in a food source.

The health of deer and elk stands and their access to proper grazing are a concern of the many tribes which possess meadows and access to forests. Even bugs, both the harmful and the beneficial varieties, receive attention from almost every group that have botanical interests (above).

WHO: Coastal environment: Wishtoyo (see Chumash), Sinkyone Salmon fisheries: Klamath/Trinity watershed: Karuk, Yurok (including Resighini), Hupa, Pit River Tribes; Smith River Tolowa Wild animal herds: Hupa and Yurok (especially maintaining up-country meadowlands with controlled burns); several Foothill Mono, Miwok, and Yokuts tribes; Chemehuevi (wild burros)

Other reservations have been lived in and, once again, only lightly touched by the hand of the inhabitants, consisting only of a few homes and sometimes tribal buildings lying at the edges—Manzanita, Mesa Grande, Morongo, Fort Bidwell, old Sherwood Valley, among many others. These are places where the natural round continues, the land is not despoiled, and the people have been able to give their respect to the land.

LAND USE

TO DEVELOP OR NOT is a serious question. Is tribal self-sufficiency, rather than termination of communal ownership and allotment to private individuals a worthwhile goal? In the past, groups that have elected development have always required external financial support—sometimes a single grant, sometimes continuing support. And that support has seldom been easy to obtain. In the north, only the large reservations have had any chance of on-reservation self-help programs: lumbering, some fishing, a little tourism.

The reservations of southern California are nearly all much larger than the dozens of tiny rancherias of the north. Once barely self-sufficient, since most of the land is practically desert, the technology of irrigation has increased the commercial value of several areas immensely. Further, the scarcity of any developable land in California increases its desirability, especially in the national rush to the "sun belt."

"Develop" can take several faces: agricultural use, waste disposal sites, or tourist attractions. Although it may seem that groups of destitute people would jump at the chance to make money, there are deeper principles involved. The concept of working the land to make it pay is foreign to native traditional uses. The relation of Indians to the land is not to force it to yield, but to cooperate with what nature has supplied, and take only what is immediately needed.

Because of this basic ethic, Indians have been reluctant modern-style farmers, often hesitating even to harm Mother Earth with a hard steel plow. Once the land is tilled or despoiled; the sacred relationship is disrupted.

In the 1920s, the Ft. Yuma Reservation acquired the ability to install a large irrigation system along the lower Colorado River. Since that time it has been able to lease its productive agricultural land to farmers in California and Arizona. The income improves the living conditions of tribal member, at the same time providing a large food supply to the nation. Winter crops in this very warm climate are especially valuable.

(dhc, 1990)

THE STRONGEST REASON for slow development, until recently, has been that the economic backing and marketing techniques for large-scale farming have not been available. The Colorado River peoples are among those most pressured by the dilemma, since their historic legal claims to water rights are now usually acknowledged. The "use it or lose it" saying has not always applied; they seldom used their full allotment, but hadn't lost it, either. Traditionally these river tribes have been cautious and prudent agriculturalists, with appreciation for their stewardship of the land. However, the urgency of survival and the availability of capital have dictated a departure from the old ways.

On the huge Colorado River Tribes Reservation and the Ft. Yuma Reservation, both of which sit astride the Colorado River, nearly 100,000 acres of once open desert are under cultivation on the Colorado River Reservation, using a complex of 250 miles of irrigation canals. Ft. Yuma's extensive irrigation complex was begun in 1934, and has been expanded recently. During winter months, a large greenhouse and hydroponics business has provided tomatoes, cucumbers, and other vegetables for national consumption.

"DEVELOP" may also mean putting in a casino or gaming establishment where feasible. It is important to note that such places are almost always placed at the remote edges of a reservation or rancheria, so that the gaming operations interfere with the daily life of the

reservation as little as possible. It is almost as if it is an embarrassment or annoyance. But then the income is directed most often toward housing and improvement of the daily lives of the people. This, too, requires development.

Development may also be directed toward natural resources—a development not attainable without money. Most disturbing is an insistent Federal government Department of Energy, along with some Bureau of Land Management and state officials who insist that there is "nothing in the desert".

For instance, they say that Ward Valley, lying right in Chemehuevi ancestral heartland, is a marvelous place to dump nuclear waste, without needing so much as a barrier between the waste and the soil below. If you pick up a topographical map of the area, it is plain to see that the desert drainage passes directly from the proposed dump directly across the Colorado Aqueduct (supplying the Coachella Valley and San Diego from the Colorado River) along Homer Wash, and right into the Colorado River via Rice Valley at the Colorado River Reservation. The surface and underground water route is immediately adjacent and accessible over a low saddle to drainage into the Chemehuevi Reservation.

TRIBAL ETHNOBOTANICAL ACTIVITIES

WHAT: Growing and collecting basketry material, medicinal plants, edible herbs, forestry (timber & firewood), agricultural, traditional foods (including acorns and nopal cactus)

WHO: Tolowa, Pit River, Maidu (Mountain, Konkow, Nisenan), Yurok and Hupa forestry, Tsungwe, Sinkyone, various Ohlone (Mutsun and others), various Pomo (Kashaya, Ya-Ka-Ama, and others), Wintun (Wintu, Patwin), Southern Sierra Miwok and other Miwok, Mono, Wukchumni (Yokuts), Chuckchansi (Yokuts), Tule River Reservation Natural Resources, various Chumash, (Oakbrook, Wishtoyo), Tongva, Cahuilla (Malki Museum), Kumeyaay (Barona, Campo), Quechan, Colorado River Tribes, Mohave, the California Integrated Hardwoods Project.

This wide desert wash is quite dry most of the year and most years, but the huge rogue hurricanes that occasionally drift through this area cause extensive flooding. Moreover, the small yearly rains soak into the ground water, as would nuclear waste. None of these facts are lost upon the local Indian tribes, who are maintaining a constant vigil against such insanity.

Another southern California tribe suffered the indignity of allowing hundreds of tons of solid sewage waste to be dumped on its land (through some devious deals), before tribal and public outcry forced removal of the stuff.

"Development" in these instances was definitely retro. Highly encouraging, however, are the great efforts that a number of tribes are taking to improve their own ethnobotanical situations—most often with casino-derived funds.

TRIBAL CULTURES

Mark Acuña, Tongva dance captain, sings and dances to tell a story at Satwiwa, the Chumash and Tongva demonstration site in the Santa Monica Mountains National Recreation Area.   (dhe, 1998)

WHAT'S A "CULTURE"? We use the term all the time: "Celtic culture", "Navajo culture", "Miwok culture", but what is it, really? The word deserves a better interpretation. In fact, most of this book is devoted to the numerous aspects of the Native American *cultures* of California. *Tribes* or *people* are not good synonyms, though these groups possess many aspects of a culture. One dictionary defines culture as ideas, habits, behavioral patterns, with language as the principal bonding agent. Jack Forbes, Native American Studies professor at U. C. Davis defines it as "living". **FOLLOWING ETHNOGRAPHIC USAGE,** we shall use *language* as the major indicator of an *original* cultural relationship. In California few descendants of the original peoples speak their old language. English or Spanish has replaced this "bonding agent"; yet there are still unmistakable ties among the peoples. I think we have to consider the word "culture" in two senses: the older sense (as tools, weapons, clothing, art forms, burial customs, etc.) and the broader sense (as what characteristics the members of any group might have in common).

HERE ARE SOME of the characteristics of any culture that may bind individuals to it.
- immediate family ties
- clan or tribal ties
- language—speakers of the old language, accents in their spoken English
- music and musical instruments
- home life—rural, urban, economic circumstance
- employment—rural, urban, regular or part-time
- education—public, home, tribal
- art—designs in basketry, painting, woodwork, architecture
- food—kind and preparation: home-grown, store-bought, government-supplied commodities
- religion—adaptations to religions: Native, Catholic, Protestant
- beliefs—shamanic, sources of spiritual strength, tribal dance (entertainment or religion?)
- beliefs—myths, superstitions, "sayings"
- loyalty priorities—to self, family, friends, tribe or clan, country
- person-to-person relations:
  —attitude towards men, women, young, elders, outsiders (other tribes, races)
  —personality: e.g., assertive or taciturn
  —sharing: "potlatch", powwows, gifts to others
  —attitude towards war, concept of "warrior"
- games—Indian handgames, casino patron

LOOKING AND LISTENING carefully and sensitively, you may find many of these traits and qualities of an older culture persisting in the tribal cultures of today, though always colored by the dominant culture. Throughout the pages of this book, you may find some of the rich diversity and unity of Native California cultures.

STORIES, LEGENDS, MYTHS, MAGIC

AS I SEE THEM applied by Native Californians:

A *story* is usually a tale told to illustrate a point, attitude, allegory; or indeed it may be someone's factual account of a happening, even though it may have occurred many generations earlier.

A *legend* is a story of long standing—changed, embellished, and colored by attitudes and addition of ethics

A *myth* is an admittedly fanciful story that deals with supernatural beings or ancestors. With some interpretation, we can extract much "truth" or even history from the mythological accounts.

Magic implies exercising supernatural control over natural forces, frequently manipulating nature with evil intent.

WITHIN THE MANY Indian communities it is possible to hear valuable traditional storytellers who are are particularly gifted at remembering the many stories, legends, and myths of their people. Fortunately, several books of their collected stories are now being published for future generations, for after all, most of the storytellers are elders. When you find an opportunity to listen to the stories from the elders, consider yourself very fortunate.

Among Native Americans who live in continuous and consistent contact with nature, special persons are recognized who have the gift of deeply knowing the properties of nature. These persons possess an intrinsic power to use both human nature and the nature around us to improve or change our condition—they are the "traditional" doctors of our well-being. Sometimes they are called "doctor", sometimes "shaman", sometimes "medicine man or woman", sometimes Bill or Agnes. When these persons use their talents, many persons acquainted only with "Western medicine" are often not accustomed to their methods, so are tempted to call their methods (including songs, chants, and rites) "magic". Resist that temptation, unless the use of sulfa drugs or nylon joint replacement is also magic.

Coyote tells of Procuring Fire from the Valley People. In the earliest stories animals spoke.   (M. Lee, WPA, 1930s)

STORYTELLING
CALIFORNIA Indian Story-telling festivals have been held annually at varying locations: Indian Canyon (Hollister) 1996 & 1997, Satwiwa (Thousand Oaks area) 1998, Indian Canyon and Ohlone College (Fremont) 1999.

CALIFORNIA INDIAN STORYTELLING ASSOCIATION
37930 Palmer Dr, Fremont, CA 94536
(510) 794-7253 texeira@ccnet.com

LANGUAGE
"...Our relations are coming around because we are calling to them in languages they understand."
—*L. Frank Manriquez*, Ajachemem

IN MÉXICO, a tribe (ethnic group) that loses its language loses its government entitlements, since it has been presumed to have lost its culture. In the U.S., entitlements and tribal continuity are determined through lineage and descendency. Of course, the former is only excuse to reduce services; however, language has long been a gauge of the health of any culture.

In California language recovery and dissemination has become a *cause*, almost a *necessity*. Even an incongruous Congress has joined in supporting language recovery. (Well, some members advocate English only, while others enthusiastically endorse financial support for disappearing languages and cultures.)

Congress aside, almost every issue of *News From Native California* bears an article relating to the latest developments in California Indian languages. Some of the developments: locating Native speakers; recording on tape and paper their speech and their recollection of words, phrases, and expressions; establishing language classes in many reservations and reservation schools; holding language camps—total immersion sessions lasting several days—for kids and adults; promoting the use of Native languages within the home setting.

LANGUAGE PROGRAMS
California Indian Language Speakers in 1994: In Our Own Words,
Leanne Hinton and Yolanda Montijo,
News From Native California, Vol. 7, No. 4, 1993 and subsequent issues.

ADVOCATES FOR INDIGENOUS CALIFORNIA LANGUAGE SURVIVAL
(A project funded by Native California Network)
P.O. Box 664,
Visalia, CA 93279
(209) 627-1050

MASTER APPRENTICE LANGUAGE LEARNINGPROGRAM (MALLP)
Breath of Life/Silent No More /Circle of Voices,
California Languages Conference
(annually since 1992)

NATIVE CALIFORNIA NETWORK,
Community Grants Program
This very aware group has been accepting grant requests for support of a broad range of Native activities with cultural continuity. Some of the subjects have included: basketry (ethnobotany, materials collection, weaving), big times, language, traditional skills, culture camps, regalia re-creation.
NCN
Adobe Cultural Center,
10 Jolon Rd., King City, CA 93930
(925) 473-4921

(These data may change with the address of the director, but forwarding may be expected.)

ART, WHAT IS IT?
MORE THAN ARTS & CRAFTS

Miwok

ART COMES TO US from many directions. For a long time, we were told that "art" consisted of paintings and sculpture to be found in museums, churches, and homes. In recent years this narrow concept of "art" has been broadened to include the form and appearance of all the things we make for ourselves and our decoration of them, for whatever reason, from bowls and clocks to tables and cars.

*Art*icles made by *art*isans, *art*ists and more.

In ancient or modern art, baskets or pottery or stoneware may be severely plain or highly decorated—in any instance they were touched and cared for by human hands and shaped by the artistry of their makers. An arrow was once a rock and a stick and sinew, but the human touch made them not only functional, but changed their forms into objects with a different beauty. Of course, not every crude pounding rock or chipping blade is art—functional and old, yes, but not necessarily artistic.

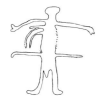
Hakataya?

Beyond the beauty of the function itself, decoration with color, incision, or carving is something especially added to say, "Look at me!" The artist may decorate hunting tools, personal clothing or ornaments, and utensils, or for a religious purpose, alter wood or rock surfaces. In ancient times, these purposes were not separated, as they tend to be today. Religion, hunting, and living were all part of an harmonious natural being.

Pomo

HANDIWORK
OF ALL HUMAN OBJECTS, those that a person has worked by hand are the closest to their creator. A basket, whatever its source, was touched, worked, formed of grasses and twigs and fibers into a piece of artistic design—often today only to be admired for its presentation, but in earlier days created to serve a further purpose. California is blessed with the richest variety of basketry in the world—a grand variety of materials and a grand imagination and inventiveness. Not merely woven, they were filled with meaningful designs, symbols, even stories, after tribal traditions. Beyond tradition, the weavers exercised their artistic freedom, leaving their own individual marks. (*p.60*)

For the pure enjoyment of the senses, the ornament and jewelry makers left their marks. California's early peoples were not gold or silver workers; they worked with sinew, shells, bone, abalone, seeds, feathers, and a few pretty stones. The works of art they produced have a quiet glow, not glitz. Well, some of the modern ones have glitz, at the craft booths.

Care went into forming tools from wood, antler, bone, and stone—handles, levers, arrows, bows, and beautifully chipped projectile points. The artistic content here consists mostly of the beauty of the form itself, although a few tools were lavishly decorated, such as fancy spoons, scoops, and acorn mush paddles carved by northwest California artists.

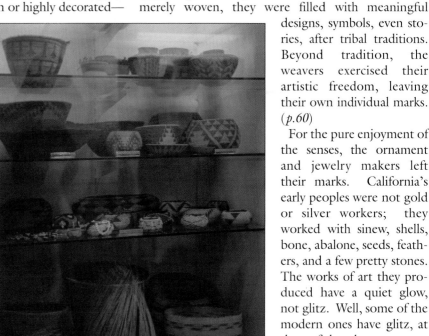

A sampling of the large collection of baskets from the Southwest Museum in Los Angeles. Most museums with any Native artwork show baskets of the tribes native to their region. (dhe, 1989)

Many of the objects that early people made for themselves became buried—either as grave goods to honor the deceased, or lost in the debris of village life. Archaeologists have determined what tools and ornaments people made. We can see them today in many museums throughout the state. (*Appendix I*)

ART is music, dance, carvings, weavings, acting, storytelling. ART IS CREATING.

Boats were objects worthy of particular artistic attention. The traditional art of carving a canoe for a northwestern river is nearly lost, but has been preserved by a few Yurok boatmakers. A rare opportunity to watch the creation of a redwood canoe occasionally presents itself at a reservation or national park festival. A Chumash and Tongva *tomol* and *ti'at* festival of boatmaking and testing and riding is given frequently in the Los Angeles area (*p.196, 211*). These are events not to be missed.

A form of basketry went into boatmaking in lakes and estuaries of central California—the tule reed boat. Used for transportation or fishing, they were nearly identical to those of the Quechua and Aymara of Lake Titicaca in South America, more a reed raft with turned-up bow and stern. A few modern reconstructions of Ohlone and Pomo design exist in museums. All of them have been found to be water-worthy.

HANDIWORK IS something which fascinates people of all cultures. Just about every community in the U.S. has a festival of arts and crafts—county fairs, block fairs, state fairs, Indian powwows, Big Times, art shows, antique shows, markets of all sorts.

Indian arts and crafts have a particular interest, because of this unusual intimate relationship of the artist with the buyer—it's not just something manufactured or made in Asia you pick up at the store. For this reason, arts and crafts is a big business and a substantial contributor to Indian income. A very partial list of sources is to be found in Appendix V.

Maidu

The cradleboard weaver here is Ms. Florence Silva, leader in the Coastal Pomo group, Bo-Cah-Ama. Ms. Silva demonstrates her basketweaving talents at the group's annual festival and dances in Mendocino every summer. (dhe, 1997)

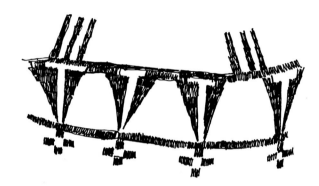

Central Valley

Jacinta Serrano, a well-known weaver of Misión San Gabriel, shown grinding cornmeal in her metate.

(Photograph # N 20055, courtesy of the Southwest Museum, Los Angeles, by C. C. Pierce, 1898)

Miwok

BASKETS, WEAVING, & INDIAN LIFE

WITHOUT DOUBT, the most widespread Indian activity throughout California, both artistic and practical, is weaving. **Fabric** is a powerful analogy for the fabric of all Indian life, of all Indian tribes; the history of tribes is wrapped in the history of the cultural crafts, the arts, the handiwork. A woven object speaks of the care and spirit put directly into it, coming from its maker. The object shows the mind of the maker and the tradition from which he or she came. Baskets are made today virtually the same way as they have been for hundreds of years. The earliest baskets, of course, are highly prized, and those of today bring high prices to a skilled basketmaker.

THE MATERIALS

WEAVERS USE STRAW, grasses, reeds, stems, fibrous leaves, vines, roots, fur and hair. They decorate with beads, shells, stones, feathers, quills, even bark and bone bits.

They may color the materials with infusions of bark, ground nuts, plant sap, sometimes seaweeds, already-colored stems of differing materials, or aniline dyes when they wish; they fix the dyes with inorganic materials like iron-rich soils, rusty nails, or other minerals.

To make them waterproof, baskets are treated with asphalt from seeps, resins and sap from various trees, and in many cases, they are woven so tightly that a little water swells the fibers so that liquids cannot pass through.

THE USES

THERE ARE OPEN weaves as well, so large that burden baskets can carry firewood, large stones, any large object. Huge bins are woven to store acorns and nuts through the winter. Quivers are woven to carry arrows, pouches to carry medicine and herbs and doctoring materials. Woven cradleboards carry infants in almost all cultures. Tight baskets can be used to cook acorn mush, with hot stones for the heat, or to carry pulverized minerals for cooking or painting or healing.

Wide straw or reeds make a very good material to weave a boat, as seen on Clear Lake or in the tule lakes and streams of the Central Valley. The same straw can make a very good water-tight home, sometimes huge ones, bigger than a typical garage, and are woven in the southlands and in the drylands. For the roof of a roundhouse, huge grapevines are woven in and among saplings to support the roof shingles of cedar or redwood. In the desert, woven straw mats fend off the sandy winds and baking sun. Woven straw mats (though seldom made by California Indians today) are still a frequent article on California beaches or any sandy, loose soil.

Baskets carry roots and tubers, household articles, hunting catches; basket beaters knock the seed from plants without destroying the plant, then other baskets carry the seeds. Baskets catch fish, hold grasshoppers. Soft grasses or fur strips are woven for clothing, such as skirts and aprons, and for protection against the elements.

Elaborate straw hats are worn in almost every part of California, especially by the ladies. Gorgeous baskets are woven for gifts—decorated with quail or owl or other feathers. Abalone and shells and pretty stones make for good decoration.

THE DESIGNS & STYLES

THE TWO MAJOR STYLES of basketweaving are twining and coiling. Description of these two methods is beyond the scope of this book, but I would like to refer the reader to the references below to learn about them. See below to know where to learn first-hand or to witness the work being done. The designs range from simple to the most elegant and intricate possible with fine fibers.

In the most infinitesimal weaving, some weavers want to show their fantastic skills by making a tiny basket (3-4 mm) that holds only a single poppy seed. See some of these in the State Indian Museum in Sacramento—but only under their high-powered magnifying glass. Tribal designs can be incorporated into these works of art that are smaller than an apple seed. I am told that the weavers must put themselves into a dream state to be able to "see" their work.

Every tribe has its special designs, though many designs can be almost universal. Where there are mountains, a mountain motif is popular. The desert peoples don't really see that many quails, but they do have Gila lizards. So stylized quail designs are popular up north, Gilas in the south. On the tribal center of the Redding Rancheria you can see the motifs of flying geese of the three resident tribes, taken from their traditional basket designs. They are not they same, but have similar elements.

Design elements include a quail front feather (an inverted L), eagle, bird shape, tree, cornstalk, sheep,

Basketweavers Gladys McKinney (Mono) and Lois Conner Castro (Mono/Chuckchansi) are displaying and selling their basketry at the annual California Indian Basketweavers Association festival, in Reno. More than a hundred other Native American basketweavers from Alaska and Canada to Hawaii and Mexico assembled in June, 1999, the first of many such gatherings. (dhe)

horse, steer head, horns, human figure (male or female with skirt), lizard, zig-zag, lightning, flame, rain, mountain (steps or jagged), star or many-pointed flower, butterfly or hourglass, cross, diamond, rattlesnake (series of diamonds), square, bowl, arrowhead, stacked arrowheads, swastika, "L", "Z", squared spiral or "Greek"-style, motifs within motifs, geometric repetition of a motif.

PROBLEMS FACED BY WEAVERS

BASKETWEAVING TODAY is a rapidly expanding cultural and remunerative art. It is not a craft, it is an art. Obtaining the proper materials is not easy. Since most Indian land has been removed from Indian control, simply finding a stand of grasses or stems has often become an adventure. The U.S. Forest Service is becoming very helpful in most ancient gathering places, though it has not always been that way. Private landholders tend to be more difficult to approach, and must be approached one by one.

Both highway and timber interests have been very insistent that chemical spraying is the only way to have a weedless roadside or a "productive" forest. However, chemical herbicides and pesticides are not exactly the most desirable ingredients for baskets, especially since it is necessary to handle the materials wet, and even to moisten and hold them by mouth. Persuading agricultural interests to practice organic means is not easy, but it is being accomplished. Some cooperation in abandoning harmful spraying in sensitive areas is slowly being offered by both CalTrans and timber interests.

FIELDS OFTEN BECOME overgrown, smothering the grasses that are the materials of choice. In earlier days, Indians carefully cultivated or burned many fields in order to produce the right grasses for baskets (and/or to provide fodder for wild game). Many earlier harvesting areas have been lost to creeping forests, but today forests are being managed in a much more sensitive way. Plants are handled in a very respectful way. Only a thoughtless clod would come in and cut every branch or frond. Weavers select only of the best and most useful fronds. With some sensitivity, practice, and proper advice, you, too, can see which leaves or roots a plant is presenting to you. The point is to leave some for the future. With advice from an experienced gatherer, you may even carefully take a few roots to a new location. This begins a new source.

BASKETWEAVING TODAY

BASKETWEAVING IS probably the most important cultural thread in the entire state, a thread that carries with it traditions and ideas, and a grand respect for the land and its produce. (Note that this subject is being written in the present tense.) We are highly favored by having a strong and energetic statewide organization to promote the creation of baskets and woven articles: the California Indian Basketweavers Association. This organization not only promotes its annual gathering in June (*see Calendar, p.283*) but also sponsors in almost every region of the state classes in basketweaving, demonstrations at major and minor events, presentations at museums and cultural centers. All of this is done for the love of creating weaving—of doing something very difficult, but artistic, with one's hands. Such pride in the product, such continuity of tradition of tribal history, arts, and culture! **CIBA** accepts new members and supporters. Call.

**CALIFORNIA INDIAN
BASKETWEAVERS ASSOCIATION,**
16894 China Flats Rd., Nevada City, CA 95959
(530) 292-0141

**MIWOK ARCHAEOLOGICAL
PRESERVE OF MARIN** (MAPOM)
(415) 479-3281 or MAPOM2255@aol.com

**SAN FRANCISO BAY AREA
URBAN INDIAN BASKETWEAVERS**
(510) 785-2845 or HSuri85519@aol.com

REFERENCES: 1. Three volumes: *American Indian Basketry of* I. *Northern* (1989), II. *Central* (1986), and III. *Southern California* (1993), by Chris Mosher, Riverside Museum Press, 3720 Orange St., Riverside, CA 92501 Photos and diagrams of baskets and their makers of nearly every tribe in the State. Carefully described techniques of coiling and twining. Discussions of the tribal environs.
2. *Indian Basketry of Western North America*, Charles W. Bowers Museum, 2002 N. Main St., Santa Ana, CA, 92706. Descriptions and color photos of their California collections.

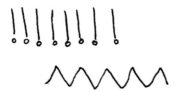

ROCK ART

Remember the ancestors... plan to be one. —anon

FOR A LARGE, high-visibility, permanent work, an artist will frequently turn to stone. This is especially true where the stone is exposed, smooth, and durable; and granite, sandstone, and metamorphic rocks of California were particularly well-suited for ancient rock art messages.

Early rock artists used two methods almost exclusively: painting (pictographs) and incision, or "pecking" (petroglyphs: *petro*, rock + *glyph*, carving). Can you imagine a painting or carving that has lasted out-of-doors for nearly a thousand years? Surprisingly, many have; California is fortunate to have the greatest number and variety of ancient rock art examples in the United States.

Paintings that endure for long periods of time need two features, durable painting materials and protection from the elements. Those that we see today have these characteristics—paintings whose colors are amazingly bright. The pigment materials were minerals—carbon (black), iron or mercury oxides (reds), clays (white, yellow, brown), or copper compounds (green, blue)—while the original binding material most likely was egg or other sticky animal or plant organic matter. The binding material has long since decomposed, but left the enduring pigments in place. The makers' technology was superb for the task at hand. The best-preserved paintings, as expected, are found in caves and overhanging rock shelters in almost all parts of the state where such rock features occur. The Central Valley is nearly devoid of rock art, owing to the scarcity of such features.

Petroglyph art was achieved by carefully chiseling with a very sharp cutting stone into a rock surface that has a natural polish or "varnish" worn by wind and weather. Thousands of elegant carvings have been found from Lava Beds National Park in the north to the Anza-Borrego Desert in the south.

If you observe any weathered rock surface, you can see that there is a variation of coloring. The darker colors come from centuries of leaching out of lighter mineral pigments dissolved in rainwater, then wicked to the surface and deposited there by evaporation of the water. These minerals then oxidize to a darker color. Where the rock has been broken off, the "real", light color of the rock is exposed. Chemists can determine the approximate age of carvings by the amount of weathering on the newer-exposed surface.

What messages did the artists want to leave? First of all, never consider any of these to be idle graffiti; they are serious writings meant to convey information or emotion. For instance, some of their meanings* might be: *trail symbols* (a spiral can mean to look up or down for some topographic feature, such as a spring or a shelter), *historical* (recording of an event, a trip, a map, a story, a myth or mythological crea-

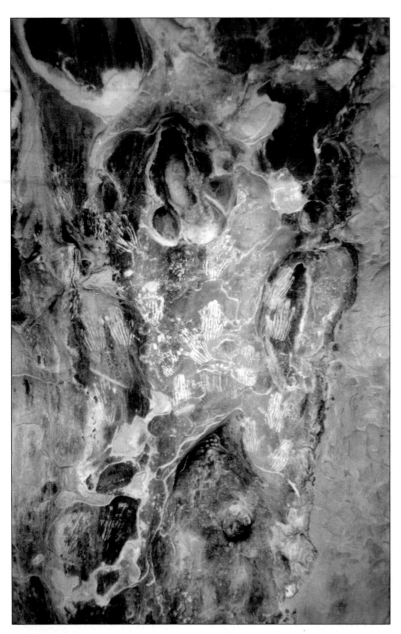

The Esselen ancestors of the Ventana Wilderness area painted the walls of their most sacred cave with black and white hand prints of the warriors accepted into adulthood by the tribe. This cave, itself a beautiful natural feature, is lined with more than three hundred prints, as well as other painted diagrams and symbols.

(photograph ® courtesy of Trudy Haversat and Gary Breschini, 1995)

ture), a *religious* invocation or homage to a spirit (especially an animal or rain spirit), or a *representation* of a diety.

All religions use symbols, and a society that devotes itself to the natural world uses many symbols from nature, much as other religions use symbols for worship: the cross, lamb, or fish (Christian), the spoked circle (Buddhist), the six-pointed star (Semitic), the crescent (Islam), the swastika (Hindu, Buddhist, Pueblo, Aztec).

IN CALIFORNIA INDIAN art, one finds quite a few animal designs, most of them pretty obvious; but then there are symbols of sun (a bright compass-like spray, or concentric circles), rain (a series of parallel straight or slanting lines), a series of "X"s in a tube (rattlesnake), a large rectangle with crisscross line inside (a medicine bag, often with other decoration), a cross (usually of broad, equal-length lines, the four directions). Then there are the strange fish-bone or centipede-like creatures and other beings of the spirit world (unknown or indescribable).

Other symbols are facsimiles of or are derived from Indian sign language, which was universally used in North America. Some designs are reproduced in basket designs, as well. (*Basketweaving p.60*) Still others are simply artistic decoration.

As Martineau points out, the Native American use of so many symbols for so many purposes should indicate to everyone that the North American Indian civilizations were not without a form of writing, contrary to the claims of some anthropologists.

One other form of rock art remains to be mentioned—the intaglios. This form of expression has only a few examples. In eastern Riverside County, huge outlines of figures have been scooped out of the desert stone "pavement." Recent research suggests that these figures were used by Colorado River shamans for symbolic representations of creation stories (*p.246*).

A design similarly made in the desert stone surface is found in the Mohave tribal territory near Needles— a maze to confound and divert evil spirits which might try to follow spirits of the dead down the Colorado River. Both of these sites have been partially mutilated by thoughtless persons who lack respect for the heritage of their country.

Stone circles occasionally found in the desert are not really art. They were "sleeping circles" erected to protect hunters from the wind and sand. Please protect them, as well.

See LeVan Martineau, Appendix VII

A few "rain" rocks survive early northern California cultures. This one is in the Presidio of Monterey, another is at the Shasta County Museum in Ft. Jones. The carved pockmarks served to help control rain—they were covered if rain was too abundant, or filled with water in drought. These stones are also called "baby" rocks—the holes filled with chosen herbal solutions when a child was desired for a woman. (dhe, 1999)

No person may excavate, remove, damage, or otherwise alter or deface any archaeological resource located on public lands or Indian lands...
—*Archaeological Resources Protection Act of 1979, Public Law 96-95*

In the Carrizzo Plain east of San Luis Obispo lies a huge rock, naturally cleaved in the center. Ancestors of the present-day Chumash and Yokuts chose this site for special ceremonial paintings (pictographs) and carvings (petroglyphs). The meaning of most of the figures here are unknown; however, the sun, or web center has meaning to many native ceremonial spiritual leaders. (dhe, 1996)

CALIFORNIA INDIAN ARCHITECTURE

An Owens Valley Paiute "haystack"-type straw dwelling from Inyo County, circa 1900. (State Parks)

~ONE RESTORED BUILDING IN
THE HUPA RESERVATION,
USED FOR RELIGIOUS PURPOSES,
OCCUPIES A SITE THAT IS
SOME 5,000 YEARS OLD!

A Chemehuevi straw house with granary and olla *storage on top, circa 1890.* (State Parks)

THE OLDEST STRUCTURES

IN NORTHWESTERN CALIFORNIA, where winds, rain, and fog make indoor living preferable much of the year, the early peoples built reasonably permanent structures resembling a sunken garage with a crown and a small round door. Patio stones were used to pave the doorway, as mud can get deep in a wet river plain. The door shape and size were to discourage bear visits; the living area inside was split-level with a shelf-deck around the walls wide enough for sleeping and for storage, while the cooking and chores were done in a central deeper area, around a fire pit. Several reconstructions of these buildings can be visited today: the *Yurok* homes at Sumeg, *Hupa* dwellings carefully rebuilt directly over several centuries-old sites on the reservation near the town of Hoopa, and the model demonstration homes at the Health Village near Arcata. The community structures were similar—one restored building in the Hupa Reservation, used for religious purposes, occupies a site that is some 5,000 years old!

A traditional dance structure is built by the Klamath River tribes: the *Karuk*, the *Hupa*, and the *Yurok*. It consists of a rectangular sunken pit, sometimes covered with a shed-like top, open at the sides, with bleacher-like benches alongside for spectators. Participants enter down a long ramp at one end of the pit, which has a small bench and a firehole. Examples may be seen at *Sumeg* Yurok Village, *Weitchpec* (private!), and *Djistandin* (Hupa Reservation).

FURTHER SOUTH, central California tribes often built a form of cedar slab tipi—a large conical semi-permanent structure. Other peoples built a round, slightly sunken, rock-lined house, covered with mud or long strips of cedar or redwood bark. Mud-covered roofs aren't known for their permanence. Examples of the tipi may be seen at *Chaw-Se Indian Grinding Rocks State Park*, *Wassama Roundhouse State Park* (Ahwahnee town), *Ahwahnee Village* in Yosemite Park (occasionally used by participants at ceremonies), and *North Fork Mono Museum*. Two others are used as shelters during the North Fork Mono Festival in the local park.

In the desert areas, the most popular shelter was made of reed or woven sapling—branches; these were left open-sided in hot climates, close-woven in higher, cooler places. Woven reed over a sapling frame was the material of choice in the southeastern region also, while impressive, large tule reed-covered sapling houses up to 20 feet in diameter were built in the *Chumash* and neighboring *Tataviam* and *Tongva* areas. A full-sized reproduction has been built at *Satwiwa* in the Santa Monica Mountains National Recreation Area. Reconstruction of a reed home may be seen in the *Los*
continued on page 70

The largest sapling and straw structure in California is at Satwiwa in the Santa Monica Mountains N.R.A., built by Friends of Satwiwa and national park personnel, according to traditional Chumash and Tongva designs.   (dhe, 1998)

Desert straw might consist of strands of palm, yucca, or other coarse fiber. This thatched house, built around 1900, is typical of of those built by Ipai people of inland southern California.
(State Parks)

THE EARLIEST PEOPLES fashioned dwellings from the most available and serviceable materials at hand, as anyone would. In central and southern California, the material of choice was straw or reed, with a framework of saplings or branches. In wetter, colder climates the choice was more sturdy wood—with log frames and covering with either planks or long bark strips of redwood or cedar.

When abundant straw is not available, as here in the Colorado River delta, the building materials are a woven sapling framework, covered by a mud stucco (wattle and daub). The relatively open walls allow necessary fresh air circulation, where temperatures often reach 110° F.   (dhe, 1985)

A foothill tipi made from sapling frame and cedar slabs. This Mono woman shows the common method of carrying a burden basket.   (State Parks)

The larger structure (top left) was a former roundhouse at Kule Loklo, a Coast Miwok and Wappo site in Point Reyes National Seashore.   (dhe, 1985) The smaller (top right) is a house structure at a village site (Ohlone) in Coyote Hills Regional Park, Fremont, Alameda County.   (dhe, 1995)

As dwellings and ceremonial structures became more complex and more interior space was desired, a framework of heavier wood was brought into use. These frameworks were later covered by either saplings and sod or reeds and bark.

A SIMPLE, BUT STURDY STRUCTURE took the shape of a tipi (like a Plains Indian tent). A cone of small tree trunks held a sloping cover of long bark strips or planks. These are surprisingly spacious places; examples are seen and sometimes used today at the Ahwahnee Village (Yosemite Park), the Sierra Mono Museum (North Fork, between Kings Canyon and Yosemite), Kule Loklo (Point Reyes Natl. Seashore), Chaw-Se Indian Grinding Rocks State Park (Amador County, near Jackson).

A tipi of cedar bark slabs with a covered entrance, offering protection from the winter storms, is seen at the North Fork Mono Museum.   (dhe, 1982)

This sweatlodge uses a framework of willows woven in a traditional Great Basin pattern, and is covered with tarpaulins, canvas, or blankets to keep out light and contain the steam generated inside. Photo at the Maidu Weda, Lassen Co.   (dhe, 1999)

At Patricks Point State Park, near Trinidad, the public can visit a Yurok sweat lodge (foreground) and a much larger house structure (background). (dhe, 1994)

Several ancient Hupa village sites still bear remnants of earlier structures, most of which were abandoned in the early 1900s. At two of these sites, visitors are allowed to observe reconstructed dwellings. This is a xonta (house) complete with stone patio, to prevent tracking in the ever-present mud. (dhe, 1984)

THE COLDER, WETTER NORTH COAST of California required substantial structures for shelter. Most frequently, dwellings and ceremonial shelters were rectangular in shape, and were usually partly below ground level. The surrounding earth furnished protection from the cold, and gave reflection of heat from the central hearth fire. Smoke was let out by raising a roof board.

The sod cover is a roof style occasionally seen in central California (Coast Miwok, Esselen, Maidu). The Esselen roundhouse seen in the springtime. (dhe, 1997)

The interior of a traditional semi-subterranean Yurok house (see above) with hand-carved ladder. The sleeping ledge and storage shelf jutting inward from the exterior wall, surround a central fireplace. (dhe, 1998)

An early construction of the roundhouse at E-lem in 1930. The newest roundhouse (below) is presently about 25 yards away, but is much larger, and is mostly above ground.

(State Parks)

BY FAR THE MOST ELABORATE STRUCTURES BUILT BY THE CALIFORNIA INDIAN PEOPLES ARE THE DANCEHOUSES OR ROUNDHOUSES.

The roundhouse at E-lem has been rebuilt or remodeled several times. The intricate carpentry on the roof was done in the early 1990s.

(dhe, 1998)

from page 66

Angeles Museum of Natural History, the *Lakeport Museum,* and the sapling frame at *Vasquez Rocks County Park* (near Lancaster). A reconstruction of the early wattle-and-daub (mud over sapling branches) homes of the Colorado River Quechan people is alongside the *Ft. Yuma Reservation Museum.*

A structure seen on and off many reservations, the sweatlodge (*p.88*), is frequently a frame of willow woven in a careful, traditional manner, then covered with blankets of every description. The blankets serve to confine the steamy heat and block out all light, so the frame is hidden. A traditional mud-covered sweatlodge is found at *Pachepus,* the *Esselen ceremonial center.*

BY FAR THE MOST elaborate structures built by the California Indian peoples are the dancehouses or roundhouses. From the northern Sacramento River Valley, along the Coast Range and the Central Valley to the southern Sierras, these traditional centers have been erected for tribal religious rites. But they are not just "churches". On reservations they serve as a community hall—for meetings, making important decisions, serving shared meals, socials, instruction, and singing, as well as the sacred tribal rites—all under the guidance of the spirits. Each roundhouse differs in its architectural specifications, but the importance of the place calls for careful design dictated by tradition. Participation in a roundhouse ceremony is a particular and very special privilege.

> •ROUNDHOUSES MUST NEVER BE ENTERED
> WITHOUT PERMISSION, AND MANY ARE
> PRIVATELY OWNED.

ROUNDHOUSES (dancehouses) may be seen at the following locations:

Ahwahnee Village (Yosemite Park), *Sierra Miwok*
Big Valley Rancheria (Private), *Eastern Pomo*
Chaw-Se Indian Grinding Rocks State Park, *Sierra Miwok*
Colusa Rancheria, *Patwin Wintun*
E-lem, *Southeastern Pomo*
Grindstone Creek Rancheria, *Nomlaki*
Manchester Rancheria, *Central Pomo*
Kashaya Rancheria (Private), *Kashaya Pomo*
Kule Loklo (Point Reyes National Seashore), *Coast Miwok, Pomo,* and *Wappo*
Pachepus, *Esselen*
Tuolumne Rancheria, *Sierra Miwok*
Wassama Roundhouse (town of Ahwahnee), *Sierra Miwok* and *Chukchansi Yokuts*
West Point Mi-wuk Village (Private), *Sierra Miwok*

NOTE: For directions to the sites of existing or reconstructed structures, see the appropriate tribal sections of this book.

NEW PATTERNS:
THE MISSION ERA

WITH THE COMING of Spanish settlers from central Mexico, a new and very different set of architectural visions was introduced. The California Indians are accustomed to artistic expression in a free form—structures and materials blend with nature and allow the eye to join the object with irregularities of trees and stone. The padres and Spanish had other concepts—to make a building stand out from the countryside.

Made of adobe bricks and shaped stone, the walls, dwellings, churches, and civic buildings took the form of straight lines, sharp angles, and studied arches. They all demand to be seen. Within and without the buildings and their arcades, the lines converge to near infinity. In contrast, the free and open Indian way of life requires use of temporal thin or open reed structures. Once the Spanish had

Carvings over the entrance of Misión Santa Barbara Indian cemetery are sobering and severe. (dhe, 1988)

imposed a more sedentary life upon the Native people, they adopted and adapted the use of adobe brick over most of southern California. It was available, cheap, long-lasting, and comfortable. A few adobe homes and structures from that era are still in use today, modified and modernized, especially on *La Jolla* and *Pauma*.

Adobe techniques were used to full advantage by the rancheros, the well-to-do Spanish and acculturated Spanish-Mexican Indian who came to California to settle. Several of their elegant homes, built with Indian labor, survive. (*See Appendix III, Ranchos.*)

For the mission churches, the cloisters, the compounds, and their complex waterworks, elaborate stonework was required. During this era, a number of Indians became distinguished as stonecarvers, creating fountains, columns, statues, and other stone artwork, but never in their own tradition, rather in the tradition of old Mexico, derived from the Italian baroque. We must never forget that these romantic, beautiful buildings were constructed entirely with Indian labor; the tribes responsible are recognized in Appendix II.

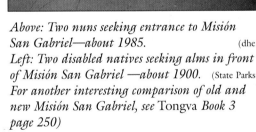

Above: Two nuns seeking entrance to Misión San Gabriel—about 1985. (dhe)
Left: Two disabled natives seeking alms in front of Misión San Gabriel —about 1900. (State Parks)
For another interesting comparison of old and new Misión San Gabriel, see Tongva *Book 3 page 250)*

The famous Petaluma Adobe built by Mexican General Mariano Vallejo maintains the Spanish long-lines concept. It was constructed and maintained with Wappo labor in a very autocratic and cruel manner. (dhe, 1985)

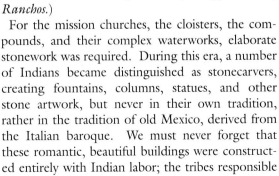

LATE 19TH CENTURY
EARLY 20TH CENTURY

THE AMERICAN MINERS and settlers brought with them a new and different concept of buildings. Mostly from the poorer parts of the Eastern United States, and expecting their tenure would be very short, they lived under extremely primitive conditions. So lived the Indians they displaced, who were trying to survive and to raise families. The Americans built their crude, initial dwellings of the styles they had known— log cabins and wooden clapboard shacks. Using available materials Indians copied the style, especially toward the end of the century, when life had settled down somewhat. A few of these simple turn-of-the-century dwellings, built in nearly every California Indian community, are extant and even occupied, though modified over the years. Examples should be preserved for their historical value, so that Indian and non-Indian alike remember the conditions of living not so long ago. A building still in use, is in the Indian Village in Yosemite Park.

AT THIS TIME in history, the many Christian churches also made their impression on the California Indian countryside. Their architecture was copied from that of the nearby towns, in turn derived from the eastern United States. Consequently, in the far northwest we find a tidy *Shaker church* on the *Smith River Rancheria*, a one-room rectangular *Pentacostal worship hall* on the *Bishop Reservation*, lovely one-room clapboard *Catholic chapels* at *Jamul* and *Sycuan Reservations*, and an unusual old *Moravian church* on the *Morongo Reservation*.

At the time of American incursions, Natives built homes of whatever was available, often from discards of the miners and ranchers. The style was as simple as a rectangle covered with a roof. These cabins were continuously occupied from the 1920s until 1994 at the formerly remote Cortina Rancheria. They are still preserved (as storage) in a recently modernized community, see page 135. (dhe, 1985)

MODERN STRUCTURES

THE TWENTIETH CENTURY rush of life and the upheavals of Indian existence forced a transient and mobile way of life upon the Native population, especially upon the men who were required to leave home for work for long periods of time. They had a small parcel to occasionally return to, where they might erect a simple shack or park a trailer, as early as the 1930s. Many an early trailer is still parked on many a reservation; some are still serviceable.

In the past decade government grants have enabled many of the people to purchase "mobile" homes, to attach to their earlier inadequate places, or to live in separately. Other Department of Housing and Urban Development grants have allowed construction of larger tracts of homes. The ugly prize goes to a rectangle of tiny, boxy sweat houses jammed into the Rincon Reservation. However, most new houses are fairly substantial homes with basic services, erected with some care in attractive settings, often on newly acquired land, such as *Robinson* and *Rumsey Rancherias* (near Clear Lake), *Table Bluff Rancheria*, two-storey homes on the *Santa Rosa Rancheria*, or single-family homes on the *Round Valley* and the *Chemehuevi* Reservations. Strikingly unique are the new homes with high windows set to gather in the winter sun under the soaring White Mountains

This fort's straight lines reflect European architecture at Russian and Pomo-built Ft. Ross. (dhe, 1992)

The historic Catholic church on the Hopland Reservation, about 1910.   (dhe, 1997)

in the mile-high valley of the *Benton Paiute Reservation.* At this writing, the majority of Federal Trust Lands have seen new housing built in the 1990s (*see Index, U.S. Government, HUD*).

Tribal centers and community buildings with powerful architectural designs are an especially welcome discovery in an age of mediocrity. Extraordinarily pleasing designs, with careful consideration of tribal tradition and natural features can be seen in the *Hupa Tribal Hall,* the *Karuk Tribe offices* (two very different sites in Happy Camp), the tribal complex of *Table Mountain Rancheria* and the tribal center of *Table Bluff Rancheria.* Outstanding, too, are the tribal office building of *Redding Rancheria,* the *Barona* tribal offices and *Kumeyaay Culture Center,* the *Bishop Tribal Center* and *Paiute-Shoshone Museum,* the old *San Manuel Community Center,* the *Campo* tribal complex, and the *Quechan Tribal Hall* (Fort Yuma), among several others.

The transient and marginal nature of Indian employment in the decades before 1970s required mobile housing. This is on the Santa Rosa Rancheria, 1985. (dhe)

Several health services buildings have been aesthetically designed, such as the modern *Pit River Health Center* (Burney), the *Health Village* (Arcata) with its outstanding gesture toward traditional tribal buildings, the traditional look and feel of *MendoLake Indian Health* (Calpella/Ukiah), *Round Valley,* and the southwest architecture of *Southern Indian Health Center* just west of Alpine. I wish I could say the same for the numerous gaming palaces erected around the state. Most look like partly-dressed warehouses, notable exceptions being Rumsey Rancheria's *Cache Creek* (fits the hilly setting), *Sherwood Valley* (Willets— a quiet, woodsy feeling) and *San Manuel* (Riverside— What, A Palace?).

Health care in the form of hospitals and clinics in areas of high Indian populations has been improving in the last decade. An example of an environmentally sensitive clinic is this Mendo-Lake clinic near Ukiah, constructed and landscaped with many natural materials. Inside, the staff provides a wide coverage of health care to several Indian rancherias of the area. (dhe, 1997)

This home on the Utu Utu Gwaitu Reservation looks strange, but it is an ecologically-designed structure, maximizing winter sun, minimizing summer heat. The White Mountains preside over all. (dhe, 1990)

WHAT DO INDIANS EAT?

ONE OF THE strongest traditions shared by any cultural group is what they eat. As you might expect, Indian food traditions in California vary widely.

In early times, before widespread abuse and neglect of oak groves, acorns were a staple food, as chestnuts were in Europe. Acorns had to be dried, stored, shelled, ground, leached of tannic acid on a layered bed of sand covered with pine needles or fern leaves, then cooked with pre-heated rocks in a waterproof

Cahuilla Indian woman grinding corn in the Mojave Desert, 1890s.

(Huntington Library, San Marino)

basket. Yes, people still do all this, and you can find acorn "mush" at most central California Indian gatherings. Personally, I think "acorn" needs some salt and seasonings, but some like it straight.

Almost all California tribes used these nuts, though some types of acorns are sweeter and less tannic than others—the tan and valley oaks, in particular. Many of the best trees have been lost, but the California Integrated Hardwoods Project (of which Ya-Ka-Ama Indian Nursery is a member) is seeking to restore a dwindling supply.

Salmon are almost a luxury to us these days, but before dams, silt-choked streams, agricultural poisons and overfishing, they ran in nearly every stream in California, often twice a year. It is no wonder, then, that to the early peoples, the salmon run became a reli-

gious symbol of the renewal of the world. Indians of northwestern California have a traditional and delicious way of baking salmon—spiking the fish on sticks, then arranging them like paddles arrayed around the fire. Once in a while the public can be treated to this specialty at festivals. Smoked salmon, or jerky, is a more common traditional fare, although genuine Indian jerky can usually be found only around Klamath, where the Yurok people produce a small amount for sale. Because of major abuse of the state's waterways, the salmon industry is fading; however, the Klamath River tribes have been struggling with the courts to preserve their traditional and legal treaty access to the source of their income and subsistence.

In central California, especially among the Pomo and their neighbors, we find another ritual food, the strawberry. Symbolizing the first fruits of spring, it is to this day honored in April ceremonies.

Deer hunters are about the only people familiar with venison, yet for some special Indian events, deep pit-roasted deer meat is provided. For such occasions, the deer spirit has been asked by the Indian hunter to provide food for the people, and is thanked for its "contribution", a practice which keeps us all in harmony with the earth as provider.

Further south, especially at powwows, you'll probably find Indian tacos. These are like Mexican tacos, except that the bread is fry bread. Fry bread could best be described as a puffy pancake, rapidly deep fried to a golden brown, frequently eaten by itself, dribbled with honey and cinnamon. Indian fry bread is now found throughout the entire state. Popular in most of the southern areas are common foods of indigenous origin introduced from south of the border—the tortilla and salsa foods. On some reservations, such as Rincon, residents have planted prickly pear cactus, from whose leaves are made nopales, not exactly a common food.

Lately, we have seen Indian "imports" into California—buffalo and blue corn products. Neither is a Native California food, but they are of Native American origin, and they are to be enjoyed.

Some tribes bordering on the Sierra obtain (with some difficulty) piñon nuts from the sticky piñon pine cones of the higher and drier slopes. The are roasted as a dietary staple or as flavoring. These nuts are one-half of the ingredients in Italian pesto sauce, basil is the other half.

Actually, at many Indian feasts and potluck meals, you are likely to find several delicious, almost gourmet, very healthy dishes, including wild rice and specially-bred potatoes, both of Native American origin. A lot of the people are paying attention to healthier foods these days.

Pretty much everything else from the local grocery, is what Indians eat.

Lizzie Enos and Mrs. Potts prepare traditional Maidu "acorn" from leached acorns. Cooked to a "mush" in watertight baskets with hot rocks, as shown here, the meal also can be made into bread by wrapping and baking over coals. "Acorn" is still served at Indian gatherings. (photo Norman Wilson, 1958, State Parks)

Pete Crowheart Zavala, chef, shows the traditional northwestern California way of cooking salmon: filleted fish skewered on a cedar or redwood staves surround coals. The fillets are roasted for 15 minutes each side. Shown at the 1994 California Indian Conference at the Blue Lake Community Center. (dhe)

Chef Kyle, cooking huge cauldrons of stew and grilling beef and salmon at the annual Mountain Maidu gathering. (dhe, 1999)

At every Indian gathering cooks serve up fry bread and Indian tacos. Above: Calaveras Mi-wuk Big Time, West Point. (dhe, 1994)
Below: Chaw-se Big Time, near Jackson. (dhe, 1989)

In the Ukiah Valley, circa 1904, a Pomo woman and her family displaying their meal of roasted caterpillars. Indians no longer eat caterpillars. (Photo S.A Barrett, Phoebe Apperson Hearst Museum
of Anthropology, University of California, Berkeley)

THE MUSIC & THE DANCE

...you descend from those who danced...
—*Shaunna Oteka-McCovey*

WITHOUT MUSIC there is no dance. The reverse is almost true, though the rhythm may be be in your head. No one ever went to a California Indian ceremony or celebration without both. (Seductive flute solos don't count.) Ceremonial rites almost always require accompaniment with instruments.

The dancer always makes contact with the earth with a bare foot.   (dhe, 1988)

Although percussion holds the prize here for possessing the greatest variety of instruments and the greatest variety of uses, we can hear samples of other modes of music.

WIND

THOUGH WE SELDOM hear them these days, every tribe and group had flutes—some wooden, some cane or elderberry stem, some of bone. These were the melody makers. When they are played, we hear plaintive and nostalgic songs, often mixed with influences of later times. The simplest of flutes, the whistle (often doubled), is still played at many ceremonies all over California. The whistle is sometimes the sound of wind, sometimes of birds.

There is one truly wind instrument, the bull-roarer. This is a wooden blade, attached to a long cord or thong, and twirled round and round, producing a zzzzz like a cicada, like a mammoth bumble-bee, like thunder. Some shamans use this instrumental sound for a danger signal, others for summoning the people to events. Kids use it, too, just for amusement.

STRING

A RARE D-SHAPED one-string bow, finger-picked, placed in front of the open mouth for resonance, sometimes accompanied individuals in meditation, but this is not heard at all any more. The padres, however, formed small orchestras with homemade violins and some winds, so that they could hear sounds approximating those heard back home in Spain.

PERCUSSION

THESE INSTRUMENTS are struck, slapped, shaken, or banged in some manner. Most of them are fairly easily made, except some drums, and their sounds usually evoke natural sounds.

The most commonly seen and heard instrument is the split-stick clapper, made from a hollow resonant elderberry or cane stalk. The stalk is slit lengthwise, with an opening for a more resounding clack! This is the basic rhythm section; the slap of the stick is like a small drum. Vibrated softly, the clapper is an introductory attention-getter. But vibrated vigorously, the clapper becomes the rattlesnake, and is the Native way of paying respect to the animal that moves with ease between the earth and the underworld, and is respected by all other animals.

In the roundhouse, the big drum is formed from a trench in the floor covered by a nearly flat section of a very large hollow tree trunk or (today) with a sheet of plywood and struck by a large pole with a tip of burlap or leather. This drum is placed off-center, where the sound best reverberates within the room. In the symbolism of all things in the Native world, this drum is the sound of the bear, to whom respect is paid by drumming.

An unusual instrument used by some Chumash singers and storytellers consists of two large, polished hardwood sticks, which give a loud, sonorous click! very much like those used in Japanese dramas and Caribbean bands. Used with storytelling, the sounds can give a sense of suspense, hurry, or foreboding.

The smaller skin-covered drums we see at almost all Indian ceremonies and at handgames are considered "imports" from east of California, although they arrived here more than a hundred years ago. Their use has become nearly universal these days, since their resonance and tone quality are more "musical" than most of the other more traditional rhythm-makers. One other banger is the log and drumming sticks used frequently at handgames. It allows many people on the front row to drum in unison.

The huge "bass" drums that are laid on their sides are more recent imports from Plains Indian tribes. You can certainly tell the difference from California music in the songs that are sung with them as well. The drums we see played most energetically in California today are those of the Nahuatl-speaking Aztec dancers. Their tall, tight-skinned drum and the syncopated rhythmic style came from Mexico quite recently. Many, many Native Americans from south of the border are familiar with the power these drums radiate.

Individual dancers enhance their movements with rattles made of many resonant materials—gourds and pottery (from southern California, their sharpness depends on the inner particles—seeds, stones, or beans); turtle shells (fairly resonant); deer and goat toenails (loud); moth cocoons (very subtle); kelp seaweed (also subtle), and seed pods (often sharp). Groups of smaller objects like deer hooves are bound together to give larger, even louder sounds.

Gourd playing is not the simple shake, shake that kids do. There are three types of beat: single, double, and tremolo. The force of the shake imparts drama to the volume, as does the number and hardness of the contents; tempo, rhythm, and meter are obvious technical variations to be used. See, it's not that simple.

VOCALS

EARLIER, I mentioned that few instruments are played solo; instead, they accompany singing and/or dancing. The singing of songs in the ancient languages is not a lost art, and it is an art being regained. With some tribes, much has been lost over the past century, but with nearly every tribe major efforts are being made to teach the old songs and traditions to the children and younger tribal members. In a few rare instances, very old recordings of songs on cylinders like dictaphones have been discovered mouldering away in libraries or storehouses. Most of these can be, and have been enhanced using modern electronic methods; ancient tunes and songs have been brought to life again, and another bit of the fabric of the ancients is unfolded.

There are songs that tell stories, usually accompanied by a clapper stick or gourd rattle. Bird Songs (below) fit this category. Sometimes an epic song may be sung. Songs most seldom heard are medicine songs, especially those sung by the doctor treating a patient; however, the Brush Dance songs (sung in public) are a form of medicine. Most commonly heard songs are those that accompany hand games, usually sung in the old language; most are simple tales, but others can be satirical, others just provocative, since the main reason for the song and rhythmic accompaniment is to throw off the concentration of the guesser (*p.129*).

SONGS & DANCE

SONGS WITH instrumental accompaniment at larger gatherings are generally classified as secular or social and ceremonial or religious. Here, the captain or leader normally informs spectators of the nature of the song/dance coming up, so that improper actions (taking photos, coming and going, walking in the wrong place, etc.) won't embarrass anyone.

Songs, the right songs, accompany the Jumping Dances, the Brush Dances, the Cahuilla, Mohave,

The Hupa White Deerskin Dance virtually disappeared in the early 1900s. With the resurgence of Indian pride, portions of the White Deerskin Dance are performed again. (photo by A.W. Erickson, 1897, State Parks)

Cupa, and Quechan Bird Songs, the Big Head, the Flathead, the Shakehead, and some other dances from the Kuksu and Hesi traditions. Bird Songs derive from a traditional sung "geographic map". While the singer walks, repeating a well-learned song, various landmarks, geographic features, or bird populations come into view, as one elder puts it, " weaving stories into the cultural tapestry". This is exactly the method Australian Aborigines use to navigate their otherwise trackless lands (see Bruce Chatwin's Songlines). Only parts of these songs survive today.

There are songs for Bear Dances—very different ones for the bears of the Maidu, the Sierra Miwok and the all-California bear dancers. There are dances honoring basketmakers, hunters, rainmakers, animal spirits—deer, mountain sheep, eagle, other birds, the rattlesnake, the salmon, the dolphin.

And there are dances honoring the Great Spirits—the most sacred of dances: these include the Big Head, the Shakehead, and the Flathead. *continued*

THE MUSIC & THE DANCE

REGALIA REPRESENT the most intense and intimate connection of the Native with "art". The regalia itself of the most sacred dances is revered, as well. Spiritual leaders dreamed their aspects many, many years ago, and the tradition is kept as closely as possible. These traditional designs are exclusive to the tribe and the family of the maker. The objects made are *very* sacred, having been prayed for, blessed, and cared for, mended, restored. When not being "danced", the regalia is kept in a very safe place, often for generations, and must be honored from time to time by "dancing" it. Regalia and musical instruments must be *used*. They were not made as museum pieces or show objects.

Unlike the arts and techniques involved in basketweaving, in which almost all the procedures have been studied and are known to the public, the making of regalia is a most private and personal art. Most California Indian regalia are seldom seen outside the dance arena, although a few museums care for special gifts. As sacred objects, they are not copied and offered for sale. Even the regalia for the secular or "less sacred" honoring dances have been drawn from tradition as closely as possible, down to the body painting designs. Body painting designs are one more part of the entire presentation of a dance, and again, are seen only during the dance, and are as specific for a tribe as are basket designs.

The feathered regalia of an Ipai-Tipai dancer from southern California Mesa Grande Reservation.

(Panorama Magazine, State Parks)

Shakehead dancers at Chaw-Se facing the seated singers with clapper sticks. Note the thick grapevine binders holding the roof poles.

(dhe, 1979)

The Yurok dance arena at Weitchpec, alongside the Klamath River, seen from Highway 169. (dhe, 1996)

THE SONGS ARE REMEMBERED by the elders; the younger people learn and continue them. Where there is a will to survive, there you will find music. Where you find music, there is dance as well. Dance is the ultimate expression bonding Native Americans to their tradition and culture. Dance is so strong a tie that leaders of non-Native religions have tended to wish ill upon the dance, even to the point of extinguishing it. The dancers, however, continue. They are the threads from past to future.

Any comment on dance would not be complete without some acknowledgment of modern interpretations, those dancers who express traditional Indian symbols in a decidedly new form. For example, once in a blue moon we can be treated to a performance by James Luna, Luiseño, who dances ritual and symbol in an intense, very personal, modern manner.

Indian musicians, not surprisingly, also play modern music. Because of their rural background, a number of Natives have become good country/western musicians—all-Indian bands appear occasionally in Bishop and Winterhaven, for example, and quite a few individuals are members of bands. Is it surprising to find several accomplished guys playing jazz and blues? The blues come naturally. Rock bands are out there too, but pinning them down is pointing to flying birds.

European-style music was introduced by the Spanish church. Local Indians quickly learned the styles and became well-known for their talents. Here are William Levy and his brother, Cahuilla Indians, with their instruments near Indio. (Photographed by A.L. Kroeber, 1907)

BRUSH DANCE

Warmth comes from a distance, from a sculpted hollow
  —borne by a cold night breeze and smoke.
The fire is divided.
Embers and flames sustain one fire and its onlookers.
A smaller glow vaporizes the healing herbs.
The family gathers
  —all in the feathers and furs of tradition
  —for the healing dances and songs.
The elder medicine woman presides.

Earlier, an assistant withdrew from a large bag
  long, dark, wooden cylinders
  adorned with feathers and leathers,
  laid them lovingly upon the counter of an old vendor's booth
  right in front of me.
What did I know? My first time at an event like this.
One particularly compelling staff
  caught my impulsive and naive hand.
I gingerly raised one end.
Not for sale, came a soft counsel.
Carefully laying it down,
  I wandered down to the dark river.
My offending inquisitive fingers refused to move.
Five minutes, ten minutes…

The smoke beckons.
The healing songs begin.
A disturbed child is being restored to health.
My fingers move.
Health, new knowledge, and new respect,

        this evening.

Nontraditional, but medicine nevertheless. Brush Dance is an ancient ceremony of curing and and alleviation of suffering, held by members of the Yurok, Hupa, Karuk, and Tsnungwe tribes of Northern California. Some of these ceremonies are public, especially those held on July 4, at the centuries-old dance grounds below the airport on the Hupa Reservation.

        —dhe, 1997

THE MOVIES, & TV, & RADIO

OF ALL THE MODERN persuasive devices, the moving image is the most pervasive, if not the most influential, albeit, hardly the most comprehensive.

The image of INDIAN, to the American public, is most commonly formed by what is seen in movies and TV. Certainly, the concepts of earlier eras of subjugating the savage (John Wayne, John Ford, etc.), fixed an already warped image in the minds of America, outside of Indian families and supporters.

The image is changing, but image still is not reality. *Little Big Man, Dances with Wolves, Geronimo, Powwow Highway, Smoke Signals,* characters in TV shows, such as "Twin Peaks", "X-Files", "Dr. Quinn, Medicine Woman", "Northern Exposure"—all have had a large part in acceptance of Indian as people, one way or another.

Then there are the actors, many of whom are not known in Indian roles: Tantoo Cardinal, Iron Eyes Cody, James Garner, Chief Dan George, Graham Greene, Will Sampson, Jay Silverheels, Wes Studi, Floyd Red Crow Westerman, many more.

How does California fit in here? Apart from the fact that Hollywood lies in Tongva and Tataviam territory, the state does produce some Native film writers, for example, most recently, Greg Sarris, author of *Grand Avenue* (so far, only in HBO). All aspects of Native Americans in films—actors, producers, in short and full-length films, from U.S. and Canadian sources—are honored with several film festivals in California:

San Francisco's American Indian Film Festival at the Palace of Fine Arts in November—a full week of presentations and entertainment, drawing persons and films from both Canada and the U.S.;

Pasadena's Southwest Museum Native American Film Festival in January;

San Diego's Museum of Man Native American Days film presentations;

Sacramento's State Indian Museum Native American Film Festival in late November. Many museums feature film presentations on a more irregular basis. Check 'em out.

TV & RADIO

PBS TV STATIONS sometimes pick up national "feeds" to give us longer Indian-made documentaries or features, usually during National Native American month (November-December). However, no station has dedicated time or programming.

One Indian reservation has its own tribal radio station, KIDE, 91.3-FM, Hoopa Reservation. In Santa Rosa, KBBF, 89.1, has been broadcasting indigenous/Indian programming for 25 years in English, Spanish, and Mexican Native languages. Programs are musical, cultural, and informational. Radio Bilingüe, KSJV, 91.5-FM, Fresno, broadcasts 2 hours in the Mixteca language on Sundays and Wednesdays, and other indigenous news and music in Spanish and English throughout the week.

Public radio stations may occasionally broadcast programs originating from larger organizations such as Western Public Radio (San Francisco), Public Radio International (Minneapolis), KQED (San Francisco), or any of several college campuses listed below. The stations in Arcata, Hoopa, Philo, Redway, and Willets broadcast the daily National Native News.

Other stations (all FM, Public Radio) carrying spo-radio or occasional Native American news, programs, or music (alphabetical by community or the larger listening area):

Arcata (Humboldt State University), KHSU, 90.5;

Bakersfield, KPRX, 89.1;

Berkeley, KPFA, 94.1;

Chico (California State University), KCHO, 91.7, and KZFR, 90.1;

Fresno, KFCF, 88.1, and KVPR, 89.3;

Groveland (CSU Sacto), KXSR, 91.7;

Long Beach (California State University), KLON, 88.1;

Los Angeles, KPFK, 90.7; (University of Southern California), KUSC, 91.5

Monterey Bay (Pacific Grove), KAZU, 90.3; (Santa Cruz), KUSP, 88.9;

Palm Springs, (USC), KPSC, 88.5;

Parker, Arizona (adjacent to Colorado River Tribes Reservation), KLPZ 1380 AM;

Pasadena Area Community College District, KPCC, 89.3;

Philo, KZYX, 90.7;

Redding, KFPR, 88.9;

Redway, KMUD, 91.1;

Sacramento, California State University, KXJZ, 88.9, and KXPR 90.9;

San Bernardino Community Valley College, KVCR, 91.9;

San Diego, San Diego State University, KPBS, 89.5;

San Francisco, KQED, 88.5;

San Luis Obispo, KCBX, 90.1;

Santa Barbara (USC), KFAC, 88.7

Santa Rosa, KBBF, 89.1;

Stockton, University of the Pacific, KUOP, 91.3;

Thousand Oaks (USC), KCPB, 91.1

Ukiah and Willets, KZYZ, 91.5.

We could not locate any AM or FM commercial radio stations carrying Native American news or programming in California. Casino ads don't count.

We welcome any calls or letters that can add to or change this list.

NATIVE CALIFORNIA GUIDE
NATIVE CALIFORNIA GUIDE
NATIVE CALIFORNIA GUIDE

BOOK TWO

NATIVE CULTURES
NORTHERN CALIFORNIA

THE PEOPLE AND TRIBES OF NORTHERN CALIFORNIA

Dolan H. Eargle, Jr.
Trees Company Press
San Francisco

AN EXPLANATION
OF THE TERMS USED IN THIS BOOK

GROUPING PEOPLE BY their ancestral language has become a universal custom among anthropologists and ethnologists, and I will follow that usage in this book. Map 1, p.13 shows the linguistic relationships of the early inhabitants of the state, to the best knowledge of researchers. A few groups otherwise similar in cultural respects spoke different languages, and some similar dialects were spoken by rather different peoples, but early language remains the best basis for cultural correlation. A thorough knowledge of some the early languages is not available, owing to the imposition of Spanish or English by the early Europeans. However, enough is known about their structure to classify them fairly accurately.

Most Native groups in California were not organized into large tribal entities, such as Lakota, Hopi, or Cherokee; rather, the people here existed in smaller, self-governing groups, in territories usually determined by geography and ecology.

This situation has resulted in a confusion over the term "tribe". The word tribe in California is seldom used in the same sense as it is applied east and north of California. The Bureau of Indian Affairs (BIA) has seen fit to call the residents of a specific rancheria or reservation a tribe, even though its people may be close family to an adjacent reservation.

For larger language groupings we will use peoples, as in the Pomo or Cahuilla peoples. Tribe is thus usually reserved for the residents of a particular community, as in the Coyote Valley Pomo Tribe or the Santa Rosa Tachi Tribe. There are exceptions to these usages, as in the Mohave Tribe (*Hamákhav*), applied to both the people and their reservation.

PEOPLE: Groups which speak (or spoke) a specific language or similar dialects. [*Outside California this grouping is usually called a tribe.*]

TRIBE, BAND, COLONY, COMMUNITY: The group of persons residing in a particular reservation, rancheria, or community, sometimes of mixed peoples. A Federally recognized tribe has a tribal council; others may or may not. [*Not the usage outside California, such as Lakota (Sioux), or Diné (Navajo).*]

TRIBE: A term frequently used by any organized language group, Federally recognized or not. (Tsnungwe Tribe)

NATION: A term originally used by several recognized tribes (east of California), increasingly used by Federally unrecognized groups, conveying the meaning of the sovereignty of this people. Usually, the language of the people is included in the title. (Shasta Nation, Tongva Nation)

CHAIRPERSON or **SPOKESPERSON**: The presiding member of a tribal council, including some tribes without land (chief is seldom used).

RESERVATION: Federal trust land, the term may also be applied to rancherias. Several larger reservations may have residents drawn from more than one people, or tribe (Hupa, Tule River, Pala, Morongo, etc)

RANCHERIA: A small reservation, usually large enough only for residences and tiny garden plots. Originally, Spanish for an Indian village.

TRUST LAND: Indian land held by the Federal government (BIA) in "trust" for the people.

ALLOTTED LAND: Land lying within the boundaries of a reservation that is "owned", under direct control of an Indian individual or family, as opposed to communal ownership.

TERMINATED LAND: Former trust land that passed into private, usually non-Indian ownership. When Indian land is terminated and deeds are issued to the resident Indians, they generally lose certain rights afforded reservation residents, such as housing assistance, education, tax exemption, health services, utility connections, and certain welfare and unemployment benefits. *(See "Short History of Land", p.46)* In 1984, numerous formerly "terminated" lands were returned to trust status, owing to government mishandling of the termination process. This land is now referred to as un-terminated or de-terminated.

NOTES:

- Certain places mentioned in this book are private land, and they are so indicated here. Respect the privacy of the residents; do not trespass.
- Other places are **OFF LIMITS** to visitors. On most Indian lands, the tribal police are the authority!
- Vandalism and desecration of many ancient sites on Indian, government, and private land is a serious problem, so readers are asked not to trespass on any of these sites.
- Some rancherias have changed their names recently to reflect more of their heritage than earlier BIA-assigned names.
- As elsewhere in this book, the numbers in **boldface type**, (e.g. **388**), refer to California Historical Landmark numbers. More complete descriptions are found in the State Parks and Recreation handbook, *(See App. VII)*.
- Map numbers follow language affiliation within a geographical proximity. You may wish to refer first to the maps and the "vocabulary" of denominating California Indian peoples.

BOOKS 2 & 3 are divided into geographical sections; Book 2 is Northern California, Book 3 is Southern Central and Southern California.

Each of the books are further divided into sections representing geographical areas of that portion of the state. Each section opens with a listing of the area tribes (by language, usually), opposite a Map of the area, and followed by a general environmental description of the area covered.

Finally, each individual section discusses the peoples, their lands (reservations) and organizations. The many tribal histories follow.

TRIBAL HISTORY

Tribal history may have to do with determination and establishment of lineages and descendants.

Tribal history may treat with major events, inner or outer conflicts, and/or tribal contributions to the outside world.

Tribal history may tell of everyday life in earlier times or today.

Tribal accounts may be of contemporary and recent activities, dreams for the future, and hopes for the future.

Tribal entries are indicated in **BOLDFACE TYPE**, below each tribal entry is a brief description which designates an example of one of the many circumstances that tribes find themselves: recognized or not; small, large, or no land holdings, etc.

BUREAU OF INDIAN AFFAIRS

Current addresses and telephone numbers for all active reservations (except those listed below) may be obtained from the following Bureau of Indian Affairs (BIA) offices:

BIA SACRAMENTO AREA OFFICE (jurisdiction and technical support for Northern, Central, and Southern Agencies) in the Federal Building.
BIA, 2800 Cottage Way, Sacramento, CA 95825
(916) 979-2555 (voice mail only, no live persons)
or (916) 979-2600.

NORTHERN CALIFORNIA AGENCY, serving the northwest counties, northeast counties, and locations north of Red Bluff.
BIA, P.O. Box 494879, Redding, CA 96049-4879
(916) 246-5141

CENTRAL CALIFORNIA AGENCY, serving Central Valley South of Red Bluff—Sacramento and San Joaquin Valleys, central coast, Owens Valley).
BIA, 1824 Tribute Rd., Ste. J, Sacramento, CA 95815
(916) 566-7124

SOUTHERN AGENCY, serving Santa Barbara, Los Angeles, Riverside, San Bernardino, San Diego Counties.
BIA, 2038 Iowa Ave., Ste.101, Riverside, CA 92507
(909) 276-6624

CARSON CITY AGENCY,
serving the Alpine-Washoe Reservation:
BIA, 1677 Hot Springs Rd., Carson City, NV 89706
(702) 887-3500

PARKER AGENCY, serving the Fort Mojave, Chemehuevi, and Colorado River Reservations:
BIA, Route 1, Box 9-C, Parker, AZ 85344

FORT YUMA RESERVATION: BIA, P.O. Box 1591, Yuma, AZ 85364

AGUA CALIENTE TRIBAL RESERVATION OFFICES, 600 E. Tahquitz Canyon Way, Palm Springs, CA 92262
(760) 325-3400

> *Many things will change; many things will happen which need writing about. Some parts of this book will become outdated; a few errors will creep in; others will stand out. PLEASE, take it upon yourself to write, call, or see me in person about any subject here. I will try to respond.*

RESERVATIONS, RANCHERIAS & OTHER

THESE ARE THE NUMBERS USED ALSO IN THE TRIBAL ADDRESSES OF BOOKS 2 AND 3

TOLOWA
1 Smith River Rancheria†
2 Elk Valley Rancheria

HUPA
3 Hoopa Valley Reservation†

TSNUNGWE
4 Tsnungwe Tribe

EEL RIVER TRIBES
5 Bear River Band, Rohnerville Rancheria
6 InterTribal Sinkyone Wilderness†

CAHTO
7 Laytonville Rancheria

YUROK
8 Yurok Reservation
9 Resighini Rancheria
10 Big Lagoon Ran. (Okét-oh)
11 Sumeg, Patricks Point St. Pk.
12 *Tsurai* Rancheria, at Trinidad

WIYOT
13 Blue Lake Rancheria†
   [& *Yurok* & *Tolowa*]
14 Table Bluff Wiyot Reserv'n

KARUK
15 Karuk Tribe, Happy Camp
   & 6 locations

SHASTA & KARUK
16 Quartz Valley Reservation†

NORTHERN PAIUTE
17 Ft. Bidwell Reservation
18 Cedarville Rancheria

PIT RIVER TRIBES
19 Burney, Pit River Tribes
20 X-L Ranch Reservation
21 Likely Rancheria
22 Lookout Rancheria
23 Big Bend Rancheria
24 Roaring Creek Rancheria
25 Montgomery Creek Ran.
26 Alturas Rancheria†

KLAMATH, MODOC, PAIUTE
27 The Klamath Tribes†

MAIDU
28 Susanville Rancheria†
   [& *Northern Paiute*]
29 Greenville Rancheria
30 Berry Creek Rancheria
   (Tyme Maidu) *2 locations*
31 Enterprise Rancheria
   (Estom Yumeka Maidu)
32 Mooretown Rancheria,
   2 locations
33 Mechoopda Maidu Tribe
   of Chico Rancheria
34 Auburn Rancheria

WINTUN
(WINTU, PATWIN, NOMLAKI)
35 Redding Rancheria†
   [& *Yana* & *Pit River*]
36 Paskenta Rancheria &
   Nome Lackee Monument
37 Grindstone Creek Rancheria
38 Cortina Rancheria
39 *Cachil Dehe* (Colusa Ran.)
40 *Yocha Dehe* (Rumsey Ran.)

WAPPO
41 Alexander Valley Rancheria

42 Round Valley Reservation†

POMO (*7 groups*)
43 Sherwood Valley Rancheria
   (*Mato band*), *2 locations*
44 Potter Valley (*Balo-Kay band*)
45 Redwood Valley Rancheria
   (*Kacha band*)
46 Coyote Valley Reservation
47 Pinoleville Rancheria (*Yamó*)
48 Guidiville Rancheria
49 Scotts Valley Rancheria
50 Stonyford Community
51 Upper Lake Rancheria
   (*Xa-bé-mo-tolel*) (*Mátuku band*)
52 Robinson Rancheria
53 Big Valley Rancheria
54 Yo-Ka-Yo Rancheria
55 Hopland Reservation
   (*Shánel*)(*Shókowa-ma band*)
56 Manchester & Point Arena
   Rancherias (*Bóya band*)
57 E'lem Indian Colony
58 Cloverdale Ran. (*Khalanhko*)
59 Dry Creek Rancheria
60 Kashaya Rancheria
   (*Cu-nú-nu shinal*)

61 D-Q University
62 Ya-ka-ama Education Center

MIWOK, MI-WUK
63 Federated Coast Miwok Tribe
   of Graton Rancheria†
64 Kule Loklo,
   Point Reyes Nat'l Seashore
65 Olómpali State Park
66 Middletown Rancheria
   (*Wí-lokyomi*)
67 Wilton Rancheria
68 Buena Vista Rancheria
   Ione' Band of Miwok Indians
69 Shingle Springs Rancheria
70 Jackson Rancheria
71 *Chaw-Se*, Indian Grinding
   Rocks State Park
72 Calaveras Band of Mi-wuks
73 Sheepranch Rancheria
74 Tuolumne Rancheria
75 Chicken Ranch Rancheria
76 Ahwahnee Village, Yosemite
77 Wassama Roundhouse
   State Park † [Chukchansi Yokuts]

OHLONE
78 Mutsun Ohlone
   Indian Canyon Nation
78A Ohlone Cemetery
   Coyote Hills Regional Park

E & W MONACHE
79 Mono Lake Indian Comm'ty
80 North Fork Rancheria
   Sierra Mono Museum
81 Auberry (Big Sandy) Ranch'a
82 Cold Springs Rancheria

YOKUTS, YOKOTCH
83 Table Mountain Rancheria
84 Picayune Rancheria
85 Santa Rosa Tachi Rancheria
86 Tule River Reservation†

ESSELEN
87 Esselen Nation of Monterey

SALINAN
88 Salinan Nation

CHUMASH
89 Santa Ynez Reservation
90 Oakbrook Chumash People
91 Satwiwa, Santa Monica Mtns.
National Rec. Area [also Tongva]

92 Tejon Ranch and Fort Tejon†

TATAVIAM/FERNANDEÑO
93 Vasquez Rocks County Park
   (sacred site)

TONGVA/GABRILEÑO
94 Kuruvungna Springs
   (sacred site)

AJACHEMEM/JUANEÑO
95 San Juan Capistrano,
   Center of Ajachemem Nation

LUISEÑO
96 Pala Reservation†
97 Rincon Reservation
98 La Jolla Reservation
99 Pauma-Yuima Reservation
100 Pechanga Reservation
101 Soboba Reservation

KUMEYAAY, TIPAI, & IPAI
102 Barona Reservation
103 Sycuan Reservation
104 Capitan Grande Reservation
105 Viejas Reservation
106 Jamul Indian Village
107 *Ewiiaapaayp* (Cuyapaipe)
   Reservation
108 Campo Reservation
109 Manzanita Reservation
110 La Posta Reservation
111 Inaja-Cosmit Reservations
112 San Pascual Reservation
113 Santa Ysabel Reservation
114 Mesa Grande Reservation

WASHOE
115 Alpine Washoe Reservation

PAIUTE & SHOSHONE
116 Antelope Valley
   Paiute Indian Community
117 Bridgeport Indian Colony
118 Utu Utu Gwaitu Paiute
   (Benton) Reservation
119 Bishop Reservation
120 Big Pine Reservation
121 Fort Independence Reserv'n
122 Lone Pine Reservation
123 Timbishá Shoshone Tribe

KAWAIISU
124 Kern Valley
   Indian Community
125 Tomo-Kahni State Park
   (sacred village site)
126 China Lake Petroglyphs &
   Koso Hot Springs

SERRANO
127 San Manuel Reservation

127 Sherman Indian High School

128 Calico Early Man Site

CAHUILLA
129 Cahuilla Reservation
130 Ramona Reservation
131 Santa Rosa Reservation
132 Los Coyotes Reservation
133 Torres-Martinez Reservation†
134 Augustine Reservation
135 Cabazon Reservation
136 Agua Caliente Reservation
137 Morongo Reservation†

MOHAVE
138 Fort Mojave Reservation†

CHEMEHUEVI
139 Chemehuevi Reservation
140 Twentynine Palms Reserv'n

141 Colorado River Tribes
   Reservation†

142 Giant Desert Figures
   or Intaglios

QUECHAN
143 Ft. Yuma Reservation†

†Shared by more than one tribe

NDIAN LANDS OF CALIFORNIA

MAP 3

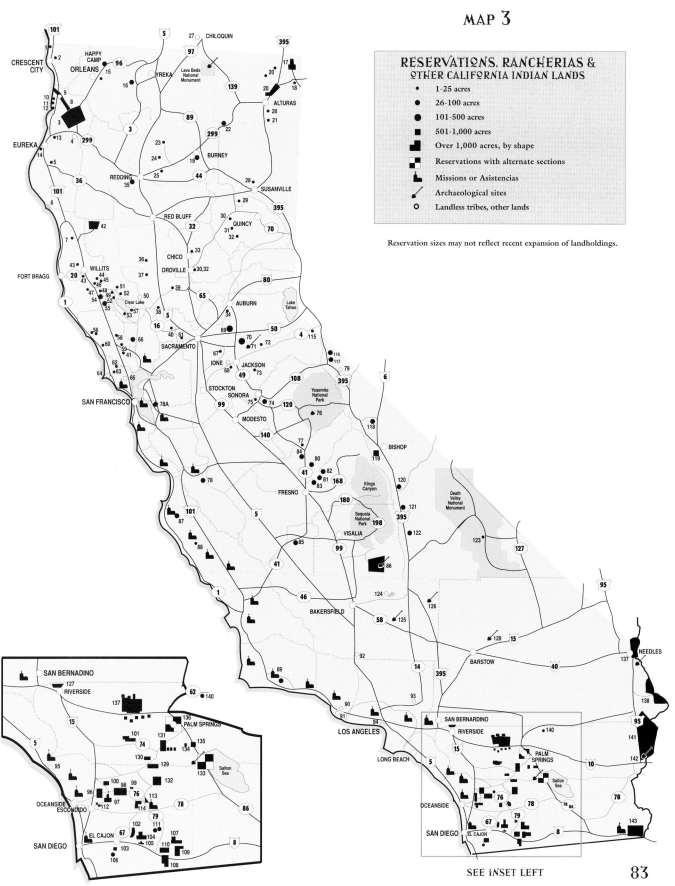

RESERVATIONS, RANCHERIAS &
OTHER CALIFORNIA INDIAN LANDS

- • 1-25 acres
- ● 26-100 acres
- ⬤ 101-500 acres
- ■ 501-1,000 acres
- ◼ Over 1,000 acres, by shape
- ◻ Reservations with alternate sections
- ◼ Missions or Asistencias
- ⌐ Archaeological sites
- ○ Landless tribes, other lands

Reservation sizes may not reflect recent expansion of landholdings.

SEE INSET LEFT

83

Original Map Prepared by Mike Mosher, 1992, for California Indian Country: The Land and the People.
Revised by Dolan Eargle, 2000, Native California Guide: edition 2000.

NATIVE
CALIFORNIA

PEOPLES OF NORTHWESTERN CALIFORNIA

THE LANGUAGE GROUPS
  THE PEOPLE
    The Reservations and
    Organizations

ATHAPASKAN SPEAKERS ‡
  TOLOWA
    Smith River Rancheria* and Elk Valley* Rancheria
    organization: Tolowa Nation

  HUPA/CHILULA/WHILKUT
    Hoopa Reservation

  TSNUNGWE
    without trust lands
    organization: Tsnungwe Tribe

  MATTOLE/NONGATL/LASSIK/ SINKYONE/ WAILAKI: THE "EEL RIVER TRIBES"
    Round Valley* Reservation, Rohnerville* Rancheria (Bear River Band), but largely without trust lands

  CAHTO
    Laytonville Rancheria

HOKAN SPEAKERS ‡
  SHASTA
    Quartz Valley Reservation* but largely without trust lands
    organization: Shasta Nation

  KARUK
    Karuk Tribe of California, Happy Camp Tribal Center, with seven other parcels

  CHIMARIKO
    without trust lands

ALGIC LANGUAGES ‡
  WIYOT
    Table Bluff Reservation, Rohnerville Rancheria*, and Blue Lake Rancheria*

  YUROK
    Yurok Reservation; Resighini Rancheria, Big Lagoon Rancheria, Tsurai (Trinidad) Rancheria ,
    Smith River Rancheria*, Elk Valley Rancheria*, Blue Lake Rancheria*

*Shared with other groups

‡ *See Languages, Tribal Origins, and Tribal Relationships discussion on page 12*

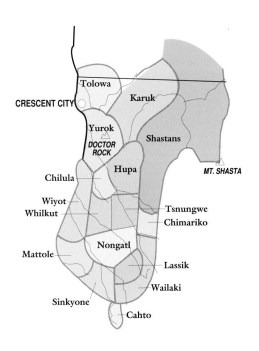

Tolowa

CRESCENT CITY

Karuk

Yurok

DOCTOR ROCK

Shastans

Hupa

MT. SHASTA

Chilula

Wiyot

Whilkut

Tsnungwe

Chimariko

Nongatl

Mattole

Lassik

Wailaki

Sinkyone

Cahto

Hokan	
Athapascan	
Algic	

NORTHWESTERN CALIFORNIA
THE ENVIRONMENT

"THE NORTH COAST is a cold coast, and a wild one," said a poet of the English shores. The description could be of this coast. Up from the sands and bluffs lie the conifer-blanketed slopes and great river valleys, so often layered-over with a soft gray ceiling of fog, the forest more mottled by the deciduous trees of the warmer uplands. Then the land opens to wide oak savannahs. This most varied ecological assortment in California is the northwest—abundant with salmon and eel, shellfish, shorebirds, deer and elk, reeds and rushes, redwoods and fir and oak—everything from nature's stores only a short walk from home. This is the land that the ancestors called home thousands of years ago. These are the lands where hundreds of the native peoples of California still live today.

Life in the villages was as varied as the topography. The Tolowa people built huge seagoing canoes for fishing and trading. The Yurok had a tradition of great river canoe-building. The people of the lower river and seacoast villages built sturdy wooden homes, partly sunken for protection from weather and bears (*see p.67*), and manifestly earth-oriented. Imagine yourself an explorer of the early 1800s coming upon a northwestern California Indian village. The homes are rectangular, built of well-trimmed planks, with low-pitched roofs and flagstone patios out front. You might guess that this design must have been borrowed from European houses. Wrong. This design has been with the Tolowa, the Yurok, the Hupa, the Shasta, and others for many hundreds of years. Athapaskans to the south didn't construct such elaborate homes: they preferred a bark or plank covered "tipi"-like structure.

Most villages built and used sweatlodges, also partly sunken, smaller than a house. Not saunas, but places that served as village community centers: for inspiration, tribal decision-making, meditation, relaxation, workshop, purification, and health. They were generally male-dominated, but sometimes opened to women for urgent or important occasions. The sweatlodge is found not just in California, but earth-oriented California natives made of it more of a tribal institution than other North American peoples. The sweatlodge of today continues to function this way, usually liberalized to include women.

Each village would require the services of a shaman—the Indian equivalent of doctor, priest, and pharmacist. Often there were two types of healers: an herbalist and a "sucking" doctor, who could suck the "pains" or ills from ailing persons. The herbalist knows plants and their curative powers intimately. The doctor uses herbs also, but in addition uses has a variety of quite different techniques for curing.

Various peoples ascribed different functions to their "medicine" persons—but pains or diseases were withdrawn by sucking in highly specialized rituals by especially inspired shamans. The feminine healing capabilities were honored in that most of the doctors in the northwest were women, or men who had "crossed

over" and adopted women's ways (*wergern*) to become doctors. It is said that some shamans in the neighborhood were able to work either evil or good, and were held to account for their deeds. Among the Yurok, it is said that young women wished to become doctors in order to become rich. Those shamans who could work evil were often held to account for it. Some things don't change.

AT THIS POINT I must be careful not to generalize. Most villages of the northwest had many features in common, so these descriptions will be of "typical" villages, but bear in mind that not all peoples or villages possessed these characteristics.

These little villages, seldom of more than 200 persons, were never part of any big "tribal" organizations. There were more like little village-states, and groups held themselves together through kinship ties, common language, and customs. Around an encampment or village we certainly would have found basketweaving, net-making, shell and woodworking—he chief vehicles for fine geometric artistry and ornamentation.

Nearly every native culture has a means of expressing art—Inuit (Eskimo) with soapstone carving, Northwest peoples in woodcarving, Southwest peoples in pottery and sand painting, Plains peoples in beadwork and tent painting. Here, in California's north, the artistic specialty is basketry. *(See Basketry, p.60.)*

Baskets are, of course, a necessity for holding goods, but here the art was developed in a way that substituted even for pottery! A fine, tight weave was developed that would swell with moisture and create watertight buckets and water bottles. Since pottery or stoneware was not known much north of the Big Sur area, liquids and mush were cooked in baskets by dropping hot stones into them. Other baskets were fashioned to carry everything from seeds to fish. Even woven hats were popular.

The basketmakers utilized a wide variety of both coiling and twining techniques. Their designs are also generally conceded as North America's finest. Countless roots and stems and grasses provided an assortment of basic colors and materials, while beads, bright bird feathers, or shell were inlaid for decoration. California Indian baskets have become valuable collectors' items, occasionally to the chagrin of some tribal groups, who find another piece of their heritage dispersed. Even today, those who practice the art of basketweaving can command high prices for their beautiful art. The **CALIFORNIA INDIAN BASKETWEAVERS ASSOCIATION** is a statewide organization that promotes the knowledge and teaching of basketry in all California styles and designs. The organization holds public meetings and demonstrations of their work throughout the state. Theirs is one of the most pertinent toward retaining California Indian cultures. *continued*

Other artists were makers of beadwork, a form of decoration and money. Beads were obtained from a variety of materials: olivella, clam, dentalium, or abalone shells, magnesite (an iron rock), bone, antler, and obsidian. Also, the Indian artists designed their finely-colored, feathered headdresses. In California they were generally like wide, flat belts with loose ends, rather than the eagle feather war bonnets of Plains peoples.

TRINITY RIVER VALLEY

The secluded Trinity River Valley was undisturbed by outsiders until 1850 when gold was discovered. Many of the village and settlement sites within the 12-mile square of the Hoopa Valley Reservation have been in continuous habitation for up to seven thousand years—not in the fashion of the permanent pueblos of the Southwest, but in the manner of the semi-subterranean wooden homes and dancehouses of northern and central California. The town of Hoopa might thus be considered among the oldest continuously inhabited villages in North America.

The people of the reservation have kept or restored a number of original homesites along the Trinity River: among them *Ta'kimildin*, a religious center, a mile north of the town of Hoopa; *Medildin*, a residential and now, ceremonial site; and *Djistanadin*, a residential site (spellings variable).

There were twelve of these villages. Vestiges of eleven remain. At the restored sites there are four or five structures typical of this region. Unlike the rounder homes further east and south, the Hupa and their neighbors built rectangular homes of hand-hewn planks, covered with sloping planks, much like the standard modern clapboard home. Outside the front entrance is a a stone terrace, and paving stones are also used in other places that are likely to become muddy.

Inside, however, I lost any feeling of being in a modern home. The entrance is a small round hole to discourage entry by bears and to afford easy access to the almost-basement room inside. The room itself is a sort of cellar for living area and hearth, with a wide earthen ledge around all four sides for sleeping.

At the *Medildin* site there are homes for women and girls and separate sweatlodges for men only. Outside are several work tables for the daily chores and an open dance pit for ceremonies. Exploring the villages gave me a profound feeling of "being there," though without people I had to synthesize my visions of old photographs with the reality at hand. The whoosh of the wind from the evergreen tips on the mountainsides and the quiet gurgle of the river easily drew me back in time. (*See also Architecture, p.64*)

DURING QUIET TIMES, while fishing, or sitting together in firelight, myths, legends, and tales of unseen spirits were often told, especially stories of Coyote*, who managed to get himself and humans into much mischief. Of all the animals of the wild, Coyote became a folk hero because he was such an unpredictable character, such a trickster: humorous, sly, deceptive, lecherous. Coyote twisted the expected world, and everybody laughed.

Find "Tales of Coyote" in the book, The Way We Lived*, See App. VII*

For the listener: if the present tense is used, the earlier traditions continue; past tense implies that the tradition is seldom, if ever, followed.

THE FAVORITE PLACE for the telling of tales was in the quiet of night by the fire of the roundhouse. Darkness masks distractions and allows the mind to better fashion a reality for phantoms. The roundhouse or dancehouse is the community center—for dancing, storytelling, almost any village meeting. These are the largest structures built by the California Indians and are built according to strict tribal specifications.

The ceremonial dancehouse and the sweatlodge are the most obvious symbols of the earth-orientation of the California natives. The dancehouse is usually sunken into the earth, covered with long beams and branches. In the center is the fire, the opening to the earth's center. Once inside, you are in the womb of the Earth Mother. We can experience this return, since occasional ceremonies are open to the public. In many ways it is like the kiva of the Pueblo peoples, whose central fire is the eye to the earth. (*See Architecture, p.64 and Dance, p.74.*) Another structure built by the Klamath River peoples is the dance pit, usually reserved for Brush Dance (*p.77*). It is rectangular, about 10 feet by 15 feet, and about 5 feet deep, covered by a tall, above-ground pitched-roof shed with open sides. A ramp at one end gives access to the bottom; a fire hole is in the center. Spectators watch from "bleachers" along the sides.

NEARLY EVERY VILLAGE held dances; today only a few communities do so. People in those communities which do not hold dances usually travel to the events of places that continue their traditions. Some are performed in dancehouses, others out-of-doors. Some of the dances are "pleasure" or secular dances; others are highly religious, such as the World Renewal dances (something like a New Year's Day-Easter ceremony). As do all cultures, the earliest Californians developed religions. They are not elaborate, but they embody respect for the life-force, the natural world, and human needs. Even though cultures and tribes were separated by language and geographic divisions, with only slight variations, religious thought and practice are somehow common to very large areas of California and the Northwest. And everywhere the shaman commands respect as the holder of the supernatural power; the one whose altered states of consciousness can influence the nature of all things.

DANCE IS A CEREMONIAL MEANS of expressing respect toward nature. Dance is a ritual, a rite. Dance honors the coming of the salmon, it honors the deer, its rites assure the renewal of life. In many dances the spirits become personified in the dancers, much as they do in the Kachinas of the Pueblo and Zuñi peoples. Most prominent of these dances are the Brush Dance, the Jumping Dance, and the White Deerskin Dance, which are performed with exquisite care today.

NORTHERN GROUPS seemed to haggle as much for a pastime as a way to strike a bargain. One such negotiation would be over the prices for brides—with the haggling being between the prospective husband and the father-in-law-to-be. Such an "arranged" marriage might actually be a result of mutual attraction, although such arrangements may have been calculated—to enhance wealth, family or tribal alliances, or some other object of clan advancement.

Violence within a tribe was certainly not productive, and in the California societies inter-tribal strife was minimal. (To my knowledge there was not a single defensive structure in the state.) Territorial disputes were not frequent, since natural boundaries delineated lands very well. Personal confrontations, however, were bound to arise, and resolution could take many forms—bewitching was popular, as was personal revenge. Personal conflict was known to expand into clan feuds, but open warfare was expensive: the winner was expected to pay reparations for dead and injured. Haggling over redress and fines for misdeeds could take years, a shrewd substitute for continued warfare.

There was always plenty of work to do: building boats, making baskets or tools, fishing and hunting, then cleaning the catch, smoking the meat, preparing the hides, cutting wood for homes and fires. Though these cultures were not big agriculturalists, planting the necessary herbs, grasses, and foods was important, too. The earth provided sustenance, but also time for relaxation. When people weren't that busy, someone would be playing games of archery, dice, a hand-guessing gambling game (a sort of "which hand?"), or a stick game something like shinny or hockey.

The favorite recreation was, and still is, the deeply psychic hand-guessing games. At almost any Indian gathering, except the most serious, one may expect the drums and chants to begin in the afternoon and not end until late at night, when the best team wins. (*See Hand Games, p.129.*)

THE COUNTRYSIDE is rugged, but the meandering rivers have shaved off numerous flats—places where oaks grow and where a village might sit. They were independent and in harmony with nature and the land; there were no big overlords or threats by powerful peoples, or conquests by power-mad bands—until the white man. Most things have markedly changed now, but a remarkable store of cultural traits remain.

The ancient Yurok village Wahsekeo along the Klamath River. These three-pitched, plank roofs were distinctive to this region one hundred years ago. The Yurok fashioned this planks mostly from redwood timber.
(State Parks, 1890s)

PLACE NAMES

Northwest California place names derived from Indian sources (translations approximate):

WIYOT TALAWA: a Wiyot name for the Tolowa people; WEOTT: English spelling of Wiyot name for the Eel River delta; MATTOLE: "clear water"

YUROK KLAMATH, ORICK, place names; WEITCHPEC: from *wéchpus*, "meeting of the waters", i.e., the Trinity and Klamath Rivers; REQUA: *rék-woi*, "creek mouth"); HUPA: a Yurok name for the Hupa people, HOOPA is English re-spelling

WINTU WAILAKI: a Wintu name for their western neighbors

KARUK PICK-AW-ISH: the sacred place of Clear Creek

SHASTA SHASTA: from *chasta*, unknown origin

POMO CAHTO: "swampy lake"

EARLY POPULATIONS

Estimated Northwestern populations before 1830:*
EEL RIVER GROUPS: MATTOLE 1,200; WAILAKI 2,800;
  NONGATL 2,300; LASSIK 1,400; SINKYONE 4,200;
  BEAR RIVER 1,300
HUPA *ca.* 1,000 (incl. TSNUNGWE); CHILULA 500- 600;
  WHILKUT *ca.* 500
TOLOWA 1,000
CAHTO 1,100
SHASTAN *ca.* 3,000 in 4 groups
KARUK 2,700
CHIMARIKO *ca.* 250
WIYOT 1,000-3,000
YUROK 2,500-3,000

The numbers given here are early estimates; they are doubtless low. Later estimates show that early counts did not include many persons absent at the time, whether in a mission village or in a settlement.

ATHAPASCAH LANGUAGE FAMILY

Peoples of northwestern California who spoke these related languages are: Tolowa, Hupa/Chilula/Whilkut, Tsnungwe, Mattole, Nongatl/Lassik/Sinkyone/ Wailaki, and Cahto.

TOLOWA

A people with two rancherias (partly shared with other groups) and a large non-recognized off-reservation population.

THE TOLOWA PEOPLE are related to a large group of Northwest Coast tribes, and in language, Athapaskan, are related to their Hupa and Eel River neighbors to the east and south. Like the Hupa, Karuk, and Yurok, their dwellings *(see p.67)* were rectangular and semi-subterranean. They resembled a plain version, not as brightly decorated, as those of their cousins in the northwestern U.S. and Canada. Nevertheless, the architecture of this area was rather elaborate, and most unusual. The homes were windowless, with only a round hole through which to crawl. "Imagine living in a village where bears would roam. You'd really appreciate one small hole, then," one elder pointed out. Ventilation—air and light in, smoke out—was easily accomplished by propping up one of the roof boards. Most of their subsistence was from the rich coastal and riverine resources, indeed, the Tolowa were noted for their unique large sea-going dugout canoes.

The Tolowa people of today, as long ago, live in the northwest corner of California and the adjacent southwest corner of Oregon. Their livelihoods are largely related to the river and maritime industries of Del Norte County. Tolowa commitment to their community is evident in their maintenance of the historic 1930 Guschu Hall (see below) and public traditional festivals.

As in many places throughout California, the descendants of the original peoples live partly on-reservation, with many persons living off-reservation as well. In California there exists a peculiar double use of the phrase tribal council. A tribal council may consist of either the leaders of the language group or culture (tribe), or it may be the governing board of a reservation (or rancheria). One or more culture groups may reside there. For example, we find the Smith River Rancheria tribal council may have persons of both Tolowa and Yurok descent.

TOLOWA NATION
Tolowa

An organization of off-reservation Tolowas, is not Federally recognized as a tribe.

CHARLENE STORR:

"Tolowa Nation is an indigenous California Indian tribe whose 200 members still reside in the present day county of Del Norte. Collectively, Tolowa ancestors called themselves *Huss*, the people. As original inhabitants of this territory, the Tolowas (a name from Yurok) occupied permanent village sites in areas which were best suited for habitation. The redwoods (*guschu*, 'gehsh´-chu') grew tall in Tolowa territory and the salmon ran twice a year.

"By the 1850s, Euro-American settlement became intense, as a result of gold mining and the founding of Crescent City. After contact, Tolowa population declined until the early 1900s. The pattern parallels the decline in Indian population throughout California, though the pattern was more severe here. The reasons: measles, diphtheria, and cholera, along with military engagements and genocide *(see p.33)*. The last major blatant attack upon the Tolowas occurred at Etchulet [Lake Earl] during the midnight hours of the last day of the year of 1855.

The Tolowa people of Smith River, along with many other fishers, are partaking of the annual salmon run in the Smith River in Del Norte Co. (dhe, 1985)

"ORIGINAL FEDERAL RECOGNITION of the Tolowa community disrupted the tribe through the establishment of a series of reservation policies in the 1850s and 1960s. Even though the first of these policies didn't last, the community endured. Then, in the early 1900s, portions of the tribe were settled on the Smith River and Elk Valley Rancherias and allotments in trust status in Gasquet. (Elk Valley initially was a donation of approximately two blocks from a private citizen for the Indians living in Crescent City.) Elk Valley and Gasquet accepted the Indian Reorganization Act (IRA) of 1934 by default; Elk Valley formally approved it, but Smith River Rancheria residents rejected federal recognition at that time.

"Since individuals with allotments in the rancherias terminated themselves [accepted private ownership of land and separation from government administration], the Tolowa never enjoyed the benefits of Federal recognition as a tribe. Piecemeal recognition of portions of the community as separate communities through untermination again leaves a large number of Tolowas still as a sovereign community, but one split and splintered by federal policy. That leaves Tolowa Nation, therefore, as the originating and surviving source of the populations of the rancherias.

"The Elk Valley and Smith River rancheria governments can exist apart from Tolowa Nation as daughter groups of the original tribe, composed of aggregates and descendants of the Tolowa towns. But Tolowa Nation, as a people, must be recognized by the Federal government if the tribal identity and duly constituted sovereignty of the Tolowa Nation is to be assured.

"IN THESE TiMES, Tolowa Nation is making a great effort to preserve our cultural heritage. We invite all Tolowa to our Annual Indian Observance Day celebration (Saturday following California Indian Day), 'Drums On The Beach' festival (Crescent City). We hold our annual Tolowa Language Camp at the Howland Hill Outdoor School, a week-long camp for all ages, rounded off with a Tolowa dance. On New Year's Eve is a candlelight vigil to honor our ancestors who perished with the coming of the Euro-Americans. Dressmaking and regalia making classes are held at Guschu Hall, followed by a traditional dance practice after each session.

"Recently renovated Guschu Hall was built by the Tolowa in Smith River in 1930 with help from local Methodist missionaries. Del Norte Indian Welfare Association, founded in 1936, the only Tolowa, and oldest Indian organization for the county, is housed here. [See also Tillie Hardwick case, p.47)

"Our hope for the future, of course, is that Tolowa Nation be granted Federal acknowledgement, and the two rancherias of Del Norte County confederate with Tolowa Nation. We see as a positive force for confederation the fact that both of these rancherias cooperate along with the Tolowa Nation in various events and functions sponsored by each."
—Charlene Storr, Council Member, Tolowa Nation
(Portions of the preceding were also contributed by Janice Bowen, Council Member)

TOLOWA NATION
P.O. Box 213, Ft. Dick, CA 95538

SMiTH RiVER RANCHERiA
Tólowa and *Yurok.* (1908) Del Norte County
In the far northwestern corner of California, the salmon run twice a year. In the old, old days, the rivers were fished only by Indians. Today there are others who fish also, but the salmon are still caught by the descendants of the early Tolowa and Yurok natives.

This historic Indian Shaker church, one of the few left in the west, is located on the wind-swept coast of the Smith River Rancheria. (dhe, 1984)

The refurbished Guschu Hall (1996) in Smith River serves elders and tribal gatherings. (photo furnished by Janice Bowen, Tolowa Nation)

The homes, at the edge of the sea, on the ancient site called *How-on-quet*, look out upon the windswept, offshore, rocky islands of the Pacific.

On the 160-acre rancheria are a notable historic 1929 Shaker church and a well-kept burial ground, where the sounds of surf and wind in the pine and fir quiet the soul. The Tolowas here are the remnants of a coastal people whose original lands included the extreme of northwestern California as far south as Crescent City and north into southwestern Oregon. Income from a gaming center on Hwy. 101 has vastly improved the well-being of the residents.

1 *In Smith River, Mouth of Smith River Rd., to South Indian Rd., right in a loop via North Smith River.*
SMITH RIVER RANCHERIA,
400 North Indian Rd., Smith River, CA 95567

Elk Valley Rancheria hosts runners from Journeys for Peace and Dignity in 1996 as part of their wider community relations.

(photo by Elk Valley Rancheria)

ELK VALLEY RANCHERIA

Tólowa and *Yurok.* (1909) Del Norte Co.

One day in 1985, I went searching for the Elk Valley Rancheria east of the docks and lumberyards of Crescent City. At that time there were only about five or six homes of a people who had been scattered by governmental abuse. I found a man, disabled from lumbering accidents, who told me that his family had lost medical, educational, and welfare rights, and, most importantly, land tenure. There was little or no help from federal or state agencies for improving even their sewer connection, without which the county could take their land from them. These are the fruits of the governmental policy of termination. He was, however, hopeful that the newly-acquired status of un-

The Tolowa tribal community center at Elk Valley in Crescent City.

(dhe, 1996)

termination might help. (*See Termination, p.47*)

Since that time, de-termination and un-termination (1983) have indeed reversed the fortunes of the Elk Valley people. An account of their difficulties and successes is presented to us by John Green, Tribal Council Chairman of the Elk Valley Rancheria:

JOHN GREEN:

"The Elk Valley Rancheria was formed as a cultural and political entity in 1934 under the Indian Reorganization Act by the vote of the eight members eligible to vote at that time. Then, in 1958, the Federal government passed the Rancheria Termination Act, which in effect tried to eliminate tribal organizations in California. In 1960, one hundred acres of land were purchased by the Federal government, just east of Crescent City. It was to be allotted (*see p.80*) to the original American Indian families who were residing on the Rancheria in 1934. Twenty parcels of five acres each were allotted to 'original distributees', as established by action of the Bureau of Indian Affairs.

"Since the government did not live up to its obligations under the Rancheria Termination Act, in 1983 under the Tillie Hardwick case (*see p.47*), it un-terminated many of the California rancherias, and established these organizations as federally recognized tribes (*see above*), authorized to exercise full governmental powers and responsibilities through their tribal councils.

"In 1983, an interim tribal council was appointed with the assistance of the BIA, to advance the governmental, cultural, and social status of the Rancheria for its members. From 1988 to 1986, over $300,000 has been contracted and spent on housing improvement on the Rancheria; in 1988 a HUD contract for $250,000 built four new homes on the reservation for members. A HUD contract in 1991-92 for $639,000 was used to build seven new homes; and a HUD contract in 1994 raised a Community Center with room for a United Indian Health Service clinic, a Head Start program, and a community meeting room. Designs of the new homes have been furnished by Habitat for America. A final version of the Constitution of the Tribe was approved by the Secretary of the Interior, and adopted by the members in November, 1994.

"An Indian gaming establishment opened in November, 1995, employing approximately 100 persons; the tribal office employs seven persons; and there are six employees at the tribally owned urn and casket manufacturing company.

"In 1996, the tribe was host to and participant in the 'Journey of Peace and Dignity'. This is a run through the Hemisphere, from Alaska to Argentina, celebrating resistance to cultural extermination and to asserting indigenous survival.

"Lately, the tribe has been able to purchase 16 acres of community land for the benefit of its members of the Rancheria. Presently (1997) the tribe has an enrollment of 87 members. There are 16 American Indian families living on the Rancheria, a total of 40 persons, and 60 of the 100 acres are owned by American Indian families. An additional 73-acre ranch adjacent has been purchased, to be used in part for the raising of bison."

—John D. Green,
Tribal Chairman, Elk Valley Rancheria

2 *From Crescent City, take Elk Valley Rd., about 2 mi. to the fork where Howland Hill Rd. will take you to the tribal gaming center and the nearby tribal center.*
ELK VALLEY RANCHERIA,
P.O. Box 1042, Crescent City, CA 95531

HUPA/CHILULA/WHILKUT

THE COAST RANGE MOUNTAINS of Humboldt and Trinity counties are a series of great straight folds running north to south. The rivers and creeks follow the folds, occasionally breaking through the mountain barriers to run toward the sea, like the Klamath. These natural barriers imposed or reinforced divisions among the bands of people living in the dense forests of this region—from the Klamath River to Mendocino County.

The settlements and villages had to be along the water's edge because of the need for level, open ground, fishing, and access to the other places. Since the remaining forests are thick, they don't support the abundant wildlife one might think would live there. One of the agricultural practices of these tribes was to maintain open space within the forest by controlled burns. This gives light and clearing for bushes and grasses for wildlife forage and basketry. The Hupa and Yurok still use this method in the Bald Hills area, west of Orick, adjacent to Redwood National Park.

The ridge lines of the mountains were the obvious geographic divisions for tribal boundaries. Actually, as described under Tsnungwe (*p.94*), trails ran along the ridge lines like a highway from tribe to tribe. Early tribes here were the Whilkut to the west along the upper Mad River, the Redwood Creek Whilkut (south), the Chilula (north), and the Hupa from the Klamath confluence for some 20 miles south. The Tsnungwe are related, and live further upstream (south) on the South Fork of the Trinity. In the 1860s, these peoples along with Yurok were all herded together into the Hupa Reservation. Not long afterwards, the Yurok managed to get their own riverside land, called at that time the Hupa Extension Reservation. The Tsnungwe also decamped to their homeland, but without benefit of reservation status. However, over the decades, the three other groups have merged their similar identities.

Basketry and decoration of everyday objects among these peoples was highly developed; where the river was wide, they built *weirs* (porous wooden dams) to trap the salmon that ran twice a year; they fashioned

Fog creeps in at sunset over the Burnt Hills on the west side of the Hupa Reservation. The meadows here are periodically burnt by the local Indians to produce appropriate grasses—that attract game and stimulate the growth of special basketweaving materials. (dhe, 1998)

dugout canoes. They sang songs at several celebrations, which are are still observed today. Their cedar homes were of large sunken rectangles (like the Yurok) covered with planks supported by a ridge pole, looking much like a standard modern garage. The small round entrance hole, as with other nearby Indians, was meant to protect from the bears in the hills. Several of these homes are kept in good condition, on the Hupa Reservation and at Sumeg (*p.105*).

HOOPA VALLEY RESERVATION
Hupa, Whilkut, Chilula, Yurok
(1864) Humboldt County

The Hoopa Valley Reservation, at 86,728 acres, is the largest reservation in California, both in size and population. It is also the only one that can come anywhere near adequately supporting its people with its resources, which consist mainly of timber, some fishing, and some farming.

The people residing here are not just Hupa from the Trinity River Valley, but also peoples of the Klamath River, Redwood Creek, and other tributaries of the region—brought here in the 1860s from Whilkut, Chilula, Chimariko, and Yurok territories. It is said that there probably are few purely Hupa people left, because the amalgamation with the other area peoples has been so complete.

Numerous ancient village sites may be visited (*see p.88*), and I unhesitatingly recommend this reserva-

The very lush green center of both ancient and modern Tsunungwe tribal life is here at the confluence of the South Fork Trinity (viewing straight ahead) and Trinity Rivers, flowing into the canyon from the left at Salyer.

(dhe, 1998)

tion as one of the valuable places to gain a feel for native living today and yesterday. The reservation has a fine rodeo grounds, a very informative Indian museum, a complete health care center, K-12 schools, and a tribal office center, whose low, wide, brown architecture is in harmony with the early structures of the region. A casino in the town of Hoopa, next to the museum, draws tourists from both the coast and the Central Valley. Here also are some of the buildings of old Fort Gaston (*see also App. IV*)—some now occupied by various government-related agencies. An old adobe fort building of 1853 is preserved. The fort was built because of frequent hostilities between the Army and the natives which lasted until 1892.

[*Spellings: Hupa, tribal; Hoopa, 19th cent. American*] —*ed.*

3 *From Willow Creek on State Hwy. 299, 40 mi. E of Arcata, take State Hwy. 96 twelve miles through the spectacular Trinity River gorge into Hupa Valley. Another yet more scenic approach is from Redwood National Park at Orick, over Bald Hills Rd. (10 mi. of good gravel) to Martins Ferry, on the Yurok Reservation. R turn to Hupa, L turn to a dead end at Johnsons on the Yurok Res. Campgrounds for visitors are available at Tish-Tang (Forest Service) on Hwy. 96, S of Hupa.*

94

HOOPA VALLEY RESERVATION,
P.O. Box 1348, Hoopa, CA 95546
(916) 625-421

TSNUNGWE

(*tse:ning-xwe*) (formerly called South Fork Hupa) Trinity County. A Federally unrecognized tribe without a land base

IMAGINE A DEEP RIVER VALLEY, long and straight, with steeply sloping banks up to a shelf, wide enough for only a house or two and a narrow road. The banks are covered with thick green forests of cedar, oaks, and maples that form bright yellow-orange splotches in the fall. Mountains up to 4,000 feet line the valley, often exposing steep walls of dark, bare, live rock. This is the home of the Tsnungwe Tribe, whose people have been speakers of a variant of Hupa, an Athapascan language. This tribe has a long and continuous history, and since governance is traditionally family-based, the succession of leaders is well-known. They were recognized as a band/tribe by the BIA in 1927. The BIA has recently confirmed that the Tsnungwe were previously recognized by the Federal government through an 1864 treaty. Yet, current official Federal recognition is still being withheld.

We were at the home of Danny Ammon, who lives near Salyer on the bank at the confluence of the Trinity and the South Fork Trinity Rivers—both clear, flashing, and noisy. It was a profound pleasure to watch him point outside the door, describing his place, naming his environment in his native language, and telling us of his people.

DANNY AMMON:

"This is the village of Hleldin (*le:ldin*) [he gestures out the door] that's all the way from up here, down across the highway, over there, way down where that mill is. There's another village right across the river, *ta:ngay-q'it*. Then there's another one right over here. This was one of the main places for us. Hleldin is "where the rivers flow together." [*Points east up the long valley*] This one is the Trinity River, coming in this way, and the South Fork Trinity comes this way [*points to the stream intersecting at a right angle*]. (*See photo above left*)

"We had some 70 place names, not all villages—but this area had many villages—the closest thing to a city in those days—a town center with suburbs, you might say. Your highway would have been the South Fork Mountain Ridge, the longest continuous ridge trail in northern California. Figure that all the modern roads up there on the ridge were trails. The Ridge Trail was our Highway #1 artery —you can drop down to many of the other neighboring tribes.

"The South Fork Mountain Ridge drops right down into Hleldin. In 1987, a new bridge was built over the South Fork Trinity River. We monitored this area during the building of the bridge to insure sensitive areas were not disturbed.

"By the time they started writing down censuses and things like that, the villages here had been destroyed in battles, and the people from here had been removed to the Hoopa Valley Reservation [about 25 miles north]. So, when we went back into our history, we explained, "This is where we're from, it's part of our oral history." This is why we came back to live here. Today, we all live around here. Our great grandparents came back to here—and that's why we live here—it's home.

"When I first started doing research on our history, I was kind of surprised that the fighting with the miners and settlers went on for so long. We knew the land so well that we knew where to go to hide out from the battles. Our family went up to New River which comes in [to the Trinity, 10 miles southeast] at Burnt Ranch, where there are a series of caves. They were able to hide out there. It wasn't until 1864 that essentially everybody had been removed from here to Hoopa, where they were forced to stay. The years of fighting began in 1849, lasting until 1864, a total of 15 years of conflict.

"OUR HOUSES were like the Hupa's—sunken, covered with cedar slabs. We haven't rebuilt any yet. We may at some point in the future. Here, when they would travel around in the summer, they'd put up cedar bark houses in the mountains when they would camp out away from home. This is not redwood country. Also, cedar is not very abundant. It's mostly fir, madrone, oak, maple here. Some trees that grow around Hleldin are buckeye and pepperwood [shows several of the trees in his yard]. There's locust trees around where the villages are, but the Indians don't have a name for them—the Chinese planted them.

"Our tribal name comes from *tse:nung-ding*, which is Ironside Mountain [on Hwy 299 at Burnt Ranch]. From: *tse*, rock, *nung*, a sloped face, *ding*, place. We are the people of Ironside Mountain, *Ts-nung-we*. Our territory is from the Willow Creek watershed to Grouse Creek towards Burnt Ranch and takes in New River. Hleldin and Ironside are both important places in our society.

"MY GRANDMOTHER'S grandpa was Saxey Kidd. He was from here, Hleldin, and New River. He was famous because he spoke so many languages including Chimáriko, which he could speak fluently. Most people in this area spoke both languages, our dialect of Hupa and Chimariko, but with a Hupa accent. With no r's, for example, they said "chimal-xwe". The Chimariko word for person is *chimar*, pronounced with a Hupa accent becomes *chimal*. The anthropologist Powers talks about this word used by people in the 1870s. People up in here were Hupa speakers—probably a very long time ago it was Chimariko territory. After the removal of the Tsnungwe people, some of the people who settled back in there [upriver to the south] were Chimarikos, so it became very mixed.

"We have a lot of contact with Chimarikos. In fact, a lot of people consider us Chimariko, they even say that Saxey Kidd was. But the people at Hoopa [Reservation] would say that because, in addition to Hupa, we also speak Chimariko. Enrollment in the tribe is about 160 now, and maybe about 70% live right around here.

"SOME PEOPLE participate in dances with other tribes. Also, one of the things we have coming up is a ceremony renaming Madden Creek [Forest Service lands] to Old Campbell Creek. The Campbells are one of our families. At the renaming, we will also be displaying some of the baskets that we have made in our ongoing basketry classes. There will also be a feast with salmon, eels, and acorns.
The people up here had a lot of regalia and were considered wealthy, but with all the removal, chaos, and violence after that, for some reason dances were discontinued. There were Deer Skin, Brush, and Jump Dances. Some of our people today can and do take part in these [at other places].

Every July 4th, the Hupa Reservation sponsors an all-Indian rodeo, where the cowboys are Indians. (dhe, 1985)

"One thing going on here that's really positive is basketry classes being taught by Susan Burdick, Yurok, who is living over here now. The class is cross-generational, which is nice, and involves gathering materials throughout our aboriginal territory.

"I did the Master Apprentice program under the Native California Network for three years. Language up here is considered a dialect of Hupa, very close. There's minor differences in the pronunciation of certain words; other words are completely different but still understandable. We used to do informal classes— mainly using 'Total Physical Response', putting things on a table and identifying them. Now we're really teaching the classes formally in the high school. At Hupa High School, this is the first year [1997] they're teaching Hupa, Yurok, and Karuk.

"I'm teaching the Hupa class. Master teacher Calvin Carpenter will be in the classroom with me.

It's an elective course for grade levels 9-12—30 people, and we had to turn away 25. Next year there will be a second year of Hupa, but maybe not the first year unless we're successful. How to measure success: you can understand and speak it.

"We are writing it now—symbols are pretty much the same as English, but we have some letters like ł (with a bar) in Hleldin. A few others are hard "q" and "x" for other sounds. Hupa writing is not a phonetic system; it is a new system. There's a new book and tape out, *Now We're Speaking Hupa*, with phrases and the writing system.

"My grandmother spoke Hupa. But like a lot of other people, she was sent to Chemawa Indian [boarding] School near Salem, Oregon. They were taught harshly not to speak their language. So she didn't speak it to her kids—trying to protect them from what she had been put through in boarding school.

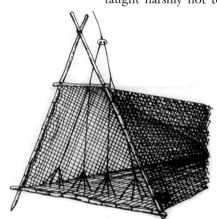

"I feel like this is a renaissance, a rebirth. We are focused on things that are really important to us. I think things will start coming back to us. Right now it's baskets and language; in the future it'll be land and fishing rights. It's heading in the right direction. We've taken the attitude that even if the Federal government never does recognize us, these are positive just for us. Our identity is well established.

Klamath River fish trap

—Danny Ammon, member of the Tsnungwe Tribe

4 *Tribal territory is centered around Salyer, at the confluence of the S. Fork Trinity and Trinity Rivers. Ironside Mountain is prominent at Burnt Ranch. Both towns on Hwy 299.*
TSNUNGWE COUNCIL,
P.O. Box 373, Salyer, CA 95563 (916) 629-3356

EEL RIVER TRIBES

MATTOLE/NONGATL/LASSIK SINKYONE/ WAILAKI

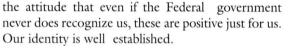

ON THE HIGHWAY MAP, U.S. 101 loops east around a large patch of land between Leggett on the south and Ferndale on the north. Only one little winding road traverses this region, and one penetrates to the coast at Shelter Cove. Beyond, to the east of 101, nearly to the South Fork of the Trinity River, embracing most of what is now the Six Rivers National Forest, lies more forest—partly government controlled, partly owned by private lumber companies.

From what is known of these peoples, their riverine way of life was not unlike those of the Hupa and Yurok to the north, but in many was was similar, too, to their neighbors to the south (Wintu and Pomo). Dwellings were mostly conical tipi-shaped, bark covered, and slightly sunken, like those their southern neighbors built. However, a few rectangular houses were built, a simpler variation of the Klamath River peoples' style.

The local environment, of course, governed their food supply. The rivers gave fish and attracted the game. The uplands were drier and offered acorns, as well as the fish and game of the wetter coast. As in most of California, textiles in the form of basketry and netting were developed in artistic forms, woven from roots and shoots and grasses.

The expanse of these lands today is very sparsely inhabited, with only a few tiny town centers. True, but in the middle of the 19th century, a vicious invasion of white settlers swept the region. This was the land of five small Athapaskan-speaking tribes: Mattole, Nongatl, Sinkyone, Lassik, and Wailaki. A few survivors eventually were gathered in and intermixed with other peoples on reservations. A small group of Wailaki maintain their identity as an entity of the Round Valley Reservation, some 50 miles east by road. Some of the Eel River descendants live on the Rohnerville Rancheria, both locations.

Finally, a number of families remain to this day on private holdings scattered about the small towns and dense forests, especially along the Mattole, Eel, Bear, and Van Duzen Rivers. And owing to the scatter, most of the old ways are fast-disappearing. As one elder of Rohnerville told me, his mother was the last of his family to have medicine powers, and she knew of the hour of her death days earlier. These peoples have been designated the Athapaskan "Eel River tribes", from the name of the largest river.

BEAR RIVER BAND, ROHNERVILLE RANCHERIA

(originally *Wiyot*) largely *Eel River Tribes*
(1910, 1989) Humboldt Co.

A victim of termination in 1958, since un-termination was achieved in 1983, several families have acquired homes on some 60 acres near their old site, on a bluff overlooking the Van Duzen River. The band includes members of the Athapaskan Eel River tribes, as well as some Wiyot residents. Homes of the old rancheria are very tidy, with gardens and orchards; the new homes near Fern Bridge at Ferndale are very comfortable.

5 *Old area: From Fortuna, access is from Rohnerville Rd. to the south entrance of Loop Rd. Go east 1/4 mi. up a zig-zag road to the top of the bluff. Identifying the Rancheria is difficult, as the area is interspersed with non-Indian homes. New area: Ferndale Exit from U>S. 101, go over the flats before Ferndale to Bear River Dr. The Rancheria tribal office and new housing is here.*
BEAR RIVER BAND OF THE ROHNERVILLE RANCHERIA,
32 Bear River Dr., Loleta, CA 95551

INTERTRIBAL SINKYONE WILDERNESS

Sinkyone (1996-98) Northern Mendocino Co.

In the remote forest west of the Mattole River northwest of Leggett, below Shelter Cove, is the area called the Sinkyone Wilderness. A unique organization from 10 Northern California tribes, the InterTribal Sinkyone Wilderness Council has been granted the supervision and resource management of a spectacular 3800-acre park just south of the State Wilderness.

The ancient land of the Sinkyone people is finally returning to Indian control. The history of the area is most keenly told in the 1850s story of Sally Bell, who hid in nearby brush, while her parents were murdered by settlers. Even after the occupation by whites, the Sinkyone managed to continue to utilize the resources of their lands—berries, medicinal plants, and fish. That is, until clear-cutting by Georgia-Pacific logging destroyed most of the forests and the cultural heritage with it. A lawsuit filed by the International Indian Treaty Council, the Sierra Club, and the Environmental Protection Information Center succeeded in preserving 7100 acres. Joined by the California Department of Parks and Recreation, Save the Redwoods League, the California Coastal Conservancy, and the Trust for Public Land, the Sinkyone Wilderness State Park was rescued and purchased from lumbering.

A 3,800-acre part known as the InterTribal Sinkyone Wilderness will be under complete Indian control, and restoration of the land to "persons with a bond to the land" is proceeding. Absolutely all usage of the land will be environmentally proper and in accordance to ancient tribal guidelines.

6 *The land is difficult to access, and runs along Usal Creek and its tributaries, S of Shelter Cove and N of the coastside dogleg on St. Hwy. 1 W of Leggett.*
INTERTRIBAL SINKYONE
WILDERNESS COUNCIL,
Info: 1190 N. State St. #333, Ukiah, CA 95482
(707 463-6745

CAHTO

THE CAHTO PEOPLE are a people in between: they descend from Athapaskan speakers (like the Eel River peoples to their north), but are adjacent to Yuki lands, and observe traditions not unlike their other neighbors, the Nomlaki, Yuki and Pomo. Their ancestral lands occupy a small spot in the drier parts of the Coast Range, just west of Laytonville. Their traditions seem to have been governed by the similar climate and geography of their neighbors.

LAYTONVILLE RANCHERIA,

Cahto [Käto] and *Pomo,* (1908), Mendocino County

This little enclave of 250 acres holds the remnants of a small band of people of the Coast Range, linguistically related to the Eel River tribes. It is located in their original territory of lightly-forested interior mountains and valleys.

On the rancheria, a quiet hillside cemetery overlooks the Cahto Creek Valley community of some very old homes and dwellings, a large cluster of substantial new homes with wide yards and trees, and a gaming center. Life here is not particularly exciting, but some advances in education have been made. The residents are not all of Cahto descent, but this is the only place where any of the old traditions can be preserved.

7 *From U.S. 101 in Laytonville, take Branscomb Rd. west through a left "S" turn, then a slow westward turn, about 2 miles. The Rancheria is on the south, as the road straightens.*
LAYTONVILLE RANCHERIA,
P.O. Box 1102, Laytonville, CA 95454

HOKAN SPEAKERS

The word "Hokan" is Atsugewi for "two."
Northwestern California speakers of this group,
which has many related languages around the state are:
Shasta, Karuk, Chimáriko.

SHASTA

Shasta Nation is a non-Federally recognized tribe, although their language is recognized. The Shasta Nation has a partial claim to a small rancheria.

ANCESTRAL SHASTA TERRITORY occupies the central part of northern California (mostly Siskiyou County) and southern Oregon. This magnificent land lies from Mt. Shasta westward. Below the mountain spreads the open, easily habitable plains of the upper Scott Valley and the upper Klamath River. Further to the west and south it is a land of steep, rugged mountain terrain, with several peaks above 6,000 feet. Villages in this region were to be found on the several flats along the streams.

Shasta culture is of the rivers—the upper Rogue, the upper Klamath and its tributaries, the Scott, the upper Salmon, the Shasta. Mt. Shasta is a place revered by all its surrounding peoples—Klamath and Modoc to the east, Wintu to the south, Shasta to the north and west, and Karuk further west. The Shasta peoples occupied a unique place in the state, as a trading center through which many goods passed east, west, north, and south. The trade was of buckskin and wolf skins, obsidian and blades, processed acorns, pine nuts, salt, shell money (dentalium and clamshell), and smoked fish—all of which was either products of their own or from adjacent peoples.

The discovery of gold in their valleys as early as 1850 began the rapid shredding of the fabric of the people. A disastrous war arose from events of a treaty of 1851 in Scott Valley, California, and a treaty with the Rogue River Shasta and other Oregon tribes at Table Rock, Oregon in 1853 (*see below*). Much later, two very small reservations, the Quartz Valley and the Ruffeys were established, but even the latter was extinguished in the termination push of 1958. The accounts below, from the Shasta tribal historian, Betty L. Hall, tell much of their story, which is not unlike that of many other California peoples.

BETTY HALL:

"The ancestral tribal divisions of the Shasta people are: *Kahosadi* (Rogue River), *Kamatwa* (Upper Klamath River), *Ahotireitsu* (Shasta River), *Iruaitsu* (Scott River), *Konomihu* (Salmon River), New River Shasta, *Okwanuchu* (Squaw Creek, McCloud, and Upper Sacramento Rivers). Some of these Shastan groups were named by anthropologists for their geographic division, usually rivers, but all these people spoke the same language. [*Betty Hall shows us a treaty, signed by a government agent known as Commissioner M'Kee and local Indians in 1851*]

'Treaty Made and Concluded At Camp, in Scott's Valley, Shasta County, State of California, November 4, 1851. Between Redick M'Kee, One of the commissioners On The Part of the United States, and the Chiefs, Captains, and Head Men of the Upper Klamath, Shasta, and Scott's River Tribes of Indians'.

"Commissioner M'Kee, sent by President Fillmore to negotiate treaties with the California tribes, signed a treaty with thirteen Shasta chiefs representing these Shasta groups. A reservation was set aside for the Shasta people in this treaty, but the treaty was never ratified and the terms were never observed by the U.S. Government, although the Shasta Indians kept their part of the treaty.

"To celebrate the treaty, a feast of meat and bread was prepared by local whites—poisoned with strychnine. [Many Wintus had also enjoyed a similar feast.] After most of the three thousand men present had died, white vigilantes swept through and burned all the Shasta villages and slaughtered the people. Thousands were murdered. Approximately forty Wintu runners had been sent by chiefs from near Shasta City to warn the Shasta of the dastardly plot. But the Wintu reported that when they got here, there were dead Indians everywhere—they were too late! Five Shasta couples (husband and wife) survived; twenty-eight Shasta women survived, because they had been kidnapped and were living in scattered locations with miners. To this day, all Shastas descend from these 28 women and the five couples. There are no Shastas left in Oregon, and only six Indians live in the Rogue River Valley. It was reported that about 175 warriors had fled to the mountains, but we are not sure of where they went. Some names appear on the census rolls in the Jacksonville, Oregon, area, and I believe many may have married into surrounding tribes.

"The Rogue River Shasta signed a treaty at Table Rock, in Rogue Valley in 1853, and a reservation was set aside for them and other Oregon tribes, but it was to be only temporary. The Rogue River War raged for a short time, after which all Indians on that reservation and in the vicinity were marched to the Siletz Reservation. Only six Indians were allowed to remain in Rogue Valley at this time. Shasta Indians who were being held prisoner at the military fort at Fort Jones, California, were also marched to Siletz along with the Rogue River Shasta at this time. This separated many families; many perished on the way. This was the Shasta Indian Trail of Tears in 1856. The Siletz Indian Reservation is located west of Corvallis, Oregon—later disbanded. Its status is now restored with full Federal recognition.

"My mother, Nana Kintano, was a full-blooded Cahuilla from Southern California, and my father, Fred Lee Wicks, was Shasta. They met at Sherman Institute, the Indian high school in Riverside, California. After graduation they returned to Quartz Valley during the Depression era and found housing conditions for the Indian people here horrible.

These people were living mostly in abandoned mining shacks up the gulches, with few land titles. People then just lived lives, worked every day, some were indentured, worked all summer in the mines, no pay, just a meal and a bed. They also worked on ranches and in the timber industry. Of course, we all had family contacts and had some discussions about establishing a reservation.

"My father, with Harry Burcell to help him, established the Quartz Valley Reservation, under the provisions of the Indian Reorganization Act of 1934. This Act and the Baker Roll (Indian census of 1928-33) were the bases for applications for a reservation "for the benefit and use of Shasta and Upper Klamath Indians." [Referring to Shastan peoples living along the Klamath River from Clear Creek to Klamath Lake.]

"QUARTZ VALLEY Indian Reservation is located within the aboriginal territory of the Shasta Indians. There were 160 to 170 applications from Shasta families (which were known and later named by Mr. Fred L. Wicks and are now included in our tribal roll). My own great, great-grandmother, Jennie Wicks, was born on what is now the Quartz Valley Indian Reservation in the 1820s. My family: Fred & Nina Wicks, my grandfather, Fred Wicks, and great aunts, Misses Clara Wicks and Bessie Wicks Harrie.

"Only thirteen families were accepted, and most were Karuk, read on! Correspondence among some of the Indian agents was found to show that they had decided not to give allotments to any family with a non-Indian spouse, male or female. That made it difficult to include Shasta families, since we are all are descended from those 28 women and their non-Indian spouses, and due to the genocide of 1851, there were very few Shasta people to intermarry with. Consequently, most Shastas had non-Indian spouses, and they were rejected. Actually, most of the families who applied to Quartz Valley Reservation were full-blooded Karuk couples, misrepresenting themselves as Upper Klamath. But, [in characteristic BIA ignorance of tribal differences] they were accepted by the Bureau, because both spouses were Indian. So both tribes are now there by allotment.

"Quartz Valley Reservation was terminated along with many others in 1958, then restored to Federal status by the Tillie Hardwick decision in 1983. The Ruffys Reservation (Shasta), located south of Etna, CA, was also terminated, but was not reinstated. There is no one living there now, but we still have contact with the Ruffys family. I went there a few years ago with family members, Mr. Floyd Smith and his son. I was very excited—there was a signal tree there. The tree was trimmed in a way that signifies a Shasta chief's residence. It is not there now.

We have about 1400 members on the Shasta and Upper Klamath Tribal Roll, and the BIA agents still try to tell us we're extinct. No, we don't have fluent

Shasta Nation territory once occupied the rolling high plains looking south to the Shasta and Shastina Peaks as seen here from the north. (dbe 1998)

language speakers left, but all families know place names, phrases, and such in the Shasta language, and there are recordings taken by Shirley Silver, a linguist, of Miss Claire Wicks and Sargent Sambo speaking the language. It is a difficult language, not related to our neighbors'. Many of the dances and songs are lost, as a direct result of the 1851 genocide. Shasta Indians were shot if caught speaking their language. Still, it seems that every Shasta family has kept some artifacts that great-grandma had. This way the Shasta cultural identity has been passed down through individual families.

"WE MUST GET OUR FEDERAL recognition first. We are working hard at this. Some larger tribes have their recognition and money and are against enlarging the recognition list, but others want to help. The Department of the Interior has its bureaucrats, anthropologists, ethnologists, and genealogists. For 15 years we have made many trips to visit them; they won't accept our packets of information as being "enough", and pick them apart. They visit us, but don't reply. We are being put off as usual. Our Congressman has not helped; on the Mt. Shasta development issue he even ridiculed us about the mountain not being sacred to the Indian people. I don't believe that anyone can presume to tell the American Indian people what their beliefs are.

"Why can't the government acknowledge our past and current existence and just say, 'Yes, you are a people.'?"

—Betty L. Hall, Tribal Historian, Shasta Nation

QUARTZ VALLEY RESERVATION.
originally *Shasta*, now also *Karuk*
(1937) Siskiyou County

A few Shasta and Karuk people live on this de-terminated land, which was originally organized by Shastan people themselves during Depression years. The reservation is located in a rather dry, remote valley of the Scott River, adjacent to the Marble Mountain Wilderness (near Fort Jones). The Shasta people here are members of the Shasta Nation, at this time a Federally unrecognized tribe. Many of the Karuk here are active in the Karuk council center in Happy Camp. The Reservation has recently purchased additional acreage close by.

16 *From Fort Jones, take the road toward Hamburg. About 8 miles out, go toward Mugginsville. The settlement is about 2 miles further, before the second crossing of Shackleford Creek. There are only some homes to see, but to give one a feel for the nature of Shasta ancestral lands, camping is possible in the neighboring Marble Mountain Wilderness Area.*
QUARTZ VALLEY RESERVATION,
GENERAL COMMUNITY COUNCIL,
9117 Sniktaw Lane, Fort Jones, CA 96032

SHASTA NATION
Shasta
Siskiyou County
A Federally unrecognized tribal organization of some 1400 Shasta people.
Info: Mr. Roy V. Hall, Jr.,
10736 Quartz Valley Rd., Fort Jones, CA 96032

KARUK

Since the very old times, the Karuk people have lived along the margins of the Klamath River and its tributaries, from its confluence with the Trinity up to its confluence with the Scott River, a few miles west of Yreka. More than a hundred settlements and towns sprinkled along this hundred-mile-long stretch in pre-contact times have been identified.

The spiritual center of these people rises in the form of a pyramidal mountain at the confluence of the Salmon River. In this place known to the Karuk as *Katimín*, and map makers as Somes Bar, the people have observed their ceremonies of "World Renewal" for centuries. The ceremony was almost lost for nearly 90 years, but thanks to the efforts of both elders and determined young members, the people are undergoing a major recovery of their identity—this is one example.

THE OCCASION OF "WORLD RENEWAL," is the fall running of the salmon of the Klamath. The riches of the life of the river are the life and livelihood of the Karuk people. When the salmon begin their struggling migration to their spawning grounds, it is the strongest symbol of the yearly cycle of life. Dancers dance; the spiritual leaders offer prayers; a feast is given, and thanks is offered to the salmon for providing sustenance. People are urged to gather their bad thoughts, release them into a rock, then hurl them

The Karuk Tribe's offices are located here in Happy Camp, a central hub for the dispersion of tribal residents up- and downriver. (dhe, 1997)

away in the stone to the river. Or, remembering their bad attitudes and thoughts over the past year, give them over to a bundle of herbs, and cast them into a bonfire to get rid of them forever.

KARUK TRIBE

Karuk, Siskiyou, Trinity, Del Norte Counties
A formerly landless tribe with Federal recognition—
granted after acquiring their own land.

In a most unusual move, in 1979, some Karuk people living in the rugged mountains of the middle Klamath River Valley bought seven acres of land for a reservation for themselves. Their chairman at that time shared with me some of their enthusiasm for the new projects: not only did the people themselves provide their reservation, they also built a spacious community center with a grant from a local church; moreover, the center was built to be shared with non-Indian groups from the town of Orleans. Homes have been provided on this small, new reservation. All this for a people who have never had a reservation, or even a center of their own until that time.

This was the first in a series of bold moves by the Karuk people. About that time, in Happy Camp, some 45 miles upriver, the Karuk Tribe of California was organized to provide a center for their nearly 700 native people of that portion of the river. There is here a most unusual spirit of industriousness among the leaders of the center.

The people demanded and received homesites in seven areas of the Klamath basin, all near their ancestral territories, plus some land in Yreka. In the meantime, Federal recognition has been restored to the tribe, enabling the acquisition of grants and funds for purchase of additional land and homes. Karuk Tribe has maintained that it is not necessary to resort to a casino in order to provide for the welfare of its people, but it still remains an enticing prospect. Judging from the number of homes and the general success, the policy of buying the property themselves, then placing it in Federal trust seems to be working exceptionally well here. Employment in the area, steady though not booming, is sufficient to support their efforts.

The teaching of both basketweaving and Karuk songs and dance classes (public) are part of a wide-ranging cultural program that extends throughout the Karuk region. Schools and education have become a major part of the revival of the people, some even offering Karuk language courses.

Here, too, in the beautiful and substantial stone tribal hall alongside Hwy. 96, is the administrative center for the several smaller Karuk parcels, including homesites in Yreka and Orleans. Happy Camp is earning its name with the Karuk people.

Slopes of the pyramidal sacred Karuk rock mass of Katimin, direct the joining of the waters of the Salmon River with the Klamath River. Katimin is the Karuk's center of the earth, near Somes Bar.

(dhe, 1996)

Although not as upset by gold miners of the last century as some tribes, the people have had considerable trouble preserving their sacred sites (such as Titus Ridge and the Clear Creek dance area) from desecration by lumbering. Many persons of the modern world have lost touch with the sanctity of natural places, having acquired some sort of "edifice complex." A sacred site seems not to be recognizable as such unless it has had some "constructive improvement" made upon it. *continued*

101

Traveling along the river highway you can see that several sacred Indian sites have been marked—an ancient ceremonial area and spiritual trails among them. The Katimín area has been secured for the tribe by two unexpected happenings. First, part of the land was taken earlier by the government and later sold to a resort "developer." The parcel was seized by federal authorities—the developer/owner was cultivating marijuana. Then, the other part run by the Forest Service as a fire station and equipment depot began to slide downhill toward the river. The Forest Service decided to return all the land to the tribe, and the tribe, in return, now manages the fire station. Other outbuildings can slide on down.

The middle Klamath is a truly spiritual region—it is isolated, with few roads, many forests, and much solitude. Along the river's edge is one of the few places in California where it is nearly impossible to pick up even a radio signal in the daytime. The isolation seems to have been a benign protection for this people.

Some of this information was taken from an article in the Los Angeles Times, July 12, 1996, by Richard Paddock, and furnished to us by Mr. Dion Wood of the Karuk Tribal Office.

15 *Karuk Tribe offices are located on the W side of Happy Camp in a long stone-based building facing St. Hwy. 96. Other equipment for maintenance of tribal homes and facilities is here also. At another site near the top the hill above a shopping center is a residential area for the Karuk people of Happy Camp. The housing office there is of a particularly interesting ecological architecture with Native American design features. In Orleans, the reservation area is just E of the Klamath R. bridge on Hwy. 96. Other parcels of homes are in Yreka, Somes Bar, Forks of Salmon, Scott Valley, Seiad, and Quartz Valley (shared with Shasta Nation).*

KARUK TRIBE OF CALIFORNIA
P.O. Box 1016, Happy Camp, CA 96039
(530) 493-5305

CHIMARIKꝎ
(Chimáriko)

CHIMARIKꝎ

A very small group lives in the remote upper reaches of the South Fork of the Trinity River, in contact with the Tsnungwe people of that region (*see p.94*). These people live quiet lives on their own lands. Their past history and living habits are quite similar to those of the Tsnungwe or the Hupa, although their language is related to the Shasta further east.

A Wiyot woman shows a variety of weaving materials, circa 1900, near present-day Eureka.

(photo by A.W. Erickson, State Parks)

ALGIC LANGUAGES

Wiyot and Yurok peoples spoke distantly related languages — also distantly related to Algonquian languages of eastern North America.

WIYꝎT

FROM JUST SOUTH of Trinidad south to Cape Mendocino and eastward for ten or so miles, you will be in Wiyot ancestral land. This is, essentially, Arcata and Humboldt Bays and the deltas of the Mad and the Eel rivers — fertile, green marshes teeming with birds and fish and game, an abundance of sea life, and a garden of edible and medicinal plants. The riversides and the sheltered coast-sides were practically lined with villages, supporting a large population. A solid line of mountains delineated their lands to the east.

The Wiyot did much basketweaving; their beautifully-woven basket hats being among the finest on the coast. World Renewal ceremonies and Jump dances were celebrated.

Because their land was so prolific and thus desirable by whites, the Wiyot suffered some of greatest atrocities in California. The Clarke Museum in Eureka displays many of their artifacts; the Indian Museum at Ft. Humboldt State Park was prepared under the supervision of local Indian personnel. Its most moving display is the account by Bret Harte of the massacre on Indian Island in 1860.

TABLE BLUFF WIYOT RESERVATION
Wiyot [Wie-ott] (1908) Humboldt Co.

The embers of Wiyot culture glow in these acres, set on an open, foggy, and windswept terrace above the Pacific Ocean. It is amazing that they do at all, for it was the Wiyots, with two other groups, who were nearly wiped out by the 1860 massacre on Indian Island in Eureka. The group annually honors the memory of lives lost in years past with a vigil on Woodly Island (adjacent to Indian Island) the last Saturday in February.

For years the Wiyot quietly and carefully kept their culture on a tiny spot of land on an isolated, grassy plain in small, old, and austere homes, sheltered a bit by windrows of low trees. But, in the 1990s, owing to a massive effort, the tribe has expanded its lands and includes a busy economic development program.

When lands become available, homes are built, the scattered people of a tribe come home and once again become a community. This one is no exception. Thirty pleasant and well-equipped homes are grouped around a spacious, lofty tribal hall, like a family.

14 *South of Eureka about 10 miles, take Hookton Rd. exit off U.S. 101 (in the direction of Humboldt Co. Beach Park) to Table Bluff Rd. The old parcel (private) is at Indian Reservation Rd.; the new parcel occupies the top of a rise on the W side of the road, 1/2 mi. further on.*
TABLE BLUFF WIYOT RESERVATION,
P.O. Box 519, Loleta, CA 95551 (707) 826-4701

BLUE LAKE RANCHERIA
Wiyot later also *Tolowa* and *Yurok*
(1908) Humboldt Co.

Blue Lake, like many small rancherias, has undergone change in the last ten years. The original 26 acres were once reduced to only 4, interlaced with non-Indians, as the residents were forced to sell. The remaining residential area is rather jumbled, with

Below, left & right:
The Table Bluff Wiyot Reservation opened its environ-mentally-designed tribal center and housing project in 1996. Overlooking the spectacular Pacific coast, and frequently visited by fog, Table Bluff requires high, open ceilings for natural light. (dhe, 1996)

many mobile homes and small houses, although the surrounding countryside along the Mad River is attractive in its tree-covered low-mountain greenery. It is still a lumber mill town. Blue Lake was terminated in 1958, but is once again in federal trust., and new housing is provided on an additional 10 acres nearby.

13 *From the center of Blue Lake, take Chartin Rd. SW several blocks to Rancheria Rd.*
BLUE LAKE RANCHERIA,
P.O. Box 428, Blue Lake, CA 95525

Functional, not decorative, the hearth in this old Yurok home smokes skins, while providing heat and cooking. (State Parks)

YUROK

The Yurok lived on fish, well, a few other things, too. But they are of two backgrounds — the river people and the sea people. Yurok villages span the lower Klamath River from the confluence of the Trinity River at Weitchpec to the Pacific, then down the coast south to Trinidad. All accounts tell that they had much trade with all the various tribes along their two routes, and shared some customs with each.

Today, many Yurok place names dot the map: Weitchpec (*wechpus),* Orick (*'orekw),* Requa (*rekwoy),* Tsurai (*churey,* name of Trinidad Rancheria's casino), Sumeg (village at Patrick's Point State Park).

Dances included the Deerskin, Jumping, Brush, and today, these ceremonies are occasionally observed. Society had "layers" that generally corresponded to the wealth of the family. Wealth could include power status, control of a fishing ground or an oak grove, objects made with considerable labor, strings of shell beads, etc. Curing doctors (women) were well-known and respected, usually acting as the curer in a Brush Dance.

Yurok woodcarving, shell carving, and basketry were among the finest of arts in northwestern California. Carving a dugout canoe was (and still is) an almost sacred work. Every so often the public can witness Yurok canoe artists at work at Aquatic Pier in San Francisco.

An older wood and stone building in the village of Klamath serves as a Yurok tribal building.

(dhe, 1996)

YUROK RESERVATION
Yurok (1891) Humboldt County

Although the large Hoopa Valley Reservation (*see p.93*) was established for the Hupa, Chilula, and Whilkut peoples of the Trinity/Klamath region in 1864, the Yuroks were generally not included because of the traditional antipathy between Hupa and Yurok, and because that region was originally not Yurok. Nevertheless, their land was administratively tacked on to Hoopa as the Hoopa Extension reservation. Yuroks won recognition of much of their ancestral land in 1891 (*see also Resighini Rancheria, below*). Since 1989, the reservation has been administered from the town of Klamath, occupying, in part, a large old stone mansion.

The reservation is rather large (7,028 acres), rich in timber and a scenery of forest and rivers. Originally, it officially occupied a mile on either side of the Klamath, from its confluence with the Trinity to the Pacific, but that was whittled away to a fraction of that portion. Later, Yurok authority was again acknowledged over the entire stretch of river from the Trinity to the Pacific, including the mile on each bank. Lumber companies had muscled illegal "deals" to clearcut much of the banks, but after they departed with the wood, the land was put back under tribal resource management. Non-Indian in-holdings are, of course, respected as private property.

The whole stretch is dotted with small settlements, some in continuous habitation for several thousand years. A ceremonial center is near Weitchpec, where an outdoor arena on a beautiful riverbank setting is used on special occasions such as the famous Brush Dance in mid-October. The other Yurok centers of activity on the Klamath are around Requa and the Resighini Rancheria.

8 *Some tribal offices in Klamath, but the reservation extends for some 30 miles up the north-flowing Klamath to Weitchpec. Johnson's is reached on a local paved road off State Rt. 96 from Weitchpec. Or, approach via Redwood National Park from Orick over Bald Hills Rd. (10 mi. of graded gravel). No paved roads connect the eastern with the western portions. In the exceptionally beautiful and historic Indian village of Requa is an entrance to Redwoods National Park and on both the north and south shore roads toward the ocean, there are several tourist facilities, including a boat launching ramp.*

YUROK RESERVATION
Main Tribal Office
1034-6th St., Eureka, CA 95501
(707) 444-0433;
Satellite local office:
15900 Hwy. 101, Klamath, CA 95548
(707) 482-2921

RESIGHINI RANCHERIA
Yurok (1938) Del Norte Co.

The Yurok have always been fishers. They still are. The salmon on the Klamath run twice a year, but the fishers are out year-round—the Yurok have nominal control over the lower Klamath fishing, but conflict with U.S. Fish and Game over the size of the take is always just under the surface. Much of the Yurok catch is dried in little smoke sheds for their own consumption, but some salmon "jerky" is sold in shops along Highway 101 at Requa and Klamath.

Resighini (its 228 acres named for an early French settler) smoulders over white interventions in its lower Klamath homelands. Consequently, non-Indian visitors are not welcome on inner reservation lands proper. However, the public is most welcome to a small gaming establishment and a campground just at the Klamath River Bridge south exit.

9 *South shore of the mouth of the Klamath River at the U.S. 101 bridge.*

COAST INDIAN COMMUNITY OF THE RESIGHINI RANCHERIA,
P.O. Box 529, Klamath, CA 95548

BIG LAGOON RANCHERIA ('OKET'EY)
Yurok (1918) Humboldt County

The ocean, in its ceaseless effort to sculpt the shore, many centuries ago formed the sand bar creating Big Lagoon. The still, brackish, black water is a perfect place for settlement—it provides an abundance of fish and shellfish, birds, tule, evergreen forest, and fresh water.

A band of early coastal Yuroks found this perfect also, because for many centuries the village of 'Oket'ey has been here. A couple of families reside there now, maintaining privacy on their nine acres. The north shore of this lagoon is spoiled by a lumber company presence, but the seaward side of U.S. 101 is idyllic.

To visit the lagoon is to experience the ambience of an ancient coastal village, an example of a type that once dotted this entire coast. (Tsurai and Smith River remain, but are greatly changed.) The village itself is off-limits, and *very private*.

10 *Roundhouse Creek Rd. from U.S. 101 to Lynda Lane comes near the rancheria, but do not take the roads beyond. The setting of the quiet rancheria may be viewed from a short distance from U.S. 101, on the south shore of the lagoon. More importantly, go to Sumeg, next entry.*
BIG LAGOON RANCHERIA,
P.O. Drawer 3060, Trinidad, CA 95570

SUMEG VILLAGE
PATRICKS POINT STATE PARK
Yurok demonstration and ceremonial village.

A few years ago, the California Department of Parks and Recreation, along with some Yurok leaders decided that this site would be an excellent place to show the public how the early villages were built. This place then appeared, built to exact traditional specifications under careful supervision of the leaders. There are various structures here, including an example of an early Yurok house, which you can climb into. This house is similar to those of other tribes of this region along the Klamath. One small building was found not to be to traditional Yurok specifications, so its use was changed into a Hupa dressing room, as Hupa dancers are often invited to dance at the ceremonies here. (*See Architecture, p.67.*)

The Park will tell you the schedule of dances and ceremonies at this very authentic place.

11 *Location: 5 mi. N of Trinidad, on U.S. 101. Camping, admission.*
PATRICKS POINT STATE PARK,
Trinidad, CA
(707) 677-3570

TSURAI (TRINIDAD) RANCHERIA
Yurok (1917) Humboldt County

Trinidad Head is a "natural" place for settlement—it has a well-protected harbor, numerous fishing sites, fresh water, and plentiful forests, supporting both game and plants. The original site of Tsurai (Chu-rey) in the town of Trinidad is even commemorated by State Landmarks plaque **838**, which mentions the first

Modern Churey (Trinidad) Rancheria lies above the jagged rocks to the left. (dhe, 1998)

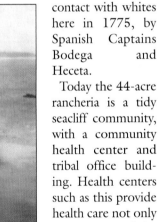

Historic photo of Trinidad Bay and the village of Tsurai (Churey), abandoned in 1916. (State Parks)

contact with whites here in 1775, by Spanish Captains Bodega and Heceta.

Today the 44-acre rancheria is a tidy seacliff community, with a community health center and tribal office building. Health centers such as this provide health care not only to residents of the rancheria, but to nearby off-reservation Indian families in the area.

The Rancheria is also proud owner of its Cher-Ae gaming establishment, well-marked.

12 *From U.S. 101, west at Trinidad exit, and then first major road (the coast road), south about 1 mile to a road (opposite a large rocky island) leading up the slope to the offices and health center. The casino has its own entrance.*
TRINIDAD TSURAI RANCHERIA,
P.O. Box 630, Trinidad, CA 95570
(707) 677-0211

PEOPLES OF NORTHEASTERN CALIFORNIA

THE LANGUAGE GROUPS
>THE PEOPLE
>>The Reservations and
>>*Organizations*

SHOSHONEAN SPEAKERS ‡
NORTHERN PAIUTE
>Fort Bidwell Reservation, Cedarville Rancheria, Susanville Rancheria*
>*organization*: Wahdatkuht Band of Northern Paiutes of Honey Lake Valley

HOKAN SPEAKERS ‡
PIT RIVER TRIBES
>Tribal Center (Burney); Big Bend Rancheria, Likely Cemetery, Lookout Rancheria,
>Montgomery Creek Rancheria, Roaring Creek Rancheria, X-L Ranch Reservation
>(in several parcels);
>Bands: Achomawi, Aporige, Astarwawi, Atsuge (Hat Creek), Atwamsini,
>Hammawi, Hewisedawi, Ilmawi, Itsatawi, Kosalextawi, Madesi
ALTURAS RANCHERIA*

YANA Some residents on Redding Rancheria* (*See p.131*)

PENUTIAN SPEAKERS ‡
KLAMATH & MODOC
>Tribal Center (Chiloquin, Oregon), Modoc Tribe (Miami, Oklahoma)
>without trust lands in California

MAIDU (MOUNTAIN MAIDU OR NORTHEASTERN MAIDU)
>Susanville Rancheria*, Greenville Rancheria, Berry Creek (Tyme) Rancheria*,
>Enterprise (Estom Yuymeka) Rancheria*
>*organizations:* Northern Maidu Tribe (Susanville, for Lassen Co.)
>Plumas Co. Indians (Taylorsville/ Greenville)
>United Maidu Nation (Susanville, for SE Plumas Co.& NE Butte Co.)

KONKOW (NORTHWESTERN MAIDU)
>Mooretown Rancheria, Meechoopda (Chico Rancheria & Burial Ground),
>Berry Creek (Tyme) Rancheria*, Enterprise (Estom Yuymeka) Rancheria*

NISENAN (SOUTHERN MAIDU)
>Auburn Rancheria

*Shared with other groups

‡ *See Languages, Tribal Origins, and Tribal Relationships discussion on page 12*

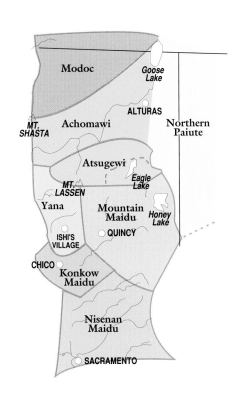

Modoc

Goose
Lake

ALTURAS

MT.
SHASTA

Achomawi

Northern
Paiute

Atsugewi

Eagle
Lake

MT.
LASSEN

Yana

Mountain
Maidu

Honey
Lake

ISHI'S
VILLAGE

QUINCY

CHICO

Konkow
Maidu

Nisenan
Maidu

SACRAMENTO

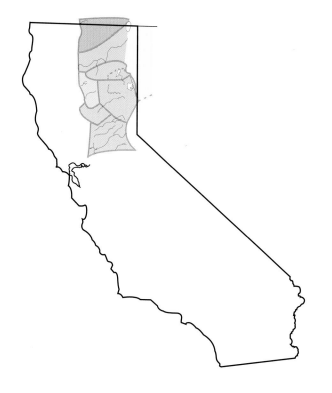

Hokan						
Penutian						
Uto-Aztecan						

NORTHEASTERN CALIFORNIA
THE ENVIRONMENT

THE MODOC PLATEAU covering a large part of northeastern California is a high, relatively flat expanse, ranging around 3,000 to 5,000 feet in altitude but sharply sculpted by a few rivers, lava beds, and long spines of mountains that form the lower Cascades and the northern Sierra Nevada. Occasional spectacular volcanic cones such as Crater Peak, Crater Mountain, and Lassen Peak rise like pencil points held under a brown sheet.

For the most part it is cold in winter and cool in summer. Pines and fir cover the loose soil where they can find a foothold. The meandering rivers are frequently deterred by natural dams, forming swamps, marshes and vast meadows that support waterfowl, fish, and grasses. Not many oaks, that staple source of so many other California peoples, are found in these upland meadows—the territory of the Modoc (of the lava beds), the eleven Pit River bands, and the Maidu (of Plumas and Lassen Counties).

Along the western edges of the Plateau lie the downslopes toward the Central Valley—a region of fairly dry, rugged foothills, scratched by creeks flowing down to the flat floor of the Sacramento River Valley. The groups seeking the water of the streams and the oaks of the flats along them were the Maidu called Konkow and Nisenan, and the Yana (*Ishi's tribe, see p.115*).

Over the Warner Mountains and the northern Sierra peaks on the far eastern border lies the country of the Northern Paiute. That desiccated terrain, striped with high mountain ranges, is called the Great Basin. The Paiute, although not part of what the anthropologists like to call "California culture," were and still are found all along that imaginary line that separates California from Nevada.

The Paiute, like their Shoshone cousins, were partly nomadic, as one must be when food supplies are sparse. It was necessary to spend much time in the daily tasks of preparing for winter. Dwellings tended to be only the most temporary wickiup of arched branches covered with brush. Winter quarters were located in more sheltered valleys and the dwellings were more permanent, often in tipi-like structures made of wooden slabs, or in tightly-woven reed huts. Dancing and dances were rare. In this Great Basin climate there was kinship with Sky and Father, unlike the "Californians", whose more sedentary spirits were more directed toward Earth and Mother.

Up on the high plateau, where the forests and marshes provided sustenance and the life was tranquil (except for occasional outbreaks of intertribal hostilities), the people wove nets for fishing, but made few canoes, because the water is usually quite rapid. As almost everywhere in California, the people demonstrated their artistic powers in arrow points, woven baskets, and feathered ornaments.

In this cold climate, however, they differed from others in collecting root and tuber species (from the marshes) for winter storage and in fashioning articles of fur and skins. In fact, the Pit River got its name from the local Indians' method of trapping deer—digging a pitfall.

Over all this land Lassen Peak stands sentinel—it is at the "corner" of several peoples' territories—the Pit River peoples, the Yana, the Maidu. In their active days both Lassen and Shasta must have been truly religion-inspiring phenomena, and their continuously seething hot springs are proof that Mother Earth is alive even when the mountains are dormant.

Dwellings on the plateau needed to be strong against the cold winds, but not so elaborate against the rain as in the northwest. For this, it was convenient to make an insulated house of cedar bark or slab strips, laid in a conical shape and supported inside with a slightly off-center pole. The dwelling was set

Lassen Peak, from the high plains to the north, Atsugewi territory. (dhe, 1999)

into the ground for better protection from the howling winds. Access was usually through a loose plank on the roof, since snow packed deeply around the sides. (The elders tell me that the winters were much colder many years ago.) Dance houses were of the same general architecture, but much larger. However, other less substantial structures might be built of brush, tule, or thatch for a temporary summer shelter, a fishing blind, or a hot weather sun-shelter. Some Yana and most Maidu and Konkow people preferred an earth-covered semi-subterranean home, especially for those who dwelt down at lower elevations.

OTHER BANDS of these peoples in geographically northeastern California dwelt at or near the alluvial fans of the eastern Sacramento River valley—the places where Sierra streams course through thick lava beds and steep foothills, then begin levelling out onto the plain. Bands of Yana, along with some Konkow and Nisenan Maidu, lead lives somewhat different from their mountain-dwelling kin.

The climate here is warmer, the ecology different, as were the foodstuffs; moreover, food was available year-round. Seasonal harvesting obviously was necessary, especially for the acorn, grass, and herb crops that came from the dry lower plains in summer, and the salmon that ran in the spring.

In this region of the margins of the plains and mountains, game was abundant—deer, antelope, elk, even an occasional black bear. Grizzlies, however, were respected and feared for their size and ferocity. Many tribes paid deference to this largest of native California mammals in their Bear Dance.

One other common practice of valley and plains peoples (common, because of abundance) was to have grasshopper and cricket roundups. Dried, these insects (and many others) made a healthy, tasty (we're told), and easily available food source that could be stored for long periods. Modern humans might consider taking advantage of this potential food source. After all, the not unsimilar shrimp and crayfish are considered delicacies.

The peoples of northeastern California were not too different from those of the northwesterners in their abilities and desires to exhibit their artistry in handiwork, especially basketry. Their legends, myths, tales, and medicinal practices, likewise were similar, but seldom identical, to other central and northern California peoples. Those who hear the tales say that Coyote, for instance, was downright lewd, and the myths were more storylike and less tied to ethics.

It is said that the people of this region respected ability and personal attainment, and paid much less obeisance to wealth and position than some northwesterners, for example, the Yurok. Perhaps this is because these bands were required to move about more for their subsistence, so accumulating things would have become a burden.

It was via the Paiute people that an unusual religious movement came to the California peoples—the Ghost

Dance. Ghost Dance began in 1870 as a dream by a Nevada Paiute, Wovoka, in which the dancing would return ancient Indian spirits to earth, whites would disappear, and Indians with Ghost shirts would be effectively protected from bullets.

The illusions were a last hope. Not from the white man's justice, legal systems, nor the religions was any help or comfort offered. As the Ghost Dance idea moved through the rapidly declining and discouraged California peoples in the 1870s, it picked up characteristics of Kuksu (see p.24), infusing it with an almost pentecostal character. The dream it represented died when salvation of the natives failed to occur. Still, some say that in death the longed-for peace was finally found.

Sutter Buttes, a revered Maidu landmark in the central Sacramento River Valley, stand out markedly above the extremely flat floodplain. Flooding of crop areas in winter, a recently introduced practice, begins to reproduce the effect of winter rains before European alteration of the land. (dhe, 1999)

PLACE NAMES

Although nearly every river flat, every mountain, and every river in Northeastern California had its local Indian name, hardly a single original place name remains—possibly a few do in translation, as in **Goose**, **Eagle**, **Coyote**, **Sage**, **Willow**, or **Big**. Most of the tribes still have their own names for the features, but they are never on maps.

MODOC **MODOC:** *móatokni,* "southerners," i.e., south of the Klamath people
NISENAN **YUBA** (City): *yupu;* **COLOMA:** *koloma,* village names

These are about the only prominent names left. The attempted obliteration of the culture by denying its historical reality was nearly total, but not successful.

EARLY POPULATIONS

Estimated original populations before 1830*:
ALL PIT RIVER BANDS including ATSUGEWI: *ca.* 3,900
YANA/YAHI: 1,500-1,900
MAIDU/KONKOW/NISENAN: 9,000
MODOC: *ca.* 3,000 (California and Oregon)
NORTHERN PAIUTE: the majority were residents of northwest Nevada and southeast Oregon; California figures not available.

* The numbers given here and in other sections are early estimates, and they are doubtless low. They are presented to show the relative populations of various groups.

SHOSHONEAN LANGUAGES

Shoshonean is one of a large group of Uto-Aztecan languages spoken in the Great Basin, including eastern and southern California, also by the Comanches, and the Aztecs of Mexico. The tribe of northeastern California is the Northern Paiute.

PAIUTE

THE PAIUTE PEOPLES of the West occupied ancestral lands of the Great Basin from Idaho and Oregon eastward through Nevada to Utah and Arizona. Closely related in language and customs to these peo-

To subdue Paiutes not anxious to part with their lands, Ft. Bidwell in the extreme northeast of California was established. This detachment of Troop "C", 4th Company (Cavalry?) is on a march near Ft. Bidwell in the Warner Mountains in 1893, the year the fort was decommissioned to become an Indian school and reservation. Note the ancient shoreline of the Upper Lake salt lake. The fence pictured surrounds an American cemetery.   (State Parks)

ple are the Shoshone, whose territory in California is to be found as far south as the Panamint Valley and whose remnant people are settled in the Owens Valley reservations. In fact, Paiute or Shoshone tribal bands are to be found bordering the entire eastern edge of California down to the Colorado River. In addition to their two Northeastern California reservations, Paiute and related peoples reside in Susanville, Woodfords, Carson City and Gardnerville in Nevada, the Mono Lake area, and at least two of the Owens Valley reservations. Several larger reservations are scattered about Nevada and eastern Oregon.

LIFESTYLES OF THESE PEOPLES demanded mobility, since their food supply of deer and wild sheep game was rather mobile. Summers are hot and dry here, and food had to be sought where the mountains snatched some rain from the seldom-seen clouds.

Winters were ruggedly cold, and sheltered places were indispensible. When horses became available from the Spanish, they became an absolute necessity.

Modern festivals and dances ("powwows") of the Great Basin peoples resemble those of the Plains Indians far more than those of the central and western California peoples.

FORT BIDWELL RESERVATION
Northern Paiute (1897) Modoc County

The piney eastern slopes of the Warner Mountains don't attract a lot of water from the passing clouds, but enough to keep a 5,000-foot-high desert valley green. About 175 Paiute people reside on the 3,335-acre reservation and several more live in private homes of the vicinity. These are a people of the desert—with a plains history rather different from that of the Modoc Plateau and the secluded Coast Range peoples.

Their lives, once semi-nomadic, now are sedentary; they live on ranches and small farms at the edges of the desert along the California-Nevada state line. In various patches on the panorama of desert and mountain we find an ancient cemetery, an old town center ghosting away, modern government-built homes grouped around cul-de-sacs, and green to gold alfalfa pastures surrounding the wooden barns of ranches. Horses and cattle give the place an old-West atmosphere.

The fort itself (State Landmark **430**) was established in 1866, to subdue the Modoc, the Paiute, and the Pit River peoples. The fort was turned into an Indian school and the lands given reservation status in 1897, after subjugation. All that is left of the fort now is the ruins of its hospital. An old school building has been converted into residences.

Schooling is not offered on the reservation—the Indians must use local white facilities in Cedarville—but there is a plain, more modern community services and tribal office structure and a 1984 health clinic. There is little employment in the local Forest Service office, because, as one ranger told me, the Indians don't trust anyone in a federal agency.

17 *From State Rte. 299 at Cedarville, take the county road north 20 miles (good, scenic road) to Fort Bidwell community.*
FORT BIDWELL RESERVATION
P.O.Box 129, Fort Bidwell, CA 96112

A view of the Cedarville Rancheria from the Warner Mountains slopes out over the salt flats of Middle Alkali Lake and the Nevada hills beyond. (dhe, 1982)

CEDARVILLE RANCHERIA
Northern Paiute (1915) Modoc County

In the little historic town of Cedarville at the edge of the Nevada desert, with infinite vistas of the desert, distant mountains, and salt flats, a couple dozen Indian people dwell on a little rectangle of 17 acres. As on a number of other rancherias, the residents include people who have married into the Paiute group from other places from Montana to Arizona. What employment exists is mostly in ranching.

18 *Behind the county fairgrounds and up against the water tank foothill in Cedarville.*
CEDARVILLE RANCHERIA
P.O. Box 126, Cedarville, CA 96104

A Paiute woman dressed in formal 1890s attire for her portrait. Even today, some elderly Paiute women maintain this fashion. (State Parks)

HOKAN SPEAKERS
The word "Hokan" is Atsugewi for "two."
Northeastern California speakers of this group,
which has many related languages around the state are:
Pit River Tribes and Yana.

PIT RIVER

PIT RIVER COUNTRY is among the most varied of any in California—from Mt. Shasta to desert, with deep forest, lava beds, and swamps in between. Present-day Pit River Indian land is, of course, only a fraction of that, but much of it is picturesque. Here, the high, dry hills are covered with scrub oak and pine, capped with lava flows like the spines of huge, fossil dinosaurs spread over 8,000 acres. The name of the river itself comes from the Indian practice of trapping deer by digging and disguising a pit along deer trails.

SEVERAL SEPARATE PARCELS of Federally recognized Indian land are highly dispersed about the countryside north and west of Alturas along the Pit River and Hat Creek in their ancestral territory of Shasta, Modoc, Lassen, and Siskiyou Counties. Members' homes are likewise dispersed, and they belong to no less than eleven bands of the Pit River people. Some homes are still quite rough, some lodged among huge piles of crumpled lava; others are quite modern.

Other settlements, not Federally recognized, exist in small pockets around the area. One such group, primarily associated with the Hat Creek, or Atsugewi, is gathered around the Hat Creek Full Gospel Church in the pleasant agricultural valley. The settlement has been here since the 1950s; the church itself is a picturesque historic wooden clapboard structure, formerly a dance hall.

Their organization includes a number of formerly independent rancherias, off-reservation groups, and individuals who, though autonomous, have long needed a collective group to deal effectively with their interests. Burney, a Modoc County mountain town, was selected as the center of Indian administrative activity for the tribes. Located here are their tribal offices, a modern health facility, a gaming establishment, and an elder/children's center.

THE PIT RIVER TRIBES OF CALIFORNIA is the name the Pit River rancherias, bands, and members adopted in the 1980s for their umbrella organization. Burney was selected to be their community center, and Federal funds began to improve the lives of this people, who had long been neglected.

Deep in the forest north of St. Hwy. 299 is the site of the Pit River Indian land claims movement. In 1938 some 9,000 acres of these forested lands were set aside for Indian lands, but the Pacific Gas & Electric Company grabbed it for timber. PG&E already has control of the local water for hydroelectric purposes. This land is actively contended over, but the intensity of the conflict has depended on its organizers.

PIT RIVER TRIBES OF CALIFORNIA

Pit River (1938) Modoc County
A Federally-recognized grouping of 11 autonomous tribes, related by similar languages and ancestry.

ONE DAY IN JUNE, 1997, we were given the opportunity by the tribal chairman to speak with some of the staff of the tribe and the clinic. The following account of the Pit River Tribe was graciously furnished by Jessica Jim, Ajumawi Band member of the Pit River Tribe, as was the interview with Roberto Dansie, Director, Pit River Health Service.

JESSICA JIM:

"The Pit River Tribe, a tribe of eleven traditionally autonomous bands [*numbering nearly 1,000 persons*] was first organized as a "Provisional Government" in 1964. On August 15, 1987, all entities adopted a formal Constitution which was signed by the Assistant Secretary of the Interior on December 3, 1987. The purpose of this Constitution was to secure our rights and powers to claim our ancestral lands, known as the "100 mile square", in which we have resided since time immemorial. [*The "100 mile square" is located in parts of Shasta, Siskiyou, Modoc, and Lassen Counties, referred to on July 29, 1959, as Pit River Docket No. 347, 7 Indian Claims Commission 815-844, Appendices A & B pages 1-49.*]

"THE PIT RIVER TRIBE claims the title to all lands within the 100-mile square (3.4 million acres) under Docket 347 as our ancestral area. The Pit River Tribe has never signed away its title or claim to its ancestral area. [*After interminable legal wrangling, various Commission incarnations purport to have "given" the Indians of California a "settlement" of $37M to 65,000 Indians for 64M acres.*]

"The Pit River Tribe's eleven autonomous bands are governed by the Pit River Tribal council on behalf of its members. Nine bands speaking dialects of *Ahjuma* language are: *Ajumawi, Astarawi, Atwamsinawi, Hammawi, Hewisedawi, Ilmawi, Itsatawi, Kosalektawi,* and *Madesiwi.* Two bands speaking *Atsuge* language are *Atsugewi* and *Aporigewi.* ["*-wi*" means "the people of..."]

"The 100-mile line begins at Round Mountain (Shasta County) to Alturas (Modoc County), bordering Lassen and Siskiyou counties. The land boundaries are fondly known as the (almost) square area bounded by "Mt. Shasta, eastward by Medicine Lake to Fandango Pass (above Goose Lake), south along the Warner Mountain crest to Eagle Lake, west to Mt. Lassen, northwesterly by Magee Peak and Burney Mountain, Round Mountain, by Grizzly Peak and Black Butte, back to Mt. Shasta, aka: the 100-mile ancestral area. This tribe is the only one in California which is Federally recognized as autonomous bands organized under the one government known as the Pit River Tribe and, therefore, an historic tribe.

An unpretentious Pit River Tribes office overlooks the tribal casino and Burney Peak. (dhe, 1998)

"OUR RESERVATION is located in Alturas, known as the XL Reservation, a 9000-acre parcel. The government calls it the XL Ranch; however, it is really the Pit River Tribes Reservation. This property was acquired in 1936 for the Tribe. A lawsuit was entered into stating that this reservation was to benefit the whole Tribe and its members, not just to be enjoyed by a few families. The lawsuit lasted for a period of approximately 17 years. During this period the Tribe and its members did not have access to the Reservation, so in the early 1980s we acquired the 79-acre parcel of land in Burney, northeastern Shasta County, under a Department of Housing and Urban Development (HUD) grant as its land base until such time as the XL Reservation was determined to be for the benefit for all members. It was eventually declared by the Court that the XL Reservation was to benefit all members of the Pit River Tribe.

"In 1982-83 another HUD Block Grant was awarded to build a Tribal Health Building to provide quality and sufficient health care to the members of the Pit River Tribe. Prior to the Tribal Health Facility, we had to travel from Burney to Susanville in Lassen County to receive health and medical care. It took all day to get to Susanville.

"This was a major success for the Pit River Tribe and its members, and since then the 79 acres have been developed to meet the demands of its members for our Tribal Office, Health Facility, and more recently, our Tribal Casino.

"MUCH OF THE XL RESERVATION is prime land for agriculture and grazing. This could be developed on one side of the 9,000-acre reservation, and the other side could be developed for housing. In the 1970s, the Tribe exercised its right to claim title to its ancestral land, the 100-mile square, against major shareholders in companies like PG&E, Kimberly Clark (lumber), etc. Our leaders were up against major companies for the fight for our ancestral land, and a confrontation occurred known as the "Battle of 4-Corners". The remnants and scars of this confrontation can be seen today 5 miles north of Burney off the intersection of Hwy. 299 and Hwy. 89. This confrontation exploded after the US Forest Service and local law enforcement agencies proceeded to remove a "quonset hut" that had been erected by the tribal leaders and supporters to signify their claim to the land. Elders were billyclubbed, children were crying for their mothers and fathers as law officers hit and pushed their parents. An elderly man with one leg was hit and lay bleeding on the land which he felt was his. They arrested a lot of young and elderly people and put them into buses, then drove them [60 miles] to Redding and put them in jail for felony trespass.

"The 1970s brought the Tribe into national headlines, and people from all over the country came to aid Pit River people to support their right to claim their ancestral area. People like Richard Oakes (a leader of the 1969 Alcatraz occupation), Grace Thorpe (daughter of James F. Thorpe, Olympic runner), and several medicine men were here in Pit River country.

"The Tribal territory land base today includes the 9,000-plus acres of XL Reservation, the Rancherias of Montgomery Creek, Roaring Creek, Big Bend, Lookout, and Likely. The 79-acre parcel is in trust for the Pit River Tribe and is known as our second land base. Individual allotments and individual trust property also are within the Tribe's territory, but we do not have any expressed right to the individual member's allotments or trust properties. In addition, two individual fee properties were donated to the Tribe in the early 1970s and are located in Modoc County. Any and all other property that may be purchased in the future will be considered additional Tribal land base.

"Sleeping Giant" is what the Pit River Tribe is called by other tribes. This may be implied by the thought that Pit River country is surrounded by dormant volcanoes. In 1998, the Tribe is progressing to move into the second millennium. We are currently seeking assistance for housing for our members. The membership has determined that to be the priority for any economic development of the Tribe. Education is the second highest priority of the peo-

ple. One comment I recently heard was that the government does not put enough money aside for education because, if they educated the Indians, then they would be out of a job.

"Gaming is the big issue now facing the Tribe. Once again, the Tribe has to fight the very agency that was intended to protect it. Once again, the Tribe has to fight for its right for economic development. Once again, the Tribe has to fight for its sovereignty. Is it not enough that the Casino employs 60% of its members? Is it not enough that we have reduced the welfare and unemployment rate by 85%? Is the future once again being clouded by the test of sovereignty?

"Finally, I say that as a Pit River Tribal member, I remain active in our political structure and choice of government. I remain proud of my heritage, the government cannot take that away with a flick of their finger. They already tried that by termination and genocide...but, here I am, a proud Pit River..."

—Jessica E. Jim,
Ajumawi Band Member, Pit River Tribe

Roberto Dansie:

"A serious governmental commitment to health care began in 1983 with construction of a health and dental clinic, under the tribal administration. This was followed by purchase of some 40 acres upon which to expand the entire administrative center. A casino followed, which brings sorely needed employment to nearly 50 tribal members, and needed resources to the tribe.

"In 1997 a community services building, *Munik-Chun* (Deer Child), was opened. We had the opportunity to observe its first few days of operation. Following a unique and thoughtful plan, the structure combines senior services (including mid-day meals) with a day-care center. Here elders, youngsters, and parents have contact, and the continuity of tribal customs is strengthened. Careful attention is given to encourage the unity of all the bands."

—Roberto Dansie, Director,
Pit River Health Service:

We learned of the tribal ethnobotanical project in the creekside and meadow adjacent to the clinic—part of the Shasta-Alturas Cultural and Health project. Though the challenges are very great for such a spread-out tribe, within the clinic, motivation and enthusiasm for new efforts are very high. This means health outreach to the X-L clinic, services to the new

> "I REMAIN PROUD OF MY HERITAGE, THE GOVERNMENT CANNOT TAKE THAT AWAY WITH A FLICK OF THEIR FINGER. THEY ALREADY TRIED THAT BY TERMINATION AND GENOCIDE... BUT, HERE I AM, A PROUD PIT RIVER..."

homes at Roaring Creek, Montgomery Creek, and Alturas. (We're looking at a spread of 100 miles!)

We heard of appeals for traditional medicine from the tribal traditionalists (estimated at some 40% of treatment) to be blended with "western" medicine, as needed—mutual respect and understanding between the two. The Health Service sponsors programs of Native traditional singing, dancing, along with healing. To have healthy children means encouraging healthy life-style and attitudes. So what is more appropriate than a very large and respected first class karate team directed by eager and intense leaders?

19 *The Pit River Tribes center of community activity is located just S of St. Hwy. 299 in the center of Burney. Here are the tribal office, the casino, the health clinic, and the tribal community services building.*

PIT RIVER TRIBES TRIBAL OFFICE
20265 Tamarak Ave., P.O. Drawer 70,
Burney, CA 96013
(530) 335-5421

Originally a roadhouse and dancehall, the Hat Creek Full Gospel Church has occupied this building since the 1950s. These lands were once considered to be uninhabitable and unsuitable for any agricultural purpose. Local Indians, never given trust lands, settled here in the lava beds along Hat Creek and nearby. This area has been an Atsugewi gathering place since being ousted from their homelands. (dhe, 1999)

The rancherias briefly described below belong to the Pit River confederation.

20 X-L RANCH RESERVATION
(1938) Modoc County
Both sides of U.S 395 for about a mile either side of the Hwy. 299 junction plus little squares nearby constitute this portion. Pit River Tribe satellite services are by BIA

Road 76, north of the State Quarantine Station on U.S. 395. Other portions of X-L are near Goose Lake, Big Sage Reservoir, and Fairchild Swamp.

21 LIKELY RANCHERIA (1924) Modoc County
Once a small rancheria of 40 acres, only one acre remains —a burial ground. About 1/2 mi. south of Likely, from U.S. 395, a dirt road east crosses the railroad tracks. About 3/4 mile to the lonely place marked only by old trees.

22 LOOKOUT RANCHERIA (1913) Modoc Co.
This quiet 40 acres, looking out over pastures and fields toward the low mountains of Modoc National Forest, was primitive residence and a tiny ranch for some 60 years. Then came electricity in 1973 and several new homes. Electricity in 1973? This is Indian country.

23 BIG BEND RANCHERIA (1916) Shasta Co.
The town of Big Bend is remote—at the end of pavement of Big Bend Rd. off Hwy. 299 . In summer, there is fishing and hunting in the wilderness beyond. A few residents of the 40 acres of Pit River bottomland enjoy their surroundings (just the other side of the river bridge) . Hot springs are here, a basketweaver lives here, and some employment in lumbering is seasonally available.

24 ROARING CREEK RANCHERIA
(1915) Shasta County
Deep in the pine forest, by a turbulent tributary of the Pit River, 3 miles north of Hwy. 299 on Cove Road, live the Lego family members. Their place is in reality a self-sufficient, 80-acre family farm—pond, geese, cows, pigs. Some car repairing is done. But the family prefers no uninvited guests. The last big uninvited guest was Pacific Gas & Electric Co. (see above).

25 MONTGOMERY CREEK RANCHERIA
(1913) Shasta County
The countryside is pretty, so dry that a single intense forest fire wiped out the rancheria and the forest in 1992. Some of the local Pit River fire fighters managed to save several local homes. New construction replaces ancient structures. It is on the south side of Hwy. 299, 2 miles north of Fenders Ferry Road.

ALTURAS RANCHERIA
Pit River and *Modoc* (1924) Modoc County
[Not affiliated with the Pit River Tribes]
About 3/4 miles east of Alturas on the south side of County Road 56 lie twenty acres of a few dwellings in a dry rectangle at the edge of the 4,400-foot- high northeastern desert. A local health clinic is also located in Alturas on Hwy. 299, serving the Alturas and Cedarville Rancherias, and scattered members of the Modoc and Pit River peoples.

26 ALTURAS RANCHERIA
P.O. Box 360, Alturas, CA 965101

The Yana people of the high country and foothills above Chico suffered the reputation of being an extinct tribe—that is, until the people emerged from near obscurity. Most of the people are today associated with the Redding Rancheria. In 1913, one member, Ishi, was given this rock shelter on the University of California, San Francisco, campus as a retreat. A brief tale of his story is in the text. (dhe, 1997)

YANA

THE YANA, a people of the foothills just to the south of the Pit River and west of the Maidu and Mt. Lassen, have ceased to exist as a culture in their ancestral homelands, although several of the tribe are quite active not far away. The last of the independent-minded Yana, a band of Yahi, fled to the bush in 1865. Hounded by whites, they were killed or captured, one by one, until one of the last of their band, Ishi, surrendered to the Butte County sheriff in 1911. Ishi was taken to San Francisco, where, at the University of California, he taught whites his Hokan language and his ways of survival in the wild. His exposure to European disease resulted in his contracting tuberculosis, and for this was admitted to the University of California medical school for treatment.

I RECENTLY READ Ishi's original University of California Hospital records. It is one of the saddest things I have ever read—it rates along with the *Diary of Anne Frank*. Ishi was persuaded to sing his healing songs in some of the wards by his physician, Dr. Saxton Pope. He did so with great relish, knowing that his efforts just might be of assistance. He died of tuberculosis in 1916. His story must be read by everyone. (*See Kroeber, T., App. VII*) So that this story might not be totally grim, the story notwithstanding, descendants of a few survivors of Ishi's family live today in the Redding area. In fact, the logo of Redding Rancheria bears the "flying geese" design motif of Yana basketry, out of respect for these Yana descendants who live on the rancheria.

Penutian languages probably arose in California; they are found largely in the central and northern parts of the state, and are related to some languages of Oregon and eastern Washington. Maidu peoples belong to the Penutian language group, Modoc and Klamath are probably related.

MODOC & KLAMATH

THE MODOC of northeastern California and southern Oregon were a feared and often hated people because of their slave raids on nearby peoples. The Warm Springs tribes to the north in Oregon to this day boast that a tribal member led the U.S. Cavalry to the capture of the most famous Modoc, *Kintpuash* (called Captain Jack by the whites).

IN 1864 the Modocs were herded onto the Klamath Reservation* with their enemies, the Klamath tribe. Intertribal friction rose to such a level that Kintpuash, with his people, decamped to their former homelands. The struggle of the U.S. Army to return them to the reservation resulted in the Modoc War (1872-73). In the rough, black, jagged lava beds of Tulelake[†], Kintpuash and 60 Modocs heroically defended themselves under the siege by 600 Army troops for four months.

Eventually, the band was forced to surrender; Kintpuash and five of his group were hanged. Much of the Modoc tribe was shipped to a tiny enclave in northeastern Oklahoma. Today, however, descendants of several Modocs that escaped the dragnet are slowly reviving their heritage. *continued next page*

CAPTAIN JACK.

I certify that L. HELLER has this day taken the Photographs of the above Modoc Indian, prisoner under my charge.

Kintpuash, Modoc leader, was called Captain Jack by the American Army. He was hanged shortly after this photograph was taken in 1873. See p.35. (State Parks)

continued next page

* *The Klamath Reservation was set in a forested, wide flat area between Upper Klamath Lake and Crater Lake, OR. This economically viable and model reservation was forcibly terminated in 1955! The Native American Rights Fund (NARF, p.261) is presently working on legal means to restore some of the former reservation lands to the Klamath Tribes.*

[†] *The battle site, "Captain Jack's Stronghold", is located in Lava Beds National Monument, and his story is told with sympathy and admiration toward the Modoc people. Within the Monument are also two examples of ancient Modoc abstract painting, and Northern California's most extensive example of petroglyphs, carved on the cliffs of an ancient lakeside.*

Annual gatherings are held in Lava Beds National Park honoring Kintpuash and his band. Some 200 Modocs take part, mostly coming from their homes in Oregon, but some from Oklahoma or scattered places about California—a tribute to the endurance and spirits of the Modoc tribe. Some Modoc people are affiliated with the Alturas Rancheria of Modoc County.

An Indian Museum at Chiloquin, Oregon (*see below*), displays Modoc culture. The people are being taught their language, native plants furnish food and materials for basketry, ceremonies and dancing are revived, and "once again there are spiritual people".

THE KLAMATH TRIBES

Klamath, Modoc, and *Paiute* Chiloquin, Oregon

Modoc ancestral lands lay on both sides of the California-Oregon state line around Klamath and Tule Lakes; Klamath land was adjacent to the north. Although officially "terminated" in the 1953, Klamath Tribes is comprised of a provisional, administrative alliance of descendants of Klamaths, Modocs who escaped the 1873 roundup and removal to Oklahoma, and Yahuskin Paiutes. The three groups may be soon detached from each other in order to preserve distinctive customs and family ties. Some land is still in Indian hands near Modoc Point on Upper Klamath Lake.

27 THE KLAMATH TRIBES
P.O. Box 436, Chiloquin, OR 97624

MAIDU FAMILY

MOUNTAIN (NORTHEASTERN) MAIDU
KONKOW (NORTHWESTERN) MAIDU
NISENAN (SOUTHERN) MAIDU

General preference today is simply to use the term Maidu for all the similar language groups of this region: *Mountain, Konkow, Mechoopda, Tyme, Nisenan*. Note: *maydi* = Maidu = person

MOUNTAIN (NORTHEASTERN) MAIDU

Mountain Maidu are those who live(d) in the more mountainous uplands of the region.

IN JUNE OF 1997, answering our request for a contribution to this book, we received a call from Susanville from a genial and expressive voice, which turned out to be Ron "Comanche" Morales, a leader of Lassen County off-reservation Maidu people, spokesman for the Honey Lake Maidu of Lassen County. Mr. Morales has been remarkably active in safeguarding and promoting the causes of the Mountain Maidu in his area. His family and his Maidu tribe are solidly versed in the knowledge of history, culture, and the extent of their lands. We spoke to him at his home in Susanville and on Maidu ceremonial grounds.

RON "COMANCHE" MORALES:

"We are identified by our myths, burials, trails, and stories. The knowledge of these show us our boundaries and our history."

Morales places great confidence in the words and descriptions of his grandmother, Roxie Peconom, and his uncles, especially George Peconom. Roxie told Fritz Riddell and William Evans in 1949 [*anthropologists, published in the1960s*] some of her recollections of the history, customs of her Maidu heritage and a lot of names of the Maidu families of the region. As a young woman, she recalls giving information to a young anthropologist by the name of Stephen Powers.

"ANTHROPOLOGIST RIDDELL spent about 20 to 30 hours asking my old and blind grandmother questions that have been long forgotten, some names that reflected geographic places. She was unsure of the area and names because of the language barrier of the two. The anthropologist was thinking and asking questions in a white man's way; Roxie Peconom gave her answers to Mr. Riddell on what she interpreted in Maidu. Most of the original camp locations, areas such as lakes and faraway places were known only to the hunter, the men. Questions relating to mountains, rivers, or wild forest was in the Maidu man's vocabulary, not in the woman's vocabulary at all. Most of the hunter's questions should have been asked to the 50 or 60 Maidu men that were still living in Honey Lake Valley when Riddell and Evans did their work on the Maidu ethnography in July and August, 1949.*"

Several topics arose in our conversations. Morales is concerned that the ancestral Maidu boundaries in Lassen County are properly delineated—it is important to the Maidu to protect the ancient and more modern burial sites of their people. Recent Bureau-created tribes, such as the Paiute people that are in this area, have caused disputes over land, and, in his words:

"Although it hasn't become animosity, it is serious. The Maidu are not a Bureau-created tribe, but are the aboriginal tribe of Lassen County. Our story of the Maidu is more updated than the work of Roland Dixon or Francis Riddell on the Maidu territory boundary and history."

Portions of history and Maidu life emerged. Morales has in his home a model of an earlier Maidu home—of cedar bark, with a center pole—a visual piece that is far more descriptive than any writing. Other artifacts, objects, and photos add to his bank of memories. He named the boundaries of the Maidu land, spoke of the lands to the north shared with the Pit River people, the *Achumawi* and *Atsugewi*. He gave me the original names of the lakes of the region. Ancient trails across the region are not only known, but are still used. He told of marriages then and now among these peoples mentioned above.

He told of his efforts to restore (Federal) tribal iden-

*William S. Evans, Honey Lake Maidu Ethnography, *Carson City, NV. Abstract, Part I, p. ii.*

tity to the 600 Maidu who have no connection to the rancherias. He teaches his son, grandson, and family these things, so that the traditions will be passed down. He encourages the Maidu language to be taught and preserved. He has written ethnographic articles with Professor William Simmons (University of California, Berkeley), local historian Steve Camacho and his older sister Viola Williams. He and his sister Viola have also devoted time in local schools talking about the Maidu traditions and beliefs, so that the Susanville community will know their early history.

WAS VIOLENCE part of Maidu history?

"Not so much as elsewhere. The Maidu were not warlike, so they did not suffer so much in terms of massacres in Lassen County, yet there were several killings. You know what was the biggest threat to the Maidu way of life? Ranchers. They brought their cattle and sheep, put up fences, changed the crops, took over our land, destroyed the edible plants of our people and gradually a large population of Indians died. It was a rather benign assimilation— they showed us how to plant potatoes and such, then gave their names to us, and took our land."

WE WENT SEVERAL MILES to a quiet pine forest, beside a creek in Lassen National Forest.

"This is Roxie Peconom Creek Campground, in honor of my grandmother. It is a sacred gathering place, *Jamam Maidu Wedam*, of the Maidu people. People come here from the Washoe, Pit River, Maidu, Paiute, Modoc, Shoshone, Hat Creek, Navajo, and many other tribes."

The center is a large, round ceremonial area in the shade of the pines; to one side is a beautifully-crafted wooden shelter (no metal) engineered and constructed by Mike McCourt and others, for either cooking or preparing for dancing. Nearby, across a small stream is a sweatlodge. Parking and a spacious camping area are alongside the creek. The campground is on Forest Road 29 , off Hwy. 36, 2 1/2 miles west of the junction with Hwy. 44.

With the expertise of Mike McCourt, and many friends from the community, plus close friends in the Forest Service, Morales has designed this outstanding effort to honor his people:

"For the public, the second weekend in June, we hold our *Wéda*, a ceremony that celebrates the coming of Spring—most people call it the Bear Dance."

Yet unaccomplished, his main goal is obtaining tribal recognition of the Honey Lake Maidu of Lassen County in the Federal registry. This is the most important part of his life. "We have a history together."

Information: Ron Morales, Chair
YAH-MONEE MAIDU
BEAR DANCE FOUNDATION
(Honey Lake Maidu)
1101 Arnold St., Susanville, CA 96130
(530) 257-3275

Ron Morales is extremely proud of the success of his efforts to honor his people and his mother at Roxie Peconom Campground in the Lassen National Forest. Mr. Morales led a great effort on the part of tribal members and enthusiastic local helpers to establish a remarkable dance arena and ceremonial site deep in the quiet forest. (dhe, 1997)

SUSANVILLE RANCHERIA
originally aboriginal *Maidu*, today
*Maidu, Washoe, Shoshone, Pit River Achumawi,
Northern Paiute*, and *Modoc* (1923) Lassen Co.

The rancheria is five blocks long and two wide, typical of many near-urban California rancherias. Just off the west side of the rancheria lies a shady Indian burial ground surrounded by a white picket fence that was first established in 1923 for California Indians. The first Indian buried there was Charlie Fox, a Pit River Indian. There are Maidu, Pit River, Washoe, Modoc, Shoshone, and Paiutes buried there.

Of further interest is the Indian Heights Gospel Church. Four Maidu families put up the homes for collateral to purchase this former roadhouse during the 1940s (*see photo next page*).

The hub of the rancheria is a tribal office-community center building, gym, and some playground equipment for kids. Here, too, are 25 or so homes, some better than many of the surrounding community, with a good feel of unconfined space on 150 acres.

A few Maidu reside here, yet most of the hundreds of Maidu of the county have never been part of the rancheria. The Maidu's annual public event is the *Wéda*, spring ceremony, or Bear Dance, currently held the 2nd weekend in June at Roxie Peconom Creek Campground in Lassen National Forest (see above). Sponsor: **LASSEN YAH-MONEE MAIDU BEAR DANCE FOUNDATION.**

28 *North side of Susanville on Chestnut St.*
SUSANVILLE RANCHERIA,
Drawer U, Susanville, CA 96130

The historic Indian Heights Full Gospel Church was built by Maidu hands on the Susanville Rancheria in the 1930s.   (dhe, 1997)

INDIAN VALLEY

Once upon a time, the beautiful, mountain-locked meadow valley named "Indian" was a Maidu valley. After the Americans came, the Indians were herded into two rancherias of about 375 acres—Greenville and Taylorsville. Since 1966, one of the reservation lands has totally disappeared, the other almost, but not the Maidu people. The valley is mostly farmland and ranches, with a sawmill intermittently furnishing some of the local employment to white and Indian alike.

One evening I met Tommy Merino, organizer for the Plumas County Indian Association. He told me some of the problems of his people, many of which stem from the difficulty of getting recognition, not as Indians, not as needy persons, but as a tribe. His dislike for the bureaucracy of BIA and government isn't unique, but it sure is there. He has been active in obtaining needed care for the children of his group, the local off-reservation Maidu

NORTHERN CALIFORNIA MAIDU SINGERS help celebrate the Mountain Maidu Wéda at a remarkable dance arena and ceremonial site built deep in the quiet of Lassen National Forest.   (dhe, 1999)

Mr. Merino told me, "When General George Custer was leaving the fort for Little Big Horn, he gave himself a grand parade, lining up officials from the BIA on one side of the parade ground, the other side with bureaucrats. Rearing back on his horse, just as he departed, he roared, 'Now remember, don't do anything until I get back!' His instructions are still being followed."

IN A LIGHT DECEMBER SNOWFALL, I wandered among the wood slab-marked graves of the ancient hillside burial ground, listening to the spirits, watching the flakes fill the sky above the flat valley floor, as though it were the smoke of a hundred village fires of 150 years ago.

A few miles away in the shade of an enveloping and protecting pine forest, the Forest Service says it "protects" the decaying slabs of the fallen roof of Satkimi Watum Kuimhu, an ancient Maidu dancehouse and an adjacent sweathouse. These sites were once the center of life for the band who dwelt on the wide, green meadow that is now Quincy.

GREENVILLE RANCHERIA
"INDIAN MISSION"
Maidu (1897) Plumas Co.

A remnant of Maidu activity in Indian Valley is situated in a corner of Indian Valley, the land of an old boarding school, once given over to the Rancheria, but since almost lost to parcelization on earlier termination. Only some four lots are still in Maidu hands.

Greenville Rancheria has been brought back into trust status, but most of the tribe has scattered. Nevertheless, the main center of activity is the tribal office in Red Bluff. The tribe has hardly been inactive, however. It employs some 70 persons to staff three community health clinics—two in Red Bluff and one in Greenville. The Red Bluff office handles matters of 70 tribal members from the site listed below.

EVENT: Northern Sierra Indian Days Powwow in Greenville, mid-September (*see Calendar*)

29 *Old Taylorsville Rd., 4 mi. E of Greenville, at a place called the "INDIAN MISSION"*

GREENVILLE RANCHERIA,
645 Antelope Bl., Ste.15, Red Bluff, CA 996080

PLUMAS CO. INDIANS, INC.
Maidu Plumas Co.

This is an organization of off-reservation Maidu living in northern Plumas County. Presently it serves a social administrative and function, as well as being a small repository of tradition.

PLUMAS CO. INDIANS, INC.
c/o Tommy Merino,
Box 102, Taylorsville, CA 95947

ROUNDHOUSE COUNCIL OF GREENVILLE

various Plumas County

There is here an educational group mostly for kids, but others are welcome. Tutorial sessions are offered for after school, and facilities include computers, a library, and a video collection. Emphasis is mainly on Indian culture (Maidu). (Sorry, no roundhouse, only the concept of a community center of learning.)

ROUNDHOUSE COUNCIL OF GREENVILLE
330 Bush St., Greenville, CA 95947
(530) 284-6866

KONKOW (NORTHWESTERN) MAIDU

Konkow people are from the lower foothills of the upper Sacramento Valley. The designation by early anthropologists as *Konkow* (or *Concow*) comes from *ko-yun-koy-i* = people of this region.

ARCHAEOLOGICAL EVIDENCE confirms that this group of people is known to have been present in the foothills along the Middle Fork and South Fork of the Feather River around 1200 BC. Their pre-white contact area is centered in Butte County and parts of Yuba and Sutter Counties

Uses of animals and local plants for food, medicine, tools, and clothing were well-developed. They planted and tended seeds and bulbs in appropriate growing areas and traded extensively with coastal peoples (west), Nisenans (south), and to the east (Nevada). A highly developed social order of etiquette and religion promoted a peaceful lifestyle, common among California peoples.

The first known contact with the Spanish, Gabriel Moraga, occurred in 1808. An increasing trade with trappers into the 1830s resulted in deadly exposure to European diseases, followed by massive epidemics, massacres, and killings. (*See P.33*). Gold discovery brought a swarm of intruders: as the gold fever wore off, packs of settlers came, appropriating land for timber, agriculture, and railroads.

The Indians negotiated treaties in good faith, but none were honored, and they were left homeless and landless. Four hundred sixty-one Konkow people were herded into Chico on September 4, 1863, and force-marched to Round Valley (75 miles across the Sacramento River, a dry plain, and a 3,000-foot mountain range). Only 277 survived the two-week ordeal. —*The above information is taken from the Mooretown Rancheria tribal bulletin.*

BERRY CREEK RANCHERIA

Tyme Maidu (1916, 1990s) Butte Co.

Tucked away in a corner of a dark, remote forest, watered by a little stream channeled into an aqueduct, with no electricity for miles, hides a 33-acre tract, once property of the Central Pacific Railroad. It must be close to the ultimate solitude, because not even their nearest neighbors know that Indians live here—it took me two tries to find it. Their seclusion is obviously appreciated.

The people of this tribe, however, decided on a grand plan to improve their lot and gather the tribe, which, by the way, prefers the name Tyme Maidu (from *tá-yim-k'oyo*, the old village site).

"Improvement" is acquisition of land (32 acres), building of modern housing, erection of a gaming house—all in the city of Oroville. This produced an awareness of the necessity for education: building a site for Headstart, a library, and computer lab.

30 *The old rancheria is near Berry Creek on Bean Creek Rd., off Hwy. 162, up against Plumas National Forest. The new tribal site is off Olive Highway (Hwy. 162) in Oroville. The casino is at 4020 Olive Hwy.*
BERRY CREEK RANCHERIA
5 Tyme Way, Oroville, CA 95966
(916) 534-3859 (casino 534-9892)

ENTERPRISE RANCHERIA

Estom Yuymeka "Middle Ridge" Maidu (1915)
Butte County

The rancheria perches on a hillside, in a foothill region of small oaks and pines, laced with a labyrinth of little roads, serving a growing number of folks fleeing the urbs. It has been called home by a few Maidu for many decades; today its 40 acres are occupied by numerous residences.

The tribe has grand plans to acquire more acreage nearby, to furnish more homes for its growing and dispersed population of 360 members. (Significantly, gaming is not in the plan.)

31 *From the Oroville-Feather Falls Rd., one mile NE from the Feather River bridge, take Oregon Creek Rd. 1 1/2 mi. in the direction of Toyon Hills, past a tire repair depot and several old buildings. Left, uphill to the homes.*
ENTERPRISE RANCHERIA TRIBAL OFFICES
2950 Feather River Blvd., Oroville, CA 95965

As late as 1985, the Mooretown Rancheria consisted of less than 40 acres of agricultural and forest land in the foothills near Feather Falls. Since that time, more than 250 acres have been acquired for an impressive complex of housing, casino, public space, and community center. These comfortable homes are part of the ingathering of that Konkow Maidu tribe.

(dhe, 1998)

MOORETOWN RANCHERIA

Konkow (Northwestern) Maidu (1894) Butte Co.
A formerly terminated tribe, reinstated, with new land acquisition.

Many years ago several Indian residents near Feather Falls took private ownership of an 80-acre parcel of land which had already been been their home for some 50 years. Later, a second 80-acre parcel was purchased by the government for 53 members of the **TAYLOR BAND OF INDIANS**. However, government services were terminated to these people in 1961. This action caused great disruption of the tribal community, and some land had to be sold off. The Tillie Hardwick de-termination action of 1983 (*see p.47*), allowed those families living in the Feather Falls area to return to trust status. Lorrie Frazier, Chairperson of the Mooretown Rancheria Cultural Resources Committee spoke with us on the phone.

LORRIE FRAZIER:

"This tribe had been terribly dispersed, but we were also terribly anxious to reestablish our presence in our home territory and to re-acquire a land base. First, the tribe reorganized in 1987 to take advantage of the newly-reacquired trust status. The opportunity to improve their lot came in the form of the Indian Self-Determination Act of 1993 that pro-

vided monies for tribal governance, start-up money for projects, economic development, and housing.

"**PERSEVERANCE OF** the tribal committees on one such project got us a tract of 35 acres, then 50 homes in a quiet, rural setting, then a modular building to house a casino employing more than 230 persons. A large new casino replaces the earlier building, with a (somewhat diminished) replica of Feather Falls at the entrance, to remind the people whence they came. Centerpiece of the Rancheria in a pretty, wooded grove is a pleasing community center, which houses tribal offices, childcare facilities, a multi-purpose room and kitchen. The residences are available for tribal members. An additional adjoining 25 acres for 25 more homes comprise the next development— and an RV park and campsites are possibilities.

"**REESTABLISHING CULTURAL** traditions of the tribe and establishing a neighborly presence in the Oroville area are very important factors in its present activities. People are working hard on community projects in preserving history. For instances: the old Post Office in Feather Falls is in need of historical documents and preservation; a Maidu presence at the Feather River Nature Center (Oroville) will include a demonstration village, native plants, and interpretive talks; participation at the annual Oroville Salmon Festival includes a booth, entertainment, and traditional dances. (*Admission is free, camping is available nearby.*)

"Participation is popular in a Konkow Language Preservation Group, which meets in the library with elder speakers, and is associated with linguists; several Maidu artists are featured regularly in exhibitions; training with the Forest Service is available for monitors at regional archaeology sites; planning is underway for a Maidu Heritage Center."

—Lorrie Frazier, Chairperson of the Mooretown
Rancheria Cultural Resources Committee

All of this is a truly outstanding, ambitious program to regain pride and a culture, once dispersed and disunited, now close.

32 *Old site: One mile S of Feather Falls, 1/2 mi. N of Island Bar Rd., off Lumpkin Rd., on a dirt road going east. Nice homes.*
New site: S of Oroville on Hwy 70, E on Ophir Rd. 3 mi. to the Rancheria complex on N side of road.
MOORETOWN RANCHERIA
Tribal offices: #1 Alverda Dr., Oroville, CA 95966
(916) 533-3625

MECHOOPDA TRIBE OF THE CHICO RANCHERIA

Maidu (ca. 1902) Butte County

A Federally recognized tribe with a parcel of land measured in square feet. Pete Ramirez is the Chair of the Mechoopda Tribe of the Chico Rancheria. We spoke him and he told us the story of his people.

PETE RAMIREZ:

"The Chico Rancheria occupies a unique historical position. Yes, it was officially terminated in 1955, when there was considerable pressure to do so. However, the cemetery remained sacred ground, and was essentially the one remaining un-ceded plot of land in the Rancheria. When the Scotts Valley untermination cases came along in 1986, the Chico Rancheria was, under the name of the *Mechoopda* tribe, brought back to Federal recognition. So here we are, a recognized tribe, but with only a cemetery and an empty house lot to call our own.

"In a way, it's pretty amazing that we're here at all. Of course, the land Rancho Chico sits on had been taken from us by the Army, and when General James Bidwell* came to town in 1847 he needed laborers to run his Rancho. Most of the other Maidu in the area had been rounded up and taken off 300 miles to Covelo [*Round Valley Reservation*], but the *Mechoopda* were available for serfdom. So he took over the village of some 250 Maidu living here and made them his work force. In one sense he "protected" the people—from being killed or relocated.

"Nevertheless, Mrs. Bidwell saw to it that Indian culture was eliminated. Traditions were replaced with Christian ideas; the original homes were replaced by wooden clapboard houses; the language became English. When she died, Bidwell's Indian village was deeded into the hands of the local Presbyterian church. But it was an unwanted gift for them, and the government was asked to take over. It did, but did absolutely nothing else. The place was nearly uninhabitable—no water, sewer line, no roads.

"Eventually, the *Mechoopda* had to abandon the 12-acre parcel of remaining land, and mostly for taxes, it was sold to Chico State University in 1955. The tribe scattered. Many went away to find work. Many remain landless, others unemployed, others have low incomes. Finally, in 1992, tribal operations were organized to arrange an action plan for the future welfare of the tribe. Some want restored reservation land, others are already settled far from here. But we do need health care, good housing, a return to our culture.

"One thing we have wanted is housing, but we have had many problems with some of the whites in Chico and the suburbs when we have tried to set up land for our people. Problems with [racist] kids harassing our kids, problems with uninformed [hostile] supervisors. We have 400 descendant members,

"General" was a self-appointed rank for the leader of the first wagon train into Native California.

but only 70 live in the Chico area, so we need something for economic development, maybe an orchard—and we're not really that interested in gaming.

"We have a project to collect the history, especially the language. Dorothy Hill is doing a lot of collecting of audio and written work. The Butte County Indian Council [intertribal, in Chico] is working on a project to get the remains of Ishi (*see p.115*) back here to his homeland. We're asking anyone who has any Ishi information to send us a letter and tell us about it. For togetherness, we have our annual picnic, which is our annual membership meeting and fun day. The future's wide open for us."

— Pete Ramirez, Chair of the Mechoopda Tribe

Once, Berry Creek Rancheria consisted of a couple of primitive houses far up and away in the Feather Falls National Scenic Area. Today the tribe has once again gathered itself in Oroville at their new Rancheria site with modern housing. (These homes have been landscaped since this photograph was made.) (dhe, 1992)

of the Chico Rancheria.

CHICO RANCHERIA

Mechoopda Maidu, Wailaki (1939) Butte Co.

All that's left of the original 25 acres of the Chico Rancheria is a well-kept cemetery, shaded by tall old trees, squeezed in between the buildings of Chico State University student housing. It can be found on West Sacramento, 1/2 block east of the railroad tracks, on the north side of the street; the oldest stones date back to 1895, and include some Hawaiian names. (One of the early members was married to an Hawaiian princess.) The grounds are maintained by a local Maidu family. However, the Chico Rancheria families recently forced re-recognition of the tribe, and are actively seeking housing on a new land base.

**33 MECHOOPDA INDIAN TRIBE
OF CHICO RANCHERIA**
1907-F Mangrove Ave., Chico, CA 95926
(916) 899-8922

Maidu dancers offer their songs and dances to many gatherings throughout northern and central California. Here, in 1995, the men and the women proudly present to the public their regalia at the Calaveras Mi-wuk Big Time in West Point. (dhe)

This sun-speckled mural in the Nisenan Maidu Village at Effie Yeaw Nature Center in Ancil Hoffman Park, Carmichael (Sacramento-area) explains the functions of the actual structures pictured, for more information see bottom right, opposite page. (dhe, 1997)

BUTTE COUNTY INDIAN COUNCIL
Intertribal Butte County

This council was formed of representatives from the Mooretown, Estom Yumeka (Enterprise), Tyme Maidu (Berry Creek), and Mechoopda (Chico) Rancherias, as well as other interested Native Americans of the region, to address the need for an intertribal council to deal with Indian affairs in the area of Butte and portions of Shasta and Tehama Counties. Cooperative efforts in education, transportation, festivals, etc., are given special attention. Improvement of cultural connections and traditions are explored through the associated Butte County Native American Cultural Committee.

Information specifics not available, but contact:
MECHOOPDA TRIBE OF CHICO RANCHERIA COUNCIL OFFICE
1907-F Mangrove Ave., Chico, CA 95926
(916) 899-8922
Also see Jules Pavalon, Oroville, Chair

NISENAN (SOUTHERN) MAIDU

FROM THE LOWER REACHES of the Yuba (all forks), the American (all forks), and the Feather River, to the east bank of the Sacramento and to the 10,000-foot Sierra crest, the Nisenan people were the managers of the land. Acorns, nuts, berries, game, fish, grasses, feathers were there (they still are). A map of the early times shows village sites lining the many streams, very few in the woods. *Pu-sú-ne* was the chief village at the confluence of two great rivers; its name today is Sacramento.

When Johann Sutter came to this place, he recruited local Indians to be his mercenary army in his big European fort. He had trouble finding enough men, for the epidemics of the lower Sacramento River were especially severe. Then the gold rush swept most Indian people out of the area. A few foothill rancherias (Nevada City and Colfax), were refuges, but they too disappeared during the termination era.

Dance houses were well-known and well-used, similar to the Miwok one at Chaw-Se (*p.140*). Kuksu was the religion (*p.24*); many other dances throughout the year were celebrated—a Flower Dance in spring, a dance to the first fruits, a Coyote dance, a Big Time in the fall. Nisenan baskets, large and small, were beautifully woven, designed, and decorated. State Indian Museum in Sacramento features a good collection.

AUBURN RANCHERIA
Nisenan (Southern) Maidu (1916) Placer County

On a high Sierra foothill covered with oaks and grass, squeezed between the Southern Pacific tracks and the old Auburn-Folsom highway, is the little 20-plus acre rectangle of the rancheria. It is one of the last refuges of the people known as Nisenan, the people who once occupied the area from Sacramento to the Placer

County foothills.

Succumbing to the coaxing and blandishments of the bureaucrats, Auburn residents forced their own termination in 1958, but at least six or seven families held on to this land. Termination prevented the people from being able to receive many benefits otherwise available to other Indian groups; consequently, most of the homes here remained aged, with much cooking and heating by that ecologically touted fuel, wood. A visit here puts one back in time. Much of the land looks like an encampment, separated by some well-kept and well-used homes. Except for autos, it has not changed much in 50 years.

Nevertheless, after many years of litigation, Auburn has regained its trust status, though all land is totally apportioned and "private". Presently, cultural development is not particularly evident, although the people here participate in several ways through outside activities in the Sacramento area— the October Maidu Indian Day (*see the Calendar, p.280*), and in the Maidu Interpretive Center in Roseville. Other Auburn residents are active in the Auburn Nutrition Center and *Chapa-De* Indian Health Clinic and Health Program (*see Indian Health, p.252*). An historic old Protestant church mission, recently rebuilt, serves some residents. Associated with and near the rancheria is an ancient Maidu Burial Ground, once used as an all-Indian burning [cremation] ground.

Sensing the Need for a more rapid recovery from termination, the tribe has appointed a tribal administrator (in 1998, John Johnson) to assist with the many hurdles of modern business affairs, including a Department of Housing and Urban Development (HUD) grant that is on its slow way from Washington, to help with sorely-needed housing.

The tribe is at the point of purchasing new land in the vicinity of the old Rancheria for both residential and casino construction. As a fine example of inter-tribal cooperation, assistance in funding for this project would come from a loan from a nearby rancheria whose casino is quite successful. Auburn is, in turn, sharing its knowledge of recovery of trust status with Wilton Rancheria, a nearby Miwok rancheria. Eventual success is predicted.

34 *About 2 miles S of Auburn, at Indian Hill Rd., just off the old Auburn-Folsom Highway.*
The Burial Ground is about 1 mile N of rancheria, on Maidu Rd. Tribal office at the I-80 Exit at Newcastle Rd., across the parking lot from Denny's.
AUBURN RANCHERIA
P.O. Box 418, Auburn, CA 95604.
(916) 663-3720

MAIDU INTERPRETIVE CENTER
Maidu Placer County
About a mile south of I-80 in the southeastern part of Roseville we come upon Maidu Park along a creek called Strap Ravine. The Park is about 30 acres in

area; in the Park are very old petroglyphs, 500 rock mortars, and ancient village middens (discard poles)— that tell us that this was an old Maidu village site. Specific archeological evidence such as this is quite rare in the Sacramento area. Realizing its significance, the City of Roseville's Parks and Recreation Department acquired the area a few years ago,

Remodeled, and somewhat modernized historic Protestant church, Auburn Rancheria. (dhe, 1998)

but did not develop it as a park, awaiting proper help. That help has been forthcoming in the form of the Maidu Interpretive Center Foundation, a non-profit organization.

Entering the Park, we find ballfields, a school, and most importantly, a Big Round Building—the Center. The round building shape symbolically reflects the Maidu roundhouse. Inside are exhibits of Maidu artifacts, a community room, and arts & crafts workshop areas for kids. Much of the effort of the Center is to direct the community to an awareness of Native Americans as a living heritage as well as to foster a sense of stewardship for natural and cultural resources. Part of the function of the Center, also, is to serve as a gathering place for local Indian groups, most of which are without local resources. Importantly, the site has been blessed through Indian ceremonies.

Location: *NE of Roseville, Douglas Blvd. E Exit from I-80, right turn onto Rocky Ridge Rd., to Maidu Dr*
MAIDU INTERPRETIVE CENTER AND FOUNDATION
P.O. Box 657, Roseville, CA 95678
(916) 791-0887

NISENAN MAIDU VILLAGE
Maidu Sacramento County
This site is a replica of a Maidu camp, really smaller than a village, alongside the American River in Carmichael (just east of Sacramento), constructed and maintained by local volunteers. It features reconstructions of some rush-covered summer houses, as well as a huge grinding (or pounding) rock and cooking holes and a pond and garden of local native plants. The location is ideal for school demonstrations, as well as a local Maidu gathering in October (*see Calendar*).

EFFIE YEAW NATURE CENTER
6700 Tarshes Dr., Ancil Hoffman Park, Carmichael
P.O. Box 759, Carmichael, CA 95609

NORTHERN CENTRAL COAST & SACRAMENTO VALLEY

THE LANGUAGE GROUPS
THE PEOPLE
The Reservations, *Organizations*

YUKIAN SPEAKERS ‡

YUKI & COAST YUKI
Round Valley Reservation*
HUCHNOM (none)
WAPPO
Alexander Valley burial ground
organization: Mishawal Wappo Tribe

PENUTIAN SPEAKERS ‡

WINTUN FAMILY: WINTU, NOMLAKI, PATWIN
Round Valley Reservation*; Redding Rancheria*, Cortina Rancheria, Grindstone Rancheria*,
Colusa Rancheria (*Cachil Dehe*), Rumsey Rancheria
organizations: No'r-El-Muk Band (Hayfork), Wintu Tribe of No. California, Wintu Tribe-Shasta Co.
MIWOK LANGUAGES:
COAST MIWOK
dedicated land: *Kule Loklo* (Point Reyes National Seashore);
organization: Federated Coast Miwok Tribes
LAKE MIWOK
Middletown Rancheria
PLAINS MIWOK
Wilton Rancheria
NORTHERN SIERRA MIWOK, CENTRAL SIERRA MIWOK, SOUTHERN SIERRA MIWOK
(N) Shingle Springs Rancheria, Jackson Rancheria, Buena Vista Rancheria,
(C) Sheep Ranch Rancheria, Tuolumne Rancheria, Chicken Ranch Rancheria
dedicated lands: (N) *Chaw-Se* Indian Grinding Rocks State Park;
(S) *Ahwahnee* Village and ceremonial site (Yosemite Park)
organizations: (N) Ione Band (Amador Co.); (C) Calveras Band of Miwuk Indians (West Point);
(S) Mariposa Co. (Yosemite) Council

HOKAN SPEAKERS ‡

POMO FAMILY—Seven languages
NORTHERN
Sherwood Valley Rancheria (*Mato*), Potter Valley Rancheria (*Balo-Kay*), Redwood Valley Rancheria (*Kacha*),
Coyote Valley Rancheria, Scotts Valley Rancheria, Guidiville Rancheria, Pinoleville Rancheria (*Yamo*)
NORTHEASTERN
Stonyford community (private land)
EASTERN
Upper Lake Rancheria (*Matuku*), Robinson Rancheria, Big Valley Rancheria
CENTRAL
Yo-Ka-Yo Rancheria, Hopland Reservation (*Shokowa-ma*), Manchester-Point Arena Rancherias (*Boya*)
SOUTHEASTERN
E'lem (Sulphur Bank Rancheria)
SOUTHERN
Cloverdale Rancheria (*Khlankho*), Dry Creek Rancheria
KASHAYA
Kashaya (Stewarts Point) Rancheria

ROUND VALLEY RESERVATION
SUSCOL INTERTRIBAL COUNCIL

*Shared with other groups
‡ *See Languages, Tribal Origins, and Tribal Relationships discussion on page 12*

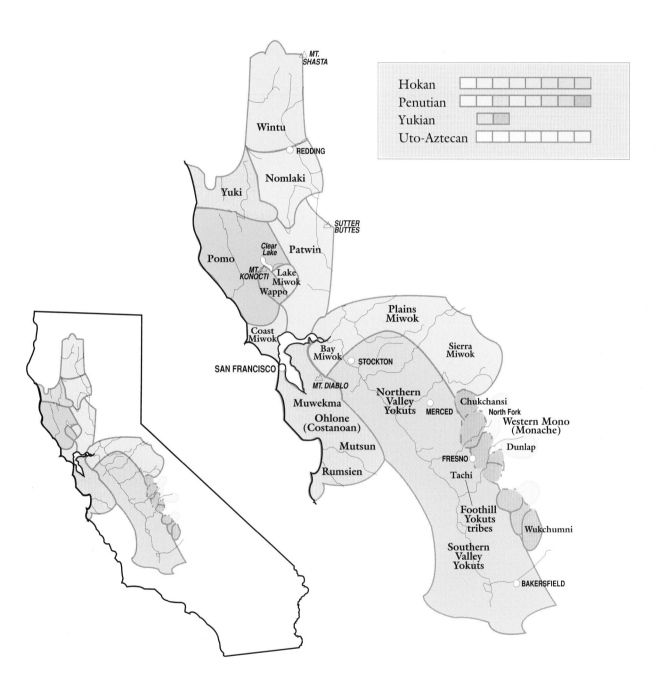

Hokan
Penutian
Yukian
Uto-Aztecan

△ MT. SHASTA

Wintu

○ REDDING

Nomlaki

Yuki

SUTTER BUTTES

Clear Lake

Patwin

Pomo

MT. KONOCTI △

Lake Miwok

Wappo

Coast Miwok

Plains Miwok

Bay Miwok

○ STOCKTON

Sierra Miwok

SAN FRANCISCO ○

MT. DIABLO △

Northern Valley Yokuts

Chukchansi

MERCED ●

North Fork

Muwekma

Western Mono (Monache)

Ohlone (Costanoan)

Dunlap

Mutsun

FRESNO ●

Rumsien

Tachi

Foothill Yokuts tribes

Wukchumni

Southern Valley Yokuts

○ BAKERSFIELD

SAN FRANCISCO BAY,
SOUTHERN CENTRAL VALLEY
& SIERRA FOOTHILLS
(SEE PAGE 157)

NORTHERN CENTRAL COAST & SACRAMENTO VALLEY
THE ENVIRONMENT

THE WESTERN CENTRAL portion of California, north and west of the Sacramento River is characterized by Coast Range mountains, their valleys, the coast on the west, and the Central Valley on the east.

Within this area were the territories of the Wintun peoples—Wintu, Nomlaki, and Patwin— extending from north of Redding to Suisun Bay, along the western slope of the Coast Range mountains. (*Note the larger class Wintun, and the tribe, Wintu.*)

Of all these peoples, the Yuki possessed at least two unusual characteristics— a unique language not related to any other, and physical features more slender than any of their neighbors. As we might expect, the Coast Miwok and Pomo groups living along the coast spent more time in littoral (shoreside) occupations than their inland kin.

THE EASTERN slopes of the Coast Range are on the leeward side of the mountains; thus, the heavy rainfall of the Pacific coast doesn't reach these rocky hills. Even so, the mountains slowly release their water even in summer, so that in earlier days there was plenty for sedentary bands of Indians camped in the broad, sheltered valleys. There was water, there were fish, there were oaks and grasses and game. Within a designated range, camps would be moved as game and food sources dwindled. Whites now have most of those flats, while the Indians are relegated to the drier places and small plots where even a short migration is not possible.

Nevertheless, the people of this region followed similar customs, often called the "Central California culture". The culture is not confined to this area, though, and is found generally in the Central Valley and its margins, seen earlier with the foothill Maidu and some northwest California tribes (*p.108, 119, 122*)

The countryside was provident year-round, and the topography between valleys rough enough that bands tended to be fixed in their locations—both influences making residences and territories fairly rigidly defined.

The dwellings of the people varied

A beacon and outlook, Mt. Kanocti, stands far above Clear Lake in ancestral lands of Wappo, Lake Miwok, Pomo. Mt. Kanocti is a long dormant, but not extinct volcano.

(dhe, 1999)

Amid the rugged countryside, we find a rather surprising number of broad, somewhat protected valleys between the mountain ridges. The Pomo, Yuki, Wappo, and Coast and Lake Miwok peoples settled into these valleys. Clear Lake, a huge fresh water feature in one such valley, was particularly attractive to a large group of tribes, because it was considered an incomparable source of sustenance.

a little, but would consist of, for temporary habitations, a few slab or bark tipis. In more permanent villages, the usual lodging might be accompanied by a circular dancehouse, excavated two or three feet down, with a bark roof set on long logs and supported by heavy vertical beams. These might also serve as sweatlodges. Village sites would be moved within the valley when food sources became scarce in an area.

In most of California the sweatlodge was an institution for social, community, and health purposes (*p.88*). As we have seen in the north, the dancehouse, or roundhouse was the community center. Dances in this region tended to be more complex and numerous than other parts of the state, although much knowledge of dance in southern California has been lost, owing to Christian eradications of "pagan" customs.

As in northwestern California, many of the dances were, and in some places still are, related to the religious concept of existence called World Renewal, mentioned earlier (*p.24, 100*). In central California these dance rituals evolved into what was then called the Kuksu or Hesi belief system, in which the dancers represent, and may embody, the spirits of deities whom they impersonate in exotic feathered regalia. Their vision of transformation is akin to that of the Kachinas of Pueblo and Hopi peoples.

The dance also maintains the world renewal purpose. Most religions incorporate the idea of yearly renewal into their system—spring, regeneration, Easter, etc. The dancers and, indeed, many of the participants in the ceremonies, were required to be members of various secret societies. Anyone with any aspirations of leadership, be it tribal or medicinal, found it indispensable to be a member. Such societies not only passed down many of the secrets of power, but also had ties to their counterparts in other tribes in one of the rare intertribal connections.

Many dances held in the fall season (acorn festivals) give thanks for the harvest and convey requests for the fall rains. This is in high contrast to the ceremonies of cold-climate religions, where fall brings a symbolic dying with the winter snows. In central California the fall rains bring life and green. The reader may sense the depth of these perceptions in the ceremonies at Chaw-Se (*see p.140*) and other fall Big Times.

Had we been in the villages of earlier times, we might have heard tales of Coyote and a whole society of animal spirits, each having rather human characteristics. In such places where wealth was less important than clever and wise leadership qualities, the legends of Coyote also changed their emphasis. Here, tales dwelt less on tricks and chicanery, and Coyote became more lusty and even lecherous. Stories and tales were more for pure entertainment than for teaching principles. But who would say that any tale doesn't include some kind of ethic?

THE MAP OF THIS REGION includes many rancherias, most in Coast Range areas, fewer in the drier eastern slopes. As with other tribes, language and customs among the groups were similar, but not their governance. The fortunes of these rancherias vary from progressive (an intense interest in cultural preservation) to practically extinct. Some were swallowed by engineering projects—Lower Lake (Pomo) is an airport, old Coyote Valley lies under Lake Mendocino, part of Shingle Springs (Miwok) is a freeway; some were overrun by urban sprawl. The latter are, in reality, urban subdivisions—the towns have grown to meet them. Actually, a majority have resurrected themselves and

The sweatlodge was, and is a center of the village. It serves a health-giving function—physically in purification of the body, mentally, as a religious meditative place. Central California sweatlodges are frequently sod covering a sapling framework, as is this one at Kule Loklo (Point Reyes National Seashore). Others, more modern and adaptive of Great Basin and Plains peoples, use a variety of blanket, tarpaulin, or canvas covers. (Vibhakar Shah, 1995)

found funds at least to build new homes and sometimes schools; their stories are told here.

The old acreage, all laid off in square streets, looks like any other group of houses at the edge of town. The older rancherias are mostly non-Indian, since they were once terminated and most plots of the dry, flat land were sold off. Though distant hills and some open fields lie nearby, few were particularly scenic attractions, nor did they have anything environmentally special to offer. But as Indian centers of culture they are no more.

Native culture does remain in the homelife, in family connections, and often in dances and get-togethers at more active centers.

Artistic conception of early Pomo life, Anderson Marsh, Clear Lake. (by archaeologist Paul Peterson, 1995)

BASKETS, WEAVING

Although everyone made functional utensils and tools, it was in the Pomo villages, more than in any others in California, that the artistry of basketry was demonstrated at its finest. Not only were the two major techniques of coiling and twining used, but also exquisite designs were incorporated, and baskets of rare shapes and functions were and continue to be fashioned. (*Also see Baskets, p.60*)

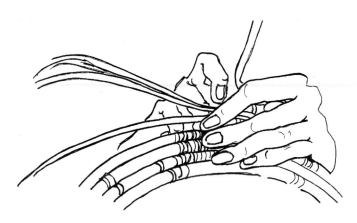

The older weavings were so well made and are of such intrinsic artistic value that even fragments of old ones have become expensive collectors' items. A few examples: finely woven caps with multi-colored designs, a funnel-like bowl with a round hole in the bottom for preventing spillage from a mortar, an incidental container laced with bluebird feathers, a headdress with crimson woodpecker feathers, a coarsely-woven cone some two feet across for carrying wood and heavy objects (a "burden basket"), an open-weave cradle with hood, a seed beater, a woven watertight bottle sealed with pine pitch. You may see many of these marvelous art objects at the City Museum in Lakeport or the State Indian Museum in Sacramento. Probably the best collection is in the Phoebe Apperson Hearst (formerly Lowie) Museum of Anthropology, University of California, Berkeley, but they are mostly squirreled away from public view.

Such a variety in design could only be matched in the United States by the pottery of the Pueblos. Many baskets of all Indians of California had to be woven to a watertight fineness, since much cooking was done by placing hot stones directly into the liquid mush.

All peoples of Clear Lake fashioned a sturdy reed boat, amazingly like those of the Indians of Lake Titicaca in the Peruvian-Bolivian Andes. Of course, fish nets were woven to accompany these fine fishing craft, as well as nets for fishing in the local streams. The tules* gave them their basket raw materials, shelter material, clothing, and tule shoots even supplemented their food supply.

THE BASKET

begins at the navel of the center

grows to a sunburst of twigs

spirals outward

reveals row by row the makers's intent

gathers slowly the fibers towards the center

enfolds and shepherds the sunburst

interlaces the rays into the border, which

infers outside and inside

    and then

contains a part of the weaver.

          —dhe, 1998

A unique Central Pomo shell and feather basket ornamentation. (drawings on this page by Nancy Record, 1999)

*Tule is a round, common marsh reed with a cluster of small seed pods at the top. The new shoots are edible and taste a bit like asparagus. Cattail is flat with a round cat tail-like seed pod. Both species have many uses: roofing, woven boats, floor covering, mats, fuel.

PLACE NAMES

SACRAMENTO VALLEY place names derived from Indian sources (translations approximate):

NOMLAKI PASKENTA: *paskenti*, "under the bank"

WINTU YOLLA BOLLY: *yola boli*, "high, snow-covered peak"; YREKA: name for Mt. Shasta

WINTUN TEHAMA: a place name; SONOMA: *sonom*, "nose"

PATWIN SOLANO: Spanish name for a Suisun chief, *Sem-yeto*; NAPA: *napato*, "bear shaman", or *napo*, "house"; SUISUN: a place or local tribal name; PUTAH: *putato*, a place name; CAPAY: *copéh*, "stream"; COLUSA: *coru*, a place name

POMO CALPELLA: a chief's name, "shell bearer"; UKIAH: *yo-kia-ya*, probably "deep valley"; P'OMO: "at red earth hole", a mine for red clay for sweetening acorn bread; GUALALA: *wa-la-li*, "meeting place of waters", i.e. Russian River and Pacific Ocean

MIWOK ACALANES: a place name; BOLINAS: *baulines*, a place name; TOMALES: *tamals*, "westerners"; TAMALPAIS: probably "tamals of the mountain"; OLEMA: *olemaloke*, "coyote valley"; PETALUMA: "flat place"; HOOKOOEKO: tribal name

EARLY POPULATIONS

Original populations of West Central peoples, 1830*:

POMO: *ca.* 8,000

WINTU/NOMLAKI/PATWIN: 12,000 -14,000

COAST MIWOK: *ca.* 2,000

YUKI/COAST YUKI/HUCHNOM: 2,000

WAPPO: 1,000

LAKE MIWOK: 500

THE GRASS OR HAND GAME

Two teams sit facing each other, along two rows about four feet apart. They are equipped with the following: two sets of two "bones" (traditionally antlers or bones, about the size of wine corks), one of each marked with a ring; a set of ten or twelve playing sticks (like pick-up sticks); an object to drum upon (either a small hand drum or, more traditionally, a log and sticks), and usually, a scarf to cover the bones. At one time, the bones were hidden with a hand-held sheaf of grass, but today the players normally use the shawl. The objective is to obtain all the playing sticks and the bones by guessing which hand holds the marked bone in each set. Meanwhile, an elaborate process of passing the sticks back and forth occurs.

Before the game begins, supporters and members of each side place cash bets. (All bets must be covered by equal amounts from the opposing sides, and are recorded). The winning side takes all: it's a double or nothing game. The bets are tied in a bundle and tossed to one end of the "playing field".

Distributing hand game winnings at Chaw-se Big Time.   (dhe, 1983)

A side will choose its "guesser," always someone known to have great powers of accuracy in guessing, since a lot of money may be riding on the outcome. On the other side, two persons are chosen to conceal the bones; it is hoped they will have sufficient thought powers to deflect the other team's guesser. (In my experience, a good guesser can always "see" through anyone who is neither serious nor sober.)

The side holding the bones begins drumming and chanting. The songs are almost always in the ancient languages, and are frequently amusing or sarcastic; "You couldn't guess your way—out of an open tent." The music sets up a psychic shield, deflecting the mind of the guesser from the "truth" of the marked bones. The guesser takes plenty of time to be sure, and then…

The moment of truth: The guesser subtly indicates, through direction of the thumb or a playing stick, the positions of the two marked bones in the hands of the two hiders—there being four possible outcomes (right-right, left-left, right-left outside, and left-right inside). Watch carefully, for a sly holder can sometimes fool the guessing team. Whoever "wins" gets either bones or sticks. If the guesser fails, his side surrenders bones, if he succeeds, sticks are surrendered to his team. It is always an advantage to be the guessing side, since all the sticks must eventually be obtained.

With two teams of nearly equal power, a game can go on for an hour or more, and the sticks change sides many times. (One tactic is to partly conceal the sticks, so as not to show the current standing of the team.) Gaming frequently goes on until dawn, or until one side is psychically or financially depleted. Sometimes the stakes can run into the hundreds of dollars.

Definitely not casino stuff.

---

* The numbers given here and in other sections are early estimates, and they are doubtless low. Later estimates show that early counts did not include many persons absent at the time, whether in a mission village or in a settlement.

YUKIAN LANGUAGES

The word "Yukian" encompasses a language used by three coastal and mountain groups, Yuki, Coast Yuki, and Huchnom, plus Wappo, a distant dialect.
Yuki is a Wintu word meaning "enemy".

YUKI

THE YUKIAN LANGUAGE is entirely unto itself, not related to any other family. The people occupied a mountainous area just north of Ft. Bragg, eastward to just north of Willits, and north into and including Round Valley and along the various forks of the upper Eel River.

THE NECESSITIES DEMANDED by their environments led these bands to styles of living very similar to the adjoining tribes: Pomo, Cahto, and Nomlaki. Coastal people did much like the Eel River people to the north; while inland, they lived much like the other Coast Range inland people. Basketry samples survive, resembling the coiled type used by the Cahto. Music and ceremonial dress was similar to the Pomo.

The Indian roundups of 1856 caught almost everyone of these peoples into its snare, putting them all onto the Round Valley Reservation (*p.154*), where white settlers proceeded to try to exterminate them.

Those who survived at Round Valley tended to have their tribal identities merged with the other tribes there. Even so, some families still maintain Yuki as their primary tribal affiliation.

WAPPO

WAPPO SHARES in the Yukian languages the distinction of being unique. Wappo is slurred Anglo for Spanish *guapo*: handsome, brave, and severe, characteristics that the Spanish soldiers apparently thought fit these people. The people's name for themselves, not in common usage, is *'ona'cátis*.

ANCESTRAL WAPPO LAND is the Napa Valley northward, along Mt. St. Helena to Cobb Mountain and west to the Alexander Valley of the Russian River. A second "bubble" of Wappo territory is at the edge of Clear Lake, called Lile'ek. Henry Mauldin, historian of Lake County for many years, says that the Wappo came here only in summer or during fish runs; they apparently were not at this place when the Bloody Island Massacre roundup occurred (*p.36*).

Life by life, the Wappo disappeared from the Napa Valley, until only a few small families were left, scattered in mobile homes here and there. The Alexander Valley Rancheria, originally 54 acres, was pared down to none. Nevertheless, as have several other tribal groups on the edge, the remnant population gathered strength and confidence and legal power to demand replacement land.

A few Wappo are members of dance groups sponsored by other tribes, primarily Pomo. Traditional Wappo dances are said to have originally been similar.

The next few years should show much increased Wappo presence, since tribal leaders are active in pressing de-termination claims.

ALEXANDER VALLEY RANCHERIA
Wappo (1909, 1913) Sonoma County
A formerly recognized tribe awaiting reinstatement.

A mile or so on Soda Rock Rd. alongside the Russian River stand some old buildings of the former rancheria, now owned by non-Indians. The last old man's wife died, his children all went away, so Jim Adams left, possibly to rest now with his ancestors in the old Wappo burial grounds hidden (but not forgotten) in the forests of Alexander Valley.

This rancheria, between Jimtown and Healdsburg, was the last of the Wappo reservations; but its termination certainly wasn't the last of the Wappo. Several are active in Indian affairs in the region around Healdsburg and Santa Rosa.

The Mishewal Wappo people are considered to be among the three most eligible tribes in California for reinstatement of tribal status because the condition of their termination was among the most unlawful. Reinstatement will bring new, replacement land and access to replacement housing. Then the tribe can re-gather.

**41 MISHEWAL WAPPO TRIBE
OF ALEXANDER VALLEY**
(no other information available)

PENUTIAN SPEAKERS

Penutian languages probably arose in California; they are found largely in the central and northern parts of the state, and are related to some languages of Oregon and eastern Washington.
Wintun, Miwok, Ohlonean, and Yokuts languages belong to the Penutian language group.

WINTUN FAMILY
WINTU, NOMLAKI, PATWIN
WINTU

THE WINTU PEOPLE held the territory from Mt. Shasta southward to Redding—eastward past the McCloud River—westward to Hayfork. Rugged mountains, cold at the top, hot at the bottom, plenty of water, made up a very diverse ecology. Some nine bands inhabited this bountiful area.

Here, the earthlodge served as dancehouse and sweatlodge—it was semisubterranean, had one center pole with a network of smaller saplings for roof support. The smokehole was also the entranceway, an uncommon feature in California. Basketry was rather unusual in the use of many materials—grapevine, redbud, maidenhair fern, willow, pine root, and/or porcupine quill. Fish and game were plentiful, though rare in mountain winters; acorns, buckeye, roots, and berries were plentiful.

Poisoning (*p.98*) and epidemics triggered by the gold rush decimated the people. Despoiling of the land through mining, clearcutting, and dam building brought the ultimate destruction of tribal unity.

The Redding Rancheria, completed in 1998, bears the flying geese symbols of its three peoples: Yana, Pit River, and Wintu. (See opposite page)   (dhe, 1998)

REDDING RANCHERIA

[originally] *Wintu,* later also *Pit River, Yana*
(1922) Shasta Co.

A Federally recognized reservation with three resident tribal groups.

FIRST SETTLED as a Wintu community, this dry, flood plain of a creek shaded by many oaks, became a refuge for other tribal peoples of the upper Sacramento Valley. In 1985, I noted the following: "A few ancient wooden houses remain, among modern suburban houses and trailers, homes for 11 Indian families. Nothing unusual to see."

Amazing things have happened since then. In 1993 gaming was approached slowly with bingo, then LARGESSE happened. There's a lot to see now. The mammoth gaming house isn't the source, only the means. The source is the diligent application of the idea that tribal people can make gaming work. The big sign on the highway pointing to the Win River Casino is the roadsign to the Rancheria.

Most of those vintage houses are still here; most have been painted and expanded, because there is limited space, and because people really like their old homes. Some new ones have been added, too. The most outstanding structure is the beautiful tribal and community center, with its spacious rooms and active staff. Like an engraved belt around the whole center are painted the symbols of flying geese (illustrated right), from the basketry of the three tribes that make up the rancheria: Wintu, Pit River, and Yana. Reminders to the people of their origins. Down the street you can find the children from the rancheria and the local community in busy Headstart classes.

MS. STACEY GREER, tribal Chief Operating Officer of the Redding Rancheria Tribal Center, met us in the spacious reception area of the architecturally elegant Rancheria Tribal Offices and Community Center, built in 1997. The gaming building was our first stop. Inside, we see a gym-sized hall filled with table and chairs—the bingo section. One end is glassed off, for the non-smokers. (I wondered if it was big enough.) But then there is a second tier around a balcony, where lighted machines add an atmosphere of perpetual Christmas trees. Every part of

flying geese basket symbols
Yana
Wintu
Pit River

the interior is wheelchair-ramped. There's no shortage of fortune-seekers, who seem to come from just about everywhere.

The Rancheria sought its fortune, and this is it. The casino employs some 400 persons from all over the local area. About 30% of Rancheria adults are included in this total.   *continued on next page*

131

We took a stroll down the shady street to the Head Start buildings. Shiny yellow school buses waited for the two rooms of 20 kids each to finish their play and learning. These kids are not just rancheria residents—this is a service area, open to all comers from the community. The same is true for the tribally owned Redding Rancheria Indian Health Clinic in another part of town. Casino income supports both these community efforts. How is it done?

We came to the office of Barbara Murphy, the tribe CEO, who was fresh from a budget meeting. The casino budget is carefully apportioned by a Rancheria committee—part obviously goes to operations, part to the residents, but then part of the income goes to support a variety of carefully considered programs, such as the ones above.

The future will involve purchases of land. The first acquisition of 8 acres will give the rancheria ownership of both sides of Clear Creek and create a park alongside. Then another 30 acres north of Redding provide additional homes for the residents because little rancheria has run out of space for its 227 members. Construction of a mini-mart and a hotel began 1998. Some time in the near future there will be a roundhouse, which according to tradition, must have a permanent leader and caretaker. And then traditional language classes. The newest program is a prominent space in the California Welcome Center alongside Interstate 5, in Anderson, that will explore subjects related to white/Indian relations; agriculture, how each approach differs; timbering and its management; effects of ancient and modern technology on the Indian.

OTHER TOPICS. The second weekend in September, Redding Rancheria is a sponsor of the Stillwater Powwow, named for the ancient traditional Wintu gathering ground. Associated with this is the annual health fair at the Convention Center .

Redding Rancheria maintains college-level relations with the D-Q University satellite (*see p.261*) and Shasta College, especially on computer training, and at the secondary education level and other levels with LIFE (Local Indians For Education).

Not long ago the Rancheria sponsored a conference on mapping its strategic goals and future tribal actions through a thorough self-assessment. This meeting appeared to us as an unusual and successful approach to tribal government. Future conferences are intended to be repeated annually.

Redding Rancheria is very proud of its environment and achievements and welcomes visitors.

35 *On Hwy. 273, about 3 miles S of Redding, at Clear Creek bridge, ironically stands a plaque of State Landmark* **78**, *a gold discovery site. The tract behind the plaque is the rancheria.*

REDDING RANCHERIA
2000 Rancheria Rd., Redding CA 96001
(916) 225-8987

NOTE:
The author would would like to append a few statistics that will answer a lot of questions people have of the size of casino incomes—and where the money goes. This is one such report. These figures for 1997 are from the Rancheria Tribal Office.
Employees: 325, 41% female. Of these employees: Rancheria members: 26, Native American: 197, other minorities: 21, others: 81.
Annual payroll: $4,072,000. Taxes: $442,000. Vendors to the Rancheria: 500.
Prizes: $3,7000,000+.
1961 per capita annual income: < $5,000; welfare dependency: 30%.
1997 (casino) income: $12,000, welfare: 0%.
Charity donations to date: $225,000.
Mandated expenditures for tribal programs to date: $2 million—for education, housing, health care, community projects, economic development.

WINTU TRIBE & TOYON WINTU CENTER
Wintu Trinity, Shasta, Butte, & Tehama Cos.
A Federally unrecognized, off-reservation tribe.

MORE THAN 1,000 Wintu descendants live off-reservation, that is, they have no real connection with the Redding Rancheria enrollment. They are seeking Federal recognition on their own as an independent tribe. The council holds regular monthly meetings to deal with matters such as assisting with personal problems, planning sessions for the various activities of the tribe, the convoluted bureaucracy of recognition, or contact with the many members.

The tribe has experienced several problems over the Toyon Wintu center—a former government installation that was acquired by the tribe after the government stopped using it as an administrative center for the Shasta Dam building project. At that time, some years ago, the tribe had expected Federal recognition quite soon, but interminable delays set in. Some government official decided to demolish the quite serviceable buildings, leaving the Center with only a barn-like structure on its 61 acres. The tribe still holds the property, but is not allowed to make improvements...yet.

The Wintu Tribe is very active in sponsoring a number of activities. An annual Big Time is held the first weekend in April jointly with the Redding Museum. Other ceremonial gatherings are held regularly at sites very sacred to the Wintu people—Bear Mountain, just south of Mt. Shasta, early in April, and at Dekka Rock (north shore of Lake Shasta) in August.

The Tribe also sponsors Local Indians For Education (LIFE) (*see Education, p.263*). This is a very important tribal function— both for retaining traditional customs and also preparing its members to live in the real world. Courses in history (from a Native point of view), English, business, and basketry and beading are offered, among others. Seminars and conferences on Indian-related subjects are offered.

Another extremely important effort within the tribe is the 4-Winds Charter School of which Ms. Caleen Sisk-Franco is a director. The School is a project of several members of the Wintu Tribe, which serves Indian people of three counties and several Indian tribes.

A charter school is a non-profit which features a special direction—in this case for Indian children. They get a special grounding in Indian traditions and customs, as well as the state-mandated educational requirements. In this case many parents can't afford child care or special private education, so the school's grant allows it to give these kids that particular Native American approach they wouldn't get in the usual public school. There are about 140 kids enrolled—in K through 10. Many of the children are bused in from Mooretown Rancheria and some from Berry Creek Rancheria, both a few miles south of here. The program is so successful that they are enlarging both their space and materials.

THE WINTU TRIBE has an enrollment of about 1,000, but there are an estimated 3,000 more Wintus who are not enrolled, for a large variety of reasons. The tribe is currently working hard on language recovery, and is preparing a standard pronunciation, grammar, and vocabulary guide.

—Information on 4-Winds from
Caleen Sisk-Franco, Tribal Member,
—other information from
Carol Martin, Tribe Secretary

Very dedicated persons may attend the Wintu Winyupus ceremony at Coonrod Flat on Mt. Shasta, usually the first week of August. The sacred fire is lit, prayers for all are offered, dances for Mt. Shasta and the sacred ones are offered, then a journey to the *Sawal Mem* (sacred spring) is undertaken.

[*Ms. Sisk-Franco has recently had the honor of having passed down to her much cherished, traditional medicine from the most revered spiritual leader of the Wintu people, Ms. Florence Jones. Traditional medicine is passed on only to the most worthy of persons, and is invaluable in preserving traditional ceremonies and in the ability to perform healing. —ed.*]

WINTU TRIBE & TOYON WINTU CENTER
P.O. Box 71036, Project City, CA 96079
WINTU TRIBE OF SHASTA CO.
Charlene Ward, Gloria Gomez, Secretary.
303400 Argyle Rd., Redding, 96022
(916) 241-7267

HAYFORK BAND OF NOR-EL-MUK WINTU INDIANS
Wintu Trinity County

A federally unrecognized, but very persistent band.

Hayfork is a small town in the western end of Trinity Co., in Wintu country, deep in the Trinity National Forest. The Wintu Indian community here has been organized for many decades, most lately under the guidance of Mr. Raymond Patton; their petition to be recognized languishes with the many others in the bureaucracy.

HAYFORK BAND
OF NOR-EL-MUK WINTU INDIANS
P.O.Box 673, Hayfork, CA 96041

NOMLAKI

THE NOMLAKI ARE THE CENTRAL of the three Wintuan-speaking groups—Wintu to the north and Patwin to the south. Drive along I-5 from Red Bluff to Corning along the Sacramento River, then look west up over the grassy foothills of the Coast Range to the 7 and 8000-foot peaks of Yolly Bolly and Black Butte Mountains of Mendocino National Forest. You are in Nomlaki country. It's pretty and valuable country—as the whites thought who poured into here in the 1850s, taking over the lands of the Indians who had died of the devastating epidemics that had ravaged these people.

The Valley was very hot in summer, and the land very dry (*see Paskenta, below*), so the people made summer treks to the mountains to hunt and be cool. Life was much like that of their kin to the south, the Patwin (*p.135*). Their villages had to be along the few creeks that ran all year, coming from those tall peaks in the forest. Nomlaki are still here—in Paskenta and Elk Creek; a few other Nomlaki live in Round Valley.

PASKENTA RANCHERIA
Nomlaki (originally 1870s) Tehama County

After suffering the abandonment of the large Nome Laki Reservation and deportation to Round Valley in 1863 (*p.154*), settlement of their own rancheria in Paskenta, then termination of their 260-acre rancheria in 1958, the Paskenta Band of Nomlaki in 1995 has finally regained Federal tribal status. Two abandoned shacks remain in their hands as private land in the town of Paskenta.

The original Paskenta Rancheria was settled by those who categorically rejected resettlement in Round Valley with their ancient enemies, the Yuki. It is located at foot of the high, prominent Williams Butte just west of the town and only yards from Thomes Creek. The still-used and well-protected burial ground is nearby.

When the Rancheria was first abandoned through termination, the land was bought for a pittance by the Louisiana-Pacific Lumber Company, which immediately burned all the dwellings and covered all signs of prior Indian occupation. When Louisiana-Pacific failed to plant trees on the land, the tribe managed to get their land back.

36 *Go W for 20 mi. on County Rd. A9 from Corning to Paskenta [enroute (unpaved) to Round Valley, some 60 mi. beyond]. The old/new rancheria is at the western foot of the large, flat-sided butte 1 mi.W of Paskenta.*
PASKENTA RANCHERIA
P.O. Box 339, Williams, CA 95987

The roundhouse became the community gathering place, a shelter from the elements, and a proper place to hold ceremonies. Each tribe has its own traditions for the design of these sacred places. This roundhouse at Grindstone Rancheria, a Nomlaki community in the range of hills west of Chico, is over 100 years old.   (dhe, 1998)

NOME LACKEE RESERVATION MONUMENT

At Flournoy, 10 miles west of Corning on County Road A9, turn north 2-1/2 miles to the No-me La-ke Reservation monument, at the end of pavement, on a rise behind a barn on the west side of the road, behind an openable closed gate. Muse about what opinion the displaced people must have had when first "presented" with this piece of near desert. The tiny creek is often dry, even after the rains. *The Smithsonian Vol. 8 (App. VII, p.279)* claims that "the Indians accepted the mode of life, learned farming and other crafts, and …prospered." Even today there are no "farms"; it is so dry that ranching is "dry ranching" and cows are trucked in only for the winter green season. Many people suffered and died here. (*See photo p.50*)

GRINDSTONE CREEK RANCHERIA
Nomlaki (Wintun), Wailaki, **and others (1906)**
Glenn County

With the exception of a new water supply, some modern homes, and a tribal hall, I expect that the Grindstone residents live pretty much as they have for decades—in a depressed and isolated place, but with a good hold on the old culture and ways. Modern life has made few inroads here to lure the people into its culture bleach.

At the center of these 80 acres is the village and a venerable roundhouse, at 100-plus, the oldest in California. On a lower level are a few destitute homes. Looking upward to the higher terrace, however, things are different. The BIA-green water tank presides over all, but 1997 government funds brought many new homes and paved roads.

Continued existence here depends on the ugly demand for water. In 1978, the California Water Project (known also as the Peripheral Canal Project) wanted Elk Creek, the nearby town, for a lake and the Grindstone Rancheria as a dam site. All persons involved would be paid well for their land, said the commission in charge. Then the Louisiana-Pacific Lumber Company closed their Elk Creek mill suddenly and permanently, throwing Indians and whites alike out of work and the town into financial chaos. Louisiana-Pacific even dismantled the community ballpark. Few communities are ever threatened with this kind of annihilation. But the final destiny rode on the tribal decision of Grindstone: stay here poor, or leave the land and heritage, but with money. After all, Federal land is guaranteed to them, and the decision rests with the tribe.

THE IRONY—many of the local whites remember that their grandparents took possession of this land from the Nomlaki, who now have the final say-so. The Grindstone Nomlaki aren't overly concerned with the whites' distress, since it was, in 1863, their immediate grandparents whose children were dashed against stones and whose parents were shot by the U.S. Calvary for lagging behind in the forced march across the mountains from Nome-Lake.

The Grindstone people aren't jumping at the chance to become economically comfortable. They and their forefathers were born here, their roundhouse is sacred ground, their roots are deep here. To be uprooted would likely disperse the tribe and its culture forever. They are quite aware of this risk. Yes, the roundhouse could be moved, but only by water, say the elders. Too, the people might be allowed to prosper elsewhere. The tribe elected to stay, the new homes were built, and the tribe continues.

The dam project was scrubbed; Peripheral Canal fever is dormant, though menacingly unforgotten, as governments and attitudes change.

Several families are currently highly involved in maintaining traditions through dance. Indeed, they almost complain of having more requests to dance from other tribes near and far than they can respond to.

NOTE: *The old L.-P. mill grounds are now being used by a horticultural group to experiment with various types of trees for the local environment.*

37 *About 3 miles N of Elk Creek on Hwy. 162 (W of Willows, off Interstate 5), right at the confluence of Grindstone Creek and Stony Creek. Campsites at the impressive Stony Creek Reservoir.*

GRINDSTONE CREEK RANCHERIA
P.O. Box 63, Elk Creek, CA 95939

PATWIN

PATWIN BANDS, the southernmost of Wintuan speakers, occupied the west bank of the Sacramento River, the "river people", and the dry eastern slopes of the Coast Range, the "hill people"—from near Willows to Suisun Bay in the Sacramento Delta. Their countryside extended from dense marshlands at the foot of Sutter Butte (Maidu country) to dense marshlands in the south and were part of the Pacific Flyway of migrating birds. This is good for birds, but then, as now, this part of the river floods in winter (and before dams, again at the June Sierra meltoff), making permanent homesites impossible.

The riverine environment gave much to the people in the way of materials for weaving—so much that they traded switches, roots, and rushes for cordage with other tribes. Baskets were exceptionally strong, bearing distinctive designs unlike their neighbors'. Food was fish, fowl, deer and elk, bulbs, berries, acorns, and seeds collected from large grain fields.

Being a river people, they made tule reed boats, reportedly up to 20 feet long. Sod-covered roundhouses served as ceremonial sites for the dances that can be seen today as *Hesi*, or *Kuksu* (*p.24*).

White influx occurred early, causing the epidemics so tragically described along the Sacramento River. Mexican Gen. Mariano Vallejo was among the first invaders. He selected as intermediary and overseer a local Indian particularly skilled at people-manipulation, one Solano, who encouraged slave-taking and other coercive actions. Vallejo made him a prime assistant, calling him "Chief", but there was resistance and several major protests by the people at this insult to them.

CORTINA RANCHERIA
Patwin (*Wintun*) (1907) Colusa County

For its first 60 years, 17 miles of dirt road and several gates (one locked, at the entrance to an intervening private ranch), would get one to Cortina. It was not recommended as a place to visit. In 1986, the Wright brothers, Edward and Amos, along with a few farm animals, had lived here alone for decades. (*See p.70*)

Earlier, however, this dry and inhospitable place was home for many more. It had one salty well, no electricity, two tiny clapboard houses, a tiny sweathouse,

and, a long time ago, a dancehouse. There is no way for food to be grown here—it must be brought in, except for the chickens and lots of squirrels. It's too dry even for deer. But things have changed.

In the early 1990s, in preparation for more new residents, a new well was dug with solar panels to run the pump. A new $40,000 prefab meeting house and tribal hall was brought in. New streets were built and paved in an oak-leaf cul-de-sac design. An easy access road to Highway 20 was opened. Then a cluster of neat, substantial homes were built, and the former isolation ceased. The residents who work in nearby places can easily reach their destinations, and several are involved with Patwin tribal dancing.

It's still rather remote, but from the ridge above the center, there are vistas of Mt. Shasta (northernmost Wintu country), Mt. Lassen, and the sharp crags of Sutter's Butte.

These clapboard one-room houses were once the homes of two elder Wright brothers, before a recent government project which brought housing, public services, and paved roads to the Cortina Rancheria.   (dhe, 1998)

PASSING THOUGHTS: When Amos Wright first heard of the new plans, he wasn't happy to have his many years of solitude disturbed. A possible advantage of such remoteness is that it is old, traditional land where near-total isolation can keep a culture alive. But, how is a culture to survive if only old men practice it and no families can share it? Continual isolation is death on tradition.

38 *6 mi. W of Williams on Hwy 20, turn S 2 mi. onto Walnut Dr., 1 mi. to Spring Valley Rd. and R 7 mi. into the Rancheria.*

CORTINA RANCHERIA
P.O. Box 7470 , Citrus Heights, CA 95621-7470

continued

COLUSA RANCHERIA (CACHIL DEHE)

Patwin (Wintun) (1907) Colusa County

Cachil Dehe is original Patwin name for this village in Wintun, and the place still bears that name. The 273 acres of the rancheria occupy a flat floodplain bordering on the Sacramento River and alongside a section of the river designated for riparian restoration. The rancheria occupies two bends in the river—one on Reservation Road is strictly residential, the other, behind the casino, also enfolds the roundhouse. Dances are held once or twice a year, and the people—old and young alike—come from miles away to dance.

Modern homes supplement the old on both parcels. The western portion of the south part is farmed in fields of safflowers, the eastern part of both are groves of ancient oaks with the inevitable tangle of vines along the river. Along the highway is the unmistakable gaming facility that provides a good source of income for the tribe.

39 *About 3 miles N of Colusa on State Hwy. 45, to Indian Rd. (BIA)155, alongside the casino; the second parcel lies about 1-1/2, mi. N., E on Reservation Rd.*
COLUSA RANCHERIA
P.O. Box 8, Colusa, CA 95932

RUMSEY RANCHERIA (YOCHA DEHE)

Patwin (Wintun) (1907) Yolo County

Clear Lake, one of the largest natural bodies of fresh water in California, sends year-round torrents of clear water down Cache Creek, through the otherwise desiccated eastern Coast Range mountains. The Rumsey Rancheria lies along this creek, in two sections (the oldest part in Rumsey itself was sold off). An older section of a few acres is irrigated, and three exceptional homes grace the banks along the well-shaded creek. Hot summer visitors pass by on cool Cache Creek float trips. In 1982, an additional 100 acres were purchased at Brooks, two miles south. Later, more land was added, landscaped, and several dozen homes were constructed to bring the tribe back home. Roads were paved, a community hall built, an adequate water supply was provided, even the local state highway was resurfaced. In 1998, there are numerous individualized homes set on spacious lots, with iron fences, by open fields and orchards, with forested low mountains, all with a prosperous look to this reservation.

All this improvement came about owing to one of the most successful gaming establishments in Northern California, the Cache Creek Casino. As is the case in most reservations, the gaming activity (although quite bustling) is set at one end of the rancheria. A California Department of Forestry Fire Station sits in the other corner.

40 *"Old" rancheria is at Road 75 at Tancred (Tan Creek) on State Rte. 16. The new rancheria is in Brooks and impossible to miss, about 15 mi. W of Woodland.*
RUMSEY RANCHERIA
P.O. Box 18, Brooks, CA 95606

MIWOK (MIWUK) FAMILY
COAST, LAKE, BAY, PLAINS, NORTHERN, CENTRAL, & SOUTHERN SIERRA

A CRESCENT OF MIWOK PEOPLES curves across the north of San Francisco Bay and the northern San Joaquin Valley. The Coast Miwok are found north of the Bay in Marin and Sonoma Counties, while the Lake Miwok reside just to the northeast of them. South, along the Carquinez Straits is the land of Bay and Plains Miwok. Then the three Sierra groups (labeled, conveniently, Northern, Central and Southern) stretch from the Cosumnes River to the Yosemite Valley and the Fresno River. These groups live(d) in widely differing environments—from the cool coast through the mild to hot Central Valley, to the more temperate valleys of the Sierra foothills.

THE MIWOK PEOPLES shared a common language (with several dialects) and many customs and traditions. Basketry, however, differed in style from group to group, and was somewhat similar to the people most near them, notably the Pomo, but also the Patwin, Ohlone, Yokuts, and Mono. Styles varied with the availability of nearby fiber materials. Examples: the Plains people had best access to tule and marsh grasses, while the Sierra dwellers had alder and redbud at hand.

ROUNDHOUSES were (and are) built by all the groups; their ceremonies are similar, though distinguished by differences—in regalia, such as the type of leggings, body paint, types of feathers used, and of course, in their songs.

BAY AND PLAINS MIWOK were the first to come into serious contact with the Spanish missionaries; many of their members were drawn into the San José and San Francisco missions. The Plains people were defiant, but suffered their greatest losses from devastating epidemics, which nearly destroyed them. Although their only land today is the small Wilton Rancheria, south of Sacramento, small communities are active in Indian affairs in their region. Bay Miwok have no identifiable groups today, though in 1986, I spoke with a motorboat repairman in Richmond, who said he was a native Miwok from the area.

The Sierra Miwok have fared somewhat better, being further from the center, though unfortunately in the middle of the Gold Rush. Many were used as laborers at that time, many were murdered, and some survived. The survivors regrouped, won small enclaves to which they could withdraw and recover, and have revived in recent years with a powerful spirit to become well-known and respected as keepers of tradition.

Their survival and revival can be seen in the profiles of the various rancherias below.

COAST MIWOK

The anthropologist Isabel Kelly wrote in 1976, "Effectively, [the Coast Miwok] people and culture have disappeared." It was the Coast Miwok people who once inhabited Marin County and southern Sonoma County in the Sonoma River Valley. However, as we can see so frequently around California, descendants of supposedly "extinct" Indian groups are appearing out of their long obscurity.

GRATON RANCHERIA [GRĀTON]
originally *Southern Pomo*, later *Coast Miwok*
(1920) Sonoma County

Years ago, tucked away in a forest along a creek near Sebastopol, Mr. Frank Truvido lived on his one acre of "terminated" land, all that remained of an original fifteen. Many years before, he had brought his family here from Tomales Bay. The other acres were sold off, bit by bit, for taxes. When he passed on a few years ago, his land and the ancient wooden clapboard house with its few possession, went to his daughter, who had remained "unterminated", through some marvel of bureaucracy. All around the house where his daughter now lives are apple ranches—and whites who covet this land. What to see? Only the old frame house.

BUT THE EXTENDED FAMILY is not content to let past injustices go. To regain Indian trust status (eligibility for numerous Federally funded improvements of life and existence), more than 300 surviving Coast Miwok of both Marin and Sonoma Counties, as the Federated Indians of Graton Rancheria, have petitioned for Federal restoration, and have excellent grounds for such action.

The various small groups of Coast Miwok, especially those families around Bodega Bay and Tomales, and the Santa Rosa area have pooled their strength into this organization, which is dedicated to restoring Federal recognition. The tribe assists many public activities, including MAPOM (*see below*) and the Kule Loklo village, a booth at Kule Loklo Big Time (July), an annual tribal gathering the second Saturday in July (*see Calendar*), as well as the annual Day Under the Oaks at Santa Rosa Junior College every summer (*see Calendar*).

63 *From Sebastopol, N on Hwy. 116 to Occidental Rd. at Molino, left past Mill Station Rd., about 1/2 mile to Cherry Lane. The old rancheria is on the left*
FEDERATED INDIANS
OF GRATON RANCHERIA
Graton, CA
Info: Mr. Gene Buvelot
(member Marin Museum of the American Indian),
P.O. Box 481, Novato, CA 94948
(415) 241-3942

Lanny Pinola, Kashaya Pomo and interpretive ranger for Point Reyes National Seashore, along with his family and friends, dance and sing for the appreciative public at Kule Loklo's Big Time every summer.

(dhe, 1999)

KULE LOKLO
POINT REYES NATIONAL SEASHORE

Ancestral *Coast Miwok* land, (1960s) Marin County
Kule Loklo ("Bear Valley") is the Coast Miwok name for a meadow near the Point Reyes Seashore headquarters—it was never a village site. But an Indian village characteristic of that people is being developed here, so that visitors may feel what life was like in a coastal village before white people came here.

Entry to the sweatlodge is encouraged—imagine the pungent smoke opening your pores. Grind acorns into the Indian's staple food; watch it being cooked in a basket with hot stones; taste it. Smell the fresh tule reeds of the dwellings. Let the mystery of the dances permeate all your senses, as Indian dancers present to the public a sample of their ceremonies.

The National Park Service and the Miwok Archaeological Preserve of Marin (MAPOM) maintain this village, the only other being Ahwahnee, in Yosemite Valley. The structures are built to the best of current anthropological, cultural, and archaeological knowledge. The Park Service employs an Indian interpretive ranger to help visitors understand what they are seeing. They welcome questions on Indian life.

AT KULE LOKLO, descendants of the Coast Miwok, nearby Kashaya Pomo, and adjacent Wappo people emerge from their private lives to dance or take part in local festivals. Since the dancehouse has been scrupulously constructed following Miwok custom, local Miwok and others feel that they can dance in an authentic setting.

The second Saturday in July has been set aside for the well-attended Annual Native American Celebration here.

64 *Marked trail to Kule Loklo, 1/4 mi. from the Visitor Center.*
PT. REYES NATIONAL SEASHORE VISITOR CENTER,
Pt. Reyes, CA 94956
(415) 663-1092

OLOMPALI STATE HISTORIC PARK

Ancestral *Coast Miwok* land, Marin County

A Coast Miwok rancheria was once here, spread over nearly 100 acres. The site overlooks a rich marsh of the Petaluma river, and was supplied with ample year-round fresh water from springs on Mt. Burdell. Some people alive in 1995 remember the place as an occupied village. In the latter 1800s, an adobe stage stop was located here, by the village. Later yet, a rancher took over the land, building a large ranch house, barns, and ponds.

Regrettably, although remains of the village with its sunken house-sites was mapped out by an archaeologist several years ago, and artifacts removed, the State Parks people have not had the resources to bring this information to the public. Other, later historic buildings are adjacent.

A Heritage Day is presented the first weekend in May, with talks and storytelling.

65 *Olompali State Historic Park is 1 mi. N of Novato on the W side of U.S. 101, but may be approached only from the north. From S.F., go N to an appropriate turnaround, and return. Adm. to the Park.*

LAKE MIWOK

This band of Miwok occupied a patch of land north of and separated from the Coast Miwok of Marin and Sonoma Counties. Their rather small area extended from the northern foot of Mt. St. Helena, Cobb Mountain, and Pope Valley northward, through rather dry hilly country, to the edge of Clear Lake, at Cache Creek. Most of their early traditions closely resemble those of other Miwok peoples.

Along with many Pomo from the western shores of Clear Lake, this group suffered first the Vallejo and Andrew Kelsey and Charles Stone occupation of their lands, then the massacre of Bloody Island (*see p.36*).

MIDDLETOWN RANCHERIA
(WI-LOKYOMI)

Lake Miwok (1910) Lake Co.

The pines of the north slopes of Mt. St. Helena (near Calistoga) shade the dwellings of *wi-lokyomi*, the one

Middletown Rancheria, is the only trust land of the small band of Lake Miwok people. The shape of their tribal council offices imitates that of a roundhouse.

(dhe, 1999)

rancheria of the Lake Miwok. The residents of the families who live here wish to better their world. Most of the homes are very old; in San Francisco, some would have landmark status. Very little improvement of the tribes living conditions has occurred in past decades.

SOME BASKETRY is woven here; but of most importance, the tribe has established a tent-shaped gaming center at the edge of the highway. Their tribal hall is roundhouse-shaped, located next to the site of the ancient roundhouse of this Lake Miwok center. Other projects are planned. A block grant for new homes is providing funds for some of the 75 members (1998) to "come home".

The site is pleasant, the clouds pushed up by the mountain drop some rain here in the otherwise dryish valley. A famous old roundhouse is gone, but residents say that, perhaps someday, another will rise.

LINDA KNIGHT, a young resident, pointed out a large, spreading oak tree that was a former shelter and prop for a canvas-covered wooden frame that had been her grandmother's home. She was delighted that the proceeds from the casino and the help of the governmental block grants allowed much-needed improvement in living conditions. However, several residents, she added, were wary of overdevelopment, and were cautious to keep changes in their way of life at a minimum.

66 *About a mile S of Middletown, on Hwy. 29, at Rancheria Rd.*
MIDDLETOWN RANCHERIA
P.O. Box 1035, Middletown, CA 95461

PLAINS MIWOK

WILTON RANCHERIA

Plains Miwok (1927) Sacramento County

The land here is flat, so flat that once, when it had only grass, it was called plains, and the local Miwok residents were given that name. Today, on these now-irrigated plains, a variety of crops are raised.

The town of Wilton is a couple of stores and a small agricultural depot on the railroad, under the shadow of the defunct Rancho Seco nuclear plant—no more than that. And the rancheria, though terminated, has stuck together. Consisting of 39 acres, its appearance is what is almost "typical" for the small rectangles of rancheria parcels. About ten families, young and old, live here in neat, comfortable homes. Flowers, tall trees and gardens grace the community.

In spite of its terminated status, more than 300 Plains Miwok people still live here and not far away. The Wilton Indian Miwok Community is one of three tribes in the state declared most eligible for reinstatement of tribal status.

(The names and addresses given below are subject to change, since this is a tribe whose present in flux.)

67 *From SE of Sacramento and Hwy. 16, take Grant Line Rd. (2 mi. W of Sloughhouse) SW about 6 miles to Wilton Rd. In Wilton, Rancheria Drive leads to the place.*
WILTON MIWOK PROTECTIVE ASSOC.
9425 Rancheria Dr., Wilton, CA 95693
Tribal Office: 1020 19th St., Sacramento, CA 95814
(916) 492-2855

NORTHERN SIERRA MIWOK

IONE BAND OF MIWOK INDIANS

Northern Sierra Miwok Amador County
A formerly, now once again Federally recognized tribal band, without land.

THIS VERY ACTIVE GROUP of people was once recognized by the Federal government as a local Miwok tribe with land. Then some bureaucrat decided to eliminate them from the Federal roles by hiding their official papers in an obscure drawer of files in Washington. As far as the BIA was concerned, they had been successfully ignored—a sort of termination by illegal abandonment. But it is difficult to eliminate a whole tribe. After continued personal, legal, and moral pressure, the papers were uncovered, and the reluctant authorities were forced to reaccept the tribe.

Within the tribe is a well-known Miwok dance group, frequently asked to perform in public. Also, they are the hard-working Indian sponsor (known as the **SIERRA NATIVE AMERICAN COUNCIL**) of the Chaw-Se Big Time (*see p.140*).

The Northern Sierra Miwok are highly organized, and their Miwok dance group is publicly seen frequently at central California Indian events.
nr. **68**
IONE BAND OF MIWOK INDIANS
2919 Jackson Valley Rd., Ione, CA 95640

BUENA VISTA RANCHERIA

Northern Sierra Miwok (1927) Amador County
In the early days after its establishment, this rancheria was a well-known ceremonial center, though only 70 acres. Today, all is in private hands, and only a handful of people remain in a dry oak-shaded parcel—watching over a lonely burial ground.

The Indian land is relegated to the dry margins of a green and fertile valley—flanked by the industrial desolation of a gravel pit and a major coal mine It is an heroic outpost of survival.

68 *South of Hwy. 88 near Ione lies the junction corners of Buena Vista. The rancheria is by an old coal strip mine, about a mile SW. Don't enter; the land is private, and the residents are not cordial to outsiders.*
BUENA VISTA RANCHERIA
#6 Glynis Falls Ct., Sacramento, CA 95831

SHINGLE SPRINGS RANCHERIA

Northern Sierra Miwok (1916) El Dorado County
Once this 160-acre expanse of a few oaks and pines on low chaparral-dotted foothills was the homesite for a few people shunted away from white society. It was too undersupplied to support anyone and lost its population, but the people persisted in their demands for proper living conditions. Presently, the land, with the amenities of water, electricity, and paved road, provides living space for several families, courtesy of a gaming hall.

69 *Shingle Springs Drive exit from U.S. 50, N on the road about 1/2 mi. into the land of the reservation.*
SHINGLE SPRINGS RANCHERIA
P.O. Box 1340, Shingle Springs, CA 95682

JACKSON RANCHERIA

Northern Sierra Miwok (1893) Amador County
As the foothills rise into the Sierra Nevada, they become more and more wooded. The Jackson Rancheria lies within the woods—of oak and pine on gentle hills. Once, lumbering within its 330 acres made life sustainable for one family here. Other members of the rancheria lived nearby on their own resources. Some tribal members have been very active in construction and maintenance of the dancehouse at Chaw-Se, a few miles away. Some members also assist in the presentation of the Chaw-Se Big Time. The Rancheria is the home of a dental clinic serving the entire area.

Today, several families live here in homes inconceivable a decade ago. They live very private lives behind a carefully guarded gate. The tasteful Jackson Rancheria casino is the reason for the elevated lifestyle of the formerly scattered Jackson Miwok people, who returned to the rancheria upon acquisition of housing. In the corner of the rancheria set aside for the casino we find also a hilltop hotel with grand vistas of mountains, foothills, and the landmark Mokolumne Hill.

70 *From Jackson, take New York Ranch Rd. 3 mi. NE to casino road, or about 1 mi. S of the Hwy. 104 intersection, 3 mi. E of Sutter Creek.*
JACKSON RANCHERIA
2200 New York Ranch Rd., Jackson, CA 95642

The Big Time at the Calaveras Band of Mi-wuks is held every September in West Point. Mr. Bill Franklin, elder of the group, designed built the roundhouse alongside an earlier smaller roundhouse.   (dhe, 1994)

CHAW~SE, INDIAN GRINDING ROCKS STATE PARK

Northern Sierra Miwok Amador County

Several hundred years ago the ancestors of the present-day Miwoks found a flat meadow in the generally hilly, wooded foothills. Acorns showered from the tall valley oaks, a continuously flowing stream gave water for drinking and acorn preparation, and several outcroppings of smooth granite projected from the ground, like the bald heads of buried gray giants.

The granite made a great place for grinding and washing the acorns, with space left over for chipping in some favorite designs and figures. There are literally dozens of grinding holes on the rocks and many of the petroglyphs are quite distinct, even after hundreds of years of weathering.

The local Miwok people have been called upon to add some of their early cultural heritage to this mystical site that has become a California state park. Some primitive homes, made of slab, have been constructed, but most importantly they erected a roundhouse, the largest in California. This remarkable structure, allwood, is used for presenting dances to the public, both Indian and non-Indian.

The "Big Time" celebration is held here during California Indian Days, the fourth weekend in

September. All during the weekend, there are Indian dances (local and invited groups), barbeque and many other foods, Indian football (something like soccer plus hockey with a big, mushy ball), and hand games tournaments. First-class Indian craft booths abound, and hundreds of Indians from miles around come to camp-meeting and to be together. Dancing continues late into the night, the time for the most serious of California Indian ceremonies.

The Indian sponsor of the Big Time is the Sierra Native American Council and the Ione Band of Miwok Indians, based in the nearby town of Ione.

71 *8 miles E of Jackson at Pine Grove, on State Hwy. 88, take the road to Volcano, N about 1 mile to the Chaw-Se entrance. Camping. Museum open 9-5, Wed-Sun.*
CHAW-SE INDIAN GRINDING ROCKS STATE PARK
& MUSEUM OF MIWOK CULTURE
Attention: Hannah Danel
14881 Pine Grove/Volcano Rd.
Pine Grove, CA 95665
(209) 296-4440

CALAVERAS BAND OF MI-WUK INDIANS

Northern Sierra Miwuk Calaveras County

Centuries ago, a group of Mi-wuk people found themselves on a spot of land in what was one day to become Calaveras County. In these gentle hills a few families lived comfortably amid abundant oak trees that bear good acorns for food and plenty of water in a creek to leach them, a mild climate (well, maybe a little snow in winter), plenty of game, and a good supply of berries and other plants, providing nearly all their requirements. A mile's walking distance is the big river (Mokolumne) that has plenty of fish. Their descendants are still here.

In the 1920s, the band was given a government parcel in which to live, but no Federal recognition as a tribe. Most people here have had little access to Federal funds available to recognized groups (they are not); consequently, their living situations are generally marginal. These people have learned to live with very little over the decades.

Nevertheless, the third weekend of every September, a week before the Chaw-Se Big Time, the Calaveras Band organizes and puts on a grand public Big Time, the largest event of its kind on Indian land in central California. The setting could not be more traditional. The large cedar-covered roundhouse nestles into the red earth hillside with a much older tiny roundhouse standing alongside, converted into the place where dancers gather for dressing and blessing.

NOT ONLY DOES the local Miwuk dance group present their songs and dances, but other Miwok, Pomo, Maidu, and central California (even Aztec) tribes may be invited. Energetic, earnest, sometimes humorous dancing and songs may continue in the firelight until dawn. Hand games can be participated in (or just heard) late into the night; booths with quality Indian food and goods are provided; camping is encouraged.

We had the opportunity to converse with Gloria Grimes, Tribal Chair, while she was slicing barbeque in the tribal kitchen at the September Big Time.

GLORIA GRIMES:

"We have been here for as long as anyone knows, but we have had a hard time keeping the land. We do have some 80 acres that are in trust, but for some reason we have not been Federally recognized, although as individuals, we are recognized—I know it doesn't make sense. For our 200 people enrolled in the tribe, we are awaiting Federal recognition so that we can apply for more land for new homes.

"Most of the people here are employed in several local industries, and lately at the casino.* I am at the MACT (Mariposa, Amador, Calaveras, Tuolumne) Health Board, a State/IHS (Indian Health Service) service area—that's a clinic that serves both the Indian and non-Native population.

"The roundhouse was designed and built a few years ago by Bill Franklin, whose 80th birthday is today [September 20, 1997]. He designed the one at Chaw-Se, too, but the State came in and made too many demands for changes, so he just quit and came here to build his own." [*Ms. Grimes took her leave to attend to her family, to the BBQ, to feed the dancers, and to assign tasks to her children and staff members.*]
— Gloria Grimes, Tribal Chair
Calaveras County Band of Mi-wuk Indians

72 *Take Hwy. 88 from Jackson 10 mi. NE to Hwy 26, E on 26 about 6mi. to West Point, E (left turn) onto Ball Mtn. Rd. about 1 1/2 mi to the Indian village (round-house on the right)*
**CALAVERAS COUNTY BAND
OF MI-WUK INDIANS**
579 Ball Mountain Rd., West Point, CA 95255
(209) 293-4332

CENTRAL SIERRA MIWOK

SHEEP RANCH RANCHERIA

Central Sierra Miwok (1916) Calaveras County
Take a winding road through the forests and the hills, through lumbering and mining communities, and find the settlement of Sheep Ranch. Find the old schoolhouse at the top of the hill (not difficult), then next to it find the 0.92 acre of this little rancheria, a postage stamp on the great parcel of the foothills. Its one resident doesn't even live here year-round. One wonders why the great white father even bothered.

A neighbor says the little government plywood house, with a cat, is host to lively parties. He spoke kindly of his neighbor, who spends some time in Tuolumne (next page).

*casino at Jackson Rancheria, 9 miles east

73 *10 miles from Murphys on Sheepranch Rd. (just off Hwy. 4, NE of Angels Camp).*
SHEEP RANCH RANCHERIA
Sheep Ranch, CA 95250
(an adjunct of Tuolumne Rancheria)

Special tribal ceremonies are held in the roundhouse at Tuolumne Rancheria. It is not spacious enough for their populous Acorn Day Gathering in September; a dance arena is used instead. (dhe, 1995)

TUOLUMNE RANCHERIA

Central Sierra Miwok and *Yokuts*
(1910) Tuolumne County
The Tuolumne, the largest of the several Sierra Miwok rancherias, is an administrative, residential, and ceremonial center. Oak forests creep to the edges of the small fields that form the large clearing in the center of the rancheria. While the fields are small—essentially small gardens or pastures—they do provide some additional support for the residents.

Of importance here are a medical-dental clinic, a fine tribal council building that includes a spacious dining room and kitchen, and a roundhouse that opens onto a festival arena. Tuolumne presents a public acorn, dance and food festival, the second weekend of September. Next to some of the homes, which are spaced over the 336 acres, some people maintain individual sweathouses. Thanks to various development bloc grants, new homes keep springing up on the reservation. It is obvious from the festivals and design of the older structures that traditions are kept here. The school even has a club for the Indian children.

74 *About a mile out of Tuolumne on E-17, the road north connecting the town with Hwy. 108, is the Rancheria sign (E).*
TUOLUMNE RANCHERIA
P.O. Box 699, Tuolumne, CA 95379
(209) 928-3475

CHICKEN RANCH RANCHERIA
Central Sierra Miwok (1908) Calaveras County

In an old gold-mining foothill region, where the lonesome steam whistle of the Sierra Railroad still echoes, a few of the people are left from a once-terminated but then partially restored rancheria. Today it is a mixed suburb of Jamestown, hardly a metropolis, but a suburb's a suburb. Most Indian activity outside of family life centers around the Tuolumne Rancheria a few miles east.

In 1985, the rancheria's restored 2.8 acres became home to a gaming hall, but the remainder of the land is still allotted, not yet back in trust. However, the tribe has made a great, probably successful, effort to acquire much more land for housing through reacquisition and replacement of its terminated and lost land.

75 *From Hwy. 108, on the western city limit of Jamestown is Chicken Ranch Rd., which leads to the top of a hill, where we find the casino and the Indian parcels remaining.*

CHICKEN RANCH RANCHERIA
P.O. Box 1159, Jamestown, CA 95327
(209) 984-4806

CALIFORNIA INDIAN LANDS OFFICE
Sonora, Calaveras County

This is an offshoot of the Central California Agency Land Acquisition Committee. Both organizations have been making great strides in identifying various California Indian groups that are eligible and who need of additional land for the many landless families belonging to the tribes of this region.

The Committee was originally set up to identify the problems and to connect the various state and Federal agencies involved in land acquisition and housing. It has since also offered strategies for the tribes to proceed with the necessary paperwork and footwork. It serves as a very necessary technical and educational resource through the labyrinth of land and housing procedures.

—Ms. Dore Bietz, Director of CILO

CILO *also publishes an informative newsletter, "Promised Land"—interviews, short articles and editorials of interest to those who respect Indian land.*

CALIFORNIA INDIAN LANDS OFFICE
Sonora, CA
(209) 588-9772

SOUTHERN SIERRA MIWOK

Almost all of the Southern Sierra Miwok villages were clustered alongside the rivers of the region: the Tuolumne, Merced, Mariposa, Chowchilla, and (northwest bank) Fresno. This group has had no rancherias Federally recognized, although one group has maintained residence in Yosemite valley up until this time. *[The Park Service persists in the autocratic attitude that Indians should not live in the Park, unless they are employed here. This presumption of ownership jeopardizes the very heart of Indian cooperation. A similar notion prejudices the Timbi-Sha Shoshone village in Death Valley Park. —ed.]*

"The sight of these fires is more beautiful
to me than any other."
—James Savage, 1891, of the fires his men had set destroying
the Ahwanichee's winter acorn provisions.

"Many of you came here to get healing. You'll get that.
But many of you didn't come here for healing,
you'll get it anyway."
—Jay Johnson, Miwok healer, 1998, to the people gathered
in the Ahwahnee Village roundhouse.

AHWAHNEE VILLAGE
YOSEMITE NATIONAL PARK
Original territory of the *Southern Sierra Miwok*
(1930s) Mariposa County

An immense subterranean granite mass rose up millions of years ago from the depths of the earth; then thousands of years ago it was carved by glacial ice into Yosemite Valley; then Native Americans came to live here; then white men came, forcibly evicting the first tenants. While protecting their homeland, the Yosemite dwellers were killed or displaced by the appropriately named Maj. James D. Savage.

NOW, IN ONE TINY CORNER of this vast waterfall-tasseled canyon, a struggling crew of Native Americans seek to show something of the original people. In an enclosure behind the **PARK VISITOR CENTER**, local Indian people perform the daily tasks of early Indian life for the thousands of visitors—curious and indifferent alike. Around the village of four conical cedar slab dwellings, a roundhouse, a sweathouse, and a few small utility and dressing rooms, they and their friends grind acorns and prepare, in 70-year-old baskets, the food that was the staple of Californians for centuries.

Erected near the site of the original village named *Awani*, the roundhouse and the sweathouse may be peered into, but not entered—for within them local tribes still hold their ceremonies. Many Miwok and other peoples from the Yosemite Valley and down the Merced Valley never had a reservation; they consider this place sacred and often make use of the village for their assemblies.

The Native facilities here are used by both Southern Miwok and Mono Lake Paiute. (Both peoples are related by family ties, since both tribes occupied the west and the east slopes of the Park in the past.) The adjacent **INDIAN MUSEUM** is open daily and staffed by Indian interpretive guides. The Museum's dioramas and collection of basketry, ornaments, and tools are excellent. You will usually find active basketweaving demonstrations, often by Julia Parker, who has lived and worked here for many years, and who generously and enthusiastically answers questions.

Certain ceremonies are given in the early spring, June, and late fall. The Bear Dances are very special healing ceremonies (led by the tribal spiritual leader) given in order to bring the strength of the bear spirit to persons in need of help and healing. The date of the June Big Time is posted in the Indian Museum.

In 1997, for the first time since the invasion of Yosemite, a contract was signed with the Park Service dedicating to Indian use a parcel of several acres west of the park's gasoline station. The new site is a ceremonial area primarily for tribal use.

There is a great spirit abroad in this awesome valley. Visit the village; see for yourself the blend of early Indian with the environment and lose the mechanical world outside. Feel the sacredness and know why the Natives are determined to remain in their land.

76 INDIAN MUSEUM
and **AHWAHNEE VILLAGE**
OF YOSEMITE NATIONAL PARK,
AT THE VISITOR CENTER
Museum: (209) 372-0304.

AMERICAN INDIAN COUNCIL OF MARIPOSA COUNTY
(the Yosemite Indian Tribe)
Southern Sierra Miwok (1978) Mariposa Co.
A statement from the Federally unrecognized tribe:

"The Indian culture which has successfully existed in Yosemite for at least two thousand years has been nearly eradicated during the years of the white man's presence in the Park. Guaranteeing the continuing presence of Indians in the Park is as important as preserving the wildlife and natural surroundings …not only for their own sake but for the benefit of future generations of visitors to the Park."

This organization is the guiding tribe for the people of Yosemite. They sponsor several public (and a few private) events throughout the year. They also make great efforts to preserve family unity with all their own people, on both sides of the Sierra. Language is preserved and used, as are basketweaving, acorn preparation, ceremonial, and healing traditions.

AMERICAN INDIAN COUNCIL
OF MARIPOSA COUNTY
Tribal Chair: Jay Johnson, 5235 Allred Rd.,
Mariposa, CA 95338
(209) 966-6038

WASSAMA ROUNDHOUSE
Southern Miwok & Chukchansi Yokuts
(1903) Madera County
[This Ahwahnee roundhouse is not to be confused with Yosemite's Ahwahnee Village roundhouse.]

THE WASSAMA STATE HISTORIC PARK is nominal guardian of this very old village site, frequented by both Sierra Miwok and Chukchansi Yokuts peoples. On this site is a burial ground of the peoples, acorn grinding rocks associated with the village, and an extremely historic roundhouse. The first was built here in the 1860s, burned with the death of the tribal chief; reconstructed with the same fate; finally rebuilt in 1903. Upon the death of Chief Peter Westphal in 1924, the roundhouse remained.

In the 1950s, a rancher bought the site (except for the burial ground), building a ranch house (now used as meeting and storage area for the Association). He eventually sold the site. Recognizing the historic importance of the place, State Parks bought the property in 1978, conveying supervision to the Wassama Roundhouse Association, a group of local Indian persons dedicated to the management of the property.

The rancher had been using the roundhouse as a barn, and learning that it was to return to Indian control, reportedly spitefully chopped down the supporting poles. With much careful consideration, local Indian leaders restored the poles, holding a very special re-dedication ceremony. A roundhouse ceremony is now held annually in July (See Calendar); the local tribes also use the site privately.

77 *From Hwy. 49, turn NE for 1/4 mi at the County Rd. 628 (Roundhouse Rd.) to the Round House Park gate.*
AWAHNEE ROUNDHOUSE ASSOCIATION
(209) 683-8194;
Cal. Dept. of Parks & Rec. at Millerton Lake
5290 Millerton Rd.
P.O. Box 2205, Friant, CA 93626
(209) 822-2332

Several times a year, the Mariposa County American Indian Council sponsors events at the Indian Village in Yosemite National Park. This special place is the Yosemite Indians' ceremonial area. The tribe's leader, Jay Johnson, is not only a healer, he is a very good chef. (dhe, 1994)

HOKAN SPEAKERS

The word "Hokan" is Atsugewi for "two."
Northern central coast and Sacramento Valley speakers of this group,
which has many related languages around the state are Pomo.

POMO

Sprinkled over the map around Ukiah and Clear Lake are twenty rancherias, mostly Pomo bands. The Pomo never were a consolidated "tribe," as were the Mohaves, for instance. Although some dialects were apparently very different, language and customs among the groups were similar, but not their governance. Some of this autonomy is reflected in the large number of rancherias of the region, and led anthropologists to name most Pomo groups with a simple geographic designation (Northern, Southern, etc.), centered on Clear Lake.

THE NAME P'OMO COMES from Potter Valley, meaning "at red earth quarry". A particularly good quality red earth, rich in iron oxide (hematite and limonite), is found in this part of the Coast Range. This earth was popular over much of Central California, because, mixed with acorn mush, it reacts with the residual tannic acid in acorns, darkening and sweetening the bread when cooked. [**NOTE***: this is not the toxic red mercury oxide cinnabar, which was sometimes used as face paint, and found at Sulphur Bank mine on Clear Lake and Mt. St. Helena— Ed.*]

Incidentally, one of the Pomo peoples (*Kashaya*) were the only California native group to make a treaty of peace and cooperation with a European power, the Russian trading company at Fort Ross. A small Pomo village sprang up next to Fort Ross to supply settlers with necessary food, timber, and labor (*see App. IV*).

An 1828 sketch of Fort Ross, established by Russians in coastal Pomo territory to hunt sea otters for fur. The Pomos were hired to grow and furnish food and to be the labor force for the Russians, who abandoned the fort after the otter population was wiped out.

(State Parks)

In the 1850s, Clear Lake had an "upper" northern portion, before the lake bed was "reclaimed" (diked and channeled) for farmland. The once-large (1000-acre) Upper Lake Rancheria, lying along a hillside above and partly among neat orchards near this land, is smaller now; much of the former land is in the hands of non-Indians. However, an original 90 acres of this land were purchased and settled as early as 1878 by the people themselves, as at *Yo-ka-yo*.

I HAVE SEEN THE PEOPLE here trying hard to make a better life for themselves, rebuilding homes, keeping as many traditions as possible. The elderly are being served (but seldom equal to the white population) by community and Indian Health Service health and nutrition centers. Though they have few resources, the strength of these bands of people is great.

For many decades, a few of these rancherias held on to some cultural identity by maintaining a remote privacy, such as Middletown (Lake Miwok), Hopland (Central Pomo), and Sherwood Valley (Northern Pomo). Native culture remained in their homelife, in family connections, and often in dances and get-togethers at more active centers; however, the attraction of establishing gaming centers near busy highways has been tempting. There are mechanisms for self-improvement. One is to acquire additional land for housing, with the land in Federal trust. This route has been available, however, only to established rancherias or reservations, who can prove that most members have been in desperate need of housing. The second has been to set up a gaming establishment on the new land. As pointed out (*App.VI*), profits from these operations can (but not always) contribute to betterment. Mismanagement, low revenue, or overextension of plans can result in problems.

For a number of Pomo (and other) rancherias, the relentless pressure to terminate became a near-death experience. Once the lands had been released from Federal trust, individual families were expected to maintain the land and become immediately integrated into the larger society. This meant bringing long substandard housing up to code, often acquiring basic utilities (electricity, gas, sewer, even water), paving roads, and worst of all, paying taxes on land which had been exempt before. It was assumed that everyone had an income, employment, and/or sufficient education to maintain their property. But this could not be so. No productive land, no skills, no education, no access to health care, no acculturation into attitudes of the main "stream", racist attitudes blocking anything gainful—hardly a way to maintain claim on a piece of land.

In a ritual like a bad movie, families found the sheriff knocking at the door with a writ of eviction for non-payment of taxes or other such violation. Parcel by parcel the old rancherias fell into the ownership of non-Indians.

When restoration by de-termination occurred, it was too late for some rancherias, and barely surviving for others—frequently surviving in name only. In 1998, Potter Valley was gone, except for two tiny parcels with no houses. Guidiville has two homes left; Scotts Valley, the same. Graton, one house, not Federally recognized, but the owner is. Nearby Lytton, all gone, but is being revived with a request for new, replacement land by an active, landless tribe. The same is true for Lower Lake, which is now an airport. Stonyford, whose handful of residents never had recognition for themselves or their land, has no spokespeople, so is dying out.

The termination era had ill-effects for several other Pomo groups, whether or not actually terminated. The people have been left bereft of most Federal support, and their cultural survival has been tenuous. Pinoleville barely hangs on (but it does); Redwood Valley does not appear to be a prosperous place (though reasonably decent); Upper Lake, whose residents acquired the land themselves many years ago, survive without seeming signs of prosperity; Cloverdale, which was sliced by CalTrans, but is trying for new land; E'lem, suffering, but dancing; Big Valley, also struggling, though its casino should indicate otherwise.

ALTHOUGH THE LAST OF THE RANCHERIAS in this region to be Federally established, E'lem is the site of an ancient village, continuously inhabited for centuries. Tule reeds sway in the gentle waves of Clear Lake; ample trees shade the several homes by the lake, a well-appointed dancehouse is used almost weekly. If this sounds almost idyllic, most of the residents are concerned about what else is happening on their 52 acres. The ugly scar of the now-silent mercury mine beside the rancheria continues to spread its vicious toxic legacy, and in the mid-90s a dark cloud of dissent descended upon the community, as we shall see.

But the culture perseveres, and culturally, E'lem is an important center in the renewal of Pomo history in Clear Lake, Lake County, and even Mendocino County. The dance house functions as a center for Pomo people, many of whom come back to the rancheria from long distances. Some dances are even open to the public.

NORTHERN POMO

SHERWOOD VALLEY RANCHERIA
Northern Pomo (Mato band)
(1909, 1990s) Mendocino County

Old Sherwood Valley is 292 acres in a remarkable remote place reached through a land of lakes, mead-

ows, fir trees, ranches, startling plugs of volcanic rock on a high mountain plateau. Its residents lived for decades in mobile homes or very primitive wooden ones. Today the living conditions have changed, but not the setting. The small older homes sprout solar panels, large and small birds, live and dead cars, trees, and idyllic rural surroundings.

The old Sherwood Valley Rancheria remains a remarkably beautiful, remote, and pristine environment on a high, partly wooded plateau. Needing to be much nearer economic activity, the tribe acquired land several miles from the old site, at the edge of Willets. The new land has been provided with attractive modern housing, again with nearby forests.   (dhe, 1997)

In the 1990s, the rancheria purchased a large tract at the southwest edge of Willets for homes of its many scattered members. Apparently the tribe values its settings, for its new homes are arranged on a hillside with ample shade trees and carefully sculpted landscapes. The small, cozy casino, which contributes to some of this betterment of life here, has a rough wooden exterior and is tucked away in a forest. This Rancheria presents a picture of well-directed programs.

The Rancheria also supports a widespread food distribution system to other area rancherias. (I found one of their large supply trucks as far south as Dry Creek Rancheria, down by Cloverdale.)

43 OLD LAND: *From U.S. 101, south Willets, go NW on Sherwood Rd. some 12 miles, past the near-urban cluster of houses on County\Rd. 311 (still Sherwood Rd. to County Rd. 419, continue left to end of pavement (the road continues on to Ft. Bragg). A dirt road loops through the rancheria.*
NEW LAND: *In town: Go 1/2 mi W of U.S. Hwy. 101 on Hwy. 20, Following signs to casino, left 1/2 mi. to the Rancheria homes and tribal office on the hill.*
SHERWOOD VALLEY RANCHERIA
190 Sherwood Hill Dr., Willets, CA 95490
(707) 459-9690

POTTER VALLEY RANCHERIA
Northern Pomo (Balo-Kay band)
(1909) Mendocino County

One small parcel remains, uninhabited. The tribe still retains its identity, presently requesting replacement land, like several other rancherias in the same situation.

44 *N of State Hwy. 20, 4 mi E of Calpella, turn N (left) on East Side Rd. to East Side Potter Valley Rd. 2.2 mi. to Spring Valley Rd. The rancheria was on the W side of this intersection.*
POTTER VALLEY RANCHERIA
417-C Talmage Rd., Ukiah, CA 95482

Redwood Valley Rancheria is a peaceful, though not imposing place near Ukiah. Its few inhabitants live quietly around vineyards and older dwellings. (dhe, 1997)

REDWOOD VALLEY RANCHERIA
Northern Pomo (Kacha band)
(1909) Mendocino County

The land is flat, pretty dry, and dotted with a few large oaks and many smaller trees. Mountains line the edges of this rather narrow valley with its summer-dry creek. Redwood Valley's return to untermination status allowed it to add land to a total of 170 acres. It has a tiny tribal hall and some 25 homes. Most are generally mobile homes or comfortable clapboards, but a few are old and austere one-roomers. A nutrition center headquartered in Ukiah serves the Valley.

45 *From Ukiah/Calpella: N on Hwy.101 to West Rd. exit [or from north: same exit], go E past stop sign @ School Way 1.4 mi., R on Rancheria Rd. or Rd. L. The Rancheria lies between these roads, on E side.*
REDWOOD VALLEY RANCHERIA
3250 Road I, Redwood Valley, CA 95470

COYOTE VALLEY RESERVATION
Northern Pomo (1909) Mendocino County

The original 100 acres of this former rancheria are under the waters of Lake Mendocino. As a result of much pressure and effort, Coyote obtained another parcel nearby, five miles north of Ukiah, alongside U.S. 101. Housing, a well-designed tribal office, playground, recreational facilities were provided on its 58 acres. Unfortunately, most of the housing was built with cheap plywood siding, and the very small houses were spaced far to closely. Consequently, the condition of most of these places is rapidly declining, though some are well-kept. It is difficult to take pride in something that was knowingly constructed using inferior designs.

The reservation offers a gaming hall, but it, too shows some signs of age. Perhaps some of its returns will be used to retard the deterioration of the housing.

Maintaining some cultural traditions, Coyote Valley sponsors a dance group, which frequently participates in many public, as well as Indian-only events.

Also, as partial recompense for taking their land, the Corps of Engineers built the **POMO MUSEUM AND CULTURAL CENTER** at a lakeside site, staffed by Reservation members. (*See App. I*)
46 *From N or S on U.S. 101, take the West Rd. Exit, E to an immediate R on North State St. 1/2 mi. to the Casino sign. The tribal office is up on the hill.*
COYOTE VALLEY RESERVATION
P.O. Box 39, Redwood Valley, CA 95470

PINOLEVILLE RANCHERIA
(YAMO)
Northern Pomo (1911) Mendocino County

Mostly non-Indian now, originally 98 acres, not scenic, partly industrial storage of pipes, heavy vehicles, fringed by auto dismantlers. This is the aspect of an extremely low economy. The one well-kept spot is the **POMO INN** retirement home. Somehow, in the midst of this unkempt place, an unlikely spark of Pomo culture kindles the Rancheria. It manages to host a summer Big Time.

47 *N of Ukiah, take Orr Springs Rd. Exit off N State St., W 2 blocks to Pinoleville Rd. The rancheria lies at the foot of a low bluff.*
PINOLEVILLE RANCHERIA
367 N. State St. Ste. 204, Ukiah, CA 95482

GUIDIVILLE RANCHERIA
Northern Pomo (1909) Mendocino County

The lower elevations of the eastern slopes of the Ukiah Valley of the Russian River are wooded with laurel; below are open vineyards. This is the setting of the Guidiville Rancheria. It once occupied 243 acres, but has shrunk to a tiny size since its termination. The two houses left are only occasionally occupied. The neighbors are unfriendly and suspicious. There are reported attempts to revive the spirits.

48 *Just S of Ukiah off U.S. 101, take the road to Talmage. R at 10,000 Buddhas (main intersection), go S 1/2 mi. on County Rd. 201, L on Mill Rd., then 1/2 mi. N to Guidiville Rd. The remains of the rancheria are 1 mi. at the road's end.*
GUIDIVILLE RANCHERIA
P.O. Box 339, Talmage, CA 95481

SCOTTS VALLEY RANCHERIA

Northern Pomo (1911) Lake County

This easternmost rancheria of the Northern Pomo consists of three homes on three acres in the shady, tranquil valley in a small canyon. Its residents successfully petitioned for a federal grant to have some of the original 57 acres returned. Their one festival is a barbeque after the annual Kelseyville softball tourney.

49 From Lakeshore Blvd., N end of Lakeport, take Crystal Lake Way 1/2 mi. to Hartley Rd, S (L) 1/4 mi. to Scotts Valley Rancheria Rd. Or, from Hwy. 29, take Scotts Valley Rd. Exit to fire station, immediately 1/2 mi. S on Hill Rd. East to L on Crystal Lake Way, 1/2 mi. to Hartley Rd., then as above.

Scotts Valley Rancheria, 149 N. Main #200, Lakeport, CA 95453

NORTHEASTERN POMO

STONYFORD (COMMUNITY)

Northeastern Pomo (W) Colusa/Glenn Counties

All year long Stony Creek flows its life-giving waters onto the flats below the mountains. A band of Pomos from Clear Lake came over the mountains many, many years ago, according to Clayton Moore, one of the surviving descendants. The band, now called the Northeastern Pomos, found Stonyford a perfect site for a village. The flats are best for oaks, homesites, and grasslands, while the mountains furnish habitats for other flora and fauna. The stream is good for water and the fish which once ran every year.

Just west of town, on private property, is the site of an ancient roundhouse. Today it appears to be a sinkhole or trash dump dug there decades ago. While we sat in his jeep, Mr. Arthur Moody described to me some later history of Stonyford.

The area was "settled" by a group of Mormons fleeing justice—conspirators in the Mountain Meadows Massacre in Utah, 1857. Attempting to discourage other immigrants from passing through Utah, they had dressed as Indians and slain nearly an entire wagon train. When they arrived here, I doubt that the native Pomos were treated with utmost respect.

At any rate, the Pomo people erected a sweatlodge. There are a large number of baked stone fragments around the site. Stones were heated, brought into the sweatlodge, and and water thrown upon them for making steam—the Indian steam bath for purification.

Mr. Moody showed me some early trenches the Mormons dug for irrigation, and a smaller trench dug by himself, with a large loop bypassing a shady flat. That flat is a former Pomo burial ground. It is still respected and the local Pomos (and Mr. Moody) know its location, but it is totally unmarked, characteristic of most California Indian peoples' burial customs. Known to the natives, but who else needs to know? Today the whole field of cemetery and sweatlodge is barren of nearly all but stones, star thistle, and drowsy cows. (Caution: the landowners are unhappy about trespassing.)

Most the very few Indian people who remain in Stonyford live in a cluster of a few primitive cabins, the size of garages, on the opposite bank of the creek, in the open chaparral, with a vista of St. John's Mountain. There is electricity, water from an irrigation ditch, and a rather prosperous Indian ranch in front. The place is in actuality a rancheria, in the early sense of the word, but its 80 acres are privately owned, with a locked gate and dirt road access. The Northeastern Pomo were never given government reservation land. Some local employment is with the U.S. Forest Service and lumbering outfits. The rancheria proper may be spotted, but not

The Northeastern Pomo people of Stonyford had one resource worth defending. They did so in a "salt war", see below.

(dhe, 1979)

entered, from a campground of Mendocino National Forest on Fouts Spring Rd., just west of Stonyford. "We're hangin' in there," says Clayton Moore, "and we're still Pomos."

Out on the main road at the Glenn-Colusa county line is the ranch, once owned by Clayton's father, Sharkey, now passed on. Sharkey's grandmother is buried in the cemetery mentioned above. Sharkey was born at the old Stony Creek rancheria, which was the Indian settlement described above. Several years ago, he spared me a few moments from his busy ranching day to tell me of one of the Salt Springs battles of the early 1800's.

"A few miles up the road there's a famous salt spring in Northeast Pomo territory that furnished salt for most of the neighboring peoples. Salt, then as like now, is very important for food preservation and health, and local people considered it their most available trading material.

It seems, though, that the spring was coveted as well by their neighbors—Wintu, Yuki, Miwok, and some other Pomo. One day some outsiders [not named] sneaked in from the south, and while making off with a load of unpaid-for salt, were killed for their insult. Some nights later, avengers from the outsiders' camp were spotted coming through a pass by a Stonyford sentry, who quickly warned his villagers. After building fires to make the place look busy, the villagers hid nearby; the avengers burned the village before dawn; and while boasting of the "victory," were ambushed. We never heard of further troubles from the south."

The salt springs are part of the Garlin Ranch, from whom permission to visit must be secured. During drought years, the springs can dry up, too. All around this region, watch out for rattlers.

50 Stonyford is 20+ mi. N of Hwy. 20, 6 mi. W of Williams, or about the same distance W of Maxwell, both on small, circuitous roads. An excellent back roads adventure.

Delvin Holder supervises reconstruction of his father's home at Upper Lake Rancheria in 1984. (dhe, 1984-99) *Mr. Delvin Holder, 15 years later.*

EASTERN POMO

UPPER LAKE RANCHERIA
(XA~BÉ~MO~TOLEL)
Eastern Pomo (Mátuku band)
(1878, 1907) Lake County

Clear Lake once had an "upper" northern portion, before the lake bed was converted to cultivation. Originally, 90 acres of this land were purchased and settled as early as 1878 by the band itself. Later expanded to 1,000 acres, lying along a hillside above and partly among neat orchards near this land, the rancheria has been carved down to 483 acres of bottomland and hillside. The people here live make a hard living with their meagre resources.

WHAT HAS HAPPENED HERE is the fate typical of a number of terminated rancherias. The band exists upon only a few of the original holdings. A second, smaller parcel, the "Woodlot", some three miles upstream, remains intact.

51 *From Upper Lake (on Hwy. 20) take the road to the Mendocino National Forest Ranger Station, continue about 1 mile N over the levees of a creek to Rancheria Rd., then right about 1/4 mi. to a settlement.*
UPPER LAKE RANCHERIA
P.O. Box 245272, Sacramento, CA 95820

ROBINSON RANCHERIA
Eastern Pomo (1910, 1984) Lake County

The old homes are mainly interspersed with non-Indian parcels, clustered on a few acres near Clear Lake, the source of their ancestors' life. The hills around appear as though giant bowling balls lay under a huge carpet. On one of these hillsides above the little valley the spirits of the ancient people must still dwell—around the marked and unmarked graves of the cemetery. It was near this site that the Bloody Island Massacre took place in 1850 (*see p.34 & p.148*).

The old pastoral locality is as different from the new one as can be imagined. First came restoration of a terminated status. Then came a tribal request for new land to build homes, which was allowed. Then came the gaming establishment, one of the best known and frequented in the area. The new rancheria location is right on the main highway and stands out almost as a landmark. On an oak savannah hillside above the casino, scattered with ample yards, are homes with good views, all utility services, as well as playground and educational services.

52 *The new 100-acre parcel is on Hwy.20, halfway between Upper Lake and Nice, about 8 miles distant from the old portion. The old location is on Hwy. 29, about 2 miles S of its intersection with Hwy 20, turn R on Mockingbird Lane. The rancheria is located at the end of the pavement.*
ROBINSON RANCHERIA
P.O. Box 1119, Nice, CA 95464

BIG VALLEY RANCHERIA
Eastern Pomo (1870, 1911) Lake County

Big Valley is really a flat, rich plain on the margins of Clear Lake, just to the north of the sacred Indian peak of Mt. Kanocti. In an effort to help the people of this place, Father Luciano Osuna bought 160 acres of land in 1870 and established St. Turibus Mission here.

In 1912, the present (Federal) rancheria was established, but much of the land was sold upon termination and turned into pear orchards. Nevertheless, a few of the people still live in a row of houses along the road, and one family has built a roundhouse to sustain their shrinking cultural roots. (The roundhouse is on private land and is off-limits to the uninvited.) Another row of houses and an historic church are at the far end of the rancheria, looking out over the waters of Clear Lake. Tules and other plants along the water's edge provide material for various weaving and ceremonial purposes.

Big Valley's tent-like gaming establishment stands in the middle of the rancheria. Grants and gaming have enabled the rancheria to construct a large facility apart from the casino. A gymnasium/community center gives an indication of progress that was lacking for decades. The gym furnishes a space not only for games of sport, but also for ceremonial events ("powwow" is not a Pomo tradition), tribal gatherings, and even local community events. Additional rooms pro-

Colorful older homes in the Big Valley Rancheria, near Lakeport. The tribe has ambitious plans: housing, community services, and environmental development.
(dhe, 1997)

vide a senior center for activities and dining. The tribal chair says of the gym: "There's also the possibility to shelter flood victims." Such a refuge would be of great benefit to local families, since the Clear Lake shores are subject to occasional flooding.

53 *South of Lakeport take the small lake-edge Soda Bay Rd. (E of Hwy. 29) about 5 mi. to the casino signboard. The Rancheria lies a few hundred yards on either side of the road to the casino.*
BIG VALLEY RANCHERIA
P.O. Box 430, Lakeport, CA 95453
[**NOTE:** *In Lakeport, Lake County Tribal Health is the health provider for some six tribes around the Lake. The complex, new in 1999, provides medical, dental Human Services, and administrative services to reservation, off-reservation, and out-of-state Native Americans. It is located at 925 Bevins Court, on the south end of Lakeport. (707) 263-8322]*

CENTRAL POMO

YO-KA-YO RANCHERIA
Central Pomo (1881) Mendocino County

This group of people was denied land even as early as the late 1800s; however, they banded together to buy this parcel for themselves in 1881. Nevertheless, the Federal government refused to recognize them as a tribe, though grudgingly accepting them as Indians. The Federal recognition hassle went on for decades. Officially it was decided in the late 1990s, but getting the BIA official acknowledgement on paper goes on... The visitor would see neat homes and farms.

54 *About 3 miles S of Talmage on both sides of East Side Rd., alongside the Russian River (just N. of huge Fetzer Winery factory).*
YO-KA-YO [UKIAH] TRIBE OF INDIANS
(No tribal office, chairperson, or telephone —governance by three trustees).
For info: Ms. Doreen Mitchell.
1114 Helen Ave., Ukiah, CA 95482

HOPLAND RESERVATION (SHÁNEL)
Central Pomo (Shókowa-ma band)
(1907) Mendocino County

The largest of the Pomo rancherias (2,070 acres), Hopland is situated in a region of rolling hills, sprinkled liberally with aged oaks. A few intermittent streams, tributaries of the Russian River, trickle through, and vineyards that were formerly hops fields line the valleys that even earlier were Indian village sites. The place is a picturesque setting in low Coast Range mountains, and the Rancheria is a success story.

Though 38 acres are in trust, nice homes for many residents here are individually owned, and are scattered about, mostly hidden behind the hills, up small back roads. If you like pretty hills with broad vistas of the vineyards and Coast Range mountains, I might recommend a scenic drive-through on East Side

> A FEW INTERMITTENT STREAMS, TRIBUTARIES OF THE RUSSIAN RIVER, TRICKLE THROUGH, AND VINEYARDS THAT WERE FORMERLY HOPS FIELDS LINE THE VALLEYS THAT EVEN EARLIER WERE INDIAN VILLAGE SITES.

Ranch Road, then loop around on Branch Road. On a hillside surrounded by moss-dripping oaks stands the very old, impeccably white-painted St. Francis Native American Catholic Church.

Or you may visit their widely advertised gaming center. Across the road from the casino is the road to the tribal center, surrounded by two- and three-story apartment-like houses and spacious ranch homes. Although there are some 200 residents, the tribal office says that about every two or three years, new parcels of land are added, and new homes are built for the ever-enlarging families.

55 *E of East Hopland wind on Hwy.175 through vineyards for 5 mi., abruptly enter a small canyon, follow Casino signs. Shanel Rd. threads N among the hills and trees.*
HOPLAND RESERVATION
P.O. Box 610, Hopland, CA 95449

MANCHESTER & POINT ARENA RANCHERIAS
Central Pomo (Bóya band)
(1909 and 1937, respectively) Mendocino County

To western eyes, the Point Arena Rancheria is probably the most neatly kept reservation in California. At the top of an ancient ocean terrace looking out over grassy fields toward the Point Arena lighthouse is a small circle of homes, each with lawns and trimmed hedges. In the center of the circle children play on swings. On the hill's summit stands a water tank, and a small clinic is available. But as Pt. Arena is modern, Manchester is the more historic; nevertheless, the same band of people lives on the 363 acres of this two-part rancheria.

At Point Arena and Manchester there are about five families, in several homes. (Remember, an Indian family can consist of a lot of relatives.) Off the road into Manchester on a quiet hillside is the ever-present reminder of times past—the cemetery. But life continues in the homes in the Garcia River Valley below. Some parcels are intensively farmed along the riverside. At the road's end rests a well-kept roundhouse, where occasional dances are held. At Chaw-Se's Big Time (*p.141*), we are often treated to dances by a group of young elegantly costumed and well-trained people from here. The people here are proud of their heritage, and are not letting it pass away.

56 *Pt. Arena: about 2 miles N of the town of Pt. Arena (on Hwy 1), E off Windy Hollow Rd. Manchester: about 1 mile E of Hwy. 1 on Mountain View Rd. (toward Boonville) to a BIA green sign, then north.*
MANCHESTER-PT. ARENA RANCHERIA
P.O. Box 659, Pt. Arena, CA 95468
(707) 882-2623

SOUTHEASTERN POMO

E'LEM INDIAN COLONY *[Ee-lem]*
Southeastern Pomo (1949) Lake County
E'lem is probably as old as any continuously inhabited Indian village on the continent. This statement is made neither boastfully nor without evidence. Borax Lake, a remnant lake of earlier, wetter times, lies a few hundred yards from the present day rancheria. Arrow and lance points of the typical elegantly fluted Clovis design have been found at Borax Lake, lending credence to the belief that this site has been occupied possibly for as long as 12,000 years.

E'lem has the characteristics of a perfect site for a settlement. The village occupies a small peninsula which juts into Clear Lake, the largest natural freshwater body in western California. Its eastern edge, a wide tule marsh, attracted birds, game, and a multitude of fish. Tule was employed for housing and boats as well as food—it is still used for carpeting the roundhouse floor.

Volcanic necks and cones surround the area, the most outstanding of which is Mt. Kanocti, the sacred mountain of the Pomo people. Volcanics such as these provided a wealth of obsidian—the natural glass for making arrow points and a source of trade income. The magnificent setting and its natural resources have made this a very desirable place. As a modern Indian community, it was organized in 1949, but nothing was done to improve the condition of the people living

here on its 52 acres. In the 1990s E'lem had fierce unrest, widely reported in the press.

But the magnificence of the place and the spiritual persistence of its people will eventually serve to restore this village to the peace, tranquillity, and prosperity that it deserves. I expect that it will take a long time, for there is a lot to do. A conversation with tribal informant Marvin Brown, in his yard under the oaks by the shores of Clear Lake at E'lem.

MARVIN BROWN:

"For centuries, all the Pomo people knew of this place as E'lem; I think it means "rock people", since it is built on rock. The [Pomo] chief was the leader of the place and the people for miles around here; he was also a cultural leader and a great organizer. *Ma-chu-chik* was the last great chief for this eastern end of the lake, and he is buried here. In the old days we had as many as 30 or 40 Indian doctors in this tribe, but we don't have one today. My dad knew powerful medicine men of his time and a few "bear men"; both protected the tribe in one way or the other. Now we use some of that medicine; being on a reservation we know what roots to get for whatever: poison oak, for example, we use Indian soap. We know some of our roots, herbs, bulbs, tule, and berries, but not all the proper names for them. My dad could and would go up the mountain and eat stuff all the way up; he knew what was edible. You know nettle, the stinging plant? My dad and uncle would cut off parts in the middle, peel the stinging outside off and eat it like a carrot. I ate some too and it was good and sweet.

"We don't have any basket weavers here now. My grandmother on my father's side, Lena Brown, Ma-chu-chik's daughter, had about 20 or 30 baskets at her house, which she had made. They were beautiful, and the designs were pure Pomo, some with feathers and some could hold water. She was real proud of her work, big and small. I believe her daughter inherited them, and they are gone now. I think the baskets were eventually sold or given away.

"*Mu-dóne* was our island; actually it was connected to us by a shallow marsh. But way back when, the new county locals took it from us by dredging the low marsh and selling the island. Now recently, they say it was sold to them for $40. The Indians here named it Rattlesnake Island to keep people off the island—and it has worked to this day. A coyote trick with flavor, if you will. There is a plant there, when the wind blows at night it sounds like a rattlesnake I've slept there many nights, I know. Once when the phone and the power companies came on our land to run lines over to the island, my aunt ran them off with a shotgun. Goats are there now cleaning out the 35 acres and keeping the brush down, but it's still not developed. When we had our casino running, the new [island] owners wanted to sell it back to us for $1 million!

"IT WAS THE NATURAL RESOURCES that brought the beginning of trouble to E'lem. First, Chinese workers for the Borax Company came to take borax and sulfur in the 1860s [from the volcanic intrusion right next to the rancheria—from which came the misspelled name Sulphur Bank Mine]. Next came the American mining company in the 1880s to get mercury from the mine, calling it "quicksilver" and taking $29 million worth out of here to save our country in WWII ...so they say. They mined for many years after the war, well into the late 1950s, leaving a 417-foot hole and putting piles of mercury tailings alongside of our village like small bare mountains, and pumping toxic waste directly into the lake. Then came the geothermal well drillers in the late 1960s, drilling holes down to 5,317 ft. deep. But the steam was too wet to use. [Some vents still steam like geysers.] When the government told them to clean it up after the companies closed down, they went bankrupt, leaving us this huge hole with a toxic mess at the bottom, which they now know is leaking into the lake. Enter the E.P.A, and the "Superfund": they are still studying the problem—and will be for years.

"It was only in 1969 that electricity was brought to the reservation, and in 1970 water and sewers along with new houses. We moved into the houses in 1972. Before that we got our water directly from the lake. We strained buckets full of water through cloth before using it, then washed our clothes, dishes, and took baths in warm, heated water. But drinking water came in big metal milk cans that we got from a very good local store owner, three miles away in Clearlake Oaks. We had outhouses and kerosene lanterns, The simple life was a happy life.

"When the new houses and new roads were being built, the government decided to grade our roads and level some old housing foundations to keep us above flood level. They used the old mercury mine tailings to build our roads and raise our new houses. We have had major health problems ever since; we were tracking the dust all over our yards and carpets without knowing that it was highly toxic. They're saying the mercury's going to kill us or make us go crazy and they want us to leave our homeland.

"The EPA came, looked, and declared it a Superfund Site, but there is always a holdup of one sort or another. They've been 'studying' it for 20 years. It took them four years to find out that mercury from the pit was getting into the lake; it's only a few hundred feet away. Maybe it's leaking through an old mine shaft, or maybe it was pumped into the lake. I'm only guessing. Hopefully, one day they will fill the hole and give us back the land that also was part of our village. A group from UC Davis came to plant over some of the bare mountains of mercury tailings that keep washing into the lake. Ironically, it seems that coyote bush thrives on the soil there, so they are planting a lot of it. They're also following the mercury levels and the health conditions here. They say the levels are going down, but I don't believe it. Because after every rain we have to avoid the flock [foam] on our lake fronts, and it has the worst mercury levels.

"We have a lot of spiritual things here, especially our great roundhouse. I believe because of this strong spirit, no one was killed in our recent casino troubles of 1995. It also has to do with the way we have treated people and the right way we try to live. We feel we have made the right choices, under the worst of circumstances. People here haven't had that much education and they sometimes don't seem to have much incentive to learn better skills. They want jobs, but they are hard to come by unless our leaders create these jobs. Before our father died, he told us to take care of our people—no one else cares for them. We hope that our troubles are now behind us, and we deserve a better day and brighter future.

"In our future we deserve new housing, but that won't happen until the EPA gets through with their dirt removal. Every time there is a change, of which there have been a few dozen, it seems they have to have an Act of Congress to get something going again. Rehab of our houses needs to be done. New homes, land, island, hotel-marina, museum, golf course, sports complex, bank, church, community center and yes, another casino are hopefully in our near future.

"Our traditional dance group is still alive and well. We still sing the oldest of the Pomo songs when our shakehead dancers perform. I like to think we have the best dancers around. We have performed all over the state and outside the state also, many times. Also the Big Head dance is performed in seasonal regularity. I believe the Great Father gave this to us to lead us down the right road, because in the end, we will follow what we know to be true."

—Marvin Brown, Tribal Informant

E'LEM IS PROBABLY AS OLD AS ANY CONTINUOUSLY INHABITED INDIAN VILLAGE ON THE CONTINENT

WE PAID A VISIT to the outstanding roundhouse in the center of the village. The ceiling has been wrought with meticulous carpentry work in an intricate design and the floor is periodically refreshed with fragrant tules to sit on. At this writing, it appears to have weathered all elements and turmoil without harm. (See p.68).

57 *From Hwy. 20, just S of Clearlake Oaks, take Sulphur Bank Rd. E about 1 1/2 mi. to the old mine tailings. The rancheria road is to the right.*
E'LEM INDIAN COLONY
P.O. Box 126, Clearlake, CA 95423

ANDERSON MARSH STATE PARK

Ancestral Southeastern *Pomo* land, Lake County

As the natural beauty of Clear Lake becomes more and more obscure owing to development, aspirations of preserving it become more difficult. Anderson Marsh is a designated preservation area. The 900-acre park is the site of an old ranch located at the outlet of Clear Lake into Cache Creek. The tule reeds of the marsh have been used by the native lake dwellers for centuries, and the park itself contains the remains of an ancient village site, partly excavated. Unfortunately, a busy county building intrudes on the south margin of the marsh.

UNDER THE GUIDANCE of some local Pomos, some model tule huts have been erected in the oak savannah adjacent to the marsh—now deserted but for the multitude of wildlife. The old ranch buildings have been converted into a small museum.

A visit here with a long walk around the marsh gave me a profound sense of going back in time to a tranquil meadow by an ancient quiet village.

Entrance from Hwy. 53 on SW bank of Cache Creek in Lower Lake.
CLEARLAKE STATE PARK
Kelseyville, CA
(707) 279-4293.

Anderson Marsh on the southern end of Clear Lake, adjacent to the Putah Creek outflow. Marshlands were, and are central to the ecological health and the sustenance of a native population.

(dhe, 1999)

SOUTHERN POMO

CLOVERDALE RANCHERIA (KHALANHKO)

Southern Pomo (1921) Sonoma County

Between a small vineyard and a sawdust-pressing factory on 20 acres of land live the families who now privately own this rancheria. It is still a Federally-recognized rancheria with more than 150 members, but no land is in trust. In the 1980s, the U.S. 101 freeway sliced the rancheria, leaving its ancient site and burial ground by the river separated from a second residential part. CalTrans promised to name a bridge for a dispossessed family and help develop the river side into a park. It never happened. Otherwise, the western part, adjacent to local industries, is in reality a suburb of Cloverdale, an otherwise pretty town in a wide part of the Russian River valley, with low mountains of the Coast Range on both sides. Progress is reserved for the future, but plans are there.

58 *S side of Cloverdale, E along Santana Rd. which is cut into 2 pieces, E & W, by Hwy.101. E part accessed from Asti Rd.. Tribal office in town.*
CLOVERDALE RANCHERIA
555 S. Cloverdale Blvd, Ste 1, Cloverdale, CA 95926

DRY CREEK RANCHERIA

Southern Pomo and *Wappo* (1906) Sonoma Co.

High, and dry in summer, on a hillside with panoramic vistas of the Russian River and Alexander Valley sits this interesting rancheria— the closest one to San Francisco. Excellent Indian artwork graces the walls of the well-kept mobile home which serves as the tribal offices and community center; flowers grace the yards of most homes; a large water tank supplies the needs of the little rural community, very much like a busy little mountain village.

HERE, ON SOME 75 ACRES (actually in ancient Wappo domain) live a number of the area's Southern Pomo people—several elderly and retired, but also a few children, who commute from home to school by bus. Tradition is preserved with the Dry Creek dancers, which pays visits to numerous local events. The Rancheria is not near Dry Creek, but the people were originally brought here from that creek valley, several miles west.

59 *About 2 miles NW of "The Geysers" exit from Hwy. 128 (between Geyserville and Jimtown) is BIA Rd. 93 onto the rancheria.*
DRY CREEK RANCHERIA
P.O. Box 607, Geyserville, CA 95441

KASHAYA POMO

KASHAYA RANCHERIA
(Cu~nú~nu shinal)

Kashaya Pomo (1916) Sonoma Co.

Some reservations are on plains or meadows, hills, or mountains. Some are in towns, but most are rural. This one, though, is the only one deep in a redwood forest, in the heart of ancient Kashaya country. It is the Kashaya's only rancheria, although many of this people live no more than 50 miles away.

The towering redwoods absorb all extraneous sounds, and the quiet solitude of these 40 acres persuades visitor and resident alike to be still. Despite the remoteness of the rancheria, there is an elementary school, where classes in the traditional Kashaya Pomo language are given.

Important for the continuance of the Kashaya culture is an active roundhouse—dances are held frequently, with very special festivals of the four seasons: Strawberry (spring), Fourth of July (summer), Acorn (fall), and Christmas (winter). Also, non-Indians are usually invited to participate in these festivities. The dancers often perform their beautifully mystical rituals at other inter-tribal functions as well.

A second, inactive roundhouse is here, too. This was the sanctuary of the very famous and influential Bole-Maru religious leader, Essie Parrish. When she passed on, the sanctuary was closed. Many of her exceptional family have been active Kashaya spiritual leaders; much of her medicine was passed on to her children.

The intense spiritual and environmental impact upon California from Kashaya is far out of proportion to its small size and small population. Without a doubt this blessing is the living legacy of Essie Parrish.

60 *From Hwy. 1, follow Stewarts Point-Skaggs Spring Rd. about 4 winding miles east, through the forests along the Gualala River to the rancheria—a hilltop clearing covered with redwoods. Or approach it 20 mi. W of Healdsburg via Dry Creek Rd.*
KASHAYA RANCHERIA
P.O. Box 38, Stewarts Point, CA 95480

BO~CAH AMA

Coastal Pomo, Mendocino County

Bo-Cah Ama is a cultural organization serving Pomo people living near the Pacific coast, many of whom are not rancheria residents. The members of this group live from Stewarts Point north to Fort Bragg. They gather in various small groups to weave baskets, practice dance, to share their history and family stories. And they gather to dance in public once a year.

The organization is currently (1999) constructing a model Coastal Pomo village on the site, which includes a dwelling circle, dance ground, and various exhibitions.

The coast is known for its magnificence; their site to hold the annual gathering in the summer partakes of

that magnificence in an open glade. On the coastal bench, high above pulsing waves, but never out of earshot, winds strike the cliff and and fly overhead—over the tall pines and redwoods bordering the glade. And the smoke from the fire first rises, then flies

The Bo-Cah-Ama organization of Coastal Pomo people hold their annual dances in Mendocino Headlands State Park, which will soon feature a model Coastal Pomo village. (dhe, 1996)

inland; the dance songs fly outward to everyone, and the camping there is the best.

28 *mi. N of 56 Location for the annual dance: Mendocino Headlands State Park—entrance off Hwy. 1 S of Big River. Continue to the Pomo Demonstration Village, Museum and dance arena. [Affiliated with the Mendocino Area Parks Association]*
BO-CAH AMA COUNCIL
P.O. Box 1387, Mendocino, CA 95460

LYTTON INDIAN COMMUNITY

Pomo, Wappo(?) Sonoma County

Not far from the Wappo Alexander Valley Rancheria was the 50-acre Lytton Rancheria (at Lytton Springs), today completely sold off to pay debts incurred after termination. The rancheria may have gone, but the people certainly have not, the Rancheria was officially designated as un-terminated in 1992. So far they have no land, but as we go to press, March 2000, Lytton is awaiting approval for the purchase of an existing casino in San Pablo. Income from the casino will enable the tribe to purchase land for housing and for re-gathering its people.

POMO MUSEUM & CULTURAL CENTER

Pomo Mendocino County

In an effort to "mediate" the submergence of the old Coyote Valley Rancheria, now at the bottom of Lake Mendocino, the Corps of Engineers has built an extraordinary building resembling a California Indian dancehouse. Inside are beautifully-displayed exhibits of Pomo arts and culture, a gift shop, and a small in/outdoor amphitheater. The Center is staffed by Pomo people mostly from the nearby Coyote Valley Reservation. An annual gathering is held in late June (see Calendar).

Just E of 46. Location: In the north shore picnic grounds of Lake Mendocino, on Hwy. 20, just E of U.S. 101 at Calpella. Open Wed-Sun, April 1st to Nov 15th.
Info: Delma Eyle
P.O. Box 53, Calpella, CA 95418. (707) 485-8685

LAKEPORT MUSEUM

Located in the old city hall/courthouse in the town center, the museum has one wing devoted to the local Pomo people and their early material ("things") culture and lifeways. An excellent collection of baskets is displayed, as well as a huge group of obsidian points scrapers, lances, etc. This is a good place to get an introduction to the local Pomo peoples. Illustrative recent tule reed work was done by James Holmes, Pomo of Finley. (*See also Appendix I, Museums*)

ROUND VALLEY RESERVATION
Nomlaki, Yuki, Wailaki, Konkow, Pit River
(1856) Mendocino Co.

Beside an overlook on the snaking canyon road leading into the quiet secluded Round Valley, there is an Historical Landmark plaque stating, "This valley was discovered… in 1854." This presumptuous sign was news to the Yuki people, who had lived there undisturbed for several thousand years. As a reservation, it is one of the oldest in California, established in 1856 as the *No-me* Cult Indian Farm. ("Cult" here means a religion, not a fanatical sect.)

Round Valley was the regional "depository" for those bits and pieces of tribes unfortunate enough to have been rounded up by the U.S. Army in sweeps of this part of the state in the decade of 1855-65.

A large sign at the edge of the reservation states that persons from "Pit River, Waylackie, Concow [Konkow Maidu], Little Lake [a Pomo band], Nomlaki, and Yuki" peoples live here. This is really only part of the story. At times, many other peoples were brought here—Cahto (from west), Modoc (from northeast), Yana and Atsugewi (from east), Huchnom and Pomo (from south), and the Wailaki's Athapaskan relatives, Mattole, Nongatl, Sinkyone, and Lassik (from northwest).

In such a melange of peoples, several cultures disappeared or became totally merged with others. In 1854, in the eastern foothills of the Coast Range, the large Nome Lackee [Nomlaki] Reservation was established (*see p.133*), and a good many remnants of peoples bordering on the Central Valley removed to it. However, no provision whatsoever had been made for support of these persons. Greedy whites immediately claimed the land (*see Nome-Laki Monument, p.50*); consequently, in 1863 these people were herded over the mountains to Round Valley, with considerable loss of life, during a two-week "trail of tears."

In spite of the large mixing bowl effect, many families continue to maintain some degree of tribal identity. It is not uncommon for someone to be identified as Yuki, Wailaki, etc.

Ownership of the 19,023 acres is a mosaic divided between reservation-controlled lands and allotted trust lands (deeded to individuals and families and often subdivided). In 1892 the land was allotted to the various families living here at that time. In 1932 a Senate committee travelled through California, attempting to note the "Indian condition" at the time, but somehow neglected Round Valley. A letter by one William Frazier, BIA official, to the California senator alerted Congress to the dreadful existing conditions. Then, in 1934 the Indian Reorganization Act abolished allotments, made new land purchases, and made available WPA (Works Progress Administration) jobs for Indians on reservations.

TODAY, THERE ARE a number of Indian farms and ranches, and dozens of newer homes, many on one- to two-acre plots, only lately furnished with electricity and water. In the area are a number of lumber camps, but no mills at the present. The reservation is generally very neat, with a 1977 clinic, a county school in Covelo (no Indian culture courses offered), a tribal center, where there are cultural programs for children. The place is very isolated; young people have few activities, little exposure to the outside world's activities, except through electronic media.

Employment here is largely with the with the Forest Service, some independent forestry work, and some dairying. The Louisiana-Pacific lumber mill closed after the company stripped the Mendocino National Forest of its best timber, the same company tactics as in Elk Creek and Ukiah.

Physically, the valley is really round—attractive, hidden, flat—something of a surprise in the rugged, oak and pine-studded Coast Range, not unlike the Hoopa Valley to the north.

Old Fort Wright, which was put here with the reservation, was abandoned in 1876 and converted to an Indian boarding school in 1883. Nothing remains of either, except for a former officer's home.

Round Valley observes California Indian Days in September with a celebration of dancing, crafts, softball, and BBQ. (See the Calendar for details.)

42 From U.S. 101, take Hwy. 162 from Longvale, through the Eel River gorge to Covelo.
ROUND VALLEY RESERVATION,
P.O. Box 448, Covelo, CA 95428

SUSCOL INTERTRIBAL COUNCIL
INTERTRIBAL

(since the 1970s), Napa County

"Songs, dance, food keep us celebrating it all.
Thanks to the Creator for the beauty
and love he surrounds us with each day.
May your eyes and ears be open to enjoy each day."

—*Charlie Toledo*

IN THE MORE NORTHERN parts of California, fewer intertribal councils are seen, since there are few large cities that have attracted tribal members from distant places. However, Napa County does have a good number of persons who feel a need for an umbrella Indian organization. In one form or another, the Suscol Council has existed for about 25 years, and is very attentive to the spiritual, social, and political needs of its diverse membership.

The council can guide persons who need assistance by means of their large network of connections: education in cultural and spiritual values; requests for clothing and its distribution; ceremonial opportunities are provided. They fulfill requirements for a Native repatriation* organization for the Napa Valley.

The Suscol Director, Charlie Toledo, tells us of their prime project: a Native Village of 20 acres has been acquired in the Napa area to be used as a cultural center for ceremonies and gatherings. Ongoing projects include fundraising for this Village and the construction of proper facilities.

Ms. Toledo also tells us of a mailing list of some 700 interested supporters, about 50 percent Native. Their Newsletter advises members and supporters of the Council's meetings, as well as nearby Powwows and Native Events. For their own part, they sponsor a Native American Crafts Fair in late September at the "Town Center" (call for exact dates). They participate in Napa College's Multi-cultural Week. The Sucsol Gathering of the People occurs in April, with songs, dances, and ceremonies. In late November, they sponsor a fundraiser and art auction.

SUSCOL INTERTRIBAL COUNCIL
P.O. Box 5386, Napa, CA 94581 (707) 226-5075

"Repatriation" is the term for ceremonially returning inadvertently excavated Native American remains to a sacred burial site.

PEOPLES OF THE SAN FRANCISCO BAY, SOUTHERN CENTRAL VALLEY & SIERRA FOOTHILLS

THE LANGUAGE GROUPS
THE PEOPLE
The Reservations, *Organizations*

PENUTIAN SPEAKERS ‡
OHLONEAN (COSTANOAN)
largely without trust lands
dedicated land: site (undesignated) in former Fort Ord, Monterey County
organizations: Muwekma Tribe, Amah Mutsun Tribal Band,
Ohlone/Costanoan Esselen Nation, Pajaro Valley Ohlone Council
MUTSUN OHLONE
Indian Canyon Ranch
YOKUTS or YOKOTCH (several tribes)
Picayune Rancheria (*Chukchansi*), Table Mountain Rancheria (*Chukchansi* & others),
Santa Rosa Rancheria (*Táchi*), Tule River Reservation*
dedicated land: Wassama Roundhouse State Park (*Chukchansi*);
organizations: Chukchansi Tribe (Oakhurst), *Choinumni* Tribe (Fresno), *Wukchumni* Tribe (Fresno County)

SHOSHONEAN SPEAKERS ‡
WESTERN MONO (MONACHE)
North Fork Rancheria, Big Sandy Rancheria, Cold Springs Rancheria, Tule River Reservation*
organizations: North Fork Mono Tribe, Dunlap Band of Mono

TUBATULABAL
Tule River Reservation*

PRESIDIO OF SAN FRANCISCO

TULE RIVER RESERVATION

CENTRAL CALIFORNIA INTERTRIBAL COUNCILS

*Shared with other groups

‡ *See Languages, Tribal Origins, and Tribal Relationships discussion on page 12*

SAN FRANCISCO BAY, SOUTHERN CENTRAL VALLEY & SIERRA FOOTHILLS

(LEFT PAGE)   MAP 6

Hokan
Penutian
Yukian
Uto-Aztecan

△ MT. SHASTA

Wintu

○ REDDING

Nomlaki

Yuki

△ SUTTER BUTTES

Clear Lake

Patwin

Pomo

△ MT. KONOCTI

Lake Miwok

Wappo

Coast Miwok

Plains Miwok

Bay Miwok

○ STOCKTON

Sierra Miwok

SAN FRANCISCO

△ MT. DIABLO

Muwekma

Northern Valley Yokuts

Chukchansi

North Fork

Western Mono (Monache)

Ohlone (Costanoan)

MERCED ○

Dunlap

Mutsun

FRESNO ○

Rumsien

Tachi

Foothill Yokuts tribes

Wukchumni

Southern Valley Yokuts

BAKERSFIELD ○

NORTHERN CENTRAL COAST & SACRAMENTO VALLEY

(SEE PAGE 125)

THE SAN FRANCISCO BAY ENVIRONMENT
FROM CARQUINEZ STRAITS TO MONTEREY BAY

SEVERAL ESTIMATES and researches into the early Indian settlement of this region indicate that it was most likely the most densely settled part of California. The reasons were the same as now. The climate is excellent, the food is good, and the people very tolerant of each other.

The extreme eastern "boundary" of this region is the 4,800-ft. volcanic intrusion of Mt. Diablo. It presides over the vast expanse of the flat Central Valley and the north and south ranges of the Coast Range. As such it became the common beacon for the north San Joaquin Valley Yokuts, the Plains Miwok of the Sacramento-Davis area, the Patwin Wintu of the southern Sacramento River, and various bands of Ohlone from Carquinez Straits, through the Livermore Valley and the South Bay. Both the North Bay and South Bay were lined with marshes, which attract flocks of migrant birds of the Pacific Flyway and offers home to thousands of non-migrants as well. Marshes offer food and shelter material, as well, and in the adjacent meadows are grass for grazing deer and elk. Dozens of species of fish were abundant (many still are), found in brackish Bay water, open ocean, and the freshwater streams that enter the Bay, the mightiest of which are the flows of the San Joaquin-Sacramento system, carrying runoff from the entire Sierra Nevada.

To the southeast are the damp redwood forests and streams of the San Mateo Peninsula, home of the Muwekma, Mutsun, Rumsien, and several other bands of Ohlone. Everything needed for sustenance was here.

Existence was neither difficult nor challenging. Concerning village life, religious life, and the daily round of the Ohlone—what is said of the Coast Miwok, the Patwin, and northern Valley Yokuts is relevant here. The accounts of contact by the Ohlone tribal members that follow are insights into life under the Spaniard, a life no longer simple or easy.

SOUTHERN CENTRAL VALLEY
THROUGH TO THE SIERRAS

Eastward through the Central Valley, regrettably most of what we can find of the peoples, both early and modern are mostly archeological sites. Once the most populous of the California cultures lived here, but the massive invasion of other cultures have nearly over-

This is the setting for the famous Painted Rock of the Tule River Reservation. All around is a plentiful supply of acorn trees, willows from which to make baskets, bedrock mortars to grind the nuts, and a permanent stream for water supply. (dhe, 1982)

Digging roots and grubs was a common occupation of foothills, Sierra, and Great Basin dwellers, so common that a common pioneer epithet for Indians was the slur "digger" (See p.31). These are Shoshonean people.   (State Parks)

whelmed the original ones. Only during the last part of the 20th century has there been a recognition and revival of the threads of the first people.

A massive effort to regain their culture and identity on the part of the various Ohlone peoples here has resulted in their increasing participation in Native American events in the San Francisco Bay Area. The acquisition of the former Spanish, Mexican, then American Presidio by the National Park Service has resulted in an expanded effort to involve Native American and indigenous peoples by sponsoring numerous events involving local indigenous groups. Similar Indian activity is expected in the area of the former Fort Ord land of Monterey County. Some 2,000 acres has been promised the local Ohlone and Esselen peoples, "as soon as the military has made the land habitable from pollution left by the Army."

One of the most exemplary efforts at recovery of their culture is that of the Esselen Tribe of Monterey County. Their efforts are described later on p.192.

Likewise, several Salinan families have made great strides in regaining their past in this region (*p.194*). Here, too, are the Chumash people of Santa Barbara county. You will read of their small but progressive reservation and active organizations later.

An ancient site of the Ohlone people (called Costanoan, "of the coast", by the Spanish explorers) is to be found at Coyote Hills Regional Park in Alameda County, near Hayward. The eastern shores of San Francisco Bay once supported one of the most dense Indian populations in the United States—some 3-5 persons per square mile. The people here of the Ohlone culture spoke a variety of language dialects—at this place, the Chochenyo. Nature was kind and provident, so the people found little reason to move about. Settled into villages of 30-150 persons, they tended to stay for thousands of years.

How do we know? They left discard piles, called middens or shellmounds. The one at San Bruno Mountain has been dated at 5,000 years old. Among the ashes and shells were found bones of deer, tule elk, antelope and some human burial remains.*

At the site, local Ohlones and volunteers have erected tule dwellings of the type common for the Bay region. At the Visitor Center, you can find grand panoramas, artifacts, photos, a real tule boat, and

Other shellmounds, direct evidence of the history of peoples before the modern society, have been seriously abused or obliterated. The shell mound of Shellmound Avenue in Emeryville has been bulldozed and built upon. The shellmound on the eastern slope of San Bruno Mountain was constantly under siege by CalTrans and developers, it's now protected. The "law" says that such sites must be protected. However, it has been ruled by courts that a simple covering with dirt and paving over is "protection". If burials are found, a better case for preservation may be made, but then the descendants of the local tribe may ask for reburial in other sacred sites and command large fees for a proper reburial. Thus, developers are reluctant to acknowledge any finds, and take great pains not to report any discoveries.

guides to the quiet, natural beauty of this bird sanctuary-marsh. The annual Gathering of the Ohlone Peoples is held here in the summer (*see p.167*).

In addition, a few Ohlone families tend their ancestors' graves at the San Jose Mission and advise on the fate of other gravesites dug up by expanding cities.

THE SIERRA FOOTHILLS
WEST OF THE SIERRA CREST
~SAN JOAQUIN AND KERN RIVER VALLEYS

South of the great San Francisco Bay and south of the delta of the Sacramento-San Joaquin River confluence, there is a marked ecological change in the state—it is drier than the northern counterparts in the northern Coast Range, the upper Central Valley, and the northern Sierra Nevada foothills. The southern Sierra are reasonably green and pine-forested.

The Coast Range is another matter. The eastern ridges of this range, called the Diablo (the Devil Range) because of its extreme dryness, could support only a very sparse human population. Only a narrow band of green appears, catching the winter rains and the summer fog along the Big Sur coast. Sparse oaks dot the valleys, the slopes are mostly brush, and only the highest peaks sprout trees. This range becomes a huge rain shield. The San Joaquin Valley would be a summer desert but for the Sierra streams that meandered (today highly regulated) across it, searching for the sea.

Plains and Sierra Miwok bands, the several Yokuts tribes, and the Western Mono (a group of Uto-Aztecan speakers who pushed west across the Sierra) occupied the San Joaquin Valley and eastern foothills. The south coast (including Santa Cruz and Big Sur) mountain region was occupied by the Penutian Ohlone and overlapped the Hokan-related Esselen and Salinan (see South Coast for these two tribes).

From San Francisco southward, we see tribal areas more and more influenced, decimated, and often totally extinguished by early Spanish occupation, even into the Central Valley. As in the north, if the reader sees no reference to the remnants of a people in present-day reservations, there is a chance that those people are culturally nearly invisible, but not necessarily extinct.

FROM SAN FRANCISCO SOUTHWARD,
WE SEE TRIBAL AREAS MORE
AND MORE INFLUENCED, DECIMATED,
AND OFTEN TOTALLY EXTINGUISHED
BY EARLY SPANISH OCCUPATION, EVEN INTO
THE CENTRAL VALLEY. AS IN THE NORTH...
THERE IS A CHANCE THAT THOSE PEOPLE
ARE CULTURALLY NEARLY INVISIBLE,
BUT NOT NECESSARILY EXTINCT.

AT THE NORTHERN END of the Valley, acorns and salmon were added to the diet, but oaks aren't found often in the swampy, marshy, often salty flats of the San Joaquin Valley. The occasional hummocks and margins did support the huge valley oaks, noted for their juicy, tasty acorns.

Dwellings here were conical, usually thatch of tule, the most common material. Many villages would have an earth-covered assembly (dance) house, half-sunken, as in the north, the earth being a good insulator from the heat.

Kuksu ideas seem not to have penetrated the religious life; instead, the quasi-religious use of *toloache** became the chief foundation of a system of beliefs. [*Anthropologists use the harsh word "cult," which I shall not. —Ed.*] As we shall see, *toloache* was used nearly universally in the southern half of California—the Yumans to the point of practicing "dreaming" frequently.

BOTH THE MIWOK AND THE YOKUTS of the valley had kin in the Sierra foothills—the latter making contact with the Western Mono, and all of the foothill peoples living more like the inhabitants of northern California than either the Valley or the coast dwellers. Today, we find pockets of these three groups scattered along the Sierra front from I-80 to near Bakersfield.

Once again, where there were oaks, acorns were eaten; where there was bark, homes were of wood; where there were streams, there was fishing; berries and seeds were everywhere. Every people exhibited their artistic skills in basketry, nearly all peoples played similar games (shinny, hand-guessing gambling (*p.129*), archery). Nearly all had tales of the animal spirits—Coyote, Eagle, Bear, Antelope, etc., and many family clans took on their symbols.

THE LOWER FOOTHILLS of the Sierra Nevada, up to about 2,000 feet, vary from rounded, grassy knolls to steep canyon-sides. Over all, there is a dappling and flecking of oaks—tall valley oaks to thorny scrub oaks. Oaks, provider of acorns, the staple protein/starch diet of most of the foothill Indian peoples.

These woodlands and meadows, dry in summer, except for the trickle of streams, easily yielded sustenance to the rather meagre bands of Yokuts and Mono. Then the gold miners surged in, but most withdrew after their despoilage and ravage of the land and its people.

The Indian peoples here, as nearly everywhere, were forced to retreat to survive. Very few reservations and rancherias were provided in this region. And today's foothills land boom has made what places were reserved even more attractive to acquisitive whites. For instance, the former 80 acres of the Picayune Rancheria became a casualty of termination. For a while, only one Indian family was left—although very active in Chukchansi Yokuts affairs. As a matter of interest, the Picayune Rancheria occupies the site of a very early Indian village. Most of the extant Chukchansi still live within a few miles of here, but now, the Rancheria is thriving and expanding.

ANOTHER CHUKCHANSI/MIWOK rancheria had existed near the town of Ahwahnee (not the one of Yosemite Park), where today there remains a burial ground, an old roundhouse, and grinding rocks. Read the story of the Wassama Roundhouse on p.143, 170.

One day I met an enthusiastic group there, planning the Wassama roundhouse restoration which had been tumbled to the ground by the former tenant in a fit of temper over the loss of "his" land. I appreciated the eagerness in the group when I recalled the Indian concept of the vitality of all things, especially ceremonial places. A roundhouse restoration is the recovery of a very ill being. The roundhouse was restored with new support poles and blessed by dancers from numerous nearby tribes: Maidu, Miwok, even Pomo from Clear Lake came to give thanks for the restoration of a large portion of the Indian fabric of history.

Since the Yokuts were probably the most numerous group in all California, occupying the entire San Joaquin Valley and its foothills, it is strange that it is hard to find the traces of this once-extensive group today.

One other Chukchansi rancheria is nearby, Table Mountain (*p.24*), and it is flourishing.

**toloache. See footnote p.170, Weaving of Tribal Patterns*

PLACE NAMES

Place names with Indian sources in Central California (San Francisco Bay and northern San Joaquin Valley).

OHLONE CARQUINEZ: *karkin*, "traders," a tribe; OHLONE: village and tribal name; APTOS: village name

MIWOK & MI~WUK (2 pronunciations) TUOLUMNE: tribal name, (*-umne*, "people of..."); COSUMNES: *kosun*, "salmon," + *umne*; MOKOLUMNE: *mugelemne*, a place name; OMO: village name; MI-WUK (from *Miwok*, the tribe; AHWAHNEE: *awani*, "deep grassy valley"; YOSEMITE: *uzumati*, "grizzly bear"; HETCH-HETCHY: *hatchatchie*, a grass; TENAYA: a chief; WAWONA: "big tree"

YOKUTS and YOKOTCH (2 pronunciations) KAWEAH: a tribe; CHOWCHILLA: *chawchila*, tribal name

EARLY POPULATIONS

Original populations of Central California peoples before 1830:

PLAINS and SIERRA MIWOK: *ca.* 9,000

OHLONEAN: *ca.* 10,000 in 8 languages

YOKUTS: 25-30,000 in 3 groupings of about 40 smaller tribes

WESTERN and EASTERN MONO: *ca.* 4,000

* The numbers given here and in other sections are early estimates, and they are doubtless low. Later estimates show that early counts did not include many persons absent at the time, whether in a mission village, or in a settlement.

PENUTIAN LANGUAGES

Penutian languages probably arose in California; they are found largely in the central and northern parts of the state, and are related to some languages of Oregon and eastern Washington. Ohloneans and Yokuts belong to the Penutian language group.

OHLONE

(COSTANOAN) [SEVERAL BANDS]

OVER THE PAST TEN THOUSAND YEARS the ancestors of the Ohlone Indians lived, gave birth, hunted, fished, harvested a great diversity of fruits and vegetables, managed large tracts of land through selective burning, married, grew old, and died within the greater San Francisco Bay region. Over these millennia the Ohlone tribes inter-married and developed complex societies which anthropologists call ranked chiefdoms.

Beginning in 1769, the evolution of these complex Ohlone societies were adversely impacted and became another casualty within the international arena of European colonialism. That year began the first of a series of contacts between the Spanish colonial empire and the Ohlone people (whom the Spaniards referred to as Costeños, or Costanoans, or Coastal People).

The early Spanish expeditions from Monterey into the San Francisco Bay region (1769-1776) encountered a number of Ohlonean tribes and villages (rancherias) along the way. Accounts of these first-hand encounters were kept by the friars and military

The following is excerpted from a summary of Muwekma Ohlone history (1997) by Alan Leventhal (Tribal Ethnohistorian), and Concha Rodriguez, Lawrence Marine, Kathy Perez, and Rosemary Cambra, all elected council members of the Muwekma Ohlone Tribe. This article describes some history and characteristics of all Ohlone people of the Monterey and San Francisco Bays, then an excellent example of the focused and exacting investigation, research, and derivation of genealogy for the Muwekma Tribe, as is required by the BIA for Federal recognition. "Muwekma" means "The People" in Tamien and Chochenyo Ohlone languages. "Ohlone" is derived from a tribal group (Oljón) in San Mateo County, and is applied to the similar language groups in lower Napa, Contra Costa, Alameda, Santa Clara, San Benito, Monterey, Santa Cruz, San Mateo, and San Francisco Counties. The Tribe also wishes to acknowledge the invaluable assistance of Allogan Slagle, Project Director for the Special Association of American Indian Affairs' Federal Acknowledgement Project in California.

Steve Cesena and son demonstrate rarely seen regalia at the Ohlone Gathering at the Coyote Hills Nature Center (Fremont, Alameda Co.) (dhe, 1995)

leaders of the expeditions, providing important information in our understanding of the nature and complexity of 18th century Ohlone societies and their world-view.

According to the chroniclers, the Spaniards were not initially viewed as enemies by the Ohlone they encountered, but, in most cases, were invited to the villages and treated as distinguished guests. An example of one such encounter occurred on April 2, 1776, near the Carquinez Straits. Father Pedro Font wrote the following account:

"We set out from the little arroyo at seven o'clock in the morning, and passed through a village to which we were invited by some ten Indians, who came to the camp very early in the morning singing. We were welcomed by the Indians of the village, whom I estimated at some four hundred persons, with singular demonstrations of joy, singing, and dancing.

A YEAR EARLIER (1775) the Spanish ship "San Carlos" was the first to circumnavigate San Francisco Bay. On board was Father Vincente Santamaria, who, after having some preliminary contact with the *Karkin* (a northeastern Ohlone tribe, from which comes "Carquinez"), decided to go ashore and visit a village located some distance inland. Father Santamaria left us with the following account:

"There was in authority over all of these Indians one whose kingly presence marked his eminence above the rest. Our men made a landing, and when they had done so the Indian chief addressed a long speech to them…

"After the feast, and while they were having a pleasant time with the Indians, our men saw a large number of heathen approaching, all armed with bows and arrows.

"…This fear obliged the sailing master to make known by signs to the Indian chieftain the misgivings they had in the presence of so many armed tribesmen. The *themi* (chief), understanding what was meant, at once directed the Indians to loosen their bows and put up all of their arrows, and they were prompt to obey. The number of Indians who had gathered together was itself alarming enough. There were more than four hundred of them, and all, or most of them, were of good height and well built."

THE REGION COMPRISING the modern city of San Francisco was the district of the *Yelamú* tribal group of Ohlones. From mission records and ethnogeographic studies conducted in 1984 and 1991 by anthropologist Randall Milliken, it appears that four people from Yelamu were first baptized by Father Pedro Cambon, others by Fathers Francisco Palóu and Santamaria between 1777-1779. Apparently the first converts from the rancheria de Yalamú into Mission Dolores also had relations living in the neighboring rancherias of *Sitlintac* and *Chutchui* (Mission Creek Valley, northeast), *Amuctac* and *Tubsinte* (Visitación

Valley, south), and *Petlenuc* (near the Presidio?). The Ohlone people from these, as well as other villages to the south and the East Bay, were missionized into Mission Dolores between 1777-1787. According to Fathers Palou and Pedro Cambon the Ohlones of *Ssalson* (to the south on the San Mateo Peninsula) intermarried with the Yelamu and called them *Aguazios* ("Northerners").

MUWEKMA TRIBE

Muwekma Ohlone San Francisco, San Mateo,
Santa Clara, and Contra Costa Counties
A tribe, one band of which (*Verona*) once was
Federally recognized.

The descendancy of the tribe from Missions San José, Dolores, and Santa Clara:

FROM MISSION DOLORES genealogical records, the Yelamu intermarried other Ohlone groups, both to the south and the east prior to Spanish contact. For example, Fathers Palou, Combon, and Noriega baptized the family of a Yelamu chief named *Xigmacse* (a.k.a. Guimas), who was identified by Palou as the "Captain of the village of this place of the Mission". Two of Xigmacse's wives, *Huitanac* and *Uittanaca* (sisters) were recorded by Cambon as coming "from the other shore to the east at the place known as *Cosopo*". (The name suffix "-*cse*" may signify a chief or distinguished status.)

Another case of cross-Bay intermarriage involved a Yelamu woman named *Tociom*. Tociom had a daughter named *Jojcote* who, according to Father Cambon, was "born in the mountains to the east on the other side of the bay in the place called by the natives *Halchis*". Halchis is in the land of the Jalquin Ohlone.

It was into this complex and rapidly changing world that a young *Jalquin Ohlone* man named Liberato Culpecse at the age of 14 years (b. 1787) was baptized at Mission Dolores, along with other members of his tribe on November 18, 1801. Seven years later in 1808 Liberato Culpecse married his first wife, who died before 1818. Presumably, after the death of his wife, Liberato was allowed to move to the Mission San José region, where he met his second wife, Efrena Quennatole. Efrena, who was *Napian/Karquin Ohlone [Lower Napa Valley is part of Northern Karkin territory]*, was baptized at Mission San José on January 1, 1815. She and Liberato were married on July 13, 1818, by Father Fortuni. They had a son named Dionisio (Nonessa) and a daughter, Maria Efrena. Both Dionisio and Maria Efrean married other Mission San José Indians. They had children who, in time, became elders in the historic Federally recognized Verona Band (Muwekma) community, residing at the East Bay rancherias of San Lorenzo, Alisal, Del Mocho, Niles, Sunol, and Newark. These elders also enrolled along with their families, with BIA under the 1928 California Indian Jurisdictional Act).

The establishment of some seven missions and two

military Presidios within Ohlone-speaking territories precipitated drastic changes within the first 25 years after contact. At contact, some estimates give the Ohlone population at about 20,000 [*others much higher, considering the abundance of resources in this region*]. However, the mission count was less than 2,000 by 1810. [*See p.39 on population counting.*] Their numbers continually declined throughout the remaining Spanish/Mexican/Californio regimes. The surviving Muwekma people eventually sought refuge (especially after the American conquest of California of 1846-48) on the six East Bay rancherias (above). Refuge was necessary as the other central California Indians were displaced and, at the time, hunted down.

Alisal (near Pleasanton), as well as the other rancherias, became safe havens for the Muwekma and members from interior tribes who had intermarried with them at the missions. This rancheria had been established on an 1839 land grant belonging to a Californio [*Hispano-Mexican landowner of former Alta California*] named Agustin Bernal.

Years later, in the 1880s, the Hearst family purchased part of the rancho containing the rancheria, permitting the 125 Muwekmas (later known as the Verona Band) living at Alisal to remain on the land. This Band became Federally recognized through the special Indian census of 1905-06, and the subsequent 1906 and 1908 Congressional Appropriation Acts designating homesites for "landless California Indians" (*see also p.46*).

During the early part of this century, the Federal census indicated the California Indian population at about 20,000 [*probably low*], a devastating decline from the estimated 1.5 million at the time of contact. Independently, several persons and philanthropic groups (e.g., the **NORTHERN CALIFORNIA INDIAN ASSOCIATION)** became greatly concerned over living conditions, precipitate decline, and concurrent loss of cultures. Among them were Mrs. Phoebe Hearst, responsible for funding the new Department of Anthropology at U.C. Berkeley, and the Department's "founding father", Dr. Alfred L. Kroeber. Kroeber and his students embarked upon the task to try to "salvage" as much memory of the culture from the surviving communities and elders as possible, in order to record their detailed aspects before they were lost. Kroeber, however, was not complete in his research. In his *Handbook of California Indians* (1925) (*see App.VII*) he wrote of the Ohlone (Costanoans):

"The Costanoan group is extinct so far as all practical purposes are concerned. A few scattered individuals survive, whose parents were attached to the Missions San José, San Juan Bautista, and San Carlos; but they are of mixed tribal ancestry and live

almost lost among other Indians or obscure Mexicans. [*The Ohlones were not alone, Kroeber also managed to "extinguish" several other tribes.*]

The surviving Ohlone people of the 1920s never read of their "extinction", nor did they embrace it. The Muwekma Ohlone continued to maintain their Indian culture. Although by this time completely landless, they, along with other Ohlone communities of the region, continued to survive as distinct Indian communities and speak their respective languages as late as the 1930s. The linguist J. P. Harrington, who worked in this region from 1921-1939 with the last fluent elderly speakers of the Ohlone languages, helped preserve much that we know of the culture. The grandchildren of those elders comprise the leadership of the present-day Muwekma Ohlone Indian Tribe of San Francisco Bay.

The Muwekma, along with some 135 other California Indian communities (most landless) were summarily dropped from Federally acknowledged rolls in 1927 by Superintendent L.A. Dorrington of the Sacramento BIA. Nevertheless, since 1979, the Muwekma have politically, spiritually, and culturally revitalized themselves according to BIA criteria, in order to seek reinstatement of earlier Federal recognition. Several thousand pages of historical and anthropological documentation have been required and submitted.

This people has left a record of approximately 13,000 years of human history, and are trying to overcome the onus of their sentence of "extinction" by continuing to educate the general public, academic institutions, and the Federal Government. In 1972, under clauses of the 1928 California Indian Jurisdictional Act, the U.S. Government made a token [*insulting*] payment of $668.51 (including interest for 1852-1972) as compensation for the illegal appropriation of Indian land, minerals, and resources.

Finally, on May 24, 1996, the Branch of Acknowledgement and Research (BAR) and BIA legal counsel made a positive determination of "previous unambiguous Federal Recognition", which dispels any myth that the Ohlones were never Federally recognized. This work of the 300 currently enrolled Muwekma of Verona descent will greatly assist the other California tribes petitioning for Federal re-recognition under the erroneous "Dorrington termination".

THE SURVIVING OHLONE PEOPLE OF THE 1920s NEVER READ OF THEIR "EXTINCTION", NOR DID THEY EMBRACE IT.

**MUWEKMA OHLONE TRIBE
OF SAN FRANCISCO BAY
COSTANOAN/OHLONE INDIAN FAMILIES
OF THE SAN FRANCISCO BAY**
503-A Vandell Way, Campbell, CA 95008

AMAH-MUTSUN TRIBAL BAND

Santa Clara, and parts of San Mateo, Santa Cruz, Monterey, and San Benito Counties

The broad, fertile southern part of San Francisco Bay that extends from north of San Jose to Gilroy, including the environs of Mission San Juan Bautista is home to another band of Ohlone peoples, the Amah-Mutsun. Some 600 in number, these descendants of families earlier drawn into the missions have held to their family traditions in the midst of the growing urban spread. Their story is sometimes nearly identical to that of the Muwekma (above).

The Spanish and American town of San Juan Bautista show characteristics of both cultures. The labor force for both early constructors was from local Mutsun Ohlone and Mexican settlers. (dhe, 1990)

The following information was furnished by Irene Zweirlein, Tribal Council Chairperson, Elvia A. Castillo, and the **AMAH-MUTSUN TRIBAL COUNCIL.**

IN THE YEAR 1797, Father Junípero Serra came to Amah-Mutun Ohlone lands to establish a mission— San Juan Bautista. His presence here was primarily to convert the Native population to Christianity. However, other purposes were revealed: including the extension of Spanish settlement of the northwest territory of México and the maintenance of a cheap labor supply for construction of the missions and surrounding ranchos.

The natives were forced into the mission system, which demanded a high price: the loss of many lives and the cessation of all cultural activities [*which define an Indian tribe*]: tradition, language, and religion.

Father Serra left Father Felipe Arroyo de la Cuesta in charge of San Juan Bautista. He acquired great knowledge of the people, writing five volumes on the Mutsun language. The Padres also maintained excellent records of their subjects for the Spanish government— in books that record births, marriages, and baptisms of the Mutsun from 1773 to 1834. These accounts became the basis for the determination of the lineages of the Mutsun people.

The 1820s saw the War of Mexican Independence, followed in 1833 by the Secularization Law, which intended to close the missions and divide the land among the natives. The plan never saw light: missions were closed, but the rancheros took the lands for grazing. The mission Indian men had to become farm laborers and vaqueros to survive, the women worked as domestics. The Indian was forced to live on the fringes of society, in small houses and huts. One such settlement was just outside San Juan, called "Indian Corners".

Then came Capt. John C. Frémont and the Bear Flag Revolt in 1847, followed closely by the gold rush of 1848. Shortly thereafter, the Treaty of Guadalupe Hidalgo was signed, in which México lost its northwest territories. This treaty, as well as the previous history of the United States, had shown government recognition of the right of Indian occupancy of their homelands. [*All too often ignored or deliberately broken, as in President Andrew Jackson's 1830s sweep of all the southeastern tribes to Oklahoma.*]

The gold seekers had little or no regard for property rights, and they were a rapacious lot, encouraged by the Manifest Destiny mania. After Statehood in 1850, the Federal government took an action in California to deal with the indigenous population. A Treaty Commission (*p.46*) was sent to California, requesting cession of Indian land for "some consideration". After the treaty commissioners acknowledged the legal competency of the California tribes to enter into meaningful political agreements, 18 agreements with 139 signatories were executed. The U.S. Senate secretly tabled the 18 treaties until 1905, and the government took all the ceded lands.

The Amah were involved in parts of five of these treaties. Not until 1905-06 was a census (never published) made of non-reservation Indians, but it did provide a count substantially larger than the BIA's 15-16,000. In 1928 compensation for lost Indian lands of 8.5 million acres of California required a Congressionally-authorized suit and an act to require Indians to apply for their compensation. Such applications required proof of lineal descent from Indians resident at the time of the 1851 treaties. After review, the final listing was called the "Approved Rolls".

In 1950 a new roll requesting additional Indian ancestry information was made. As a Result: the "Supplemental Rolls" were created. In May, 1950 compensation was issued under the two rolls— stipends of $150.00 to each Indian on the rolls. 1964 brought another roll call.

Still, today, the tribal members, although recognized on the rolls, do not have the tribal Federal recognition they desire. These people work many hours at jobs in every facet of society, in projects with Santa Clara and Alameda Counties. They have given educational seminars, lectures, and advice on their Indian history. Participation of tribal families has been welcomed in Indian schools and health clinics. Some have been elected government officials of the City of Gilroy.

John P. Harrington, a linguist and ethnographer from the Smithsonian Institution left an extraordinary collection of notes on all phases of Mutsun life, giving great credit to Ascensión Solorzano de Cervantes, Amah of "Indian Corners" (she later resided in Gilroy, then Monterey). Many of today's tribe trace their ancestry through this woman. Further, the entire tribe is documented as to Mission Indian descendency. We survive and simply ask this government for what is just and rightfully ours—recognition.

AMAH-MUTSUN TRIBAL BAND OF OHLONE/COSTANOAN INDIANS

c/o Irene Zwierlein
789 Cañada Rd., Woodside, CA 94062

OHLONE/COSTANOAN ~ESSELEN NATION

Monterey, Santa Cruz, and
southwestern Santa Clara Counties

Greater Monterey Bay includes the regions around Santa Cruz, Monterey, and Salinas. The valleys of the San Lorenzo, the Pajaro, the Salinas and the Carmel Rivers and their tributaries include fertile plains and deeply forested coastal mountains. The people of this region have always been closely associated—the Ohlone to the east and the Esselen of Carmel Valley to the west—and also with all other nearby tribes, whose livelihoods (and often families) were closely related. Much language of the Esselen was shared with the Ohlone, as we might expect.

This group of Ohlone and Esselen with mostly coastal origins had been initially drawn into the missions at Carmel and Santa Cruz. Presently with some 350 members of mission descent, they are also seeking Federal re-recognition (*see Muwekma, above*). As with other groups, these people can trace their lineages directly back to the mission era, and to the tribal groups associated with them. Tracing lineages, famility cohesiveness, and tribal continuity is almost never easy, but it must be done to comply with BIA requirements.

OHLONE/COSTANOAN—ESSELEN NATION

c/o Loretta Escobar-Wyer, P.O. Box 7383,
Spreckels, CA 93962
ESSELEN NATION OF MONTEREY COUNTY,
38655 Tassajara Rd., Carmel Valley, CA 93924
(831) 650-2153.
(*also see p.192*)
These two groups are discussing merger possibilities.

INDIAN CANYON NATION

Mutsun Ohlone (1988) San Benito County
A small tribe with trust land, requesting Federal re-recognition

Indian Canyon Ranch is the contemporary home of the Mutsun/Hoomuntwash speaking peoples whose ancestral lands comprise the area of the Pajaro River Valley at the juncture of three counties. These lands lie within about a 20-mile radius of San Juan Bautista. Indian Canyon is the original (1887) home of the Sebastian Garcia family of this tribe, whose village lay at the mouth of this canyon at Pescadero Creek. In a recent saga of struggle for Indian lands, a battle has been won to restore to Indian control 124 acres of Ohlone land. Here is a place of intensely earth-oriented feeling and passionate effort.

Ann Marie Sayers, Tribal Chair and a Mutsun descendant living here, in 1988 regained her family land (familiarly called "The Canyon") from the Bureau of Land Management through a complex campaign against bureaucracy. Still to be accomplished is Federal recognition of the tribe. Quiet and powerful Indian Canyon in the Gabilan Mountains is the only trust land for a hundred miles in any direction. She describes her stewardship of the land:

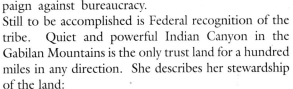

A great resurgence of the fine art of telling a good story, whether traditional, historical, surrealistic, or newly invented is occurring in Indian country. Here, Darryl Babe Wilson (Pit River) is fascinating his audience at the annual Storytelling Festival at Indian Canyon Ranch, San Benito County. (dhe, 1999)

ANN MARIE SAYERS:

"What is happening right now is what my hopes and aspirations are. That is, providing traditional lands for indigenous peoples' ceremonies. We facilitate events for more than 5,000 Native people a year.

"For example, some things happen on a regular basis—a Tlingit man (who is a sweatlodge leader) comes here every Saturday morning; a Zuñi man observes a feather-planting ceremony every full moon; the California Indian Storytelling Festival is every August. Several women's groups utilize our facilities regularly. The Canyon is used on a regular basis for academic studies—we have interns from UC Santa Cruz, UC Los Angeles, UC Davis, Stanford, and other schools.

"Some things occur unscheduled or on a one-time basis. Not long ago we had some Maori (New Zealand) visitors who sang for us—and our wild birds replied. We have many school groups visiting for a day.

"On the premises are six sweatlodges, one of which

is a traditional subterranean type, and each under the care of a different group. Also, we have a ceremonial arbor, a village house (under construction), and our very sacred site at the waterfall.

"Our Village House (*Tupen-tah-ruk*) is on Mother's home site. It has been designed in the form of a turtle, about 60 feet in diameter. We were fortunate to have Grandmother Bernice Torrez dedicate it for us. We have great support by and from the community, including some 30 California Native tribes and nations as Friends of the Village House. The estimated cost will be about $330,000—we accept donations.

"Near the Village House is our Cultural Center and tribal office. Its most important holding is a copy of the 1928 Federal Census, which contains the names of those eligible for the land claims settlement. (*See p.47*). The names in this census are supposed to be only descendants of those involved in the treaty settlements of 1851-52. The 1928 document also includes a denial list [of those denied settlement for one reason or another, often random and arbitrary]. We have lived through three generations of denial [*of our land and recognition*]. Our land was restored only in 1988 by implementation of the Indian Allotment Act of 1887!

Life-giving water sources are always a sacred places, especially in drier climates. This is a waterfall from the spring at Indian Canyon, the Mutsun Ohlone land in San Benito County.　　　　　(dhe, 1997)

"What we are doing is asking for a restoration of Federal tribal recognition for Indian Canyon Nation. We have already received restoration of trust land, but Washington's legal opinion-givers say that if we are not members of a Federally recognized tribe, then we cannot have land in trust. Isn't this a strange contradiction?

"In California there are some 3,000 Indians holding some 18,000 acres in trust, but they are without Federal recognition. The Advisory Council on California Indian Policy has asked for an extension of their own existence so that they can implement the suggestions they were created to make. [*specific recommendations to Congress on Indian problems, p.259*]

"Our greatest vision would be to be able to purchase the adjacent property, which is our old village site in the lower canyon, in trust to honor the elders. The Canyon has attracted numerous persons, pro-

grams, and projects. We are academically well-connected: community "hands-on" studies, environmental studies, workshops in ethnobotany (basket sedges, tule use, Indian use of fire, roots, medicinal herbs). Some of these environmental training sessions are conducted with California Department of Forestry sponsorship and with Federal rangers.

"We are now working through our cooperative agreement with the National Park Service on the deAnza Trail (*p.26-27*). [*In 1775 the route of Spanish explorer Capt. Juan Bautista deAnza from Tubac (just north of Nogales, Arizona), to San Francisco passed directly through Mutsun country.*] This is a hard thing to celebrate, since it was the beginning of the end for many Native cultures. With the **NATIONAL RESOURCES CONSERVATION & DEVELOPMENT** (NRC&D) program we are contacting tribal groups along the Trail. Their perspectives—whether Indian past, colonial past, or present should be presented.

"With the NRC&D, Indian Canyon is being utilized as model of how state and federal agencies can work with Indian communities successfully. The difficulty has been communicating with Native communities—a lack of rapport and knowledge of who to talk to. It is important for people to know that we are a member of the UCLA Tribal-State Working Group for creating a California Tribal and State Commission, dealing with issues of importance to both groups. There are a number of influential people in this Group from state government, universities (UCLA), and the Indian community. Twenty-eight other states have such groups; finally California has begun.

"We have many visitors here, all of whom are asked to observe three rules:
1. Observe truth.
2. Rise above negativity.
3. Take responsibility for the consequences of your actions.

"For all, and especially school children, a "payment" is requested: a Pledge of Allegiance to the Earth. This might consist of a promise to pick up so much litter, to plant so many trees, to donate funds to research.

"I'm living my dreams—exactly what I'm doing right now.

　　　　　—Ann Marie Sayers, Tribal Chair
　　　　　of Indian Canyon Nation

78 *From Hollister, W on Hwy 156, S on Union Rd. to Cienega Rd. 9 1/2 mi., then W on Grass Valley Rd. to a locked, unmanned gate. All visitors must call before arrival.*

**INDIAN CANYON RANCH
COSTANOAN INDIAN RESEARCH**
P.O. Box 28, Hollister, CA 95024-0028
(408) 637-4238
website: http://www.UCSC.edu/costano e-mail
ams@garlic.com

RUMSIEN (RUMSEN)

PAJARO VALLEY INDIAN COUNCIL
Monterey County

A family group, along with several other dedicated Indian families, is working hard to preserve some history and culture of the Ohlone tribes of southwestern Monterey County. They make frequent public dance presentations at local events and schools, along with instruction and demonstrations of *atlatl* use (a slotted sling used to hurl arrows before the bow was invented), early cooking, and living customs. *(See photo, p.17).*

PAJARO VALLEY INDIAN COUNCIL
c/o Patrick Orozco
110 Dick Phelps Rd., Watsonville, CA 95076

COYOTE HILLS REGIONAL PARK
Ohlone (Costanoan) Alameda County

An ancient site of the Ohlone people (formerly called Costanoan—from the coast) is to be found at Coyote Hills Regional Park in Alameda County, near Hayward. The eastern shores of the San Francisco Bay once supported one of the densest Indian populations in the United States—some 3-5 persons per square mile. The people here were of the Ohlone culture and spoke a variety of related languages—at this place, the Chochenyo. Nature was kind and provident, so the people found little reason to move about. Settled into villages of 30-150 persons, they tended to stay for thousands of years.

How do we know? They left discard piles, called middens or shellmounds. The one here has been dated as far back as 380 BC and was continuously used until about 1800 AD. Where there are shellmounds, there was a village. A few other mounds found in the coastal area are sacred burial grounds. They are secret and protected.

This is the only easily accessible shellmound left in

ONE SHELLMOUND
HAS BEEN DATED
BACK TO 380 BC.

the Bay Area, and it was used in the past as a student "dig". Digging was halted to preserve the rest of the mound and was restored to its original shape. Found among the debris were ashes, bones of deer, tule elk, antelope, and, of course, many shells. At the site, local Ohlones, rangers, and scouts have erected tule dwellings of the type common for the Bay region. The conical dwellings have an unusual windscreen in front of the door—to fend off the night winds of the Bay. *(See photo p.66)* At the Visitor's Center, you may find artifacts, photos, a real tule boat, and guides to the quiet, natural beauty of this bird sanctuary-marsh.

The Ohlone Gathering is an annual weekend event in October, held in the park picnic grounds. Crafts, food, and California Indian dance presentations by several regional tribes are presented. (See the Calendar for dates).

78A *Near Fremont and Newark, CA. Just N of Hwy. 84, 1st exit E of Dumbarton Bridge, N to Patterson Rd. (left). Guided tours Saturdays to the shellmound; self-guided tours of the marsh, year-round.*
COYOTE HILLS REGIONAL PARK
VISITORS CENTER
open 8:30-4:30
(510) 795-9385

Pajaro Valley Ohlone and TENA Council enjoy dedicated land by the Regional Parks Department at Mt. Madonna Park, near Gilroy. Their annual Honoring of the Elders Gathering is held every June, with Ohlone tribal dancing, powwow dancing, and Bear Dance. (dhe, 1997)

OHLONE CEMETERY
Ohlone (1797) Alameda County

Anyone wishing to pay respects to the hundreds of Ohlones buried here may do so. This is the cemetery associated with the Indian burials of the San José Mission and is tended by members of the Galván family. (Buried under much marble at the Mission are non-Indians.)

78A *Location: Off Hwy. 238, about 1 mile SW down the street directly in front of the Mission.*

THE PRESIDIO OF SAN FRANCISCO

Ancestral Ohlone land San Francisco County

The Presidio was placed at a strategic point on the Golden Gate to be a Spanish military outpost. Both built by and supplied by Ohlone Indians, it eventually served as a command and supply headquarters for the U.S. Army until the 1990s, when it became part of the **GOLDEN GATE NATIONAL RECREATION AREA (GGNRA)**. Many of the 1800s expeditions to the north against California, Oregon, and Nevada Indians originated here.

IT IS ONLY RIGHT AND PROPER THAT THE OHLONE AND OTHER CALIFORNIA INDIANS HAVE ACCESS TO A PART OF THIS LAND, NOW UNDER THE JURISDICTION OF THE NATIONAL PARK SERVICE AND THE PRESIDIO TRUST

It is only right and proper that the Ohlone and other California Indians have access to a part of this land, now under the jurisdiction of the National Park Service and the Presidio Trust (a very private corporation). An undesignated building was proposed by the Park Service to be the site of the Presidio's California Indian Museum, affiliated with the National Indian Justice Center. Later, however, the "Trust" required all building leases to be at a very high "market rate". Such reversal of intention has caused the Museum not to be located in this long-anticipated site. Also proposed was a site for California Indian ceremonies, likely a meadow or other similar location in a quiet, secluded place, suitable for the construction of a demonstration "Indian Village", not unlike Kule Loklo (Point Reyes) or Ahwanee (Yosemite). The search for appropriate places continues.

In the 1990s, several cultural programs have been presented by the Museum at the Visitor Center, and there is an active Indian participation in large cultural events in the Presidio. So far, these events have not been established on a regular basis, but the Calendar will reflect some activities.

TEMPORARY LOCATION: *Visitors Center, Bldg 102, Main Parade Ground, and offices in Bldg. 96, Presidio, Golden Gate Natl. Rec. Area, San Francisco*
CALIFORNIA INDIAN MUSEUM & CULTURAL CENTER
P.O. Box 29908 Presidio Station
San Francisco, CA 94129
(415) 561-3992 ext 5
email: cimandcc@aol.com

YOKUTS OR YOKOTCH

YOKUTS IS THE NAME of the Central Valley peoples, once numbering some 25,000 to 30,000—in as many as 40 bands or smaller tribes—before contact. These peoples lived in the upper (northern) San Joaquin Valley, the lower (southern) San Joaquin Valley (which is actually higher), and in various groups scattered throughout the Sierra Nevada foothills.

The name itself means "the people" in the language of the tribes, speaking more or less similar dialects. The gold rush, followed by the complete irradication of the winter flooding and seizure of the flat land drove many of these people to near extinction in the foothills.

Most of the bands have amalgamated or blended their cultural and familial differences. Nevertheless, it is of considerable importance that several bands still today proudly maintain their identity, their rare language, and their skills in basketry.

YOKUTS

(pronounced and spelled "Yókotch" by the Table Mountain Chukchansi)

The following historical description of this people is a contribution by Bob Pennell, Tribal Cultural Resource Director of the Table Mountain Rancheria

BOB PENNELL:

"Yokuts was Alfred Kroeber's linguistic designation for all southern Central Valley Indian people and is a kind of misnomer. Prior to coastal missionization in the mid-1700s, there were some 63 separate tribes living in the San Joaquin Valley from Sacramento to Tehachapi. They spoke dialects of a similar language. Some of them used the term *yokotch*, which means "people". This word stuck as a tribal designation for anyone living in the San Joaquin Valley. [*The language family has been designated Hokan.*]

"Northwest of the San Joaquin River lived the Chukchansi people and the Dumna tribe, no longer a political entity. [*The San Joaquin River flows from the Sierra, northeast to southwest towards Fresno, where it then curves northward.*] South of the River were the Ketchayi, Gashowu, and the Choinumni, but they called themselves *Maie* people [*not "Yokuts"*].

"**IN 1833** there was a massive epidemic that swept California. [*The death toll is estimated at 12,000 in the San Joaquin Valley, 8,000 in the Sacramento Valley to the north. It is supposed that cholera and typhoid were the cause, since most of the dead were found near sluggish waters. See p.35.*] The tribes on the southwest and west sides of the Valley were completely wiped out. People on the east side were hit hard, but remained intact. In 1940-41 when the Millerton Dam went in down here, some of the elders from Picayune Rancheria were interviewed. The elders told the story of what they knew of the epidemic at that time. There had been a mass burial in Millerton of about 400 people, but the flood of 1868 took out that mass grave. So the epidemic did hit here, but the tribes seemed to survive.

"INDIAN AGENTS Wozencraft & McKee [*see p.46*] came through here in 1850-51. They set up two treaty sites, Camp Barbour (near Ft. Washington School—four miles downriver from here), and Camp Belt on the Kings River. [*Treaty sites were set up by the treaty negotiators, accompanied by about 200 soldiers who were to bring in the leaders of any Indians in the region.*] Chief negotiator for the tribes along the San Joaquin was Tom Kit, spokesman for the Pitkatchi and Dumna tribes.

"In 1851, each tribe numbered in the hundreds, still pretty strong, because mining had come down the Valley only to about Millerton. The chief for the tribes on this [*south*] side of the river past Dry Creek to the Kings River was named Pascual, chief of the Choinumni. He was looked on as headman by several other bands as well and was the signer at Camp Belt.

"A 22-year-old Indian, Bill Wilson (*Pah Mit*) (1828-1936), was present at the 1851 signings. He knew names of all the tribal leaders in the area, and was able to recite them to several anthropologists in the1930s. [*This was important because it would establish connections between the treaties, later census names, and tribal histories.*]

"Fort Miller was active from 1851-56 [*ostensibly to protect the miners/settlers and the Indians from each other*], deactivated, then reactivated from 1861-65 to counter secessionist talk during the Civil War. By that time, the Native population was nearly all gone. Really gone—dead from disease, moderately heavy mining gold activity, and some shootings.

"We have a photo of Bill Wilson in front of an old building at Ft. Miller, now removed to Roeding Park, Fresno. The old log building, built with forced Indian labor, was rededicated in 1945 by people from Cold Springs, Big Sandy, and Table Mountain Rancherias.

"IT WAS A DIM PERIOD of history between 1870 and 1910, when most of the rancherias were created. It's the toughest time to find information on. It was in 1861 that the people were first removed to the Fresno Indian Farm and another reservation on the Kings River. [*These were on government-leased land near Visalia—the owners made a bundle.*] Then they were all moved to the Tejon Reservation [*see p.238*], and finally to the Tule River Reservation in 1873.

"The best information on people of the area at this time is from the Kelsey census of 1905. [*In 1905, C.E. Kelsey, Secretary of the Northern California Indian Association and a special agent of the BIA, was assigned to survey and report to Congress on Indian conditions and make recommendations for action.*] J. W. Hudson gathered material here in 1901-02, talking with several elders. Frank Latta's information [*Handbook of Yokuts Indians, 1949*] is good only for the treaties and Ft. Miller.

"Millerton Rancheria was established in 1907, but terminated in 1941 when the dam went in. The people were forcibly removed, and there was no compensation for those living on land held in common. Families which lost allotments got a little compensation. They left for Friant, Sanger, some temporarily came to Table Mountain."

—Bob Pennell, Tribal Cultural Resource Director
of the Table Mountain Rancheria

Bob Bautista, a Yokuts medicine man, presents his basketwork and some of his feather equipment in 1920.　　(State Parks)

TABLE MOUNTAIN RANCHERIA
(SHISH~LI~U)

Chukchansi (and other) *Foothill Yokotch*
(1916) Fresno County

For ten years I had been accustomed to drive by Table Mountain Rancheria on a return to San Francisco from foothill events. Each time I noted the warm character of the place and the changes it had gone through over the years. In the mid-1980s, the Rancheria consisted mainly of a 3/4-mile loop drive off Friant Rd. It was a place that was marked by an old church just off the highway, then a series of well-spaced homes, where basketball was played in driveways, and an occasional farm animal strolled by. Things were very quiet, neat, and rather dry. The flat-topped mountain rose to the west over potato-shaped boulders and oak-dotted hills.

Invited dancers help rededicate the restored Wassama Roundhouse at the town of Ahwanee (not Yosemite). The roundhouse and adjacent lands are honored by both Miwok and Chukchansi Yokuts peoples.   (dhe, 1992)

THEN, ONE DAY I spotted a bingo hall alongside the highway, topped by a tall satellite dish. Billboards told us that this was a home for "MegaBingo". And cars began arriving every day for the All-American bingo hookup. Still, the loop was quiet.

The next year that I paid a longer visit, 1997, I was astounded at the changes. The casino had grown; many cars grouped around it like orderly cows at a dairy trough. Roads were paved, new roads that led up to the Table; new, larger buildings were present. The loop was still there, but many of those homes had extensions. Up the hill a side road turned at the proudly waving tribal flags and carved road signs. This is a very private place, to be entered only by persons with a reason for being there—an iron gate says so. After explaining my purpose to a smartly uniformed guard, I was directed to my destination through a web of trail-like roads. Behind the gate are

marvelously landscaped and sculpted hillsides with several handsome buildings.

A most enjoyable and helpful visit with Mr. Robert Pennell, Tribal Cultural Resource Manager for the Rancheria, resulted the following details on Table Mountain. Mr. Pennell is well informed depicts a people who have lived on or very near their ancestral land, have struggled, and are still there.

Our discussion was in two parts: first, a background of the Foothill Yokuts/Yokotch people of this region and the people of the Table Mountain Rancheria (above). Second, he gave a short review of more recent history of the Rancheria, and the eager expectations of its people in a brand new, improved setting.

BOB PENNELL, AGAIN:

"Table Mountain Rancheria was founded in 1916, 'for landless California Indians'. The people in this region had been living in the open or in cabins, frequently on their own traditional properties and were working for the ranches or farms—for the very people who were taking over their lands. Actually, I'm not positive that the Table Mountain people who had been here in the area in the late 1800s were ever really removed. There were still scatterings of families in their traditional lands. When I came here six months ago, doing research on tribal history, I was surprised at this and the later continuity of the people. What happened was that the government came in, purchased a few acres, and pulled in some people living near here.

"There was no real advantage to being listed on early censuses (1905). It wasn't until 1928 for the class-action lawsuit [*a suit against the government for compensation for lands taken in the 1850-51 treaties*] that a pretty accurate count was made. Most people here today trace their ancestry to *Chukchansi* or Western Mono (from Auberry). However, the 1928 census shows descendancy from almost every river tribe that lived around here at that time—*Táchi, Dumna, Ketchayi, Gashowu*. According to ethnographic material, it appears that there were several villages at Table Mountain, and the tribe that occupied the area was *Ketchayi*. There were a couple of families of that tribe here until the 1930s.

"From the 1920s to the 1940s there was a pretty steady population of 55-80 residents. Water was always a big issue. We were not allowed to get it from the lake. Until 1941 three families had lakefront property—it was taken then by the Bureau of Reclamation [*the dam builder*] for $2000 for 160 acres. Water today comes from wells, but the underground stratification is not good for us, although we now have a new, good well source.

"Residents today number 53 adult members, with children, 150. We originally had 160 acres, trimmed down to 44 in 1950 to pay for a viable well and to reconfigure the road. We had one hand-pump until the 1940s. Today the tribe has taken income from their businesses to get their original land back plus more for housing and economic development—now to a total of 400 acres.

"The economic developments are, of course, Number One, the casino. We employ almost 800 people. Everyone on the rancheria is employed—in tribal government, and some outside the rancheria. Our people come from Auberry, Friant, Clovis, all around us.

"Kids go to school at Foothill Middle School, Fresno Christian School, Auberry Elementary, and Sierra High up by Prather. At Auberry, the Eastern Fresno County Historical Society is restoring an old elementary school next to the high school for a museum. Their exhibits include both Indian and pioneer history, along with their excellent photo collection.

"Table Mountain is investing in their kids. We have hired the Cullinan Institute to help with after-school tutoring; we have a spacious and well-equipped tribal youth center with computer room; we have hired a GED specialist. The Medical-Dental-Vision Clinic is at the top of the hill. [*This facility is open to employees and tribal members.*] Other facilities: a well-appointed tribal government office, a gaming operations center, a tribal meeting hall, a social services building.

"We are publishing a tribal history book; we publish a newsletter to and for all tribal members. We have a tribal museum, native village, and cultural center. The core building is a restored building amazingly salvaged from Ft. Miller and stored disassembled in a barn for 50 years, and an additional three officers quarters have been rebuilt as museum buildings. Interpretive exhibits are concerned with the Ft. Miller era and its impact upon the Native American community of this area. The approach to the cultural center is a loop trail planted with native plants and, especially, with whiteroot, redbud, sourberry, and grasses to be used by basketweavers. A recent (1998) bonus is the discovery of a very old village site on a hilltop that was being prepared for housing. Artifacts from the contact era were found, and the round depressions of ancient dwellings were discovered. Visitors are very welcome.

"Finally, as yet, we do not yet have public events, but our people take part in the ceremonial events and activities at North Fork, Coarsegold, Ahwanee, and the Fresno Powwow.

—Bob Pennell, Tribal Cultural Resource Director
of the Table Mountain Rancheria

83 *Go N of Fresno on Hwy. 41 to Friant Rd. and follow signs NE, about 15 mi. to the Table Mtn. Casino.*
TABLE MOUNTAIN RANCHERIA
P.O. Box 410, Friant, CA 93626
(209) 822-2587

PICAYUNE RANCHERIA
Chukchansi
(1912) Madera County

After the depredations of the miners and then the settlers, the Indians of this region had few reservations and rancherias in which to take refuge. And today's foothills land boom has made what places were reserved even more attractive to acquisitive whites. For instance, the former 80 acres of the Picayune Rancheria was a casualty of termination in 1958 and was reduced to half of that as private, parceled land.

In the 1990s, though, the tribe has revived, is thriving and expanding, and with great energy has begun to re-form itself. New housing is being constructed on 40 acres in the very center of Coarsegold. It has begun an admirable program to support the educational needs of its younger members, and it has as a goal of sending many of its younger 1025 members to college.

A tribal administrative center and gaming establishment are under construction (1999) on an additional 27 acres just across the road from its old site. As a matter of interest, the "old" Picayune Rancheria occupies a very early Indian village site. Family ties are important here; most of the extant Chukchansi still live within a few miles. These people prefer not to be called "Yokuts", which is a nonspecific term applied by anthropologists (see above). The tribe sponsors a powwow every fall, the first weekend in October, in Coarsegold.

Ms. Linda Saw, Tribal Enrollment Specialist, has kindly provided the above information.

84 *Rd. 417 leaves Hwy. 41 about 2 miles S of Coarsegold, and about 1/2 mile down the road are the old rancheria parcels. Across the road is the new tribal administrative center and casino. New homes were provided in 1998 in the center of Coarsegold.*
PICAYUNE RANCHERIA
P.O. Box 269, Coarsegold, CA 93614
(209) 683-6633

WUKCHUMNI (YOKUTS)

WUKCHUMNI TRIBE
Tulare County
A Foothill Yokuts people, not Federally recognized

THE WUKCHUMNI are a tribe of the San Joaquin Valley, acknowledged early-on by the treaty-makers (see previous). This group has never had a rancheria to call its own, but the people continue, nevertheless. As long ago as 1988, they indicated their intention to petition the BIA for recognition. Jennifer Malone, a member of the tribe, tells more.

JENNIFER MALONE:

"Our Wukchumni Tribe now has about 240 persons enrolled, but our petition request isn't being worked on right now because the great demands of time and expenses involved have really handicapped us from pursuing our goals.

Our ancestral area extended from Lake Kaweah ("Goweah" is the Native name), down the Kaweah River bank to near Visalia and then to Porterville. [This farming and foothill area is just southeast of Sequoia-Kings Canyon National Park, and includes the towns of Exeter, Lindsay, and Three Rivers.] Our cemetery in Three Rivers and the pictographs at Rocky Hill [near Porterville] are two of our sacred sites.

"We continue to follow as much of the traditional ways as we can: We hold the "End-Of-The-Year" fall ceremony, and have our spring ceremony, too. Many of our children are enrolled with the California Indian Education Association's (Indian) language courses. They have space for 12 children. This is also supported by the Native California Network for language grants.

"We have a project of collecting, preserving, and planting as many of our original plants as we can locate. These are useful in basketweaving and herbal medicine, especially since many of these plants are quite rare and hard to find.

"Several of us do beadwork and basketwork. As members of the San Joaquin Basketweavers we have classes at Tule River Reservation weekly.

"In addition to attending the annual Porterville Powwow, we take part in the Three Rivers Powwow (Venice-Hill Valley Tribes) on Labor Day weekend. "The Indian" restaurant there gives land for the powwow. [Members of the tribe may often be found at public events serving at their excellent food stall.]
—Information from Jennifer Malone, member of the Wukchumni (Yokuts) Tribe

WUKCHUMNI TRIBE
932 Spruce Rd., Exeter, CA 93221
(209) 592-4589

Several tribes from the Southern Sierra and the Tehachapi Mountains were rounded up and deposited in the high valley, today known as the Tejon Ranch and many acres at the foot of the "Grapevine" on Interstate 5. The peoples included Yowlumni (Yokuts of the

CHOINUMNI (YOKUTS)

Choinumni (or *Choynimni*) Yokuts people live in or near their ancestral territory alongside the Kings River, below Pine Flat Reservoir, the Sierra National Forest, and Kings Canyon National Park. Fresno seems to be the big catcher for the remnants of these Foothill peoples. Their existences as tribes, or at least as large, cohesive, extended families seems pretty obvious to me, if not to the BIA. The people know who they are, and they are here.

YOWLUMNI (YOKUTS)

The *Yowlumni* (also called *Yawelmani*) lived on the southern fringes of the Central Valley, occupying land at the mouth of the Kern River, near the present city of Bakersfield. The lands of their range also included some hunting and harvesting areas in the mountains above the end of the Valley.

In the army's removal of Indians in the 1850s, most of the Yowlumni were taken into the mountains to Ft. Tejon, to live with tribal people quite different from themselves (*see Kitanemuk and Ft. Tejon: p.238*). Descendants of the Ft. Tejon peoples are still with us, and have risen to claim their affiliation with their ancestors. We will be hearing more from them in the very near future.

Central Valley, Kitanemuk (from the western Mojave Desert), Kawaiisu (from the Southern Sierra Kernville area), Paiutes (from the Owens Valley area), Chumash (of the high mountain area near Lebec and Mt. Pinos).
(Drawing by W. Philly? attributed to Charles Koppel, 1853)

TACHI (YOKUTS)

The *Táchi* are a band of Yokuts who frequented the lower half of the San Joaquin (Central) Valley around old Tulare Lake—definitely not Foothill people. That lake is now mostly a series of salt and mud flats along the Fresno Slough, although several square miles have been designated "Tulare Lake Bed", which lies south of Stratford and east of Delano. Parts of the lake bed have been diked into duck ponds and the Kern National Wildlife Refuge. Buena Vista Lake and County Park, west of Bakersfield, is also a part of the once-huge marsh.

Imagine all of this, including the present-day cotton fields, as the territory of the southern valley Indians. Plenty of marsh birds, fish, deer, small mammals, salt-tolerant plants of all sizes, heat, and water only from the river. They lived primarily along the San Joaquin River in summer and along other watercourses flowing from the Sierra the rest of the year. Unlike other northern California peoples, the Valley bottom dwellers were not at first displaced by the gold miners, because the gold was not there. When the gold in the hills ran out, so did the miners, who turned to farming, seizing Yokuts lands, killing or driving the Native peoples away.

The displacement from the Valley was nearly complete. The one existing Valley community, Santa Rosa Rancheria, is relegated to a salty field, bordering on once-vast Tulare Lake. For decades, the people struggled to survive in this place, mostly as farm laborers. But things are different now.

SANTA ROSA RANCHERIA
Táchi Yokuts (1921) Kings County

On a clear day you can see the distant Coast Range to the west or the Sierra to the east. Otherwise, the only visible terrain is the very flat floor of the San Joaquin Valley. A mile or so from the rancheria, the lazy Fresno Slough meanders behind cattail and tule-lined banks, or rather, mud flats. A few miles south are the diked-in marshes of the bird sanctuary that comprises what's left of Tulare Lake. This is the country of the Táchi.

The rancheria land is, as usual, the worst of the land hereabouts. The soil is salty, practically useless for farming. Nevertheless, some people have tried small gardens or keep a cow or horse. In this little 170-acre rectangle live some 30 families. Only a few years ago, the only jobs were in the canneries or in the vineyards or walnut orchards. Today, their fortunes have turned around. "Gold" is returning. Carefully distanced from the residences is a casino, The Palace. Casino money has given the families reasonably spacious and comfortable air-conditioned homes. Many persons are employed there, almost everyone benefits from the improved facilities—a good tribal hall, improved nutrition, a good school on the reservation, good roads, and a good water supply, and a first-class ballpark. The tribal center is attractive, around a little cul-de-sac of Southwestern-style architecture. Kids play in the green, well-kept park, or go to school right there under the landmark water tank.

However, Santa Rosa isn't isolated, so preservation of the "old ways" is difficult, although a strong sense of tradition can be found among many members, many of whom have relatives at other reservations in the foothills. At the end of August the Rancheria sponsors a festival—baseball, horseshoes, dances—another in March. It's good for the kids.

85 *Between Lemoore and Stratford off Hwy. 41; between Jersey and Kent Avenues, and W of 17th Ave, follow signs to the Palace Casino.*
SANTA ROSA RANCHERIA
16835 Alkali Dr.,
Lemoore, CA 93245
(209) 924-3583

SHOSHONEAN LANGUAGES

Shoshonean is one of a large group of Uto-Aztecan languages spoken in the Great Basin, including eastern and southern California, also by the Comanches, and the Aztecs of Mexico. The tribe of northeastern California is the Northern Paiute.

(EASTERN) MONO

The desert Eastern Mono peoples who speak a Shoshonean language, are related to the Shoshone and Paiute peoples to their north, east, and south. They have no reservation home and are widely scattered in the region around Mono Lake. There is some family affiliation with the Southern Miwok people in Yosemite Valley, and with the Western Mono (see below).

An intertribal organization in Lee Vining (of Paiute and Mono) serves the Native community there.

79 MONO LAKE INDIAN COMMUNITY
P.O. Box, 237, Lee Vining, CA 93541

(WESTERN) MONO (MONACHE)

The mix of three peoples who live in the foothills in and below the Sierra National Forest (south of Sequoia National Park) are these: various Yokuts bands—Chukchansi and Wukchumni; Southern Miwok; and Mono or Monache—all living in in close proximity to each other.

The Western Mono people sponsor an annual summer Fair, with California tribal and powwow dancing, along with many other activities, plenty of unusual crafts and special foods. Camping and swimming on site.

(dhe, 1997)

These Sierra Mono people are separated from, but related to, their desert Eastern Mono cousins across the mountains to the east. The fact that their language is Shoshonean leads to the story that, early on, some bands of the Eastern peoples migrated easily over to the west. These groups settled along a series of river valleys—the Kings, the Kaweah, and the north bank of the San Joaquin—but their affiliation was loose. In earlier days, as today, families intermarried with other tribes in the area.

In earlier days, too, there was considerable trade across the mountains in summer—the Mono Lake people had access to the best obsidian for arrow points in the whole state. Since this natural glass had very few bubbles and was uniform in quality, it became as valued as money.

On the other side, the Western Mono had access to more food from the riverine environment: acorns, fish, deer and to bear skins, woods and basket materials. The westerners had access to steatite, but it was not widely used. [*Luckily, for steatite has a large quantity of asbestos in it. Steatite, or soapstone, is easily carved and does not crack when heated. It was widely used by the Chumash.*]

A great variety of beautifully-designed basketry was produced. The North Fork Sierra Mono Museum has a magnificent display of baskets of many types, shown as they were used.

NORTH FORK RANCHERIA

Western Mono (or Monache) (1916) Madera County

The rancheria is a small, peaceful settlement of 80 acres of cabins and small homes scattered under the trees of a mountainside. The setting is a little foothill lumbering town, too small even for the usual fast food chains. The temperature varies from hot to snow. In winter the green mountains get neatly sliced off with snow-bearing clouds. In summer, the town is a stopover to nearby Bass Lake.

Give yourself a tour of the old rancheria, now all private land. Many people still live in the wooden cabins with vertical siding, and gray wood smoke dribbles out of the chimneys, although more modern homes are seen noe. You might talk with busy people at the museum, then seek out a local restaurant dinner.

80 *Rancheria: take County Rd. 22 south toward Mamouth Pool, 1/2 mi. past lumber mill to Cascadel Rd. 233, then 1/4 mi. to BIA Rd. 209 at a church.*
NORTH FORK RANCHERIA
P.O. Box 929, North Fork, CA 93643

SIERRA MONO MUSEUM
Western Mono Madera County

Visit the Sierra Mono Museum, between North Fork and South Fork. It is also the tribal council headquarters for non-rancheria residents and features excellent descriptive tableaux and a fine display of Mono baskets.

The museum sponsors one of the state's most intimate and genial and sincere Indian events. The August festival features dances from many tribes, sports competition, crafts, even fashion shows, and great food. Camping. (*See the Calendar.*)

80 SIERRA MONO MUSEUM
From North Fork, take County Rd. 22 S toward South Fork about 1 mi. the Museum and tribal office is on the right.

NORTH FORK MONO TRIBE
Western Mono (or Monache) Madera County

This council organization is intended for those Mono people of the North Fork region who have not had ties to the rancheria. So far, they are Federally unrecognized, but prospects for recognition soon for its 600 members are good. Land has been scouted out and is expected to be acquired after the recognition process is completed.

The Tribe has many members who are basketweavers; they offer classes occasionally, and some 45-60 people clamor to attend.

The North Fork area has some three dialects of the Mono language—with small variations in the way the people speak using added syllables and/or letters. Ron Goode offers the information that there seems to have been two different routes to the various pockets of Mono settlements (*see the map, p.157*) from the Northern Paiute tribal groups. One would have been through the Yosemite valley from the Lee Vining area, the other from further south and then up the San Joaquin River Valley. For instance, the Auberry group speaks mostly the same dialect that is spoken in the region south of North Fork to the San Joaquin River. Doubtless, when the Monache intermarried with their several neighbors, they also traded parts of their languages.
Info: Ron Goode, 133 Sierra, Clovis, CA 93612

DUNLAP BAND OF MONO INDIANS
Monache Madera County

This is another band of Mono people isolated from their kin, with neither Federal recognition nor trust land. Their lands were from here into the canyons of Kings Canyon/Sequoia National Park.

DUNLAP BAND OF MONO INDIANS
P.O. Box 342, Dunlap, CA 93621

Ivadell Mowery, a member of the North Fork Mono Tribe and the Sierra Mono Museum, helps in the kitchen at the annual Museum-sponsored summer Fair.
(dhe, 1994)

AUBERRY (BIG SANDY) RANCHERIA
(Western) Mono (1909) Fresno County

Auberry occupies some 245 acres of a quiet foothill valley. The homes are scattered around the acreage on several parcels of a few acres each, and today all are individually owned. Family connections keep Indian consciousness alive. The people here take part in many activities centered around North Fork. Tribal offices have moved to a small building, where not much space is needed. They converted a beautiful former tribal office building into a small gaming hall. Is this competition for Table Mountain? not really, just cozier.

81 *From the town of Auberry, about 4 miles up Huntington Lake Rd. to a Sierra National Forest signpost, left to the valley floor, signs to (Baptist Church) Mission Rd.*
AUBERY (BIG SANDY) RANCHERIA
P.O. Box 337, Auberry, CA 93602

COLD SPRINGS RANCHERIA
(Western) Mono (1914) Fresno County

Of all the Sierra reservations, Cold Springs is the most hidden and remote. Green mountains surround the beautiful, secluded valley. Small homes, some mobile, others old, hide beneath the many trees, not interrupting the expanse of green. Here, there is only a quiet life on the 101 acres. On moonlit evenings, only shadowy figures attract the comments of the neighborhood dogs. Deer bounce across the path of the steep lane out of the valley.

82 *South of Tollhouse, on Hwy. 168, to Burroughs Valley Rd., go 5-6 miles E to Watts Valley Rd. (don't take it). Left on (unmarked) Sycamore Rd. across meadows, down a grade.*
COLD SPRINGS RANCHERIA
P.O. Box 209, Tollhouse, CA 93667
(209) 855-8459

TULE RIVER RESERVATION

Yokuts, Western Mono, Tubatulabal, Kawaiisu,
Wukchumni, Kitanemuk, Tejon, and others **388**
(1873) Tulare County

The Tule River Reservation was one of the first reservations in California. Because it was so large, it became a refuge for the fragments of numerous Southern Sierra and Central Valley peoples. The people were brought here by Army units in charge of "clearing out" the Indian peoples from their former lands in the Southern Sierra. The most numerous were various tribes and bands of the Yokuts, the people of the southern San Joaquin Valley. Original populations from other tribal groups of the Tehachapi mountain region were not large, and those taken to the Reservation were similarly quite few in number. Owing to their proximity to each other on the Reservation, they have intermarried, effectively diminishing the variety of cultural influences. Nevertheless, consciousness of tribal and family identity still can be found in this very spacious place.

The Tule River Reservation extends from the alluvial fans of Sierra rivers upward into cool, pastoral, mountainous countryside. (dhe, 1992)

TULE RIVER RESERVATION is the second largest in the state, at 54,116 acres, occupying the Tule River Valley between the lowest part of the foothills up to the Sierra forests at 7,000 feet. Lumbering was once a valued income producer, but now logs are brought down only sporadically. The tribe has been concerned that the forests not be overlogged, as earlier.

The lower elevations, where most of the 700 residents live, consist of rocky, nearly treeless dry and mountainous slopes, with the green river valley providing water and sustenance. A number of small farming operations with horses, cows, and sheep contribute to survival. Fortunately, there is room to spread out, and in many places the people live in new, modern, wooden homes.

Clustered about the population center are tribal offices; community center; housing and road services headquarters; firehouse; medical, dental, and optical health services; a church; a school. Some distance away on a flat above the river, the tribe has established a gaming hall, which is said to provide the residents with a reasonably good income supplement.

Tule River holds the Gathering of Elders the third week of August. This is an occasion to hold a small feast, with songs and dancing by invited groups and local singers. Drum groups are well-organized and are in demand for their services in many places throughout the year, but there is no roundhouse, only a large dance arbor. Sweatlodges are used. The California Bear Dance has been held here in the early spring, as well as a Wildflower Festival.

THIS IS A REGION OF archaeological interest. At the Natural Resources Department in the community center, visitors can arrange a tour to the Painted Rocks, accessible and well-protected magnificent examples of ancient Southern Sierra pictographs. Several walls of a cave are painted in both fantastic and realistic designs in white, yellow, red, and black. The colors have been well preserved for hundreds of years, representing animals and geometric designs, most probably for shamanistic purposes. Outside the cave, the Tule River tumbles over granite, watering the numerous oaks of the valley which once supplied acorns for the old grinding rocks there. A short stay to explore this placid, rustic setting will take you back in time many years.

The hills around Porterville bear a number of pictographs (rock paintings) and petroglyphs (carvings)—examples of early California art. High in Inyo National Forest above the reservation I spotted grinding rocks—in a pine forest. Obviously, the early peoples here brought acorns up from the torrid summer valley for summer "campouts".

THE NEW NATURAL RESOURCES Department has begun to appraise the many assets of the Reservation—such as the growth of Sierra redwoods and oaks (and acorns), various wild plants, the fishing, and other wildlife, and tourism. For many years the resources were overexploited, but eventually the people found it necessary to put a halt to this and to reassess their environment.

Life today is pretty much as it has been for many decades, though it has been only fairly recently that services to the population have improved the quality of life—the clinics, schools, paved roads, and electrification to all parts of the valley. As in most Indian communities, the people maintain very close relations with their families both here and outside the reservation.

— Much of this information was kindly furnished by Mr. Isidore Garfield and Mrs. Louise Williams, elders of Tule River, both born and raised here.

86 *From Porterville, take Hwy. 190 to County Hwy. J-42 to the reservation. For visitors, the Chollolo campground (10 miles upstream—basic, for fishing) is frequently open (ask the Natural Resources Department at the community center. Other campgrounds are available in the nearby PG&E Lake Success area and Sequoia National Forest above Springfield.*

TULE RIVER RESERVATION
P.O. Box 589, Porterville, CA 93258
(209) 781-4271

CENTRAL CALIFORNIA INTERTRIBAL COUNCILS

Intertribal councils and Indian Centers are frequently the first stop for Native Americans go to for information concerning health, education, housing, social services, socializing, well-being, and employment. This section is a listing of of councils, often providing the information as to where such assistance is found, but mainly providing a social setting for Native peoples outside their home areas. A listing of several specific services may be found under Services to the Indian Population, p.252.

CITY OF BAKERSFIELD

United American Indian Involvement, Inc., is a referral agency for health matters, education center, and general information center for spiritual and social as well as physical matters.

UNITED AMERICAN INDIAN INVOLVEMENT, INC.
1830 Truxton Ave., #210, Bakersfield, CA 93301
(805) 850-2940

FRESNO COUNTY

No Indian center as such here, but many services and a council (which is somewhat indefinite) are available, if somewhat diffuse. The most helpful agency is Central Valley Indian Health, which is helpful in directing inquiries. The California Employment Development Department (EDD) has an Indian representative, the California Indian Manpower Consortium and California Indian Housing both have offices in Fresno.

CENTRAL VALLEY INDIAN HEALTH
20 N. DeWitt, Clovis, CA 93612
(559) 299-2578)

NAPA COUNTY
SUSCOL INTERTRIBAL COUNCIL
See **INTERTRIBAL COUNCIL**, Napa Co., p. 155

CITY OF OAKLAND
INTERTRIBAL FRIENDSHIP HOUSE
523 E. 14th, Oakland, CA 94612
(510) 452-1235;
UNITED INDIAN NATIONS
1320 Webster St., Oakland, CA 94612
(510) 763-3410

SACRAMENTO COUNTY

No specific Indian center. Various services available through state and Federal agencies. See also Services to the Indian Population, p.252.

SAN JOAQUIN COUNTY
CITY OF STOCKTON

Central California Indian Tribal Council Intertribal San Joaquin County is an organization for the Stockton area that provides social and educational services (through the local Indian center) and for the more spiritual part of life by sponsoring a well-known powwow (see Calendar).

NATIVE AMERICAN INDIAN PROGRAM,
(Title IX)-Education)
1425 S. Center St., Stockton, CA 95206

SAN JUAN BAUTISTA INTERTRIBAL AMERICAN INDIAN COUNCIL
San Benito County

The San Juan Bautista Intertribal American Indian Council (SJBIAIC) furthers spiritual, cultural, and social interactions among the Native peoples of the large surrounding area. It is dedicated to the preservation and perpetuation of the Native cultures of North, Central, and South America, through a membership which reflects the peoples of these places. Says Sonne Reyna: "It is a colorful whirlwind—many faces, many feathers, many cultures."

SJBIAIC
c/o Elaine or Sonne Reyna
P.O. Box 1388
or 311-3rd St. San Juan Bautista, CA 95045-9786

TENA COUNCIL
Santa Clara County

"TENA" is a multilingual acronym bearing the idea of "promise of the spiritual lands"—based upon the objective that the land may become more spiritually inclined. TENA Council was chartered in Santa Clara County in 1981 by Indian activists from a wide range of backgrounds—as Diné, Lakota, Apache, and Ohlone. Although today's membership resides mostly in Santa Clara, Monterey, and San Benito Counties, their tribal origins remain widely based. Directions and orientations of the Council have changed over the years to become focused on issues and specific actions. TENA Council has supported the well-known 500-mile run (organized to bring public attention to promoting and protecting Indian rights), Native fishing rights on the Klamath River, funds for Oglala ambulances, the Big Mountain cause against corporate takeover and abuse of Indian land. They also sponsor participation in certain Sun Dance and Bear Dance ceremonies; they sponsor food drives when and where needed.

The small (20-member) Council sponsors the annual Honoring of the Elders Powwow and Gathering at Mt. Madonna, on ancestral Ohlone land near Gilroy, every June (see Calendar). This event is organized largely by the Candelaria family with help and support from many other sources. The drum group Lost Boyz accompanies many events. Members are active in programs with teenagers such as Barrios Unidos, promoting campaigns against and alternatives to violence, gang activities, and drugs. Local school presentations are frequently given, as well as special ceremonies at prisons in central California for Native American inmates.

Emphasis among members is on preserving and respecting traditions of many tribes, and aiding and assisting rites of passage among their people and others who need their help. Consequently, they are occupied providing sweatlodge ceremonies, vision quests for drug-freedom, help at many powwows.

—Information was provided by Chemo Candelaria, former spokesperson for the Council.

TENA Council may, at any given time, be active or dormant, depending upon the circumstances of the leaders and council members.

TENA COUNCIL
San Jose-San Juan Bautista-Salinas area
contact location varies with the residence of the leader.

THREE RIVERS INDIAN LODGE
All-Indian San Joaquin County
A quiet, rural retreat for chemical dependence rehabilitation. Sponsor of July 4th Powwow. Sponsors a local Christmas dinner for everyone.

THREE RIVERS INDIAN LODGE
13505 Union Rd., Manteca, CA 95336
(209) 858-2421

NATiVE CALiFORNiA GUiDE
NATiVE CALiFORNiA GUiDE
NATiVE CALiFORNiA Guide

BOOK THREE

NATiVE CULTURES
SOUTHERN CALiFORNiA

THE PEOPLE AND TRibES OF THE SOUTHWEST

EAST OF THE SiERRAS

& THE SOUTHEAST—THE MOJAVE & COLORADO RiVER

Dolan H. Eargle, Jr.
Trees Company Press
San Francisco

SOUTHERN CALIFORNIA ENVIRONMENTS
COASTS, MOUNTAINS, DESERTS & RIVERS

ONE GLANCE AT THE MAP might lead to saying that Southern California is the region of the Indians of Dry California. And, as always, the climate and ecology lead to certain similarities in ways of life, but not in all ways. Here is a great variety of language families, probably resulting from both very long-term separation of bands of a single group, and from the intrusion of other families. Extreme geographic isolation of a group is likely to further the differentiation of language.

What is the makeup of this land? An ocean lies at the western extremity, warmer than in the north, outlined by a coastal zone of small and large marshes—today the sections of Marina del Rey of Los Angeles and the harbors of Long Beach and San Diego. Mountains rising to 10,000 feet capture winter rains and snows. Chaparral-flecked hills shelter oak-tufted stream beds. Deserts here are among the driest and hottest in the world; the high plains that neither deflect nor retard the hot and cold winds. Rivers bring streams of water to deep, highly colored valleys and canyons—and end there. This is Dry California.

WHO WERE HERE FIRST, who were the early peoples? As we look first at the northern part, then toward the south, we see an increasing complexity and structuring of life and village organization, as well as formalized rituals. As A. L. Kroeber observed, there are fewer dances, less use of the dancehouse, less regalia and paraphernalia, and an "increase of personal psychic participation, of symbolism and mysticism, of speculation or emotion about human life and death, and of intrinsic interweaving of ritualistic expression with myth."

Many of the people in southwestern California, followed the spirit *Chi-ngich-ngish* erecting to him small, sacred temples with a small skin and feather image—surrounded by ornamentations with elegant geometric sand paintings of symbolic spiritual references to the heavens and earth.

Here, too, the shamans had more power and functions than shamans in the north—they might be rainmakers as well as doctor-priests; they might transform themselves into bears; they might use hypnosis; or they might use something like the "voodoo" of Haiti and Brazil, casting spells upon others.

We find that climate dictated differences among the peoples "The changes in attitude with changes in latitude," as Jimmy Buffet calls them. The peoples of the north, though restricted in movement by weather and climate, were interlinked by an "elite" of multilingual traders and religious leaders. Traders disseminated the goods of diverse cultures. More importantly, the religious leaders established a vast network among the groups,

The coastal environment of the central coast tribes consists of steep slopes of the Coast Range plunging directly into the Pacific, with only a few creek canyons for access. This is the beautiful, inaccessible coast at Point Lobos. (dhe, 1995)

182
NATIVE CALIFORNIA

SOUTHERN CALIFORNIA
SOUTHWEST, EAST OF THE SIERRA.
SOUTHEAST~THE MOJAVE & COLORADO RIVER
MAP 7

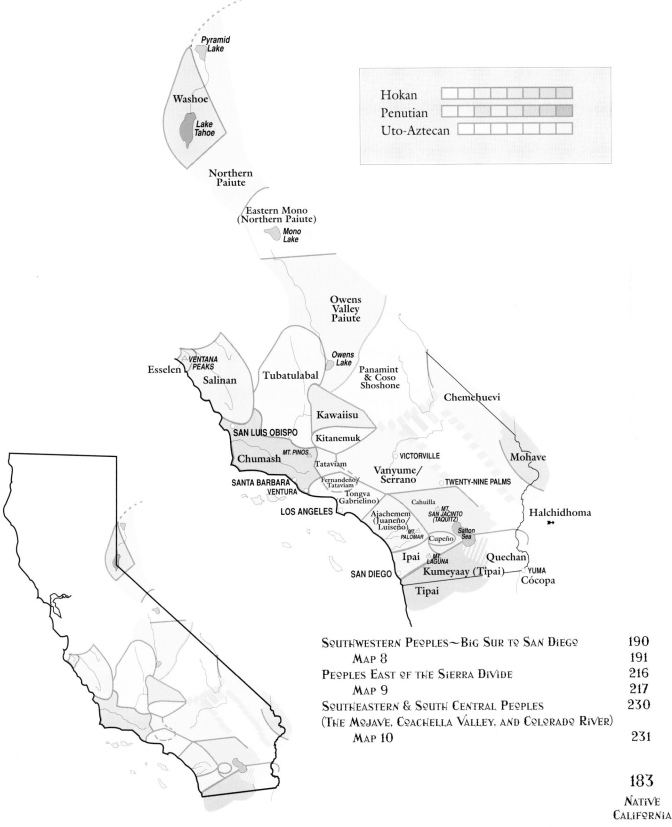

Pyramid Lake

Washoe

Lake Tahoe

Northern Paiute

Hokan

Penutian

Uto-Aztecan

Eastern Mono (Northern Paiute)

Mono Lake

Owens Valley Paiute

Esselen

△ VENTANA PEAKS

Salinan

Tubatulabal

Owens Lake

Panamint & Coso Shoshone

Chemehuevi

Kawaiisu

SAN LUIS OBISPO

Kitanemuk

Chumash

MT. PINOS

Tataviam

VICTORVILLE

Vanyume/ Serrano

Mohave

SANTA BARBARA VENTURA

Fernandeño/ Tataviam

Tongva Gabrielino)

TWENTY-NINE PALMS

LOS ANGELES

Ajachemem (Juaneño/ Luiseño)

Cahuilla

△ MT. SAN JACINTO (TAQUITZ)

Halchidhoma

△ MT. PALOMAR

Cupeño

Salton Sea

Ipai

△ MT. LAGUNA

Quechan

SAN DIEGO

Kumeyaay (Tipai)

YUMA Cócopa

Tipai

allowing their religions to spread and enabling inter-tribal alliances to keep the peace.

In the south, the people engaged more widely in trade, sharing their mutual traditions, moving about more freely. Paradoxically, however, intergroup conflict was more widespread, possibly because the religious network, though extensive, was less effective, and more "border conflicts" erupted.

To those not ready for the desert, it can appear a hostile place. How many times have we said, whizzing down the freeway, "There's nothing there." To its inhabitants, though, the desert was home, and they

Many inland southern California reservations have the quality of Ewiaapaayp Reservation—dry, hot, and remote. Because these lands were considered undesirable by the early settlers, these people were never forced from these mountainous lands.

(dhe, 1998)

found ways to deal with its rigors. The Paiutes and Shoshones of the Owens Valley, the Mojave Desert, and the ranges and basins around Death Valley weren't many in number, but they found the rare water, painted magnificent pictures on the dry rocks, and lived in temporary brush and frame houses, for they were frequently on the move. Remember, before the horse, people traveled on foot.

THE FURTHER SOUTH AND EAST ONE GOES, the more skilled the potters became. *Cahuilla, Quechan* (lower Colorado River peoples), and the *Hamakhava* (Mohaves) showed the greatest proficiency, with their artistic skills in pottery and basketry coming from a Southwestern (Arizona) *Hakataya* influence. North of the southern Sierra, pottery apparently was not made—inventive basketry served the same function.

Over along the Colorado River, peoples such as the Hamakhavas, Chemehuevi, and the various Yumans were living their lives somewhat differently from their neighbors across the desert. Their source of being, the huge river in the midst of a wide desert, gave them the reason to be more sedentary (growing crops and harvesting the riverine abundance), although there seems to have been a good bit of shifting of territories up and down the river.

These peoples acquired many of their modes of life from further east and south: (**1**) earth-covered dwellings, likely related to the pueblos and kivas or wattle-and-daub (interlaced branches or reeds covered with mud, as seen at the Ft. Yuma Reservation Museum); (**2**) pottery making and decorating; (**3**) cultivation of corn, squash, and beans—the only intensive agriculture known in California;* (**4**) a "dreaming" form of inner religious experience; (**5**) a more "political" tribal organization with a sense of a whole people, more like central North American (e.g., Cheyenne or Pawnee) or central Mexican (Zapotec or Yaqui) peoples and unlike the small, compact northern California tribes.

Over Dry California, then, ranged three rather distinct groups: (**1**) the coastal peoples usually related in language and customs to those further north; (**2**) the Shoshoneans, who were more kin to the Great Basin peoples; and (**3**) the Colorado River Hokan speakers, with language related to central and northern California, but with traits borrowed from further east. Each group adapted a set of ancient customs to their ecology, but differentiated by following their own individual inclinations over the centuries.

SOUTHERN SIERRA

The Southern Sierra are not known for a ready water supply, but the height of the ranges and the fact that they are close to the Pacific draw an adequate amount of rain and snow to support flora, fauna, and humans. Tribes, though not populous, were indeed here. The only reservation land was the old Tejon Reservation, guarded by Ft. Tejon, which was dissolved in the mid-1800s, to become today's private holding, the giant Tejon Ranch. Most of the peoples were removed mostly to the Tule River Reservation, north of here, or left to fend for themselves.

Tribes of the Southern Sierra-Tehachapi region are emerging from seeming oblivion. The names of *Kawaiisu, Tubatulabal, Koso,* and *Kitanemuk* peoples are becoming known again, and their leaders are making great efforts to have their tribes recognized in the Federal rolls. Public ceremonies and public activism are bringing these names back into the public consciousness from which they have long been absent. Although the Army roundups of the 1850s seem to have cleared this region of natives and their cultures, many never left, or didn't go far, and they surely did not forget their past.

Unlike other parts of the state, the desert does not support many oaks or their seed, acorns.

SOUTHWESTERN COAST

The other peoples on and around the southern slopes of the Sierras, in the southern coastal mountains of what is now the metroplex of Los Angeles to San Diego, were fortunate to have more water—and more grass for seeds, piñon pines for nuts, oaks for acorns, animals for game, and for those directly on the coast, fish and shellfish.

These people lived variously under what has been described as large, thatched domes, or less imposing conical structures or in summer, simple open sheds (see examples at the Morongo Reservation). Earth-covered sweatlodges and large ceremonial dancehouses were used, and there was often a fenced-in temple (see *Chi-ngich-ngish*, above).

In the midst of the metropolitan colossus of greater Los Angeles, a tribal group is performing a remarkable feat of survival. *The Smithsonian's 1978 Handbook of North American Indians* declared that as of 1900 "Gabrielino culture is now only in the minds of a few people." This would be news to the 1500 descendants of the original *Tongva* (Gabrielino) groups now thriving in the San Gabriel Valley and to other hundreds of *Fernandeño/Tataviam* from the San Fernando Valley.

Characteristic of many emerging groups, other non-reservation southern California groups in San Juan Capistrano (*Ajachemem*) and in San Luis Rey are presently seeking formal tribal recognition from the BIA. "Recognition", even though without land, greatly facilitates a tribe in obtaining government assistance and many entitlement benefits.

THE INDIAN PEOPLE of southern San Diego County were once called "Diegueño" by the Spanish, as if they belonged to the San Diego Mission. In actuality, two culturally similar groups traditionally occupied this land, the Ipai and the Tipai. In recent times the more southern Tipai have used the name *Kúmeyaay* (kú-me-yai) or *Kámia* for themselves.

The Kumeyaay people have a long history of fierce independence even among themselves. During Spanish occupations 200 years ago, many fled to the coastal mountains to hide and to evade capture. When the U.S. Cavalry tried invasion and roundup, they had to repeat the evasions. But now most reservations have a new-found public presence, especially where gaming establishments are successful—Sycuan, Viejas, and Barona.

When, in 1848, politicians and military drew the

A natural rock formation in the Ventana Wilderness, not far from the Esselen Cave of the Hands (below). The Esselen ancestors painted the walls of their most sacred cave with black and white hand prints of the warriors accepted into adulthood by the tribe. This cave is lined with more than three hundred prints, as well as other painted diagrams and symbols.

(photographs ® courtesy of Trudy Haversat and Gary Breschini, 1999)

boundary between the United States and the Mexican State of Baja California, some families of six Tipai reservations were affected by the partition of their lands. A few residents possess a singular the right of dual citizenship in the United States and Mexico—the right to move freely between family lands.

A rare winter snowfall brings badly needed moisture to the Los Coyotes Reservation of the Cahuilla people. The elevation here makes this portion of desert a little more tolerable in summer. (dhe, 1991)

All through the southern valleys and mountains I see the ancient with the old and with the newer. The oldest is the undisturbed land—the bare mountains and the piney mountains, the clumps of oak where they can find water, the stiff green-gray chapparal, the brown and red rocks. Older things appear to the informed eye: the fish traps dug on the banks of a lake from a cooler, wetter age, rocks carved by long-gone ancestors—as long gone as 10,000 years. Along the Pacific coast can be found the remains of ancient villages and their middens of shellfish and deer bones. These peoples traded their especially colorful and best-shaped shells to the inland peoples as money. How do we know? In some of the older villages in the mountains sea shells have been found as funeral offerings, shells that certainly were not from nearby.

Mission and early 19th century relics remain as useful homes and chapels and cemeteries in places like Sycuan, Campo, Jamul, Santa Ysabel, and Pala. Neighborhoods have the permanent and settled look of old towns, which they are.

Here also are new mobile homes and new HUD homes, and cars, horses, cattle, and chickens.

All these sites are part of what the Indian environment is today. To know the Indian people of today, go to some of these places with a spirit of learning and curiosity to better understand their life.

TRY A VISIT TO THE PAUMA VALLEY—the valley of the San Luis Rey River and its tributaries, lying in the shadow of Mt. Palomar. On the north, orange orchards checkerboard the gentle western slope of the mountain. The valley bears a strong Indian character, presence, and permanence, very different in feel and appearance from the white suburbs not far away. The Pauma Reservation is a settlement that has much of the aspect of a Mexican village with the adobe walls adding a red-brown contrast to the green orchards.

Two miles down the road the scene changes in the Rincon Reservation. Things are more active here within a cluster of buildings that have an architectural unity with the grand countryside. Improvement in housing services and the quality of life and living are noticeable, as in health services, fire protection, education, tribal affairs, personal services action. All are signs that the people are striving hard to better themselves.

Throughout Southern California the mania for crashing about through fields with motorcycles and four-wheel drives has been a serious problem. The people here want none of it, so they have posted militant prohibitions on off-highway travel, another sign of ecological awareness.

To go east, up the valley, is to travel back in time. The word "La Jolla" (pronounced hóy-a) is a corruption of Spanish for either "the jewel" or "the hollow" and fits both descriptions. The reservation hugs the wooded, southern slopes of Mt. Palomar and descends in cascading terraces to the cool forests of the upper reaches of the San Luis Rey River. Along the creek are campgrounds and access to stream fishing. The public campgrounds here and at nearby Los Coyotes are superb locales to explore and experience these ancient Indian lands.

ALMOST HIDDEN IN THE FLANKS of the mountain is a scattering of homes, many with orchards and small cattle ranches. From the highway, a careful eye can pick out several adobe homes with yards adorned by flowers and cacti. The quiet, undeveloped beauty of these shady acres truly makes this a jewel.

At the valley head, Lake Henshaw covers the lush marshes that once sustained bands of *Luiseño, Ipai,* and *Tipai,* and *Cupeño,* whose permanent village of Kupa was at the bubbling hot springs. These became Warner's Hot Springs after acquisition by Jonathan Trumbull (alias Juan José Warner) in 1844. The Cupeños were removed in 1903 to Pala Reservation.

In spite of their past tribulations, some 60 *Cahuillas* now live (mostly in summer) on the spacious 25,000 acres of low mountain-land above the hot springs, and have made part of their magnificently scenic homeland of Los Coyotes Reservation available to the public for year-round camping and exploring. Follow the paved, winding road leading up into the mountains overlooking the Valle de San José and Mt. Palomar in the distance. At the top of a hill, further in, sits a tiny, solitary chapel with its separate bell tower, reminiscent more of Peru than California.

From Los Coyotes, up over the hill crest to the south, more Native history is encountered at Santa Ysabel. This pleasant place has been a well-known center of Indian activity for many years, due to the presence a mile down Highway 79 of the Santa Ysabel Asistencia, founded here in 1818, and rebuilt in 1924. The adjoining cemetery, the Campo Santo, dates back to the 1820s.

The reservation spreads over the slopes and woodlands on the northeast side of the road, overlooking the fertile valley above the Sutherland Reservoir. In just such valleys, so characteristic of the southern Coast Range, that a little creative dreaming can unveil the blue smoke from the ancient hearths of Native villages layering the air. Not now. The Native homes only overlook the valleys. The best land is no longer theirs.

Several times I have camped in the Pala valley, feeling the coexistence of two civilizations. A quaint suspension footbridge crosses the river from a cool oak grove to the heart of the town. Amid the very old homes, a young man remarked on one resident's shiny new car: "The finest on the rez." I have the lasting image of an old man leading his saddled horse and dog across a road made white by dust blown from large, whirring quarry trucks.

COAST RANGE MOUNTAINS

The government-abrogated treaties of 1851 set aside as reservation land a huge swath of the southern Coast Range in Riverside and San Diego Counties from the present Interstate 10 to the Mexican border. Today over thirty reservations make up the small fraction of this area that actually became Indian land.

Very little of this barren mountain and desert countryside is habitable without expensive or unobtainable irrigation. So, although they form an undisturbed preserve of Indian territory, several lands are unoccupied: the (hot desert), Ramona (high chaparral), Twentynine Palms (rocky desert, the part the casino isn't in), Capitan Grande and Mission Reserve (barren mountains), and *Inaja-Cosmit* (remote valley) Reservations.

UNTIL RECENTLY, many of this region's peoples were quite content to exist with moderate, small changes in improved housing and community facilities, their standard of living being somewhat higher than most northern Indian land. Typical were Cahuilla, and Pechanga. But not now. Pechanga has found its casino to be a medium of change, and has used its resources to upgrade the living status of its people.

One striking exception to slow reservation development in this region is the Agua Caliente Reservation, which is a large chunk of Palm Springs. Looking about the city, realizing that much of it is Indian land, it is easy to see that finding an oil field here would have been less fortunate for the tribe. Oil makes a mess; leasing land to a city is much more attractive. Another exception to slow growth is the San Manuel Serrano Reservation. Its castle-like casino is the closest one to the gold mine of Los Angeles. Homes and their appurtenances here are large.

An unusual wet spot below Mount Boney, this waterfall is in Sycamore Canyon in the Santa Monica Mountains is near Satwiwa. (dhe, 1990)

EAST OF THE SIERRA DIVIDE

When the maps were made delineating California, the line drawn just east of the Sierra Nevada mountain range, left only a tiny strip of the Great Basin within the State. This high, rather dry ecological area presents a startling contrast to the Central Valley and the Sierra, and we would rightly expect the life of the original peoples here to have been markedly different from those to the west.

THE SHOSHONEAN SPEAKERS of this region are descended from an extremely widespread group: the Shoshone and Paiute of the Great Basin, to the Ute of Utah and Colorado, and even to the Nahuatl (Aztec) of Mexico. They are significant to California because the peoples of this language group not only touch the Sierra on the east, but also occupy Indian country through the Owens Valley and almost the entire Mojave-Los Angeles Basin area.

The narrow strip of Great Basin in northeast California adjacent to Nevada is the country of the Northern Paiute, a people whose lands extend into Oregon and Idaho as well as into central Nevada. Their California lands are included in the discussion of Northeastern California peoples (*see p.110*). Other of these Shoshonean peoples whose lands are within California include the *Mono* (relatives of the Western Mono or Monache), from which we get the name Mono Lake; the Owens Valley Paiute; a portion of the Western Shoshone people (in the Panamints and Death Valley); the *Kawaiisu* of the lower Kern River; and a portion of the Southern Paiute, including the

Chemehuevi (a California Colorado River people). These last three groups will be discussed in the next section.

Generally, the Great Basin groups lived on land that, characteristic of high desert, is very warm in summer, and can be extremely cold in winter. The land is not devoid of water, but one must know where to look for it, and the Paiutes made full use of what there was.

The upper Owens Valley and the White Mountains is home to families of the Utu Utu Gwaitu Paiute Reservation. Beyond the abandoned early buildings are modern homes, many environmentally designed for the high desert climate.   (dhe, 1990)

ONE OF THEIR STAPLE FOODS was fish from the many lakes and mountain streams. Piñon pine nuts were another staple, found on almost any mountain slope. (Paiutes still gather and sell these excellent nuts, indispensible for pesto sauce.) Rabbit roundups were popular, and the deer and the antelope gave sustenance. The many marshes attracted migratory birds.

Clothing and dwellings were of course made from available materials; the most interesting structures were large ten-foot-high domed shelters made from pliable willow trunks, covered with reed mats and/or skins. This design, not unlike Buckminster Fuller's modern domes, provides shelter from powerful desert winds, sand, and cold.

ARTIFACTS OF INDIAN ACTIVITY in this region have been recovered dating from at least 5,000 B.C. Numerous beautiful rock art paintings are known throughout the desert regions of the West, though their meanings remain a mystery. Some of these impressive carvings and exquisite paintings are to be found in California.

Of the few ceremonies that were practiced, an annual mourning for the dead, the "Cry" ceremony, occasionally accompanied by cremation, is still observed in several communities (*see p.235*). In addition, the Sun

Dance and Bear Dance have been introduced from the Great Plains and Northern California tribes. The Ghost Dance (*see p.109*) originated with the Northern Paiute nearby in Nevada.

One activity of the Great Basin peoples that impressed the "anthros" and continues today is the ever-popular hand games (*see p.129*). Few Indian gatherings are held without avid Paiute participation.

SOUTH OF THE Northern Paiute peoples is country of the Washoe (also spelled Washo), who inhabited the Lake Tahoe and upper Truckee River region. These people speak a California Hokan language. They served as intermediaries between the California and the Great Basin peoples, trading salt, fish, and acorns from Maidu country. Today, Washoe land consists of the Alpine-Washoe Reservation, a relatively new site with full-service homes and tribal center near tiny Woodfords, near Markleeville, California; a reservation called the Dresslerville Colony; and a small reservation near Carson City (the Carson Colony), Nevada.

The Mono people occupy a small corner of former Northern Paiute homelands. They have no reservation lands, but are well organized in Lee Vining as the Mono Lake Indian Community, and are seeking use of part of their traditional lands for ceremonial purposes.

Further south, the Owens Valley Paiute people had set up an unusual society in an unusual place: a long, deep, and narrow valley. Somewhat like the peoples of northern California, they too found it difficult to move freely across their landscape.

The Shoshone people here come from the Panamint Valley and the desert country to the east of the Owens Valley. The Paiute-Shoshone Museum in Bishop presents the cultures of both these peoples.

To the north of Bishop, on the Utu Utu Gwaitu Paiute Reservation in Benton several unusual new homes are designed for sun-catching in winters that can be quite cold. Members of the tribe own a gas station/RV park at the main intersection (Highway120 and U.S. 6) with a restaurant noted for its homemade soup. To the south, small reservations can be found at the edge of the towns of Big Pine, Lone Pine, and Independence. Paiute-led horse pack trips to the Sierra may be hired at the Lone Pine Reservation. The Eastern California Museum in Independence presents several artifacts of early Paiute life.

The Kern Valley Indian Council (in Kernville) currently represents landless Kawaiisu, Tubtulabal, Coso Shoshone, and Southern San Joaquin Valley Yokuts living in this area.

The Western Shoshone people once occupied a large region from the Panamint Valley and Coso Range, through central Nevada, into northwestern Utah. In California their remnants are to be found in the Owens Valley reservations, in a tiny reservation in the arid Panamint Valley, and in Death Valley National Monument as the Timbisha Shoshone Band who reside at aptly named Furnace Creek. Their history is in part presented at the Visitors Center.

PLACE NAMES
(Often with Spanish spellings)

SHOSHONEAN (UTO-AZTECAN):
TAKIC
CAHUILLA AGUANGA: a "leader"
SERRANO MORONGO: Serrano family name;
YUCAIPA: "wet or marshy land"; PECHANGA: place
name; PALA: "water"; PALOMAR & SOBOBA: place
names; TEMECULA: "rising sun"
TONGVA AGUANGA [awáanga]: "dog place" (--NGA,
"place of"); AZUSA: "skunk"; CAHUENGA (source
unknown); CUCAMONGA: "sandy place";
MALIBU: "deer"; PACOIMA: "running water";
TOPANGA (source unknown); TUJUNGA: "mountains"
LUISEÑO ANAHUAC: a place name (not Aztec)

NUMIC
CHEMEHUEVI tribal name, corruption of në-wë-wë;
COSO, "fire", a spelling of the Koso Shoshone;
INYO, "dwelling place of a great spirit";
MONO, from monache: "fly people";
OLANCHA: tribal place name; PAH, "water":
IVANPAH: "good water"; NOPAH: "no water"
PIUTE & PAIUTE PIUTE and PAIUTE: PAH + UTE,
"water Utes", i.e., those from wetter places
SHOSHONE SHOSHONE: tso + sóni, "curly head";
TECOPA: TECOPET, "wildcat"
KAWAIISU TEHACHAPI: "frozen creek"

NAHUATL
AZTEC TEMESCAL: TEMA + CALLI, "bath house" or
"sweatlodge"

UNCLASSIFIED
YAQUI: YAQUI: a Sonora, Mexico tribe with names in
Anza Borrego Desert

HOKAN:
ESSELEN ESALEN or ESLENES village name
SALINAN JOLON, CHOLAME, place names;
SALINAS, corruption of e'n-ne-sen, main tribal village
CHUMASH The following are place names, although
slightly altered versions of the original Chumash:
ANACAPA: ANIAPA, the island; ANAPAMU: ANAPAMU
"ascending place"; CALLEGUAS: "my head";
CASTAIC: CASTAC "our eye," a tribe; CUYAMA:
"clams"; HUENEME: "place of security"; LOMPOC;
MATILIJA: "poppy blossom"; MUGU: MUWU
"beach"; NIPOMO; NOJOGUI; OJAI: a'hwai, "moon";
PISMO: "tar"; SATICOY: "I have found it";
SESPE; SIMI; SISQUOC: "quail"; SOPMIS; ZACA

KUMEYAAY/TIPAI CUYAPAIPE: (ewiiaa + apaayp)
"rock lie on" [CUY- is the Spanish respelling for ewiiaa]; CUYAMACA: (ewiia + amak), "rain above";
GUATAY: "large"; JAMACHA: a wild squash; JACUMBA:
"hut by the water"; JAMU: "foam", a village name;
OTAY: "brushy", a village name; SYCUAN, a species of
bush
WASHOE TAHOE: "lake"
MOHAVE and MOJAVE, corruption of hamákhava,
"three mountains" or Pipa Aha Macav, "people
who live along the river" [MOHAVE is used for the
people, esp. the Needles band,
MOJAVE for geographic names]
QUECHAN YUMA: "sons of the river"

EARLY POPULATIONS
Southern and Eastern populations before 1800*

Peoples of Southwestern & Southern California:
ESSELEN 500-1,000
SALINAN 2,000-3,000
CHUMASH 10-20,000 in 6 languages
TONGVA (GABRIELINO & FERNANDEÑO/TATAVIAM)
up to 5,000
AJACHMEM (LUISEÑO~JUANEÑO) 5,000
CAHUILLA 6,000
CUPEÑO 500
SERRANO~VANYUME and KITANEMUK 3,000
TUBATULABAL 1,000
IPAI, KUMEYAAY/TIPAI, including some of
Baja California 2,000-3,000

Peoples of Eastern California:
SHOSHONEAN and HOKAN peoples with territories
mostly or partly ranging outside California are:
NORTHERN PAIUTE/BANNOCK, WASHOE, SHOSHONE,
CHEMEHUEVI, HALCHIDHOMA, HAMAKHAVA (Mohave),
QUECHAN.
Plus two California-only groups:
OWENS VALLEY PAIUTE & KAWAIISU

California total about 5,000,
more in Nevada and Arizona

EASTERN and WESTERN MONO 4,000

*The numbers given here and in other sections are early estimates, and they are doubtless low. Later estimates show that early counts did not
include many persons absent at the time, whether in a mission village, or in a settlement.

SOUTHWESTERN CALIFORNIA PEOPLES BIG SUR TO SAN DIEGO

THE LANGUAGE GROUPS
   THE PEOPLE
      The Reservations, *Organizations*

HOKAN SPEAKERS ‡
   ESSELEN
      without trust lands
      organizations: Esselen Tribe of Monterey Co., Ohlone/Costanoan-Esselen Tribe
   SALINAN
      without trust lands
      organization: Salinan Nation
   CHUMASH
      Santa Ynez Reservation
      organizations: Oakbrook Chumash People, Coastal Band of Chumash, Ventureño Chumash, *Wishtoyo, Mishkanaka*
   IPAI
      Inaja-Cosmit Reservation, Santa Ysabel Reservation, Mesa Grande Reservation,
      San Pascual Reservation, Pala Reservation*
   KUMEYAAY (KAMIA) or TIPAI (formerly called Diegueño)
      Jamul Village, *Ewiiapaayp* (Cuyapaipe) Reservation, Campo Reservation, Manzanita Reservation,
      LaPosta Reservation, Sycuan Reservation, Viejas Reservation, Barona Reservation, Capitan Grande Reservation

SHOSHONEAN (UTO-AZTECAN) LANGUAGES ‡
   TAKIC:
   TONGVA (GABRIELINO)
      without trust lands
      organization: Tongva Nation
   FERNANDEÑO/TATAVIAM
      without trust lands
      organization: Fernandeño/Tataviam Tribe
   LUISEÑO
      Pala Reservation*, Rincon Reservation, La Jolla Reservation, Pauma-Yuima Reservation,
      Pechanga Reservation, Soboba Reservation*
      organizations: San Luis Rey Band of Mission Indians, Atahun Shoshones of San Luis Rey?
   AJACHEMEM (JUANEÑO)
      organizations: Ajachemem (Juaneño) Nation, Juaneño Band of Mission Indians
   JUANEÑO
      organization: Atahun Shoshones of San Juan Capistrano
   _____

   TONGVA, CHUMASH, & ALL SOUTHERN CALIFORNIA TRIBES
      dedicated land: Satwiwa* (in Santa Monica Mountains National Recreation Area)

*Shared with other groups

‡ *See Languages, Tribal Origins, and Tribal Relationships discussion on page 12*

SOUTHWESTERN CALIFORNIA
BIG SUR TO SAN DIEGO
MAP 8

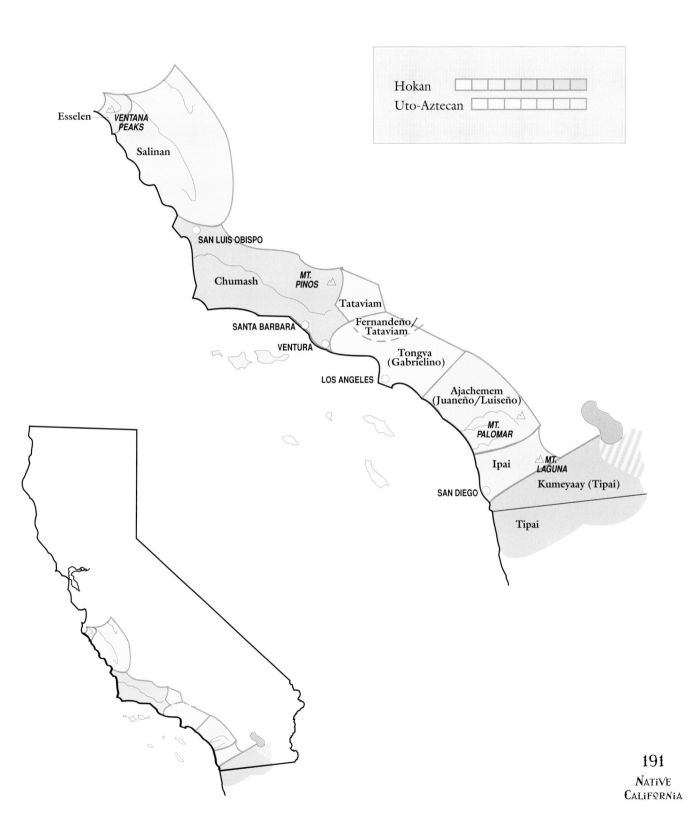

Hokan
Uto-Aztecan

Esselen

VENTANA PEAKS

Salinan

SAN LUIS OBISPO

Chumash

MT. PINOS

Tataviam

SANTA BARBARA

Fernandeño/
Tataviam

VENTURA

Tongva
(Gabrielino)

LOS ANGELES

Ajachemem
(Juaneño/Luiseño)

MT. PALOMAR

Ipai

MT. LAGUNA

Kumeyaay (Tipai)

SAN DIEGO

Tipai

SOUTHWESTERN PEOPLES
BiG SUR TO SAN DiEGO

HOKAN SPEAKERS

The word "Hokan" is Atsugewi for "two."
Southwestern California speakers of this group, which has many related languages around the state are: Esselen, Salinan, Chumash, Kumeyaay.

ESSELEN

The Esselen homelands comprise the land of Big Sur and the Ventana Wilderness area, from the Carmel River, east to the Salinas Ridge, and south almost to the San Antonio Mission—the rugged Santa Lucia Mountains of the Central Coast.

The Esselen Nation has recently acquired the site of an ancient village of Cuchún, along Arroyo Seco in Monterey County.   *(dhe, 1999)*

A FAMILY OF ENGLISH TRADERS, the Nasons, who had rounded Cape Horn five times even while Monterey was Spanish intermarried with the Esselen family of Tomasa Maria in the 1800s, maintaining many of the Indian traditions. The Nason family of today is one of the original ranchers; they hold title to some 1,200 acres of ranch and woodland, and in addition, the rights to graze cattle in some of the 30,000 adjacent acres of Los Padres National Forest. Raising cattle in such rugged country requires much effort, but they run a few cows, and keep two stables with 75 riding horses and pack mules that are used for pack trips into the adjacent Ventana Wilderness, ancient Esselen territory. These trips not only keep the family together and help them retain the land, but also offer great opportunities for spiritual enhancement—for the tribe and for its many visitors.

THE VENTANA PEAKS (in the Wilderness area) form a distinctive geographic feature on the western horizon of Big Sur, and are cherished by the Esselen as a particularly sacred place—the exit to the spirit world, the western "Exit to the Dead." Other coastal tribes have recognized the significance of this place, and have traditionally offered prayers there. Even the Spanish settlers recognized the exceptional quality of the place, calling it "Ventana" (window).

Among many other unusual artistic acts, ancient Esselen placed white and black painted hands upon a cave wall in a nearby canyon, then and now a very sacred and very beautiful place (*see p.185*). From this inspiration, four hands in four directions form the design of the tribal banner.

The Nason ranch is situated on a prominent 3,400-foot mountain saddle, with spectacular views. It abounds with ancient oaks and has a good water supply. The ranch serves as an occasional gathering place of the tribe and is also used as a ceremonial and camping ground.

ESSELEN NATION OF MONTEREY COUNTY

Esselen Monterey County

Stories of the Esselen lands, its people, its accomplishments, and its spiritual leader were given to the author by Tom Little Bear Nason:

A week before the fall equinox in 1991, the first Esselen roundhouse to be built in modern times was dedicated at *Pach-hepus*, Monterey County, California. Only one other Esselen roundhouse site is known, at a remote village in the Los Padres National Forest, abandoned probably in the late 1700s, after the establishment of the Carmel Mission in 1770. This dedication represents one in a series of immense efforts by the 38-year-old spiritual leader of the Esselen people, Tom Little Bear Nason, to revitalize his tribe.

AT THE AGE OF 8, Little Bear had an insight that a spirit was telling him that his future would not be commonplace. As he grew, he realized that his life was following a different direction. With his father and brother, he began first to explore the ancient lands of the Esselen, learning the places and the spirits that surrounded him. Eventually, taking advantage of their ranching experience and intimate knowledge of their tribal land, the Nason family established Ventana Wilderness Trips—horseback pack trips into their ancestral lands on the backcountry trails.

LITTLE BEAR BEGAN TO UNDERSTAND that in order for the dream of tribal revival to become real, he would have to accept leadership, and that deep spiritual growth was to become his privilege. A massive effort is presently underway to renew and recover the shreds of the culture that remain. These are being carefully woven into a renewed culture. Part of the dream consists of an energetic and powerful effort throughout the Monterey County and central California to educate all people about the reality of the Native American presence and heritage.

Always with proper dedication ceremonies, a roundhouse, a large covered dining area and kitchen, and dance arbor have been completed with the labor, support, and cooperation of a great number of persons who have chosen to assist the Esselen people in realizing their dream. Events in this sacred place are held regularly with the contributions of numerous dancers and spiritual leaders, and as all roundhouses should be, it is truly a gathering place for members of all tribes.

THE TRIBE IS LOOKING forward to the rehabilitation of nearly a square mile of nearby ranchland on Arroyo Seco, a not-dry river. The newly-acquired land (1999), lying in ancient Esselen territory, contains decaying structures of original ranch houses (under reconstruction) and archaeological sites including the ancient village site of *Cuchún*. Also, they are highly active in identifying many other archaeological sites throughout their ancestral lands, most of which have been undisturbed for 100 years. Altogether, more than 100 persons of Esselen descent have been located so far, and this small, highly dispersed tribe is striving hard to gain Federal recognition, after having been called the first "extinct" California tribe.

87 *From Carmel Valley, take Carmel Valley Rd. SE about 10 mi. to Tassajara Rd. Follow this road W about 10 mi. uphill to the Ventana Wilderness Ranch and Pa-che-pus*
ESSELEN NATION OF MONTEREY COUNTY
38655 Tassajara Rd., Carmel Valley, CA 93924
(831) 650-2153

See also p.165
OHLONE/COSTANOAN—ESSELEN NATION
c/o Loretta Escobar-Wyer
P.O. Box 7383, Spreckels, CA 93962
This group and the Esselen Nation of Monterey County are currently negotiating a possible merger.

WINDOW TO THE WEST is a unique foundation, sponsored by this tribe, which offers a number of unusual cultural and outdoors experiences to the public. The variety of offerings includes numerous Native American study courses and cultural explorations in wilderness lore, environmental studies, archaeology (of the ancient Esselen homeland), most involving hikes and/or trail riding. Other activities offered are Big Sur Trail Rides on the coast. Ventana Wilderness Expeditions is the contact group: 38655 Tassajara Rd., Carmel Valley, CA 93924. WTTW is at 1780 Prescott, Monterey, CA 93940. Call (831) 625-8664 for programs and fees.

Visit their website at www.nativeguides.com

The sod cover is a roof style occasionally seen in central parts of the state (Coast Miwok, Esselen, Maidu). Tom Little Bear Nason stands in front of the Esselen Nation's roundhouse. To see a different view of this roundhouse in the spring, see page 67, Architecture, Book 1. (dhe, 1992)

SALINAN

THE NAME OF THIS PEOPLE comes from the Spanish "Salinas", or the river of that name that flows from the high plains above San Luis Obispo to Monterey Bay. "Salinas" implies salt, or salt flats, but there are few, if any, such places in the entire region. Even the Salinan people are reported to have traded sea shells for salt from Yokuts just across the Diablo Mountains to the east. A more likely source for the name, from C.H. Merriam, would be an alteration of *e´n-ne-sen*, the main tribal center, near present-day Salinas.

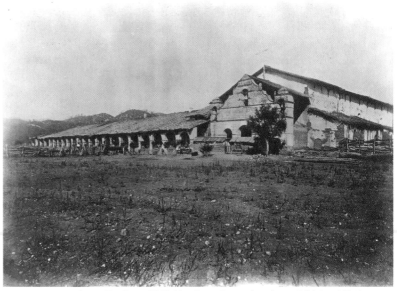

Ruins of Misión San Antonio about 1906. All the missions have been restored to some extent through cooperative efforts of government and Catholic Church historical preservation programs. (State Parks)

The Spanish mission style of architecture, long associated by Hollywood with romantic, bucolic places, was all accomplished with Indian labor, brick by brick. At this attractive Misión San Antonio, Salinan people were exploited to build and maintain the mission, its fields, mill, and cattle. (dhe, 1985)

SALINAN PEOPLE LIVED in a variety of ecological climates: primarily in the Salinas River valley and its tributaries (warm to hot and dry in summer) with breezes from Monterey Bay but also in the valleys of the Coast Range and along the steep ocean cliffs of the Pacific. Livelihood in this region was harder to obtain than to the north, but it was adequate. The Salinan people of today live in these same places, of course, but are scattered and few. Their homeland is characterized by the abundance of oak trees which, over thousands of years, led to their name for themselves as the "People of the Oaks".

The early homes were round with thatching set on a pole frame, somewhat smaller than the Chumash to the south. Sweatlodges were (and are) known. Examples of their basketry and other craftwork in flint can be seen in local museums, including the Cultural Center in Jolon.

The Spanish occupation drew Natives into, first, Misión San Antonio (Jolon), then Misión Soledad and Misión San Miguel. Though the mission "system" effectively extinguished the Indian lifeways, some songs, language, and customs survived in the lives and minds of the elders, who have passed them on to their descendants. As with so many other Indian tribes, revival of the culture has been made extremely difficult by the pronouncements of "cultural extinction" by anthropologists. They apparently did not sufficiently scour the countryside nor the minds of their informants to find that the fabric of the culture had not been obliterated.

Leaders and family of the Salinan Nation's Adobe Center, now tribal headquarters and refreshment stand on Jolon Rd. In front, meet Salina Castle, Donna Haro, Linda and Nathaniel Castle. (dhe, 1999)

SALINAN NATION
Salinan
Monterey and San Luis Obispo Counties

As mentioned above, the Salinan people still live in the country of their ancestors. The tribe of today numbers some 800 persons, of whom two-thirds live within the ancestral lands. And there is much visitation back and forth. The tribe itself gathers annually at San Antonio Mission in Jolon the last Saturday of September to contribute more segments and shreds from the fragments of their history. Their cultural fabric once again is taking shape and design.

The tribe is seeking Federal recognition, and to this end finds a great need for the recollection of historical elements, but as Gregg Castro, a tribal leader says, "The gathering of history has value in itself. We seek to avoid 'recognition' as a single focus." The tribal organization has gained a form of de facto recognition— the authority to monitor and supervise culturally sensitive sites in the counties of their origin.

Fort Hunter-Liggett was placed over 50 years ago on 280,000—now reduced to about 160,000—acres of Salinan lands previously taken by the Hearst family. The Army has recently been attempting to reduce their land holdings in this area, a situation that has not gone unnoticed by the Salinan Nation. A proposal to establish a 25,000-acre National Historical Landmark District, to include Misión San Antonio and its burial ground of the Salinan peoples has had much attention, especially from the "Friends of the San Antonio Mission". The Salinans strongly oppose this project as another attempt to grab their beloved, irreplaceable cultural heritage by a misguided society. They insist on primary jurisdiction over this land.

The Salinan Nation has acquired a landmark store in Jolon to create a Salinan Cultural Museum that will acquaint the public with their history and the rich archeology of the area. They are arranging to have a nearby "home"—the Salinan Nation Adobe Cultural Center—for the tribe members to use as a meeting place, classroom, tribal office, and activity center. The Salinan Nation will be heard from much more in the future.

—information from
Gregg Castro, Vice Chair,
Tribal Council

88 SALINAN NATION
Adobe Cultural Center
10 Jolon Rd.,
King City, CA 93930
(408) 385-1538,
FAX (408) 385-3436

The historic old Tidball Store in Jolon is the new cultural center for the Salinan Nation. (dhe, 1999)

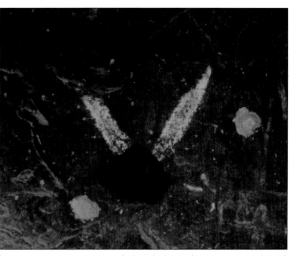

A short distance in the mountainous region behind the Salinan Nation's Adobe Tribal Center are ancient paintings, protected by the Army in Ft. Hunter-Liggett. (dhe, 1996)

CHUMASH (schú-mash)

"AMONG THE CHUMASH, there are many circles. Some overlap, some don't," as one leader advised. This is the way it was in earlier times, as now.

Chumash-speaking tribes once stretched from San Luis Obispo to Thousand Oaks and inland to Castaic and Mt. Pinos. The coast here is mountainous, except for a few coastal flats—at San Luis Obispo, Santa Maria, Santa Ynez, and Ventura.

Coastal livelihoods depended in large part on the bounty of the ocean and its marshes. In summer the land is without rain, so villages were located where the creeks ran all year. Inland, the people sought out and utilized the springs and continuously-flowing streams. These are places where there is often a town or ranch today.

Within the southern San Joaquin Valley and in several lateral valleys alongside, rainfall is only about five inches in the winter, with an intense summer sun drying everything to a crisp. Plants here put out a great spring display, to encourage seed production. This is the Carrizo Plain, Chumash and Yokuts country, known for its wildflowers. The only native trees grow along sheltered feeder streams.   (dhe, 1997)

THE CHANNEL ISLANDS of San Miguel, Santa Rosa, Santa Cruz, and Anacapa are ancient Chumash land, and several dozen small fishing villages once lined accessible sites on the coasts of these islands. The Spanish padres, however, had a strange notion

that all the natives should be gathered into their missions. The last Island Chumash were removed to the mainland missions in 1830. (*See Juana Maria, p.28*)

SEVERAL CHARACTERISTICS DISTINGUISH the Chumash from other Californian tribes: steatite*, asphalt**, canoes (*tomols*), large thatched houses, and a rare form of rock art. Chumash tribes are probably best known for their manufacture of steatiteware, used both for artistic carvings and cookware. The mines for the best steatite, however, are located on Santa Catalina Island and belong to the Tongva.

For marine fishing and transport to the islands, the Chumash used large ocean-going transports, called *tomols*, to haul the raw steatite, large fish and marine mammal catches, and passengers. Twenty-foot-long tomols were made of planks stitched with sinew and sealed with asphalt; the bow and stern were decorated with designs of abalone mother-of-pearl glued on with asphalt. Whereas other California Indians used pine resin for glue and sealing, the Chumash took advantage of asphalt seeps all along the coast. They used asphalt for sealing water baskets, as well as for sealing their tomol canoe planks and for glue. Tomols can be seen today in a ground floor hallway of the Santa Barbara City Hall and a small one in the auditorium of the Santa Barbara Museum of Natural History. The **CHUMASH MARITIME ASSOCIATION** of today is dedicated to building and decorating these traditional beautifully-shaped boats.

THE LARGE, ARCHED CHUMASH HOUSES, as much as 50 feet in diameter, and were made of woven thatching of long grass or reeds, covering a frame of saplings. Not unexpectedly, the Chumash excelled in the arts of basketry, as well as weaving their thatched roofs. Smaller replicas of these perishable structures can be seen at Satwiwa, the Los Angeles Museum of Natural History in Exposition Park (at Figueroa and Exposition) and sometimes in a park on the Santa Ynez reservation. A fine Chumash basket collection is on view at the Santa Barbara Museum of Natural History.

Some of the fascinating, wonderfully fanciful apparitions of Chumash rock art are discussed below under Chumash Painted Cave.

Steatite is the mineral name for soapstone, a "soft" carvable rock composed of many fine layers. It feels soapy to the fingers. This is one of the few natural rocks that can be heated and cooled without cracking, so it became the material of choice for cooking, where it could be found. Unfortunately, unknown to its carvers, it also contains a harmful amount of asbestos.

**Oil residues on the beaches of the Santa Barbara Channel are a natural and ancient feature. Coal Oil Point near Isla Vista and the many offshore oil platforms in the Channel indicate the extent of these deposits. Unfortunately, the present-day oil seepage is much greater than early times, owing to the excessive extraction of underground oil. Asphalt (tar, pitch) has also been used by the Tongva to the south. The Rancho La Brea Tar Pits in Hancock Park by the Los Angeles County Art Museum at Wilshire and Fairfax, near Hollywood, presents some of the story of natural asphalt seeps.*

SOME CHUMASH PEOPLE of today live on the Santa Ynez Reservation. Many more are associated with several Federally unrecognized councils and several organizations. Many persons following traditional ways have chosen to affiliate for specific aspects of their culture, for examples, the Chumash Maritime Association builds tomols; the **OAKBROOK CHUMASH PEOPLE** in Thousand Oaks educate through a beautiful museum and demonstration village; some councils sponsor traditional dance and ceremonies; some are members of the California Basketweavers Association. Many are activists in environmental preservation, especially necessary in this part of the state, to conserve landmarks, village sites, beaches, and marine life.

SANTA YNEZ RESERVATION
Chumash (1901) Santa Barbara County

There is but one small Chumash reservation, though Chumash lands extended along the coast for 200 miles. This reservation is situated on 126 acres of an original "grant" by the Bishop of Monterey to Chumash families living near the Santa Ynez Mission.

Located in the Santa Ynez Valley below the 3,000-foot Santa Ynez Mountains, it has been the recipient of housing grants and gaming assets to upgrade its facilities and homes. Several older homes and a large number of newer atypical (non-HUD) homes dot the banks of willow-lined Zanja de Cota Creek. At the entrance is a very large, handsome tribal office, community center, a grand casino, and an office for a commodious public trailer park.

89 *Adjacent to Santa Ynez (E of Solvang), just south of State Hwy. 246. Nearby is the old Misión Santa Ynez (see App.II).*
SANTA YNEZ RESERVATION
P.O. Box 517, Santa Ynez, CA 93460
(805) 688-7997

OAKBROOK CHUMASH PEOPLE
Chumash Ventura County

A group seeking Federal recognition, highly involved in community work

Under the leadership of Paul Varela, a dedicated circle of Chumash have come together to preserve their traditions, to educate large groups of the public to Chumash and native traditions in their own community, and to be a center for Ventura County Chumash people to gather.

To do this, they have located a rare oak savannah park (everything else around is "developed") to present the early native aspect this land. Here they have acquired the resources to erect a 1000-sq.ft. museum, construct a nature walk in the park, staff an educational program for thousands of local school children, work with local wildlife, and present programs to prisons. A group dedicated to raptor rehabilitation works nearby, giving frequent presentations at the Museum. A rock art site is also on the premises.

This is a significant demonstration of Chumash concern for the public knowledge of Indian ways.

90 *Chumash Interpretive Center, West Lake Exit off Hwy. 101, 3 mi. N to Lang Ranch Pkwy. (R, 2 blks) to 3290 Lang Ranch Pkwy. and sculpted iron gate.*
OAKBROOK CHUMASH PEOPLE, and
CHUMASH INTERPRETIVE CENTER
3290 Lang Ranch Pkwy., Thousand Oaks, CA 91362 (805) 492-8076

Chumash kitchen and food preparation utensils on display at the Chumash cultural center in Thousand Oaks. (dhe, 1998)

COASTAL BAND OF CHUMASH OF THE CHUMASH NATION
Chumash Santa Barbara County

A Federally unrecognized band of the Chumash linguistic group

One of the more active Chumash groups in this region, the Coastal Band, with present center in Lompoc, is an interregional Chumash tribal organization made up of some 750 persons from San Luis Obispo, Santa Barbara, and Ventura Counties, and includes persons from the Ventureño and Candelaria bands. The non-profit Lompoc office coordinates several functions—social services, cultural resources, and community activities. Health services are coordinated with the American Indian Health Services in Santa Ynez. A summer camp at Gaviota and a flower festival in Lompoc are among their most visible public events. Cultural resource preservation is one of their prime activities; they are "site savers".
Info.: Aggie & Larry Garnica, Hutash Consultants, 604 E. Ocean Ave. #G, Lompoc CA 93436

SAN BUENAVENTURA INDIAN COUNCIL

Ventureño Chumash and others, Ventura County

A fairly active group seeking to preserve artifacts and remnants in the neighborhood of the Misión San Buenaventura. Other details not available.

Information: Carol Pulido, Santa Barbara.

CANDELARIA INDIAN COUNCIL INTERTRIBAL.

Santa Barbara and Ventura Counties

An organization which handles affairs of all tribal people in these counties. Other details not available.

SANTA BARBARA

Barbareño Chumash are somewhat loosely organized and meet sporadically. Other details not available.

CHUMASH COUNCIL OF BAKERSFIELD

Chumash Kern County, other details not available.

MISHKANAKA TRIBAL COUNCIL

Chumash affinity, Ventura County

Red Star, leader. Other details not available.

Petroglyph carvings and pictograph paintings: Chumash Painted Cave, symbolizing the cosmic sun and the four directions, and unknown glyphs.

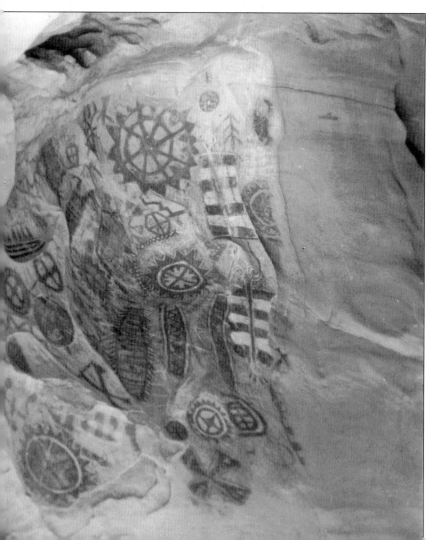

WISHTOYO

Chumash affinity, Western Los Angeles County

An organization deeply concerned with the environment from a traditional native point of view. The members are involved in "gathering, preserving, and using traditional beliefs, practices, songs, stories and dances to create self-respect and a greater awareness of our connection with, and dependence upon, the natural environment." This group of people support many native gatherings in the region.

WISHTOYO
3625 Thousand Oaks Blvd., Ste. L,
Westlake Village, CA 91362
(805) 7798-1526

CHUMASH MARITIME ASSOCIATION

This group seeks to preserve the ancient, somewhat different, Chumash and traditions of building boats: the Chumash boat is called a *tomol*; the Tongva boat is a *ti'at*. Both groups give names to their boats in the old languages.

Their efforts are supported by grants from the Channel Islands National Marine Sanctuary. A clever, fanciful tomol sculpture is located at the entrance of the Chumash Interpretive Center in Thousand Oaks.

CHUMASH MARITIME ASSOCIATION
5700 Via Real #73, Carpinteria, CA 93013
(805) 684-7783

CHUMASH PAINTED CAVE

ancient *Chumash* Santa Barbara County

In the midst of the dry Santa Ynez Mountains above Santa Barbara are dozens of small caves bearing ancient multi-colored paintings and carvings, known only to a few archaeologists, locals, and the Chumash. The caves are in yellowish sandstone, reminiscent of the caves of the famous Mesa Verde in Colorado. One of these is accessible to public view, although barred to protect it from vandals and usually dark. Still, its brilliant reds and yellows, whites, and black are as vivid as when they were painted. Apparently, they were created between 1000 and 1800 AD, and have the reputation of being some of the most beautiful and singular examples of Indian rock art in the United States. Look at these fantastic spoked cogwheels, centipedes, striped humanoids, and eerie animals. Imagine yourself in a trance with a shaman—perhaps introducing you to the secrets of power—power with natural things and the animals of the hunt which will be your sustenance. Deeper reasons for the paintings are unknown to the uninitiated.

From Santa Barbara and St. Hwy. 154, go E on Camino Cielo Rd. off Hwy. 154 two mi. to Painted Cave Rd. Turn right, go past a huge "Painted Cave" sign (indicating a housing development) about 1 mi through a winding one-lane road in a wooded area alongside a stream to the cave.

RED WIND RANCH

ancient *Chumash* land, San Luis Obispo County

Although the southern central coast region seems to have little evidence of modern Indian presence, there is one striking exception. Some years ago a sensitive and energetic Chumash man looked about him and disliked what he saw happening to his modern Indian brothers and their white cousins. After devoting many years of hard labor and stubborn effort, Grandfather Semu Huaute (elder leaders are often called "Grandfather"), established a 200-acre sanctuary in the La Panza Mountains of his ancestry. He named it Red Wind (now Red Wind Ranch). This retreat-like area near Santa Margarita under the shadow of Black Mountain in the Los Padres National Forest, has undergone several changes in direction, but still exists as a refuge for Native Americans. It is very private and deliberately remote—it is not for the casual visitor.

SATWIWA
RANCHO SIERRA VISTA,
SANTA MONICA MOUNTAINS
NATIONAL RECREATION AREA
Chumash and *Tongva* (*Gabrielino*)
(1978) Ventura County

Within the Rancho portion of this huge national park, a segment has been dedicated as an American Indian Natural area, an ecological and ceremonial preserve of both Chumash and Tongva (Gabrieleno) peoples. Called Satwiwa (bluffs), it is sponsored by the National Park Service and the **FRIENDS OF HUTASH AND TUGUPAN**. *Hutash* is Chumash for Mother Earth, and *Tugupan* is Tongva for Sky. A small visitor center is provided.

The Satwiwa public program is rich with talks on the natural features of the Park; skilled Indian storytellers weavers their tales on Sundays; Native dances occur on special days.

Satwiwa is a remote, wild location set aside for everyone (especially urban dwellers) to appreciate the natural environment, and for Native Americans to perpetuate their traditions in a place of spiritual beauty. Come, park, walk the land through relatively untouched ecological areas. Mountain lions and golden eagles live here.

91 *Access from Ventura Fwy. (U.S. Hwy. 101) at Wendy Dr., W of Thousand Oaks. West on Potrero Rd. to Rancho Sierra Vista—continue to trailhead and Satwiwa. Or stop at the SMMNRA Visitor Center.*
SATWIWA—SANTA MONICA MOUNTAINS NATIONAL RECREATION AREA
30401 Agoura Rd., Ste. 100,
Agoura Hills, CA 91301-2009
(818) 597-1036

The treeless hills of the southern Coast Range exhibit a unique ecological beauty every spring. This yucca blooms on the unpopulated backcountry of Viejas Reservation.
(dhe, 1992)

KUMEYAAY (kú-me-yai)
also KÁMiA (Spanish spelling)
[Ed. note: ..aa.. has a long i sound, as in "eye"]

THE INDIAN PEOPLE OF southern San Diego County were once called "Diegueño" by the Spanish and anthropologists, after the San Diego Mission. In actuality, two culturally similar groups traditionally occupied this land, the *Ipai* and the *Tipai* (local names for person). In recent times the Tipai especially have preferred the name *Kumeyaay* or *Kamia* for themselves. (The Ipai designation is for the reservations and people of the northwestern corner of San Diego county—between La Jolla and the San Luis Rey River.) The name Tipai is still preferred by the Kamia families living in Baja California Norte, México.

The Kumeyaay people are located on Campo, *Ewii-aa-paayp* (Spanish, Cuyapaipe), Barona, Viejas-Capitan Grande, La Posta, Manzanita, Sycuan, and Jamul Reservations. The bands (or tribes, in California BIA nomenclature), although geographically practically adjacent to one another, have maintained considerable independence, owing in no small part to their historic isolation and rivalry. Consequently, though in a similar ecologic region, and bearing a common history and families, temperaments among the bands have varied vastly.

The Kumeyaay people have a long history of fierce independence. Even when Spanish troops were rounding up natives for the coastal missions some 200 years ago, those who could fled to these desolate hills. The same was true of their avoidance of the U.S. Cavalry.

SOUTHERN CALIFORNIA TRIBES suffered the same American rejection of the terms of the 18 treaties of 1851 (*p.47*), similar to the rest of the state. Originally, a large portion of the south had been set aside for reservation lands. The lack of their legal status caused Native American claims not to be recognized. Settlers moved into Indian lands with impunity, knowing that their land patents were quite "legal". Struggling along on their own for decades, land was finally acquired, or rather, restored, in a series of suits against the government (*see Land, p.47*).

> THE PADRES ATTEMPTED TO OBLITERATE THEIR CUSTOMS & TRADITIONS, BUT WERE NOT COMPLETELY SUCCESSFUL.

They have emerged from relative seclusion with much difficulty and without much enthusiasm. Considering the massive assault on Indian life for those 200 years, we can see why it's appealing to disregard the temptations of modern life and live unmolested on a remote reservation. That is, until certain entitlements and opportunities of modern life like casinos present themselves.

In a new-found spirit of cooperation, three of the Kumeyaay reservations with large casinos have begun to unite their peoples in a common economic bond. Barona, Sycuán, and Viejas all have very popular gaming establishments, and as reservations operate in complementary fashion to each other. For instances, when the Barona Labor Day weekend Powwow is swarming with thousands of campers and participants, the well-equipped and well-respected Sycuán Reservation Fire Department joins the Barona fire crew with full gear. One small reservation has been the grateful recipient of help from other well-off reservations—after all, many family members share relatives on all of them.

SOME RESIDENTS OF THE Kumeyaay reservations exercise a right that few other Native Americans possess—dual United States and Mexican citizenship. The original territory of the Tipai peoples straddled the political division of these two modern nations, so their descendants are free to move about from homes of relatives on either "side" of the border.

The Kumeyaay continue ancient cultural ties with the Colorado River peoples, who, in earlier times would often move toward the Jacumba Mountains through the dry Imperial Valley to avoid the blistering heat. Occasional fiestas are held at Campo, usually tied to church festival days such as the All Saints Day Barbeque. Many older tribal customs are still kept, such as native languages, gourd dances, and epic songs (bird songs). Archeological sites in the area are known and revered, but since they are undeveloped and unprotected, they must remain confidential.

THE COASTAL VILLAGES first felt the impact when the inhabitants were forced into the Spanish domain. The padres attempted to obliterate their customs and traditions, but were not completely successful—especially since many of the people fled to mountains and arid areas outside the mission system, where language and traditions could persist. When the American period began, the people were still in remote places that had few resources. Since gold prospecting was not a factor, they were left pretty much alone, except when the better land became coveted by the American settlers. Assimilation was never complete.

I see old churches and missions with their burial grounds—the clapboard chapels of Sycuan and Campo and Jamul, the Spanish missions of Santa Ysabel, La Jolla, Barona, and Pala. And I see the flower-decked adobe homes of La Jolla and Pauma, the many little wooden houses erected so long ago, where the heritage of tribe and tradition continue. New mobile homes and new government-built homes add to the air of progress. Off the main highways, new cars, and sometimes horses, cows, and goats compete for road space.

THIS IS THE KUMEYAAY environment. To know the Indian people of today, go to some of these places to better understand their life. Attend a Powwow to learn the songs and dances and the culture. Go with an attitude of wanting to learn. Someone will help you; it is amazing the number of people eager to show you. It was my distinct pleasure to share a bleacher bench at the Barona Powwow with Larry Banegas, Southern California Resource Consultant and Barona Tribal Council member.* Larry was kind in sharing his knowledge of his people with me.

Kumeyaay comes from a word meaning "the ledge"—the people at the edge of the ocean. Mr. Banegas told me of culture classes on Barona—he wants to make his a living culture. To help do this, he leads a very popular summer school course on the Indian history of the region.

Some of the above information was drawn from literature furnished me by Mr. Banegas, including articles by Florence Shipek: "An example of intensive plant husbandry: the Kumeyaaay of Southern California", from Foraging and Farming, D.R Harris and G. C. Hillman, Eds., Unwin Hyman, London (ca.1984) and "Mission Indians and California Land Claims", American Indian Quarterly, Vol. XIII, No. 4, (1989).

Many of the exhibits in Barona's outstanding Kumeyaay museum, as much as a third of the collection, come from the Squier family of the Cuyamaca area. Mr. Squier was a collector from 1914 to the present, initially in an era when few people respected the ancient Indian objects found in the area (mortars, pottery, etc.). Once people realized what he was doing, he was presented with many artifacts, and the collection grew, but had no home. [*Aside from the occasionally-displayed artifacts at the Museum of Man in San Diego.*] This is now the place to come for specific information on the Kumeyaay tribes.

He told me of the people's use of acorns, *shawee,* a preparation somewhat different from that of northern California. Agriculture, as practiced by the Kumeyaay, consisted largely of plant husbandry, the "manipulation of the natural ecosystem by substituting domesticated for wild species, especially where a new species would produce food". This required a complex knowledge of plant biology and experimentation to determine in which eco-niche a species would thrive. Stream banks were planted with erosion-reducing trees, and fire was used to control excess growth. Plants used in the essential art of basketry were carefully planted and maintained. They still are. Grapes, agave, yucca, and sage required special supervision because they are fire susceptible.

LARRY TOLD ME of the traditional tribal structure of the Kumeyaay peoples. The setup was notably different from other peoples of California, partly in response to the climactic and geographic differences. For instance, there were a series of runners for maintaining joint communication between the bands. The primary subjects for conferences were on agriculture and the resolution of political disputes. The meeting had a *kwaaypaay,* headman, and each band was represented by a *kuchut kwataay,* or second-in-command. In addition, there were persons with special talents who adopted certain tasks, like one in charge of arranging ceremonies, one to care for the fires, one to direct the planting and harvesting of crops (especially agave), one to give medicine.

Each village had at least one storyteller, someone to recount long songs—the thread which preserves traditions and entertains. And still today, fragments of the old culture remain, and the tribe is making every effort to preserve what it can of these customs.

BARONA RESERVATION
Kumeyaay (Tipai) (1932) San Diego County

The Barona Reservation, like the Viejas, occupies a wide, fertile, highland valley of 5,181 acres near the Cleveland National Forest. (*See p.202, Capitan Grande for an early history of the land.*) This is not the unproductive wasteland pawned off on powerless people—here are several ranches, much cleared land, some small farms, clusters of comfortable homes for its 300 residents, a mission-style chapel with meeting

This complex of the Barona Reservation Kumeyaay Cultural Center and tribal office is designed to fit the character of the place and to serve both the public and tribe. (dhe, 1998)

hall, a tribal office and community center (built in 1997) of remarkable southwestern style architecture, indoor and outdoor recreational facilities, including a fine ball park, used also for the Powwow. I had never seen the host drum on a pitcher's mound before, and when the Grand Entry began, the bases were loaded.

Much of the new construction is a result of the huge success of the equally huge casino on the south end of the Barona Valley. Here, as on all Indian reservations, the gaming activities (consisting of a gymnasium-sized central arena, with operations wings and two or three ballpark-sized parking areas) are confined to a specific, remote segment of the reservation. It is always clear that this is a separate function, not part of the community life.

Located in the tribal offices and meeting building is the striking **KUMEYAAY CULTURAL CENTER**, a museum and center for learning of the Indian peoples of the region. You will find signs of prosperity, comfort, and respect for the older times as you traverse the eight miles of Barona/Wildcat Canyon Rd.

102 *Northbound: from El Cajon, Hwy. 67 to N side of the San Diego R. arroyo, right at casino signs onto Willow Rd., left at Wildcat Cyn. Rd., then about 5 mi to the reservation on Barona Rd. Southbound: from Ramona, San Vicente Rd. 5 mi to Wildcat Cyn. Rd., R to Barona.*

BARONA RESERVATION
1095 Barona Rd., Lakeside, CA 92040
(619) 443-6612

Las Viejas Reservation (Kumeyaay) is probably best known for its large gaming establishment along Interstate 8, but its chapel offers a place of meditation and quiet beauty away from the highway bustle. (dhe, 1998)

SYCUAN [sy-quón] RESERVATION

Kᴜᴍᴇʏᴀᴀʏ (*Tipai*) (1875) San Diego County

At the head of a narrow, chaparral-coated valley, surrounded by a scatter of sun-seeking tract developments, lies this, the oldest reservation of the Kumeyaay. The center of tribal activity is on a small hill overlooking the several older homes and trailers. Nearly hidden by a clump of trees is a pretty clapboard chapel; nearby is the large gaming hall and a couple of fire engines. The fire department is operated in conjunction with the regional fire protection network, and the firefighters at Sycuan and Barona Reservations are well-known for their skill at extinguishing summer brush fires. The community center and tribal offices for the 640-acre reservation are on the hill, too. Down the far slope of the quiet valley is the ever-present reminder of the past, the cemetery.

103 *E of El Cajon on I-8, take the Alpine-Tavern Rd. Exit, go S on Tavern Rd. to Dehesa Rd. Then about 3 mi to the Dehesa Fire Dept., R on paved road following the casino signs.*
SYCUAN RESERVATION
5459 Dehesa Rd., El Cajon, CA 92021
(619) 445-2613

CAPITAN GRANDE RESERVATION

Kᴜᴍᴇʏᴀᴀʏ (*Tipai*) (1875) San Diego County

The large, bare mountainous region east of Barona Reservation is the uninhabited Capitan Grande. This 15,753-acre mass of dry mountain and chapparal was judged uninhabitable by the bands which now live in the lower, wetter, fertile valleys. The countryside to the east and south of the San Diego River was the land of group known as the *Guatay* or Los Conejos; the land to the west were the *Coapan* (Spanish "capitan").

Capitan Grande, situated in the center of the present Cleveland National Forest, west of the 6,500-foot Cuyamaca Peak, is bisected by El Capitan Reservoir, taken from the Kumeyaay by forced sale for water for San Diego, and whose construction submerged the little habitable land here. With the money from the sale, the Coapan group bought the land today called Viejas; the Guatay group bought the land today called Barona. (An early ranchero occupying this region was named Baron Long.)

Capitan Grande itself is presently jointly administered through the Viejas Reservation and the Barona Reservation. As an essentially undeveloped area, it is a continuing portion of ecological preserve.

104 *Capitan Grande: N of Alpine (off I-8), flanking the upper stretches of El Capitan Reservoir.*

VIEJAS RESERVATION

Kumeyaay (*Tipai*) (1939) San Diego County

The upland plateaus and wide valleys of the Coast Range east of San Diego inhabited in the past by impermanent bands of Native Americans—small groups that camped for a few years or less, while foraging for local plants and animals. Occasionally, however, certain areas make excellent long-term living sites. The 1,609-acre Viejas Reservation occupies the end of one such place. Oaks dot the valley floor with open green to brown pastures. Farther up the slopes of the low mountains, scrub oaks appear, then give way to chaparral and live granite rock. On the back loop road stands an old, very attractive church and the reservation cemetery. Alongside, a dirt road winds into the far distance toward Capitan Grande, apparently occupied by no humans.

The Spanish named it El Valle de Las Viejas ("The Valley of the Old Women"), for when a party of them approached the valley, searching for persons to populate the coastal missions, they found only old women. The men had fled to hide and fight another day. (*See above, under Capitan Grande Reservation, an earlier history of the people here.*)

Today, back in the oaks of the valley head, residents run an RV park and campground for the general public. Occasional cows and other tame animals wander the area, while wild ones forage the hills beyond. The RV management can point out *Ma-Tar-Awa*, an ancient archaeological site.

Along Interstate 5, the most evident indication of change is the large casino complex on the frontage road. The casino has funded both the modern homes sprouting up all over the valley, and a short distance away, the very attractive and well-equipped southwestern-style Indian Health Service clinic—built as a cooperative effort for the nearby tribes.

The tribe holds two annual ceremonies: "Clearing of the Cemetery", a time when the members clean and tend to their two cemeteries, and Dia de las Animas, "All Souls Day".

105 *East of San Diego, from I-8, the E. Willows Rd. Exit (between Descanso and Alpine).*

VIEJAS RESERVATION
P.O. Box 908, Alpine, CA 92001
(619) 445-3810

JAMUL INDIAN VILLAGE
Kumeyaay (Tipai) (1912, 1975) San Diego County

Sixty-five years ago a small band of Kumeyaay found six acres upon which to settle—a tiny plot in the rolling hills east of the town of Jamul. The village is a random assembly, and most of the houses are old; nevertheless, there is a great feeling of community.

The winter Sunday I first arrived, the sky was cold and wet, the one dirt road nearly impassable. But in the air was a feeling of excitement—these friendly people were gathered in an old meeting hall to hear what new things their newly-attained status was to bring them. The village had just become a full-fledged reservation, and everyone seemed pleased that 65 years of "squatting" and tenacious endurance were finally being rewarded. This was 1981.

In 1997, the picturesque chapel of St. Francis Xavier (1926) still stands, carefully repainted, and is a tribute to the labors of the past; its colorful cemetery will not slide down the hillside, thanks to a new retaining wall. Sadly, the old meeting hall was lost to fire. Nevertheless, the roads are now paved; the tribal office and new meeting hall are in a real office building, and things are a lot more prosperous than 16 years ago.

One summer afternoon in 1997, I snagged Kenny Meza, Tribal Chair, Jamul Band of Mission Indians, from his seemingly perpetual duties to tell me a little bit about Jamul and its plans.

Mr. Meza told me that Jamul's new council of 1997 is changing things for the better. [*I noted that many things were already different. He concurred.*] Jamul is able to share a certain amount of revenue from sister Kumeyaay reservations with large casinos—Barona, Viejas, and Sycuan. Jamul's people have very little access to Federal funds. Although some are forthcoming, it is hardly enough to do anything other than simply survive. The extra amount helps a lot to fund the everyday running of this small band of six or seven families, which consists of about 20 persons.

The place is run like the large family that it is. Mr. Meza was involved in procuring a bookcase for one resident, seeing about getting some plumbing installed for another, trying to rectify some bookkeeping mistakes for another, and answering my questions all the while.

THE LAND UPON WHICH THE ORIGINAL residents settled was owned in the late 1800s by Klaus Spreckels, sugar baron and builder of the San Diego & Arizona Eastern Railroad. He gave back the 6-1/2 acres to the Indian tribe in 1912, but the Federal government refused to recognize its existence until that cold day in 1981. The only adequate thing they had had all that time was a water supply.

Jamul is trying for a grant for land acquisition to expand its tribal housing. But the locals are opposed,

Left & Below: Jamul, a small village at the edge of a former Adolph Spreckels ranch, is the most southwestern of the Kumeyaay reservations. St. Francis Xavier Church and its cemetery are San Diego County historic sites, overlooking a small group of homes and fire department, acquired in 1999 as part of the county fire protection system. (dhe, 1998)

Kenny Meza, tribal leader of the Jamul village, keeps busy solving the problems of his village and has been known to call the bingo numbers at the Barona Reservation casino. (dhe, 1998)

saying it will just bring another gaming establishment into the area. Meza counters, saying that although they might not like it, gaming seems to be the only solution to providing sufficient housing for the 30 tribal members still without space on the reservation.

Mr. Meza also said funding earmarked for Native American education in the local schools is not always properly applied. Kids seldom get any information about their heritage there. Kumeyaay language teaching is, however, available at Sycuan, some 10 miles north.

AS I LEFT, I NOTICED a large bulletin board filled with flyers of Native American activities in the region. Yes, Meza said, many of our tribal members are very involved in a lot of these activities and gatherings.

[*In February, 1998, Meza was very happy to tell me that the tribe had acquired 4 additional acres, including the fire station next door.*]

The culture is far from vanishing.

106 *E of San Diego on Hwy. 94, one mile E of the Jamul junction with Proctor Rd. and one block E of Jamul Fire Station.*
JAMUL RESERVATION
Box 612, Jamul, CA 91935
(619) 669-0301

EWIIAAPAAYP RESERVATION
[eweé-aa-pipe]
[Spanish spelling: Cuyapaipe (quí-a-pipe)]
Kumeyaay (1893) San Diego County

The pines and evergreens of the south slopes of Mt. Laguna overlap a bit onto the remote lands of the Ewiiaapaayp. The three families who live here are hidden in the shade of a remote, wooded valley, surrounded by low, rocky mountains. As with much other reservation land, this place was at one time considered nearly valueless, but the real value, solitude and fastness, has been preserved for centuries. The land is as it was from the beginning—beautiful. Its 4,100 acres, as is true of many reservations, are not "developed".

One can only walk in—on paths that are known only to the families in residence and a few locals of Mt. Laguna. It is obviously private. Do not enter unless you call beforehand.

MR. JIM PENNEY, Business Manager of the Ewiiaapaayp Reservation was kind enough to fill us in with a few comments. The 13 residents at the ranch live in 7 houses on the expansive 4,100 acres. The main enterprise that has supported the people here for many years is breeding horses. This is an occupation of long hours and tedious work, but one that continues to provide a profitable existence on the wide expanse of the reservation.

However, the tribe is beginning a new venture. This place is endowed with a good, pure, and tasty water source. Bottled H2O from their well will be marketed under the name "Leaning Rock", which, not incidentally, is the translation of that long vowel-rich word that is the name of this place. The spelling is the true phonetic rendition of the name. We honor their request. Yes, there is a leaning rock nearby.

This small band of people opens their gates to the public once a year for a free three-day gathering, complete with camping, birdsongs, demonstrations of medicinal herbs, basketweaving and *shawee* (acorn) demonstrations, *peon* (hand) games, and barbeque.

107 *For the annual (public) Ewiiaapaayp Gathering, the last week in July, the gates at the Thing Valley ranch toward the end of La Posta Truck Trail, 10 mi. off old U.S. Hwy. 80 are opened. Other times, the gates are locked. Call if you have business.*
EWIIAAPAAYP (CUYAPAIPE)
RESERVATION TRIBAL OFFICE
P.O. Box 471, Alpine, CA 92001
(619)445-6315

The Ewiaapaayp Reservation is extremely remote, hot in summer, cool in winter. The tribe has one valuable economic resource—a pure, clear water source, which is being developed. (dhe, 1998)

CAMPO RESERVATION
Kumeyaay (Tipai) (1893) San Diego County

The 15,000-acre Campo Reservation lies high on a 4,000-foot plateau in the Laguna Mountains east of San Diego, endowed with powderings of winter snow and cooler breezes in summer. The hills are rocky and naturally covered with chaparral, but many clearings offer land for grazing and small farms; taller oaks shade the valleys.

On the north part of the reservation are a motel, store, and trailer park in Live Oak Springs (some businesses are non-Indian owned). The tribal administrative center is on the south end of the reservation, where one finds a neat, modern community center, health services, and tribal office, adjacent to an exceptionally colorful old church and Indian cemetery. A visit to this site might give one a good experience of the patterns of life in the Kumeyaay community.

NOTE: The scenic San Diego & Arizona Eastern Railroad main yard is in the town of Campo, on Highway 94, and winds through the rez.

108 *Tribal offices are located on a hillside on Church Rd., right alongside State Rte. 94, between Campo and Jacumba. Some dirt roads traverse the reservation, but it must be remembered that this is private property!*
CAMPO RESERVATION
36190 Church Rd., Campo, CA 91901

Kumeyaay (Tipai) (1893) San Diego County

The Manzanita, named for the brushy bush so common over drier California, occupies a 3,580-acre rectangle of infertile upland valleys and meadows in the western part of the Carrizo Desert.

Homes of the residents are widely scattered, tucked behind boulders and hillsides for protection from the uncompromising summer sun. As residents have been troubled by inconsiderate and trespassing scofflaws, they prefer no off-road visitors.

109 *E of San Diego, Live Oak Rd. from Live Oak Springs is a southern public access road to parts of Anza-Borrego State Park, passing through the reservation, but heed the preceding sentence.*
Information: Chairperson,
MANZANITA RESERVATION
P.O Box 1302, Boulevard, CA 91905
(619) 766-4930

Campo Reservation (Kumeyaay) is not very densely populated, but the people keep many early traditions. Their tribal center is built in a very low, southwestern style that fits the countryside environment. (dhe, 1984)

Quero Santo, an Ipai-Tipai dancer of the Mesa Grande Reservation, photographed 1907. (See opposite page for more.) (photo by T.T. Waterman, Phoebe Apperson Hearst Museum of Anthropology, University of California, Berkeley)

IPAI LANGUAGE

Ipai language is a northern dialect of the Ipai-Tipai language group, known further south as Kumeyaay. Sketches of Ipai reservations follow.

INAJA~COSMIT RESERVATIONS

Ipai-Tipai (Kumeyaay) (1875) San Diego County

These are two parcels of rather remote and inaccessible land under the silhouette of Cuyamaca Peak. At present there are no permanent inhabitants of these 852 acres, although some remodeling of older homes is underway on Inaja. Deep winter snows and lack of facilities make these locations inhospitable to all but the hardiest.

Many years ago, I am told, there were residents on Cosmit, and once there were fiestas and dances. Time has changed modes of existence.

111 *W of the intersection of Hwy. 79 with County Rd. S-1, N of Cuyamaca Reservoir, 7 mi S of Julian.*
INAJA-COSMIT RESERVATIONS
P.O. Box 186, Santa Ysabel, CA 92070
(619) 789-8581

SAN PASCUAL RESERVATION

Ipai (1910) San Diego County

Although one of the later-acquired reservations in southern California, much of this reservation has been removed from its original location. The original parcels are now occupied by Lake Wohlford and by an organization dedicated to the preservation of nature, the San Diego Wild Animal Park.

COMPENSATORY LAND is now in five parcels, totalling 1,500 acres, on the dry, scrub oak hills east of Valley Center. At least the lake provides the residents with some water that they would not otherwise have had. Other compensations include a large tract of modern homes to replace the tired dwellings of the early 1900s.

Indian activity is centered at the pleasantly constructed tribal hall and education center, marked with a fine carved-wood sign.

112 *Take the Lake Wohlford exit from County Rd. S-6 on the north end of Valley Center, about 1-1/2 mi. to the San Pascual Tribal Hall sign. The other parcels nestle nearby.*
SAN PASCUAL RESERVATION
P.O. Box 365, Valley Center, CA 92082
(619) 749-3200

LA POSTA RESERVATION

Kumeyaay (Tipai) (1893) San Diego County

Under the shadow of 6,270-foot-high Mt. Laguna and at the eastern edge of Cleveland National Forest lies this 3,672-acre park-like highland. La Posta has occasional residents, who value and guard their privacy. The one entry road is dusty or muddy, and is fenced off from intruders.

110 *The almost vacant countryside with grand vistas of mountains and valleys, E of San Diego, may be seen only by taking the La Posta Rd. Exit N off I-8 (the same exit S is Hwy. 80 E to Live Oak Springs). Vistas from a nearby hilltop overlook.*
Information: Chairperson
LA POSTA RESERVATION
P.O. Box 154, Boulevard, CA 91905
(619) 561-9294

Santa Ysabel Reservation is home to an Ipai group, with a long history of Catholic traditions. Their church is decorated for Christmas. (dhe, 1984)

SANTA YSABEL RESERVATION

Ipai (1875) San Diego County

Santa Ysabel occupies the slopes of the wooded and rugged Volcan Mountains, rising to nearly 4500 feet. This rural area is home to numerous wildlife, and the people here enjoy solitude.

The homes on these 15,527 acres are mostly older ones, as are the tribal and educational buildings. An old wooden structure standing near the highway is for the Indian equivalent of ceremonies like "wakes and showers", one resident told me. November 14th is the big feast day for the mission, founded in 1818. [*See App.II for a description of the early mission asisténcia and its location.*]

113 *Entrance is E off Hwy. 79 on Schoolhouse Cyn. Rd., 1/4 mi N of Mesa Grande Rd. intersection and about 2 mi N of the town of Santa Ysabel (NE of Ramona).*

SANTA YSABEL RESERVATION
P.O. Box 130, Santa Ysabel, CA 92070
(619) 765-0845

MESA GRANDE RESERVATION

Ipai (1875) San Diego County

Although closely related to and only a couple of miles distant from Santa Ysabel, the Mesa Grande band is one of those groups that cherishes a singular independence. The reservation land itself has been disputed among its families. In any event, the place is rather remote, very quiet, and scenic, high on a group of hills above the forests of Black Canyon (part of Cleveland National Forest). In winter it is often covered with a mantle of snow.

For their living during the year, the thirty-odd residents keep some horses, cows, and a few simple farms in mostly wooden structures—on the 120 acres of land (2 parcels).

114 *From Hwy 79, 1-1/2 mi. N of Santa Ysabel, go W on Mesa Grande Rd. about 5 mi to intersection with Black Canyon Rd. at several abandoned stone buildings. Black Canyon Road, a steep, winding, dirt road, passes through an unoccupied portion of the reservation by the National Forest. The habitations, on private land, are off a paved farm road 0.7 mi E of this intersection.*

MESA GRANDE RESERVATION
P.O. Box 270, Santa Ysabel, CA 92070

Mesa Grande Reservation (Ipai) is very isolated—located next to the Cleveland National Forest, and high enough to collect winter snow. Its rural setting is everywhere evident. (dhe, 1984)

SHOSHONEAN LANGUAGES

Shoshonean is one of a large group of Uto-Aztecan languages spoken in the Great Basin, including eastern and southern California, also by the Comanches, and the Aztecs of Mexico. The tribes of Southwestern and South Central California are the Kitanemuk, Fernandeño/Tataviam, Tongva/Gabrielino, Ajachemem (Juaneño). Takic is a subgroup of the Shoshonean languages as spoken by a large and diverse group of California native peoples.

TAKIC:

FERNANDEÑO/ TATAVIAM

DESCENDANTS OF THE ORIGINAL PEOPLE from the upper San Fernando Valley around Sylmar and the San Fernando Mission are organized to continue many of their traditions. Some 580 members plan for their annual three-day California Gathering at Rockwell Park in West Hills (Canoga Park) the second weekend in June. Their 12-member board meets monthly.

The Vasquez Rocks County Park occupies ancestral lands of the Tataviam/Fernandeño Tribe. Los Angeles County maintains this place of great natural beauty, history, and ecology.

(dhe, 1998)

The Fernandeño/Tataviám people's efforts at preserving their culture results inspires the teaching of their own Indian history at schools and clubs. The language has been lost, but it has been determined to be related to Shoshonean languages.

Several members have dedicated themselves to the Bear Dance; they also provide ceremonies and attend sweats and prayers at the Vasquez Rocks caves at Agua Dulce. This is a sacred site of the Tataviam, off Highway 14, some 8 miles east of Newhall in their ancestral territory. It is remarkable that any sacred sites survive anywhere near the great urban bulldozer.

FERNANDEÑO/TATAVIÁM TRIBE
Information: Chief Little Bear (Rudy Ortega, Sr.), 11640 Rincon Ave., Sylmar, CA 91342-5455 (818) 361-0680

VASQUEZ ROCKS COUNTY PARK
ancient *Tataviam* land, North Los Angeles County
Few unspoiled sites of Native villages can be found around the vast city of Los Angeles. However, one in ancient Tataviam land, has been preserved by the startling nature of nature here. The rocks rise and tilt steeply, providing shelters—not so much from rains as from the searing desert sun. In the extremes of temperatures, sandstone rocks crumble slowly into the sandy soil that holds enough water for desert bushes and small trees to take root and grow.

Such conditions are adequate for desert dwellers like the Tataviam people who were here for thousands of years. They built cool, domed thatch shelters under these shady, overhanging rocks, harvested and ground acorns for their primary source of food, and hunted the desert animals that also fed off the grasses. They danced in special places amid the rocks, and painted pictures, which are still there.

EVEN WHEN EUROPEANS came and sent the Indians away to Misión San Fernando, the strange rocks invited protection. Spanish rancheros took over, followed by Americans, but none permitted trespass. When Hollywood was snooping around for a good "Western" setting for many movies. This was it. (See Gunga Din, Charge of the Light Brigade, Bonanza, Flintstones, Maverick, many more.) Hollywood kept the place in good order. Finally, the ranch owner gave the place to the County Parks Department.

IN THE MID 1800S a bandit (or a "Robin Hood", depending on your point of view) named Tibúrcio Vasquez took refuge here. However, after years of rough escapades, he was shot in a gunfight on the highest rock, later captured at Cahuenga Pass (in Hollywood of today), then executed in San José.

Today, the Tataviam/Fernandeño tribe and its adherents still come to its ancient, protected, sacred sites to perform ancient, sacred ceremonies, and to honor the past, the present, and the future.

93 *Access from Hwy.14, 7 1/2 mi S of Palmdale, Agua Dulce Exit N to Escondido Cyn. Rd., about 1/2 mi to Park.*
VASQUEZ ROCKS COUNTY NATURAL AREA PARK
10700 W. Escondido Cyn. Rd.,
Agua Dulce, CA 91350
(805) 268-0840

ANTELOPE VALLEY INDIAN MUSEUM TAKIC
ancient *Serrano* land, Northeast Los Angeles County

This museum featuring western Great Basin Indian tribes (east and southeast of the Sierra), and many others, should be visited for an orientation also to the local tribal areas. Active crafts include firemaking, beadmaking, basketry, along with an extensive collection of Indian craft materials of stone, leather, basket-making grasses and sedges.

Near **93** *Access from St. Fwy. 14: E on Palmdale Blvd. 17 mi. to 170th St. East. Left, (north) 2 mi. to signs at Ave. M.*
ANTELOPE VALLEY STATE INDIAN MUSEUM
P.O. Box 1171, Lancaster, CA 93584

Rogerio Rocha of Misión San Fernando harvesting nopales (prickly pear fruit).

(Photograph # N 20020, courtesy of the Southwest Museum, Los Angeles, by C.C. Pierce, 1898)

TONGVA
(GABRIELENO & FERNANDEÑO)

LIFE AMONG THE TONGVA peoples (Gabrieleno or Gabrielino and Fernandeño—names taken from Missions San Gabriel and San Fernando) probably did not differ much from that of the Chumash (see *p.196*), for their ecological and biotic zones cover quite similar environments.

Above: Native dwellings adjacent to Misión San Gabriel. In southern California, local Indians were often allowed to live in their own places, near the mission. Note the round reed hut and the mud walls and galvanized roof sheets of the larger building. (photograph # N 20098, courtesy of the Southwest Museum, Los Angeles)

Right: Viewed one hundred years later, the same imposing Misión San Gabriel as viewed above was designed by a Spaniard with a knowledge of Arabic Moorish mosques in his homeland. Consequently, it is not so Italianate or overly simple as other missions of California. Nevertheless, the Tongva people of the Los Angles basin were required to make the brick and do the labor. (dhe, 1985)

THEIR ANCESTRAL LANDS stretched roughly from the San Fernando Valley eastward through the Los Angeles Basin to near San Bernardino. The geography varies from a warm coast to the high Coast Range mountains. Since the tribal culture has been so decimated since the arrival of Spanish intruders, archaeological and early anthropological investigations are probably the only means of making comparisons. Their spoken languages, though similar, could be best described as close dialects of one another. Since this is a rich agricultural area (even today), the populations of most villages was rather high—food was plentiful, easily obtainable, and relative peace reigned throughout the region. Among these groups, dwellings and articles of village life also seem to have been similar. As with the majority of southern California peoples, they were skilled at sand painting; they held puberty ceremonies for both men and women; and in trading they used a form of counting by knots in a string, like the *quipú* of the Incas, a device not seen in other North American Indian cultures.

THE GREAT SPREAD of Spanish settlement and diseases decimated the villages and towns in the San Fernando and Los Angeles areas in the late 1700s and early 1800s. Then the great intrusion of Americans nearly smothered the remaining people.

A hiding place need not be in the remote fastness of a forest; it can be in the vastness of a spread-out city. For many decades, Tongva families kept their heritage quiet, their relationships known only to themselves and to a few others. It was often dangerous to do otherwise. They had no land base at all. Within the last decade, they have found that organizing can yield numerous benefits and pride in being Native American.

In the midst of the metropolitan colossus of greater Los Angeles, a remarkable feat of survival of tribal groups of California Indians is even today developing. The Smithsonian's 1978 Handbook of North American Indians (*App. VII*) declares that as of 1900 the Gabrielenos "had ceased to exist as a culturally identifiable group." This may be news to the Handbook readers, but not to some 1800-2000 descendants of the original groups from the San Fernando Valley and the Los Angeles Basin.

In 1983, having read accounts such as the one above, I was surprised to find a newspaper article about an ancient Gabrieleno village site near El Segundo. It was being dug up for a new Hughes Aircraft complex, yet the excavation was being carefully observed by a "local Gabrieleno", present to make certain any burials were not disturbed. (None were found.) Soon thereafter I noticed that the new Santa Monica Mountains National Recreation Area (SMMNRA) was preparing a cultural center near Thousand Oaks (*see p.199*) for Chumash and Gabrieleno peoples. It seemed that Gabrieleno people must still be around.

I then located the SMMNRA Gabrieleno guide, who enlightened me on the situation of his people. Since 1900, the native people had disappeared into the rapidly expanding metropolis, where they could, at the very least, maintain family ties, often using the San Gabriel Mission as another basis of contact.

AMONG THE SEVERAL NEGATIVE effects that a large metropolitan area has on the history of any indigenous people is the near obliteration of any distinctive or unique geographical sites. Los Angeles Basin is no exception, but there are scattered miraculously preserved and jealously guarded sites. Indeed, the Tongva-Gabrileno people have arranged to allot certain areas and sites near their homes for special preservation, ceremonies, and honors.

Springs in very dry regions have always carried a special relation to indigenous peoples. *Hoahoamonga*, for example, is a very special spring located along the Gabrieleno National Recreational Trail just north of Pasadena near the Jet Propulsion Lab site. The trail itself to the summit of Mt. Wilson is of special Indian interest. A second special spring is *Kuruvugna**, where sacred ceremonies are held every year. Still another center of a great struggle is to preserve *Puvungna*, an ancient village site and birthplace of *Chinig-chinix* (*see p.182*), the greatest spiritual leader of the Tongva people. California State University at Long Beach holds title to this ancient site, and was recently prepared to ravage the place with yet another mall. As of 1999, the land is still undeveloped (though disturbed), the all-important spring still flows water to a grove of trees, and ceremonies are held on the village site, from which many Native Los Angelinos trace their ancestors' homes. Why does it seem so important to destroy the few ancient vestiges of our earliest peoples?

*Kuruvungna Springs is an oasis amid the bustle of the city. Carefully preserved, this is the site of an ancient village, which lasted into fairly recent historical times. Well-protected in the grounds of the University High School in Westwood (near UCLA), clear water bubbles from two well-cared-for springs into pools where fish swim. Tall palms and old trees shade the pools, rimmed with green grass and shrubs. Benches are provided for resting. Most of the time during the week, the springs may be visited by first checking in with the high school office on Texas St. at Barrington. Tours are offered the 1st Saturday of every month, at University High School, led by Native guides, and are available to all who wish to learn of the presence of Tongva ancient sacred sites. Cultural displays and hands-on crafts for children are provided, if you make prior arrangement. (Donations accepted.)

Pímu (Catalina Island) is the annual site for the *Ti'at* Plank Canoe Culture ceremony in honor of the boats that carried residents from the mainland back and forth. *Humaliwa* village on the mainland (Malibu) was the probable landing site from Pimu. Rancho Santa Ana Botanic Garden (Claremont) is the site of hundreds of native plants that have wondrously survived the onslaught of the city (See below). Rancho Los Cerritos (north end of Long Beach) is the site of an ancient Tongva village; the only remains there are shell fragments. One particular site has, however, been preserved, though laced with overhead wires— and that is the stone cliff called Eagle Rock. Even CalTrans was persuaded to curve Highway 134 around it. The shadowy image of Eagle landing with widespread wings can best be seen from across the freeway about noon.

WHERE CAN ONE SEE ANCIENT OBJECTS (called material culture) of the Los Angeles Basin peoples? The Southwest Museum in Pasadena is a good starting place. Los Angeles Natural History Museum by the University of Southern California campus is another. For some reason, the Antelope Valley Museum near Lancaster has a good collection of artifacts. The City Hall at Eagle Rock features a diorama of the area before settlement. San Dimas (just west of Claremont) presents a large mural of Juana Maria, a very famous Tongva ancestor. An annual festival is held in her honor.

Curiously, Missions San Fernando, San Gabriel, and Asisténcia de San Bernardino, give very little attention to the people who built these impressive and well-known missions in the first place. Go there and pay your respects to the ancestors who were the workers. The Serra Mass at San Gabriel is always attended by Tongva in full regalia who stand in silent witness.

MANY OF THE EARLY remembered traditions continue to be practiced and taught to youngers by a small core of elders (though some are very infirm). Gatherings tend to be within the extended families, though some larger meetings are held in halls. One group, known as the Gabrieleno-Tóngva Nation, holds regular meetings. The tribe selects a chief, supports an active dance company, sponsors several public gatherings annually, gathers for story-telling, supports the ceremonies and cultural activities at Satwiwa, and frequently is in demand at other neighboring events. Remarkable activities for 1800 people who have been considered "culturally extinct."

94 GABRIELINO/TONGVA SPRINGS FOUNDATION
P.O. Box 602043, Los Angeles, CA 90064
(310) 397-0180

GABRIELENO-TONGVA NATION
Tongva (Gabrieleno/Fernandeño)
Los Angeles, Orange, San Bernardino Counties
A tribe without land, never Federally recognized.

The vivid descriptions of this tribe are presented by Anthony Morales, Chief, and Mark F. Acuña, (*see p.56*) Tongva Nation Dance Captain

ANTHONY MORALES & MARK F. ACUÑA:

"A MAJOR ASPECT of our history is our tenacity. Despite the almost complete extermination of language, culture, traditions, music, land base, and presence, we have survived to surface in the 1990s. While other cousin and brother tribal nations have managed to hang on to bits and fragments of land, we have none. Yet we are here. We have begun an extensive language reconstruction (with eight language lessons and the start of a dictionary) and cultural retrieval program, including the return to traditional spiritual beliefs of our ancestors.

"Our dance company performs in full regalia and body paint. We have sung our songs anew from Satwiwa to San Diego, from San Gabriel to Catalina. We have danced at the annual Grunion Festival in San Diego and have performed for the Ti'at Festival on Catalina (Pimu). We sing songs and tell stories at Satwiwa and hold the annual Piñon ceremonies in the San Gabriel-San Bernardino Mountains.

"DESPITE EVERY EFFORT of nation, state, city, and county to turn blind eyes on our existence, we are here. Some 200 very active members of this Nation are with us; many hundreds more are active in various other Indian activities in the Basin. We have finally won state and county recognition. Even San Gabriel (Mission) has acknowledged our continuous existence. Presently we are working our way through the Federal labyrinth. Thanks to the Dance Company, our existence is even more obvious.

"A special group of Tongva people in cooperation with Rancho Santa Ana Botanic Garden (Claremont) botanists have recently published a guide for the original Tongva names and uses of these plants. The group helps with docent training there, also.

"WE PARTICIPATE IN OUR annual "Naming Ceremony" in August. We serve as silent witnesses in full regalia at San Gabriel Mission's Serra Mass. We gather on *P'imu* (Catalina) for the *Ti'at* Festival celebrating the Tongva Plank Canoe Culture. [*Catalina was a major site for mining steatite, or soapstone, from which fireproof ware can be made. See p.211.*] We hold the "Before Columbus" ceremony at the sacred springs of *Kuruvungna* in October. We join other groups in November at Heritage Park in Santa Fe Springs. Satwiwa is our final site of the year for dancing in November.

"The tribe is the Gabrieleno-Tongva Tribal Nation; the land is Tovangar; the language and the people are Tongva. Extant sacred sites are Kuruvungna,

Doc Con, Captain of Sheepshearers at San Juan Capistrano. (photograph #N 37182, courtesy of the Southwest Museum, Los Angeles, by Charles F. Lummis, ca. 1900)

Puvungna (on the grounds of California State University, Long Beach—under great threat of 'development'), and Eagle Rock (in the town of the same name)."

—Anthony Morales, Chief, and Mark F. Acuña, Tongva Nation Dance Captain

GABRIELENO/TONGVA TRIBAL NATION
196 E. Arrow Hwy., Claremont, CA 91711
(909) 624-2539

OTHER GABRIELINO/TONGVA GROUPS

GABRIELINO/TONGVA INDIANS OF CALIFORNIA
(largely west side, Los Angeles Basin)
Tribal Council Information: John Lassos
5450 Slauson Ave., Ste. 151,
Culver City, CA 90230-6000
(310) 390-4798

GABRIELINO BAND OF SOUTHERN CALIFORNIA INDIANS
Tribal Council Information: Vera Rocha
3451 Remy, Baldwin Park, CA 91706
(818) 962-8546

AJACHEMEM & LUISEÑO
(AJACHEMEM ALSO KNOWN AS JUANEÑO)

PRACTICALLY INDISTINGUISHABLE from their Luiseño neighbors in custom, tradition, and language, the Juaneños do have differing family backgrounds. The names of both groups derive from the missions San Juan Capistrano and San Luis Rey. Both territories shared a coastal environment, and dwellers settled along the low coastal shelf into the Santa Ana Mountains. Both lands extended up into this loose chain of Coast Range mountains.

The variety of wildlife and flora allowed the people to settle into relatively small areas and remain more or less in one village, without having to roam for food. As reliable water supplies were necessary, most villages were located on higher knolls of the flood plains of the rivers. These rises turned out to be ideal locations for the Spanish ranchos, since they did not flood in the winter rains. Today, among the few vestiges of early Indian presence in the L.A. Basin are the sites of these ranchos, in whose gardens can be found large sprinklings of abalone and clam shells from the middens.

Clan and family were extremely important, as was the territory of each family. Owing to various functions, such as monitoring and use of sensitive archeological sites, the knowledge of these territories and their boundaries is still important. *Ching-ich-ngish* was and is their revered supreme being (*see p.182*).

JUANEÑO

Juaneño territory extends up the coast more or less to the Santa Ana River, though the springs at Puvungna, on the northwest corner of the grounds of California State University, Long Beach (alongside the San Gabriel River) are held sacred by both the Juaneño and the Tongva. San Mateo Canyon (by Camp Pendleton), Bolsa Chica, and Aliso-Wood Canyon are areas carefully watched by the Natives (Juaneño and Luiseño alike) as pristine vestiges of their ancestral heritages. Acjacheme is the name of the main Native village near Misión San Juan Capistrano; the name is preserved by a street sign on the north side of the mission complex.

AJACHEMEM NATION (AK-HÓSH-MEM)
Juaneño Orange, Riverside, and San Diego Counties

For many reasons, many Natives of this region have grown up here without benefit of reservation status. That leaves them without much say in the councils of those who have land. Therefore, the Ajachmem Nation was organized to give assistance to these people and to provide a group in which to retain traditions and customs of their ancestors.

Most of these families are descendants of both the Spanish settlers and equally, the local Indians. Consequently, most are connected to both cultures.

Here, as in the rest of Mexico, the Indian religious system was transformed by name and function into the Spanish religion. *Ching-ich-ngish* took on the appearance of the Catholic God, and names of other religious beings and ceremonies changed.

The chair of the Ajachemem Nation, David Belardes, told me of his dual, rather than conflicting, faith. One half of his family is descended from two of the original Spanish (one of whom arrived with Portolá), Belardes and Yorba, the other half is Juaneño Indian. During a *Velório* (candelight ceremony), he recalls the songs of his father and grandfather—Indian songs translated into Spanish, but Indian nevertheless.

Tribal applications have been submitted for Federal recognition, but the BIA is making glacial progress.

The tribe does its best to attempt to preserve what few remnants of the past are still extant. They volunteer to help with Native American interpretation at the Blas Aguilar Museum, located in an old building across the street from the San Juan Capistrano Mission. They gather at the Puvungna Spring and village site in public ceremonies that observe spring and fall equinoxes. Belardes' son has learned a number of Indian dances (including intertribals).

95 AJACHEMEM NATION
David Belardes, Chair,
32161 Avenida Los Amigos,
San Juan Capistrano 92675
(714) 493-0959

LUISEÑO

The Luiseño people suffered less from Spanish rule than the Ajachmem. For some reason the padres allowed the Luiseño to live normal lives in their own villages. Nevertheless, when other whites arrived, they were evicted from their lands, and ended up in a few settlements, which eventually became the reservations of today. Large numbers of the people were left outside the reservation, where their descendants still live.

PALA RESERVATION
Luiseño, Ipai, and *Cupeño* (1875) San Diego County

Groups from three distinct people live on the ancient Luiseño territory that is the Pala Reservation: the Luiseño (named for their proximity to Misión San Luis Rey, and includes some people from Misión San Juan Capistrano (earlier called Juaneño); the Ipai (part of a group earlier called Diegueño, from Misión San Diego) are descendants of people brought here from several miles to the south; and the Cupeño (*p.243*) whose fathers were tragically dispossessed of land in and around what is now Los Coyotes Reservation (*see p.240*), about 40 miles to the east of here.

In family customs, ceremonies, and language, the three groups maintain some distinctiveness to this day. Intermarriage, proximity, and common religion have tended to blur most differences, however.

Burials at Pala Reservation (Luiseño, Ipai, and Cupeño) are often marked with a small carved-wood enclosure, with family objects inside. (dhe, 1985)

The interesting village consists of a large assemblage of older houses gathered about the reconstructed Misión San Antonio de Pala Asisténcia (*App.II*, **243**), decorated with ancient Indian motifs and flanked by the Indian cemetery. In the village center are small stores and the Cupa Cultural Center, focus for activities of the Cupeño people, and an adult learning center. Further out in the 11,600-acre reservation are a ballpark, school, and various government (HUD-type) homes, mobile homes, and small farms. Some income is derived from avocado farming and a gaming hall. Cupa Days Festival is the first week in May.

The former Mission Reserve Reservation, a rocky, chaparral-covered uninhabited mountain of 9,500 acres is attached to and part of the east side of Pala Reservation. Who knows what some early bureaucrat thought when he assigned such an uninhabitable rock for a reservation?

96 *The village of Pala is at the intersection of Hwy. S-16 and Hwy. 76, about 25 mi E of Oceanside.*
PALA RESERVATION TRIBAL OFFICE
P.O. Box 43, Pala, CA 92059
(619) 742-3784

LA JOLLA RESERVATION
Luiseño (1875) San Diego County
State Highway 76 passes through La Jolla and its verdant forest, a contrast in this dry region of brush and chaparral. In the valley, we go back in time. La Jolla Reservation hugs the wooded, southern slopes of Mt. Palomar and descends in cascading terraces to the cool forests of the upper reaches of the San Luis Rey River.

Along the creek, the reservation offers public campgrounds, access to river fishing and swimming/splashing at the cool San Luis Rey River water park. The campgrounds here and at nearby Los Coyotes are superb locales to explore and experience these ancient Indian lands.

Almost hidden in the flanks of the mountain are the scatter of homes, many with orchards and small cattle ranches. From the highway, a careful eye can pick out several adobe homes with yards adorned by flowers and cacti. The quiet, undeveloped beauty of these shady acres truly makes this a jewel, one of the original meanings of the Spanish La Jolla.

At milepost 40, a small dirt road leads up the mountainside to the reservation center—a small mission with its ancient Indian cemetery, a tribal center, and recreation fields.

98 *About 2 mi E of the Mt. Palomar Observatory road on both sides of Hwy. 76*
LA JOLLA RESERVATION
Star Rte. Box 158, Valley Center, CA 92082
(619) 742-3771

RINCON RESERVATION
Luiseño or *WA$XAYAM* (1875) San Diego County
Probably the best term for this reservation is "bustling." Although the reservation is more than a century old, there are new buildings for Health Services, an Indian Action Team (security), a fire department, and an Indian Education Center and Tribal Hall, entitled *wa$xayam pomki* ("Place of the Washxayam"—the Luiseños' name for themselves). The orthography (writing and spelling) above is theirs.

Scattered over the 3,960 acres are old and new homes, athletic fields, Catholic and Protestant chapels, and, in this green valley of spectacular vistas of Mt. Palomar, orange orchards, small farms, and even prickly pear cactus cultivation. Signs marking the reservation boundaries bear prohibitions against trespassing off the highway; the reservation has had trouble with people seriously damaging their fragile ecology. Roads and buildings are strictly for persons on business. However, the public is invited to the gaming hall.

At the La Jolla Reservation a deep southwestern flavor shows in adobe homes and cactus flowers. (dhe, 1984)

97 *Both sides of County Rd. S-6 (Valley Center Rd.), about 10 miles NE of Escondido. Signs mark entrance to reservation lands.*
RINCON RESERVATION
P.O Box 68, Valley Center, CA 92082
(619) 749-1051

PAUMA-YUIMA RESERVATION
Luiseño (1892) San Diego County

The area of these two segments of Mt. Palomar totals nearly 6,000 acres. Yuima is high on the Mt. Palomar slope; it has no residents. Pauma's ninety-odd residents live along Pauma Reservation Rd. The reservation is a settlement that has much of the character of a Mexican village—an earth-brown stucco chapel and Spanish-style tribal hall, all set in citrus groves and dissolving adobe ruins.

The Pauma Valley, the valley of the San Luis Rey River and its tributaries, lie in the shadow of the huge mountain. The seems to be of another era, not so touched by modernity. On the north, orange orchards striping the gentle western slope of the mountain produce some agricultural income.

99 *On Pauma Reservation Rd., off State Rte. 76, 1 1/2 mi. N of the town of Pauma Valley (30 miles E of Oceanside).*
PAUMA-YUIMA RESERVATION
P.O. Box 86, Pauma Valley, CA 92061
(619) 742-1289

PECHANGA RESERVATION
Luiseño (1882) Riverside County

The broad, highland mountain basin, sometimes gently watered and sometimes inundated by the Temecula River accommodates several ranches, some housing developments, and the 4,094 acres of the Pechanga Reservation.

FOR MANY YEARS ALL "development" was strictly individual, with some comfortable homes, many tiny ones, and some clutter. The roads were mostly unpaved, winding around the old clapboard chapel on a low hillside and the picturesque old wooden tribal hall. The residents wanted it this way—they'd rather not be saddled with paved roads and bulldozed countryside. It was this way for a century, so why change?

But the lure of the casino took over. The building rose like a modern mammoth, as did the income. Now much of the place looks not unlike Rancho Murietta, just up the road. But it is still comfortable.

On the west side of Highway S-16 lies the Pechanga burial ground and the remains of Juan Diego, hero of Helen Hunt Jackson's novel "Ramona"—an exposé of the terrible Indian conditions of the last century.

100 *Pechanga Rd. (47,000-block) off County Rd. S-16, just S of the intersection with Hwy. 79 (at Rancho California).*
PECHANGA RESERVATION,
P.O. Box 477, Temecula, CA 92593

SOBOBA RESERVATION
Luiseño and *Cahuilla* [ka-wé-a] (1883) Riverside Co.

Where the San Jacinto River at one time spread out over this wide valley, its currents cutting terraces at the edges of the low mountains, we find the Soboba Reservation's 5,036 acres. The arroyo bears enough water to support a few feathery trees, but not much else. However, the rough, colorful banded-rock countryside gives the eye plenty to admire. Although first a Cahuilla reservation, most of the people who live here now are Luiseño, quite a distance from their original territory and the other Luiseño reservations.

Along the rocky mesa are a few horse ranches, some newer and some elderly homes, an old chapel and cemetery, and fine offices in the *Ahmium* tribal hall and education center. Here, as well, are located dental and medical clinics. There are some archaeological displays in the tribal hall—relics retrieved from the hills and mountains of the area.

Soboba is the site for occasional powwows. A few miles away at Ramona Bowl, in April and May the Ramona Pageant tells the story of the terrible struggles of southern California's native population in the last century.

Probably the most obvious part of the rez is the gaming center. Don't stop there if you want to experience the reservation.

101 *East on Main St. in San Jacinto, cross the arroyo to Soboba Rd., R 1 mi to tribal center.*
SOBOBA RESERVATION
P.O. Box 487, San Jacinto, CA 92581
(714) 654-2765

SAN LUIS REY BAND OF MISSION INDIANS
Luiseño San Diego County

In the late 1800s, the Natives of northern San Diego County were being gathered up by the American government to put onto reservations. However, a very large number (about 4,000) of those known as Luiseño were missed or overlooked in the big sweep. These people stayed prudently quiet for many decades, but have decided that now is a good time to come forward to be recognized.

The tribe's annual public offering is their festival Powwow on the San Luis Rey Mission grounds, 2nd weekend in June, on the green in front of the mission, near the Lavanderia, the old Indian laundry facility on the banks of the San Luis Rey River.

The Misión San Luis Rey de Francia is located 5 mi. E of Oceanside (nr. Camp Pendleton) on St. Hwy. 76.
SAN LUIS REY BAND OF MISSION INDIANS
Carmen Mojado, co-chair,
Oceanside, CA
(760) 724-8505

PEOPLES EAST OF THE SIERRA DIVIDE

THE LANGUAGE GROUPS
THE PEOPLE
The Reservations, *Organizations*

SHOSHONEAN (UTO-AZTECAN) LANGUAGES ‡
NORTHERN PAIUTE
Ft. Bidwell Reservation[1], Cedarville Rancheria[1], Susanville Rancheria[1],*,
Antelope Valley Band of Paiutes (Coleville), *Utu Utu Gwaitu* Paiute Reservation
EASTERN MONO
no trust land
organization: Mono Lake Indian Community (Mono Lake/Lee Vining)
OWENS VALLEY PAIUTE
—with NORTHERN PAIUTE:
Bridgeport Colony*
—with WESTERN SHOSHONE:
Bishop Reservation*, Big Pine Reservation*, Lone Pine Reservation*, Fort Independence Reservation*
SOUTHERN PAIUTE [2]
Chemehuevi Reservation, Colorado River Tribes Reservation*
PANAMINT (WESTERN) SHOSHONE
Timbisha Shoshone Tribe (Death Valley)
KOSO PANAMINT SHOSHONE (China Lake)
Indian Ranch (terminated, some residents remain) no trust land
KAWAIISU (TEHACHAPI), KOSO and TUBATULABAL
organization: Kern Valley Indian (Kern River) Community
TUBATULABAL—residents on Tule River Reservation (*see Sacramento Valley, p.170*)

Other nearby Paiute communities in Nevada, closely related:
Pyramid Lake Reservation (Nixon), Reno-Sparks Colony (Sparks), Walker River Reservation (Schurz),
Yerington Reservation and Yerington Colony (Yerington)
Several other Northern Paiute communities are located in Oregon and Nevada.

HOKAN SPEAKERS ‡
WASHOE
Alpine Washoe Reservation,
Washoe Tribe of Nevada and California
(four locations Woodfords, California; Dresslerville Colony, Carson Colony, Reno-Sparks Colony, Nevada)

---

*Shared with other groups

[1] These reservations are discussed in "NORTHEASTERN CALIFORNIA" (*see Book 2, p.110 ff*)

[2] These tribes are discussed in "MOJAVE DESERT, COACHELLA VALLEY & COLORADO RIVER" (*see Book 3, p.236 p.246*)

‡ *See Languages, Tribal Origins, and Tribal Relationships discussion on page 12*

EAST OF THE SIERRA DIVIDE

MAP 9

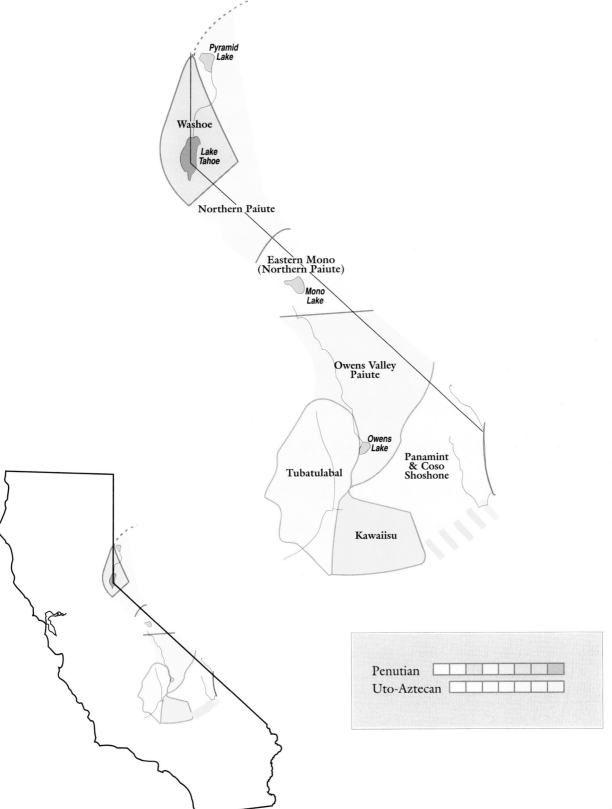

Pyramid Lake

Washoe

Lake Tahoe

Northern Paiute

Eastern Mono
(Northern Paiute)

Mono Lake

Owens Valley Paiute

Owens Lake

Tubatulabal

Panamint & Coso Shoshone

Kawaiisu

Penutian

Uto-Aztecan

EAST OF THE SIERRA NEVADA
THE ENVIRONMENT

WHEN THE MAPS WERE MADE delineating California, the line drawn just east of the Sierra Nevada mountain range, left only a tiny strip of the Great Basin within the State. This high, rather dry ecological area presents a startling contrast to the Central Valley and the Sierra, and we would rightly expect the life of the original peoples here to have been markedly different from those to the west.

The Sierra Nevadas do a good job of enticing moisture from the Pacific storms that pass overhead. Little is left for the eastern slopes, giving the land a scrubby desert, fiery hot in summer and windy-icy in winter. Nevertheless, it is home for many people. The earliest people here at the "crook" in the California borderline with Nevada were Washoe, who had plentiful food sources all around.

Their land surrounds Lake Tahoe and extends on all sides for several miles, giving them an unequalled variety of terrain. They had a knack for trading and an ear for languages, too, since they traded with Maidu to the west, and the Northern Paiute to the east.

The Shoshonean speakers of this region are descended from an extremely widespread group: the Shoshone and Paiute of the Great Basin, to the Ute of Utah and Colorado, and even to the Nahuatl (Aztec) of Mexico. They are significant to California because the peoples of this language group not only touch the Sierra on the east, but also occupy Indian country through the Owens Valley and almost the entire Mojave-Los Angeles Basin area.

The narrow strip of Great Basin in northeast California adjacent to Nevada is the country of the Northern Paiute, a people whose lands extend into Oregon and Idaho as well as into central Nevada. Their California lands are included in the discussion of Northeastern California peoples (*see p.110*).

Walker Valley Paiute, once scattered, now have a village, the Antelope Valley Indian Community, in Coleville. It's a little HUD-style village, an enclave of people who had been looking for a homeland for many years. They are now trying to establish their right to Federal recognition. At first, the place seems remote and isolated, it is, but the people here have something to call their own, along the beautiful and cold Walker River, with a reliable water supply and better access to education and health care than their former scattered desert shacks. Today they are a community.

IT TAKES A LOT OF HOMELAND attachment and spectacular Sierra scenery to overcome the desire to flee a destitute existence. The Indian people of Bridgeport have not fled. My first visit to the Bridgeport Reservation in 1979 was a shocker—the majority of the people were existing in dilapidated clapboard houses more than half a century old. Years later, one can find one or two of those run-down houses, but they are deserted. Today there are more than thirty comfortable homes on the 40-acre reservation on a low bench overlooking the old town of Bridgeport and its lake. The sights of the Sierra Nevada from here are of the postcard, travelogue, calendar quality. These Paiute people have existed as a community for hundreds of years, and now have an even more desirable place to call home.

Down U.S. 395 shines Mono Lake, once drying up because of Los Angeles' thirst and political power, now rising, owing to the concern and action of people from many walks of life. The lake is sacred to the Eastern Mono people, now scattered and without reservation land. East through pine-rimmed glass craters is the jagged land where Mono and Paiute and Shoshone once picked up the natural obsidian glass for making the finest arrow points. They traded this essential resource far and wide for hundreds of miles. At mile-high Benton Hot Springs the modest collection of homes to the south is the Utu Utu Gwaitu Paiute Reservation.

Minerals deposited from the underwater springs at Mono Lake form the odd formations seen here. The lake is within the Eastern Mono ancestral lands, but now tribal members associate with other Native peoples living in the region, mainly Paiute.   (dhe, 1989)

An Owens Valley vista of the Inyo Mountains is inspiring. These rocks bear inscriptions probably carved there by hunter shamans, hoping to inspire their students to a proper relationship with their food source—antelope. (dhe, 1985)

UPON A DESERT HiLLSiDE is a community of environmentally designed modern homes, overlooking a few abandoned wooden shacks that have tumbled into the tumbleweed. To the north of Bishop, on the Utu Utu Gwaitu Paiute Reservation in Benton several unusual new homes are designed for sun-catching in winters that can be quite cold. Members of the tribe own a gas station/RV park at the main intersection (Highway120 and U.S. 6) with a restaurant noted for its homemade soup. The White Mountains tower above it all, silently, as they always have.

Other of these Shoshonean peoples whose lands are within California include the Mono (relatives of the Western Mono or Monache), from which we get the name Mono Lake; the Owens Valley Paiute; a portion of the Western Shoshone people (in the Panamints and Death Valley); the Kawaiisu of the lower Kern River; and a portion of the Southern Paiute, including the Chemehuevi (a California Colorado River people). These last three groups will be discussed in the next section.

GENERALLY, THE GREAT BASiN groups lived on land that, characteristic of high desert, is very warm in summer, and can be extremely cold in winter. The land is not devoid of water, but one must know where to look for it, and the Paiutes made full use of what there was. Food supplies of the Great Basin peoples were reasonably plentiful. Although the desert is to the east of the mountains, the Sierra streams flow eastward from melting snow, and flow year-round into the Mono Lake basin and the Owens Valley. The wetter upper slopes of the mountains offer moisture for

piñon pines and their tasty nuts. Fish are plentiful in the mountain lakes and streams. Deer and antelope frequent the grassy slopes, the marshlands are excellent stops for the many migrating birds.

THE ENViRONMENTAL SETTiNG did not require periodic migration, as would living in a wide, dry, dusty desert. Consequently, Owens Valley people became more settled than their Paiute and Shoshone desert cousins. They erected large frame domed structures, often with a sunken room area to offer better protection from the rain and cold, then roofing them with reeds or skins. These people were known to practice a form a farming, with large irrigated sloping fields.

Religious practices were similar to the other Paiute peoples. the "Cry" mourning ceremonies were, and are observed in several places. Hunting was a form of religious activity, requiring the shaman to offer thanks to the hunted animal for its sacrifice, but also obliging the hunter to know the trails frequented by the animals. Thus, we find elaborate glyphs carved into certain rock formations, for the probable purposes of instructing the hunter and influencing the deer.

Today's Paiute people are of two groups. Those from the drier parts of Nevada and eastern California live in small, scattered reservations or live individually off-reservation. Those from the Owens Valley find themselves in a rather provident area, on the Bishop Reservation and three other small enclaves.

THE OWENS VALLEY PAiUTE were promised 66,000 acres of the valley for a reservation in 1910— land that, of course, was theirs to begin with. However, thirsty Los Angeles "bought" the land from white possessors and took over the cascading waters of Bishop Creek and the Owens River from the local farmers to build the Los Angeles Aqueduct in 1913.

The 875 acres of the Bishop Reservation, with an additional total 872 acres of Big Pine, Ft. Independence, and Lone Pine Reservations to the south, are all that are left of the grand promise. Early guidebooks speak of the great fertility of the Owens Valley. The few farms and dried-up rows of trees that are left reveal what it must have been. The Bishop Reservation retained some water rights, as numerous irrigation ditches gurgle through green pastures.

The reservation, like most of the base of the Owens Valley, sits on the dry, high river floodplain, a region of sagebrush and rounded stones. Although the valley is nearly 4,000 feet in elevation, it lies low between the Sierra Nevada and the White and Inyo Mountains— both ranges towering 10,000 feet above.

In this extraordinarily tranquil setting, the people of the Reservation—Paiute, from this valley, and Shoshone from over the White Mountains in the

Panamint Valley—live, farm, and do the tasks of survival. Homes on the reservation are spaced in parcels—like tiny farms. Cows and horses graze, along with other farm animals.

The Washoe people inhabited the territory around Lake Tahoe, trading both sides of the Lake; to the east, the Paiute desert people, to the west, Maidu. This positioned the Washoe in an excellent trading situation. Salmon and other river fish and deer hides from the Maidu—obsidian and desert game and birds from the east. Today, they live almost entirely on the eastern, drier side of the Sierra along the California-Nevada state line.

Other peoples of the region have fared only marginally as tribes. The Mono people maintain a well-organized group in Lee Vining at Mono Lake. Kawaiisu people are a large part of a small community around Lake Isabella, the Kern Valley Indian Community. Those Tubatulabal people not on the Tule River Reservation have also associated with this group, as well as some southern Central Valley Yokuts. Other off-reservation Coso Shoshone down the Owens Valley associate with various Owens Valley reservations.

THE WESTERN SHOSHONE people once occupied a large region from the Panamint Valley and Coso Range, through central Nevada, into northwestern Utah. Present day California residents live in or around the Owens Valley reservations, in the terminated Indian Ranch Rancheria, and in Death Valley National Monument as the Timbisha Shoshone Band. Their history is in part presented at the Visitors Center.

ANCIENT PETROGLYPHS

NOTE: Many of this area's thousands of ancient rock carvings have been and are being vandalized at an alarming rate. Please report any violations of these sacred sites to tribal or sheriff's police. Destruction of our ancient heritage is forbidden.

Rabbit skin capes and blankets were a specialty of the Washoe people. The cold, dry, windy winters of the eastern Sierra slopes made warm clothing a necessity. This man is curing and stretching the skins. (State Parks, date unknown.)

PENUTIAN LANGUAGES

Penutian languages probably arose in California; they are found largely in the central and northern parts of the state, and are related to some languages of Oregon and eastern Washington. The Washoe people belong to the Penutian language group.

WASHOE

WASHOE COUNTRY surrounded Lake Tahoe and the upper Truckee River region. These people speak a California Hokan language, and served as friendly trading intermediaries between the California and the Great Basin peoples. Their language is related to their California neighbors, and they used the Shoshonean languages. Trade from the east consisted largely of salt from the salt lakes of Nevada, fish from Tahoe and Pyramid Lakes; from the west trade included acorns (the Indian delicacy) from Maidu country and basketry materials, not abundant in the desert. [As the Washoe were reported to be friendly and well-supplied, it is unfortunate that the Donner Party, which bogged down in their territory, pridefully and arrogantly refused Indian assistance, preferring to starve, and worse. —ed].

Washoe bands were, in the old times, fairly stationary, living near the green mountains east of Lake Tahoe that sustain the the fertile Carson River Valley. From the 10,000-foot peaks to the mile-high desert below, food sources were quite plentiful. Their twined and coiled woven baskets are splendid.

From the wet winter storms of the Pacific, first the Coast Ranges, then the mighty Sierra Nevada wring rain and snow. Little moisture is left for the eastern slopes—it is desert, just about where Nevada begins. So it isn't too unexpected that the government "found" this type of land appropriate for Indian habitation. This is where the Washoe centers are today.

The Washoe Tribe sponsors a gathering and basket-weaving display at Tallac Historical Site on the southwest shore of Lake Tahoe every year in July (usually the third weekend). The *Wa She Shu It Deh* Festival invites both California and powwow-type dancing, vendors of excellent Indian wares and foods, hand games, as well as weavers who weave and sell their marvelous baskets. On the site also are a small Washoe Museum and a Washoe Native plants garden.

ALPINE-WASHOE RESERVATION

Hung-a-Lel-Ti Washoe (1970s) Alpine County

In the mid-1970's a sturdy tribal council hall and education center were put up on a plot of 80 acres in a field on the desert. A well was dug, streets laid out and paved, a modern school was built. This is today the home for 44 families—people from the adjacent Dutch Valley. Some 300 Indian families live in the valley now, in the place which had since early times been a small Indian village.

Solitude reigns over their desert, with seven ice-cream-cone peaks of Alpine County as a backdrop to the California Washoe community near Woodfords. Their other community is in Gardner, Nevada, a few miles away, shared with some Paiutes. The Indian land is pure desert, but with a network of paved roads, water, electricity, and a tribal center with a child education group.

William Dancing Feather, Director of the summer gathering of Washoe people presides over the tribal information booth. Tallac Historic Site, South Lake Tahoe. (dhe, 1998)

115 *From Woodfords, CA, (at Hwy. 4 intersection, go E 3 mi on Hwy. 88, S of Lake Tahoe) to Diamond Valley Rd. (before the Nevada state line. Go S about 1 mi over the Carson River on to the settlement on the next mesa.*

WOODFORDS COMMUNITY COUNCIL, SOUTHERN BAND WASHOE TRIBE
2111 Carson River Rd., Markleville, CA 96120

DRESSLERVILLE COLONY AND CARSON COLONY

Nevada Washoe, Douglas & Washoe Counties, NV

Today, the majority of the Washoe people reside in these two smaller reservations, just over the state line in Nevada. The main tribal office for all the Washoe is on U.S. 395 in the area known as Dresslerville, across from the famous Smoke Shop. A health clinic is next to the Shop. The settings of the reservations are beautiful; the places themselves seem to be comfortable.

The Gardnerville, NV, reservation is alongside the Carson River on both sides of U.S. 395, S of town. Signs for both Tribal Office (E side) and Health Center (W side) of U.S 395. Carson Colony is near Stewart Indian School at the S edge of Carson City.

WASHOE TRIBE OF NEVADA-CALIFORNIA
919 Hwy. 395-S, Gardnerville, NV 89410
(Dresslerville)

SHOSHONEAN LANGUAGES

Shoshonean is one of a large group of Uto-Aztecan languages spoken in the Great Basin, including eastern and southern California, also by the Comanches, and the Aztecs of Mexico. Shoshonean tribes of Eastern California are the Paiutes, Owens Valley Paiutes, Koso Panamint Shoshone, Kawaiisu, and Tubatulabal.

PAIUTES
(OF EASTERN CALIFORNIA)

ORIGINAL NORTHERN PAIUTE lands occupied a huge triangle from eastern Oregon and Idaho on the north, southward along the Sierra front range to Mono Lake in California, and on the east through the western third of Nevada. Of necessity they moved fairly frequently, from summer to winter grounds, never far from water sources. The high mountains and crags of the Humboldt and Sierra ranges are good at snagging moisture from the sky; the runoff gathers in a few rivers and creeks; the grass and trees on the mountainsides give sustenance. Some of the water even seeps far underground to bubble up unexpectedly from distant springs. Utah Utes recognized the proximity of their western cousins to water; hence, *pah-ute* (pah, water).

Paiute ponies do the hardest work on the Lone Pine Reservation. (dhe, 1982)

Early Paiutes knew where to find these places of sustenance, honoring and distinguishing the sacred grounds with some of the most exquisite and ingenious pictographs in the country. The immigrants and miners who have plundered the countryside for a hundred years likewise mutilated many of these rare sites. Fortunately, some of the most valuable places have been protected, often through good luck, as in the China Lake Naval Weapons Station. Some sites are still esteemed ceremonial centers for Paiute spiritual leaders.

The Paiutes nearest California were (and are) more fortunate in having rather reliable water sources, from the Warner Mountains in the northeast, the Sierra's Truckee, Carson, and Walker Rivers—the many clear and cold east-flowing streams along the mountain front, fed all summer by reserves of melting snow.

The Northern Paiute reservations north of Lake Tahoe are discussed in the section Northeastern California. South of that lake are several small communities: Bridgeport Colony, Antelope Valley in Coleville, and Utu Utu Gwaitu Reservation (in the upper Owens Valley).

AROUND MONO LAKE a dialect of Paiute developed that was different enough so that that linguists call it Mono, or Monache. Some of their people found it easy enough to cross over the mountains in summer, establishing small enclaves of Mono peoples on the western slopes of the Sierra. They are discussed in the section on Central California. The Indian people remaining on the eastern side, the Eastern Mono, never were given a chance to establish a land base; nevertheless, they maintain an organization, the Mono Lake Indian Community, made up of Paiute, Yosemite Mono, and other Native peoples in the locality of Lee Vining.

OWENS VALLEY'S NATURAL attractions brought groups speaking a dialect of the Paiute/Shoshone language. Although these bands had names for themselves, we usually refer to them by their (Celtic) geographical name Owens Valley Paiute. Their relative isolation and sedentary existence allowed them to develop aspects of culture unlike their Great Basin cousins. Water sources were much more plentiful and more reliable; their climate was gentler; their land was more susceptible to a variety of methods of cultivation; animal life was more confined. Their reservations are sketched later in this section.

ANTELOPE VALLEY INDIAN COMMUNITY

(mostly) *Northern Paiute*, Mono County

A few years ago, the United States Department of Housing and Urban Development (HUD) used an old military plot of land called Camp Antelope for the construction of 32 homes for a number of Indian people (mostly landless Paiutes), who had been living in grossly inadequate places along the eastern slopes of the Sierra. Its houses are arrayed about a desert hillside, overlooking the oasis-like Walker River Valley, with vistas of lofty mountains to the west.

The community looks like a HUD suburb—most homes are alike, but some are beautifully tended with gardens, while others are ill-kempt, depending on the mind of the keeper. In spite of its faults, the project is exemplary. I have seen many HUD reservation homes. There appear to be about two or three house plans; one or two bedrooms, universally made with those brown plywood sheets. Though sturdier than 50-year-old clapboard boxes, and comfortable if kept up, they are not the easiest to maintain. In any event, finally these people have a village, and are trying to gain Federal recognition for their status as a Paiute community.

116 *Off U.S. 395 at Coleville, Eastside Lane (S side of town), 1 mi to Camp Antelope*
ANTELOPE VALLEY INDIAN COMMUNITY
P.O. Box 119, Coleville, CA 96107

BRIDGEPORT INDIAN COLONY

Northern Paiute (recognized in 1974, settled long before) Mono County

Stand by one of the now-empty paintless little cabins here, looking at majestic mountains, and try to imagine what a zero-degree windy winter across these 40 acres must have been like. This, too, is all a part of Indian existence in California. About two of these relics exist as mementos of the past, but today 30-odd comfortable homes replace the clapboard shacks I first encountered here in 1984.

THE OCCUPANTS OF these new homes and mobile homes have one of the most enviable spots in California—a community on a mesa overlooking a wide, round, 6,700-foot-high valley with Bridgeport Lake as its heart, surrounded by 10,000-foot peaks. Finally, a people who have suffered privation for so long have a decent community to call home. The people do have occasional gatherings, around the thatched ramadas lining the edge of their recreation field.

For the public, the tribe sponsors a Native American Crafts Days in Bridgeport Park with live crafts demonstrations, workshops, Indian dancing and music, and vendors, the second weekend in August, an excellent time to escape the heat of the rest of California.

117 *From Hwy 182 (close to the intersection with U.S. 395 in Bridgeport), take Aurora Canyon Rd. The reservation is immediately to the S of this road.*
BRIDGEPORT INDIAN COLONY
P.O. Box 37, Bridgeport, CA 93517
(760) 932-7083
Crafts Show (760) 934-3342

A cluster of comfortable homes on an open mesa with vistas of the town, the reservoir, and the snow-cones of the Sierras. This is the Bridgeport Colony Reservation—home to many Paiute peoples of Great Basin origins. (dhe, 1992)

OWENS VALLEY PAIUTE

THE OWENS RIVER follows a long, deep, formerly well-watered valley between the foot of the eastern slopes of the Sierra Nevada and the western slopes of the Inyo and White Mountains.

In this space they developed the only known irrigation systems in early California. Streams falling from the Sierra were diverted into communally held meadows for seasonal watering of large crops of tubers. After harvest, crops were replanted. The Owens Valley people also harvested two crops of bugs: one a huge pine-eating caterpillar that is high in protein value and keeps well when dried; the other a brine fly larvae which collected in drifts on the ancient Owens Lake. Apparently both creatures were used much as Asian chefs use their prized dried shrimp.

OTHER FEATURES that distinguished Owens Valley Paiutes from Great Basin peoples were use of a very large, 25-foot-diameter semi-subterranean sweat-lodge-community house, something like the round-house of the north. They also made and used a simple pottery.

An excellent place to appreciate much of the early culture of this 80-mile-long valley is the Paiute-Shoshone Museum and Cultural Center on the Bishop Reservation. The building ornamented with startling designs, has outstanding displays and a crafts shop. On the reservation itself are many historical older and newer buildings, in a magnificent setting.

UTU UTU GWAITU PAIUTE (BENTON) RESERVATION

Owens Valley and *Northern Paiute* (1915) Mono Co.

At the desert intersection of U.S. 6 (which once connected L.A. with N.Y.) with Highway 120 (that connects I-5 with U.S. 6 through Yosemite), is mile-high Benton Hot Springs. This is near the reservation. Look south. Only a few years ago, in 1985, a few primitive homes sat lonely upon the desert hillside alongside a few abandoned wooden shacks; and the White Mountains towered above it all, silently, as they always have. Nearly everyone left, but the place was not forgotten. The scattered tribe worked hard to get funds to return. Some 100 persons now live comfortably on their 400 acres, in homes environmentally designed by a Sacramento firm especially for this place. The gas station and RV park at the intersection are owned by tribal members.

118 *From Hwy. 120 (2 mi W of Benton) at Benton Hot Springs, 1/2 mi. S up Yellow Jacket Rd. The reservation lies on both sides of the road for 1 mi. You are invited to have a look; the people are proud of their place.*
UTU UTU GWAITU (BENTON) PAIUTE RESERVATION
Star Rte. 4, Box 65-A, Benton, CA 93512

The Bishop Reservation (Owens Valley Paiute and Shoshone) provides spacious residence parcels for many families in this spectacular setting. Although much water was appropriated from the Valley by the Los Angeles Water Department many years ago, the reservation has held on to most of its water rights—irrigation ditches are normally full. (dhe, 1977)

BIG PINE RESERVATION
Owens Valley Paiute and *Panamint Shoshone*
(1912, 1937) Inyo County

What is said of the Bishop Reservation previously in terms of its setting in the spectacular Owens Valley may be said also of Big Pine. Here the valley is narrower; the mountainsides don't slope, they plunge.

The reservation consists of dispersed homesites in rectangular parcels, occupying most of the eastern side of the town of Big Pine. Many homes have been erected under the auspices of OVIHA, the Owens Valley Indian Housing Authority.

On the rather dry 279 acres there is simply a small community, a gathering of people of like background. A few horses can be found that are raised for pack trips into the Sierras.

120 *On U.S. 395, in the town of Big Pine, both sides of Bartell Rd. (E of highway), and tribal offices on U.S. 395 near Blake Rd.*
BIG PINE RESERVATION
814 S. Main, P.O. Box 700, Big Pine, CA 93513
(619) 938-2003

BISHOP RESERVATION
Owens Valley Paiute and *Panamint Shoshone*
(1912) Inyo County

The Bishop Reservation is a remarkable place. The setting is unusual—dry valleys, massive green mountains on one side, and massive bare ones on the other. The reservation itself is not unusual, but it's important to appreciate that they were mostly a hunting and gathering people, used to the open range, who have only recently been forced to settle into a farming lifestyle. Realize, too, that 65,000 acres were taken from them only 70 years ago (*p.219*).

THE MOST STRIKING building complex houses the tribal offices and community center. Crafts, history, and artifacts of the Paiute and Shoshone peoples are displayed in their impressive museum, open April to October. A tour around the reservation will reveal a day care center, an historic old multi-story former tribal office, and a couple of clapboard churches that have served some of the people for many years.

119 *W side of the town of Bishop. Hwy. 168 passes through it.*
BISHOP RESERVATION
P.O. Box 548, Bishop, CA 93514
(619) 873-3584

Members of the Paiute Pentecostal Church on the Bishop Reservation prepare lunch for others in need of spiritual and physical nourishment. (dhe, 1977)

FORT INDEPENDENCE RESERVATION
Owens Valley Paiute (1915) Inyo County

Ironic as it may seem, several California reservations occupy the land of the conqueror. In 1862, at Fort Independence (349) in the center of the Owens Valley, the U.S. Army dug some caves (some still here) in a dry wash embankment for the enlisted men to stay in, and put up tents for the officers, who later moved into wooden quarters (one remains). The fort, or "camp" as it was then called, was to subdue the inordinately active Paiutes, who had a certain natural attraction for their long-time valley homes. The camp was soon abandoned, but later occupied by the local Indian people in search of a new place to call home, unoccupied Federal land. Today a few of the people make a scant living on 356 acres of the old fort grounds. Pastures stay green from an irrigation ditch. A couple of ancient buildings shelter some families, newer homes others. It is very quiet.

The sawteeth of 14,500-foot Mt. Whitney loom right down into the Owens Valley upon Ft. Independence; the clouds pass over, very high, seldom even watering the Inyo Mountains, just to the east. To understand the words "splendor" and "grandeur" and why the Paiutes wanted their valley, go five miles up the side road toward Kearsarge Pass. Look back and lament their loss.

TO GAIN A WIDER UNDERSTANDING of the history of the Valley's Native peoples, the Paiutes and the Shoshones, visit the Eastern California Museum on Grant St. in town. Although intermittently open, the Indian campgrounds along U.S. 395 are in a magnificent place to spend time.

121 *About 2 mi N of the town of Ft. Independence on U.S. 395. Take Schabell Rd. about 1 block (to cave sites in a dry wash). Reservation extends over both sides of U.S. 395.*
FT. INDEPENDENCE RESERVATION
P. O. Box 67, Independence, CA 93526
(619) 878-2126

LONE PINE RESERVATION
Owens Valley Paiute and *Panamint Shoshone* (1937), Inyo County

As what is left of the Owens River dribbles towards its end in Owens Lake, it passes Lone Pine. It is lonely, but only if one doesn't care for grand mountains, quiet, desert, and solitude. The railroad ended here. Pack trips begin here, often on Indian horses.

The reservation of 237 acres is rather new (1937). New homes appear, courtesy of OVIHA. In the town of Lone Pine is a trading post at 137 S. Main. Some diligence may reward you for finding sales of piñon nuts, once a staple of these peoples.

122 *On U.S. 395, just S of Lone Pine—tribal office on W side of the highway*
LONE PINE RESERVATION
Star Route 1, 1101 S. Main St.,
Lone Pine, CA 93545
(619) 876-5414

OWENS
VALLEY
PAIUTE

From the road up to Kearsarge Pass, just under Mt. Whitney, the town of Ft. Independence is visible. The Owens Valley Paiutes found places such as this worth fighting for, obliging the Army to erect its fort. Today, the fort is an Indian Reservation. (dhe, 1977)

SHOSHONE

As discussed previously, Shoshonean is the name given to Uto-Aztecan languages spoken in the Great Basin and eastern California. The group called Numic is found in Nevada and Utah. Great areas of the west from Oregon, Idaho, Utah and Nevada are either Paiute or Shoshone land. (Further discussion later) The eastern mountain front of California, north of Mono Lake and south to Mammoth, is Paiute country. Shoshone tribes extended mostly into the Koso, Panamint, and Death Valleys east of the Inyo Mountains in California.

Three arroyos of hard volcanic rock are well-preserved by the military within the China Lake Naval Weapons Station in the Mojave Desert. On the walls of each of these are carved hundreds of petroglyphs, left there by generations of students of weather and bighorn sheep (and other topics). This is a "teaching" site, where those seeking to become predictors and controllers of rain come to receive their visions.

PANAMINT (WESTERN) SHOSHONE (ALSO KOSO OR COSO)

THE ANCESTRAL WESTERN SHOSHONE people occupied a huge area from northwestern Utah in a swath across modern-day Nevada to Death Valley and the Panamint Valley, at the southern end of the Inyo Mountains. This is DRY country, scorched in summer, freeze-dried in winter. Nevertheless, the early people found springs, protected valleys, even a few streams. Of necessity, they had a closer relation to the land than most peoples, since they were obliged to stay close to their sources of sustenance. They cultivated mesquite, piñon pine nuts, oaks, managed wildlife, fuel, and food plants. Parts of Death Valley and Panamint Valley are just such places that this tribe inhabited and maintained.

IN THE BIG SWEEPS OF INDIAN TRIBES to reservations in the 1800s, most Panamint Shoshone people were gathered into the Owens Valley reservations of Bishop, Big Pine, Lone Pine, and Fort Independence. These places are discussed in the previous section.

Other Shoshone managed to escape the sweep, and lived independently in the Panamint, Koso, and Death Valley areas. A small settlement around a water source was once designated Indian Ranch, near Wildrose, Death Valley National Monument. Federal trust was terminated in the 1950s; however, several Indian families still live there on their parcels. Other of these Shoshones have lived scattered about the area, but have retained ties as a tribal family for a very long time.

IN 1933, upon creation of **DEATH VALLEY NATIONAL MONUMENT**, the government decided to remove the Indians of Panamint and Death Valleys from their settlements near their springs and sources of sustenance. A place was made for them (now the Timbisha Shoshone Tribe) in Furnace Creek amid a shady grove of salt cedar and salty water. Even so, as this spot was envied by RV-ers, they were moved again to the most barren southern margins of the Furnace Creek settlement. The people were "offered employment" producing handicrafts for the trading post, washing Park Service employee's clothes, or being put on display outside of the trading post's door

The bighorn sheep is used as the rain symbol, since it inhabits desert land where the most rain falls. The sheep is seen as being pierced by an arrow, falls apparently dead, later rising and running. The vision-seeker may also fall unconscious, to rise again with power. The analogy in Christianity is apparent. Honor and respect is also devoted to the rattlesnake, as seen by numerous representations of the snake and its diamond-like designs. The area has been used by mostly Paiute shamans for centuries, drawing learners from as far away as Idaho and Montana.   (dhe, 1994)

as "guides". Even the laundry was run by the Park Service. This situation was soon abandoned, as tribal members refused to submit.

IN 1999, situations reversed with a change of attitude by the Park Service. Death Valley National Park became expanded on nearly all sides, absorbing much land formerly controlled by the Bureau of Land Management and private sources. At the same time, not only the existence of the Timbisha was recognized, but also their claims to land. The Tribe itself has been "invited" to be a working partner in environmental caretaking of a large bloc of the Park. The original idea had been explored and put forth by the Tribe earlier, but only recently has the Park Service responded favorably. These tribal efforts are supported by environmental groups such as Greenpeace.

TIMBISHA SHOSHONE TRIBE
DEATH VALLEY NATIONAL PARK
Panamint Shoshone (1933, 1983) Inyo County
A Federally recognized tribe with a newly-negotiated claim to their ancestral land base.

The tribe is comprised of some 300 members, some 50 of whom live and work in Death Valley and the surrounding area, the rest not having been allowed to reside in the Valley. But with great determination, this little group of descendants of the original Western Shoshone has managed to survive borax miners, 20-mule wagon trains, and government takeover. A long succession of demeaning and arrogant policies has attempted to deny the *Timbisha* any permanent access to any portion of their ancestral lands. ("They are not compatible with Park purposes.")

Federal recognition as a tribe was obtained in 1983, but this did not guarantee their land holdings. The tribe has since requested a land restoration program, with the tribe responsible for preserving traditional cultural and land uses over a portion of Death Valley. (Within the Park boundaries a cyanide-extraction gold mine continues to function—a condition of an earlier Park expansion.)

The Timbisha will be able to have land claim over several parcels both within and at the edges of the Park for several purposes—housing and various economic developments, cultural resource protection (including mesquite and piñon harvest areas and land management), tribal government offices, and a museum/cultural center. Timbisha persistence has resulted in an impressive cultural revival.

Finally, the Park Service has come to understand that it was the Shoshone whose land was taken away in the first place. Native American stewardship of land that has been illegally removed from their control should be managed in a traditional and ecologically sound

way, and will be once again. The process of restoration takes much time and effort. [*See also Yosemite.*]

Much of this information has been furnished by the Timbisha Tribal Office and the *San Francisco Chronicle*, July 11, 1999.

123 *Tribal land in 2000 is on 40 acres, called the "Indian Village", on the S edge of the Furnace Creek complex and is the planned center of the newly acquired land.*
TIMBISHA SHOSHONE TRIBE
P.O. Box 206, Death Valley, CA 92328

KAWAIISU (ka-waí-ee-su) & TUBATULABAL (tu-bá-tu-labal)

A RESURRECTION OF IDENTITY among groups of the Southern Sierra-Tehachapi region is happening. Some years ago, just as I was about to accept the anthropologists' writings of the "disappearance" of the Kawaiisu and Tubatulabal peoples, I learned of a powwow in Tehachapi. From Ron Wermuth at that gathering, I found out about a newly-formed council representing some 400 Indian families who live scattered about that region.

He told me of a number of families living in secluded areas of these rugged Sierras that still speak the old language—in fact, they hardly know English. Three groups of this region identify themselves as branches of Paiute: *Kawaiisu* (Tehachapi), *Tubatulabal* (Kern River/Lake Isabella), and *Koso Panamint Shoshone* (China Lake area). Since linguists consider the Paiute and Shoshone languages as nearly identical Uto-Aztecan groups, this self-description is quite logical. The people themselves maintain close ties with the Paiute groups of Owens Valley and with the Mono (also Shoshonean-language people) of the foothills further north. Their annual late-June powwow is usually held in a high, cool, green mountain valley near Tehachapi.

IMAGINE A WIDE BAND across the southern Tehachapis continuing northeastward across Owens Valley into the Inyo Mountains and the Panamint Valley inhabited by these three tribes.

The Tubatulabal territory originally was an area from near the Grapevine at Kitanemuk country, across the Tehachapis to and including the Kern River. All these, Kawaiisu, Tubatulabal, and Koso had considerable similarities in lifestyles, governed as they were by similar ecologies of high mountains and dry foothills or plains. The Tulatulabal, however, had the added generous advantage of the Kern River from which to draw water and fish.

The Kawaiisu lands occupied the more remote southern Tehachapis, eastward to the Owens Valley from the Mojave Desert to about Lone Pine. No rivers here and very few streams; springs sustained life.

The Panamint Koso were desert and dry mountain dwellers, consequently, they had to move with the seasons more often. Their lands began just above the Kern River, over the mountains, through China Lake Basin, into the Mojave Desert and up to Death Valley. Their prime survival means was hunting. Their basketry has been described as plain but very functional. Their art was reserved for other media.

IN THIS AREA STAND SOME of the most fascinating examples of rock art known, the Koso Pictographs. Within the China Lake Naval Weapons Station, and under the visitation supervision of the Maturango Desert Museum in Ridgecrest, are three canyons whose walls are laden with pictures carved into the dark brown walls of desert "varnish".* This was (and continues to be) a Paiute school for the training of shamans majoring in the invocation of the water spirits, drawing students from as far away as Utah. (*See Rock Art, p.62*)

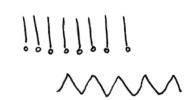

WATER, with a rain symbol ||||||||| , is linked with the bighorn sheep, ¥ , which are found in the mountains within the Paiute/Shoshone Great Basin and Plains range (Idaho to California). Portions of this region are frequently in need of more rain, so practicing this invocation is a most necessary skill. These motifs abound, along with drawings of the medicine pouch, rattlesnake patterns, and human/humanoid figures. The hunt is figuratively pictured, but only of the bighorn. (Antelopes were the hunted animal, and are pictured in other canyons, none here.) Since the bighorn was seldom hunted, what is shown here is the figurative killing and resurrection of the sheep. [*Does this bring to mind other religions?*] Along the upper portions of the canyons are meditation niches for the initiates to occupy during their vision quests. The rattlesnakes are watching and are friendly, so long as they are not disturbed.

Just down the slope (off limits to all but tribal members with passes) bubbling and gurgling springs vent hot, steaming water into channels lined with red algae—the female complement to the more male locale upslope. Deep rumbling sounds come from within the earth. Female spiritual leaders make their offerings here.

Over in the Panamint Valley are intaglios, like those along the Colorado River (*q.v.*). Five miles east of Tehachapi, the Sand Canyon Rd. exit off of Highway 58 leads in about 10 miles to a new state park, the ruins of an ancient Kawaiisu village.

Today, most of the members of these tribes live in their private homes around the region, though some, especially Tubatulabal, live on the Tule River Reservation (*p.176*).

KERN VALLEY INDIAN COMMUNITY
Kawaiisu, Tubatulabal, Koso Shoshone, Yokuts, and others, Kern County

This council attends to the necessities of Native American people of the groups (see above), living in the Kernville area, and to those from distant tribes who live here as well. These duties include sponsoring the annual public Monache Gathering the third weekend of May, high in the mountains above the Kern River, in a place very sacred to the tribe. The tribe helps sponsor the Tehachapi Powwow in June, as well.

Duties also include watching over the physical and spiritual well-being of the many families scattered over this very large and rugged area, some of whom have no roads to their homes.

The tribe oversees a dedicated dance ground within a lakeside park, courtesy of the U.S. Forest Service, on the east shore of Lake Isabella. It is occasionally used for dances and special events.

The tribe is actively seeking Federal recognition.

124 KERN VALLEY INDIAN COUNCIL
P.O. Box 168, Kernville, CA 93238

TOMO-KAHNI STATE PARK
Kawaiisu, Kern County

An ancient Kawaiisu village site here on 240 acres is now protected with a State Park designation. Elder Andy Greene of the Kawaiisu people in Tehachapi is monitor of this sacred place. Guided tours are available through Nick Maris of the Mojave Sector headquarters, California State Parks and Recreation.

125 *Tomo-Kahni State Park is found off Hwy. 58, about 5 mi E of Tehachapi. It is off of Sand Cyn. Rd. a few miles, but no signs indicate its presence in this highly built-up area.*
TOMO-KAHNI STATE PARK
Nick Maris
California State Parks and Recreation
(805) 942-0662.

*"Desert Varnish" is the brown coating on lighter rocks, usually hard, fine-grained sandstone. The occasional rains cause dark minerals deep inside the rock to seep to the surface by capillary action, where the hot desert wind evaporates the moisture deposited there. Finally, windy sandblasting polishes this to a glassy surface. Chipping the surface into designs is called "pecking" by archaeologists.

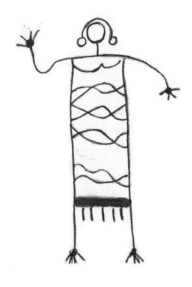 

Opposite Page Top: A pictograph, perhaps indicating the length of a journey (eight days, eight stops or eight springs. Opposite Page Center: A pictograph, also a journey record or possibly a snake, a powerful and revered animal to the desert dwelling Shoshone people.
Above Left & Right: Anthropomorphic figures taken from pictographs, perhaps Shoshone Creation Spirits.
Below: A Paiute-Shoshone elder at an Indian gathering in the early 1980s still reflects "pioneer" dress. It is not uncommon to see older Indian women wearing similar attire today. (dhe, 1985)

PEOPLE OF THE MOJAVE DESERT, COACHELLA VALLEY & COLORADO RIVER

THE LANGUAGE GROUPS
    THE PEOPLE
        The Reservations, *Organizations*

UTO-AZTECAN LANGUAGE SPEAKERS ‡
  SHOSHONEAN (NUMIC)
    CHEMEHUEVI (SOUTHERN PAIUTE)
        Chemehuevi Reservation, Twentynine Palms Reservation, Colorado River Tribes Reservation*
  SHOSHONEAN (TAKIC)
    SERRANO & VANYUME
        San Manuel Reservation
    CAHUILLA
        Cahuilla Reservation, Ramona Reservation, Santa Rosa Reservation, Los Coyotes Reservation,
        Torres-Martinez Reservation, Morongo Reservation*, Soboba Reservation*, Augustine Reservation,
        Agua Caliente Reservation, Cabazon Reservation
    CUPEÑO
        Pala Reservation*, Morongo Reservation*
    KITANEMUK
        no trust lands
        organization: Kitanemuk Tejon Indians

HOKAN SPEAKERS ‡
  MOHAVE (*HA-MÁK-HAVA*)
        Fort Mojave Reservation, Colorado River Tribes Reservation*
  QUECHAN
        Fort Yuma Reservation

  COLORADO RIVER TRIBES RESERVATION*

Shared with other groups

Note the spelling of Mohave—English for the tribe, Spanish for the Fort and Desert.

‡ *See Languages, Tribal Origins, and Tribal Relationships discussion on page 12*

MOJAVE DESERT, COACHELLA VALLEY, & COLORADO RIVER

MAP 10

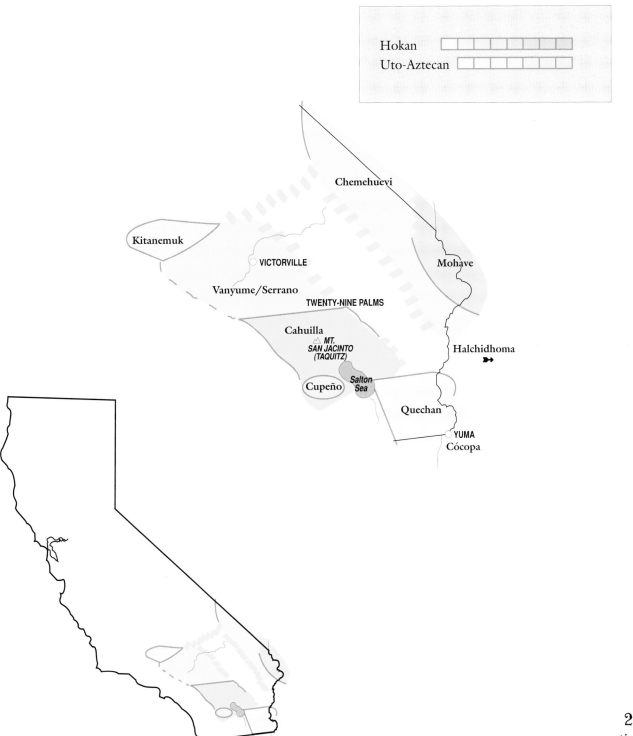

Hokan

Uto-Aztecan

Chemehuevi

Kitanemuk

○ VICTORVILLE

Mohave

Vanyume/Serrano

TWENTY-NINE PALMS

Cahuilla

△ MT.
SAN JACINTO
(TAQUITZ)

Halchidhoma
➤➤

Salton
Sea

Cupeño

Quechan

○ YUMA
Cócopa

THE MOJAVE DESERT, COACHELLA VALLEY, & COLORADO RIVER ENVIRONMENT

THE MOJAVE DESERT

The Mojave is a true desert, ranging in altitude from the 2,000-foot Lower Sonoran zone to the 5,000-foot Upper Sonoran zone, with several mountain ranges and peaks much higher. It is speckled with fascinating and colorful volcanic cones, peaks, dead volcanos, red and black and green mountains. Strange plants like the Joshua tree and other yuccas rise like quiet, inert spirits. Lizards, snakes, tortoises, birds, mice, rabbits, foxes, and even fish scurry through this land. Water rises from springs in unexpected places, then vanishes. The land often shakes from the San Andreas Fault, which passes through the southern part.

The ancient ones knew this land well and where to find sustenance—food, water, shade, shelter. They passed this knowledge down for countless generations, sometimes in graphic form by painting and carving or chipping rock faces. Thanks to the isolation and dryness of the desert, many of these works remain for contemporary shamans to use—sometimes for everyone to contemplate.

A huge part of the lower elevations were once part of a system of great lakes which extended from Lancaster and Palmdale to beyond Victorville, surrounded Barstow, and lapped the flats around Ridgecrest. The Mojave River, now just a trickle, was the overflow of Lake Mojave, the largest lake, cutting its way down through the great plateau above Los Angeles Basin and eventually draining the lake.

The early Indians camped and lived by the many lakes of this earlier, wetter time, left some traces of their handiwork in stone, then adapted as the climate grew drier. Their new homes continued to be located near water and sustenance; their languages and tribal patterns developed into those we know today. Their descendants still live here, still adapting to changing times.

Some tribes interacted with adjacent peoples through trade, especially those who shared hunting grounds in places like mountain ranges. These would include the *Tataviam*, the *Kitanemuk*, and the *Kawaiisu*, dwellers of the southern Tehachapi/Sierra Ranges (discussed earlier). The *Vanyume* and *Serrano* peoples ranged the Mojave Desert itself, occasionally interacting with *Chemehuevi* from the east. In the southernmost extension of the Mojave, the *Cahuilla* occupied the extremes of climactic territory—from the heights of snowy Mt. San Jacinto (*Tahquitz*) to the desiccated Coachella Valley. The Cupeño were tucked away in a corner of Cahuilla land, only to be removed much later to a Luiseño reservation.

In the driest desert, few tribes called this "their" territory, for no one could live year-round in this place of winter ice and summer dust storms. Instead, they chose appropriate times to hunt, harvest desert plants for basketry, or choose rocks and minerals for tools and ornaments.

THE COACHELLA VALLEY

West of Fort Yuma and east of the Coachella Valley we encounter the Colorado River Desert dunes and the Chocolate Mountains, uninhabitable and among the world's driest regions. The Coachella Valley, however, has been host to Native peoples for many thousands of years. The evidence is there for those who bother to look: 200 feet above the sump of the Salton Sea, the shore of ancient Lake Cahuilla lines the edge of the mountains, and in the rocky "beaches" small depressions three to four feet in depth have been hollowed out. When the lake was full, some 10,000 years ago, fishermen would shoo fish into these little ponds and trap them. The lake dried up and the descendants of the fishermen remained—they are (in part) the Cahuilla people of today.

The Cahuilla are essentially a desert people, but this

desert rises in places to over a mile in elevation, capturing enough rain and snow for extensive pine forests and green meadows. Their food included items such as cactus buds, corn, beans, and melons from the lowlands; plus piñon, acorns, berries, seeds, mountain sheep, and deer from the uplands. Towering over all is the 10,800-foot San Jacinto Peak and behind it to the west the immense granite pylon *Tahquitz* (tá-kwish), the Cahuilla earth center. Tahquitz, the source of storms and lightning and rain and sustenance and the power of the spirits. (The pylon's English name is Lily Rock, near Idyllwild.)

Though the Cahuilla have always been a desert people, the desert has changed, and so have the Cahuilla with it. Who would have guessed in 1875 that the desert would be as popular as it is today? So long as it has any water, there are demands for the land. With some irrigation (and a few water pipes for residents), large tracts of Torres-Martinez Reservation have been leased. Agua Caliente, whose land is a large part of the city of Palm Springs and the historic Palm Canyon, the source of the city's water, has profitably sold or leased its resources. But most of the Cahuilla desert lands remain as they always have been, now an ecologically unspoiled island. The most publicly culturally active Cahuilla center is the Morongo Reservation, the home of the **MALKI MUSEUM**, a repository for Cahuilla artifacts and the site of festivals, ceremonies, and feasts.

THE CAHUILLA and their neighbors to the west and south, the Kumeyaay (Kamia, Tipai) and Ipai, originally were granted by treaty a very large bloc of land in Imperial, San Diego, and Riverside Counties. Before long, the usual axing away of Indian land occurred, and today's Indian land is but a small fraction. Nevertheless, their southern California Indian country is fairly ample—the Cahuilla occupy some ten reservations including two that they share with other tribes. Most of this land is undeveloped or sparsely settled, as in the Cahuilla and Los Coyotes Reservations, making them nearly pristine examples of ecological preservation (*see p.53*).

The shapes of the Torres-Martinez, Soboba, Morongo, and Agua Caliente Reservations were the bizarre result of government land policies—land "awarded" in a checkerboard of alternate square miles. The accidental flooding of nearly half of the Torres-Martinez in 1905 (*see p.201*) did not result in a compensatory grant of land; only a few persons live on the many remaining flat, deserty acres, although a large number of acres are leased to agricultural enterprises. Most of their people are housed in a community against the Santa Rosa Mountain front.

Several reservations are making various enterprises pay. The Cabazon is right on I-5 in Indio, and one of its members is the originator of California Indian high-stakes bingo. The Morongo, up the road, also sports a casino, as does Soboba, over the mountain. The largest Native enterprise in the area, though, is Palm Springs. Half the city is Indian land leased by the Agua Caliente tribe, which owns every other square-mile section. The tribe also jealously preserves the Palm Canyons, the source of their culture and the water supply and a unique ecological niche.

To gain an appreciation of the Indianness of the Cahuilla culture, a visit to the Morongo Reservation and the small, informative Malki Museum is imperative. The Morongo is in a beautiful, peaceful setting.

The Cahuilla section of the Palm Springs Desert Museum is informatively presented, and the Agua Caliente tribe itself is readying plans for a culture center of its own. Additionally, the Palm Canyon Trading Post (at the extreme south end of Palm Canyon Dr. in Palm Springs) serves as a book and crafts shop and trailhead for a tour of the Canyon. The Agua Caliente Tribe sponsors an Indian Market in March.

continued on the next page

The Santa Rosa Mountains as seen from the Torres-Martinez Reservation located on the western edge of the Coachella Valley. The majesty of this awe-inspiring land encompasses desert and cool mountain environments, home to many tribes and hundreds of Cahuilla people.(dhe 1990)

233

NATIVE CALIFORNIA

A family enjoys the shade afforded by cottonwood trees beside a small irrigation ditch in the Mojave Desert.   (Huntington Library, San Marino)

BEYOND THE CITIES AND HIGHWAYS and bordering the desert, lies the ancient Cahuilla land of Los Coyotes. The camping facilities are primitive, but the vistas of Mt. Palomar and the desert are superb in this nearly unspoiled Indian country. The Cupeño are a small group whose language is a variant of Cahuilla. They once lived in a few villages grouped around the Warner Springs adjacent to what is now Los Coyotes. Acquisitive whites demanded ownership of the springs and forced the removal of the Cupeño to the Pala Reservation. Cupa Days honors the people and is celebrated the first weekend in May at Pala.

The people of the lower Mojave desert and San Bernardino Mountains just to the north of the Cahuilla were small groups of *Serrano* and *Vanyume*. Much the same can be said of their desert and mountain mode of life that was said of the Cahuilla. The Vanyume were totally dispersed before 1900; the San Manuel Reservation is the present-day home of the Serrano, with a magnificent casino that finally provides a comfortable income for the people.

THE COLORADO RIVER

The Colorado River is a provident year-round life-giver to the desert. Even when is wasn't dammed, its waters were reliable. Especially important are the broad flats and marshes of the lower river, caused by the narrows at Needles and Yuma. One of these special places is home to the Mohave (*ha-mák-ha-va*), who utilized a long stretch of river from Nevada to what is now Parker. This group of Hokan (California-

oriented) speakers were bordered on the south by another, the Quechan people. Both groups were unlike other California peoples: they had a strong tribal organization; they made wide use of pottery, a technique they seem to have borrowed from the early Hakataya culture to the east; and most unusual, they were and still are farmers.

The Colorado, much like the Nile, flooded once a year, covering the flatlands with a fertile layer of silt. Maize (corn), beans, and several types of melons were then planted in this soil. Later, the Spanish arrival in Arizona in the 1600s brought the introduction of wheat, which the Colorado River peoples adopted as a winter crop. The searing desert and barren mountains on both sides can't support much large game, so they relied on fish, rabbits, other rodents, and marsh birds for meat.

Open brush shelters* (*see p.64, 239*) were easily devised to counter the intense summer sun and let the breezes in, but winter homes were earth-covered dwellings made of saplings plastered over with mud. A replica of this wattle and daub construction has been erected on the grounds of the Fort Yuma Reservation Museum.

Between these two peoples, the Chemehuevi people settled in the Lake Havasu area. They are a branch of Southern Paiute who, in very early times, shared some farmland with the Mohave, though they were mainly desert dwellers who preferred to migrate with the seasons to where food was most plentiful. Their contemporary territory is in an area formerly occupied, but vacated over 150 years ago, by the Halchidhoma, who migrated eastward up the Gila River to live today with the Maricopa. Transient residents on the lower Colorado of California were the Cocopa, now settled in Somerton, AZ, and the Yaqui, who came into the Anza-Borrego area for game and water (hence, the place names) and spent some time here. No doubt Apache raiding parties found their way here, too.

THE NATIVE PEOPLES OF THE COLORADO develop their lands in various ways. Like other Native populations, they did not escape the devastation and economic debasement of the Indian peoples during the

This arbor is called a ramada *in Spanish, but don't tell the modern innkeeper this.*

past century and so are now finding ways to better themselves. Since the three largest of the reservations—Fort Mojave, Fort Yuma, and the immense Colorado River Tribes— have managed to keep most of their water rights through all the political shifts of the last two centuries, they have been able to lease much of the fertile, arable land for a significant boost in their per capita incomes. There always looms the great open threat of the developers, however, who sometimes have considerable influence on legislators. The rocky, sloping Chemehuevi Reservation isn't arable, so the tribe is exploiting the white migration into the sunbelt by developing long-lease homesites on Lake Havasu, accompanied by a marina, restaurant, and other amenities, including a tribal craft shop and beach.

If you are interested in visiting large farms, try any of the Big Three above (all of which straddle the state line). On the Colorado River Reservation you will find thousands of miles of canals, and at Fort Yuma, hydroponics for winter crop development.

In 1858 the United States Government sent the steam sternwheeler Explorer *up the Colorado River to observe the lands of the Quechan, the Chemehuevi, up to the head of navigation at Needles deep in Mohave territory. The Needles is a lava dike perpendicular to the Colorado, forcing it into dangerous rapids. The dike is also a barrier causing a wide, fertile floodplain to spread out upstream in what is now the Mohave reservation.* (from a Currier & Ives print, 1858)

Mourners attending a Mohave cremation. These ceremonies are called a "cry" ceremony, and are occasionally held today in several California tribes, such as Mohave and Maidu. (Phoebe Apperson Hearst Museum of Anthropology, University of California, Berkeley photo by E. H. Kemp, 1926)

PEOPLE OF THE MOJAVE DESERT, COACHELLA VALLEY, & COLORADO RIVER

SHOSHONEAN LANGUAGES

Shoshonean is one of a large group of Uto-Aztecan languages spoken in the Great Basin, including eastern and southern California, also by the Comanches, and the Aztecs of Mexico. The tribes of Southeastern California are the Chemehuavi (Southern Paiute) (Numic). Takic speakers (a subgroup of the Shoshonean languages) are spoken by Serrano, Vanyume, Cahuilla, and Cupeño peoples.

NUMIC

CHEMEHUEVI (SOUTHERN PAIUTE)

THE CHEMEHUEVI are a branch of the Southern Paiute. Their ancestral land extended from the Colorado River (in California) up to the Las Vegas area of Nevada, and westward into the desert a hundred or so miles, as far as Death Valley. As a Paiute people, their traditions were almost identical to bands further to the east. However, their Colorado River lands in California were once Mohave, who were displaced in the last century. Indeed, vocabulary and several customs, such as semipermanent houses and riverine farming, were seen similar to the Mohave of earlier days.

As a people at the edge of the desert, the Chemehuevi found it necessary to hunt in the outlying lands, bringing them in cultural contact with the bordering peoples. As a desert people, they also needed light travelling materials, so their basketry became an important part of their culture.

One of the most important Paiute ceremonies is the "Cry" or "Mourning", which is sung in honor of the dead of the past year, and is accompanied by cremation and ceremonial burning of wealth. As in other desert tribes, many of the songs came from "dreaming", a trance state assisted by datura (*p.24*).

Spanish incursion into Arizona only marginally affected this part of the Colorado river peoples. The worst effect was that of the introduction of European disease epidemics. That was followed by slave raiding into Paiute country by both whites and Utes. Mormon settlements stopped this practice, but their presence also unravelled Paiute traditions, as did removal to reservations.

The Chemehuevi had a reputation for not being overly pleased with reservation life, either on the the Colorado River Reservation, where they were in too-close contact with the Mohave, or in Twenty-Nine Palms, where there tended to be very little water (see

A portable brush, cloth, and skin dwelling, and the designs of their caps tell us that these ladies are nomadic dwellers of the Mojave Desert.

(State Parks 1890s)

below). Some persons did remain at Torres-Martinez Reservation (Cahuilla, at the Salton Sea).

CHEMEHUEVI RESERVATION

Chemehuevi [Ché-me-way-vy] Paiute or *në-wë-wë*,
(1870s, 1930s) San Bernardino County

This is ancient territory of the *Halchidhoma*, who abandoned it in the early 1800s. It was subsequently occupied by the Mohave, then more recently by the Chemehuevi in the late 1800s. Most of the reservation as such is relatively new. In 1938, as the backwaters of the newly-constructed Parker Dam on the Colorado River began flooding the rich, flat lands south of Mohave Canyon, the residents of this remote stretch of river, the Chemehuevi, were obliged to disperse. Some went to Los Angeles, some to the Colorado River Reservation in Parker, Arizona, others to Torres-Martinez Reservation, a few to Twentynine Palms (who later left there for other reasons) and a very few remained on the dry, forbidding, higher terraces nearby.

Things have radically changed for them in the last few years. Between 1970 and 1982, more than $6 million of development was invested in the reservation, now called the west bank of Lake Havasu, the upgraded backwaters of Parker Dam. Since the sandy, sloping, and mountainous land is unsuitable for agriculture, development has been in the form of recreational facilities for the general public—long-lease, fully-equipped homesites, marinas, campgrounds, a motel, restaurant, store, and even a passenger ferry to Lake Havasu City, Arizona, and London Bridge, across the river. These sun belt developments have enabled the Chemehuevi to become highly self-sufficient, so much so that many dispersed families are returning to their homeland.

Although it is good to see the welfare of the people improving, with "progress," little time is left for tradition—no dances or festivals are held here. There are activities for the Chemehuevi people, but they are held to the south on the Colorado River Reservation. What will happen to the Chemehuevis as a people, a tradition, when "civilization" takes over?

Developed only along the Colorado River bank, the reservation occupies some 28,000 acres of mostly dry desert and treeless mountains. Though not available to the general public, such features as petroglyphs, pictographs, grinding rocks, turquoise mines, and sleeping circles (low, round rock walls for wind and weather protection) abound, both on reservation land and in ancestral lands. Birds, coyotes, and wild burros roam free, but too many of the burros are destroying the few trees and spoiling wells and water holes.

Project offices and a wildlife protection and security office are near the new boat landing, but modern council offices and most Indian homes are located on a secluded northern end of the reservation. A visitor gets no feeling of "Indian-ness" here, but the realization that human needs are being cared for as never before is welcome.

An extremely important development is happening in the desert just west of the Chemehuevi Reservation: the possible installation of a nuclear waste dump. Details are in the section on land use (*p.55*).

139 *The tribal offices and development area: an unnumbered turnoff with sign to "Lake Havasu", on U.S. 95, about 17 mi S of Needles. Proceed E about 15 mi to a guardhouse at the boat landing. Maps of the reservation are available at the Reservation project office.*
CHEMEHUEVI TRIBE
P.O. Box 1826, Havasu Lake, CA 92363
(619) 858-4531

One doesn't usually think of a marina on an Indian Reservation, but this one is on the Chemehuevi Reservation at Lake Havasu City on the Colorado River, just across from London Bridge, Arizona. (dhe, 1990)

TWENTYNINE PALMS RESERVATION

(originally *Serrano*) *Chemehuevi*
(1895) San Bernardino County

This is a 402-acre rocky hillside reservation, settled in 1868 as a Chemehuevi refuge from a war with the Mohave, far from their Colorado River home, on land that was formerly a Serrano camp. Currently there are no residents; after the famous Willie Boy incident in 1909,* residents drifted away to other nearby reservations. The oasis which supplied their water is now part of the Joshua Tree National Park. A few persons associated with the tribe use the land for gatherings. On Adobe Street in the town is a well-kept Chemehuevi

*Tell Them Willie Boy is Here *is a 1969 movie with Robert Redford and Katherine Ross. The story was faithfully based on an incident in 1909 on the Morongo Reservation in which a young Chemehuevi man from Twentynine Palms killed the father of his lover in self-defense. Nearly the entire county sheriff's office went on a manhunt for the boy and his girl, who had fled into the hills, evading capture for many weeks. Because the President was travelling through the area, the press whipped up a massive anti-Indian campaign, claiming all Indians to be dangerous. An Indian was found (who was not Willie Boy), shot, and his body shown in triumph. Most Chemehuevis in the area found subsequent life uncomfortable, and fled to Torres-Martinez. Willie Boy stayed hidden.*

burial ground with unmarked graves, as tradition dictates. Although unsettled, the land is not unoccupied. The Twentynine Palms gaming hall is prominent on the site, bringing sorely-needed income to the tribe.

140 *Adobe Rd., S of Hwy. 62, to a corner of Joshua Tree National Monument.*
TWENTYNINE PALMS RESERVATION
c/o Dean Mike
555 S. Sunrise Hwy., Ste. 200,
Palms Springs, CA 92262

TAKIC:
KITANEMUK

KITANEMUK TRIBE
OF TEJON INDIANS

Kitanemuk & Tejon Indians,
Yowlumni, & "Interior" Chumash (Kern County)
A previously Federally recognized tribe seeking re-recognition.

Ft. Tejon and the Tejon Reservation were the "repository" for Kitanemuk along with a group of Chumash from the interior regions around Mt. Pinos (a Chumash sacred place, from which a immense land area can be viewed) and the Cuyama area. Other tribes of the Tehachapi Mountains were gathered here too, including Yowlumni Yokuts. (*See Military Posts, App. IV.*)

The small Kitanemuk tribe occupied a region in the Tehachapi Mountains from about the Grapevine (on I-5) eastward into the Mojave to about Lancaster. Their traditions and customs were quite similar (though their language was not) to the nearby tribes of Chumash, Yowlumni Yokuts, Tongva, and Tataviam. The Yowlumni (*Yawelmani*) were the Valley people just to their north, occupying the Tehachapis to the Kern River Valley.

Following the dissolution of the reservation in 1864, many of these people migrated northward toward Bakersfield, whence many went or were sent to the Tule River Reservation. Still others dispersed into the countryside. Nevertheless, 450 modern descendants of predominantly Kitanemuk and Yowlumni families from Tejon have been able to trace their lineages to the present. They were recognized as a tribe early in this century by the BIA, but like eight others, were "administratively ignored", then required to resubmit all their papers, as if they had never been recognized.

THE TRIBE has been intensely interested and involved in ecological protection in and of their ancestral area. The former San Emigdio Ranch land just to the west of the Grapevine is currently owned and administered by a nature conservation organization. As a number of members are basketweavers, one project involves restoration and planting of basketmaking material on this land which was formerly used for cattle.

The same area is adjacent to the Sespe Condor Sanctuary, also of intense interest to the tribe. The large Tejon Ranch (the former Tejon Reservation, bought from the government by its first supervisor, Lt. Beale) is the site of a Kitanemuk cemetery and numerous rock art sites. The Kitanemuk need special permission to visit their old lands. Tejon Ranch says that the condors are not welcome either.

Yet another concern is an attempt by Occidental Oil Company to drill in the old government Elk Hills Petroleum Reserve—reserved for emergency use during World War II, but never completely exploited. Occidental wants to punch wells in this land, despoiling much of the remaining Yowlumni lands and artifacts next to what is left of the old Buena Vista Lake.

Several elder speakers of Kitanemuk have contributed to a written language dictionary.

—much of the above was contributed by Ms. Dee Dominguez, whose grandparents were residents on the Tejon Ranch.

92 *Tejon Ranch is located on the SE side of I-5, just N of Lebec, Kern Co., Ft. Tejon State Park is 1 mi. N of the Ranch, Ft. Tejon exit.*
TEJON RANCH: former Kitanemuk, Yowlumni, Interior Chumash reservation lands.
KITANEMUK TRIBE OF TEJON INDIANS
Chair: Dee Dominguez
981 N. Virginia, Covina, CA 91722

SERRANO & VANYUME

A long tongue of Shoshonean language-related peoples, reaching from the Great Basin into the Los Angeles Basin, includes the Serrano people of the San Bernardino Mountains and its northern hills, plus the small band of Mojave River dwellers, the *Vanyume*. Serrano is Spanish for "people of the mountains"; indeed, the early Serrano people lived among the peaks, valleys, and deserts of the San Bernardino Mountains, from Victorville to Twentynine Palms. The Vanyume survived the Mojave Desert only along its one intermittent river, from Victorville to Barstow.

As Dry California dwellers, existence of both groups was difficult—acorns and piñon or cactus for the main course; roots, bulbs, chia, maybe dates or mesquite berries for side dishes. Of course, villages were only where water was available. Deer, antelope, birds, and various rodents of the desert were fair game. The mountains (some 11,000 feet) furnished a source of water for people, plants, and game, with the latter two furnishing housing, food, and craft materials. Basketry was a fine craft among the Serrano, and many examples survive.

Today's Serrano live predominantly on the San Manuel Reservation near by Patton, and the Morongo Reservation (along with Cahuilla, and others) in Banning. Other tribal members live in nearby communities. The Vanyume people have long been absorbed into the larger communities.

SAN MANUEL RESERVATION

Serrano (1893) San Bernardino County

Most present-day Serrano live on or near their ancestral lands on San Manuel or Morongo reservation.

The 653 acres of San Manuel are arrayed along a foothill of the San Bernardino Mountains near Riverside. The approach to the hill is lined with ancient eucalyptus shading the southwestern rancho-style Serrano Cultural Center at the base of the foothill. However, the first man-made structure you see is the colossal casino and its asphalt-ocean parking lot. As the gaming hall closest to L.A., it is consequently the most immense. The fortunes of the tribe have changed in the last decade. Once San Manuel was an isolated refuge; today fortunes flow into this reservation.

On the slopes and the terrace above are older homes, as well as much larger, newer homes, a few adobe ruins, an ancient functioning acequia [canal], some storehouses, and the quiet of a burial ground—all with vistas of mountains to the north and the orange smog-veiled valley of San Bernardino to the south.

The cultural center displays some articles of archaeological and ethnological interest. Educational and tribal functions are also held in the building, while well-cared-for are athletic fields and sports areas are outside.

127 *In Highland, take Highland Ave. to Victoria Ave., go uphill to the Center.*
SAN MANUEL RESERVATION
P.O. Box 266, Patton, CA 92369
(714) 862-8933

CAHUILLA

The Cahuilla have occupied a large portion of San Diego County forever. Their assortment of geography, though in Dry California, gave them a decided advantage—a extensive variety of climates and its accompanying benefits. The highest mountain in the region is above 10,000 feet, the lowest basin below sea level. The Cahuilla sacred center is 8,900-foot *Tahquitz* (pronounced "tá-kwish") Peak, an outstanding granite cone near Idyllwild.

The location of the tribe between the coast and the Colorado River was ideally situated for trade in both directions. Food was probably not plentiful, but their skillful land management made it much easier to obtain. The Cahuilla were clever people (still are).

Too often we read about "hunter-gatherers" as if the people simply went out and took what they could find. The Cahuilla did hunt, but took great care not to deplete the game and carefully watched over the grazing lands. They gathered, but so does anyone who picks their garden produce. Even today, remnants can be seen in Cahuilla territory of their hillside erosion

prevention techniques—stones and branches used in arroyos and gulches to stem the washing of soil, forming a small dam, and diversion channels dug to collect and distribute water to their plantings. These barriers become habitats for small animals and birds, as well as giving a little more water for their thickets of bushes and trees to grow.

Indian camps, such as this one in Riverside County, probably Serrano, were established adjacent to reliable water and nearby employment. (Huntington Library, San Marino)

THE CAHUILLA PRACTICED WATER conservation in other ways not commonly seen among California tribes. Utilizing the art of pottery-making, they made large cisterns for water storage, and dug deep wells for access to the desert's deepwater sources.

Many hundreds of years in the past they built fish traps along the shores of ancient Lake Cahuilla (*see p.240, p.246, Antiquities*), the huge forerunner of the Salton Sea. This lake was full in a much wetter age, and its shoreline can still be detected along its western shore near the modern reservoir also called Lake Cahuilla.

Cahuilla-made baskets are among the finest and most diversified. Baskets were and are made for daily subsistence uses and other uses: acorn leaching, sifting, seed gathering, brush gathering, bowls, scoops, jars, dry food storage, hats, memorials, gifts. They are also commonly a source of income when sold to the public as beautiful artwork. Their designs include Cahuilla cosmological symbols, anthropomorphic figures, many stylized animal forms, and imaginative abstractions.

CAHUILLA RESERVATION
Cahuilla [ka-wé-a], (1875) Riverside County

Many high, upland plains of the southern Coast Range are dry, as is the Cahuilla Reservation. At 4,000 feet, it is relatively cool—between the towering hulk of Mt. Palomar (6,126 feet) to the west and San Jacinto Peak (10,800 feet) to the east. The Cahuilla people here are one group among many who have preferred to allow their 18,272 acres to remain more or less as they have always been.

The scrub brush, granite boulders, gentle hills, and dry washes support several dozen persons on a few widely-scattered ranches. A few dirt roads wind about the desert-like landscape; the silence is broken only by the wind, a few birds, and the whine of high-speed motors on the highway.

A primitive old schoolhouse in a clump of pines beside the road is the tribal hall. I took refuge behind a large rock at the adjoining burial ground one windy day to feel the spirits. They were there.

129 *Four mi W of the settlement of Anza on Hwy. 371 (about 30 mi W of Palm Desert).*
CAHUILLA RESERVATION
P.O. Box 391760, Anza, CA 92539-1760
(909) 763-5549

RAMONA RESERVATION
Cahuilla administration (1893) Riverside County

Out on that big plain mentioned earlier in the Cahuilla Reservation (above) lie 560 uninhabited acres of this reservation, mostly chaparral. It is administered by the Hamilton family of the Cahuilla people.

130 *Access by dirt road, NW from Hwy. 371, about 1 mi W of the intersection of Hwy. 371 and Hwy. 74.*
RAMONA RESERVATION
3940 Cary Rd., Anza, CA 92539-0439

SANTA ROSA RESERVATION
Cahuilla (1907) Riverside County

Ten miles east of here in the Coachella Valley lies one of the hottest, driest deserts in California. But the 5,000-foot altitude of the Santa Rosa Valley is watered by some rain and snow snatched from the clouds passing around nearby 8,000-ft. Santa Rosa Peak, one of several in the San Bernardino National Forest.

The 11,293 acres of the Santa Rosa Reservation are thinly populated, with a few ranch houses scattered along a dirt road in a long, narrow valley. The mountainsides are dashed with Jeffrey, sugar, and yellow pines, as well as other greenery— a refreshing contrast to the desert in the surrounding lowlands. The people here are in concert with the conservancy groups trying to keep the Santa Rosa Plateau a wilderness. Beautiful as it is, the people want to keep it that way, so have subtly suggested that the public stay away by erecting a series of unmistakable "No Trespassing" signs.

131 *Private road about 4 mi E of intersection of Hwy. 371 and Hwy. 74 (E of Palm Desert). Hwy. 74 actually passes right through the reservation, but there are no signs indicating it.*
SANTA ROSA RESERVATION TRIBAL OFFICE
325 N. Western St., Hemet, CA 92343

LOS COYOTES RESERVATION
Cahuilla (originally partly *Cupeño*)
(1889) San Diego County

In spite of their past tribulations, some 60 Cahuillas now live (mostly during the summer) on the spacious 25,000 acres of low mountain land above the hot springs (which were the Cupeño life-blood until 1903), and have made part of their magnificently scenic homeland accessible to the public for year-round camping and exploring. Follow the paved, winding road leading up into the mountains overlooking the Valle de San José and Mt. Palomar in the distance. At the top of a hill, further in, sits a tiny, solitary chapel with its separate bell tower, reminding me more of Peru than California. In a high valley on Los Tules Rd., a ranch house serves as tribal hall.

132 *Warner Springs, on Hwy. 79. Entrance sign on the highway, 6 mi to a campground via Camino San Ignacio and Los Tules Roads.*
LOS COYOTES RESERVATION
P.O. Box 249, Warner Springs, CA 92086
(619) 782-3269

The level bench on the side of the mountain at right is an ancient beach of Lake Cahuilla, west of Indio. Around 5-6,000 years ago there was a freshwater lake here, but as the climate warmed, the water slowly dried up. Today, the Salton Sea depression is all that is left of the lake. (dhe, 1982)

TORRES-MARTINEZ RESERVATION
Cahuilla (1876) Riverside County

In the last century, in the course of making large land allotments (e.g., railroad grants, national forests, public lands, certain Indian reservations), it was popular to set aside alternate sections of land, that is, every other square mile (640 acres). That is why the Torres-Martinez, Ft. Mojave, Morongo, and Agua Caliente Reservations look like checkerboards (*see Map 3, p.83 inset*).

In this very flat, hot, dry (if it's without irrigation), scrubby portion of the Coachella Valley, the Cahuilla people have elected (or have been forced by economics, as in many other places) not to develop much of their checkerboard reservation. In the midst of shady, stately rows of date palms with citrus groves on all sides, brown Chocolate Mountains rising up close by, the Torres-Martinez remains much as it always has been, a desert. More than 10 square miles lie under the waters of the Salton Sea, flooded by accident in 1905. The flooding Colorado River broke a weak levee constructed by the Southern Pacific Railroad, forming the below-sea-level lake before the levee could be plugged. Most of the rest of the dry land is covered with only greasewood scrub, although some land is leased to agribusiness—dates, alfalfa, other legumes. A few people seem to work the land of the reservation's 24,823 acres.

The tree-shaded ruins of the old government Indian Agency, a national landmark, are interesting in their decrepitude. In the same yard under some palms is a little brick tribal hall with grinding rock relics out in front. A well-staffed Riverside-San Bernardino Indian Health clinic serves the region from here. A baseball field and swimming pool adjoin.

This reservation has also been refuge for several Chemehuevi families for many years. When conditions became bad for them along the Colorado River and later at Twentynine Palms, they settled here.

There has been some progress. On a westerly bloc of land against the mountains, near the Fish Traps (*p.247*), the tribe has acquired 40 modern permanent homes with magnificent vistas of the stark Santa Rosa Mountains. This is the first real community of the reservation in many years.

133 *North of the Salton Sea, off 66th St., between Mecca and Valerie Jean at a point halfway between Hwy. 86 and Hwy. 195, is the paved entrance, S, to ancient palms of the Agency and the tribal office. The homes are W of Valerie Jean. Date shops are near here.*
TORRES-MARTINEZ RESERVATION
66-725 Martinez Rd., Thermal, CA 92274

Rural Los Coyotes Reservation in the winter.   (dhe, 1991)

AUGUSTINE RESERVATION
Cahuilla (1893) Riverside County

Lying between 54th Ave. and Airport Blvd., State Highway 86 and Van Buren St., south of Coachella, is a square mile of nearly uninhabited chaparral, called a reservation. Yet, it is reserve land, an ecological preserve of sorts (*see p.53*).

134 AUGUSTINE RESERVATION
1185 N. Hargrave St, Banning, CA 92220

CABAZON RESERVATION
Cahuilla (1876) Riverside County

Cabazon shares with Agua Caliente the dubious distinction of being an urban reservation—a real oddity in California. There's not much to look at—but the 1,452 acres (in two parcels) are extremely neat, made up of a collection of homes-in-a-grove lying at the edge of Coachella. That's it for this side of I-10.

The most prominent part of the rez, however, is the Cabazon Indian Casino, right on I-10. You can't miss it. After a tough dual with the law, this became California's first tribe to successfully introduce high stakes (and tribal income-producing) gaming. Their continuing business acumen established, they are venturing into other areas such as energy co-generation, if permits can be obtained. Gaming income produces health and education benefits for all.

135 *Interstate 10 at Dillon Rd. is Cabazon. Residences just E of railroad tracks.*
CABAZON INDIAN RESERVATION
84-245 Indio Springs Drive, Indio, CA 92201

AGUA CALIENTE RESERVATION
Cahuilla (1896) Riverside County

Many centuries ago, the Cahuilla found the springs that greened some of the few native palm stands in the West. From watering holes like these have come the life source of all desert peoples. But in the 1930s, a life force alien to this desert came here—the wealthy, who wanted a winter playground. Thus, an Indian reservation came to be in the middle of one of the richest communities in the state, Palm Springs.

How do you tell reservation from the rest of the town? Sometimes you can't. The reservation was established in 1876 and is a checkerboard of 50 one-mile squares, totalling 24,463 acres. Some portions have been sold off, but nearly half of what you see in Palm Springs is on long lease land, making this tribe possibly the best off in California.

Come and visit the well-preserved ancient canyons of the region: Andreas, Murray, Palm (with Trading Post), and Tahquitz (by permit). These resources are administered by the tribal office (see below). Hiking, horseback riding, and picnicking are encouraged in these superb palm oases. The tribal office is a big building, and the tribe is rather independent of the BIA.

Realizing that the tribe was fast losing its cultural traditions, one of the families now sponsors a public festival in mid-April with Cahuilla and other Indian dances and traditions (*especially "bird songs", a type of song in which a story is told, see Music and Dance, p.75*). The festival, which is held on the tribal dance ground on Palm Canyon Rd., includes an Indian Market for local and visiting crafts makers.

136 *Location: Palm Springs.*
AGUA CALIENTE RESERVATION
960 E. Tahquitz Way #106,
Palm Springs, CA 92262

MORONGO RESERVATION
Cahuilla, Serrano, Cupeño, and *Chemehuevi* (1877) Riverside County

The Morongo is one of the few reservations in California that is impossible to miss. Interstate 10 passes right through it at Banning and San Gorgonio Pass (2600 feet). Signboards point out the local casino and the Malki Museum. I had the distinct honor of visiting the former director of the museum, Mrs. Jane Penn. She came from her sickbed to tell me of names. "*Malki*," she said, "was a sly way for the people here to fool the Indian agents, who asked what their tribal name was. In reality, 'Malki' means 'dodging'. Even '*Morongo*,'" she added with a twinkle, "is a misnomer." In their haste to name the place, the agents gave it the name of a family who lived some distance away. With Mrs. Penn's untiring help, this museum became one of the more complete collections representing local Indian cultures in California. [*Jane Penn passed on about a year after I spoke with her.*] Her work was pursued by Ms. Katherine Siva Saubel, the most valuable person imaginable.

The 32,248-acre reservation is a well-developed community of some 300 persons, with a good-sized health clinic, tribal offices and hall, substantial homes, ranches, farms, and an historical Moravian church dating back to the 1890s. Movie and TV films are made here occasionally, owing to the very scenic nature of the location. Gaming at the Morongo is prominent, but isolated, right on the Interstate.

In May the residents present a festival and barbeque with some ceremonies and dancing centered around the adobe Museum, which is situated in the dry, often windy, open fields looking up to the towering 10,800-foot San Jacinto Peak.

Morongo has become home for Cahuilla, Serrano (from the north of here), Cupeño (from Los Coyotes and Pala), and Chemehuevi (from the Colorado River area), enriching the variety of traditions to be found in this part of California.

137 *Field Rd. exit from I-10 at Cabazon is the road to the Malki Museum. Potrero Rd. is where the tribal offices are.*
MORONGO RESERVATION
11581 Potrero Rd., Banning, CA 92220

SOBOBA RESERVATION
originally *Cahuilla*, today is shared predominantly by *Luiseño* people (*see p.215*).

Palm Canyon is a part of the Agua Caliente Reservation. The springs which originate here and at other sites along the San Jacinto Mountain front, belong to the tribe, which carefully protects their purity and ecology. (dhe, 1991)

CUPEÑO

Near the head of the San Luis Rey River, Lake Henshaw covers the lush marshes that once sustained bands of Luiseño, Ipai, and the Cupeño, whose permanent village of Kupa was by the bubbling hot springs. The hot springs (today, Warner's Hot Springs) at the edge of Los Coyotes Reservation (*map# **132**, p 240*) have occasioned several episodes of relatively recent history.

The Cupeños were a very small tribal group; they spoke a Uto-Aztecan language somewhat related to Cahuilla. They have in common some religious customs related to their Luiseño neighbors to the west, principally *Chi-ngich-ngish (see p.182)*.

Originally the center of Cupeño life, the springs and adjacent fertile lands were appropriated by the San Luis Rey and San Diego Missions. Later, one Jonathan Trumbull (aka Juan José Warner) acquired possession and established a ranch here in 1844, giving succor to Col. Stephen W. Kearny (on his way to take Los Angeles from the Mexican Army, 1846), and later to Butterfield stages passing east-west. Fed up with appropriation of land and resources, one Juan Antonio Garrá, a Cupeño clan leader attempted a revolt against the white oppressors in 1850. The revolt failed; the village of *kupa* was burned; Garrá and followers were executed.

After this time the Cupeños had been "allowed" to live nearby, and somehow felt this was still their land. But, by a California Supreme Court decision in 1903, they were removed in one of the State's many "trails of tears" to Pala Reservation (*p.36*). Meanwhile, a resort was built at the springs, and today, the valley's water quenches throats and yards of San Diegans and their suburbanites.

The Cupeños survive today on the Pala Reservation (map# **96**, p.213) somewhat apart from the other two tribal entities there. A Cupa Day celebration is held the first weekend in May.

Village in the dry San Bernardino Mountains, Riverside County. Careful inspection of the upper left of the photo will reveal a small burial ground. Dogs, live poultry and a "people's wagon" are part of daily life, as in most Indian communities of this era.
(Huntington Library, San Marino)

The hated Ft. Mojave along the Colorado River, in Mohave territory, was abandoned in 1890, then converted into an Indian school until 1935. In 1942, the buildings were razed, the tribal offices moved across the river into Needles—all that was left were the sidewalks to nowhere. Just behind the photographer is a fertile complex of irrigated fields, leased by the tribe to farmers.

(dhe, 1987)

HOKAN SPEAKERS

The word "Hokan" is Atsugewi for "two."
Eastern California speakers of this group,
which has many related languages around the state
are Mohave and Quechan.

MOHAVE

Like the Quechan, the Mohave are a desert riverine culture, whose ancestral lands occupied a ribbon of the Colorado River from southern Nevada about 70 miles south to South of Parker, Arizona. They never relinquished control of their lands to Spanish control, and only did so amid great strife to the American Army in 1859. They were farmers of the floodplain, which flooded every year, renewing the topsoil, like the Nile.

The culture had no big villages, only small clusters of houses, but a tribal identity was present. They lived by hunting (rabbits, rodents, deer) in the hills and desert nearby, fishing in the river, and planting (corn, beans, squash) after the annual flood.

Mohave language is a Yuman-Hokan language, related to Quechan, and distantly related to other much more northerly California languages. Perhaps it was among the original languages of the state—unlike the Uto-Aztectan languages that surround the Mohave.

FORT MOJAVE RESERVATION*
Mohave (ha-mäk-háv) (1870)
Clark County, Nevada; Mohave County Arizona;
and San Bernardino County, California

The Mohave are one of the peoples along the Colorado River in California which still occupy some of their traditional tribal lands. Nearly 400 *Hamakhavas* live on some 38,000 acres of their reservation, which lies in three states.

At the north end of the reservation is the site of old and hated Fort Mojave (*see App. IV*). Nothing is left but sidewalks to nowhere. Beyond the southern end of the reservation, along Interstate 40, are the remaining acres of an ancient furrowed field, called Rock Maze (see below).

The spacious tribal office-library-community center and gym are situated at the north edge of Needles, CA. On the Arizona side of the river are leased agricultural lands, and several public RV parks. The southern boundary of the reservation is also the boundary of the Havasu National Wildlife Refuge, a wide, flat marsh of the Colorado River. The reservation itself covers an even wider flood plain, flat enough for intensive farming.

One finds a businesslike bustle at the tribal office that administers the many acres leased to agri-businesses. The income has enabled the children to have a decent library and gym; it has enabled the tribe to pull down hot, stuffy crackerboxes and build more than 150 substantial homes on tree-lined streets; and it has given the people a reasonable standard of living.

A gaming casino also contributes to the tribal resources; the tribe never had a problem with the California gaming controversy, since part of the Fort Mojave Reservation lies in Nevada, where gambling is quite legal.

Traditional dances are open to the public in September, and the tribe supports a famous marching band that tours all over the U.S.

138 *In Needles, take the River Rd. Exit from I-40, south 4 blocks on W. Broadway to I-40 overpass. North to tribal offices in Needles. Maps of the reservation are available there. The casual visitor can drive the length of the reservation along Arizona State Hwy. 95 from Topock to Bullhead City, Mohave County, AZ.*
FT. MOJAVE TRIBE
P.O. Box 798, Needles, CA 92363
(619) 326-4596

* *NOTE: Mohave Tribe (English), but Fort Mojave (Spanish)*

ROCK MAZE

early Hamakhav, San Bernardino County

At the south end of the Ft. Mojave Reservation (see previous entry) are about two acres of a field that appears to be plowed or furrowed in a maze-like fashion. From the north, the Colorado River has been flowing through a wide flood plain, but here it hits narrows caused by needle-like projections of ancient lava rock.

Whites who first observed the labyrinthine maze realized its uniqueness and noted it in early accounts. Most of the furrows have been rather miraculously preserved. They were created to confuse and entrap evil spirits pursuing spirits of the dead floating down the river. Until recently the Hamakhav have been using this holy place for funereal ceremonies. Some of the field has disappeared, but thanks to the efforts of many people, the adjacent Interstate and pipelines have sacrificed little of it. (*See photo p.49*)

138 *East of Needles, take Park Moabi Exit off I-40. At mile 1.7, keep to left and at mile 1.9 ("Road Closed" sign), before a pipeline pumping station, find a parking lot for viewing the maze.*

QUECHAN

The Quechan people are a very settled desert river tribe who have always been accustomed to planting and farming—and enduring a very hot summer. Many of their cultural roots and necessities derive from the desert *O'Odham* (Pima and Papago) and Pueblo neighbors to their east.

In 1781 the Quechans (one of the Yuma language groups) and their allies of the lower Colorado River launched an assault on the year-old Spanish mission and fort at what is now Ft. Yuma. These peoples were ungrateful for the harsh servitude offered them by the Spaniards. They were successful in maintaining the independence won in this battle—though under considerable pressures from all sides—until the American invasion around 1850, when they lost their freedom.

FT. YUMA RESERVATION

Quechan and others (1884) Imperial County

After many skirmishes and struggles, a reservation was established in 1884 at the site of the old mission. An Indian agency and a new church were erected on the California prominence overlooking the city of Yuma, Arizona. Today the refurbished buildings of the old fort (*see App. IV, p.274*) and agency school appropriately are used for tribal functions.

In 1934, a large irrigation complex was begun that crosses the reservation. Nevertheless, establishing their water and land claims has been difficult for the tribe, at times resulting in clashes with both government and non-Indian intruders. Only lately has full advantage been taken of the water rights, resulting in much agricultural development (*see p.55*).

Fort Yuma Reservation is the southeast corner of California, and is essentially a warm weather agricultural community. It's a fine place to be in January, if you don't like snow. The pueblo-like Quechan Tribal Center, the old Officers' Mess Hall of 1851 (now a museum open only sporadically), and two venerable churches perch on a promontory overlooking the Colorado River and the reservation to the north and east. From this hill you may gaze out upon miles and miles of vegetables destined for the plates of America. Around the 25,000 acres are at least two RV parks (camping, also) and high-stakes gaming halls. As in all reservations, tribally issued licenses are required to fish in the many canals.

The life? Busy, quiet. Traditions are subtly kept; songs are still sung and some ceremonies still performed. One day I found an elderly Quechan man searching for a horse, property of an Indian dreamer-lady who had walked the animal all the way from Oregon, only to lose it here. I found at a club in Winterhaven a good Indian band playing country/rock music—a style that is very popular among the Indian peoples of California. Annual pow-wow is during September Indian Days, and the first week in March is the time for a powwow in Winterhaven hosted by San Pascual School.

Water rights along the Colorado have largely been preserved by the Quechan on the Ft. Yuma Reservation (California, and Arizona). This situation has allowed a complex irrigation system to be constructed, beginning in the 1920s. Most of the farming operations, such as this, have been leased to private interests, the proceeds going to members of the tribe.

(dhe, 1990)

143 *Off I-8 the Winterhaven Exit (from W) will lead to a road N toward Imperial Dam/Picacho. A few hundred yards down the highway is the road up the hill to the tribal offices (maps available), museums, and old missions.*

QUECHAN TRIBAL COUNCIL
P.O. Box 1352, Yuma, AZ 85364
(619) 572-0213

COLORADO RIVER TRIBES RESERVATION

Mohave (Hamákhava), Chemehuevi (Nëwëwë), Hopi, Diné (Navajo)

(1865) Yuma County, Arizona, and San Bernardino and Riverside Counties, California

Around 1865 several bands of peoples from southeastern California and western Arizona were settled into this sixty-mile portion of the Colorado River, which is the ancestral home of the Halchidhoma people. After World War II, they were joined by a large group of Hopi and Diné.

Relaxing in the ramada, this fellow seeks protection from the fierce sun of the Colorado River valley in a traditional, temporary shelter. Early 1900s

(State Parks)

Although the reservation's 2500 residents present a melange of five peoples, they all practice and maintain their individual languages and cultures. Dances are held periodically; potters and basketmakers are active; cultural classes are available. You will find access to an excellent "working museum", which sponsors various cultural classes for all ages and an excellent library in the Parker (Arizona) headquarters amid the large complex of tribal offices and community center.

National Indian Day, the last Friday of September, is observed in a big way on the reservation, with thousands of people coming long distances to participate. A campground is available for public use year-round.

The Bureau of Indian Affairs and other governmental agencies maintain a large complex of health, housing, and maintenance facilities just south of Parker. In and around the several communities on the reservation, there is an air of the progressive spirit of expanding agricultural areas. For those who wish to experience life in a large Native American community, this is probably the most impressive in the southern California area, although the headquarters lie just across the river in Arizona.

Visitors to this area will marvel at the striking ancient Giant Figures scooped into the desert floor centuries ago, located on the southwestern edge of the reservation (see below).

141 *Extending S for 60 mi on both sides of the Colorado River from Earp, CA (State Hwy. 62 and U.S. 95) and from Parker, AZ, to near Ehrenburg (BIA Rd. 1). Reservation offices and museum are about 2 mi S of Parker on Agency Rd., past the BIA-hospital complex, in modern buildings. Reservation maps available there.*

COLORADO RIVER TRIBES ADMINISTRATIVE OFFICE
Rte. 1, Box 23B, Parker, AZ 85344
(520) 669-9211

GIANT DESERT FIGURES
(OR INTAGLIOS)
Riverside County, **State Landmark 101**

Off U.S. 95, 15.3 miles north of the intersection of Interstate 10 and U.S. 95 in Blythe are found several huge figures (95 to 167 feet) on an alluvial terrace, "carved" into the desert pavement. The "pavement" is of small dark brown pebbles resting on a light-colored sand, the "carving" is as though scooped with a shovel. The figures are stylized animals and anthropomorphic figures. One set of figures honors the ancient spirit of creation, *mastambó* and his spirit helper, the mountain lion (*see p.58*). Since early survival depended largely on finding game, other figures were made by shaman artists to better the fortunes of hunters. These figures are similar in nature to the more famous Nazca Lines of the dry Peruvian coast.

Jeeps and motorbikes have defaced some of the surface, but the figures still appear almost newly-made, although they pre-date local Indian knowledge of their origin. The significance of the figures is known, however. This site is currently protected by a fence, though occasionally it has been cut. [*See also* National Geographic Magazine, *January, 1998, p.26, for an aerial photograph;* Smithsonian Magazine, *September, 1978; and* New West Magazine, *January 29, 1979 for articles on the deliberate defacement of Indian antiquities, this included.*]

Just SW of 141. Giant Desert Figures are 15.3 mi N of I-10 (Blythe) on U.S. 95. on State-protected land.

ANTIQUITIES
Sites in Southern California suitable for public viewing

The reader will note that within most areas of California, there exist a number of sacred sites of pictographs, petroglyphs, and other ancient works. Vandals with a notion of greed have despoiled many. This book will not divulge areas not protected or otherwise well-known. Sometimes state, Federal, private, or Indian authorities have "protected" sites by denoting them, but have otherwise provided no real protection. RESPECT OUR HERITAGE

FISH TRAPS
Ancient *Cahuilla*, Riverside County

In the ancient days when the Mohave Desert had water, some four to five hundred years ago, and the Salton Sea, the Imperial and the Coachella Valleys were Lake Cahuilla, some of the early Cahuilla Indians were fishers. But their fishing methods were unique.

Taking full advantage of a rock slide at the edge of the old lake, they arranged the large, loose stones to form fish corrals two or three feet deep at the water's edge, whence they drove the fish to an ultimate capture. The traps consist of 8 to 10 ft. diameter circular stone walls along the lakeshore, with the tops just above water level and with a small gap in the top edge, allowing fish to be enticed or herded into the trap from outside, then the gap was closed.

About four hundred years ago, the Colorado River, which fed the lake, changed course, isolating the depression. The lake dried up over about 60 years, according to Cahuilla stories.

It is remarkable that this process must have been carried out over many years, as the lake level dropped, for the traps are to be found from the highest level to some twenty to thirty feet down.

The old beach levels of ancient Lake Cahuilla are quite evident; up against the mountainside is the rock slide in which the traps are to be seen. Absolutely do not disturb the loose rocks!

Near 133 From State Rte. 86 at Valerie Jean (8 miles S of Coachella) take 66th Ave. W to Jackson St., then go N two blocks.

CALICO EARLY MAN SITE
probably ancient *Serrano-Vanyume*
San Bernardino County

In 20,000 BC, the Mojave Desert was wet, and was inhabited by distant ancestors of the California Indians. In 1942 AD, San Bernardino County Archaeologist Ms. Dee Simpson, and later, Dr. Louis S. B. Leakey, the famous archaeologist of Kenya, took an interest in the culture of these people, mainly because Ms. Simpson had discovered the site of a stone tool factory belonging to them. The public is invited to tour this superb archaeological "dig" and displays of thousands of arrowheads, mallets, choppers, scrapers, lance heads, etc. Wednesday through Monday, 8-5.

128 *Fifteen miles NE of Barstow, access by Minneola Rd. exit from Interstate 15.*

HEMET MAZE STONE
ancient *Cahuilla*, Riverside County
state landmark 557

Before the days of preserving an artifact by not disturbing it, the State of California installed a bronze plaque on this large granite boulder, bearing an incised pictograph maze, about 1 1/2 by 2 feet, probably an ancient Cahuilla relic.

557 *Near 101. Five miles W of Hemet off State Rte. 74, on California Ave. 3 miles N to small park.*

Nadyne Gray sits in an ancient Cahuilla fish trap to show the scale of these low tech collectors.   (dhe, 1982)

KOSO PICTOGRAPHS
ancient *Panamint Koso*, South Inyo County

Extremely well-protected are the pictographs in three canyons located in the present-day China Lake Naval Weapons Station in Ridgecrest. Guided tours from the Maturango Museum in Ridgecrest, watched over vigilantly by armed guards, are available for visiting two weekends in the spring and fall. That's it.

These pictographs, mostly carved in very early times, are still visited, comprehended, and revered by contemporary spiritual leaders. (*Details on pp.226, 228*).

126 MATURANGO MUSEUM
Ridgecrest, NE Kern County

ROCK MAZE

early *Hamakhava*, San Bernardino County
Ancient and modern, this is a sacred site. **DO NOT TRESPASS UPON THE MAZE** (*Details, p.245*).
Adjacent to the Ft. Mojave Reservation
Needles, California

GIANT DESERT FIGURES
(OR INTAGLIOS)

Riverside County, **State Landmark 101**

These are figures carved into the desert surface, much like those of Nazca, Peru. The sacred site to the ancient god *Mastamhó* and his spirit helper is a state historic site. (Partly desecrated by vandals.) Details, p.246.

101 *Off U.S. 95, 15.3 miles N of Interstate 10/U.S. 95 intersection in Blythe.*

EAGLE ROCK

Tongva natural site, Los Angeles County

Freeway 134 curves around this natural phenomenon, best seen around noon, when the shadow of a landing eagle is obvious. The community of Eagle Rock is named for this hill, which was saved from freewayization by CalTrans.
Just W of Pasadena, in the town of Eagle Rock

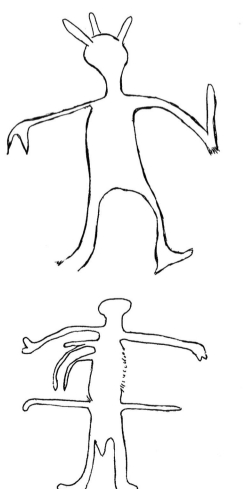

EARLY MAN SITE

Out beyond Barstow about ten miles on I-15, next to the reconstructed ruins of Calico Mine, is the Early Man Site. Maybe as far back as 20,000 years ago, someone was out here in a village on a wet, piney lakeshore making arrow and lance points, scrapers, and the like. It is a searing desert now, but the arrow work is beautiful and clean.

A university group supervises the archaeological dig, and under a small shed there's a showcase of some of their diggings. The first finds nearby were thought to have been washed in from another source, but this particular site seems to have been a factory site.

It's possible that they are ancestors of the Vanyume/Serrano, but who knows?

128 *Fifteen miles NE of Barstow, access by Minneola Rd. exit from Interstate 15.*

FORMER RESIDENTS

On the map of Ancestral Homelands there is one group along the Colorado River that I have not yet mentioned—the Halchidhoma. Their tribal narratives tell that, owing to pressure from other peoples from the north and south, they began a retreat from this region long before 1830, possibly as early as the 1500s. They migrated up the Gila and Salt Rivers of Arizona and became partially amalgamated with Maricopa groups to the east. Their descendants now live near Tempe, Arizona, and their old lands along the Colorado are today occupied by the Chemehuevi people.

Finally, one group of Indian people who once were at least occasional residents in extreme southeastern California areas are the Cócopa. However, today their reservation is in Somerton, Arizona, near Yuma, in the center of their ancient lands. In Anza-Borrego State Park along Highway 78 we find places bearing the name Yaqui: Yaqui Wells, Yaqui Meadows, and Yaqui Ridge. They too paid visits here for water and forage. After all, this part of the world was within the Yaqui region of vigilance, so say some of their knowing elders.

NATIVE CALIFORNIA GUIDE
NATIVE CALIFORNIA GUIDE
NATIVE CALIFORNIA GUIDE

Book FOUR

NATIVE CULTURE
RESOURCES & REFERENCES

CONTEMPORARY SOCIAL SERVICES
AVAILABLE TO NATIVE PEOPLES IN CALIFORNIA

APPENDICES & INDICES

Dolan H. Eargle, Jr.
Trees Company Press
San Francisco

Cultural Indian education includes learning how to drill beads for necklaces. Big Time, Kule Loklo (Point Reyes National Seashore)

(dhe,1985)

INCREASINGLY, CONGRESSIONAL and parsimonious Congressional attitudes towards the well-being of just about everyone has resulted in budget cuts impacting Indians. Among the worst of these were those that forced the closing of small town and urban Indian Centers that had provided or administrated many services. These are the places to which people in need come for a centralized source of assistance and direction through the maze of bureaucratic paperwork and for direction to the sites of various services available. Indian Center staff often provide the services themselves. Within the larger reservations, it is the tribal office that usually provides these functions.

Outside reservations, there exists a well-defined need for the centers and for the services they offered. It is only common sense to see that there is a great need for a central location to serve small and rural towns, as well as urban areas. The diversification and dispersal of Indian services causes much confusion and results in denial of expected and entitled help.

TYPICAL SERVICES

- medical aid, psychological assistance, pharmacy, dental, child care, elder care, nursing care
- organizations for in-family abuse
- councils for alcohol and drug abuse
- social programs: festivals, powwows, dances, talks, gatherings, parties (for children and adults)
- social work
- education: scholarships, special programs, special help, school curricula
- legal: family, tribal, civil, criminal
- guidance in finding services: Indian Centers
- employment (Job Training Partnership Act, **JTPA**)
- housing assistance: construction, renting, buying, repair
- welfare assistance in filing for and receiving money
- cultural (*see Tribal Culture, p.56*)

HEALTH & RELATED SERVICES
A SHORT HISTORY OF INDIAN HEALTH

The general health of the enrolled (Federally recognized) Indian population has been the nominal responsibility of the Federal government for more than 150 years—ever since reservations were established. However, in yet another abuse of the word "trust", Indian health has been at best ignored, or worst, suppressed—until recently.

Insistence on health and persistence in efforts on the part of many concerned persons—doctors, lawyers, Indians, politicians, health workers, anyone cognizant of injustice—has resulted in several Congressional acts designed to improve the well-being of Native Americans. But Congress is not always dependable.

INDIAN HEALTH, as any American's health, has not always been conceived of as a "right", an "entitlement". The concept of universal health as a right has only slowly found acceptance in the minds of Americans. Early on in the history of this country, "health" was always ignored or seen as subordinate to other rights: legal, economic, religious, shelter, land and property, education, or provisions.

During the 1830s, when Indians in the eastern United States were being removed to western locations, the government took no responsibility for anything Indian, much less rights. When the Commissioner of Indian Affairs post was set up in 1834, the only thing that was even remotely health-oriented was the governmental concern for Indian consumption of whisky—and then only as it affected the stability of the Indian communities.

A series of treaties defined Indian obligations, but no concern was demonstrated for the welfare of the Indian people. In 1869, as reservations were established after the Civil War and following massive campaigns against the western tribes, Congress finally responded with some minimal concern—this time for alcoholism, hunger, sanitary facilities, and disease, but showed no general concern for human well-being on or off the reservations. Decline in their general situation continued to the point that the death rate exceeded the birth rate of all American Indians. The decline was duly noted in Congress, and some minimal health and medical care finally were provided. For every Indian? Hardly.

In 1928, as a result of the Meriam Report to Congress, the first responsible action on the government's part became law.* A glimmer of perception of health and medical services to everyone as a right had begun.

Southern Indian Health Council clinic near the Viejas Reservation provides medical, dental, and optical services for southern San Diego county in a pleasant setting of southwestern architecture. (dhe, 1998)

Shortly afterwards, Great Depression attitudes acknowledged all people's misery. Treatment of some problems began to be provided, at least upon the larger reservations. Even then, off-reservation Indians had to take their chances, as they were directed to their often non-existent local community providers.

IN 1955 THE BIA DECIDED to discharge health from its responsibility, passing it to the Public Health Service, through a sub-agency, the Indian Health Service (IHS). At that time, Federal allocation for Indian health increased significantly, but neglect and persecution for over a century made catch-up very difficult. Eventually, Indian health professionals began to emerge; training in academic circles for IHS personnel was beginning.

California in the 1950s had the strange notion that both education and health could/should be provided only by counties and local communities. The idea was badly applied and was soon abandoned. Rural rancherias and remote communities were simply ignored or had no funding.

Today in California, clinics aware of special Indian needs can be found in most places that have even a small Indian presence. Providing this care came about from great pressure on the various governmental levels by Indian health personnel, along with increasing budgets for health care in general. (HMOs are seldom seen on reservations.)

I have seen a number of poor to well-staffed clinics in most parts of the state—clinics that may sometimes be understaffed, but generally well supplied and that are on a par with the community in general. Several of these clinics have been generously funded by local Indian gaming establishments, which have seen a great need for them. Following is a partial list.

Redding Rancheria has joined with the local public health group to purchase a clinic in the neighborhood, which supplies many needed services to everyone who needs them. Table Mountain Rancheria, similarly, provides a clinic on their own land, for themselves and the wider community. **UNITED INDIAN HEALTH SERVICES, INC.**, a cooperative of nine northwest coast reservations, provides complete health services for its larger area (see below.)

Near the Viejas Reservation in southern California, the very attractive **SOUTHERN INDIAN HEALTH COUNCIL** clinic provides numerous services for several reservations in the area, including picking up people who cannot come in by themselves. Tule River Reservation has developed a complex of clinical services for its members, including medical, dental, and optical needs. Likewise, similar services are found in Round Valley Reservation in Covelo and Pit River Tribes tribal center in Burney. All of the larger cities in California have urban Indian Health Service-funded clinics.

SOMETIMES YOU COME ACROSS a particularly complete facility. An example of an IHS clinic complex that serves a four-county-wide community is *CHAPA-DE* (People of the Foothills) **INDIAN HEALTH PROGRAM**, located in Auburn, just east of Sacramento. This is a set of clinics, really, offering medical treatment, dentistry, optician, pharmacy, mental health services, podiatry, maternal and child care, health-related youth and family activities, and family health education—an amazingly broad range of services. The area covered comprises the rural areas of Placer, Nevada, Sierra, and Yolo counties—many

*The Lewis Meriam Report by the Brookings Institution, 1928, was highly critical of the BIA's handling of Indian affairs and the administration of Indian tribes, urging greatly increased appropriations for Indian health and education. (Ref. **X**, Vol. **4**, App. **XX**)

square miles. The complex itself, including an extension in Grass Valley (*YOCHA-DE-HE* **MEDICAL AND DENTAL CLINIC**), was founded as an IHS facility, but services are available as a managed care system to the entire community.

Health Village of the United Indian Health Services provides full medical services for tribes in the Eureka-Trinidad coastal area. The complex is built in traditional northwestern style, and is flanked by restored marshlands.

(drawing from UIHS)

HOW DO THEY DO IT? With much dedication and hard work. Plus additional funding from the State and billings to clients. Its services are available to Native persons with enrollment documentation, at a lower cost than the general public. The buildings (24,000 and 18,000 square feet) were built by and are owned by the Indian Health Program. Some 48% of its clients are Indian, not all of whom come from the 4-county area.

Are Indians better served by this type of facility than before? "Definitely, yes," says Carol Irvine, Director, who has been with *CHAPA-DE* for nearly 15 years.

What about the neighborhood? Adjacent to *CHAPA-DE*, but serving other areas, are the **SHINGLE SPRINGS TRIBAL HEALTH CLINIC**, which covers El Dorado County and Mother Lode country (mostly rural), and the **SACRAMENTO URBAN INDIAN HEALTH PROGRAM**.

ONE OF THE MOST IMPRESSIVE "bootstrap" operations undertaken by Indian health organizations is in Arcata—Health Village of the United Indian Health Services, Inc. UIHS serves an area of Tolowa, Yurok, and Wiyot peoples in nine reservations (Smith River, Elk Valley, Yurok, Resighini, Big Lagoon, Tsurai, Blue Lake, Rohnerville, and Table Bluff) and Tolowa Nation.

Some 20 years ago, visionaries in Del Norte and Humboldt Counties decided that a centralized modern health clinic would best serve their Indian population—especially attractive would be the ability to have

all medical and health services under one roof. Forty acres of land was found at a traditional scenic meeting place of tribes, on the north side of Arcata, on the Mad River delta. An architect was engaged who had an especial awareness for tribal traditions.

The resulting **HEALTH VILLAGE** incorporates a superb blend of north coast tradition with modern health. Fifteen segments are connected by an arcade around an open courtyard garden; each segment bears a roof gable in the style of the ancient northwest house (*see p.67*), and a restored marsh wetland is the vista below the windows.

The blend consists of a Wellness Garden, sweat lodges, a demonstration old-style house and dance pit with day care facilities, with a medical complex offering full medical, optical, dental, physical therapy, nutritional, mental health, and pharmacy services. Satellite clinics are in Fortuna, Klamath, and Smith River.

Though all this health coverage sounds marvelous, parts of California clinics have had to close or cut back services, owing to lack of funding and growing Congressional pressure to cut human services to just about everybody.

AVAILABLE HEALTH SERVICES

IT IS FAR BEYOND THE SCOPE of this book to include the contents of the excellent manual of the California Area Office of the IHS, but listed starting at the top of the next page, are the locations of all the California Indian Health clinics, Rural and Urban; most rural sites serve more than one area, often with several satellite clinics.

Mendo-Lake Health Center is an inviting, comfortable, conveniently located and environmentally and architecturally sensitive complex serving Native peoples in Mendocino and Lake counties. (dhe, 1999)

All listings are from north to south.
Abbreviations used: HS=health service; HP= health
project or program; C=clinic, center, or council

RURAL
• *Trinidad-Del Norte & Humboldt*
(in Hoopa Valley)
UNITED INDIAN HEALTH SERVICES
• *Happy Camp*
KARUK TRIBE HP
• *Redding*
REDDING RANCHERIA IHP
• *Burney*
PIT RIVER HS
• *Alturas*
MODOC IHP
• *Ft. Bidwell*
WARNER MOUNTAIN IHP
• *Plumas County (Greenville)*
GREENVILLE TRIBAL HP
• *Ukiah*
MENDO-LAKE HS
• *Covelo*
ROUND VALLEY IHC
• *N. Sacto. Valley (Willows)*
NORTHERN VALLEY IH
• *Lake County (Lakeport &* Clear Lake Oaks*)*
LAKE COUNTY TRIBAL HC
• *Oroville*
FEATHER RIVER IHC
• *Susanville*
LASSEN IHC
• *Auburn*
CHAPA-DE IHC
• *El Dorado County (Shingle Springs)*
SHINGLE SPRINGS TRIBAL HP
• *Santa Rosa*
SONOMA COUNTY IHP
• *Tuolumne*
TUOLUMNE RURAL IHP
• *Clovis*
CENTRAL VALLEY IHP
• *Bishop*
TOIYABE IHP
• *Tule River Reservation*
TULE RIVER IHC
• *Santa Ynez*
SANTA YNEZ TRIBAL HP
• *Morongo Reservation (Banning)*
RIVERSIDE-SAN BERNARDINO COUNTY IH
• *N San Diego County (Pauma Valley)*
INDIAN IHC
• *Viejas Reservation (Alpine)*
SOUTHERN IHC
• *El Cajon*
SYCUAN IHC.

URBAN
• *Sacramento*
URBAN INDIAN HEALTH PROJECT
• *Oakland/San Francisco*
URBAN INDIAN HEALTH BOARD'S
NATIVE AMERICAN HEALTH CENTER
• *San José*
INDIAN HEALTH CENTER
OF SANTA CLARA VALLEY
• *Fresno*
INDIAN HEALTH ASSOCIATION and
CENTRAL VALLEY INDIAN HEALTH (Clovis)
• *Bakersfield*
BAKERSFIELD EDUCATION CENTER
FOR NATIVE INDIANS
• *Santa Barbara*
AMERICAN INDIAN HEALTH & SERVICES
• *Los Angeles*
UNITED AMERICAN INDIAN
INVOLVEMENT, INC. and
AMERICAN INDIAN HEALTH PROJECT
• *San Diego*
AMERICAN INDIAN HEALTH CENTER

As an example of the types of services offered:

NATIVE AMERICAN HEALTH CENTER
San Francisco (415) 621-8051
Located near the 16th & Mission BART stop, the Center is not restricted by residential, tribal, or ethnic requirements for use of its services. Among the many medical services available are women's health and pre-natal care, dental care, family and child guidance, and access of care to the homeless. Located next door is the **FRIENDSHIP HOUSE OF AMERICAN INDIANS OF SAN FRANCISCO** (see next page).

Both the Native American Health Center-San Francisco and the Native American Aids Project, 1540 Market St., are clinics of the Native American Health Center-Oakland, 3124 International Blvd., divisions of the United Indian Nations (see Oakland)
SAN FRANCISCO NATIVE AMERICAN HEALTH CENTER
56 Julian Ave., San Francisco 94103
(415) 621-8051.

Ft. Mohave, Chemehuevi, Colorado River Tribes, and
Ft. Yuma are served from Arizona offices in Phoenix.

continued next page

ALCOHOL/SUBSTANCE ABUSE TREATMENT CENTERS

•*HOOPA*
HOOPA VALLEY BUSINESS COUNCIL
•*EUREKA*
UNITED INDIAN HEALTH SERVICES
•*MANTECA/STOCKTON*
SACRAMENTO URBAN INDIAN HEALTH PROJECT and
SAN JOAQUIN COUNCIL FOR AMERICAN INDIANS
•*OAKLAND*
AMERICAN INDIAN FAMILY HEALING CENTER
•*SAN FRANCISCO*
FRIENDSHIP HOUSE ASSOCIATION OF AMERICAN INDIANS
•*SAN JOSE*
AMERICAN INDIAN CENTER OF SANTA CLARA VALLEY
•*FRESNO*
SIERRA TRIBAL CONSORTIUM
•*LEMOORE*
SANTA ROSA RANCHERIA
•*PORTERVILLE*
TULE RIVER TRIBAL COUNCIL
•*Los Angeles*
UNITED AMERICAN INDIAN INVOLVEMENT.

For further information concerning the listings here:
CALIFORNIA AREA OFFICE, INDIAN HEALTH SERVICE
1825 Bell St., Ste. 200, Sacramento, CA 95825-1097
(916) 566-7020, FAX (916) 566-7053

As an example of services provided in many communities, here are extracts from a San Francisco bulletin:

FRIENDSHIP HOUSE OF AMERICAN INDIANS OF SAN FRANCISCO
Residential Alcoholism and Substance Abuse Treatment Program

"The mission of the Friendship House is to provide a culturally sensitive, highly-structured, therapeutic treatment and prevention program in which personal change and recovery from alcohol and drug addiction are made possible for American Indian men and women.

"We treat each client with care, respect, responsibility, and knowledge in order to restore them to joyous, sober and productive living in our community.

"We believe and we have demonstrated that we can treat the ravages of addiction in an environment that is culturally supportive of the rich but shattered lives of American Indians who are battling addictions.

"While emphasizing American Indian Values, the House provides residential and aftercare follow-up

treatment, counseling, prevention services, employment readiness training, and clean and sober community events.

"Twelve steps toward admission are required (not the AA 12-steps), including commitment to the program and a 30-day in-house restriction."
[*Ed. note: The director, Helen Waukazoo, has been awarded many honors for her success with this program. Other programs in other cities use similar models for their efforts, hopefully as successful.*]

CHILD CARE

Examples of only a few of the many agencies furnishing child care. (An overwhelming majority of Indian casinos are currently supporting at least one child care center for employees and community members):
•**FOSTER FAMILY AGENCY**
•**SAFE AMERICAN INDIAN FAMILIES**
•**INDIGENOUS NATIONS CHILD AND FAMILY AGENCY(INCFA)**
405 14th St., Suite162, Oakland 94612
(510) 645-1430
(916) 492-8567 Sacramento
•**CALIFORNIA RURAL INDIAN HEALTH BOARD**
1451 River Park Dr., Ste.220, Sacramento, CA 95915
Many child care programs were engendered by the Indian Child Welfare Act (child protection, troubled families)

EDUCATION

NUMEROUS SOURCES OF FUNDING are available for Indian education at all levels. The problem is how do students, parents, and teachers find out about them? This book cannot even begin to list these sources, but to let you know of their existence, there are JOM (Johnson-O'Malley) programs, "Even Start", "Head Start", tutoring, cultural classes in tribal languages, parenting skills, employment skills, GED preparation. Title V and Title IX programs are also available in most cities and many towns.

One example is the San Francisco Title IX, Indian Education program for students, K-6. A large part of an older school building is used for this program, to boost the learning skills of Indian students who have been underserved in the past.

Information is usually available through at tribal offices, and every urban Indian Center should have information (if the center in your city is still open).

One example is Stewart Indian School near Carson City, Nevada, this is available to some California students, through Paiute or Washoe and other tribal affiliations.

A special section of this book is devoted to higher education—high school and college. (*p.260*).

LEGAL SERVICES

CALIFORNIA INDIAN LEGAL SERVICES (CILS) has been an extraordinarily important factor in defending Indian rights and issues in the State. In the late 1990s, funding has been decreased because, I believe, of its great successes—which irked the governor and influential groups in the legislature antagonistic to Indian progress. Issues: sovereignty, child welfare, acknowledgement, environment, cultural resources, fishing, water, family disputes, tribal status, sorting out federal vs. state issues. CILS has offices in Oakland, Escondido, Eureka, Ukiah, and Bishop.

CALIFORNIA INDIAN LEGAL SERVICES

510-16th St., Ste. 301, Oakland, CA 94612
(510) 835-0284.

Native American Rights Fund is national organization that serves the entire U.S. Indian community in cases with major legal issues. Various California cases have been considered (natural resources, sovereignty, human rights). Most have been resolved in favor of the Indian communities. Many of their cases end up in arguments before the Supreme Court. Specialties: development of Indian law, governmental accountability, preservation of tribal existence.

NATIVE AMERICAN RIGHTS FUND (NARF)

1506 Broadway, Boulder, CO 80302
(303) 447-8760.

BUREAU OF INDIAN AFFAIRS (BIA) (*see below*). This agency has handled some legal aid for its constituents, often on land and housing issues. Owing to its continuing shortages of funding, however, it is often relatively powerless to force decisions.

The Special Association of American Indian Affairs Federal Acknowledgment Project in California has been extremely instrumental and effective in cases involved in Federal acknowledgement, religious freedom, and tribal law cases. Specialty: investigating, uncovering, interpreting, and acting upon attitudes and deeds of officials in Washington.

SPECIAL ASSOCIATION OF AMERICAN INDIAN AFFAIRS FEDERAL ACKNOWLEDGMENT PROJECT IN CALIFORNIA.

Allogan Slagle, project director

Private sources. Most Indian tribes in California have found it necessary to hire lawyers, experienced in Indian law and familiar with Indian problems. The BIA lists the law firms representing various tribes in their directory of tribes. Issues: gaming, housing, land and water rights, issues of civil/criminal jurisdictions, enforcement of legal obligations of other entities

THE BUREAU OF INDIAN AFFAIRS (BIA)

A HUNDRED YEARS AGO the Bureau of Indian Affairs was known as "Indian Service", but changed to this more realistic label. This agency is charged by the Department of the Interior with the supervision, protection, and administration of the welfare of the Indians of the United States. For most of its existence, its reputation has been to do just the opposite.

Realistically, the "Federal government" as used in this book, is the direct political control of the Native peoples, exercised through the BIA. Until the 1930s, the Commissioner of Indian Affairs and the regional Indian Agents followed the often vague dictates of Congress and the Secretary of the Interior, as interpreted through their own personal prejudices. Scores of instances of incredible injustices, murders, torture, removals, criminal impositions of oppressive government policies are told in every proper history book.

There are some persons in the Bureau today struggling to do the right thing, but they must put up with high-level Interior and Bureau incompetence, not to mention the difficulties of maintaining a balance between conflicting political and legal policies. There is so much to do, and so little to do it with. There are many who believe that Indians, not whites, should be at the highest levels of the BIA—but to carry out the misdirected white men's policies? Native people have given it a try, at all levels, but often resign in the face of these obstacles.

The short history at the beginning of this book of "government" interference or neglect is essentially the story of the BIA in California. Tribes protest that even today there is little legal protection for them or defense on their behalf. Reservation sizes and populations are consistently under reported, following strict, unrealistic government dictates of lineage. There is almost no protection or services for off-reservation Indians or for those without tribal recognition. BIA is reluctant even to acknowledge Indian names for their reservations, rather than imposed English names. Little wonder that Indians have so little confidence in the BIA.

In the early 1990s, the once-monolithic California BIA office was divided into regional offices, but the regions are very uneven in size and makeup, and relations between them does not appear cordial. The BIA now has northern, central, and southern regions, but retaining an earlier delegation of supervision of the peripheral Modoc, Paiute, Washoe, and Colorado River tribes to out-of-state agencies. Such divisions can hardly foster cooperative work and common enterprises.

> THERE ARE MANY WHO BELIEVE THAT INDIANS, NOT WHITES, SHOULD BE AT THE HIGHEST LEVELS OF THE BIA

When I dialed the Sacramento offices (moved from the old Federal Building offices in Sacramento to the IRS!), I got an idea of what they are up against these days, in terms of what they have to supervise: "Press 1 for credit, education, Social Security, appraisals, roads. Press 2 for forestry, realty, tribal operations, and natural resources. Press 3 for contracting, trusts, finance, budget, and ATD. Press 4 for the director's office." Note that housing and health are now relegated to other agencies.

Can they do it all?

INDIAN CENTERS

Most activities in this part of the state are handled by specific agencies or tribal offices (*see above*). However, social activities and specific programs may be handled by certain local councils. See also Butte Intertribal Council, *p.122* and Central California Intertribal Councils, *p.177*

OAKLAND (for greater San Francisco Bay)

The **INTERTRIBAL FRIENDSHIP HOUSE** (**IFH**) is the oldest Indian social services institution in the Bay Area, founded in 1955 by the American Fiends Service Committee, (Quakers). It functions today as an agency supported by United Way, foundations, and donations. In addition to its social services and counseling, IFH also offers cultural programs and community functions.

INTERTRIBAL FRIENDSHIP HOUSE
523 E. 14th, Oakland, 94612
(510) 452-1235

Since 1979, **UNITED INDIAN NATIONS** (**UIN**) has been offering job training and placement, social services, health center, charter schools, rehabilitation programs, and direct attention and help to personal situations for Natives from all over the United States who have found themselves in the SF Bay Area. From their pleasant offices in downtown Oakland, UIN serves an East Bay urban community of more than 20,000 individuals and families. The atmosphere here feels to me like tribal council offices for a very large tribe, and I believe that this is on purpose—to create a feeling of community center and Indian identity for the widely disparate urban aggregation from so many tribes.

One room at the front of the UIN Oakland center is a cultural gift shop—articles from the Bay Area's American Indian Arts & Crafts Cooperative. The public is quite welcome.

In 1996 the United Indian Nations created a special branch called the Community Development Corporation for identifying, planning, and management of larger projects. Then, in 1999, the UINCDC was able to grasp and exploit a most unusual situation that arose near Oakland—three military bases closed

offered land for use by Native American organizations. UIN CDC was on the scene with timely and excellent proposals for all three—to provide their community with institutions that re-establish the Indian pride of supporting their own people:

1. Rehabilitation of former Navy housing of the former Naval Air Station in Alameda has been accomplished as residences for persons and families in transition—mostly those jobless or very low income, or homeless. This project is now **UNITY VILLAGE**; a project of the Homeless Collaborative in a campus setting. The work is performed with Native American labor and furnishes single families (at present, some 60 persons) a temporary place to call home for up to 24 months while they are securing work and/or while they are at substandard income levels.

2. Establishment of a **NATIVE AMERICAN MUSEUM AND CULTURE CENTER** at the former 3-3/4 acre Oakland Naval Hospital site in east Oakland. A unique museum, this undertaking is dedicated to the "depiction of the urban Indian experience". Interior space includes a gift shop, with on-site artisans at work (weavers, artists, carvers, potters, etc.), some permanent exhibits, and some traveling exhibits. It is primarily (but not exclusively) oriented to North American Indian tribes.

3. Utilizing some 200-plus acres of the former Oakland Army Base (along with two non-Indian development agencies) in the creation of an eco-industrial park. This eco-park is to employ as many as 2,000 low-income American Indians and Oakland residents in ecologically significant projects.

—information from Rick Lewis,
Senior Project Manager
and UINCDC brochures

UNITED INDIAN NATIONS
1320 Webster St., Oakland
(510) 763-3410

There is at present no Indian center as such in San Francisco. However, health service and alcohol/drug rehabilitation is available at the San Francisco Native American Health Center (*see Indian Health services, above.*)

SOUTHERN CALIFORNIA INTERTRIBAL CENTERS
Los Angeles, Riverside

SOUTHERN CALIFORNIA INTERTRIBAL CENTERS (**SCIC**) is a group of centers that arrange, manage, and administer various programs for all Native Americans (mostly off-reservation) in Los Angeles and Riverside urban areas. Their specialties are job placement, senior services, health placement, commodities distribution, social services, and information on most Native activities.

SCIC
12755 Brookhurst, Garden Grove, CA 92642
(714) 663-1102

Three satellite **SCIC** offices:
Los Angeles, (213) 387-5772;
Commerce, (SE of downtown), (323) 728-8844;
Riverside, (909) 682-8684

Los Angeles City/County Native American Indian Commission
Los Angeles City/County

LOS ANGELES CITY/COUNTY NATIVE AMERICAN INDIAN COMMISSION manages local, tribal, state, and Federal governmental concerns for American Indian residents of the county: funding, legislation, information, conferences, advising officials and agencies.

LOS ANGELES CITY/COUNTY NATIVE AMERICAN INDIAN COMMISSION
500 West Temple, Rm. 780, Los Angeles, CA 90012
(213) 974-7554

Indian Human Resource Center, San Diego
The **INDIAN HUMAN RESOURCE CENTER, SAN DIEGO** is *THE* Indian Center for San Diego. They offer advice, help, programs.

INDIAN HUMAN RESOURCE CENTER, SAN DIEGO
4040 30th St. Ste. A, San Diego, CA 92104
(619) 281-5964

EMPLOYMENT

The **NORTHERN CALIFORNIA INDIAN DEVELOPMENT COUNCIL** advertises available jobs and receives applications for Native Americans from the entire state.

NORTHERN CALIFORNIA INDIAN DEVELOPMENT COUNCIL
241 F St., Eureka, CA 95501
(707) 445-8451

The **CALIFORNIA INDIAN MANPOWER CONSORTIUM** (CIMC) offers statewide services through their Community Services division, including emergency block grants for off-reservation persons (housing, utilities, food). Other programs include employment, utilities, food resources, education, consumer education (counseling on non-Native community requirements to obtain various services). They have satellite field offices and connections in every tribal headquarters to deal with situations statewide.

CALIFORNIA INDIAN MANPOWER CONSORTIUM (CIMC)
Central office, Sacramento (916) 920-0285
Sacramento field office: (916) 564-4053
Field offices: Bishop, Escondido, Hoopa, Redding, San Bernardino, San Jacinto, Stockton, Ukiah

The **ADVISORY COUNCIL ON CALIFORNIA INDIAN POLICY** (ACCIP) is not really an "Indian Service", although it has definitely been of service to most tribes. In early 1994, some members of Congress, highly disturbed by the hodge-podge of conflicting laws, policies, treatments, and official attitudes toward California Indians, conceived the idea of listening. Funds were provided. A board of 18 persons was appointed, which convened many sessions in locations throughout the state to hear problems and possible solutions.

The Council was set up to last a probable two years. But the time required to hear all the problems, and for Indian groups to realize that this was not just another useless gripe session, required much longer (and much persuasion to get people to come forward).

They did come forward, and some in Congress listened. A bulletin was issued occasionally, informing Indians and the public and the press what was going on. Eventually many well-known tribal leaders testified. A task force was gathered that brought their recommendations to the Congressional staff. The activity eventually quieted down to about two members, who kept the phone line open. Even the phone number changed—callers complain that the old number is now the New York State Automated Phone Betting Line.

At least one of the considerations of the ACCIP has been nearly resolved— the problem of the support of gaming after the Proposition 5 initiative of 1998. However, situations change. One of the most important recommendations was requesting smoother and easier recognition process for unrecognized California tribes, giving consideration to the unique history of Indians and tribes in this state. Also considered: in education—discontinuing the BIA "assimilationist attitudes", establishment of tribal schools and contract schools; in economics—equal funding for all Indians, recognized or not; in social areas—tribal day and boarding schools involving consortia of multiple tribes; in law—transfer of tribal law enforcement to the reservation governments with funding for tribal courts. Action is still pending, but pendant questions are either dropped or are picked up. We're still waiting.

ADVISORY COUNCIL ON CALIFORNIA INDIAN POLICY (ACCIP)
(916) 568-5196
(subject to change or cancellation without notice)

If readers have any corrections or additions, please write to Trees Company Press offices at 49 Van Buren Way, SF, CA 94131, or phone (415) 334-3544.

SECONDARY & HIGHER EDUCATION

YA~KA~AMÁ (yah-keh-amáh)
All-Indian Sonoma County

In the mid-1960s, Congress passed a law stating that Indians might claim any unused federal lands. This was the basis for the famous takeover of Alcatraz Island in 1969-71, which involved Pomo people. At about the same time, an alert Sonoma County resident informed local Pomos and other Indian activists that several acres of a former (1955) government radio station site were unoccupied. Some 125 acres were then occupied in 1970 by the people and *Ya-Ka-Ama* (Pomo: "Our Land") vocational school was begun, after obtaining considerable government support.

TODAY, IN A CLUSTER of several buildings, Ya-Ka-Ama supports local Indian educational, economic, cultural, and social opportunities. Training and assistance in job development, search, referral, and placement are available as well as training in accounting and merchandising, based largely on GED requirements. An extensive nursery provides training in horticulture, landscaping, knowledge of native plants, and brings in income. Research into local educational needs is an on-going program.

Ya-Ka-Ama and the Native American Studies Program at Sonoma State University in Rohnert Park jointly maintain an ethnographic library of books and taped Indian dances for cultural and historical reference.

Ya-ka-ama Indian Education struggles to offer opportunities in several areas in which local Indians are deficient. Programs here also offer training in specialized areas, such as nursery care for native plants, economics, and office skills. (dhe, 1994)

A BULLETIN FROM Ya-Ka-Ama states: "The Ya-Ka-Ama American Indian Emporium carries a good selection of books on Native American pertaining to crafts, myth and legends, games, cookbooks, teaching guides, and much more. All of our books have been screened for bias and stereotyping... The store provides retail merchandising skills as well as encouraging local artists and craftspeople to place their works on consignment."

On the grounds are a ball field, a dance ground (with arbors), a plant nursery, and a campground for occasional events. A large Spring Festival is held in June, which draws people to California dances, an all-Indian softball tourney, crafts, food, and native plant sales. An Indian Harvest Festival is occasionally presented in October. (*Check the Calendar, p.280, for approximate dates and call for specific dates.*)

I HAVE BEEN FOLLOWING the progress of Ya-Ka-Ama for many years, always hoping that new undertakings might blossom. But the institution seems impaired by a sense of drifting. It has always been imperative that Ya-Ka-Ama offers programs that are distinctly different from those of the surrounding community and that will appeal to both Indian and non-Indian communities. This requires very strong and imaginative leadership and dedicated continuity in both staff and students. Every so often a new program engages the staff's attention, but the enthusiasm eventually fades somewhat. I expect the essential reason is lack of continuing funding.

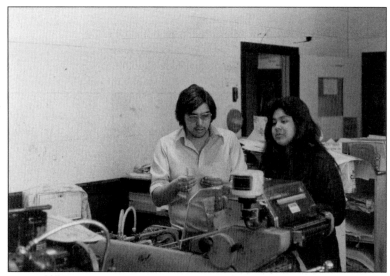

A former Yakima educational function was the teaching of the printing arts. This is Jim Helmer assisting a student. (dhe, 1984)

This institution has been very patient ever since its founding, and everything points to its continuing and enduring contribution to the community. We all must be patient, too, and find ways to assist.

62 *Take River Rd. (N of Santa Rosa) W 6 mi. to Trenton-Healdsburg Rd., turn R (N) for 1 1/2 mi. to the "wye" intersection at Eastside Rd. Follow the sign (at left) to Ya-Ka-Ama, about 1 mile.*

YA-KA-AMA INDIAN EDUCATION & DEVELOPMENT
6215 Eastside Rd., Forestville, CA 95436
(707) 887-1541

D-Q UNIVERSITY
All-Indian Yolo County

"From California, neighboring states, and a few countries outside the United States, students come to D-Q University, an accredited, two-year college. D-Q University is designated as a tribally-controlled college, which gives it a specifically indigenous flavor not found at other mainstream colleges.

"One of the reasons students come to D-Q is the personal attention they get from faculty and staff. Also, the school offers unique Native American-related courses. Twenty California tribes sanction (endorse) D-Q: students represent a variety of in-state and out-of-state tribes.

"Its 13 majors programs (Associate of Arts, Associate of Science degrees) cover a wide range of course offerings, from basic academic skills and college survival skills, to Appropriate Technology (the study of the applications of technology to problems encountered in the many environs of Native Americans), Environmental studies and related General Sciences, Social Sciences, Indigenous Studies, Native American Fine Arts, Computer Science, Business and Gaming Operations.

"In 17 specialized areas, certificates may be acquired in business economics and skills relating to such subjects as accounting. Other directions that have relevance to indigenous endeavors are gaming operations and Indian entrepreneurship.

The student body of full- and part-time students lives in campus dormitories or in nearby towns. Their tuition plus federal funding support D-Q U. The faculty is full- and part-time, also; some of the administrative staff teach classes.

"Providing financial aid for students, personal and academic counseling, and employment assistance fosters a caring, encouraging environment for many who would not otherwise make it through difficult times.

"The buildings, the site of a former military communications station, are located in a quiet rural agricultural area. The Cultural Arts Building is the site of four school-sponsored powwows a year. Ceremonial grounds are in the field to the north of the main campus. Sweats are held for students and others on a weekly basis during the school year.

Also, a California Indian Big Time as well as a Youth and Elders Gathering are held at the ceremonial grounds.

"In addition to classes at the school's main campus, located about seven miles west of Davis, programs are offered at seven affiliate sites around the state.

"D-Q U's name derives from both North American Indian and MesoAmerican spiritual names—names not publicly used, but kept in mind as reminders of the ultimate dedication of the school.

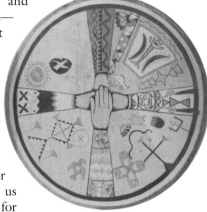

A mural at D-Q U depicting the four directions.

"Since its origins in the early 1970s, continued existence of this campus has been only through great struggle. But the school's educational philosophy and powerful regard for making Native scholars assure us that it will be educating students for a long time."

—Rick Heredia, Public Information Officer

D-Q UNIVERSITY AFFILIATE SITES

1. BISHOP [Owens Valley-Mono Lake]
OWENS VALLEY CAREER DEVELOPMENT CENTER
PO Box 1467, Bishop, CA 93515
(619) 873-4107

2. REDWOOD VALLEY [Ukiah]
COYOTE VALLEY TRIBAL CENTER
PO Box 39, Redwood Valley, CA 95470
(707) 485-1247

3. SHASTA LAKE CITY [Redding]
LOCAL INDIANS FOR EDUCATION,
PO Box 729, Shasta Lake, CA 96019
(916) 275-6290

4. Sherwood Valley [Willits]
SHERWOOD VALLEY TRIBAL CENTER
190 Sherwood Hill Dr., Willits, CA 96490
(707) 459-9690

5. Soboba [Riverside County]
PO Box 487, San Jacinto, CA 92383
(909) 654-2765

6. Oakland [San Francisco Bay]
UNITED INDIAN NATIONS, INC.
1320 Webster St.,
Oakland, CA 94612
(510) 763-3410

7. Corona [Orange County]
5000 Birch St., Ste. 4000, West Tower,
Newport Beach, CA 92660
(714) 260-2077

D~Q UNIVERSITY'S PURPOSE AND PHILOSOPHY

by Rick Heredia

D~Q UNIVERSITY BEGAN WITH A DREAM: Control our own education and we control our destiny. That's the reason one cold November morning in 1970, Indians, in a legendary act of civil disobedience, occupied a U.S. Army communications facility near Davis, California.

They wanted change; they wanted a college where eagle feathers, clapsticks, and acorn were just as important as scientific theories, mathematical equations, and term papers.

The circular dance arena at D-Q University reflects an homage to California roundhouses and to Native tribes of other states. (dhe, 1998)

IN APRIL, 1972, D~Q UNIVERSITY won a major psychological and educational victory when the federal government handed over the deed to the school. For once, instead of losing land, Indians won back land, land that, before non-Indian settlement, nurtured California Indians.

Twenty-seven years later, that dream of higher education for the tribes of this state lives. D-Q University, the state's tribal college, lives.

D-Q University has struggled. Struggled and persevered. That is the story of all tribal colleges. But from the fires of adversity, the school has forged a legacy of survival. It has learned to do much with little. It has become an expert in stretching resources to keep the doors open for its students.

D-Q University knows education is expensive, in this age of technology, the costs soar. But how can you put a price tag on human potential? On the dreams of people who hope D-Q University and the doors to other tribal colleges will be open when they are ready to learn?

D-Q believes the price is worth paying when it comes to providing cultural and academic support for its students. It is an investment D-Q makes because it knows students and their tribes will benefit. That is part of the school's mission, to help Indians and tribes bridge the gap between the Indian and non-Indian world. To give students the skills, the confidence to succeed, as Indians, in both worlds.

THE D-Q UNIVERSITY EXPERIENCE lights a flame of achievement that chases the shadows of poverty, ignorance, and low self-esteem. The circle of knowledge we weave can crush the cycle of despair. Our students will dance in the roundhouse and be heard in the statehouse.

That is the dream D-Q University will carry into the new millennium. It stands on the threshold of a new era, led by an administration that believes the past is our strength, the future our promise. Together, tribe and tribal college can build a country of the mind.

Unlike the state's community colleges, D-Q University does not get FTE (Full Time Enrollment) funds. This means that administrators have to be creative, resourceful, and improvisational in operating on a lean budget. It means that D-Q strives to provide a solid education without many frills. We are a school proud of our mission!

Our students, like many at other tribal colleges, don't have much money. So it's a challenge to keep tuition affordable to feed and nourish hungry minds.

Some students are single parents, some students don't have a high school diploma; others have dropped out of mainstream schools for various reasons ranging from no money to feeling alienated on those campuses. D-Q is doing something about this.

D-Q U is the school of last resort for many of our students. They come unsure, doubtful. They soon realize they've joined a family—one that makes education a priority.

It's the best investment going. Long-term, to be sure, requiring lots of sacrifice. As long as we exist, we will be called upon to make the sacrifices, though they are taking their toll on our campus facilities.

We need new dormitories, classrooms, offices, recreational, kitchen and dining facilities. We are understaffed and lack the money to provide the amenities that state-funded colleges take for granted.

Still, we persevere with little money because we know we can exert influence. We challenge minds, inspire scholars, instill pride and nurture a desire for knowledge. For 27 years, that has been our goal. We know we're doing a good job. Our students tell us so.

D-Q University is a community college in the broadest sense of the word. It offers hope and resources to tribes, indigenous people, and others, especially at a time when everything from sovereignty to basketmaking is under attack. It is a tribal college, unique and enduring. It can ensure, if allowed to flourish, that the dreams of a people are not delayed.

And that history—not always kind to the tribal peoples of this state—waits to be made by those bold enough to dream.

61 *D-Q U is located N of Rd. 31, about 5 mi. W of Woodland, or about 2 mi. E of I-505 (follow signs).*
D-Q UNIVERSITY
P.O. Box 409, Davis, CA 95617
(916) 758-0470

SHERMAN INDIAN HIGH SCHOOL

In its statement of purpose, Sherman Indian High School intends to "provide a safe, caring environment...to foster the academic, social, cultural, physical, and spiritual growth...in an off-reservation boarding school [aiming] for post-secondary success." The statement also expects dedicated involvement and commitment of "staff, students, parents, guardians, tribal leaders, educational coordinators, and board members."

Their impressive application packet includes a schedule of— among the usual high school curricula of English, biology, physics, chemistry, math, U.S. and world history—unusual Indian-oriented courses such as world cultures, Indian studies, tribal government, Native American traditions, museum operation, Navajo language. Then there are special course offerings in beading, needle-craft, woodcarving, ceramics, basketry, and (computer) graphics. Practical training is also included in office and computer skills, consumer math and economics. Extracurricular activities include music, drama, art, and physical education.

Special attention is given to searching for ways to support those with limited funds and with special disabilities. Maintaining or attaining students' health seems to be of great concern, considering the several forms required in the application and the number of facilities for sporting and athletic activities. The school has several liaisons with local colleges and universities.

Student behavior is rather tightly regulated, at least on paper; the academic program appears exceptional, but strict application of rules might deter some creative students. However, in my experience, quiet apparent observance of rules demands supreme creativity.

All in all, Sherman seems like a special opportunity for good students lacking resources near their homes.

The Sherman Indian Museum occupies the old administration building of the school, built in 1902. It is used largely for touring school groups learning of their heritage. Housed here are over 2,000 artifacts of Native American origin, as well as school records from the school's earliest days. (Open to the public only by appointment.)

127 SHERMAN INDIAN HIGH SCHOOL
9010 Magnolia Ave., Riverside, CA 92503
Museum: (909) 276-6719

LOCAL INDIANS FOR EDUCATION (LIFE)

Wintu and others, Shasta County

LIFE was founded in 1978 as an educational organization with the goals of increasing the educational level of Shasta County Indians. At the same time it seeks to encourage research about the unique California Native culture and to preserve and disseminate that knowledge.

The old mural on the Hupa High School wall promises rededication.
The promises are still remembered; the mural has gone. (dhe, 1984)

LIFE also is ready to make recommendations to all governmental levels programs or legislation that would improve the educational and leadership levels of Indian people.

THIS ORGANIZATION is more than a school, though it offers classes in history, English, business skills. Research in Native culture is developed and then presented in classes, for instance, in traditional basketry and beading techniques. Modern technological skills are also taught, like those necessary to operate and understand a computer.

Services of this institution are offered to indigenous people regardless of residence—reservation, urban, or rural. Affiliation with D-Q University allows LIFE to offer specialties in fine arts, community development, and general education.

The Indian Art and Design Gift Shop and Visitor Center at this address is also an economic development project for local Indian craft experts.

L.I.F.E.
P.O Box 729,
4440 Shasta Dam Blvd., Shasta Lake City 96019
(530) 275-1513
(Exit from Interstate I-5)

4-WINDS CHARTER SCHOOL
Wintu & Maidu: Meechoopda, Mooretown, Enterprise Rancherias *(see p.133)*

TRIBAL EDUCATION

Many tribal efforts are being made, some with financial help from their casino, others with their own resources—from an intense realization that education of their young people is a necessity for perpetuation of the tribe:

These are just a few that I have personally seen.

Barona Reservation; Hupa, all grades; Pit River headstart; Redding Rancheria headstart; Santa Rosa Rancheria headstart and elementary school; Table Bluff Reservation; Table Mountain Rancheria headstart, preschool, and Learning Center; Tule River Reservation

Redding Rancheria furnishes school buses for its school's children, many of whom live off-reservation, and many of whom are not Native residents.
                                                                    (dhe, 1998)

URBAN EFFORTS

Children from three years of age to high school age may be enrolled in the Johnson-O'Malley educational assistance programs located in Los Angeles, San Francisco, San Diego, Sacramento, and San Jose, and several other smaller cities and towns. Parents of prospective students would contact their reservation tribal office or urban Indian center about details. Requirements for eligibility are tribal membership or provable one-fourth Indian heritage (parents), among other things. The applicable BIA office would then arrange assistance in transportation, room and board, and other expenses, if necessary. Of course, dealing with the proof-work required is not likely to be easy, especially for city-dwellers.

Within some cities, some special educational facilities may be found. Title IV of the Indian Education Act

of 1972 provides basic educational aids for Indian students, primarily assisting students in their present schooling. Adult education in the form of GED (high school diploma) preparation is often provided. Cultural enrichment studies can sometime be found, as well—Indian history and culture.

NATIVE AMERICAN STUDIES
(AMERICAN INDIAN STUDIES)

College and university level courses in Native American subjects are often available through a specific course curriculum. Intensive courses may include history, social studies, Native American arts, health concerns, ethnic studies, or incorporated into other general cultural subjects. A few colleges have majors in AIS, and at least one offers a degree. Native student graduates in these courses are finding that more and more colleges are interested in finding knowledgeable instructors.

All the campuses of the University of California sponsor some curricula in this area, some stronger than others. Programs are offered at Berkeley, Davis, Irvine, Los Angeles, Riverside, San Diego, Santa Barbara, and Santa Cruz (none at San Francisco).

The California State Universities with major programs are (alphabetical by location) Humboldt State (Arcata), CSU Chico, CSU Fullerton, CSU Hayward, CSU Long Beach, Sonoma State (Rohnert Park), Sacramento State, CSU San Bernardino, San Diego State, San Francisco State, San Jose State, CSU San Marcos, CSU Stanislaus (Turlock).

A large number of community colleges are providing some emphasis in Native American Studies as well; some offer at least one course with an emphasis in Native American concerns. Among them (alphabetical by location):

Cabrillo College, (Aptos), Bakersfield City College, Palo Verde College (Blythe), DeAnza College (Cupertino), College of the Redwoods (Eureka), Ohlone College (Fremont), Fresno City College, Gavilan College (Gilroy), Antelope Valley (Lancaster), Merced College, Saddleback College (Mission Viejo), Napa Valley, Cerritos College (Norwalk), Diablo Valley College (Pleasant Hill), Chaffey College (Rancho Cucamonga), Shasta College (Redding), Sacramento City College, Hartnell (Salinas), Grossmont (San Diego), Los Angeles Mission College (San Fernando), Cuesta College (San Luis Obispo), Palomar College (San Marcos), Santa Barbara City College, Santa Rosa Junior College, Ventura College, Victor Valley College (Victorville).

Private institutions include Pomona College (Claremont), D-Q U (Davis), Mills College (Oakland), Chapman University (Orange and other sites), Mount San Jacinto College (San Jacinto), Stanford University, University of Redlands, and Whittier College.

Any others, or deletions, please let us know.

APPENDIX I
CALiFORNiA MUSEUMS witH INdiAN ARTiFACTS

LISTED BY REGION

For anyone pursuing an interest in the history of the California Indians of a region, a visit to a local museum is strongly recommended, and, if possible, to one of the larger all-California museums. Specific directions and museum hours may be obtained locally by telephone.

[CAUTION: Several local museums with small budgets are sometimes open only for a few days a week or seasonally.]

NOTE: Please write or telephone us any corrections or additions to this information.

LEGEND CODE FOR MUSEUM HOLDINGS
a ARCHAEOLOGY
b BASKETRY, BEADS
c CLOTHING, CEREMONIAL ATTIRE
l LITERATURE
m MILITARY ARTICLES
p PHOTOGRAPHS
s STONEWORK (arrow points, lance & spear points, grinding mortars)
t TEXTILES
OTHER ITEMS (models, dioramas, boats, etc.) Dioramas portray
   earlier times, in which objects are shown realistically, as if in use.

NORTHWESTERN & NORTHEASTERN CALIFORNIA
AUBURN, Placer Co. Museum. *Maidu* (b, c, m, s)
BLAIRSDEN, Plumas Eureka State Park. *Maidu* (b, l, s)
CALPELLA, Pomo Museum, Lake Mendocino. *Pomo* [b, c, l, p, s, t]
CRESCENT CITY, Del Norte Co. Historical Society Museum. *Tolowa, Yurok* (b, c, l, p)
DOWNIEVILLE, Sierra Museum. *Maidu* (m, s)
EUREKA, Clarke Memorial Museum. *Karuk, Yurok, Hupa, Pomo* (a, b, c, l, p, s,#)
—College of the Redwoods, Spinas/Brown Collection Main Art Gallery. *Yurok, Karuk, Kashaya* (b, c, t, #)
—Fort Humboldt State Historical Park. *NW Calif.* (p, m, s,#diorama)
FALL RIVER MILLS, Ft. Crook Museum. *Pit River, Modoc* (b, l, p, s, #)
FORT JONES, Fort Jones Museum. *Karuk, Shasta, other Klamath River peoples* (b, c, m, p, s, t, #)
HOOPA, Hupa Tribal Museum. *Hupa and surrounding peoples* (a, b, c, p, s, #)
KLAMATH, Trees of Mystery End of the Trail Museum. *Yurok* (a, b, c, l, p, t,#)
ORICK, Redwood National Park Information Center.
OROVILLE, Lake Oroville Visitor Center. *Maidu*
PATRICKS POINT STATE PARK, Sumeg Yurok Village. *Yurok* (b,s, t, #)
REDDING, Redding Museum. *Sacramento River tribes (a,b,#diorama)*
QUINCY, Plumas Co. Museum. *Maidu* (b, c, l, m, p, s)
SHASTA, Shasta Courthouse Museum. *Northeast Californian* (b, p, s)
TULELAKE, Lava Beds National Monument. *Modoc, Klamath* (a, b, l, m, p, s)
WEAVERVILLE, Trinity Co. Historical Society–J.J. Jackson Memorial Museum. *Shasta, Chimariko, Wintu, Lassik, Wailaki, Yuki* (b, c, l, p, s, t)
YREKA, Siskiyou Co. Museum. *Shasta, Karuk, Modoc* (b, l, p, s)

WEST CENTRAL CALIFORNIA
KELSEYVILLE, Clear Lake State Park Visitor Center. *Pomo* (a, b, s, #)
LAKEPORT, Lake Co. Museum. Pomo, Wappo, Lake Miwok (a, b, c, l, p, s, t, #)
NOVATO, Marin Museum of the American Indian. *Miwok, other California* (a, b, l, p, s, #; June Festival)
PETALUMA, Petaluma Adobe State Historic Park. *Miwok, Patwin, Wappo* (a, b, c, m, p, s, t, #, summer festival)

RED BLUFF, Kelly-Griggs House Museum. *Yana-Yahi, Wintu, Maidu* (b, c, p, s)
REDDING, Redding Museum and Art Center. *California and other U.S.* (a, b, c, l, p, s;) Indian Heritage Day in November)
—Shasta College Museum. *Wintu, others* (a, b, l, m, p, s)
SANTA ROSA, Jesse Peter Memorial Museum. *Pomo, Miwok, others* (a, b, c, s, t, #, Day Under The Oaks Festival, May)
SONOMA, Sonoma State Historic Park. *Wappo, Patwin*
UKIAH, Grace Hudson Sun House Museum. *Pomo, other California* (a, b, l, p, s, #)
WILLITS, Mendocino Co. Museum. *Pomo, Yuki* (a, b, c, l, p, s)

Living around a large freshwater lake such as Clear Lake, allowed Pomo peoples access to an abundance of strong reeds to build large homes—often several rooms. This model is at the Lakeport Museum; other models may be seen in the Los Angeles Museum of Natural History.   (dhe, 1995)

CENTRAL, SOUTHERN CENTRAL VALLEY & SIERRA FOOTHILLS
BAKERSFIELD, Kern Co. Museum. *Yokuts, Tehachapi and Tejon peoples, others* (b, c, l, m, p, s, t, #diorama)
BERKELEY, Hearst Museum of Anthropology, University of California, Berkeley Campus. *All California, North America*
CARMEL, San Carlos Mission. *Rumsien Ohlone, Esselen, Chumash* (a, b, m, s)
COLUMBIA, Columbia State Historic Park. *Miwok* (a)
FREMONT, Coyote Hills Regional Park. *Ohlone* (a, b, l, p, #diorama)
FRESNO, The Discovery Center. *Yokuts, other California, Plains, and Southwestern* (a, b, s, #)
—Fresno City and Co. Historical Museum. *Yokuts* (b,c,l,m,p,s,t,#)
JACKSON, Amador Co. Museum. *Sierra Miwok* (a, b, s)
LAKE ISABELLA, Kern River Valley Museum. *Tubatulabal, Kawaiisu, Koso Shoshone, Paiute* (a, b, l, p, s)
LODI, San Joaquin Co. Historical Museum. *California, others* (b, c, l)
MARIPOSA, Mariposa Co. Historical Museum. *Miwok* (b, l, s, #)
MONTEREY, Monterey State Historic Park. *Ohlone* (b, c, s, #)
—Monterey Bay Aquarium. *Rumsen Ohlone* (diorama)
NEW ALMADEN, New Almaden Museum. *Ohlone, Yokuts* (b, l, p, s, t)
HAYWARD, C. E. Smith Museum. (Cal. State Univ.) *Central California & Hopi* (a, b, p, s)

NORTH FORK, Sierra Mono Museum. *Monache, Miwok, Paiute,* various *Yokuts* (b, l, p, s, #diorama); Indian Fair in August

OAKLAND, Oakland Museum. *Pomo, Ohlone, Miwok, Wintun* (a, b, c, p, s, #diorama)

PINE GROVE-JACKSON, Chaw-Se Indian Grinding Rocks State Park. *Miwok* (a, b, c, l, p, s, #; Big Time in September)

PLACERVILLE, El Dorado Co. Historical Museum. *Maidu, Miwok* (b, l, p, s)

PLEASANTON, Amador-Livermore Valley Historical Society. *Ohlone, Yokuts* (a, b, l, p, s)

POINT REYES NATL. SEASHORE, Visitor Center, *Miwok* (diorama)

PORTERVILLE, Porterville Museum. *various Yokuts* (a, b, p, s)

SACRAMENTO, State Indian Museum. *All-California* (a, b, c, l, p, s, t, #dioramas); California Indian Days in September.

SAN FRANCISCO, Presidio of San Francisco Army Museum. *Spanish and U.S. Military* (c, m, p, #) [Presidio Indian Cultural Center has books, no displayed objects. In search of new site.]

SAN JOSE, San Jose Historical Museum. *Ohlone* (b, s)

SAN MATEO, San Mateo Co. History Center. *Ohlone, others* (a, b, l, m, p, s, #)

SANTA CLARA, de Saisset Art Gallery and Museum. *Ohlone, other California* (a, b, p, s, t, #)

SANTA CRUZ, Santa Cruz City Museum. *Central California* (a,b,l,s,#)

SANTA MARIA, Santa Maria Valley Historical Society. *Chumash* (b,l,s)

STOCKTON, Holt-Atherton Pacific Center for Western Studies. *Northwestern California, Southwestern tribes, others* (b, c, l, m, p, s, t)

—Pioneer Museum and Haggin Galleries. *Miwok, Washoe, Pomo, other* (b, c, m, l, p, s, t, #)

TAHOE CITY, (North Shore), Marion Steinbach Indian Basket Museum. *Washoe* (b)

VISALIA, Tulare Co. Museum. various *Yokuts* (b, c, p, s)

YOSEMITE NATIONAL PARK, *Miwok, Paiute, Monache, Washoe, Yokuts* (a, b, c, l, m, p, s, t, #diorama)

SOUTHWESTERN, SOUTH CENTRAL CALIFORNIA

BANNING, Malki Museum. *Cahuilla, Kumeyaay, Luiseño, Tongva, Serrano, Ipai, Taipai, Chemehuevi, Chumash, Mohave, Yuman groups* (b, l, p, s, t, #; May celebration)

BARONA RESERVATION, Kumeyaay Cultural Center , *So.California., Kumeyaay*

CARPINTERIA, Carpinteria Valley Museum of History. *Chumash* (b, c, l, m, s, t, #)

DESERT HOT SPRINGS, Cabot's Old Indian Pueblo Museum. *Cahuilla,* others (b, c, l, m, p)

FORT TEJON, Fort Tejon State Historic Park. *Kawaiisu, Kitanemuk, Yokuts, Chumash* (a, l, m, p, s)

FULLERTON, Museum Association of North Orange Co. *Southwestern peoples* (a, b, s)

JOLON, San Antonio Mission. *Salinan* (a, b, s)

–Salinan Tribal Culture Center. *Salinan* (a, b, l, p)

LAKE PERRIS, Ya I Heki', Home of the Wind Regional Indian Museum State Park. *Luiseño, Acjachmen, Cahuilla, other desert peoples* (a, b, c, l, p, s, t, #)

LOMPOC, La Purissima Mission State Historic Park. *Chumash, other California* (b, l, m, p, s, #)

LONG BEACH, Rancho Los Cerritos. *Tongva, rancho era* (b, l, m, s)

LOS ANGELES, California Historical Society. *Southern California and Southwestern* (l, p)

—Natural History Museum of Los Angeles Co. *All-California and Southwest* (a ,b, c, l, p ,s, t,#)

—(Pasadena) Southwest Museum. *All-California, North America* (a, b, c, l, p, s, t,#diorama)

—Southwest Museum. *All-California, North America* (a ,b, c, l, p, s, t,#)

—(Beverly Hills) Los Angeles Co. Museum of Art (LACMA). *North American* (a, b, c, p, s, t) and LACMA West, adjoining, a cooperative exposition hall with the Southwest Museum, California's most outstanding displays of Indian art.

—University of California's Fowler Museum of Cultural History, some California holdings, but seldom displays any Native American archaelogical material (a, b, c, l, p, s, t, #)

MISSION HILLS, San Fernando Valley Historical Society–Andres Pico Adobe. *Rancho era*

MORRO BAY, Morro Bay State Park Museum of Natural History. *Chumash* (a, l, s, diorama)

OJAI, Ojai Valley Museum. *Chumash* (a, b, c, l, p, s, t, #)

PALM SPRINGS, Palm Springs Desert Museum. *Southwest and California desert* (a, b, c, l, p, s, t,#diorama)

REDLANDS, San Bernardino Co. Museum and San Gabriel Asistencia. *All-California, others* (a,b,c,l,m,p,s t, #)

RIVERSIDE, Jurupa Mountains Cultural Center. *Cahuilla* (a, b, l, s, t)

—*Riverside Municipal Museum. Serrano, Luiseño, Cahuilla, other California* (a, b, c, l, p, s, t, #)

—Sherman Indian High School Museum. *All Indian, incl. México* (a, b, c, l, p, s, t, #)

SAN DIEGO, San Diego Historical Society. *Kumeyaay, Tongva, Luiseño* (a, b, c, l, m, p, s, t, #)

—San Diego Museum of Man. *All-California, others* (a, b, c, l, p, s, t, #diorama): June Indian Fair

SAN LUIS OBISPO, San Luis Obispo Mission Museum. *Chumash* (a, b, p, s)

SAN LUIS REY, San Luis Rey Mission. *Luiseño* (b, m, s)

SAN MIGUEL, San Miguel Mission. *Salinan, Chumash* (b, s, l)

SANTA ANA, Bowers Museum. *Southern California, other Southwestern, other U.S.* (a, b, c, l, m, p, s, t, #diorama)

SANTA BARBARA, Santa Barbara Museum of Natural History. *Californial, others* (a,b,c,l,p s,t, #diorama)

SANTA YNEZ, Santa Ynez Valley Historical Museum. *Chumash* (a, b, c, l, p, s, #)

SIMI VALLEY, Simi Valley Historical Society. *Chumash, Rancho* (s, l)

THOUSAND OAKS, Chumash Interpretive Center. *Chumash* (a, b, c, l, p, s, t,#)

VENTURA, San Buenaventura Mission. *Chumash* (b, l, p, #)

—Ventura County Historical Museum. *Chumash* (a, b, c, l, m, p, s)

YUCAIPA, Mousley Museum of Natural History. *Serrano, Cahuilla, Luiseño, Mohave, other California, other U.S.* (a, b, c, s, t, #)

EASTERN, SOUTHEASTERN CALIFORNIA

BISHOP, Paiute-Shoshone Cultural Center *Paiute, Shoshone, Owens Valley* (a, b, c, l, p, t, #diorama)

BORREGO SPRINGS, Anza-Borrego Springs State Park Visitor Center. *Kumeyaay, Cahuilla* (a, b, l, p, s, #)

DEATH VALLEY NATIONAL MONUMENT, *Shoshone.* (b, l, m, s, diorama)

FORT YUMA, Ft. Yuma Reservation Museum. *Quechan, Cocopa, other Colorado River* (a,b,c, p, s, #)

INDEPENDENCE, Eastern California Museum. *Paiute, Shoshone, Washoe* (a, b, c, l, m, p, s, t, #)

LANCASTER/PALMDALE, Antelope Valley Indian Museum *Mojave desert* (a,b,l, p,diorama)

RANDSBURG, Desert Museum. *Koso Shoshone, Paiute, Mohave desert* (b,s)

RIDGECREST-CHINA LAKE, Maturango Museum. *Koso* and *Panamint Shoshone, Yokuts* (a, b, l, p, s); arrangements to visit Koso petroglyphs

SOUTH LAKE TAHOE, Tallac Historic Site. *Washoe* (a, b, c, l, p, s, t,#)

TWENTYNINE PALMS, Joshua Tree National Monument. *Serrano, Cahuilla, Chemehuevi* (a, b, l, p, s)

Like many museums, the Southwest Museum—Beverly Hills, offers an impressive variety of handmade goods, art, and crafts of traditional and modern design. (dhe, 1999)

APPENDIX II
CALIFORNIA MISSIONS, PRESIDIOS, & PUEBLOS

THESE ARE SHORT sketches of the California Missions and other sites which impacted the California Indian. The history of the missions is detailed in numerous other places, usually highly romanticized. The order of listing is south to north, more or less in order of their founding. The reader might find them to pay homage to the thousands of Native Californians and padres who lived and died there. Other missions to the Indians, but not ones of the original "Chain of 21", still exist on reservations; some are noted here; not all are state landmarks. Most are mentioned within the reservation entry. Their commonly known names are all capital letters.

As elsewhere in this book, the numbers in Block boldface (e.g. **242**) refer to California Historical Landmark numbers. More complete descriptions are found in the State Parks and Recreation handbook (see Appendix VII). Founding dates are given in Galliard boldface (e.g. **1769**), their original Spanish name in Retablo Antiguo (e.g. MISIÓN), Indian place name, if known, and the tribal peoples affected are displayed in Galliard Bold Italics (e.g. *Nipaguay*).

1769 MISIÓN SAN DIEGO DE ALCALÁ **242, 52**
(*Nipaguay*), San Diego

Though the original site was at the Presidio, the mission was moved some distance away, so as to separate the neophytes (newly-converted) from the coarse army types (a policy followed at all the Presidios). Several times destroyed by Indian revolt, earthquake, and neglect, today it is a beautiful church overlooking the Mission Valley of San Diego. Museum. Founder: Fray Junípero Serra (Franciscan). Indian peoples: *Tipai, Ipai, Kumeyaay* (once all lumped under the term *Diegueño*).

1769 PRESIDIO DE SAN DIEGO **59** (*Cosoy*), San Diego

Of the site of the original Spanish fort at Old Town, San Diego, the only remnants are the tile floor of the chapel and some crumbling adobe walls in a green and tree-shaded park. Once the headquarters for the Spanish army occupation of the entire southern region of Alta California.

1780 MISIÓN PURÍSIMA CONCEPCIÓN **350** (See also p. 245)
At Fort Yuma, Imperial County

The original buildings were destroyed in an Indian revolt, 1781. The mission was not rebuilt until 1922, as St. Thomas Church, part of the Ft. Yuma Reservation. The first mission name was transferred to the coastal Santa Barbara County site. Indian peoples: *Quechan, Halyikwamai* [formerly all called *Yuman*], *Cócopa* [from Arizona].

1926 ST. FRANCIS XAVIER CHAPEL
Jamul Reservation, San Diego County

A clapboard chapel built for the Jamul Band on their original six acres. The cemetery predates the chapel. Indian people: *Kumeyaay*.

1898 IMMACULATE CONCEPTION CHAPEL
Sycuan Reservation, San Diego County

An attractive, historic wooden structure. (A 1980s church sits alongside.) Indian people: *Kumeyaay*.

1930s SAN YSIDRO CHAPEL
Los Coyotes Reservation, San Diego County

The feeling here is remote and of a place not California. Indian people: *Cahuilla*.

early1900s OUR LADY OF REFUGE CHAPEL
(Adjunct of Pala). La Jolla Reservation, San Diego County

A pretty little Spanish-style building, built by the tribe, with a very old burial ground. Indian people: *Luiseño*.

Kitty in the corridor, Puríssima Concepción. (dhe, 1986)

1818 ASISTENCIA DE SANTA YSABEL **369** (*Elenaman*)
Located one mile N. of Santa Ysabel,
on State Hwy. 79, San Diego County

The asistencia was a branch, or *visita*, of Misión San Diego. A pretty chapel and an Indian cemetery remain. Feast Day, see Calendar. Indian peoples: *Ipai, Tipai, Kumeyaay, Cupeño, Cahuilla, Luiseño* (?).

1798 MISIÓN SAN LUIS REY DE FRANCIA **239**
San Luis Rey, San Diego County

The church is a well-restored pastel jewel set in jade-colored grass. It probably never looked so good as today. Founder: Fray Fermín Francisco de Lasuén, Serra's successor as President of the Alta California missions. Indian peoples: *Luiseño, Ajachmen*, some *Tongva*.

1816 ASISTENCIA DE SAN ANTÓNIO DE PALA **243**
At the Pala Reservation on State Hwy. 76, San Diego County

This is one of the most interesting chapels with original Indian designs on the walls and ceilings. Hundreds of reservation residents people still worship here. The chapel cemetery contains curious grave-markers adorned with personal possessions. It was an adjunct of Misión San Luis Rey. Founder: Fr. António Peyri. Indian peoples: *Luiseño, Cupeño, Cahuilla*.

1823 ASISTENCIA LAS FLORES **616**
Located in Camp Pendleton Marine Base, San Diego County

This was a branch of Misión San Luis Rey, and was built for use as a way-station between San Luis Rey and San Juan Capistrano. Indian peoples: *Luiseño*

1776 MISIÓN SAN JUAN CAPISTRANO **200**
Town center of San Juan Capistrano, Orange County

This beautiful place once bustled with the arts and industries of the local Native. Now it is famous for its swallows which arrive annually on March 19th (St. Joseph's Day). The tourists leave; the quiet settles in. *Acjachmen* still worship here. Founder: Fr. Serra. Indian peoples: *Luiseño, Acjachmen*, some *Tongva*.

The city of Ventura takes its name from Misión San Buenaventura. The signs for spas and tonics, lack of automobile tire tracks, and abundance of fields indicate the time of this photo to be the very early 20th century. Today, the main building looks very much the same, but the porch along the side building is gone. (State Parks)

1830 ASISTENCIA DE SAN BERNARDINO 42, and the ZANJA 43, (Guachama) On Barton Rd. in San Bernardino

This was a branch of Misión San Gabriel, with an irrigation system (*zanja*) built, as always, with Indian labor. Small museum. Indian peoples: *Tongva, Cahuilla, Serrano.*

1771 Misión SAN GABRIEL, Arcángel, 158
Mission Drive in San Gabriel

Today this is a parish church with Arabic-derived architecture of short towers and buttresses. It was once one of the largest missions. Tongva honor their ancestors on Serra Day. Founder: Fr. Serra. Indian peoples: *Tongva, Serrano, Tataviam, Vanyume, Kawaiisu.*

1797 Misión SAN FERNANDO REY DE ESPAÑA 157
On State Hwy. 118 in San Fernando

What remains of the old mission is the convent; there is a new church, and the gardens are tropical and nearly silent, a refuge from Los Angeles. Founders: Fr. Lasuén and Fr. Francisco Dumetz. Indian peoples: *Tataviam/Fernandeño, Tongva, Chumash, Kawaiisu.*

1781 El Pueblo de Nuestra Señora la Reina de LOS ANGELES de Porciuncula 144 (Yangnah)
downtown Los Angeles

The second of the "towns" founded by the Spanish (the first was San José) with Indian help, as usual. Located near Los Angeles' City Hall, the tourist-oriented Olvera Street is part of the original pueblo.

1782 Misión SAN BUENAVENTURA 310
Main and Figueroa Streets, Ventura, Ventura County

Only the church structure and a little garden remain of the buildings twice hit by fire and once by quake. Founder: Fr. Serra. Indian peoples: *Chumash, Kawaiisu, Yokuts*(?).

1782 El Presidio de SANTA BÁRBARA Virgen y Martir 636 Santa Barbara

The remains of this fort are just off Anacapa St. in Santa Barbara. Excavation has been undertaken of the old Presidio walls. The most interesting intact part is the old guardhouse. After abandonment of the Presidio proper, the Covarrúbias family rancho enveloped the entire Presidio lands. The Covarrúbias adobe is an excellent present-day museum. *Chumash* land.

1786 Misión SANTA BÁRBARA Virgen y Martir 309 Santa Barbara

On a high hill in Santa Barbara, at Los Olivos and Laguna streets, is this beautiful, stately place constructed in 1815 with Indian labor. Adjacent are an elaborate irrigation system and a museum. The cemetery contains the graves of 4,000 *Chumash*. Display of artifacts. Indian people: *Chumash* (especially a band formerly called *Canalino*).

1804 Misión SANTA YNÉZ (aka *Inés*) 305
Solvang, Santa Barbara County

This small mission is at the south end of town, not far from the present Chumash reservation (see p. 197). In it are some local relics; outside are fields and impressive mountains. Founder: Fr. Estévan Tapis. Indian people: *Chumash.*

1787 Misión La PURÍSIMA CONCEPCION 340 On State Hwy. 246
near Lompoc, Santa Barbara County

Probably the most complete mission remaining, this is one of the few without fortifications. It has an elaborate water system and museum. Subjected to a month-long Indian revolt in 1824, this is the second mission of the same name (*see p. 267*). Founder: Fr. Lasuén. Indian people: *Chumash.*

1772 Misión SAN LUIS OBISPO DE TOLOSA 325 At the center of San Luis Obispo

At Chorro and Montgomery Streets, a few restored parts of one of the oldest missions remain, overlooking a small creek. Founder: Fr. Serra. Indian peoples: *Chumash, Yokuts.*

1831 Asistencia de SANTA MARGARITA 364
Near Santa Margarita, San Luis Obispo County

This was a way-station and granary for Misión San Luis Obispo; it is now a barn for a local ranch. *Chumash* land.

1797 Misión SAN MIGUEL, Arcángel 326
San Miguel, San Luis Obispo County

Along U.S. 101 San Miguel in the entire aspect of the mission gives one a feeling of the earlier era, the town is small, the hills are dry. The small cemetery conceals the remains of hundreds of Indians buried there over a few short years. Museum. Founder: Fr. Lasuén. Indian people: *Salinan.*

1771 Misión SAN ANTONIO de Pádua 232
Situated in the mountains six miles from Jolon
at the entrance to Fort Hunter-Liggett, Monterey County

The setting here is picturesque and remote; the buildings have not been altered for tourists—It's pretty much as it was, including the water works (now dry). *Salinan* people still worship here. The Mission is friendly to their tribal organization. Founder: Fr. Serra. Indian peoples: *Salinan, Yokuts, Esselen.*

1791 Misión Nuestra Señora de SOLEDAD 233
Three miles southwest of Soledad, Monterey County

All that remains are a plain reconstruction of a chapel and many crumbling walls in a field of flowers and gardens. Founder: Fr. Lasuén. Indian peoples: *Salinan, Yokuts, Esselen, Ohlone.*

1770 El PRESÍDIO DE MONTERÉY 105 Monterey

An ornate chapel is all that is left of the old Presidio, except some stone walls (Church St. at Camino El Estero, Monterey). The chapel was also part of the first mission. With U.S. military occupation, a redoubt was added in 1847 (still there, with antique cannon). The post is still active. *Rumsien Ohlone* Indian presence is evident in the soil surrounding the Serra "landing site". A "rainrock" is near the old museum (now City of Monterey property).

1770 Misión San Carlos Borromeo del Río CARMELO 135

Carmel, Monterey County

This extraordinarily beautiful mission was originally founded in Monterey (see above) in the Presidio, but moved in 1771, because of the rowdiness of the soldiers. As at all the missions, the tiny cemetery only hints at the graves of thousands of the local Indians buried there. Founders: Frs. Serra and Juan Crespi. Indian peoples: *Esselen* and *Ohlone* (mostly *Rumsien*).

1797 Misión SAN JUAN BAUTISTA 195

San Juan Bautista, San Benito County

Right in the town of the same name, the colorful chapel is strongly buttressed against the many earthquakes of the San Andreas fault that occur here. Parts of the old town coexist with the mission. Once the largest of the missions, it also bears some 4,000 Indian graves. In May and September, Indian festivals are held. Indian peoples: *Mutsun Ohlone, Yokuts.*

1791 Misión la Exaltación de la SANTA CRUZ 342

On High and Emmett Streets in Santa Cruz

A diminutive and stylistically changed replica is all that one sees at the site of the original mission, destroyed in two quakes. Founder: Fr. Lasuén. Indian peoples: *Rumsien* and other *Ohlone*. VILLA DE BRANCIFORT, **469**, on State Hwy. 1, an adjacent pueblo was founded at the same time, but without an Indian population.

1777 El PUEBLO DE SAN JOSÉ de Guadalupe 433

San José

The old town center was at Jefferson School, San Jose. Though California's first pueblo, it was not immediately populated by a large number of California Indians, they preferred to remain in nearby rancherias.

1797 Misión del Gloriosísima Patriarca Señor SAN JOSÉ 334 Located on State Hwy. 238

near Fremont, Alameda County.

Strangely, the mission isn't in the town of San José, but several miles northeast. The church was recently totally restored, with one older cloister now a museum. The Indian cemetery a mile west is tended by local *Ohlone* people. Where once was the mission compound is now an ancient grove of olives. Founder: Fr. Lasuén. Indian peoples: *Ohlone, Yokuts, Plains, Lake,* and *Coast Miwok.*

1791 Misión SANTA CLARA de Asís

First site: **250** Kifer Rd. and De La Cruz Blvd. (*soco-is-uka*).
Last site: **338** Alameda and Lexington St. (*gerguensun*), both in Santa Clara, Santa Clara County.

After the first site flooded, two other sites were chosen, the last subjected to two quakes. As a result, of the original buildings, only cloisters remain—adjacent to several buildings of the University of Santa Clara. Founders: Tómas de la Peña, Joseph Murgíria. Indian peoples: *Ohlone, Yokuts, Plains Miwok.*

1776 Misión de SAN FRANCISCO de Asís (*or* Misión DOLORES) 327 Dolores St., San Francisco

A rather oddly-colonnaded building is all that is left of the mission establishment that once covered huge tracts in what is now San Francisco. The chapel bears original Indian-painted designs on the ceiling beams. Founder: Fr. Serra. Indian peoples: *Ohlone, Miwok, Patwin.*

1776 El PRESIDIO DE SAN FRANCISCO 79 San Francisco

The military station in San Francisco has been headquarters for all military activity in northern California since Spanish time, through Mexican and Yankee rule as well. The older post is now a part of the Golden Gate National Recreation Area. One Spanish era building remains, now the old Officers' Club, whose entrance is flanked by two 1673 Spanish cannons from Lima, Peru. *See also p.168.*

1817 Misión SAN RAFAEL, Arcángel 220

Fifth and Court Streets, San Rafael, Marin County

The present structure is a very plain reconstruction of the chapel; nothing else remains, but modern buildings are all around. Founder: Fr. Ventura Fortuni. Indian peoples: *Coast Miwok, Wappo,* some *Pomo*

1823 Misión San Francisco SOLANO 3

On the Central Plaza, Sonoma, Sonoma County

Under independent Mexico, this mission was the last to be founded in the "Chain of 21", more as a political gesture toward Russia than from religious zeal. The beauty of the chapel is in its simplicity; the cloisters hold grape arbors, framing the entrance to a museum and Miwok monument in the garden. Founder: Fr. José Altamira. Indian peoples: *Coast Miwok, Patwin* (*Suisun*), *Wappo, Pomo.*

Preparations for Palm Sunday at Misión San Miguel, ancestral Salinan territory.
(dhe, 1998)

References for this Appendix
Bauer, Helen, California Rancho Days. *Doubleday and Co., Garden City, NY, 1953.*
One of those sweetly romanticized versions of early rancho days, but with a listing of extant buildings from that era.
Camphouse, Majorie V., Guidebook to the Missions of California. *Ward Ritchie Press, Pasadena, CA, 1974.*
Published research from UCLA. Lee, Gregory, California Missions, *1992. Available Bookpeople and Gem Guides. Basic statistics.*

APPENDIX III
NOTABLE HISTORIC RANCHOS OF ALTA CALIFORNIA

THE SPANISH CROWN MADE NO LAND GRANTS, only 25 settlement permits. However, the government of México, between 1824 and 1846 (first American invasions) made more than 800 land grants of varying sizes (1 acre at San Luis Obispo, 133,000 at Santa Margarita, and 3 of 48,000 each to Sutter) from Shasta County to the southern extent of Alta California (now the border). Of these, 346 were to non-Mexicans. Some of the most notable are presented below.

A COMMISSION FOR THE U.S. LAND ACT OF 1851 adjudicated claims of ownership after California's admission to the Union, approving 553 of these, for nearly 8,500,000 acres of land. All had Indian builders, workers, and vaqueros.

The listings begin with the date established, followed by California Historical Landmark numbers in boldface type, (e.g. **525**), the name of the rancho is in Retablo Antiguo (e.g. RANCHO), Founder, and Location. More complete descriptions are found in the State Parks and Recreation handbook.

EARLY COASTAL SOUTHERN CALIFORNIA

1784 **285** & **637** RANCHO SAN RAFAEL
    José María Verdugo, Glendale, Los Angeles County
1784 RANCHO LOS CERRITOS Manuel Nieto
1810 **226** RANCHO SANTA ANA
    Bernardo Yorba, Santa Ana Canyon, Orange County
1817 **308** RANCHO COVARRÚBIAS,
    Domingo Carillo, Santa Barbara County
1818 **383** RANCHO JOSÉ SEPÚLVEDA
    Palos Verdes Hills, Los Angeles County
1828 RANCHO SANTA MARGARITA
    Pio Pico, San Fernando, Los Angeles County
1834 **362** RANCHITO RÓMULO
    Rómulo Pico, San Fernando, Los Angeles County
1836 **227** RANCHO SANTIAGO DE SANTA ANA
    Diego Sepúlveda, Costa Mesa, Orange County
1839 **553**, RANCHO SAN FRANCISCOA
    António del Valle **556** Los Angeles and Ventura Cos.
1840 **372** RANCHO SAN JOSÉ
    Ygnácio Palomares, Pomona, Los Angeles County
1842 **528** RANCHO SAN BERNARDINO
    Diego Sepúlveda, San Bernardino
1842 **199** RANCHO CAÑADA DE LOS ALISOS
    José Serrano, El Toro, Orange County
1843 **425** RANCHO CAÑADA DE LOS COCHES
    Apolinaria Lorenzana El Cajón, San Diego County
1844 **102** RANCHO JURUPA
    Luis Rubidoux Riverside, Riverside County
1849 **689** RANCHO EL ENCINO
    Francisco Reyes, Encino, Los Angeles, County

EARLY NORTHERN CALIFORNIA

1820 **246** RANCHO SAN ANTONIO
    Luís Peralta, San Leandro, Alameda County
1833 **18** RANCHO PETALUM
    Mariano Vallejo, Petaluma, Sonoma County
1835 **241** RANCHO LAS POSITAS
    Robert Livermore, San Leandro, Alameda County
1835 **509** RANCHO LAGUNA DE LOS PALOS COLORADOS
    Joaquín Moraga, Moraga, Contra Costa County
1836 **564** RANCHO CAYMUSA
    George C. Yount, Yountville, Napa County
1839 **525** NEW HELVETIA (Sutter's Fort)
    John Sutter, Sacramento County
1840 RANCHO RINCOÑADA DE LOS GATOS
    José Hernandez and Sebastian Peralta,
    Los Gatos, Santa Clara County
1845 **534** RANCHO LOS PUTOS
    Juan Peña and Manuel Vaca, Vacaville, Solano County
1846 **12** RANCHO DE LA BARRANCCA COLORADO
    William B. Ide, Red Bluff, Tehama County
1846 **206** RANCHO LOS ROBLES
    Daniel Rhoads, nr. Lemoore, Kings County
1846 **10** RANCHO BUENA VENTURA
    Pierson B. Reading, Cottonwood, Shasta County
1847 **426** RANCH AT KELSEYVILLE
    Andrew Kelsey and Charles Stone, Lake County
1847 **331** RANCHO DE LAS MARIPOSAS
    John C. Frémont, Bear Valley, Mariposa County
1849 **329** RANCHO CHICO
    John Bidwell, Chico, Butte County
1850s RANCH IN FRESNO COUNTY
    James D. Savage

The major reference for this Appendix is the Historical Atlas of California, W.A. Beck and Y. D. Haase, University of Oklahoma Press, 1974, in which are more than 100 useful additional references.

APPENDIX IV
MILITARY POSTS INVOLVED WITH INDIAN AFFAIRS

ARMY OFFICERS were divided in their opinion of the so-called "Indian Problem." An officer of Ft. Mojave: "The Indians know no restraint, save the fear of a superior power, and until they are made to feel the ability of the United States to punish the outrages, they will repeat them as often as the temptation to do so arises."

Writing with perceptive sarcasm, Capt. Hannibal Day, commandant of Camp Far West proposed that the Federal Indian agent advise the local Nisenans as to "what will be their probable fate unless they discontinue their thieving and submit with a better grace to being shot down, although it may seem strange to them to be thus intruded upon by the whites...and they must vacate their hunting-grounds in favor of our gold diggers.

"From all the information I can gather, the aggression was rather on the part of the whites toward the natives..." He apparently had no taste for his duty: "...So far as the mining population is concerned they are competent for their own protection..."

THIS LIST is highly selective. It includes only those posts that served as bases for military actions against Natives before 1900. Many other posts are known to have been erected, but lasted only as brief encampments, causing little or no disturbance to the Indian population. Today, there are few, if any, remnants, and nothing to be gained from the sites, save the knowledge that they existed as severe irritants. Some of these latter have been given inflated recognition as State Landmarks.

The vast majority of these camps existed only one or two years, a few 10-15 years, and a very few to the present. Had the contest been between near-equals, one might wonder whether these short times were indicative of Army efficiency or of Indian ineffectiveness. The true reasons however, were the tragic vulnerability of the Indians to disease and their total lack of psychological preparation for organized conflict with either the Spanish or Americans.

As elsewhere in this book, the numbers in **boldface type** refer to California Historical Landmark numbers. More complete descriptions are found in the State Parks and Recreation handbook.

NORTHWEST & NORTHEAST CALIFORNIA

Ft. Humboldt (1853-66) **154** Humboldt County

One inhabitant, Capt. Ulysses S. Grant, was driven to drink here—so goes the legend. The Army spent 13 years here driving the local Indians out of this territory. Ft. Humboldt was the headquarters of northwestern California's Army activities, but the only Indians who were here were some 300 prisoners who died after being held in stockade for two months. It was not needed after the Civil War.

Remnants: Two restored wooden buildings on the old parade ground—now part of a logging museum. Though unloved by the local Indians, local Hupa have assisted in making an extraordinary Indian Museum of the old hospital building. This museum should be a first stop by all persons visiting this area.

On U.S. 101 at the south city limits of Eureka.

Ft. Tejon was established in a region common to Kitanemuk, Kawaaisu, and Yowlumni Yokuts in the southern Sierras at the Grapevine. The fort and much of its Indian labor was appropriated by its last Army commander. It became the large Tejon Ranch. (dhe, 1986)

Camp Lincoln (1862-69) **545** Del Norte County

The Tolowa, Yurok, and Karuk felt the terrible pressures of the company of soldiers based here to guard the invading miners and settlers. Remnants: Commandant's home—now a private farm house against the forest front, overlooking lush, green fields.

Three miles off U.S. 101 or 1 mile off U.S. 199, just north of Crescent City (markers on U.S. 101).

Ft. Ter-Wer (1857-61) **544** Del Norte County

A little post for "containment" of the local Yurok on the lower Klamath River. The location has been completely washed out several times by floods.

Ft. Gaston (1858-92) Humboldt County

Established on the Hupa Reservation for "gathering" and control, sometimes protection, of all Indians in the area. Several older buildings remain including some old BIA "Indian Agency" buildings. The BIA left long ago.

Ft. Jones (1852-58) **317** Siskiyou County

For six years two companies of dragoons harassed the Karuk and Shasta who were attempting to defend their homelands. Only a bas-relief brass marker featuring covered wagons and stockades remain.

One mile S. of Ft. Jones on the old east-bank Scott River road to Etna.

NOTE: **Ft. Dick** is the name of a town in Del Norte County, but it had only a very temporary encampment.

Ft. Bidwell (1866-97) **430** Modoc County

See p. QQ for details on the fort, now a Paiute reservation.

Roop's Fort (1854-64) **76** Lassen County

It's not really a fort. But in 1854 Issac Roop, a pioneer, put up a couple of little log cabins to protect himself from the Maidu upon whose land he was squatting. It saw action in 1863, when a group of pioneers had a little shootout (later dubbed the "Sagebrush War") over whether Nevada or California should "get" Susanville.

Weatherlow St., Susanville.

Camp Far West (1849-52) **493** Yuba County

Originally, a few log barracks for a small detachment to "guard" a bunch of miners who were devastating the Nisenan Maidu people's land—it lasted only three years. Remnants: A few foundations, some tumbled gravestones. Property was once Johnson's Ranch (Mexican land grant of 1845), now churned by developers' machines.

From State Hwy. 65 at Wheatland, go NE on Spenceville Rd. about 3 miles to Camp Far West Rd., then 1.5 mi. straight to the Bear River (not the Reservoir) and a locked green iron gate with concrete foundations. Walk a dirt road to the river's edge, on your right.

continued next page

Sutter's Fort (built 1839) **525** Sacramento County

Johann Augustus Sutter, a Swiss ex-army captain, took advantage of the Mexican government's offer of land grants for his 50,000-acre grant called New Helvetia. He set up a small feudal empire, using local Indians as labor and as mercenaries to run the estate and to raid other Indian areas as necessary for supplies or to keep the peace.

The huge estate (Indian-built, of course) was nearly self-sufficient and was managed in a military manner (uniforms, cannon blast at 6 AM, etc.). In addition to the adobe fort and travelers' hospice in what is now central Sacramento, he built outlying fortifications, especially one at his Hock Farm, eight miles south of Marysville on the Feather River. As happened to the Indian population of California, his estate was overrun and divided up by the forty-niners; ironically, in that it was upon his estate that gold was first found in 1848. Remnants: Primarily, the large fort, with many of the original cannon, and reconstructed interiors.

L and 28th Streets, Sacramento. This is also the location of the State Indian Museum.

WEST CENTRAL CALIFORNIA NORTH OF THE SACRAMENTO RIVER

Benicia Arsenal and Barracks (1851-present) **176, 177** Solano County

It was the Benicia Arsenal from which supplies, munitions, men, and animals were dispatched for Indian control of Northern California. Located on the north side of the San Francisco Bay, it thus had more ready access to the field than the Presidio.

Situated from high on a (then) treeless hill above the windswept tidewater's edge, this post provisioned almost all western California military expeditions against the natives, as well as Civil War and more modern operations. In 1859 an impressive stone fort with tall towers was erected to guard and oversee ship traffic in the Carquinez Straits. Other architecturally attractive structures were raised in the same decade, many of which survive, most unoccupied.

On the eastern edge of Benicia, just below the Interstate 680 bridge across the Carquinez Straits.

Ft. Ross (1812-1841) **5** Sonoma County

Russian fur-trading settlements in Alaska, mainly Sitka (founded in 1799), were in need of food that could be obtained only from warmer climes. Thus in 1812, a stockade and block-houses were erected by the Russian-American Company, a quasi-governmental business, something like the Hudson's Bay Company of England and Canada. The site is on a beautiful coastside terrace, with forests, fields, and orchards.

The Company, in a unique gesture of territorial respect, pursued a policy of cooperation with the local Pomos with whom they seemed to have had no hostilities. A large Pomo village sprang up around the fort, as most of the labor was Indian. The Company traded with the Presidio in San Francisco, but the Mexican government became wary of Russian intentions and soon founded missions at San Rafael and Sonoma as a foil to Russian expansion.

The Russians retired in 1841, selling to Sutter (see above) supplies for his fort. (The deal included a cannon captured from Napoleon's troops outside Moscow in 1813.) Remnants: A reconstructed stockade, church, original commandant's home, numerous relics of Russian, Spanish, and Pomo origin in a small museum. Some archaeological diggings in the Pomo village area.

State Hwy. 1 at Fort Ross State Park. Camping sites nearby at Salt Point State Park. *(See photo, p.70)*

This cave at Ft. Independence was dug by soldiers in 1862 in a dry wash. Officers had tents, but at first the soldiers had to make do with what they could, as tents were in short supply during the Civil War. (dhe, 1982)

Sonoma Barracks (Presidio de Sonoma) (1836-1851) **316** Sonoma County

It was Gen. Mariano Vallejo whose baronial rancho was installed near here in Petaluma, and who set up the first barracks at the tiny Pueblo of Sonoma, adjacent to the Misión Solano. His purpose were on two levels—nationally, to repel the Russian encroachment of settlers moving eastward from Fort Ross (see above) and personally, to guard and extend his fortunes, supported by Indian (Wappo, Miwok, Pomo) labor.

It was here that a group of Yankee settlers took over the town in 1846, raised the Bear Flag, and declared themselves independent of México. Indian fortunes throughout California were to change radically by this action, as Alta California passed into United States control three weeks later. The U.S. garrison abandoned the post in 1851, there being no more "Indian problem" in the area.

Remnants: Several barracks buildings, well-restored, on the Plaza in Sonoma.

Ft. Wright (1858-75) Mendocino County

This was the post for the Round Valley Reservation, not unlike those at Ft. Bidwell and Hoopa Reservation.

Post at Nome Lackee (1854-66) **357** Tehama County

This was one of those desolate places that Army policy decided was suitable for an Indian Reservation. The Indians decided otherwise and decamped *(see p. 50)*.

Ft. Bragg (1857-64) **615** Mendocino County

The fort here was only to keep the Indians of an ill-fated Mendocino Reservation "in check". As usual, the Army made no provision for support of the people it brought here. Both the reservation and then the fort folded.

Remnant: A quartermaster building, moved from its original location, now adjacent to the City Hall at 430 Franklin, Ft. Bragg. Today it is a small museum of army memorabilia of the 1850-60s. No mention of the Pomo and Yuki Indian populations.

Ft. Reading (1852-67) **379** Shasta County

From this largest of forts in northern California troops marched in all directions to quell the resistance of the Shasta, the Wintu, the Yana, and the Pit River. It is named for Pierson B. Reading, owner of the 26,000-acre Rancho Buena Ventura (established 1847). He was allocated $25,000 for protection of the Wintu in a 35-square-mile reservation in 1852, but gold miners continued to assail the Natives in spite of the Army's "protection". Eventually, the Indians who had survived periodic hunts, were force-marched to coastal reservations, removing the need for further occupation of the fort.

Six miles NE of Anderson.

CENTRAL CALIFORNIA
CENTRAL VALLEY, SIERRA FOOTHILLS

Ft. Miller (1851-64) **584** Fresno-Madera Counties

The eastern Central Valley came to have its U.S. Army fort to protect invading forty-niner miners and settlers from the Yokuts and Monache owners. This one, Ft. Miller, was established in 1851 on the San Joaquin River as it plunges out of the mountains a few miles north of Fresno. The fort was abandoned after the Civil War, the Indians having been subdued in less than seven years.

The site is totally inundated by the waters of Lake Millerton, though several buildings have been preserved by the Table Mountain Rancheria as a cultural center, and as a reminder to everyone of the terrible times of the past. (*See p. 169*)

Presidio of Monterey (1770) **105** Monterey County
(*See Appendix II, 268*)

Presidio of San Francisco (1776) **79** (*See also App. II, 168*)

The early Spanish castillo (fort) of San Joaquín was levelled in 1854 to accommodate construction of Ft. Winfield Scott (today Ft. Point), built in the style of Ft. Sumter, South Carolina. Activities at both the Spanish and U.S. forts were not primarily directed at Indians. Nevertheless, all U.S. Army operations against the indigenous peoples of northern California originated at this post.

[Note: Both the Spanish (with Ohlone and Miwok labor) and later, the United States constructed numerous defensive fortifications about the San Francisco Bay.]

Presidio of Santa Barbara (1786) **636**
Santa Barbara County (*See Appendix II, 268*)

Hudson's Bay Company Headquarters (1841) **819**
San Francisco County

This quasi-military English-Canadian company placed a trading outpost of its huge western holdings here in the little year-old Mexican village of Yerba Buena. The post, in what was to become the financial district of San Francisco, was set up for buying pelts and furs from trappers and Indians. The English were just one of the many countries interested in acquisition of California's Native lands.

Montgomery St. at Commercial St., San Francisco.

EAST OF THE SIERRA NEVADA
AND THE MOJAVE DESERT

It was a wild and desolate canyon, barren and rocky, miles from every human habitation. —A visitor to Ft. Piute in 1866

Ft. Churchill (1860-69) Nevada

Located only 40 miles from California, this largest of Nevada forts had considerable impact on the subjugation of Paiute and Washoe at the eastern edge of California. These peoples had protested in violent fashion the kidnapping of their children and seizure of their lands. Row upon row of crumbling adobe quarters bring to mind the old Latin phrase: *sic semper tyrannis*, "thus always to tyrants".

Take U.S. 50 E of Carson City to U.S. Alternate 95, 8 mi. S of Silver Springs to Ft. Churchill State Park and Museum.

Ft. Independence (1862-77) **349** Inyo County
(*See Ft. Independence Reservation, p. 225.*)

Though the Spanish never succeeded in establishing a permanent post along the middle Colorado River, Indian resistance to the push of immigrants into California in the 1850s persuaded the United States Army to establish a series of desert forts along the Government Road from Needles to Barstow. Mohave and Paiute were the peoples whose land was being trespassed upon and invaded.

Ft. Mojave was the first and largest, located near the present town of Needles, California. The others were strung out at well-spaced water holes along the parched track.

Ft. Mojave   (1859-90)
Arizona and eastern San Bernardino County, California

Originally a post for control of the local Mohaves and Paiutes, this fort on the California border became a part of the Union's southwestern defenses (though abandoned 1861-63 during the Civil War). From 1890-1935 the site was an Indian school. In 1942, the buildings were leveled, no doubt to the great satisfaction of the Mohaves, for whom the fort had been a repulsive symbol for nearly a century. Only sidewalks to nowhere and an abandoned cemetery remain.

Near Needles, on the north end of Ft. Mojave Reservation (p. 122), go 12 mi. N on Arizona State Hwy. 95 to Camp Mohave Rd., turn W to the river levee road, then N for 1/2 mi. to end of the dike. Climb the cliff to fort site.

This building of approximately 1885, was the post hospital of Ft. Humboldt in Eureka. Today it houses a valuable Indian museum, sensitively recounting the ill-treatment and massacre of the local tribes by both vigilantes and the Army. The Wiyot, the several Eel River peoples, the Yurok, and the Hupa, Chilula, Whilkut, and Chimariko peoples to the east suffered from the presence of this fort, as well as the associated Ft. Lincoln in Crescent City and Ft. Gaston in Hoopa. (dhe, 1996)

Ft. Piute (ca. 1867-68) San Bernardino County

This was the first post, some 22 miles west of Ft. Mojave, on the Old Government Road. Twelve plus mi. S of Searchlight, NV on U.S. 95, 1/2 mi. past the CalNevAz Casino, a road E to ruins is a very rocky 2 mi. around the cinder cone of Paiute Mountain.

Camp Rock Springs (ca.1860-68)
(E. Mojave Natl. Scenic Area) San Bernardino County

The ruins, next in the line of Mojave Desert forts, are 30 miles SE from Valley Wells, near Cima, in an area of several springs.

Camp Marl Springs (ca.1860-68)
(E. Mojave Natl. Scenic Area) San Bernardino County

The ruins, 18 miles west of Camp Rock Springs lie by the washed-out Government Rd.

Fort Soda (ca.1860-68) (Zzyzx Springs,
E. Mojave Natl. Scenic Area) San Bernardino County

The fort is not exactly a ruin. As all the posts on the Government Road were, this is the site of springs; and the Indians, seeing their own water sources being expropriated, reacted accordingly with several raids on the Army encampment.

The bubbling springs are rather salty, and empty onto a great, intermittently dry lake, rimmed in places by reeds, and surrounded by low, barren mountains. Once abandoned by the Army, in 1907 the Tonopah & Tidewater Railroad passed through for water. Then, in 1917, a chemical company in search of salts raised a few more buildings. Both enterprises failed. Later, in 1944, one Mr. Spenger, a very religious man, appropriated the site, built hot mineral baths, planted palms and tamarack trees, and made it a desert resort, oriented toward religion.

Finally, the Bureau of Land Management took back the original government title. Since then it has been an environmental study center for various university groups, especially for the preservation of the Mojave chubb (a fish). One or two buildings preserve the foundations of the old fort walls.

About 55 mi. E of Barstow, take the Zzyzx Springs Exit from I-15, go S about 3 mi. to a locked gate. Walk 1/2 mi. to the site.

Camp Cady Westernmost of the string of posts, it has disappeared into floodwaters in recent years. 5 mi. E of Calico Early Man Site.

Ft. Yuma (1850-83) 806 Imperial County

The cliffs of Yuma tempted Fr. Junípero Serra to found a mission here in 1769, but both church and Spanish army were wiped out a year later. Not until 1850 was the strategically valuable area wrested from Quechan hands—this time by the U.S. Army. The government's original purpose for establishing the fort at this place was the protection of pioneer and forty-niner wagon trains along the extreme southern route into California.

Only a year passed before the outsiders were ousted once again—as the Army puts it: "... provisions at the post were exhausted." However, this time Indian control lasted only for a few months.

Today, the Quartermaster Depot building (1864) on the Arizona side of the bluffs remains. On the California side, the Quechan Tribal Museum occupies the old officers' mess, and other former administrative buildings are used by agencies serving the tribe.

Top of the hill at the Ft. Yuma Reservation, California, and on the opposite bank in Yuma, Arizona.

Ft. Tejon (1854-64) 129 Kern County

In 1853, one of the first California Indian reservations was established near this site, 4,000 feet high in the Tehachapi Mountains. The fort itself was placed here in a pass to "protect the Indians", who had been rounded up from a number of sparsely populated neighboring tribes. By 1864 the reservation was deserted by its 1,000 protectees, but not before it became a stop on the Butterfield stage line and the site of the U.S. Army's first camel detachment.

Lt. E. F. Beale, reportedly a compassionate commandant of the reservation and friend of Kit Carson, bought the defunct fort and the Indian reservation for his huge rancho. The reports of compassion are suspect.

Several of the original buildings have been well-restored, and there is a local "early-days" fiesta every June. The big Rancho Tejon, a green and fertile valley in the long, high valley, sports a big sign at Lebec along the Interstate. It is the home of ancestors of some modern Kawaiisu, Kitanemuk, Yowlumni, Yokuts, and Chumash Indians.

The "Grapevine," on I-5 at Lebec, on the Los Angeles-Kern County line.

Drum Barracks (1861-66) 169 Los Angeles County

As Camp Drum in 1861, it was headquarters and supply depot for many anti-Indian and Civil War defense activities in southern California.

A two-story house remains at 1031 Cary Ave., Wilmington.

Castillo (Fort) Guijarros (1795) 69 San Diego County

One of the first of the early Spanish forts, this one, like Castillo San Joaquín (now Ft. Point) in San Francisco, was not a presidio. Neither probably saw anti-Indian activity, both being essentially national outposts. The U.S. Army's Fort Rosecrans (62), established in 1852, encompasses the Guijarros site.

San Diego-Point Loma area, near Ballast Point, off Cabrillo Memorial Dr. (State Rte. 209).

Presidio of San Diego (1769) 59 San Diego County
(See Appendix II, 265)

Ft. Stockton (1838-48) 54 San Diego County

The original earthworks here were thrown up in 1838 by San Diego townspeople anticipating Mexican civil war. The site is near that of the original Presidio. Its present name was given in 1846 by the U.S. Army. As it was abandoned in 1848 and never used in Indian campaigns.

References for this Appendix
California Department of Parks and Recreation, William P. Mott, Director, California Historical Landmarks, *1973, and later editions. Contains the wording and locations of the bronze plaques around the state.*
Frazer, Robert W., Forts of the West. *University of Oklahoma Press, Normal, OK, 1972.*
Hart, Herbert, Old Forts of the Far West. *Superior Publishing Co., Seattle, WA, 1965*
—, Old Forts of the Northwest. *Bonanza Books, New York, 1963.*
—, Old Forts of the Southwest. *Bonanza Books, New York, 1964.*

Day and night, vendors gather to enjoy the entire event, not just to sell goods.
Above: Calaveras Mi-wuk Big Time, 1998. (dhe)
Below Right: Sierra Mono Museum Fair, 1992. (dhe)

COLLECTING, owning, and wearing Indian artwork are popular with thousands, if not millions of American and people of any culture. The works become art or artisanship not just because of their intrinsic beauty, but also because of their direct connection to the maker.

To find the genuine articles, there are some rather general directions, and a few specific ones. First, I recommend one or several visits to powwows and Indian gatherings. Such festivals are never without a number of crafts booths. It is here that you may survey the types of articles for sale. Some of the smaller gatherings may even offer the more unusual artwork, not catering to the big, popular markets. In addition to well-made traditional items, some daringly new things seem to show up, if you spend the time looking.

Second, Indian fairs, markets, and trade shows are the places to find the more unconventional items, bulkier and more fragile pieces (like ceramics and weavings), and especially, antiques. Not all fairs are run by Indians, however, and the selling of an antique never profits its creator.

Third, try shops called "trading posts", stores featuring Indian arts and crafts, museum shops, reservation arts and crafts shops, and individual artist's shops and galleries. Since these places almost always buy directly from the creator or maker of the work, their process are seldom excessive.

In the past, *caveat emptor* (let the buyer beware) was the word on genuineness; how-ever, since the Indian Arts and Crafts Act of 1990 (Public Law 101-644), let the seller beware has spawned a lot of problems for some Indians. The law was intended to protect Indian sellers from non-Indian copies, forgeries, imports, and imitations, but the seller has had to possess a documentation of Indian-ness, frequently more difficult to obtain than certification from the BIA. Understand that many Natives never had a reservation to belong to, many others have never chosen to affiliate with a tribe, and others have come to California from afar and have no easy access to determine or maintain ties with their tribal heritage. Therefore, buyers may find articles labeled something like: "not guaranteed to be Indian, as defined by law" or "member of the (whatever) tribe".

SELECTED GALLERIES
(Some Indian owned, some not) (*N* to *S*)
Trinidad Trading Co.,
  460 Main St. Trinidad, CA 95570
Indian Arts Gift Ship,
  241 F St., Eureka, CA 95501
Alta California Traders,
  18149 Main St. Marengo Courtyard
  (rear of Jamestown Hotel), Jamestown,
  CA 95327 (from Tuolumne Rancheria)
Pacific Western Traders,
  305 Wool St., Folsom, Ca 95630
  (specializing in California)
Gallery of the American West,
  121 K. St., Sacramento, CA 95814
American Indian Contemporary Arts,
  23 Grant Ave., San Francisco, CA 94108
  (much California artwork)
Rising Arrow, 265-M Sobrante Way,
  Sunnyvale, CA 94066
Lee Chavez, Silversmith,
  P.O. Box 1915, Gilroy, CA 96021
Reyna's Gallerias,
  311 3rd St., San Juan Bautista, CA 95045
Ojai Indian Shop,
  318 E. Ojai Ave., Ojai, CA 93023
Buffalo Robe Indian Trading Post,
  8415 Reseda, Northridge (L.A.), CA
Indian Art Center of California,
  12666 Ventura Blvd., Studio City, CA
Wounded Knee Indian Gallery,
  2313 Wilshire, Santa Monica, CA 90403
The Indian Store,
  338 "C" W. El Norte Pkwy.
  Escondido, CA 92026

American Indian Store,
  1095 S. Magnolia, El Cajon, CA 92020

MUSEUM SHOPS
(A highly subjective list, additions invited)
Miwok Museum, Chaw-Se Indian Grinding
  Rocks State Park, Volcano/Pine Grove,
  strictly California, mostly Miwok
Yosemite National Park, Ansel Adams
  Gallery and Ahwahnee Lodge
Southwest Museum, Pasadena & Beverly
  Hills, Native American artwork and craft-
  work from the hemisphere
Museum of Man, San Diego,
  Worldwide objects

RESERVATION SHOPS
(Smaller, but authentic)
Hupa Museum
Pomo Museum @ Lake Mendocino
Ya-ka-ama Education Center
Bishop, Paiute-Shoshone Cultural Center
Fort Mojave, Needles, Museum
Colorado River Tribes, Parker, AZ, Museum
Morongo, Malki Museum
Agua Caliente, Palm Springs Trading Post

TRADERS
The magazine *Indian Trader*, publication of the Indian Arts and Crafts Asso., lists most of the trade shows here in California, as well as the West, in general. 311 E. Aztec Ave., Gallup, NM 87305

The American Indian Traders Guild in Fresno present trade shows and authenticates items by exhibitors (North America only). Membership directory available from them and public libraries. 3876 E. Teodora Ave., Fresno, CA 93762

The American Indian Index, from Denver, lists most California outlets that sell Indian goods, including many trading posts, museum shops, and reservation shops. Arrowstar Publishing, 10134 University Park Station, Denver, CA 80210-0134

APPENDIX VI
INDIAN BINGO & CASINOS

THESE ARE 43 INDIAN GAMING ESTABLISHMENTS IN CALIFORNIA
known at the beginning of the year 2000, 41 of which are members of the California Indian Gaming Association.
All gaming operations are supervised by the Federal government.
For one reason or another, some may change names, change type of operation, or suspend operations for a time.

[Listed north to south by reservation, name, and location.]

SMITH RIVER RAN., Lucky 7 Casino, Smith River, Del Norte Co.
ELK VALLEY RAN., Elk Valley Casino, Crescent City
RESIGHINI RAN., Golden Bear Casino, Klamath (town)
TSURAI RAN., Cher-Ae Heights Bingo & Casino, Trinidad
HOOPA VALLEY RES., Lucky Bear Casino & Bingo, Hoopa, E of Eureka
PIT RIVER TRIBE, Burney Casino, Burney
REDDING RAN., Win-River Casino, Redding
SUSANVILLE RAN., Northern Lights Casino, Susanville
LAYTONVILLE RAN., Red Fox Casino & Bingo, Laytonville
BERRY CREEK RAN., Gold Country Casino, Oroville
MOORETOWN RAN., Feather Falls Casino, Oroville
SHERWOOD VALLEY RAN., Black Hart Casino, Willets
COYOTE VALLEY RAN., Shodaki Coyote Valley Casino, Calpella (Ukiah)
ROBINSON RAN., Robinson Rancheria Bingo & Casino, Nice, Lake Co.
COLUSA RAN., Colusa Indian Bingo, Colusa Co.
HOPLAND RAN., Hopland Sho-ka-wah Casino, Hopland
BIG VALLEY RAN., Konocti Vista Casino & Bingo, Finley (Lakeport)
MIDDLETOWN RAN., Twin Pines Casino, Middletown
RUMSEY RAN., Cache Creek Bingo & Casino, Brooks (Davis)
JACKSON RAN., Jackson Indian Bingo, Jackson
CHICKEN RANCH RAN., Chicken Ranch Bingo, Jamestown
BISHOP RES., Paiute Palace Casino, Bishop
BIG PINE PAIUTE RES., Sierra Spring Casino, Big Pine
PICAYUNE RAN., Picayune Casino, Coarsegold (under construction nr. Oakhurst)
AUBERRY BIG SANDY RAN., Mono Wind Casino, Auberry
TABLE MOUNTAIN RAN., Table Mtn. Rancheria Casino & Bingo, Friant (E. Fresno)
SANTA ROSA TACHI RAN., The Palace Indian Gaming Center, Lemoore
TULE RIVER RES., Eagle Mountain Casino, nr. Porterville
MOJAVE RES., Mojave Indian Casino, Needles
SANTA YNEZ RES., Chumash Casino, Santa Ynez
CHEMEHUEVI RES., Havasu Landing Resort & Casino, Lake Havasu City
SAN MANUEL RES., San Manuel Indian Bingo & Casino, Highland (San Bernardino)
MORONGO RES., Casino Morongo, Cabazon (Banning)
SOBOBA RES., Soboba Legends Casino, San Jacinto
AGUA CALIENTE CAHUILLA RES., Spa Hotel & Casino, Palm Springs
CABAZON RES., Cabazon Bingo Inc. and Fantasy Springs Casino, Indio
TWENTYNINE PALMS RES., Spotlight 29 Casino, Coachella
PECHANGA LUISEÑO RES., Pechanga Entertainment Center, Temecula
CAHUILLA RES., Cahuilla Creek Rest. & Casino, nr. Anza
BARONA RES., Barona Casino & Bingo, Lakeside (NE of El Cajon)
SYCUAN RES., Sycuan Indian Bingo & Poker Casino, El Cajon
VIEJAS RES., Viejas Casino & Turf Club, Alpine (E of El Cajon)
FORT YUMA RES., Paradise Casino, Winterhaven (Yuma)

For an up-to-date listing of most gaming locations contact the
California Indian Gaming Association, Sacramento, CA (916) 448-8706.

ADVENTURES IN CALIFORNIA INDIAN COUNTRY

CASINO: FROM ITALIAN FOR A "COUNTRY HOME", IN TURN, FROM LATIN FOR "HUT".

JUST ABOUT ANY NIGHT at any of the many California Indian casinos featuring Megabingo that are tied by satellite to the nationwide Indian bingo network—you might see: "Mega at 10:35 EST nightly." Read the flyers. For stakes up to $10,000, you can try most of the other California "regular" Indian bingo gaming establishments.

There have been many modern attempts to pull "the Indian" out of the economic pit, some constructive, others destructive employment crusades, timber and mining schemes, small business development. Few of these seemed to work to the betterment of the tribe members. Until along came bingo and then casinos for the fortunate minority.

High-stakes bingo originated with the daring of a group of Florida Seminoles in 1981. Here was a way to cater to the gaming instinct of a lot of people in a big way. Along came the hurdles, also. The game had to be high stakes, but most states wouldn't allow that. But then, Indian reservations aren't state land, nor exactly federal land either. They are Indian land.

To get an audience, there has to be a nearby population base without access to big gambling. We're not talking Vegas or state lotteries or some remote rez; we're talking Miami, Los Angeles, Tulsa, or Minneapolis. The stakes have to be high enough to pull people out of the city, as big as most lotteries, and there has to be live action. Who's going to set it all up? Most enterprises capable of setting up such operations don't have noses clean enough for the Federal bureaus who will have ultimate oversight.

In 1983, two years after the Florida venture had successfully gained its legal footing, high-stakes Indian gaming (as poker) was introduced into California by an "immigrant" from the Florida venture, Mark Nichols, and his father John, an economist. A card parlor was opened at the Cabazon Reservation in Indio, sparking round after round of legal challenges to state and federal law, and to Indian sovereignty. An appeal of the case on Indian sovereignty versus state and local laws went all the way to the Supreme Court, who in February, 1987, found in favor of the tribe. Not only was their card parlor legal, so was high-stakes bingo.

Casinos found their way into this scenario almost by subterfuge. California law says that games not already sanctioned by the state must be negotiated with the governor. This meant that bingo, poker, and the like were OK, but video poker, for instance, was a no-no, until negotiated with then-governor, Pete Wilson, who was adamant about not negotiating. Most bingo halls then added some poker tables (already legal, with the house taking a fixed percent) and the far higher income-producing video slots. Presto!, a casino!

The original video machines are still in place, after the success of famous Proposition 5 of 1998. Does this make it obligatory for ALL tribes to follow suit? What about tribal sovereignty, etc., etc. At least, Prop 5 made California Indians visible, as nothing had before.

In Lotto, everyone bets against all the other players at that instant; in video, each player bets against the "house" odds at all times. California law requires that all bets be made among the players, not against the house. Since video machines are set by the house, and betting is against the house, some fancy design work in video Lotto has been devised. A very good mechanical genius devised a video slot that looks like a legal Lotto card. In fact, in 1998 four such machines were offered on one floor, but very few people chose to play them. Unfortunately, smaller halls with formerly only video poker-style games or slots may suffer from lack of players betting against one another, unless they can be hooked up electronically with others around the state.

ONCE THE LEGAL GROUNDS were laid, California Indian reservations from Smith River to Fort Yuma recognized the opportunity to raise a comfortable income for their members. Even though Indian gaming establishments undoubtedly provide income, they are not without detractors. Not long ago, a Congressionally directed investigation of several operations forced closure of four, at least temporarily. Fraud and skimming, described as "wrongly paid contracts", seemed to have been the main concern. As one reservation project director told me, so much money in one place is bound to cause things to go bad. He, for one, would rather not see any bingo on his reservation. The trouble lies in operations; although the director must be a local tribesperson, the operating skills, personnel management, security, and accounting are usually handled by an outside organization, with a payroll of from 25 to 350 persons. Some of these outside organizations have alleged ties to people with less than impeccable credentials.

ANOTHER APPROACH that some tribes take, is to handle operations virtually all tasks with tribal members. Prudent measures like

this and careful supervision over all operations have kept most halls clean.

A typical gaming establishment is a comfortable, neat, gymnasium-sized space with rows and columns of machines with blinking, tinkling Christmas lights. For those with bingo, the all-important announcer's platform stands on the center of one wall. At bingo time, anywhere from 1000 to 2500 guests are present. Other halls are rather small, homey places. Most provide a snack bar or a dining room offering American food at very reasonable prices. They operate seven days a week, most 24 hours a day, and their parking lots seem to have several tour buses of players drawn from the nearest urbs. Even the tiny establishments seem to have players who drift in all night. Security is tight and evident. It's safe there.

What does the operation generate for the members of the tribe? For a small tribe, some members can receive a monthly per capita distribution of $5000, but that varies. (See p. 132)

HOW DO INDIANS feel about gaming on their reservations? If there is any one activity common to the Indians of California, or of the U.S., for that matter, it is gambling. But their traditional kind of gambling is radically different from the high-tech, big business type seen today (see p. 129). Indian hand games or guessing games call for a deeply psychic milieu and require intense concentration, not just listening to numbers with felt tip in hand or pushing at buttons incessantly. Not many Indians regularly frequent the establishments; they would rather enjoy the fruits of the enterprise. Many casinoed reservations are now free of unemployment. The gaming halls are almost always located at the edges of the reservations, so as not to interfere with the daily life of the residents.

MARK NICHOLS notes that he recognizes about 30% of his players on any one night, and maybe 85% are returnees. In response to my query if these might be called "addicts", he pointed out that most are using bingo and the machines for pleasant socializing, and enjoy a good adrenalin rush.

The situation remins fluid, and few situations are ever definitively settled. For now, Indian economics in California are better than they have been for a long, long time.

APPENDIX VII
BIBLIOGRAPHY, REFERENCES & FURTHER READING

A Short Essay on Early 20th-Century Anthropologists

As the reader can note in my writings, I have a goodly amount of skepticism concerning anthropology in general, especially of California Native anthropology and its lack of attention to the Native point of view. However, my objections tend to be about, specifically, some of the attitudes stated by earlier anthropologists on their perceptions of California Indians.

Remember that these authors had just come out of the Dark Ages of anthropology, or rather, were early members of the field before it became a well-known science. They began with all the biases and prejudices of the age, but, actually, I think Alfred Kroeber and his associates and successors did a pretty good job of breaking out of the strict "science" mold that had been there before. Kroeber, for all his biases, was probably the first anthropologist with any cultural sensitivity. Of course these workers were loaded with Euro-baggage, but so were the philosophers, the psychologists, the sociologists (a new field), the historians, even the chemists and physicists.

Dr. Saxton Pope, the physician who treated Ishi (*p. 115*), was a good friend of Kroeber, with offices in the same building, in fact. These two men spent a great deal of time with Ishi, trying to understand his nature and feelings toward European society. Furthermore, both were extremely concerned with his health. This is hardly being culturally insensitive. For all his posturing, Kroeber was initially a pretty sensitive person. But power grew in him to an excess, and he eventually became an autocrat.

Read carefully how early anthropologists say what they say. There is practically an intentional negation between their designation "primitive Indian" and their actual description of a person, a tribe, or a practice that is most obviously not primitive. They were obliged to use the jargon of the day, at least to get the public's attention, then to tell a lot more. Moreover, they were professors, authoritarian, yes, but not journalists.

Even today, elders are revealing knowledge of such things as ancient medicinal and agricultural practices. The first California anthropologists could hardly have been expected to know all things, or to interpret everything correctly. Indeed, they admit to incomplete knowledge (but never to a mistake). Facts from all over are now being published that fill gaps, refute earlier attitudes and statements, and greatly amplify the earlier books. But this is good. Moreover, many of the tribes that are recovering their cultures and recognition readily but reluctantly concede that they are highly indebted to these first authors at least for the material that they did find.

After all, at the beginning of this century, a distressing amount of Native information had been destroyed, lost, or deeply hidden. Yes, indeed, the anthropologists' know-it-all attitudes about "extinction" of languages and cultures make recovery of a tribal recognition extremely difficult (the Esselen, Salinan, Ohlone, for examples). In these statements they show their biases, incompleteness of information, and Euro-centrism. Read these anthropologists, take the best of what they offer and with better knowledge, and correct the incorrect parts. Perhaps you might not realize it nor care to recognize it, but these early anthropologists did do a lot of good.

BIBLIOGRAPHY, REFERENCES
(used in this book), and Suggested Further Reading

Bean, Lowell, Sylvia Brakke Vane, and Jackson Young, *The Cahuilla Landscape*, Ballena Press, Menlo Park, CA, 1991. This is a publication which shows the Indian relation to the land in its most exact form—the naming and description of every object and landform in the Cahuilla area of the Santa Rosa and San Jacinto Mountains.

Bean, Lowell, *California Indian Shamanism*, Ballena Press, Menlo Park, CA, 1992. Who, what, when, occasionally how, often why.

California Department of Parks and Recreation, William P. Mott, Director, *California Historical Landmarks*, 1973, and later editions. Contains the wording and locations of the bronze plaques around the state.

Cook, Sherburne F. *The Conflict Between the California Indian and White Civilization*, University of California Press, Berkeley, CA 1976. The facts and figures of the California Indian holocaust.

d'Angulo, Jaime, *Indian Tales*, Hill and Wang, New York, 1953 and later editions. Stories from the early 1900s of and by (mostly California) Indians. Tapes available from Heyday Books, Berkeley.

Eargle, Dolan H., *California Indian Country; the Land & The People*, Trees Co. Press, San Francisco, CA, 1992. A contemporary pictorial presentation the countryside of the California Indian.

—*The Earth Is Our Mother: A Guide to the Indians of California, Their Locales & Historic Sites*, Trees Co. Press, San Francisco, CA 4th (and last) Ed.,1996. A history and detailed guidebook to all contemporary Indian places.

Forbes, Jack D., *Native Americans of California and Nevada*, Naturegraph Publishers, Happy Camp, CA, 1969 and later editions. A history of the peoples, with emphasis on Native languages and teaching of Indian history.

Gillis, Mabel, *California* (American Guide Series), Hastings House, New York, 1939. An excellent WPA guidebook, out-of-print, but available at second-hand bookstores.

Grant, Campbell, *Rock Art of the American Indian*, Thomas Y. Crowell Co., New York, 1967. A careful description of rock art, the shapes, the figures, the classification of styles (but not much meaning).

Heizer, Robert F., and Clewlow, C. W., *Prehistoric Rock Art of California* (2 vols.). Ballena Press, Menlo Park, CA, 1973.

–and Elsasser, Albert B., *The Natural World of the California Indians*, University of California Press, CA,1980. An ethnological survey of the environment and traditions of the early peoples.

–and Whipple, M. A., *The California Indians, A Source Book*, University of California Press, Berkeley, 2nd Ed., 1971. A compilation of writings about the original California Indians.

Kroeber, Alfred L., *Handbook of the Indians of California*. Orig. Bureau of American Ethnology Bulletin (78), reprinted by University of California Press, Berkeley. The first compiled, detailed description of the peoples of central California.

Kroeber, Theodora, *Ishi in Two Worlds*, University of California Press, Berkeley, CA, 1971. The true story of Ishi, a Yahi-Yana man of the Northern Sierra forests, forced to surrender after years of persecution in the forests.

Margolin, Malcolm, Publisher, *News From Native California*, Heyday Books, Berkeley, CA. A quarterly periodical that informs all aspects of the past and present. An indispensable publication for everyone interested in the California Indian people. (See below.)

—*The Ohlone Way*, Heyday Books, Berkeley, CA, 1978. Descriptions of the modes of living of many coastal and riverine California cultures; applicable to peoples other than Ohlone, this is set in the Central California environment.

—*The Way We Lived* and its children's version, *Native Ways*, Heyday Books, Berkeley, 1982. Deeply moving short stories of and by Native people of California. Anyone wishing to know the spirit of California Indians must read this book.

Martineau, LaVan, *The Rocks Begin to Speak*, . KC Publications, Las Vegas, NV, 1973 and later editions. This book moves rock art from the ambiguous or mysterious to communicative art with meaning.

Rawls, James D., *Indians of California, The Changing Image*, University of Oklahoma Press, Norman, OK, 1984. Rawls cites Stephen Powers, 1872: "Men damn what they do not understand." It is Rawls' purpose here to make us understand.

Sturtevant, William C., General Editor, *Handbook of North American Indians*: **Vol. 4** *History of Indian-White Relations*, Wilcomb Washburn, Editor; **Vol. 8** (1978), *California*, Robert F. Heizer, Editor; **Vol. 9** (1979), *Southwest*, Alfonso Ortiz, Editor; **Vol. 10** (1983), *Southwest*, Alfonso Ortiz, Editor; **Vol. 11** (1986), *Great Basin*, Warren L. d'Azevedo, Editor. Smithsonian Institution, Washington, DC. These are the primary references for the history of Native America, in which detailed information and references are given on every known group. Contemporary situations have changed over the last 25 years for most peoples discussed here, as well as some reassessments of former times. Nevertheless these volumes remain the most complete compact accounts.

FURTHER READING

Several publishers have an interest in specific tribes or aspects of California Indians. Others also have a Western and/or Native American emphasis. The reader may write for their catalogs.

BALLENA PRESS, 833 Valparaiso, Menlo Park, CA 94025. (415) 323-9261. Detailed books, biographies, and monographs on specific tribes and California Indian ecological topics.
CAPRA PRESS, Box 2068, Santa Barbara, CA 93120. Archaeology and regional topics.
HEYDAY BOOKS, Box 9145, Berkeley, CA 94709. Other details below. Excellent catalog of California Indian stories, biographies, special topics, publisher of News From Native California.
MALKI MUSEUM PRESS, Morongo Reservation, Banning, CA 92220. Topics rather specific to Southern California Indian peoples.
NATUREGRAPH PUBLISHERS, 3543 Indian Creek Rd., Happy Camp, CA 96039. (800) 390-5353. FAX 530-493-5240. Several California Indian smaller books, crafts, tribes, stories.
PIEDRA PINTADA BOOKS, P.O. Box 1376, Claremont, CA 91711. An excellent collection of rare and reprints out-of-print books. Specialty is rock art and rock art calendars.
Stanford University Press, Stanford, CA 94305. Scholarly studies of Indian topics.
UNIVERSITY OF CALIFORNIA PRESS, 2120 Berkeley Way, Berkeley, CA 94720. Numerous California Indian topics, often scholarly specialties, some from Hearst Museum.

UNIVERSITY OF CALIFORNIA, LOS ANGELES, AMERICAN INDIAN STUDIES CENTER, 3220 Campbell Hall, Los Angeles, CA 90024.
UNIVERSITY OF UTAH PRESS.1795 E. South Campus Dr., Ste.101, Salt Lake City, UT 84112-9402. (800) 773-6672. Strong on western ecological topics and archaeology.
WESTERNLORE PRESS, 11860 Pami Pl., Tucson, AZ 85704

Several book distributors maintain excellent catalogs with California Indian and American Indian titles, as well as California history

BOOKHANDLER, 3597 Lomacitas Lane, Bonita, CA 91902. (619) 472-0471, FAX 619-472-0418. Catalogued resources for California schools & libraries, good on specific tribes and story books.
GEM GUIDES BOOK CO., 315 Cloverleaf Dr., Ste. F, Baldwin Park, CA 91706. (818) 855-1611. Broad spectrum of western topics, including Native American; catalog contains catalogs from NATUREGRAPH PUBLISHERS (see above) and K C PUBLICATIONS (Las Vegas).
SUNBELT PUBLICATIONS, 1270 Fayette St., El Cajon, CA 92020. (619) 258-4911. Good list of California Native Am. titles.

Perhaps I should mention that big chains carry many California Indian books, or can get them for you: B Dalton, Barnes & Noble, Borders, Waldenbooks, &c.

Some other distributors carry a large selection of Native American titles: Baker & Taylor (Reno), Bookpeople (Oakland), Ingram Book Co. (La Verne, TN)

The internet provides access to much information, also. A few access names are given in this book, but many more are available, for the price of time on the net.

PERIODICALS & PERIODICAL REFERENCES

News From Native California. The required reading for anyone interested in following detailed accounts of the California Indian peoples. Past volumes are treasures of accounts on every topic that relates to the lives of the peoples: history, individuals, language, basketry, legal aspects, education, health, events, news. Heyday Books also sponsors or co-sponsors numerous Indian events around the state—persons interested in the News will also be interested in their programs. Published by Heyday Books, P.O. Box 9145, Berkeley, CA 94709 (510) 849-0177. Editorial offices, 2054 University Ave, Berkeley, CA 94704 (510) 549-3564.

SOUTH AND MESOAMERICAN INDIAN INFORMATION AND RIGHTS CENTER (SAIIC). The center gathers much information, and furnishes news, articles, and information on numerous indigenous peoples south of the United States. Thousands of indigenous people from these regions live in California, and have a deep interest in news of developments from their homelands—the same information which is always of great interest to anyone interested in cultural and political happenings in this hemisphere. SAIIC also sponsors a number of informative meetings, lectures, films, and gatherings in various California cities. Their journal of articles, information, and news is Abya Yala News, P.O. Box 28703, Oakland, CA 94604 (510) 834-4263. SAIIC, 12312 Broadway, Oakland, CA 94612

INTERNATIONAL INDIAN TREATY COUNCIL (IITC). The IITC, though based in California, is truly an international sentinel, which investigates, documents, and publicizes offenses against the rights of tribal or indigenous people anywhere in the hemisphere, indeed on other continents, as well. IITC sponsors Indigenous Peoples' Day on Alcatraz every October 12th, and Unthanksgiving Day, same place (see p. 288). Write for their bulletin. IITC, 2390 Mission St., Ste. 301, San Francisco, CA 94110 (415) 641-4482, (FAX 415.641.1298)

CALENDAR of CALIFORNIA INDIAN EVENTS:
BIG TIMES, FESTIVALS, FEASTS, & POWWOWS

(For exact dates and confirmation, the best source of information is the Calendar section
of the latest quarterly *News From Native California*, published by Heyday Books, Berkeley)

WINTER

MID-JANUARY
Southwest Museum, Pasadena
Native American Film Festival (213) 221-2164

FEBRUARY 19TH & 27TH
San Francisco
Honoring the Longest Walk (19th)
Recognition of Wounded Knee Occupation (27th):
International Indian Treaty Council (415) 641-4482

3RD WEEKEND IN FEBRUARY
Sacramento or central CA location
Annual American Indian Education Conference & Powwow
(no fry bread or camping)
(916) 657-3357

FEBRUARY 21ST & LAST WEEKEND IN FEB.
Concord, Contra Costa County
Mt. Diablo High School Powwow

Los Angeles, Olvera St./Lincoln Park
Cuauhtémoc Day Mexican Indian dances, entertainment.
Xipe Totec, Templo Flor, participants:
(714) 774-9803, (213) 664-6433

San Diego (call for location)
Cuauhtémoc Day Aztec dances,
Sponsor: Danza Mexicayotl.
Info: Méario Aguilar (619) 422-6433

San Francisco (location varies)
Cuauhtémoc Day Mexican Indian dances.
Xitlalli, participant (415) 586-0435

FEBRUARY 22ND
Woodley Island, Eureka-Arcata
Candlelight Vigil
In remembrance of the 1860 massacre on Indian Island
(707) 442-2762 or 733-5572

LATE FEBRUARY/MARCH
Santa Rosa Rancheria, Lemoore, Kings County
Spiritual Renewal All tribes dances and songs (all night)
(209) 924-1278

SPRING

DATE UNSPECIFIED
Location varies (usually Sacramento)
Annual American Indian Education Powwow and **conference**
(916) 277-9390 or 971-9190

1ST WEEKEND IN MARCH
Ft. Yuma Reservation, Winterhaven, SE Imperial County
Powwow and BBQ
Sponsor: Native American Indian Organization
of San Pascual School (619) 572-0213

2ND WEEKEND IN MARCH
Long Beach, California State University, Los Angeles County
Valentine Powwow
Contest and intertribal contest dancing, gourd dancing, vendors
(562) 985-8528

Turlock, California State Univ., Stanislaus County
Powwow In the gym (Sat. only) (209) 667-3598

MARCH 19TH
San Juan Capistrano, S Orange County
Ajachemem Gathering for Equinox/Swallows Day
At the Mission: dances, food
(714) 488-3484

MARCH WEEKEND NEAREST EQUINOX (21ST)
Los Angeles, Echo Park area
Changing of The Seasons
Songs and healing prayers honoring the children & the people.
Sponsor: Templo Flor (principally Maya)
2201 Park Dr., Los Angeles 90026
(213) 664-6433

Pasadena, La Villa Park
Fiesta de Primavera
Mexican tribal dances, food.
Xipe Totec (714) 774-9803

Sacramento, location varies
Spring Fiesta Mexican tribal dances, food
Quetzalcoatl/Xitlálli (916) 739-1105

San Francisco (location varies)
Fiesta de Colores (Children's Festival)
Sponsor: Xitlálli (415) 586-0435

3RD SATURDAY IN MARCH
Stewart Indian School, Carson City, NV
Mother Earth Powwow (702) 822-1808

Cupertino, Homestead High School, San Mateo County
American Indian Education Powwow (408) 522-2238

Torrance, El Camino College, S Los Angeles County
Spotted Horse Powwow Intertribal contest dancing.
Info: Chris Rodriguez (310) 532-3670

4TH WEEKEND IN MARCH
Riverside County
Eternal Flame Powwow (909) 222-8577

PRE-EASTER
Pala Reservation, N San Diego County
Holy Week services in Mission Chapel (619) 742-3784

EASTER
Quartz Valley Rancheria, Siskiyou County
Tribal Easter gathering Indian card games, music, pot luck
(916) 468-2468

1ST WEEKEND IN APRIL
Davis, call for location
Powwow, Univ. of California and D-Q U (916) 752-2027

Sacramento, California State University
Native American Culture Week (916) 278-6595

Tule River Reservation,
  Porterville, Tulare County
Wildflower Festival (Sat. only) (209) 784-3155
  Crafts, food, basketry, flowers.

2ND WEEKEND IN APRIL
Chico, California State University, Butte County
Powwow (camping) (916) 898-6485

Riverside Sherman Indian High School
Powwow Dances, cultural demos (909) 276-6719

MID-APRIL
Agua Caliente Reservation, Palm Springs, 218 S. Palm Cyn. Rd.
Indian Heritage Festival (Sat., call for date)
  Cahuilla traditional songs, arts & crafts, food.
  Sponsor: Agua Caliente Cultural Museum
  (619) 778-1079 or (619) 322-4851

Arcata, Humbolt State University
Annual Powwow
  Sponsor: Indian Teacher & Educational Personnel Program
  (707) 826-4994

San Diego, beneath Coronado Bridge
Chicano Day Intertribal (mostly Mexican)
  dances, food, entertainment.
  Danza Mexicayotl, participant (619) 442-6433

3RD WEEKEND IN APRIL
Oakland, Mills College
Bill Wahpepah Powwow (510) 430-2341

4TH WEEKEND IN APRIL
Fresno, California State University
Tewaquachi (Indian Club) **Powwow** Contests, booths, camping
(209) 278-3277

Kule Loklo, Point Reyes National Seashore, Marin County
Strawberry Festival Songs, dances, prayers (415) 663-1092

Satwiwa, Santa Monica Mountains National Recreation Area,
Ventura County
Chumash and Tongva Storytelling
  (with other California tribes, dancing)
  (805) 499-2837

Frank Kanawha and Clarence Hostler demonstrate northwest salmon cooking at the Western Basketweavers Conference, in June, 1999 in Reno. (dhe)

LAST WEEKEND IN APRIL
Long Beach, California State University
Annual Spring Powwow
  Contest dancing (Southern drum), gourd dances, food, crafts.
  Sponsor: American Indian Studies Council (562) 985-4963

1ST WEEKEND IN MAY
Cupertino, Santa Clara County
deAnza College Annual Powwow (Ina Ta Anpetu Wacipi)
  Three days of arts & crafts, hand drum singing,
  contest dancing, films
  (408) 864-5448

Los Angeles, University of California
Annual Powwow
  Intertribal and contest dancing, arts, crafts, food
  (no camping available) (310) 206-7513

1ST WEEKEND IN MAY CONTINUED
Pala Reservation, N San Diego County
Cupa Days Invited dances (619) 742-3784

San Juan Bautista, San Benito County
American Indian & World Cultures Festival (adm.)
  Tribal arts and culture presentations,
  North American & Aztec drums & dancers, singers, Indian food.
  Reyna's Gallerias & Indian Museum (408) 623-2379

Santa Rosa, Sonoma County
Jesse Peter Native Am. Art Museum, Santa Rosa Jr. College
Day Under the Oaks
  Crafts, food, tribal dancers, story-telling, children's activities
  (707) 527-4479

WEEKEND NEAREST MAY 5TH
Berkeley, Martin Luther King Park
Cinco de Mayo Invited Mexican dances, food, entertainment.
  Xitlalli, participant (415) 586-0435

2ND WEEKEND IN MAY
Stanford University
Stanford Annual Powwow (3 days) Dances, crafts, food
(650) 723-4078

MID-MAY
Kern River Sequoia Natl. Forest, above Kernville, Tulare County
Monache Gathering California tribal & intertribal drums
and dancing, elders talks, sweat lodge, Bear Dance
(619) 376-4240 or 878-2523

3RD WEEKEND IN MAY
Marysville, Sutter County
Annual Yuba-Sutter Powwow (Sat) (530) 749-6196

Riverside, University of California
Medicine Ways Conference & Powwow
Gourd dances, bird songs, food, arts, crafts.
Sponsor: Native American Student Program (909) 787-4143

San Diego, Balboa Park, Museum of Man
Annual San Diego American Indian Cultural Days
Intertribal, Kumeyaay bird singers, drums, arts, crafts, food.
Sponsor: Indian Human Resource Center (619) 281-5964

San Francisco, California State University (in the gym)
Annual Powwow (415) 338-1929

Santa Cruz, University of California
Annual Spring Powwow
Sponsors: UC Santa Cruz and
Student Alliance of North American Indians (831) 462-4167

MEMORIAL DAY WEEKEND
Casa de Fruta, Hollister, S Santa Clara County
Red Road Powwow (3 days) (adm., pkg., camping)
Sponsor: Santa Cruz Indian Council (831) 471-9155

Davis/D-Q-U, Yolo County
•**Big Time Celebration**
Traditional dances of all California, storytelling, exhibitions, sales
(916) 758-0470
•**Graduation & Graduation Powwow**
(916) 758-0470

Folsom, Sacramento County
Spring Art Show & Indian Market
Sales, music
Pacific Western Traders (916) 985-3851

Fontana, San Bernardino County
Four Moons Powwow Intertribal & California,
Northern & Southern drums, food, crafts, camping (adm.)
Native American Indian Center (909) 823-6150

Morongo Reservation Banning, Riverside County
Malki Museum Fiesta
Southern California tribal dances, bird songs, food,
basketry artisans, traditional BBQ
(909) 849-7289

Sierra Mono Museum, North Fork, Madera County
Memorial Day Gathering: Honoring of the Elders, entertainment
(209) 877-2115

END OF MAY
Sacramento, Cal. State Indian Museum, Sutter Fort State Park
Gathering of Elders (Sat. only) (adm.)
Honoring the elders, California traditional dancing, food, crafts
(916) 324-0971

The World Cultures Festival at San Jaun Bautista, sponsored by the San Juan Council, brought the entrancing Okinawa Dancers from San Jose to perform in 1997. (dhe)

SUMMER

1ST WEEKEND IN JUNE
Alturas, Modoc County
Pit River Gathering & Trade Fair
Sponsor: American Indian Traditional Preservation Committee
(541) 474-6394

Grass Valley Fairgrounds, Nevada County
Maidu Heritage Day (Sat. only) Dances, food, crafts
(916) 273-1749

Marysville, Yuba College, Yuba County
Annual Yuba-Sutter Powwow (530) 749-6196

Mount Madonna County Park— call for date.
(Hwy. 152 W of Gilroy) Santa Clara County
Honoring of the Elders Powwow (3 days)
Ohlone & intertribal dancers, food (adm. to camping)
Sponsors: Tena Council and Pajaro Valley Ohlone Council
PVOC: (831) 728-8471; Park: (831) 842-2341

San Bernardino, California State University, 5500 University Pkwy.
Four Moons Powwow (3 days) (adm. & pkg. fee)
Forum, lodge village
(909) 823-6150

San Diego, NASA, Miramar
Sound of Freedom Powwow (619) 491-9334

1ST SUNDAY IN JUNE
Pala Reservation, N San Diego County
Corpus Christi Religious festival (619) 742-3784

2ND WEEKEND IN JUNE

Napa, Napa County
Gathering of the People Napa Valley College.
Sharing, foods, crafts, and powwow dancing.
Sponsor: Suscol Council & Napa Valley College (707) 226-5075

Oceanside, San Luis Rey Mission, San Diego County
Annual Intertribal Powwow
Contest dancing, arts, crafts, food, peon games.
Sponsor: San Luis Rey Band of Luiseño Mission Indians
(760) 724-8505

San Diego, San Diego Museum of Man
Indian Fair (adm.)
Dancing, crafts, storytelling, artisans, food
(619) 239-2001

MID-JUNE, NEAR SOLSTICE

California Indian Basketweavers Gathering location varies
Demonstrations of basketry and related arts, showcase, sales,
discussions, Indian dancers.
Info: CIBA (530) 292-0141

San Francisco or Sacramento
Xilomen, Fiesta de Maiz (Corn Festival) location varies
Mexican ceremonies and dances.
Xitlálli (415) 586-0435 or (916) 739-1105

Susanville, Lassen County
Maidu *Weda*, the **Bear Dance**
Roxie Peconum Creek Campground, Lassen Natl. Forest Rd. 29,
off highway, 2-1/2 mi. W of jct. with Hwy 44.
(530) 257-3275

3RD WEEKEND IN JUNE

Oakland, Kaiser Center
Silver Star Powwow & Market (3 days) Food, vendors.
Sponsor: Native American Film Institute (415) 554-0525

Tehachapi, Kern County
Tehachapi Powwow call for exact location
Dances, food, camping.
Sponsor: Kern Valley Indian Community (760) 376-4340

Ya-ka-ama, Forestville, Sonoma County
Spring Fair
California dances, crafts, food, games, sports tourney
(707) 887-1541

Yosemite National Park Visitors Center
Indian Day Big Time
(admission fee to Park; Native American event free; camping)
Sierra Miwok dances, sweats, big dinner, handgames.
Park info (209) 372-4461,
or card to: Jay Johnson, Yosemite National Park, CA 95389

4TH WEEKEND IN JUNE

Healdsburg, Lake Sonoma, Sonoma County
Big Time Traditional dances, food, art, crafts, speakers.
Sponsor: Dry Creek Pomo Traditional Dancers (707) 837-8506

END OF JUNE

Fallbrook/West Hills, W Los Angeles County
Rockwell (Park) Powwow
Sponsor: Friends of Satwiwa
Info: weekends only (805) 375-1930

Pomo Culture Center, Calpella/ Ukiah, Mendocino County
Honoring of Seniors Day BBQ and Coyote Valley Dancers.
Info: Delma Eyle, (707) 485-8685

Trinidad, Patricks Point State Park, Humboldt County
Sumeg Village Days (Thurs-Sat) (adm., camping)
Yurok Dances, crafts, stories (Thurs)
Brush Dance (Sat)
(707) 677-3570

JULY 4TH WEEKEND

Hoopa Reservation, Humboldt County
Hoopa Rodeo, ceremonial dances following (916) 625-4110

Kashaya Rancheria, W Sonoma County
Tribal dances during week, potluck on July 4th (707) 785-2594

Manteca, San Joaquin County
Three Rivers Indian Lodge Powwow 13505 S. Union Rd.
Arts, crafts, food, invited drums, dances
(209) 858-2421

Santa Ynez Reservation, Santa Barbara County
July 4th Powwow Crafts, food, Chumash and other dances
(805) 688-7997

*An invited troupe of Hawaiian dancers delight the spectators
at the Casa de Fruta Powwow near Hollister (San Benito
County).* (dhe, 1997)

2ND WEEKEND IN JULY
Lava Beds National Monument, Modoc County
Captain Jack's Stronghold Gathering
Ceremonies, dances, songs, live crafts
(916) 667-2282

Monterey, Fair Grounds
American Indian & World Cultures Festival
Tribal arts and culture presentations,
North American & Aztec drums & dancers, singers, Indian food
Sponsor: Reyna's Gallerias (San Juan Bautista) (408) 623-2379

Pinoleville Reservation, Ukiah
Big Time Festival
Traditional California Indian dancing, crafts, food
(707) 463-1454

Wassama Roundhouse State Park, Ahwahnee, Madera County
Gathering Day (Sat) Yokuts, Miwok, & others
Dances, demonstrations, arts & crafts, sweat lodge, food
(559) 822-2332

Ya-ka-ama, Forestville, Sonoma County
Federated Coast Miwok annual picnic & tribal gathering
(Sat only) (707) 887-1541

3RD WEEKEND IN JULY
Kule Loklo, Point Reyes Natl. Seashore, Marin County
Big Time Festival Miwok, Pomo, Wappo, others (Sat. only):
Trade booths, native foods, weaving, native arts demonstrations.
Sponsors: Pt. Reyes Natl. Seashore, MAPOM,
Federated Indians of Graton Rancheria (415) 663-1092

4TH WEEKEND IN JULY
South Lake Tahoe, Tallac Historic Site
Wa She Shu It Deh Festival of Native American Arts (3 days)
Sponsor: Washoe Tribe of California and Nevada
(with US Forest Service) (702) 888-0936

Trinidad, Patrick's Point State Park, Humboldt County
Sumeg Village Day (Yurok) (Sat only) (park adm.)
Arts, crafts, food, brush dance.
(707) 677-3570

LAST WEEKEND IN JULY
Costa Mesa, Orange County Fairgrounds
Southern California Indian Center Powwow
(714) 663-1102

San Diego, Pacific Beach
Annual Grunion Festival (Sat).
Running of the grunion, stargazing, fun.
(619) 274-1326

EARLY AUGUST
Sacramento, 6th & Broadway
Annual Community Powwow (3 days)
Fri.–California dancers (adm.)
Sat., Sun.–Powwow & contest dancing
Dances, crafts, health care info
Sponsor: Sacto. Urban Ind. Health Project (916) 421-0657

1ST WEEKEND IN AUGUST
Ft. Bidwell Reservation, Modoc County
Northern Paiute Traditional Powwow (916) 279-6310

Sierra Mono Museum, Northfork, Madera County
Sierra Mono Indian Fair Days (adm.)
Dances, food, games, princess contest, crafts,
sports (archery, running)
(209) 877-2115

Smith River at Ne-lo-chun-don (S. Bank Rd.), Del Norte County
Naydosh (**Ten Night Dance**) Pot luck Fri. & Sat. nights.
Sponsor: Tolowa Nation (707) 464-7332

Lake Mendocino (Ukiah), Pomo Area B
Annual Senior Native American Day Entertainments,
traditional foods, BBQ, Pomo dances, gifts for elders
Coyote Valley Tribal Office: (707) 485- 8723

2ND WEEKEND IN AUGUST
Bridgeport, Bridgeport Park, Mono County
Native American Crafts Days (Sat., Sun., 9-3)
Arts & crafts, demonstrations, workshops, dancing, music
(760) 934-3342

Fall River Mills Buckskin Family Camp, E Shasta County
Annual Protecting Mother Earth Conference
Environmental issues: sacred sites, toxics, forestry,
Mining, fishing rights, biodiversity
Sponsor: Indigenous Environmental Network.
IEN: (218) 751-4967 or (707) 825-7640

3RD WEEKEND IN AUGUST
Klamath, Del Norte County
Annual Yurok Salmon Festival
Sports, food, cultural demonstrations
(707) 444-0433

Mendocino, Sonoma County
Coast Pomo Indian Days Celebration
Coastal Indian dances, displays, arts & crafts.
Ya Ka Ama Bo-Cah Pomo Demonstration Village,
Mendocino Headlands St. Pk., 1 mile S of Mendocino, camping.
(707) 964-3041 or (707) 964-2647

San Francisco, Golden Gate National Recreation Area
California Indian Festival Dances, food, crafts.
Info: Bldg. 102, Visitor Center, Presidio (415) 561-4323

McCloud, Shasta County, date may vary, call
Annual Wintu Spiritual Ceremony E on Hwy. 89, L on Pilgrim
Rd., 10 to Coonrod Flat.
Sponsor: friends and family of Florence Jones.
Info: (530) 275-1013 or 246-2849

ADVENTURES IN CALIFORNIA INDIAN COUNTRY

THE SAN JUAN BAUTISTA ALL-INDIAN SPRING MARKET.

SOUTH FROM GILROY, the fuzzy foothills of the Coast Range are backed by high ridges that will block the straight lines of Highway 101. Here I loop off the freeway and head southeastward through the flat pepper and tomato fields, driving on top of the San Andreas fault. My destination is in sight: perched on a little shelf above the greening fields is the little red-tile-roofed mission town of San Juan Bautista, founded by Padre Fermin Lasuén in 1797. The site is the ancient Mutsun Ohlone village of Xumontwash, but nobody in San Juan seems to know that.

I drive by the front gate of the market, partly enclosed by an adobe wall which is slowly dissolving over time; the skies above are threatening to accelerate the dissolution with a deluge. None comes. In other years, the market was held in April, and storms sent everyone scurrying inside cramped quarters. Elayna and Sonne Reyna (Comanche), the market's directors, struggling mightily to present this market for many years, moved the date later, hoping the skies would cooperate. With hope and prayers to the Great Spirit, they usually do.

The annual Indian spring market does not disappoint my expectations—rows upon rows of beautiful artistry set beside the olive-laden trees of the 200-year-old mission. The sunny skies enhance the artwork in the sixty-five stalls—sparkling and brilliant—the crafting and artistry of hundreds of Indian talents. A hawk whistles its approval overhead, always a good sign at an Indian event.

TO SAVOR THE PLACE I walk around, just quickly, looking to see what to my wondering eyes should appeal. Silver and turquoise—massive, or tiny and delicate. Black and lustrous Hopi silver. Glacier-blue lapis. Rare polished clam-shell necklaces. Fancy beadwork. Guatemalan and Peruvian Indian embroidery and patterned fabrics—new and old and made into clothing, rugs, purses. Bold and soft posters of Indian life. Tile work. Pueblo pottery. Basket weavers weaving beautiful baskets in non-traditional dark colors or in traditional California style. New ideas—amber and bamboo jewelry from Mexico, bright orange and blue mother-of-pearl in angular designs. Lakota ceremonial and battle axes. The artwork has undergone a judgement, and ribbons are awarded. A feast for the eyes.

Books on Indian lore, crafts, history. On the recommendation of a Southwestern Indian co-op merchant, I buy one on rock art interpretation, a neglected field.

Then for the rest of your body: saucy BBQ chicken, Indian tacos, fry bread, buffalo burgers. The drifting smells of food, incense, and sage enhance the art.

ALL DURING THE DAY, there is music and dancing from so many ethnic groups. The booming of drums sounds over the church cloisters. The Aztec dancers, in plumed and gilded costume are dancing their energetic, rhythmic dances, seemingly tireless. They dance because they must, they say. These dancers appear several times during the two-day market; some of the vendors grumble that they lose the buying crowd, while they go to watch. Another drum sounds—this time Lakota songs on the big bass drum—from a quartet who drove all the way from South Dakota. Feasts for the eyes and ears.

Later, while I rest in the pretty mission flower gardens, the Spanish priest happens by. "We like to let the Indians use the ground for free. It's good for both them and the church." On the other side of the church there is a simple wooden plaque: "Buried in this sacred ground in unmarked graves are 4,300 Mission Indians..."

I wander into the simply-furnished old mission before Mass time; the Indian drums boom just outside—not heard for 200 years.

Elayne (above, left) and Sonne Reyna (right), owners of Reyna's Gallerias in San Juan Bautista, sponsor a variety of cultural and artistic Indian events throughout central California, including California Indian Markets held at the San Juan Mission the first weekend in May and Labor Day. (dhe, 1990)

4TH WEEKEND IN AUGUST

Santa Rosa (city) Fairgrounds, Sonoma County
Annual Powwow
Dancers: intertribal, gourd, Pomo, Aztec
Art, crafts, raffle, food.
(707) 869-8233

LAST WEEKEND IN AUGUST

Santa Rosa Rancheria, Lemoore, Kings County
Santa Rosa Days Powwow dancing (tribal & C/W), food
(209) 924-6961

LATE AUGUST OR SEPTEMBER

Hollister, San Benito County
Annual Storytelling Festival (adm.)
Indian Canyon Ranch, call first (831) 637-4238

Hoopa Reservation, Humboldt County
White Deerskin and **Jumping Dances** (biennial) (916) 625-4211

LABOR DAY WEEKEND/1ST MONDAY IN SEPTEMBER

Bishop Reservation, N Inyo County
Labor Day Celebration Handgames, sports, picnic
(619) 873-3584

Reno-Sparks Indian Colony Nevada in Sparks, off I-80
Numaga Indian Days (702) 673-0775

San Juan Bautista, San Benito County
Annual California Indian Market
Crafts, juried art, exhibition dances
Sponsor: Reyna's Gallerias (408) 623-2379

Stockton, Stand School, Stockton
Annual Powwow
Sponsor: American Indian Education Program &
Stockton Unified School District (209) 953-4803, or 546-7569

Three Rivers, San Joaquin County
Annual Venice-Hill Valley Tribes Powwow
E of Hwy. 99 on Hwy 198 @ Three Rivers.
Info: (209) 592-4589

2ND WEEKEND IN SEPTEMBER

Avalon, South Beach, Catalina Island, Los Angeles
Annual *Ti'at* Voyage & Tongva Gathering
Celebrates the canoe *Mo'omat Ahiko* voyage
Exhibits, demonstrations, singing
(310) 510-3598, or http://home.earthlink.net/~tongva

Bass Lake, Recreation Point, Madera County
Annual Precious Sunset Powwow (adm.)
off Hwy. 41, just SE of Yosemite N.P.
Contest dancing, vendors, hand drum contest
Sponsor: American Indian Center of Central California
(209) 855-2705

Chico, Cedar Grove, Bidwell Park, Butte County
Cedar Grove Powwow
Intertribal (non-contest) & California dancers, vendors
(530) 345-5415, (530) 894-5068

Lancaster, Los Angeles County 15701 East Ave. M (adm.)
Annual American Indian Celebration on Piute Butte
California and western Great Basin traditions:
Traditional dance & music, arts and crafts, demonstrations,

Booths, food, storytelling, children's activities.
Sponsor: Antelope Valley Indian Museum
(805) 846-3055 (Museum), (805) 942-0662 (State Park)

Marin Museum of the American Indian, Novato, Marin County
Indian Trade Feast Miwok & other California dances
Crafts, food, storytelling, foods, children's activities
(415) 897-4064

Redding, Shasta County
Stillwater Powwow At the ancient Wintu gathering grounds
by the convention center; in conjunction with the Health Fair
and Redding Rancheria (916) 225-8979

Tuolumne Me-Wuk Rancheria, Tuolumne County
Acorn Festival (Big Time)
California Indian dances, food, camping
(209) 928-3475

3RD WEEKEND IN SEPTEMBER

Pala Reservation, N San Diego County
Fiesta-Pala Fire Dept. benefit Crafts, food, social dancing, softball
(619) 742-1632

Greenville, Greenville High School (Hwy. 89), Plumas County
Annual Northern Sierra Indian Days Powwow (adm.)
Crafts, booths, Maidu basketry demonstrations
(530) 283-3402

San Diego, Balboa Park, Presidents Way & Park Blvd.
California American Indian Days
Celebration: dancing, arts & crafts, education, health clinic, food
Sponsor: Indian Human Resource Center (619) 281-5964

Thousand Oaks/Newbury Park, E Ventura County
Annual Everything Is Sacred Powwow
Borchard Community Center, Reino Rd.
Sponsors: California Indian Council Foundation
and Conejo Recreation and Park District (805) 493-2863

West Point, Calveras County
Mi-wuk Big Time Roundhouse dancing
(Miwuk, Pomo, Maidu, Wintun), booths, food, camping
Sponsor: Calaveras Band of Mi-wuk Indians
(209) 293-4332 or (209) 354-0882

4TH WEEKEND IN SEPTEMBER
CALIFORNIA INDIAN DAYS
Barona Reservation, Lakeside, San Diego County
Indian Days Observance (619) 281-5964

Sacramento, California State Indian Museum,
  Sutter Fort State Park
California Indian Days
  Dances, crafts, food (location may vary)
  (916) 445-4209 or (916) 324-0971

Chaw-Se Indian Grinding Rocks State Park,
  Pine Grove, Amador County (State Park parking fee)
Big Time Roundhouse dances, games, crafts,
  Food (deep pit BBQ Sat.)
  (209) 296-7488

Colorado River Reservation, Parker, Ariz.
Combined Colorado River Tribes Fair & Indian Days Pageant
  Powwow, food, games, dances.
  (602) 669-9211

Crescent City, Del Norte County
California Indian Day
  Salmon bake, dances, arts & crafts, stick games (beachfront)
  Sponsor: Tolowa Nation (707) 464-7332

Henry Cowell Redwoods State Park, Felton, Santa Cruz County
Ohlone Day (adm. to park)
  Participation in many "old ways", making baskets,
  Arrowheads, games, storytelling, food
  (408) 335-3174

Ft. Yuma Reservation, SE Imperial County
Indian Days Powwow, food (619) 572-0213

Jolon, San Antonio Mission, Monterey County
Annual Salinan Nation Tribal Gathering
  W off US Hwy. 101 on Jolon Rd (County Hwy. G-14),
  24 mi. to Ft. Hunter-Ligget. Public invited, BBQ
  (408) 281-4459 or email:glcastro@pacbell.net

Morongo Reservation, Riverside County
Annual Casino Morongo Powwow Cabazon Exit, I-10
  (909) 849-6736 or (310) 599-6550 or (800) 252-4499

Porterville, Tulare County Fairgrounds
Annual Tule River Yokuts Powwow Indian arts, stories.
  Native American Heritage Committee (209) 784-6135

Roseville (environs), Sacramento County
California Indian Days Powwow, crafts, food, camping.
  (916) 920-0285

Round Valley Reservation, Covelo, Mendocino County
Indian Days @ Hidden Oaks Park.
  Crafts, food, intertribal & Calif. dances, camping,
  Handgames, Sun. free BBQ, softball tourney
  (707) 983-6126 or (707) 983-1026

FALL

1ST WEEKEND IN OCTOBER
Carmichael, Ancil Hoffman Park, Sacramento
Maidu Indian Day (Sat only) (adm. & pkg. fee)
  Effie Yeaw Nature Center, 6700 Tarshes Dr.
  Celebration of Maidu culture in Nisenan village, skills demos,
  Maidu dancers, food, crafts, storytelling.
  (916) 489-4918

Coarsegold, Madera County
Annual Chukchansi Powwow
  Sponsor: Chukchansi Tribal Nation, Coarsegold.
  (209) 642-6069 or (209) 683-6633

Fremont, Coyote Hills Regional Park, Alameda County
Annual Gathering of Ohlonean Peoples
  Music, dance, stories, games, foods, basketmaking and more
  (510) 795-9385

2ND WEEKEND IN OCTOBER
Sacramento, California State Indian Museum,
  Sutter Fort State Park
Acorn Day (Sat only) (adm.)
  Learning history, traditional acorn processing.
  (916) 324-0971

Ft. Mojave Reservation, Needles, E San Bernardino County
Annual Powwow
  Crafts, food, parade, gourd dances, bird songs, intertribal drums
  (619) 326-4591

OCTOBER 12TH
Los Angeles near UCLA
Before Columbus Day Festival (weekend day nearest Oct. 12)
  @ Kuruvungna Springs, University High School: songs, dances
  Sponsor: Gabrielino/Tongva Springs Foundation
  (310) 397-0180

Sacramento, location varies
Fiesta de Los Guerreros Aguilas y Jaguares:
  Aztec ceremony of transition from boyhood to manhood.
  Sponsor: Quetzalcoatl/Xitlalli (916) 739-1105

San Francisco, Alcatraz Island
International Day of Solidarity with Indigenous Peoples
  Sunrise Ceremony. Meet Pier 41, 5:30 AM.
  International Indian Treaty Council (415) 641-4482

MID-OCTOBER
Pala Reservation, N San Diego County
Children's Festival of St. Francis of Assisi (619) 742-3784

Ya-ka-ama, Forestville, Sonoma County
Indian Summer Harvest Festival (call for date)
  Arts & crafts, dances, garden harvest, elders dinner
  (707) 887-1541

Yurok Reservation, Humboldt County
Yurok dances (biennial) (916) 625-4275

3RD WEEKEND IN OCTOBER
Morongo Reservation, Banning, Riverside County
Malki Museum Fall Gathering
  Celebration of piñon and acorn harvest, weewish cook-off, foods,
  Crafts, gourd rattle-making, rabbit stick throwing
  (909) 849-7289

NOVEMBER 1-2/DIA DE LOS MUERTOS

Campo Reservation, SE San Diego County
All Saints Day Festival: Mass for the Departed (619) 478-5251

Los Angeles, Echo Park area
Songs, prayers, esp. Spanish language tribes.
  Sponsor: Templo Flor (213) 664-6433

Monterey
Infants to Elders Festival Dances, artwork, crafts.
  Sponsor: Reyna's Galerias (408) 623-4379

Sacramento, location varies
Vigil, prayers, Mexican ceremonial dances
  Sponsor: Xitlalli (916) 739-1105

San Francisco, Mission neighborhood
Velación (late night).
  Sponsors: Xitlalli, Instituto Familiár de La Raza (415) 586-0435

EARLY NOVEMBER

San Francisco, Palace of Fine Arts
American Indian Film Festival (adm.)
  Films on Native American subjects, crafts, food
  (415) 554-0525 or aifisf@aol.com

Santa Fe Springs, Heritage Park, W Orange County
Sejat Spirit Powwow 12100 Mora Dr.
  Drums, songs, arts, crafts, food,
  California dancers: Gabrielino/ Tongva
  (562) 946-6476

1ST WEEKEND IN NOVEMBER

Los Angeles, Southwest Museum
Annual Intertribal Marketplace (adm.)
  Museum is about 3 mi. N of Dodger Stadium
  (213) 221-2164 x 224

Redding Museum and Arts Center, Redding, Lassen County
Indian Heritage Days (biennial, even years)
  Dances honoring Wintu, Pit River peoples, food,
  Demonstrations, oral tradition
  (916) 225-4155

2ND WEEKEND IN NOVEMBER

Eureka, Redwood Acres, Humboldt County
Intertribal Thanksgiving for Honoring Elders
  Powwow, arts & crafts, potlatch for elders.
  Coord., Pete Taylor (707) 455-8451

Fremont, Alameda County
Annual California Indian Storytelling Festival
  Ohlone Community College
  Arts, crafts, books and Symposium Sat.
  Storytelling performance Sun.
  (510) 651-6414 or 794-7253 or teixeira@ccnet.com

MID-NOVEMBER

Pala Reservation, N San Diego County
Annual Christmas Bazaar Cupa Cultural Center
Dances, handicrafts, pottery, food.
(619) 742-1590

NOVEMBER 15TH

Santa Ysabel Mission, central San Diego County
Feast Day at the Mission church

LATE NOVEMBER WEEKEND

Cabazon Reservation, Indio
Indio Powwow & Native American Festival

Red Bluff, Tehama County
Native Peoples Gathering Tehama District Fairgrounds
  (541) 474-6394

Sacramento, Cal. State Ind. Museum
Native American Film Festival Films and live dances
  (916) 445-0971

Satwiwa, Santa Monica Mountains National Recreation Area,
Ventura County
Fall Festival and Gathering
  Tongva dancers, intertribal participation food, booths, vendors.
  Info: Satwiwa (weekends only) (805) 375-1930

THANKSGIVING DAY

San Francisco, Alcatraz Island
Un-thanksgiving Sunrise ceremony honoring sun dancers, prayers.
International Indian Treaty Council (415) 641-4482

1ST WEEKEND IN DECEMBER
Ukiah, Mendocino College
Powwow (Sat.) Pomo dances, exhibition dancing.
  Sponsor: Native American Organization (707) 468-3047

DECEMBER 12TH
San Diego location varies
Fiesta of Our Lady of Guadalupe
  Sponsor: Danza Mexicayotl (619) 428-1115

Los Angeles, Loreto Church, Echo Park
Ceremonies Dances, food.
  Xipe Totec, participant (714) 774-9803

MID-DECEMBER
Davis/D-Q U, Yolo County
Winter Powwow (916)758-0470

Folsom, Sacramento County
Annual Christmas Show
  Fine Indian arts & crafts
  Pacific Western Traders (916) 985-3851

Sacramento, location varies
Fiesta de Tonanacin (Mother Earth Festival).
  Sponsor, with others: Xitlalli (916) 739-1105

DECEMBER 21ST (SOLSTICE)
Smith River at Ne-lo-chun-don, (S. Bank Rd.), Del Norte County
Indian New Year Dances and celebration.
  Sponsor: Tolowa Nation (707) 464-7332

DECEMBER 25TH
Christmas services At all reservation churches.

DATE VARYING WITH MAYAN CALENDAR
(9-month cycle) In 2000 & 2004, March; 2001 & 2005, December; 2002, September; 2003, June

San Francisco, location varies
Mayan New Year Sunrise Celebration often Dolores Park
  Marimba music and dances
  Call Grupo Maya (415) 824-2534

ONGOING PROGRAMS
OF VARIOUS INDIAN ORGANIZATIONS

All sponsor annual meetings, classes, workshops, or gatherings, but the dates will vary. Some require fees.

BREATH OF LIFE LANGUAGE RESTORATION
Director, Native California Network,
P.O.; Box 664, Visalia, CA 93279
(209) 627-1050; aicls@lightspeed.net

CALIFORNIA INDIAN BASKETWEAVERS
CIBA,   (530) 292-0141 or (916) 324-0333

CALIFORNIA INDIAN STORYTELLERS ASSN.
Annual Gathering and local gatherings
Info: Lauren Texeira
37930 Palmer Dr., Fremont CA 94536
(408) 446-9273 or (510) 651-6144; teixeira@ccnet.com

CALIFORNIA INDIAN MUSEUM
Lectures, monthly, on a variety of topics,
Bldg. 102, Visitor Center, Presidio, San Francisco

CALIFORNIA INDIAN ARTS ASSOCIATION
Twentynine Palms office of Joshua Tree National Monument
Info: Justin Farmer (714) 256-1260

MIWOK ARCHEOLOGICAL PRESERVE OF MARIN (MAPOM)
Several classes monthly, held at Kule Loklo,
Point Reyes National Seashore
(415) 479-3281 or 883—4310; mapom@aol.com

SHELLMOUND WORK DAYS
Open Houses, Basketry Workshops
Several times monthly, various lecturers and classes.
Coyote Hills Regional Park, 8000 Patterson Rd., Fremont
Coyote Hills Visitor Center (510) 795-9385

IDYLLWILD NATIVE ARTS PROGRAM
Nat Am. art and culture workshops, mostly summer
Idyllwild Arts (*W slope San Jacinto Mtn.*),
P.O. Box 38, Idyllwild, CA (909) 659-2175

SATWIWA SUNDAYS
Guest hosts every Sunday 10-5: talks, stories, gatherings
Santa Monica Mountains National Recreation Area
Native American Indian Culture Center,
4126 Potrero Rd., Newbury Park,
(805) 499-2837 (Sat & Sun)

LET US KNOW

Many things will change; many things will happen which need writing about. Some parts of this book will become outdated; a few errors will creep in; others will stand out. PLEASE, take it upon yourself to write, call, or see me in person about any subject here.

I will try to respond.

Dolan Eargle
49 Van Buren Way
San Francisco, CA 94131

INTERTRIBAL CALENDAR of POWWOWS
REGULARLY OCCURRING POWWOWS: COLLEGES, SCHOOLS, OTHER SPONSORS

NOTE: Powwows are primarily, but not exclusively, intertribal dances, ceremonies, or festivals of Native American peoples from other states who reside in California, and who wish to maintain their tribal traditions, though many miles from home. Several of these powwows may include California dancing,as well. In addition, several of these are included in the general calendar, preceding this section.

FEBRUARY
Concord, Mt. Diablo H.S.; **Sacramento**, American Indian Education (916)237-9390 or 971-9190

MARCH
Carson City, NV, Stewart Indian School (702) 822-1808; **Cupertino**, Homestead H.S. (650) 522-2238; **Ft. Yuma Reservation**, (619)572-0213; **Riverside** Community, (909) 222-8577; **Stockton**, San Joaquin Delta Coll. (209) 474-5151; **Turlock**, Stanislaus Coll. (209) 667-3598

APRIL
Arcata, Humbolt State Univ. (707) 826-4994; **Chico**, Cal. State Univ. (916) 898-6485; **DQU with Univ. of California, Davis** (916) 752-1001; **Fresno**, Cal. State Univ. (209) 278-3277; **Long Beach**, Cal. State Univ. (562) 985-4963; **Martinez**, Golden Eagle Parent Committee (Title V) (510) 372-0547; **Oakland**, Mills Coll. (510) 430-2344; **Riverside**, Sherman Indian High School, (909 276-6719; **San Francisco**, San Francisco State Univ. (415) 338-1664; **Saratoga**, West Valley Coll. (408) 867-2200x5601

MAY
Cupertino, De Anza Coll. (408) 864-TELL; **Los Angeles**, Univ. of Calif. (310)206-7513; **Marysville**, Yuba Co.(530) 749-6196; **Riverside**, Medicine Ways (909) 787-4143; **San Francisco**, SF State Univ. (415) 338-1929; **Santa Cruz**, (831) 462-4167; **Stanford Univ.** (650) 723-4078; **Susanville**, Mother's Day Intertribal (916) 257-5222

MEMORIAL DAY
Casa de Fruta, Red Road, Santa Cruz Indian Council (408) 471-9155; **Davis**, D-Q U, Graduation (916) 758-0470; **Fontana**, (909) 823-6150

JUNE
Fallbrook/West Hills, (805) 375-1930; **Gilroy** (Mt. Madonna Park), Honoring Elders (831) 842-5411; **Marysville**, Yuba-Sutter (530) 749-6196; **Napa**, Suscol Council (707) 226-5075; **Oakland**, Silver Star (415) 554-0525; **Oceanside**, Mission San Luis Rey (760)724-8505; **San Bernardino**, Four Moons (909) 823-6150;

San Diego (Miramar), Freedom, (619)491-9334; **Tehachapi**, location varies (760) 376-4340

JULY
JULY 4TH
Santa Ynez Reservation, July 4th Powwow (805) 688-7997; **Manteca**, Three Rivers Lodge, July 4th Powwow (209) 858-2421; **Costa Mesa**, Orange Co. Fairgrounds, S. Cal. Ind. Centers (714) 663-1102; **Riverside** (Big Bear City), All Nations, SoCal (909) 585-6532, NorCal (510) 465-3267; **Sacramento**, 6th &Broadway (916) 421-0657

AUGUST
Ft. Bidwell Reservation, Traditional Paiute (916)279-6310; **Santa Rosa Rancheria**, (209) 9246961

SEPTEMBER
Bass Lake, Precious Sunset (209)855-2705; **Quincy**, Greenville H.S. (530) 283-3402; **Redding**, Stillwater (916) 225-8979; **San Jose**, Indian Youth Council (408) 971-9622; **Thousand Oaks**, Everything Is Sacred (805) 493-2863

LABOR DAY
Reno/Sparks, Numaga Days (702)673-0775; **Stockton**, Am. Ind. Ed. Prog., USD, and Cent. Cal. Council (209) 953-4803, or 546-7569; **Three Rivers** (209)592-4580

CALIFORNIA INDIAN DAYS:
Barona Reservation (619) 281-5964; **Colorado River Reservation** (602) 669-9211; **Ft. Yuma Reservation** (619) 572-0213; **Porterville** (209) 784-4509; **Roseville** (916) 920-0285;

OCTOBER
Carson City, NV, Washoe Community (702) 885-9759; **Ft. Mojave Reservation** (619) 326-4591; **Pittsburg**, Los Medanos College (925)439-2185 x802

NOVEMBER
Kernville, Kern Valley Council (P.O. Box 169, Kernville, CA 93230)

DECEMBER
San Jose, Santa Clara Indian Center (408) 971-9622

REGULAR POWWOWS
SOUTHERN CALIFORNIA
MONTHLY SCHEDULED EVENTS:
[Other unscheduled powwows are held throughout the year in Southern California. Please consult your local Indian Center for a monthly calendar.]

1ST SATURDAY OF EACH MONTH
Eagle Rock Recreation Center (or other locations), **Los Angeles** Sponsor: Little Big Horn Club

2ND SATURDAY OF EACH MONTH
Cecil B. DeMille Jr. High School, **Long Beach**, Los Angeles County Sponsor: Many Trails Club (213) 371-2026 or 372-1842

3RD SATURDAY OF EACH MONTH
Eagle Rock Recreation Center, Los Angeles Sponsor: LACCIM (Los Angeles County Concerned Indian Movement) (818) 575-3512

4TH SATURDAY OF EACH MONTH
Stanton Community Center, Stanton (nr. Anaheim), **Orange County** Sponsor: Orange County Indian Center (Garden Grove) (714) 530-0221

NORTHERN CALIFORNIA
[For a complete listing of these and other unscheduled powwows, write the **Intertribal Friendship House**, 523 E. 14th St., Oakland, CA 94606 for their annual calendar. Also see the general calendar, above]

ALMOST MONTHLY:
D-Q University, Davis, Yolo County, Sponsor: D-Q U (916) 758-1470

INDEX

italic page numbers [*124*] photos or drawings
bold page numbers [**47**], significant discussion

D

E

F

G

other publications by Dolan Eargle from Trees Company Press:

CALIFORNIA INDIAN COUNTRY:
THE LAND & THE PEOPLE

(1992) ISBN 0-937401-20-X, 180 pages, $10.00 + postage $1.60

A pictorial guidebook to Native American peoples and places of California.
Contains a brief history of California Indians, maps of original tribal lands (color-coded by language and geographical areas), approaches to various aspects of contemporary Indian life, present-day reservations, calendars of events.

CONOZCA SUS RAICES/KNOW YOUR ROOTS

(1994) ISBN 0-937401-22-6, folded into 9x12 envelope, $2.00 + postage $0.55

A Map of the Indigenous Peoples of Mexico & CentroAmerica
A full color, 18"x24" poster, bilingual Español & English with color-coded legend of contemporary ethnic homelands grouped by linguistic families., [México to Panama] Bibiliography.
(Compiled and edited by Dr. Eargle)

To Order copies send check, purchase order, or telephone order to
TREES COMPANY PRESS, 49 Van Buren Way, San Francisco, CA 94131
or call (415) 334-8352